THE OXFORD HANDBOOK OF

VOICE STUDIES

THE OXFORD HANDBOOK OF

VOICE
STUDIES

Edited by

NINA SUN EIDSHEIM

and

KATHERINE MEIZEL

OXFORD

UNIVERSITY PRESS

Oxford University Press is a department of the University of Oxford. It furthers
the University's objective of excellence in research, scholarship, and education
by publishing worldwide. Oxford is a registered trade mark of Oxford University
Press in the UK and certain other countries.

Published in the United States of America by Oxford University Press
198 Madison Avenue, New York, NY 10016, United States of America

Library of Congress Cataloging-in-Publication Data
Names: Eidsheim, Nina Sun, | Meizel, Katherine.
Title: The Oxford handbook of voice studies / edited by Nina Sun Eidsheim & Katherine Meizel.
Description: New York, NY: Oxford University Press, [2019] | Series: Oxford
handbooks | Includes bibliographical references and index.
Identifiers: LCCN 2018049752| ISBN 9780199982295 (cloth: alk. paper) | ISBN 9780199338641
(oxford handbooks online) | ISBN 9780190934590 (companion website)
Subjects: LCSH: Voice—Psychological aspects. | Voice—Social aspects. | Singing.
Classification: LCC BF592.V64 O94 2019 | DDC 152.3/842—dc23 LC record available at
https://lccn.loc.gov/2018049752

1 3 5 7 9 8 6 4 2

Printed by Sheridan Books, Inc., United States of America

CONTENTS

PART III ACTIVE VOICE:
VOICE AS POLITICS

PART IV SENSING VOICE: VOICE AS
(MULTI)SENSORY PHENOMENON

PART V PRODUCING VOICE:
VOCAL MODALITIES

PART VI NEGOTIATING VOICE: VOICE AS TRANSACTION

Acknowledgments

This volume came to fruition through the engagement and dialogue of many invaluable voices. The editors wholeheartedly thank the authors, who have each contributed a unique perspective and fascinating research, for their hard work and patience as the book developed. And we are truly indebted to Senior Editor Norman Hirschy for his vision and for his consistent encouragement, patience, expertise, and thoughtful guidance throughout this book project. We appreciate Trevor Pinch for first suggesting this project to Norm and for making the introduction. We also thank the six extremely thoughtful and helpful readers who reviewed the manuscript.

Beyond the authors, editors, and reviewers, many have worked hard on getting this volume to the finish line. The brilliant Juliette Bellocq and Jessica Fleischmann took on the challenge to render Yoko Ono's text. We owe thanks to graphic designer Gabriel Lee, who masterfully handled the broad range of figure styles across the many chapters. Additional thanks to Jonas Herbsman, Ms. Ono's legal representative, and David Leaf, who facilitated the introduction to her team. We also acknowledge Jake Johnson and Schuyler Whelden for their careful copyediting work with the book's diverse material. Devastatingly, not everyone was able to cross the finish line with us. We remember with gratitude countertenor Brian Asawa, whose chapter was unfinished at the time of his unexpected passing.

For space, staff support, funding, and more, we are also deeply grateful to the University of California Los Angeles, the Herb Alpert School of Music, the UCLA Department of Musicology, the RU Nelson Endowment, University of California Multicampus Research Group (MRG), *Keys to Voice Studies: Terminology, Methodology, and Questions Across Disciplines*, the UCLA Faculty Research Grant, and the UCLA Arts Initiative award. Without this support, we would not have been able to organize the Voice Studies Now conference in 2015, which allowed the authors to exchange ideas in person and with an enthusiastic audience. And the conference and volume would not have been possible without the further support of Deans David Schaberg and Judi Smith, Mike D'Errico, Jessica Gonzales, Luis Henao, Raymond Knapp, Anahit Manoukian, Tiffany Naiman, Barbara van Nostrand, Jillian Rogers, Jessica Schwartz, and Neal Stulberg, to whom we offer sincerest thanks. Special gratitude goes to Jody Kreiman for coteaching two seminars on voice with Nina and for answering all questions voice, as well as to her colleagues at the Bureau of Glottal Affairs, UCLA School of Medicine—especially Bruce Gerratt, Zhaoyan Zhang, Rosario Signorello, and Jennifer Long—who hosted our seminar for two vocal apparatus dissections. At Bowling Green

State University, Kathy is grateful to Ron Scherer not only for his work with her on their chapter, but for his advice and support of the project.

Finally, we thank our families and friends for their support and patience throughout this process.

The cover photo features Valeriy Mongush playing a contemporary *doshpuluur*. Photo by Vasilii Maksimovich Balchyi-ool, courtesy of the Övür House of Culture, Xandagaity, Tyva Republic.

About the Companion website

www.oup.com/us/ohovs

Oxford has created a website to accompany *The Oxford Handbook of Voice Studies*. Material that cannot be made available in a book, namely figures and audio content, are available here. The collaborative syllabus, described in chapter 23, is also provided here. The reader is encouraged to consult this resource in conjunction the chapters. Examples available online are indicated in the text with Oxford's symbol.

The Oxford Handbook of Voice Studies

Edited by Nina Sun Eidsheim and Katherine Meizel

Contributors

Santanu Bandyopadhyay, singer and teacher, Hindustani tradition (Bishnupur gharana)

Robert O. Beahrs, Lecturer in Ethnomusicology, Dr. Erol Üçer Center for Advanced Studies in Music (MIAM), Istanbul Technical University

Juliette Bellocq, graphic designer

April L. Brown, Professor of History, Northwest Arkansas Community College

Gregory A. Bryant, Professor of Communication, University of California, Los Angeles

Shane Butler, Nancy H. and Robert E. Hall, Professor in the Humanities, Professor and Chair of Classics, Johns Hopkins University

Hyun Kyong Hannah Chang, Lecturer in Korean Studies, School of East Asian Studies, University of Sheffield

Nina Sun Eidsheim, Professor of Musicology, Herb Alpert School of Music, University of California, Los Angeles

Cornelia Fales, research associate, Indiana University

Jennifer Fleeger, Associate Professor of Media and Communication Studies and Coordinator of Film Studies, Ursinus College

Jessica Fleischmann, graphic designer

Mary J. Hawkshaw, Research Professor of Otolaryngology-Head and Neck Surgery, Drexel University College of Medicine

Jake Johnson, Assistant Professor of Musicology, Oklahoma City University

Alisha Lola Jones, Assistant Professor of Ethnomusicology, Department of Folklore and Ethnomusicology, Indiana University

Alexander K. Khalil, Lecturer in Ethnomusicology, Department of Music, University College Cork

Jody Kreiman, Professor of Head and Neck Surgery and Linguistics, University of California, Los Angeles

Elias Krell, César Chávez Postdoctoral Fellow in Latin American, Latino, and Caribbean Studies and Women, Gender, and Sexuality Studies, Dartmouth College

Tom McEnaney, Assistant Professor of Comparative Literature and Spanish and Portuguese at the University of California, Berkeley

Eve McPherson, Associate Professor of Music, Kent State University at Trumbull

Katherine Meizel, Associate Professor of Ethnomusicology, Bowling Green State University

Yoko Ono, singer, composer, multimedia artist, filmmaker, and activist

Katarzyna Pisanski, postdoctoral research fellow at the University of Sussex, Brighton

Nandhakumar Radhakrishnan, Associate Professor of Speech and Hearing Sciences, Lamar University

Matt Rahaim, Associate Professor of Ethnomusicology, University of Minnesota

Shanara R. Reid-Brinkley, Visiting Scholar in the Humanities and former Director of Debate for the William Pitt Debate Union, University of Pittsburgh

Robert T. Sataloff, Professor and Chair of the Department of Otolaryngology-Head and Neck Surgery, and Senior Associate Dean for clinical academic specialties at Drexel University College of Medicine; he is also on the faculties of Temple University, Philadelphia College of Osteopathic Medicine, and Thomas Jefferson University

Ronald C. Scherer, Distinguished Research Professor in the Department of Communication Sciences and Disorders, Bowling Green State University

Jessica A. Schwartz, Assistant Professor of Musicology, University of California, Los Angeles

Rosario Signorello, postdoctoral researcher, Université Sorbonne Nouvelle and CNRS

Dan Wang, Assistant Professor in Musicology, University of Pittsburgh

Miriama Young, Faculty of Fine Arts and Music, the University of Melbourne

INTRODUCTION

Voice Studies Now

NINA SUN EIDSHEIM
AND KATHERINE MEIZEL

Introduction

"Hello." "Bonjour." "Ciao." "Hallo." Thus uttered Wolfgang von Kempelen's speaking machine as it enthralled audiences in the 1780s. Later, the creators of nineteenth-century speaking machines built on von Kempelen's success, including Joseph Faber, whose apparatus toured globally with P. T. Barnum in 1846. Unlike von Kempelen's device, which could only manage romance languages, Faber's Euphonia was said to speak any European language, sing "God Save the Queen," laugh, and whisper.[1] The voice sounds were created by fourteen keys, organized as on a piano, which controlled the jaw, lips, and tongue. A bellow and ivory reed served as lungs and larynx. The speaking machine voice were mediated to their publics through a dummy face. Though the very thrill of the invention was a *machine* that could speak, the machine's speech was mediated through a recognizable but uncanny (Dolar 2006, 7) facsimile of a living, voice-producing entity.[2]

More than two hundred years after Kempelen's speaking machine, we are accustomed to voices speaking from seemingly anywhere and everywhere. We no longer line up to be entertained by "tone test" evenings at the theater where we might guess whether the sound behind the curtain is emitted from a gramophone or from a live performance like the millions of people who participated in the ones offered by the Edison Company in the United States from 1915 through 1925 (Sterne 2003, 262). And we no longer need the assurance of a live or reproduced human face and body to be impelled to listen to and speak with voices emitting from house alarm systems, cars, telephones, and digital assistants, or "smart speakers" such as Alexa and Google Home.[3] However, vocal events still have the capacity to raise familiar questions regarding the human, the animal, the machine, and the spiritual—or in nonmetaphysical terms, questions about identity and authenticity. For example, the question of personalization and perception of synthetic voices comes to mind (Mills et al. 2014; Marshall 2014). Clearly, individuals and groups perform, refuse, and play identity through vocal acts and by listening to and for voice. Voice and its imaginary are immensely complex, and affect so many aspects of our interaction with and meaning-making in the world that they exceed study by a single discipline.

While not assigned a singular meaning, voice holds a singular preoccupation in the sound world. Independent of the source—human, animal, nature, or machine—listeners choose to judge a sound as "voice" or "not voice." We can make or break a voice and all its attendant meanings by the way we listen to it. Voice and its surrounding values represent no stable category, rather one that is negotiated with each utterance and each listening. Thus, this volume not only asks the question "what is voice?" and the underlying question "what is accomplished by evoking voice?" but troubles seemingly straightforward responses. Furthermore, we ask how we might study voice in ways that take into account the many roles voice is made to serve and the ways in which its many definitions are shaped by those needing something from it. We believe this is best accomplished outside the confines of any one scholarly area that studies voice; thus, we place the work in this volume within what we broadly conceive of as voice studies.

Voice Studies

What is voice studies? Voice studies does not make a claim to a given definition of voice, but instead suggests the limits of any one claim. Voice studies offers tools to better detect the values underpinning any definition of voice. And voice studies deconstructs not only the performance of the voice, but also the performance of claims to voice. Thus, voice studies asks questions that necessarily connect practices of and inquiries into voice. In our definition, what distinguishes voice studies as a whole from each of the many individual and overlapping strains of scholarship and inquiry that center voice is that it seeks to understand or interact with voice knowledge beyond the potential narrow confine of a defined area of inquiry.

Following that framework, voice studies scholarship recognizes the voice as a complex, often contradictory domain for cultural exchange in areas such as materiality, performance, meaning-making, and knowledge production. It recognizes that the voice is not materiality, text, discourse, or performance as such, but that any of these aspects are already symptoms or evidence of the pressures and affordances that have empowered some vocal expressions and foreclosed on others. The work is attentive to the ways in which some people's voices and vocal practices are misconstrued or suppressed, while others are heard with generosity and encouragement. Voice is so heavily inscribed with power relationships that it is often conceptually conflated with power itself, and with agency—though the English word *vote* comes from the Latin *votum* as applied to ancient Roman religious vows, in many Germanic languages such as German, Norwegian, Danish, Dutch, and Yiddish a vote is literally a voice (*Stimme, stemme, stemmen, shtimen*/שטימען—the latter also means "to fit in" or "agree"). To enter into questions regarding the voice is to enter into a complex of unequal power structures. Therefore, voice studies cannot simply ask about the meaning or technical production of the vocal sound, but must ask under which pressures, for whom, to what end, a given voice or vocal community was formed.

To us, then, voice studies scholars must be vigilant in remembering that whatever answers are arrived at are dependent on or limited by the questions asked and methodologies employed. Additionally, this means that not only do voice studies scholars carry out distinct investigations using specific disciplinary methodologies, but they also step back and take into account how a particular methodology and perspective is a performance, a domain for cultural exchange. What we can know about voice at any given moment in time is afforded and limited by the very underlying values that direct the research. We believe that voice studies scholars not only bring forward new knowledge about voice proper, but also offer tools to deconstruct that knowledge by naming the constraints and affordances through which it has been produced. The knowledge, then, cannot be construed as stable and unencumbered, but always expressing a point of view. Voice studies scholars do not only each produce an independent piece of knowledge, but also understand and can articulate the ways such knowledge is always already reproducing the precise values from which it arises.

From our perspective, however, the goal of voice studies is not to undo knowledge for the purpose of undoing knowledge. In contrast, we contend that the goal of voice studies is to recognize that we are not only carrying out the study of voice per se, but we are also in the business of defining voice. If voice studies scholarship is successful in this regard, it can make legible the interlocking and mutually affecting relations between practice, pedagogy, knowledge production, and definition. Its aspiration is to name the boundaries and alliances of knowledge as it is produced through voice. Because by doing so it does not blindly (re)produce voice, neither does it allow for any knowledge produced to automatically justify itself through replicated studies. Voice studies carries out this inquiry while also naming the kind of cultural and political work—lodged in the voice—the research produces. In short, voice studies makes and critically interrogates itself simultaneously.

To be healthy and sustainable, studies of voice must, in part, reject the very premise of a stable ontology and epistemology of voice. (see also chapter 2.) Indeed, voice studies ought to both seek to understand the many simultaneous definitions and lay bare contingent values from which such practice or understanding arises and are validated. To not reproduce such patterns itself, voice studies must disclaim any singular epistemology while it carries out its work.

Though scholars have traced a millennia-long history of interest in studying the voice, the genealogy—to us, the more immediate genealogy of this broader voice studies—can be traced to the late 1990s.[4] From the point of view of Western humanistic and social science scholarship prior to the late 1990s, voice inquiry was what we might think about as provincial—its theories and methods determined, and driven, by discipline-specific goals.[5] For example, vocal pedagogy discussed vocal aesthetics, practices, health, and acoustic processes, but its end goal was field-based and unambiguous: improved singing, performances, and interpretations of composed works. In the same way, work in linguistics was thought to serve the deepening of knowledge in that particular discipline rather than a broader concept of voice. Musicologists sought to understand vocal compositions and lyrics as literary texts, musical works, or cultural practices. On rare occasions, these scholars studied the singer on whose vocal abilities a composition might be based, or who made a particular role or piece their own. However, such inquiries were mounted mainly for the purpose of understanding the musical work, a composer's or singer's biography, or a broader cultural milieu. Meanwhile, ethnomusicological work dealt with the voice in the service of understanding the social or cultural interactions upon which a musical practice rested. Another way to say this is that while the work was interesting and valuable for the discrete fields, voice was studied for the development of a more local level understanding, rather than for seeking out the overlaps and broader points of connection. One important exception that laid the groundwork for the opening of conversation was linguist, anthropologist, and ethnomusicologist Steven Feld's 1982 study of the Kaluli people of Papua New Guinea. Feld gave prominence to the aspect of voice that goes beyond vocal cords. Indeed, the Kaluli people exemplified a continuity and interrelationship between categories that many other cultures understand as distinct from one another: that is, between human, animal, and nature, thereby bridging the humanities and social sciences.[6]

The reorientation to voice as more than the sound emitted from the human vocal cords was key to the development of voice scholarship. In the 1990s the overarching achievements in the study of voice included: the sharing of knowledge and experience among those in the arts and those in voice science; attention to the malleability of the body and its connection to the overall material environment; the recognition that the body is a site through which culture is materialized and expressed; and a focus on both singers' and listeners' performativity in any given moment with the voice as a performative expression. As the conception of voice expanded, areas that would not have been studied when, for example, the concept of "repertoire" was an organizing principle began to be considered. Moreover, what also marks these works is that they either reached far beyond their fields of origin or that they somehow were able to speak to or dialogue with multiple fields. Though ideas about vocality had been introduced to voice discourse earlier, Leslie C. Dunn's and Nancy A. Jones's 1997 edited interdisciplinary collection addressed this broader concept within Western frameworks of voice, showing the connections between different humanities fields and methodologies. Around the same time, a handful of books offered analysis of the complex relationship between vocal performance and the shaping of material vocal bodies, and of the centrality of listeners' imaginary in meaning-making processes around voice. It is also important to note that these landmark studies were based on a variety of case studies that center the roles of voice in the construction of identity, such as: African American singing of spirituals in the antebellum United States (Cruz 1999); gendered and queer listening to opera (Poizat 1992; Koestenbaum 1993); material bodies performing gendered and queered vocal acts; (Cusick 1999); the changes in singing styles historically as it relates to power and ideology (Potter 2006); and the role of the cinematic media as shaping understanding of voice, absence, and presence (Chion 1990, translated into English in 1994). These authors addressed different political stakes, including issues related to race, gender, LGBTQ+, and homeland as performed, resisted, or argued through vocal performance and its related listening practices. Considering that the voice science and vocal pedagogy side for the National Center for Voice and Speech was established in 1990, and in 1996 its director and chief scientist, Ingo Titze, defined the interdisciplinary study called *vocology*—"the science and practice of voice habilitation" (1996). This concept built on and helped to reaffirm the established research and practical relationship between voice science and everyday and professional voice users in music, theater, media, and in speech-heavy occupations such as teaching or politics, as well as those with voice disorders or other therapeutic needs. As such, Titze built on the work carried out by the National Voice Foundation (since 1969) and the Voice and Speech Trainers Association (since the late 1980s), both of which have also continued to nurture these connections in scholarship as well as practice. In 1996, Hugo Zemp and the Musée de l'Homme in France released a landmark compact disc anthology titled *Les Voix de Monde* (1996), dozens of recordings of voices around the world, accompanied by both descriptive notes and sonograms of many examples—allowing listeners to consider voices, their cultural contexts, and visual representations of the voices' acoustic content. The *Les Voix de Monde* project exemplifies transdisciplinary inquiry, crossing the performing arts, social sciences, and the acoustic and voice sciences.

Work in the 2000s built on these advances, considering the very fleshiness of the throats and mouths that form vocal sounds alongside identities and the pressures of power structures that inform vocal practices and the way listeners derive meaning therefrom. Related to this, Laurie Stras (2006), bringing in a disability studies perspective, showed us that the materiality and sound of voice is affected by the overall environment and by the types of sounds the audience wants. Such relationships between listener and singer make up another vital topic in the study of voice. Steven Feld, Aaron A. Fox, Thomas Porcello, and David Samuels (2003) present voice and its modes as a site where music and language intersect, becoming the body's chief technology of difference—a site where listeners learn to interpret individualities and aurally distinguish others' voices from their own (Feld et al. 2004). Publications by Jonathan Sterne (2003), Jean-Luc Nancy (2007), and Charles Hirschkind (2006) became models for attending to the process of vocal mediation and listening technologies. Whether technologically mediated or not, voices are reimagined in the listener's mind and thus shape vocal constructions of identity—what one of us, Eidsheim, has written about as "performative listening" (2009).

Also in the 2000s, theoretical analyses began to build on the work of previous thinkers from Aristotle to Roland Barthes (1977) to re-examine the overall role of voice in human lives. Classicist and feminist scholar Adriana Cavarero (2005) reached beyond her fields with *For More Than One Voice: Toward a Philosophy of Vocal Expression*, in which she connected humanist philosophy about voice to scenes from opera. This book offered an entry point to how philosophical history has largely ignored what Cavarero argues is its hallmark, an index of uniqueness. Like Cavarero, Lacanian scholar

Mladen Dolar (2006) reinvigorated the language and imagination of voice. Taking a historical and practice-based approach, Steven Connor (2000) thought about voice, the supernatural, perception, and fantasy through the lens of ventriloquism. Scholarship on practices outside the West slowly started to become more influential to the Western canon. For example, works such as Amanda Weidman's (2006) on voice and the subaltern in Indian music context both helped us better note Western conceptions of voice as well as the sheer diversity of non-Western conceptions. Grant Olwage (2004) offered important work on vocal timbre and colonization in South Africa. And Cornelia Fales's (2002) work on perception of vocal timbre has become a model for considering in very concrete ways how tradition and stories about sounds are at play in perception of voices.

Together, these and related works at the turn of the twenty-first century have helped diversify the entry points into voice inquiry and enable the shift toward thinking about voice through the concept of "vocality." While historically voice is often described in singular terms, Katherine Meizel has argued that vocality, in contrast, "goes beyond qualities like timbre and practice, and encourages us to consider *everything* that is being vocalized—sounded and heard as vocal—and offers a way to talk about a voice beyond simply the words it imparts or its color or production techniques. Instead, it encapsulates the entire experience of the speaker or singer and of the listener, all of the physiological, psychoacoustic, and sociopolitical dynamics that impact our perception of ourselves and each other" (2011, 267).

From the 2010s and beyond, the flow of scholarship on voice has increased exponentially. Instrumental to this development was Jody Kreiman and Diana Sidtis's (2011) brilliant synthesis of vast amounts of research from voice medicine and sciences. Other work, such as Mara Mills's (2010) work in science and technology studies on communication technologies and issues of disability, shows that much of the normative voice- and listening-related technologies we take for granted were developed for or with individuals from the disability community. Sound studies has recently become a fertile ground for voice research. Investigating the relationship between voice and ear (orality and aurality), Ana María Ochoa Gautier has written about boundaries between human and nonhuman sound by attending to ideas about voice on the power structures of modernity and European imperialism (2014). Eidsheim (2015) has argued that voice can productively be understood through the analytical lens of intermaterial vibrational practice. Connor (2014) and Brandon LaBelle (2014) have questioned the close connection made between voice and meaning-making, by considering nonword vocal sounds such as sobs, hums, babble, and coughing, as well as the oral cavities as a spatial entity as much as a sound-making chamber. Research on voice in popular music has also continued to flourish, with examples such as Duchan (2012), Goldin-Perschbacher (2007; 2015), Jarman-Ivens (2011), McKay (2013), Krell (2013; 2015), and more.

Increasingly, toward the end of the second decade of the new millennium, studies that span and interrogate the interrelations between the pedagogical, performative, corporeal, material, cultural, and symbolic dimensions of voice have moved us into what we think about as a loosely established voice studies. Notable examples from musicology, ethnomusicology, classics, anthropology, the study of improvisation, and African American literature include Bergeron (2010), Brooks (2013), Butler (2015), Davies (2014), Dillon (2012), Eidsheim (2015), Feldman (2014), Harkness (2014), Lordi (2013), Meizel (2011), Tonelli (2016), Jacobsen (2017), Jarman-Ivens (2011), McPherson (2005), McPherson et al. (2014), Utz and Lau (2013), Rahaim (2012), and other works by many of the authors in this volume. We also want to highlight another volume in the Oxford *Handbook* series, *The Oxford Handbook of Voice Perception* (Frühholz and Belin 2018), which will serve as a nice complement to this volume. In addition, a substantial number of panels, conferences, edited volumes, and special journal issues—and the recently founded *Journal of Interdisciplinary Voice Studies*—show the increasing institutional support behind work that crosses disciplinary boundaries through the connection of voice.

Why has voice historically been central to such diverse areas of inquiry? Voice has for a long time functioned as a lens of inquiry—as a sustained space of interrogation. On the one hand, studying vocal repertoires, practices, and habits helps us to understand human and animal practices and culture at a given time. On the other hand, the vocal apparatus and breathing organs that are centrally involved in vocal expression can work as tracking tools, illustrating mammalian development across large swaths of time. Elements such as the tongue, vocal orifices, and vocal cords are vital organs that participate in the regulation of eating, drinking, and breathing. Hence, the vocal organ is also a key point of interest for human evolution and physiology.

From work in literature to psychoanalysis, voice has also been understood as a portal into the unconscious. Vocal expressions and extralinguistic sounds and silences are thought to provide direct and indirect information regarding the inner life and memory of the vocalizer. However, conscious vocal communication can take many forms. Indeed, communication that is not linked to the vocal apparatus, from gesture to sign languages to typed conversation, also falls within vocal expression. For example, people in so-called vegetative states who are unable to vocalize audibly have been found to be able to respond to questions by cognitively engaging in one of two activities, for example blinking: each of the activities were set up to signify "yes" or "no," giving such patients a way to communicate (Owen et al. 2006). The study of subvocal speech—the engagement of neuromuscular speech processes without vocalization—has been combined with new technological developments, with the goal of enhancing communication in situations when vocalized speech is impossible, from military combat conditions to speech synthesis for those with speech-related disabilities. Subvocal speech occurs involuntarily in many contexts, including silent reading, the mental rehearsal of speech, and in combination with auditory hallucinations (Iddo and Jorgensen 2006). The hearing of voices in auditory hallucination, experienced only internally by a listener, can contribute to alterations in identity and sense of self. Psychoanalysis also theorizes different types of internal voices and their participation in how lived human life is felt. For example, the superego or "voice of conscience" tells us what to do, and another internal voice demands submission. The voice's ability to make sound, sometimes silenced without any clinical reason seeming to underlie an inability to speak, can manifest symptoms of an issue that may be too complex and sensitive to discuss openly, and hence to request and receive help.

Moreover, because vocal activities such as speaking and singing are processed within distinct parts of the brain, studying these communicative aspects helps to illuminate both brain function and the overlap and divergence between speech and music. Researchers and clinicians can utilize this knowledge in situations where one brain region is damaged and an alternative region may be trained to compensate for the missing functionality. And, crucially to everyday human life, the vocal folds within the apparatus that gives rise to vocal sounds also enable fundamental physical functions, such as strength (for example, weightlifters use the technique of lifting while closing the vocal cords, and thus holding the air inside, which involves the *Valsalva maneuver*) and closure of the glottis when ingesting. As Jody Kreiman summarizes it, "everything in vocalizing is repurposing something else" (personal communication, April 18, 2016). Hence, encultured expressions are entwined with biological function and human evolution.

Vocal activity is always connected with the process of feedback through self-monitoring and social monitoring. This has been studied primarily through the mode of hearing, but it is a multisensory process. Therefore, in investigative efforts into auto-hearing, attention to how others hear you, and how these cycles feed into self-image, regulation, and positioning within a social group, voice and multimodal listening are crucial.

In short, the voice is central to fields spanning medicine, science, social sciences, arts, and the humanities because the vocal apparatus is so central to basic human function, life, and culture that it always points to dimensions outside itself.[7] For these and many other reasons, we feel it is no exaggeration to posit that examining voice more broadly contributes to a knowledge of vocal epistemology, "of the ways in which comprehending voice remains central to understanding human experience" (Eidsheim, 2019).

THE THREE MEN AND THE ELEPHANT

A friend reminded us of the well-known story about an elephant and three blind men. This story, versions of which are documented at least as far back as the Sanskrit Mahayana Buddhist text Mahaparinarvana Sutra (first and fifth centuries C.E.) (Gregory 2001), is often used as a metaphor for academic study. And it is apt in our case, illustrating a problem that sometimes, without researchers' awareness, has stunted holistic inquiry into voice.[8] (We leave out the metaphor of blindness in our version, first because the metaphorization of blindness has inflicted real harm in the history of disability discourse [see Kleeger 2010], and, second, an elephant is large enough so that any human being would be hard-pressed to perceive all parts of an elephant at once at close quarters. Either version requires some suspension of disbelief.) The version we heard goes something like this: A group of three men had heard that the elephant was a very interesting animal. When they came upon one, they each approached it. The first man touched a leg. The second touched the trunk. The third touched an ear. Walking away, the first man exclaimed: "It is indeed an interesting animal, like a tree-trunk." The second man, at the trunk, protested: "No, the elephant is like a snake." The third retorted: "Both of you are wrong; an elephant is like an enormous fan." And, for the rest of their lives, they kept up a running argument within which each position ossified. Whenever they ran into an elephant, they would move along it until they came to the part they recognized as an elephant—the leg, trunk and ear—respectively. Even after they had interacted with its entirety, none of the men adapted this new information into expanded knowledge about the elephant.

Of course, each man was both correct and incorrect. They were all correct in their observation of the distinct piece of the elephant that they examined. However, they failed to grasp the bigger picture, and to understand how each of the parts together made up a whole. All three made the part stand in for the whole, each failing to understand the relationship between the parts and their sum. They misunderstood—or at least vastly misgauged—the meaning of even that part of the elephant they did know. This story has been used across disciplines to illustrate potential problems: in medical specialization (each doctor looking at one part of a human patient), international politics (each country examining a problem in terms of its own benefit), education (multiple teachers see a single student during a day of school), and countless types of research. Essentially, it is applicable anywhere that an object of study is approached from multiple, but each limited, viewpoints.

We could imagine a scenario in which the story did not end with the argument. In this alternate version, the three men went their separate ways and developed hypotheses and methodologies based on their individual understandings of the elephant: the leg, trunk, and ear, respectively. In this case, we can see how each definition would lead down a vastly different road, which in turn would further differentiate and isolate the parts of the elephant, and thus the study of it. Voice—as topic, object, and practice—is as enormous as an elephant. By virtue of the ontological and epistemological assumptions inherent in our fields, we all metaphorically, as scholars trained within a particular field, fail to grasp the world not captured by that field. Through our limited methodological platforms we are given access only to one part of voice, as the men are given access to a single part of the elephant. The result is that as the men each called the leg, the trunk, and the ear "an elephant," researchers accessing vastly different aspects of the multifaceted phenomenon of voice call each of these aspects "voice."

When a scholar of voice ventures outside her discipline and seeks to learn about additional aspects of voice, vocabularies and assumptions can clash, often creating insurmountable tensions. The first line of tension resembles the situation illustrated by the story of the three men and the elephant. Put simply, it is: "You are wrong and I am right." Other formulations of this line of argument include: "Your definition of voice is wrong; what you study is not voice. What you study is not relevant for *my* research, which *is* about voice. Your methodologies rely too much on quantification; or, your methodologies rely too much on qualification, hence I distrust any findings." Within such a dynamic, scholars will not develop an understanding of the larger whole of which the leg, trunk, and ear are part.

For example, imagine our elephant as an opera.[9] For the composer, the opera is the score; its form, rhythms, notes, harmonics, or textures; the realization of the libretto through the vocal writing; its place within opera and music history (through, say, quotations or references, or through pushing the envelope). The conventional music theorist studies the score, its internal and contextual logic and structure, and its relation to other operas and compositions. This could include the study of different versions of the score, or deciphering the seed of a musical theme and its development.

The conventional musicologist studies the role of this composition in the context of the composer's other work, perhaps considering the composer's overall agenda. Additionally, the opera is studied in relation to the historical and social environments within which it was created—it is assumed to be a product of that time and its concerns, so studying the opera would shed light on a particular era. Both musicologists and ethnomusicologists also study staging and representation: the ways in which particular singers' vocal abilities historically influenced and informed the vocal writing or subsequent direction; the placement of the vocal writing within a trajectory of vocal pedagogy; and possibly the ways in which these aspects intersect with broader vocal practices and contemporary values around vocal practice.

Vocal pedagogues and singers may consider the technical, stylistic, and interpretive skills needed to perform the opera. These topics are considered in turn in their historical, social, and cultural contexts, and a related network theory approach may map the links between voice teachers and prominent singers and their subsequent influences on the realms of culture, politics, and education. Moreover, the topic of vocal pedagogy is both considered historically and in terms of how it intersects with, and has developed alongside, medical and scientific research on voice. Scientific entry points to voice research notions may emerge from the point of view of the science of sound as well as the acoustics of vocal sound and of the spaces within which it is sounded. A critical theory or science, technology, and society (STS) approach considers the ways in which each of these so-called rational and scientific measurements is also biased. An acoustic approach seeks to understand the acoustic makeup of operatic practice, and perhaps to measure its changes over time. Optimization of vibrato and related engineering approaches consider the rate of vibration depending on the amount of airflow, flexibility, and thickness of the material components of the voice (vocal folds, etc.). The clinician may hear symptoms of disorder in an opera singer's voice, and investigate with the goal of intervention. And the psychoanalyst considers the words, emotions, and experiences the voice carries, analyzing them according to different theoretical frameworks.

Moving to the social sciences, the individual work or the general phenomenon of opera may be investigated in terms of their social and cultural exchange value: for example, the fundraising that took place around it, or the markers of racial and class status on display within the culture of opera. Such an approach might also look at the ways in which opera, as a status symbol, has changed over time. Networks of contributions to opera and the gaining of political office might be drawn. The symbolic value of the roles, costumes, and vocal play offer insight into a real-world power dynamic.

While this list is far from exhaustive, the point is that each of these approaches represents a partial understanding, only grasping that part of the elephant, or of the phenomenon of voice, that their methodologies and field-specific assumptions place them directly in front of. The aim of this introduction—and indeed the impetus behind this project—is to show the complementarity and clarity brought to each voice research project when it is clear how each is part of a larger whole.

Thus, for example, the scholar studying voice as a conceptual and cultural phenomenon may benefit greatly from gaining insight into the ways in which these concepts are lodged in the physical, material voice. The scientist might learn much from considering the ways in which actual vocal practice as *practiced* is limited to what a given culture endorses, or the ways in which a given person or group seeks to overturn these conventions. Moreover, aspects of vocal practice and culture that are considered ungraspable, and perhaps overinterpreted, are fairly easily explained from a vocal pedagogical, technical, or scientific point of view. However, this volume's overarching argument is that when we do pay attention to a given study's relation to the general topography of voice studies, we can understand much that we didn't understand before. We can see that each study is incomplete; we can note how a given study might be complemented or where previous research could take over to explain the next step in the understanding of a given phenomenon. That is, we can see the trunk, the leg, and the ear for what they are.

Viewing one aspect as part of a larger whole allows the outer boundaries of a domain to be considered, and sometimes expanded. "In order to understand the leg, I must understand its purpose for the entire animal," one of the men might have thought if they had eventually been able to perceive the entire body of the elephant. Instead of defending a domain ("This is how musicology should be carried out"; "This is the kind of methodology that is correct"), the outer boundary instead becomes a zone that is redefined to signal *opportunity* and *connection* points. These points then become spaces for new interactions, conversations, and transdisciplinary work. A viewpoint that had demarcated inside and outside and labeled ideas as correct or incorrect, relevant or irrelevant according to a given field is now a point that can be deepened, functioning as an invitation to use more than one domain at the same time.

But it has been challenging for one field to understand how its goals would be served by interacting with another. The analogy is not perfect, but it would be akin to one of men saying about the elephant, "I want to perfect my knowledge about trunks, so learning about legs is irrelevant . . . and what is a leg, anyway?" Similarly, when we entered into transdisciplinary conversations, we found that for most participating voice studies scholars it was not even clear which part of the voice some of the other fields investigated. With such a lack of understanding, it is unavoidably challenging to grasp how an alternative perspective may enrich a given area. For example, one researcher may ask, what useful information could queer theory add to acoustic vocal tract analysis? Or, how might mechanical engineering aid in formulating a phenomenological position?

If we are not embedded in one of what seem to be incompatible positions, it is easy to see how the parts fit together to serve a larger whole. Text is not understood in a vacuum, without the sense made by its performance or its author's sense of the voice. Performance is not understood separately from the sympathetic experience of the performer's physical movements. Vocal anatomy and function don't mean anything in isolation from the goals of a person with a voice. Additionally, all of these aspects take place within particular cultures and times that largely determine the extent of available knowledge. In other words, whether in the exact form we will suggest or in a different form, the coordinates of the interconnectedness between isolated areas of voice research have not, until this point, been explicit. And the significance, the limits, and the exact contribution of a particular piece of the larger project we call voice have not been fully articulated. We do not claim that this volume provides such a complete articulation, either, but hope that it offers ways of approaching the puzzle.

Domains of Inquiry

As an outside observer of their insurmountable disagreement, our advice to the three men with partial knowledge would be to get together, describe the part of the elephant they each know, and collectively create a map. In regard to the voice, we have found it useful to think about a similar map. It would not draw body parts, but would broadly synthesize a number of fields' perspectives and methodological approaches. The point of such a map is to begin to make out the contours of what different epistemological stances have created. The map is not intended to offer a new taxonomy. It is instead intended to constitute a *system* designed to help understand the relationship between (and possibly expand upon) existing taxonomies.

By synthesizing the myriad ways voice is conceptualized and researched into the broadest terms, we arrive at six modes, or domains, of inquiry. These modes are not mutually exclusive, often overlap, and is only one of many ways this material could be conceptualized. We name the domains (1) prompts; (2) product and performance; (3) material dimension and mechanism; (4) auditory/sensory perception; (5) documentation, narrativization, and collection; and (6) context. To explain how theorizing these six domains helps to explicate the interactions between various regions of scholarship, let's return to our example of opera. The score, a prompt for or set of instructions to the singer (domain 1), can be studied without considering its performance. The resulting vocal performance can be investigated (domain 2). Vocal materiality and its mechanisms can be studied in terms as diverse as vocal fach designation, vocal pedagogy, vocal hygiene, or health (domain 3). Inquiry into the sensorial and cognitive perception and sensation of the operatic performance would cover yet another domain (domain 4). Documentation, criticism, narration, reception, and stories about the piece and its performance can also be studied (domain 5). And, finally, the cultural context within which this phenomenon took place and which enabled, shaped, and limited it can be considered (domain 6).

The first domain, *prompts*, covers the texts, artistic forms, and everyday practices the voice is asked—whether explicitly or implicitly—to perform or execute. Domain 1 seeks to capture notated and non-notated vocal works, genres, styles, habits, and conventions. Typical examples include texts, scores, orally transmitted practices and repertoire, interpretive traditions, speech, and vocal conventions found outside a specific vocal art. While in some areas of scholarship what we call "the prompt" and the resulting vocal utterances are studied as one and the same, in other fields only one of these two possibilities is (primarily) considered. We divide them not only because this division may be observed in some scholarship, but also because—even for those approaches that do not divide them—we believe that considering them in isolation allows us to map their separations and interminglings—where and when they come together.

The second domain, *performance*, covers the execution of the prompt. That is, it considers what comes into being during vocal engagement, including sounds, their character, silences, and the trajectory along which these elements unfold. Thus, this domain represents the actual performance of a vocal composition as well as the myriad aspects of and considerations involved in that performance. Domain 2 concerns the performative aspects of vocal production, whether the performance is intentional (as in a concert) or unintentional (as in the unconscious adaptation of vocal habits during an informal conversation). This domain may be studied using both human and machine observation. A human observer would document a performance through memory, transcription, or other types of notation. By machine observation, we refer to technology based mainly on recording formats such as audio and video, as well as more granular transcription devices (including audio synthesis). In this way, domain 2 is closely related to domain 4, which directly addresses the documentation and transcription of vocal performance.

The third domain, *material dimensions and mechanism*, considers the physicality of the voice and its function. This domain is concerned with the nature and limits of the material vocal body and its mechanisms. For example, it considers the ways in which vocal materiality is shaped for a particular vocal outcome and also can redirect vocal intentions beyond the performer's control, as well as the material impact of vocal performance. This includes areas such as vocal tissue, its flexibility, its mechanical connection points (for example, the widening, shortening, or lengthening of the vocal tract), tongue and jaw manipulation, and vibration, hormonal, or other material changes. It can also include certain acoustic elements, especially when concerned with material dimensions and mechanics.

The fourth domain, *auditory/sensory perception*, relates to domain 3, but focuses specifically on the part of the vocal feedback cycle that is concerned with auditory and any sensory perception of voice, including auto-perception. While voice is traditionally imagined as related to vocal output, we know that vocal production is dependent on hearing or otherwise sensing voice. Hence, while domains 3 and 4 are intimately connected, it is also useful to divide them, considering each on its own terms as well as within a dependent relationship.

The fifth domain, *documentation, narrativization, and collection*, is derived from the first four domains. While domains 1 through 4 depend heavily on documentation and data collection, domain 5 seeks to describe the modes of research that focus primarily on voice in the form of these secondary forms. Recall that the term "secondary form" riffs on the notion of primary and secondary texts, considering vocal activity while including sound as the primary text. Thus, domain 5 covers any form of observation or documentation of the voice—and therefore, if studied as a secondary text, could include all scholarship on voice. The fourth and fifth domains, then, are more general than domains 1 through 3. While documentation, narrativization, and collection (as related to domains 1–4) are considered within their distinct domains, this area is so plentiful, considered, and cultivated that we find it useful to consider documentation, narrativization, and collection as together constituting a distinct domain. Descriptions of voices, critical writings, and so on may be viewed through this lens, as may transcriptions and technologically assisted recordings. Domain 5 also includes any documentation of vocal writing, traditions, practices, production of voice, and vocal culture.

The sixth domain, *context*, is the meta-context within which we understand the other domains, and, equally importantly, the domain that affords and limits insight into a given phenomenon. The studies within domain 6 identify and consider a particular epistemological and ontological status quo. Understandings of vocal repertoire or practice, interpretive options, and ontological and epistemological views on the mechanical, material, and definitional dimensions of the vocal apparatus are all dependent on this dimension. In other words, the first five domains are incomplete if they are not also considered in relation to domain 6. Here we wish to reiterate that all vocal phenomena clearly exist within broader contexts. This domain indicates merely that certain research approaches take the connection between phenomena and cultural contexts as their main area of investigation. Thinking in general terms, they examine how given vocal practices are shaped by aspects of their cultural, social, political, and economic contexts; or, to reverse this lens, how given vocal phenomena may have arisen in intentional opposition to the contexts within which the vocalizers found themselves.

While convention has dictated that researchers confine themselves to their home disciplines, allowing them to offer confinements and defense of a given object, voice's location on the map of our six domains clarifies and invites us to examine the ways in which study within these complementary regions may help to deepen knowledge within a single domain. In other words, investigating an object through alternative perspectives and methodologies does not eliminate or invalidate the initial approach. The very purpose of articulating these domains is to inspire partnerships in exploration, and to hint at where the subsequent phase of a given study might begin.

Unexpected Interconnections and New Research Areas

Initiating the process of mapping the territory and naming the six domains is only a first step in a much larger project: the collective work of charting voice-related areas of scholarship and practice for the purpose of facilitating new entry points for scholars and illuminating connections across fields. As voice studies scholars, we develop perspectives and questions that allow us to draw connections between, say, a gender studies approach to the corporeal aspects of voice and mechanical engineering work on tissue flexibility, mass, and resulting vibrational capacity. We hope that the six broad domains of voice research we have identified, in conjunction with future collaborative projects that will develop and populate such a matrix, may help to systematize—or, better, to translate—voice research, enabling it to facilitate the detection of tendencies within current work and point to a general need for additional studies. Naming these six domains is also intended as an initial step that can assist individual researchers in considering how and into which fields they might expand their own studies, or show where their contributions are needed. As such, the overarching intention of this introduction, and indeed of the volume as a whole, is to serve as a starting point for new voice studies researchers, or for any voice researcher who is unfamiliar with areas outside her own.

DYNAMICS OF VOICE

We need voice studies' collective methodological and epistemological richness and attending divergences to recognize the complex interlocking systems of power within which voice takes place. Rather than field-contained inquiries that seek coherence and conclusive stories, the hallmark of a broader voice studies is productive dilemmas, irresolutions, and suspensions. From such rich inquiry, researchers and practitioners can approach voice not as *either/or* but instead as *both/and*. Within such framework, incongruences, and contradictions—including voice's play, manipulation, complicity, and resistance—can be examined side by side.

Instead of offering a fixed definition of voice studies, we advocate for an approach within which familiarity is tested and, to use a visual metaphor, reseen in a new light that possibly expands the limits and advantages of fields and approaches. Here a given scholar is alert to very different—sometimes oppositional—definitions or methodologies in order to, again, clarify her own stance within this broad transdisciplinary field.[10] In the way that, for example, humanities-based studies have encouraged and practiced historically, socially, and culturally aware definitions for decades, we advocate for methodological, epistemological, and ontological awareness—not in defense of any particular approach, but toward clarification of the affordances and limitations of all.

When we use the term voice studies here, we use it in the broadest possible sense to describe an attitude of openness and awareness of one's position within the wider field of voice-related inquiry. Because so many assumptions and values have become lodged within the voice, an investigation from a transdisciplinary perspective wherein research into its flesh and ligaments is understood within a broader critically-, practice-, and performance-based context could range from dispelling deep-seated misconceptions to understanding voice's role in how human connections are forged. Our broader motivation to study voice, then, is to discern both the "more beautiful and more ugly" aspects of human nature (Lacy, quoted in Weiss 2006).

VOLUME SECTIONS

Based on the editors' respective performative (we are both classically trained singers) and academic backgrounds (musicology and ethnomusicology), and on our view of the field at the time of compilation, we have organized the chapters into six sections. The chapters could have been organized in many other ways, and some chapters could also fit within different sections than where they are currently placed. As organized, the sections are meant to address both how voice is used in the service of an agenda *and* how the phenomenon of voice is experienced, interpreted, and understood. While the chapters included exemplify a broad range of approaches and disciplinary perspectives, we recognize that a number of important perspectives are not included. Our hope is that along with all the exciting voice studies research that is published today, this volume is one of many that will start to suggest the immense possibilities voice offers as a field of inquiry.

Part I: Framing Voice: Voice as a Carrier of Meaning

Voice as it is made to stand in for a given meaning is regarded in terms of that meaning only, and thus the very concept of voice becomes identified with that meaning and is erroneously made to "evidence" it. As John Shepherd and Peter Wicke have noted about timbre, voice offers a "sonic saddle" upon which the listener is invited to ride in order to define a given meaning (Shepherd and Wicke 1997, 159). For example, voice is depended upon to signal a category such as gender. While listening communities have cultivated gendered vocal and sonorous clues and the voice functions in this service, voice's technical dexterity and the vocalizer's awareness of and adaptation to such cultural clues or explicit rules are hugely underestimated. Voice itself, in its material and sonorous dimensions, is not taken into account in examinations of the broader function and equation within which it plays a central role. As a result, voice is subsumed within the meaning-function it is pulled into. In this way, voice qua voice is often ignored. For example, a voice that is coded as "feminine" is made to reflect the feminine dimension of a person. Or, a voice that is understood as racialized—say, "Asian-sounding"—is made to evidence the racial essence of that person. In this way, meaning is carried on the back of the voice.

The chapters in this section examine past and present meanings assigned to voice, and how they are intertwined with understandings of identity. We begin with an interview with Yoko Ono, who possesses one of the most significant voices in American culture, titled "What Is Voice?" To honor her own long engagement with voice, language, and space, our questions and her thoughts about the meanings of voice have been graphically arranged by Jessica Fleischman and Juliette Bellocq. Next, Shane Butler's chapter, "What Was the Voice?," explores the rhetorical, etymological, and philosophical contributions of classical Greek and Latin literature to Western ideas about voice, and the ways those works have helped to shape recent understandings of antiquity itself. Butler notes that though it is today consumed primarily in print, this ancient literature was transmitted for centuries in oral form, and that its authorial voices may therefore be plural. Matt Rahaim's chapter, "Object, Person, Machine, or What: Practical Ontologies of Voice," examines the uncertainty that accompanies the recognition of diverse vocal practices and surrounding meaning-makings. Offering concrete examples in the setting of Mumbai, he explores the frameworks through which experiences and discourses construct voices. In "Singing High: Black Countertenors and Gendered Sound in Gospel Performance," Alisha Lola Jones addresses coconstructs of voice, race, and masculinity in the context of African American sacred singing. Focusing on the experiences and reception of high male voices in American black churches, her chapter discusses the ways in which high male voices affirm and challenge ideas about the performance of black masculinity, and about perceived relationships between race and music genre.

Part II: Changing Voice: Voice as Barometer

Because voice is made to perform, stand in for, and express values within a given society, it is a useful tool with which to take stock of these values, and also offers an opportunity to detect societal changes. In this way, we compare paying attention to what people make their voices do and what we believe about voice to licking a finger and sticking it in the air to determine the wind's direction. By paying attention to aesthetic values around vocal usage and timbre, voice is a useful barometer for broader movements within a given society. For example, what was considered an attractive feminine voice a century ago compared to now might constitute very different vocal performances. In this way, then, voice is made to express deep and broad values, and these values may be articulated and examined through the lens of vocal inquiry.

Valued by both medical practitioners and professional voice users, the work of Robert T. Sataloff has profoundly influenced American singing and voice pedagogy. In his chapter for this volume, "Medical Care of Voice Disorders," he and coauthor Mary J. Hawkshaw offer a summary of the physiological problems that may alter voice function, and discusses how changes in sound can facilitate diagnosis and treatment. In "Fluid Voices: Processes and Practices in Singing Impersonation," Katherine Meizel and voice scientist Ronald C. Scherer write about intentional changes of voice in the context of singing impersonation, and analyze the practices and sonic configuration in one performer's work. Tom McEnaney's chapter, "This American Voice: The Odd Timbre of a New Standard in Public Radio," addresses the phenomenon and implications of the voices on National Public Radio, focusing on their sonic characteristics. Contextualizing vocal tone, pitch, cadence, and timbre in radio history, as well as within aesthetic and political frameworks, McEnaney studies the processes that shape the reception of certain voices as representative of a "national" sound. In an analysis of two films starring Colin Firth in the chapter "The Voice of Feeling: Liberal Subjects, Music, and the Cinematic Speech," Dan Wang positions the emotional performance of dramatic speeches at the center of a "liberal togetherness, one in which a certain concept of the voice sustains and unites an idea of individual expressiveness with the promise of a collectivity magnetized by feeling."

Part III: Active Voice: Voice as Politics

Voice is also a tool used as an expression of active agency. It does not just passively express given values, but can also be actively used to push such values into the private and public realms through concerted vocal expression. Simultaneously, hegemonic vocal practices can also be rejected and refused—and, through this means, the power inherent in and represented by such vocal, social, and cultural practices may be undermined.

In this sense, voice functions both as a medium through which politics may be expressed, and as a currency in the negotiation process that takes place around values. To this end, Elias Krell offers an embodied theory of noise through a case of singer-songwriter Joe Stevens in his chapter "Trans/forming White Noise: Gender, Race, and Disability in the Music of Joe Stevens." The noise in Stevens's voice, Krell argues, encapsulates the sonic presence of social power structures imbricated in the singing of trans men. Both Krell's chapter and chapter 9 address ideas of power structure performed vocally. In his chapter, "Voice in Charismatic Leadership," Rosario Signorello proposes a set of vocal behaviors and perceptions that shape charismatic leadership in ways both universal and specific to different cultures. As Krell above in chapter 8, in "Challenging Voices: Relistening to Marshallese Histories of the Present," Jessica A. Schwartz and April L. Brown address ability and disability within the sounds of singing. Specifically, they discuss voice as a site of both hegemonic violence and resistance, in the singing of those affected by the history of nuclear testing in the Republic of the Marshall Islands—in particular, women and their families living in Arkansas today. Speech and persuasion figure in Shanara R. Reid-Brinkley's chapter, "Voice Dipped in Black: The Louisville Project and the Birth of Black Radical Argument in College Policy Debate," as well. In her case study of the University of Louisville's Malcolm X Debate Program for black students she documents the normativity of whiteness within debate competitions as well as civil society at large, discusses the courageous work of students who performed and competed against this dominant practice, and reflects on the complex reactions to this activist work.

Part IV: Sensing Voice: Voice as Multisensory Phenomenon

This section seeks to expand the concept of voice beyond the textual and the sonorous, two aspects that have constituted the major areas of inquiry into the voice within the humanistic and performing arts—the coeditors' broad home disciplines. It exemplifies inquiry into the extrasonorous voice and possible extravocal in the tactile, philosophical, scientific, biological, and evolutionary realms. Cornelia Fales addresses perceptions of the extrasonorous voice though her chapter, "Voiceness in Musical Instruments," which centers on the particular phenomenon of hearing traits of "voice," of embodied humanness, in the sounds made using musical instruments. In "The Evolution of Voice Perception," Katarzyna Pisanski and Gregory A. Bryant trace a history of listening to voices. From crying to speaking, they contextualize voice as a type of animal (human) behavior developed through adaptation. In "Acoustic Slits and Vocal Incongruences in Los Angeles Union Station," Nina Sun Eidsheim focuses on the importance of "negative space" (the spaces between structures) in the perception of voices. Through the example of the 2013 opera *Invisible Cities*, set in Los Angeles' Union Station, she demonstrates how listening to vocal acoustics can reveal information about the distribution of social space, about access, and about privilege. In the chapter "Tuning a Throat Song in Inner Asia: On the Nature of Vocal Gifts with People's *Xöömeizhi* of the Tyva Republic Valeriy Mongush (b. 1953)," on Tuvan "throat-singing," or *xöömei*, among nomadic herders, Robert O. Beahrs provides a theoretical framework of multivocality—and the ability of voice to "presence others in a relational ontology"—to situate a Tuvan cultural understanding of the relationships between language, life, soul, and nature.

Part V: Producing Voice: Vocal Modalities

Though other sections have also discussed vocal production, this section deals with modes and modulations of voice—alterations and additions in practice that create shifts in meaning. These changes may be effected through singing or speaking technique, or through technological mediation, and impact listening practices as well. In "The Echoing Palimpsest: Singing and the Experience of Time at the Ecumenical Patriarchate of Constantinople," Alexander K. Khalil discusses the act of realizing a written melody as a dialogue with past voices rendered present within the context of Ecumenical Patriarchate of Constantinople in Istanbul, Turkey. Khalil shows that this multi-layered, polyphonic experience of voice forms the context through which both personal and cultural identity are apprehended and re-negotiated. In "Laryngeal Dynamics of Taan Gestures in Hindustani Classical Singing," Nandhakumar Radhakrishnan, with Ronald C. Scherer and Santanu Bandyopadhyay, presents a physiological and aerodynamic analysis of a single vocal gesture that is iconic of North Indian classical singing, in two contexts. As *taan* is executed differently in performance practice and pedagogical training, the chapter details the mechanisms of each. Miriama Young also approaches the phenomenon of a voice sounding in separate contexts in her chapter "Proximity/Infinity: The Mediated Voice in Mobile Music." She investigates the complicated sense of intimacy conferred by microphones and headphone use, even in the experience of listening to a recording made as far away as outer space. Jennifer Fleeger's chapter, "When Robots Speak on Screen: Imagining the Cinemechanical Ideal," traces cinematic negotiations of ideas about humanity and technology, authenticity and artifice, about the envoicing of science-fiction souls in mechanical bodies. The robot voices at stake sound a set of fantasies and anxieties characteristic of the late twentieth and early twenty-first centuries, not only about what it means to be human, but also what it means to *be*.

Part VI: Negotiating Voice: Voice as Transaction

This section addresses situations in which voice—a particular vocal style, recognition, or rejection—is used in an exchange. Voice can function as a medium that expresses cultural value when performed in the expected way under a given set of circumstances. The success or failure of the outcome is dependent on the vocal quality or additional aspects of the performance. In these examples, vocal performance and presentation are—consciously or unconsciously, explicitly or implicitly—used in exchanges where the outcome pivots on the impact of the voice.

Like the last section, this one includes a discussion of technology, humanity, and the integrity of the soul—this time, though, in the context Turkey's *ezan* (call to prayer) and its controversial state centralization in the twenty-first century. In "Robot Imams! Standardizing, Centralizing, and Debating the Voice of Islam in Millennial Turkey," Eve McPherson writes about the resulting debates: "By manipulating the voice, technologically or otherwise, the state inserts itself as the interpreter of holy sound, and while some listeners celebrate the results, others do not." Voice here represents a transaction between citizen and state. Hyun Kyong Hannah Chang conducts her study, "Singing and Praying among Korean Christian Converts (1896–1915): A Trans-Pacific Genealogy of the Modern Korean Voice," in another *trans*actional religious setting, this time intersecting with the development of a *trans*-Pacific modernity. She examines the role of voice in turn-of-the-twentieth-century Korean culture, as it negotiated the growth of Christianity through the Million Movement. Chang uses voice to advance "a critical framework of modernity" that "renews our conception of the world's vocal cultures as practices constituted by complex and contested global relations." Jake Johnson addresses a different kind of transaction, in the relationship between Broadway as a tourism industry and the voices it sells. In his chapter, "Building the Broadway Voice," Johnson discusses how these voices have been critiqued as homogenized, though that process occurred first through a fusion of multiple generic styles. Johnson examines the ways in which musical theater pedagogy at the University of Cincinnati College Conservatory of Music has disciplined the singing Broadway body into a specific, *same* marketable sound.

Epilogue

As a conclusion to the chapters in this volume, Jody Kreiman, in her epilogue "Defining and Studying Voice across Disciplinary Boundaries," attempts to provide a preliminary foundation to support dialogues and promote mutual understanding between these two groups of scholars. This piece shows where these different scholarly traditions overlap, where they abut, and where they differ, with the goal of elucidating how these bodies of work might eventually combine as parts of a single discipline of "voice studies."

Methodologies and the Object of Voice

This volume is particularly concerned with methodology. Through our selection of contributions, we seek to exemplify a wide range of methodologies and analytical strategies. This was done in order to exhibit possibilities in voice scholarship and, more generally, to open up further possibilities across disciplines. Our decision was also based on observations regarding the connection between epistemology and ontology. While the relationship between them is a venerable philosophical question, we have not seen them exhaustively addressed in relation to voice. More specifically, in relation to the possibly impossible multifaceted, interdisciplinary topic of voice, these epistemological and ontological assumptions in practice form the disciplinary divides that we believe have forestalled some developments in vocal inquiry.

If the object of study comes into focus based on the methodological lens, different definitions of voice, or voice "objects"—the term used in the humanities to refer to those things that are investigated—are created. And, if different objects call for specific methodological treatments, the limit of knowledge is near. In short, these methodologically derived voice objects have led to an impasse that has created siloed areas of knowledge around voice. While the epistemological-ontological dilemma is not limited to the study of voice (see, for example, Annemarie Mol's deep insight into this topic in relation to the notion of illness [Mol 2003]), the object of voice is splintered and parsed, with each part incomplete without the others. However, because these delineations take place within the aforementioned isolated research areas, a partial understanding of the object takes on the definition of the object itself.

The solution is not to create an encyclopedia of scholarly and performative approaches to voice. Rather, this volume's goal is to provide explicit examples of the range, advantages, weaknesses, and limits of each approach, and to suggest potential connection points. Through an eclectic collection, we aim to place diverse approaches into conversation. We hope that each unique contribution will then come into clearer relief, and that the commonalities between very different and highly field-specific terminology and assumptions will be illuminated.

Synthesizing voice research from the humanities, performing arts, and social sciences to the sciences and medicine, we understand voice in the most general terms as the entanglement of six broad areas. These areas are akin to mini-universes built of epistemological and ontological assumptions, which in turn are built in opposition to each other. Each of these mini-universes carries its own centrifugal force made up of the limits, affordances, and contexts within which vocal activity takes place.

A Practical Note

Because within a truly interdisciplinary volume, authors are based in a number of scholarly traditions and conventions, we have strived to balance volume coherence while respecting distinct scholarly field's conventions with regards to citations as well as issues such as orthography and spelling. We have also deferred to individual authors' preferences regarding capitalization of identity terminology relevant to their own perspectives (e.g., "Black" or "black").

Notes

1. Joseph Faber first demonstrated his talking machine in Vienna in 1840. However, there was not much public interest at that time.
2. Additionally, in these years between the early Industrial Revolution and its subsequent effects, great ingenuity was accompanied by great fear as Europeans and Americans imagined the potential threat machines and their implications might pose to humanity, and vocal automatons both delighted and horrified those who saw and heard them. Voice, that innermost process, had been externalized through the application of scientific study, producing what seemed to be the expression of thoughts in an inanimate body unnaturally animated, as Frankenstein's monster was in Mary Shelley's 1818 novel. In fact, John Hollingshead, a London theatrical manager who saw Faber's machine, invoked *Frankenstein* in his description, guessing that Faber and his invention, with its "sepulchral voice," were "destined to live and die together" like Shelly's scientist and his monster (Hollingshead 1895, 68–9; quoted in Hankins and Silverman 1995, 214).
3. But the same fears of uncanniness and existential peril that surrounded the earlier vocal automatons continue to permeate our discourse. "Alexa and Google Home Are Getting Increasingly Creepy" (Tobitt 2017) read one headline in 2017, and "Amazon Has a Fix for Alexa's Creepy Laugh" (Liao 2018) another. The aunt of one of this volume's editors has repeatedly noted her Google Home device spontaneously speaking or responding to questions and comments not directed at it, and has referred to it as "freaky." Nevertheless, Amazon Echo (Alexa) and Google HomePod had sold more than 44 million units by January 2018 (Heatherington 2018). The automated voice, perhaps like our own embodied voices, represents a monster we have made but do not understand, which we at once love, fear, and cannot live without.

    Automated voices can be entirely programmed—as in Ingo Titze's 1992 operatic vocal model "Pavarobotti" (http://www.ncvs.org/videos.html), or the similarly named opera-singing robots described as a potential threat to "temperamental tenors" in 2017 (Sherwin 2017)—or, as in Vocaloid software (see Eidsheim 2009), other sampling libraries (see Meizel forthcoming a), and digital voices tailored to individuals who otherwise cannot speak aloud (Patel 2014), they can be created from originally embodied human voices. These technologies assist us in something more significant even than daily Internet searches or the democratization of music composition—they inspire us to question the place of voice in human nature, individual and cultural identities, and the value of human bodies and their labor. They prompt us to think about how voice is made and heard, sounded and silenced, to consider what voices means, and especially what it *is*. And they demonstrate, as did van Kempelen's Enlightenment-era automaton, the imaginative and practical progress possible when scientific, humanistic, and artistic work intersects.

4. For other reflections on the recent history of voice studies, see for example Dolan (2017), Feldman (2015), Meizel (forthcoming b), and Weidman (2015).

5. We obviously think that work beyond the Western world is equally important, so this and other references to scholarship in the West is a recognition of the limitations of the volume and the intellectual trajectories represented and presented and those omitted due to the editors' limited background.

6. Anthony Seeger's *Why Suyá Sing: A Musical Anthropology of an Amazonian People* (1987) is contemporary of Feld's study, but this work does not seem to have been picked up by voice studies scholars in the same way as Feld's work has been.

7. This voice studies overview and history is written from the authors' areas of expertise and we welcome further collaborations on more collective and integrated histories.

8. This parable has been attributed to an origin in India, but is referenced across multiple cultures and religions—for example, as early as the thirteenth century C.E., it appears in work by the Sufi poet Rumi. It has been used in numerous contexts in the natural sciences, humanities, and social sciences to describe the processes and products of academic research. In music, for example, Robert Cantrick applied it to the ethnomusicological study of popular music (Cantrick 1965); Anthony Seeger included it in his 2002 *Yearbook for Traditional Music* essay on comparative study (Seeger 2002); and Bruno Nettl notes it in his collection *Nettl's Elephant: On the History of Ethnomusicology* (Nettl 2010).

9. As with our three men, the scenarios here are more reductive than some of the studies within the fields mentioned. However, the examples are well within the bounds of reality.

10. Some colleagues who have kindly read drafts of the introduction have made the observation that it is only possible to see the limiting effect of field-held assumptions if not oneself holding those assumptions; hence that opening up between fields can only take place over generations. We respectfully do not hold the same view. Sometimes insights take place in a flash, and this volume hopes to provide such a source of energy.

WORKS CITED

Barthes, Roland. 1977. "The Grain of the Voice." In *Image, Music, Text*, essays selected and translated by Stephen Heath, 179–89. New York: Hill and Wang.

Bergeron, Katherine. 2010. *Voice Lessons: French Mélodie in the Belle Epoque*. Oxford: Oxford University Press.

Brooks, Daphne A. 2013. "Bring the Pain: Post-Soul Memory, Neo-Soul Affect, and Lauryn Hill in the Black Public Sphere." In *Taking It to the Bridge: Music as Performance*, edited by Nicholas Cook and Richard Pettengill, 180–203. Ann Arbor: University of Michigan Press.

Butler, Shane. 2015. *The Ancient Phonograph*. New York: Zone Books.

Cantrick, Robert B. 1965. "The Blind Men and the Elephant: Scholars on Popular Music." *Ethnomusicology* 9 (2): 100–14.

Cavarero, Adriana. 2005. *For More Than One Voice: Toward a Philosophy of Vocal Expression*. Translated by Paul A. Kettman. Redwood City, CA: Stanford University Press.

Chion, Michel. 1994. *Audio-Vision: Sound on Screen*. Translated by Claudia Gorbman. New York: Columbia University Press.

Connor, Steven. 2000. *Dumbstruck: A Cultural History of Ventriloquism*. Oxford: Oxford University Press.

Connor, Steven. 2014. *Beyond Words: Sobs, Hums, Stutters and Other Vocalizations*. London: Reaktion Books.

Cruz, Jon. 1999. *Culture on the Margins: The Black Spiritual and the Rise of American Cultural Interpretation*. Princeton, NJ: Princeton University Press.

Cusick, Suzanne G. 1999. "On Musical Performances of Gender and Sex." In *Audible Traces: Gender, Identity and Music*, edited by Elaine Barkin and Lydia Hamessley, 25–48. Los Angeles: Carciofoli Verlagshaus.

Davies, James Q. 2014. *Romantic Anatomies of Performance*. Berkeley: University of California Press.

Dillon, Emma. 2012. *The Sense of Sound: Musical Meaning in France, 1260-1330*. Oxford: Oxford University Press.

Dolan, Emily I. 2017. "A Note from the Guest Editor." *Opera Quarterly* 33 (3–4): 203–6.

Dolar, Mladen. 2006. *A Voice and Nothing More*. Cambridge, MA: The MIT Press.

Duchan, Joshua S. 2012. *Powerful Voices: The Musical and Social World of Collegiate A Cappella*. Ann Arbor: University of Michegan Press.

Dunn, Lesley, and Nancy Jones. 1997. *Embodied Voices: Representing Female Vocality in Western Culture*.

Eidsheim, Nina Sun. 2009. "Synthesizing Race: Towards an Analysis of the Performativity of Vocal Timbre," *TRANS-Transcultural Music Review* 13 (7). https://www.sibetrans.com/trans/articulo/57/synthesizing-race-towards-an-analy.

Eidsheim, Nina Sun. 2015. *Sensing Sound: Singing and Listening as Vibrational Practice*. Durham, NC: Duke University Press.

Eidsheim, Nina Sun. 2019. *The Race of Sound: Listening, Timbre, and Vocality in African American Music*. Durham, NC: Duke University Press.

Fales, Cornelia. 2002. "The Paradox of Timbre." *Ethnomusicology* 46 (1): 56–95.

Feld, Steven. 1990 [1982]. *Sound and Sentiment: Birds, Weeping, Poetics, and Song in Kaluli Expression*. 2nd ed. Philadelphia: University of Pennsylvania Press.

Feld, Steven, Aaron A. Fox, Thomas Porcello, and David Samuels. 2004. "Vocal Anthropology: From the Music of Language to the Language of Song." In *A Companion to Linguistic Anthropology*, edited by A. Duranti, 321–45. Malden, MA: Blackwell.

Feldman, Martha. 2014. *The Castrato: Reflections on Natures and Kinds*. Berkeley: University of California Press.

Feldman, Martha. 2015. "The Interstitial Voice: An Opening." *Journal of the American Musicological Society* 68 (3): 653–8.

Frühholz, Sascha and Pascal Belin. 2019. *The Oxford Handbook of Voice Perception*. Oxford: Oxford University Press.

Genuth, Iddo, and Chuck Jorgensen. 2006. "Subvocal Speech—Speaking Without Saying a Word." The Future of Things, October 12. http://thefutureofthings.com/3021speaking-without-saying-a-word/.

Gregory, Peter N. 2001. "Describing the Elephant: Buddhism in America." *Religion and American Culture: A Journal of Interpretation* 11 (2): 233–63.

Goldin-Perschbacher, Shana. 2007. 'Not with You but of You': 'Unbearable Intimacy' and Jeff Buckley's Transgendered Vocality." In *Oh Boy! Masculinities and Popular Music*, edited by Freya Jarman-Ivens, 213–33. New York: Routledge.

Goldin-Perschbacher, Shana. 2015. "TransAmericana: Gender, Genre, and Journey." *New Literary History* 46 (4): 775–803.

Hankins, Thomas L., and Robert J. Silverman. 1995. *Instruments and the Imagination.* Princeton, NJ: Princeton University Press.

Harkness, Nicholas. 2014. *Songs of Seoul: An Ethnography of Voice and Voicing in Christian South Korea.* Berkeley: University of California Press.

Heatherington, James. 2018. "Best Smart Speaker: Amazon Alexa Reportedly Beating Apple's Homepod in Smart Homes." *Newsweek*.com, April 19. http://www.newsweek.com/best-smart-speaker-amazon-alexa-crushing-apples-homepod-smart-homes-892313.

Hollingshead, John. 1895. *My Lifetime.* Vol. 1. Lndon: Sampson, Low, Marston.

Hirschkind, Charles. 2006. *The Ethical Soundscape: Cassette Sermons and Islamic Counterpublics.* New York: Columbia University Press.

Jacobsen, Kristina M. 2017. *The Sound of Navajo Country: Music, Language, and Diné Belonging.* Chapel Hill: University of North Carolina Press.

Jarman-Ivens, Freya. 2011. *Queer Voices: Technologies, Vocalities, and the Musical Flaw.* New York: Palgrave McMillan.

Kleege, Georgina. 2010. "Blindness and Visual Culture: An Eyewitness Account." In *The Disability Studies Reader.* 3rd ed., edited by Lennard Davis, 522–30. New York: Routledge.

Koestenbaum, Wayne. 1993. *The Queen's Throat: Opera, Homosexuality, and the Mystery of Desire.* New York: Poseidon.

Kreiman, Jody, and Diana Sidtis. 2011. *Foundations of Voice Studies: An Interdisciplinary Approach to Voice Production and Perception.* Malden, MA: Blackwell.

Krell, Elias. 2013. "Contours Through Covers: Voice and Affect in the Music of Lucas Silveira." *Journal of Popular Music Studies* 25 (4): 476–503.

Krell, Elias. 2015. "'Who's the Crack Whore the End?' Performance, Violence, and Sonic Borderlands in the Music of Yva las Vegass." *Text and Performance Quarterly* 35 (2–3): 95–118.

LaBelle, Brandon. 2014. *Lexicon of the Mouth: Poetics and Politics of Voice and the Oral Imaginary.* New York: Bloomsbury Academics.

Liao, Shannon. 2018. "Amazon Has a Fix for Alexa's Creepy Laugh." TheVerge.com, March 7. https://www.theverge.com/circuitbreaker/2018/3/7/17092334/amazon-alexa-devices-strange-laughter.

Lordi, Emily J. 2013. *Black Resonance: Iconic Women Singers and African American Literature.* New Brunswick, NJ: Rutgers University Press.

Marshall, Caitlin. 2014. "Crippled Speech." Edited by Nina Sun Eidsheim and Annette Schlichter, *Postmodern Culture* 24 (3). http://muse.jhu.edu/article/589570.

McKay, George. 2013. *Shakin' All Over: Popular Music and Disability.* Ann Arbor: University of Michigan Press.

McPherson, Eve. 2005. "The Turkish Call to Prayer: Correlating the AcousticDetails of Vocal Timbre with Cultural Phenomena." *Proceedings of the Conference of Interdisciplinary Musicology*, Montréal, Canada, March 10–12.

McPherson, Eve, Sandra McPherson, Roger Bouchard, and Robert Heath Meeks. 2014. "Some Meanings of the Islamic Call to Prayer: A Combined Qualitative and Quantitative Analysis of Some Turkish Narratives." *Narrative Matters 2014: Narrative Knowing/Récit et Savoir*, edited by Sylvie Patron and Brian Schiff. Paris: Université Paris Diderot.

Meizel, Katherine. 2011. "A Powerful Voice: Investigating Vocality and Identity." *A World of Voice: Voice and Speech across Culture* 7(1): 267–75.

Meizel, Katherine. Forthcoming a. *Multivocality: An Ethnography of Singing on the Borders of Identity.* Oxford: Oxford University Press.

Meizel, Katherine. Forthcoming b. "Sound Studies and Voice Studies." In *Theory for Ethnomusicology*, edited by Harry Berger and Ruth M. Stone. New York: Routledge.

Mills, Mara. 2010. "Deaf Jam: From Inscription to Reproduction to Information." *Social Text* *102* 28 (1): 35–58.

Mills, Timothy, H. Timothy Bunnell, and Rupal Patel. 2014. "Towards Personalized Speech Synthesis for Augmentative and Alternative Communication." *Augmentative and Alternative Communication* 30 (3): 226–36.

Mol, Annemarie. 2003. *The Body Multiple: Ontology in Medical Practice*. Durham, NC: Duke University Press.

Nancy, Jean-Luc. *Listening*. Translated by Charlotte Mandell. New York: Fordham University Press, 2007.

Nettl, Bruno. 2010. *Nettl's Elephant: On the History of Ethnomusicology*. Urbana: University of Illinois Press.

Ochoa Gautier, Ana María. 2014. *Aurality: Listening & Knowledge in Nineteenth-Century Colombia*. Durham, NC: Duke University Press.

Olwage, Grant. 2004. "The Class and Colour of Tone: An Essay on the Social History of Vocal Timbre." *Ethnomusicology Forum* 13 (2): 203–26.

Owen, Adrian M., Martin R. Coleman, Melanie Boly, Matthew H. Davis, Steven Laureys, and John. D. Pickard. 2006. "Detecting Awareness in the Vegetative State." *Science* 313 (5792): 1402.

Patel, Rupal. 2014. "Everything You Need to Know About Donating Your Voice: Why You Should Help The Human Voicebank Initiative." TedBlog, February 13.https://blog.ted.com/everything-you-need-to-know-about-donating-your-voice-why-you-should-help-the-human-voicebank-initiative/.

Poizat, Michel. 1992. *The Angel's Cry: Beyond the Pleasure Principle in Opera*. Translated by Arthur Denner. Ithaca, NY: Cornell University Press.

Potter, John. 2006 [1998]. *Vocal Authority: Singing Style and Ideology*. Cambridge: Cambridge University Press.

Rahaim, Matthew. 2012. *Musicking Bodies: Gesture and Voice in Hindustani Music*. Middletown, CT: Wesleyan University Press.

Seeger, Anthony. 1987. *Why Suyá Sing: A Musical Anthropology of an Amazonian People*. Cambridge: Cambridge University Press.

Seeger, Anthony. 2002. "A Tropical Meditation on Comparison in Ethnomusicology: A Metaphoric Knife, a Real Banana and an Edible Demonstration." *Yearbook for Traditional Music* 34: 187–92.

Shepherd, John, and Peter Wicke. 1997. *Music and Cultural Theory*. Malden, MA: Blackwell.

Sherwin, Adam. 2017. "Meet Pavarobotti—First Robot Opera is Bad News for Temperamental Tenors." *Inews*.co.uk, June 9. https://inews.co.uk/essentials/meet-pavarobotti-first-robot-opera-bad-news-temperamental-tenors/.

Sterne, Jonathan. 2003. *The Audible Past: Cultural Origins of Sound Reproduction*. Durham, NC: Duke University Press.

Stras, Laurie. 2006. "The Organ of the Soul: Voice, Damage and Affect." In *Sounding Off: Theorizing on Disability in Music*, edited by Neil Lerner and Joseph Straus, 173–84. New York: Routledge.

Titze, Ingo. 1996. "What is Vocology?" *Logopedics Phoniatrics Vocology* 21 (1): 5–6.

Tobitt, Charlotte. 2017. "Alexa and Google Home Are Getting Increasingly Creepy and Even Comlimenting Each Other." *Ibitimes*.co.uk, December 28.https://www.ibtimes.co.uk/alexa-google-home-are-getting-increasingly-creepy-even-complimenting-each-other-1652926.

Tonelli, Christopher. 2016. "Ableism and the Reception of Improvised Soundsinging." *Music & Politics* X(2): 1–14.

Utz, Christian, and Frederick Lau. 2013. "Introduction: Voice, Identities, and Reflexive-Globalization in Contemporary Music Practices." *Vocal Music and Contemporary Identities: Unlimited Voices in East Asia and the West*. New York: Routledge. 1–24.

Weidman, Amanda. 2006. *Singing the Classical, Voicing the Modern: The Postcolonial Politics of Music in South India*. Durham, NC: Duke University Press.

Weidman, Amanda. 2015. "Voice." In *Keywords in Sound Studies*, ed. David Novak and Matt Sakakeeny, 232–45. Durham, NC: Duke University Press, 2015.

Weiss, Jason. 2006. *Steve Lacy: Conversations*. Durham, NC: Duke University Press.

Zemp, Hugo (ed.). *Les Voix du Monde*. 1996. Collection du Centre dela Recherche Scientifique et du Musée de L'Homme, CD CMX 374 1010.12.

How would you define voice?	What is a "beautiful" voice?	What role(s) does voice fulfill for you in your art?	How does voice figure in your sense of identity?	What is the relationship for you between your body and your voice?	How do you think the experiences of hearing a voice and seeing the vocalist might affect each other?	How do you think public expectations of voice have changed since you began writing and performing?
An instrument to communicate with sounds.	A truthful voice.	Adding sounds to what I am communicating.	Voice reflects your emotion, your age, your experience, your health, and your understanding of the past and your hope for the future.	Voice gives me precisely what my body condition is at the time.	Voice can give you an independent experience from the visual of the vocalist. They do not necessarily affect each other.	Not much.

FRONTISPIECE. What Is Voice? Yoko Ono (with Juliette Bellocq and Jessica Fleischmann).

hat is the lationship r you between ice and nguage? hen you eak/perform different nguages, what anges, and hat stays the me?	What are the purposes of the extreme vocal sounds in your work (whispering, screaming, coughing, etc.)?	What are the limitations of voice?	What are the differences/ similarities between your voice on stage and your voice in other parts of your life?	What is the relationship between voice and silence?	How has your understanding of voice changed over time?	In 2010, you performed "Voice Piece for Soprano" at MoMA—how have your performances of that instruction piece changed since 1961?
ach language s its ique vocal flection.	**I don't think there is any set purpose for any of the expressions. It happens. And when it does, it expresses whatever emotion or intention it expresses.**	**It depends on your physical health.**	**Stage voice needs a good mike. I am sure sometimes we wish we had a good mike to speak in other parts of our lives!**	**Silence can give the rest the voice needs.**	**Now, I am not afraid of my voice going through many changes according to my emotional stage at the time.**	**Nothing changed except I had more of an audience this time. In 1961, it was for me and for my friends. Now, it is for the world.**

PART I

FRAMING VOICE

VOICE AS A CARRIER
OF MEANING

CHAPTER 1

....

WHAT WAS THE VOICE?

....

SHANE BUTLER

GIVEN that one of the stated aims of the present volume is to ask, if not definitively to answer, the question of what a voice *is*, it may be useful to pause to ask the same question in the past tense, specifically about classical antiquity—birthplace of many of the Western theories and practices of the voice that subsequent ages would inherit, adapt, and contest. Needless to say, this chapter cannot provide a survey of all that a voice could be or do in the ancient world, a vast task for any era. Our focus will be instead on antiquity's contribution to the idea of the voice, especially in relation to both spoken and written language. This narrow aim will lead us to say less than some readers might expect about music and song, though we shall begin with these. From there we shall proceed through terminology, philosophy, rhetoric (which will constitute a large part of our discussion), and pantomime. We shall conclude with some brief thoughts about the role of the voice in our idea of antiquity itself.

SIREN-SONGS

....

It is one of the key ironies of the classical tradition that it has led us to ground the history of Western "literature" (from Latin *litterae*, the "letters" of the alphabet and thus any "text" made thereof) in the *Iliad* and the *Odyssey*, that is, in works originally composed and transmitted orally, well before they took written form. Before and after their eventual transcription, the epics attributed to Homer—whose very existence, like his blindness, may be entirely fictitious—were performed by professional singers, accompanied by the lyre, and, later, by unaccompanied reciters known as rhapsodes, literally "sewers of songs," reflecting the tradition's origins in oral (re)composition and improvisation.[1] The role of these performers in the production and preservation *of* the poems is repeatedly reflected *within* the poems, most literally through the presence of actual singers, like the character Phemius, who sings, in the first book of the *Odyssey*, of the return home of the Greek heroes, until Penelope asks him to stop, or Demodocus, who sings three songs while Odysseus is a guest in the court of the Phaeacians (Homer, *Odyssey* 1.153–5, 325–44; 8.75–82, 266–366, 499–520). The most intriguing stand-ins for the singer, however, arguably are to be found in the *Odyssey*'s Sirens, who claim to know all that happened at Troy, suggesting, in effect, that they are about to sing something like the *Iliad* (12.184–91). The *Odyssey* skips the song itself, leaving the Homeric performer's own audience in the position of Odysseus's crew, whose ears had been stopped with wax. They, like us, are left to wonder whether it is the Sirens' story (which their one listener, Odysseus, firmly tied to his ship's mast, already knows well), their music, or their voices that bewitch, luring countless earlier sailors to certain death. Might their appeal even have resided precisely in the way in which their singing voices both did and *did not* tell a story, since, as Wayne Koestenbaum notes, "singing is a barricade of codes" (1993, 157), concealing even as it reveals?[2]

Our own inability to hear the Sirens' song could be said to be emblematic of our relationship to ancient singing voices generally, inaudible either because their songs were never written down, as must be the case with all but a tiny fraction of ancient song culture, or because their songs were written down but subsequently were lost, or because, as is the case with almost everything that does survive, including Homer, we have the words that were sung but not their music, beyond their meter, the natural pitches of the Greek vowels, and the language's pitch-based system of accent. Nor, certainly, do we have access to the voice of a real, live, ancient singer or even speaker—despite the fantastic suggestion of Charles Sanders Peirce that given "only a hundred more centuries" of scientific progress, we shall discover "that the sound waves of Aristotle's voice have somehow recorded themselves" (Peters 2003, 409–410).[3] To be clear, enormous strides have been made, including very recently, in the reconstruction of some ancient music, in part from the ongoing discovery and decipherment of examples of ancient musical notation, but our knowledge will never be complete.[4] What is striking, however, is the fact that lost singing voices—those of the Sirens—appeared as obscure objects of desire (and terror) already in the sung epics that unwittingly launched the classical tradition we inherit in its fragmentary textual state. From the beginning, in other words, and not just from our own belated point of view, the voice could mark an aural vanishing point, just out of earshot. For an ancient live audience, this voice that cannot be heard seems designed precisely to call attention to the one ever-present in the Siren-singing of the Homeric singer himself. But what of eventual readers with no such singer in easy reach?

For an answer, let us switch briefly from Greece to Rome. "I sing of arms and the man" (*arma virumque cano*): so begins the epic of Homer's greatest Latin imitator, Virgil, echoing the opening words of the *Iliad*, "Sing, Goddess, of the wrath." But while the *Aeneid* might be read aloud by trained "readers" (*lectores*) and famously was given moving readings to the imperial family by Virgil himself, this epic, unlike its Homeric models, was never meant to be sung (that is, its delivery would have been metrical but not otherwise musical).[5] Its first verb, however, like the general ancient tendency to call even unsung poetry "song," reflects more than a quaint habit that harkens back to the rhapsodic and other origins of poetic practice. Rather, it points—just as the written Homer's verb would come to point—to the text's own claim to be not just a linguistic artifact, but one both musical and, even more insistently, vocal. As we later shall see, ancient prose texts likewise made a vocal claim; indeed, in the section after the next, we shall adopt the expedient of setting aside, for the limited purposes of this chapter, the musical complexities of poetry in favor of the somewhat (though not entirely) more straightforward case of prose. (We shall return briefly to Virgil in a final section.) First, however, let us follow the question of the voice's presence in and as language, including its presence in and as a written text, into the ancient languages themselves, and then into various schools of ancient philosophy.

THE ANCIENT VOICE, IN THEORY

Consider, as a simple introduction to ancient vocal thinking, the principal Greek and Latin words for "voice." These were, respectively, *phōnē* and *vox*, each of which includes the ordinary range of meanings of the English word "voice," for which the latter is, of course, the etymological root, just as the former is deployed in nineteenth-century coinages for new vocal technologies like "telephone" and "phonograph." Their complexity, however, begins to emerge when we consider what *else* they designate. *Phōnē* can, for example, be used for a wide range of sounds not produced by humans or animals, but more importantly, its primary meaning in ordinary usage is not "voice" but "speech," that is, spoken human language. This is not the normal case with *vox*, which surprises the English-speaker with, instead, its frequent use to designate a single "word," including a written word, which is why we still sometimes cite dictionary articles *s. v.* or *sub voce*, indicating under which word entry the relevant information is to be found. In other words, translating "voice" into Greek and Latin gives us such a range of meanings that our question might well become, "What was the (ancient) voice *not*?" And the acuteness of the problem becomes especially evident if we narrow our focus to the speaking voice, regarding which one might be inclined to define the voice as something that enables speech but that is distinct from it, indeed, as something that becomes most audible when it is superfluous to or dissonant from speech. But try saying that in Greek, using only *phōnē*. And built into Latin is a similarly confusing obstacle to understanding the voice as the physical medium of speech, comparable to the media of written texts, since transcribed speech will still be made entirely of "voices," that is, "words" (*voces*).

To be sure, classical writers were hardly unaware of these ambiguities, nor were they unable or unwilling to use other terms in order to distinguish the voice from spoken or written language. Aristotle, for example, uses *dialektos* or *logos* for "speech" when contrasted with *phōnē* in the meaning of "voice" (*History of Animals* 4.9.535a.; *Politics* 1.1253a). And as an alternative to *vox* (and the cognate *vocabulum*), Latin had recourse to an even more ordinary word for "word," *verbum* (though it may be useful to note that this was sometimes supposed to derive from *verberare* and thus originally to have designated not an abstract linguistic concept but the "striking" either of air or of a listener's ear, as noted by Augustine, *De dialectica* 6).[6] Despite these clarifications, however, the fact that the classical languages' two primary words for "voice," *phōnē* and *vox*, themselves resist efforts to define the voice by distinguishing (linguistic) form from matter is something that remains extremely suggestive. Indeed, this resistance actually increases if we try to push beyond Greek and Latin to Proto-Indo-European, their reconstructed common ancestor. *Phōnē* derives from the hypothesized root **bhā-*, "to speak," source also of the regular Greek verb for speaking, *phēmi*; so too does *vox* derive from a root meaning "to speak," **wekʷ-*, source also of another Greek word for "voice," *ops*, as well as of *epos*, the Greek word for "word" that gives "epic" its name (Watkins 2011, 7, 100).[7] What all of this suggests is a kind of deep corollary to Derrida's deconstruction of what he calls "phono-logocentrism," the long philosophical tradition that privileges speech over writing on the seemingly common-sensical assumption that the latter is derivative of the former, even though, as Derrida shows, our very understanding of speech depends so heavily on the language and metaphors of writing as to suggest that writing is instead the primary idea, of which speech is really an afterthought (Derrida 1976). The vocal corollary is this: though we might be inclined to regard speech as something that emerges from the voice, it seems instead to be the voice that derives from speech—indeed, from the earliest words for speech, from speaking about speech. Of course, there is no question that humans had voices before they could speak, just as they could speak before the invention of writing. The question is whether, once humans began speaking, it would ever really be possible to speak about the voice without thinking about speech. The prehistoric origins of their own languages were as obscure to speakers of Greek and Latin as they are to most of us; nevertheless, their efforts to define the voice as distinct *from* speech, like our own, almost inevitably construct the voice as a kind *of* speech—originary, primitive, infantile, bestial, or even inanimate, but still expressive and even communicative in a way that is not distinct from language but, rather, something like language's essence.

Let us consider more closely Aristotle, for whom the voice was a question of recurring interest across a wide range of works. One of the fullest expressions of his views (which, like those on other topics, are not always consistent across his vast and varied *oeuvre*) comes in his treatise *On the Soul*, in which the "soul" of the title is not the disembodied entity described by his teacher Plato but, rather, the specific principles of life embodied in each kind of living thing. For Aristotle, the voice is always meaningful (else it is not a "voice"), even when it comes from a nonhuman animal, as he explains in this brief extract from the longer discussion:

> Voice (*phōnē*) is a kind of sound characteristic of what has soul in it; nothing that is without soul utters voice, it being only by a metaphor that we speak of the voice of the flute or the lyre... Voice then is the impact of the inbreathed air against the "windpipe," and the agent that produces the impact is the soul resident in these parts of the body. Not every sound, as we said, made by an animal is voice (even with the tongue we may merely make a sound which is not voice, or without the tongue as in coughing); what produces the impact must have soul in it and must be accompanied by an act of imagination, for voice is a sound *with a meaning*, and is not *merely* the result of any impact of the breath as in coughing.[8]

Aristotle approaches the same question with greater anatomical detail (though not always with full precision, especially regarding the placement of the "pharynx" and "larynx") in his *History of Animals*:

> Voice (*phōnē*) and sound (*psophos*) are different from one another; and language (*dialektos*) differs from voice and sound. The fact is that no animal can give utterance to voice except by the action of the pharynx, and consequently such animals as are devoid of lung have no voice; and language is the articulation of vocal sounds by the instrumentality of the tongue. Thus, the voice and larynx can emit vowel sounds (*phōnēenta*); consonantal sounds (*aphōna*) are made by the tongue and the lips; and out of these language is composed.   (Aristotle, *History of Animals* 4.9.535a–b)[9]

Animal anatomy is here at the service of a vivisection of language itself, for which the voice is found to be a necessary but not sufficient condition, like the "vowels" (*phōnēenta*, Latin *vocales*, whence our own word) to which it lends its name. Animals lack the anatomy, the resulting consonants, and, though not mentioned here, the human mind (*nous*) required for language; what we do not share makes what we do share—the voice—into a kind of incomplete speech.

Compare, from a very different philosophical tradition, an analogous attempt to relate human to animal voices by the poet Lucretius, Roman heir to the Greek thought of Epicurus. Rooting human language in the expressive sonic eruptions of the natural world, even as he seeks to distinguish language from such sounds, Lucretius plays along the way on the double meaning of *vox*:

> If, therefore, different sensations force even mute animals to produce different vocal sounds (*voces*), then how much more fitting is it that mortal man can mark (*notare*) distinct things with this or that word (*vox*)?
> (Lucretius, *On the Nature of Things* 5.1087–90)[10]

In Aristotle and Lucretius alike, despite their differences, the voice tends, teleologically, toward language, even in animals that anatomical or cognitive limitations keep forever mute (though neither silent nor, indeed, unimaginative). This is especially clear in Lucretius, where *notare*, the final word in the original Latin, makes human verbal pointing like writing, that is, the making of "marks" (*notae*). Giving as it takes away, philosophy bestows "voices" on animals but then makes these into little more than caricatures of human communication. At the same time, human sounds that do not work like language, such as Aristotle's troublesome cough, are banished from the very category of the voice.[11] This view provides the necessary context for understanding Aristotle's pithy definition, in his treatise *On Interpretation*, of language (*logos*) as *phōnē sēmantikē*, "signifying voice," which he carefully distinguishes *agrammatoi psophoi*, "noises that cannot be written down," including those made by animals, which may be meaningful (as he tells us in *On the Soul*) but are not the products of rational beings (1.4.16b; 2.16a). In the end, ancient philosophy drowns noisy voices of all kinds in two kinds of muteness: that of animals, in that they cannot speak, and that of humans, whose "signifying voice" survives its reincarnation as an inanimate text.[12]

An important though only partial exception can be found in Stoic thought, which exerted significant influence on the Late Antique "grammarians," teachers and writers on language and rhetoric, who would in turn shape much medieval thought on the voice's nature. Indeed, the bifurcated Stoic definition of the voice provides the opening words and point of departure for the more advanced of two rhetorical textbooks by Donatus, teacher of St. Jerome:

> A voice (*vox*) is air that has been struck and which, barring other factors, can be heard. Every voice is either articulate (*articulata*) or confused (*confusa*). An articulate voice is one that can be captured by the letters of the alphabet; a confused voice is one that cannot be written down.   (Donatus, *Ars grammatica [major]* 4.367 [ed. Keil])[13]

(This expansion of the ordinary meaning of *vox* is the result of its use here to translate the more malleable *phōnē* of the Greek sources of this Stoic tradition, where the subcategories are *enarthros*, "articulate," and *anarthros*, "inarticulate.") Needless to say, the lessons to follow would be devoted almost exclusively to the former, "articulate" voice. Nevertheless, the Late Antique grammarians preserve and expand remarkable lists of examples of the latter category, embracing everything from animal sounds to nonverbal human sounds, including musical sounds. Even here, however, the voice seems usually to be just on the verge of language. Cattle, for example, may not speak, but one can in fact approximate the sound they make with a (written) Latin word: *mugitus*, pronounced, of course, *moooooo-gitus*.

THE ANCIENT VOICE, RECORDED

For the ancient voice as something potentially not less but more than speech, we must look not to philosophy but to art. Despite the ubiquity of song (and of poetry called "song") in the ancient world, the paradigmatic vocal art for antiquity's elite was rhetoric, which provided the basis of their education and was crucial to their roles in public life. The narrowly "vocal" part of the art of rhetoric belonged to the category of "delivery" (*hupokrisis* in Greek, *actio* in Latin), which also included other aspects of embodied performance, like gesture. (Latin sometimes uses *pronuntiatio* specifically for the role of the voice, as distinct from gesture, in delivery.) Asked to name the three most important things in rhetoric, Demosthenes, the greatest of the Greek orators, famously replied, "Delivery, delivery, and delivery" (Cicero, *On the Orator* 3.213; *Orator* 56; *Brutus* 142). If delivery does not similarly dominate the extensive surviving pedagogical and technical literature on rhetoric, this is because, as the anonymous author of a Roman textbook, the *Rhetorica ad Herennium*, explains, it is a considerable undertaking "to express the movements of the body in words and to imitate voices in writing"; he has told us what he can, but necessarily "will leave the rest to proper practice" (3.27). Nevertheless, rhetorical works like this one provide our best ancient sources on vocal training and thus on the qualities expected from a practiced voice, here outlined as volume or intensity (*magnitudo*), strength or endurance (*firmitudo*), and flexibility (*mollitudo*) (3.20).

Beyond the basic training of the vocal instrument, the ancient manuals place considerable stress on matching delivery to subject matter and setting: "The most important thing...is to make the voice conform to the idea of the subjects on which we are speaking and to their corresponding emotional states," as Quintilian puts it in one of the longest surviving ancient discussions of the use of the voice (Quintilian, *The Orator's Education* 11.3.45). But while this principle clearly must have been the rule in actual practice, its emphasis in the manuals may also be a product of the role that texts of speeches, especially those by famous orators like Demosthenes and his Roman counterpart Cicero, came to have in rhetorical training. Much of Quintilian's advice is, in fact, about how to deduce from the (written) words of Cicero and others a logical form of delivery, knowing, for example, where to pause:

> Sometimes pauses without breathing are made within periods. "But in an assembly of the Roman people, performing an official function, in his capacity as master of the horse," etc., exhibits many segments (for it provides one thought, and then a different one, and so on) but just one period. Accordingly, we should pause briefly in the intervals, but the overall continuity should not be broken.   (11.3.39)

Poetry too provides useful examples of pauses, here from the first line of Virgil's *Aeneid*:

> *Arma virumque cano* is followed by a momentary suspension.   (11.3.36)

Tone as well can be deduced from the text, even phrase by phrase:

> Let us consider the beginning of Cicero's outstanding speech on behalf of Milo. Is it not the case that one's expression, though still on the same face, must be altered practically at every pause?   (11.3.47)

Quintilian's discussion of the Ciceronian passage soon turns from facial to vocal expressiveness, carefully detailing appropriate delivery. As these examples should already make clear, the rhetorical manuals, regarding the use of the voice, tend to present the art of speaking as an art of reading—itself a vocal art, since much reading in antiquity (just how much is a matter of controversy) was done aloud, either by solitary readers or by trained slaves or professionals.

The question, however, of the real, in-the-flesh voices of famous orators is rather more complicated. The natural voice of Demosthenes, for instance, reshaped by art, was an object of persistent interest in ancient rhetorical thought. First of all, we are told, he had overcome a speech defect by which he had been unable to pronounce the letter *r* (Cicero, *On the Orator*, 1.260). Later, he worked at breath capacity and control by filling his mouth with pebbles and reciting as many verses as he could on a single breath, while walking or climbing, and he boosted his power and volume by declaiming on the shore against the roar of the sea (1.261). Several authors repeat his quip about the supreme importance of delivery. But as Cicero himself remarks, an even more revealing anecdote is one about his rival Aeschines, who retired to Rhodes after failing in his prosecution of Ctesiphon for proposing an honorary crown for Demosthenes. Asked one day by the Rhodians to read his own speech from the trial, he complied, and he did the same the next day when urged to read instead Demosthenes' speech for the defense. Aeschines read the latter "in the most pleasing and powerful voice," and the resulting acclaim, Cicero reports, led him to inform the crowd, "You would be more astonished, had you heard the man himself" (3.213)![14] But Pliny the Younger preserves, in Greek, a slightly different, double-edged version of the sentence, one that strikes right at the heart of unwriteable embodied sound: "What if you had heard the beast himself?" (Pliny the Younger, *Letters* 2.310).

Where did such a voice leave the ancient reader? At least one, Valerius Maximus, was led by the story of Aeschines on Rhodes to a degree of despair:

> Regardless of how great an orator Aeschines himself was or how bitterly he had just opposed Demosthenes, he so looked up to the oratorical force and energy of his enemy that he declared himself an inadequate reader of his written texts, since he had known first hand the piercing power of his glance, the formidable severity of his expression, the sound of his voice, made to fit each individual word, and the purposeful movements of his body. Even if nothing can be added to his work, a large part *of* Demosthenes is nevertheless missing *in* Demosthenes, because he is read rather than heard   (Valerius Maximus, *Memorable Doings and Sayings* 8.10, ext.1).

Meditating on this same problem, however, Dionysius of Halicarnassus is more sanguine that the educated and sensitive reader can recreate the expressivity of Demosthenic delivery, including the emotive power of his voice, by following cues embedded in the content of each speech, on which he provides an extended lesson, analogous to that of Quintilian (Dionysius of Halicarnassus, *Demosthenes* 53–54). And regarding more formal matters, Cicero himself makes the revealing observation that the breath capacity of his famous counterpart was revealed by the length and complexity of his written periods, some of which contain "double raisings and lowerings of the voice" (Cicero, *On the Orator* 1.261). Any reader could see that sound and even hear it in the mind's ear, but it took one as good as Demosthenes (such as Cicero) to read it (aloud) properly. What Valerius, Dionysius, and Cicero seem to agree upon is this: when reading Demosthenes, one often heard, for better or worse, one's self.

The analogous case of Cicero's own oratory casts additional light on the relationship between voice, delivery, and text. In his *Brutus*, which provides, in the form of a fictitious dialogue, a historical survey of famous orators, up to Cicero himself, he pauses to provide a vocal self-portrait as a young man:

> Now since you seem to want to know me not just from a particular mole or my baby-rattle, but on the basis of my whole body, I shall embrace a few matters which may seem less important. Back then I had a body that was extremely thin and weak,

with a long and slender neck—a physical make-up not thought to be remote from mortal risk, once one adds physical exertion and strain on the lungs. Further increasing the worry of those who cared about me was the fact that I pronounced everything without decreasing or varying my intensity, with maximum straining of my voice and whole body. Even so, when both friends and doctors urged me to stop trying cases, I thought any risk worth taking rather than giving up on success as an orator. But when I decided that, by relaxing and moderating my voice and by a change in oratorical style, I could simultaneously avoid mortal danger and speak in a more balanced way, this was the reason—to change my oratorical habits—that I left for the East.   (Cicero, *Brutus* 313–314)[15]

Cicero consulted teachers and trainers in Greece, Asia Minor, and Rhodes; he then returned to Rome to resume his career:

Thus did I better myself in two years' time: not only more trained, but practically a changed man. For my excessive vocal strain had eased, my speaking style had cooled off, my lungs had gained strength, and my body, a bit of weight.   (Cicero, *Brutus* 316)

Here ends the account, though not Cicero's vocal education, since we know, for example, that he also took advice from famous actors (Plutarch, *Cicero* 5.3).

Seven years after his return to Rome, Cicero prepared his retrained voice to face that of the man who was then Rome's most celebrated orator, Hortensius, whose death twenty years later would frame the discussion in the *Brutus*, where Cicero somewhat cagily remembers his voice as "musical and pleasant" (303). In fact, Hortensius's delivery attracted fierce fans and foes alike; when one of the latter compared him to a famous dancing girl, Hortensius is said to have retorted, "in a soft and gentle voice," that this was better than what his accuser was, namely, a "Museless" brute (Aulus Gellius, *Attic Nights* 1.5.3). Cicero, as prosecutor, would win the case against the corrupt provincial governor Verres, defended by Hortensius, to enormous acclaim, but neither advocate's voice had anything to do with the result: Verres fled into exile after the presentation of the evidence in trial's initial phase, depriving Cicero of the opportunity of delivering most of the surviving *Verrine Orations* in court. Instead, Cicero "published" these—that is, he circulated written copies from which were made more copies, and so on. Hortensius published his oratory too, but it is no accident that none of his speeches have survived: Quintilian, who could still read them, complained that "his written texts fall so short of his reputation ... that it seems clear that people liked something when he spoke that we, as readers, do not find" (Quintilian, *The Orator's Education* 11.3.8). Not so Cicero, whose voice, for Quintilian and for countless other readers, seems to come through loud and clear.

Certainly, Cicero was hardly the first orator to exploit successfully the text as a vocal medium. The rhetorical text's claim that it could, under the right conditions, embody the voice had been there from the beginning, which is why, for example, it made sense to circulate written copies of speeches by Demosthenes, even though he insisted on the triply supreme importance of delivery. Nevertheless, Cicero does represent a culmination and, crucially, translation into Latin of this tradition. Two factors establish what we can call the "vocal claim" of Ciceronian texts. The first lies in his exploitation, imitating and surpassing that by Demosthenes in Greek, of sonic features that could be encoded directly in a Latin text, from simple matters like alliteration to a vast, complex system of "prose rhythm" that applied particular quantitative cadences called *clausulae* to the ends of phrases and sentences. (Regarding the latter, one cadence especially favored by Cicero, exemplified by the phrase *esse videatur*, came to be heard as such a signature part of his written voice that some orators, derided by Quintilian, thought they could sound like him simply by peppering their speeches with it; 10.2.18.) The second factor is one we already have encountered: Cicero adopted and, through his theoretical writings, further solidified the authority of the principle that vocal delivery should be a logical consequence of what was being said. Naturally, this principle depended on the presence of "media players" carefully programmed to generate more or less the same delivery from the same script: these reliably were produced, generation after generation, by rhetorical curricula soon based overwhelmingly on texts of Cicero's own speeches. To be sure, Cicero and his successors were well aware of vocal virtues that could not be represented in writing and that thus could only be appreciated *viva voce*; hence the complaint of Valerius. But this was scarcely reason to shake what had become a deep ancient habit that would be key to antiquity's ongoing legacy to vocal thinking, up to and including the present. And this consisted in a widespread assumption that the most important questions about what a voice is and does—including questions about what makes a voice moving or beautiful—could be answered on the basis of recorded voices, especially the famous voices of the dead.

WHOSE VOICE?

It should at once be said that not all ancient ears devoted this much attention to recorded voices, not least because only a fraction of the ancient population at any given time was literate. Even among educated readers of oratory, the views of Dionysus, Cicero, and Quintilian amounted to only one perspective (albeit the prevailing one), distinct from that of Valerius, for example, mourning what he could not hear of Demosthenes. Beyond oratory, other performing arts offered still other competing perspectives. Let us close with a curious anecdote about an encounter between one of those performing arts—a lost one, in fact—and two giants of the classical literary tradition.

The first giant is Virgil, who, before "arms and the man," sang instead of the lives and loves of singing shepherds. "On a delicate pipe I shall exercise the country Muse," as he himself puts it in his sixth *Eclogue*, subject of our anecdote. The poem offers a remarkable tangle of nested voices, as the author-narrator we have just heard channels the Muses in order to tell of shepherds who seize the sleeping Silenus, a regular companion of Bacchus in his revels. The shepherds force him to sing a long song that begins with the origins of the world and proceeds through stories from myth, like the disappearance of

Hylas, whose companions seek him by shouting his name, echoed back by the shore—all mostly recounted, by the author-narrator, in indirect discourse, periodically interrupted by direct speech that blends his own voice with that of Silenus, and the latter's with those of the characters in his own song. If the Homeric poems require the rhapsode singing them to ventriloquize storytelling characters within the poem, then Virgil's thrown voices take the same device to new levels of disorienting complexity. And literary scholars are surely right to find part of the reason for this in Virgil's own sense of belatedness to the poetic traditions he is inheriting, translating, and adapting, for the stories he tells us in the *Eclogues* are ones he himself has "heard," that is, read, from Theocritus, Callimachus, Apollonius, and others.[16]

But this very literary game must be balanced against the report that this particular *Eclogue* was performed in Rome, to great acclaim, by the pantomime Cytheris, called Lycoris in poems by her lover Gallus and in Virgil's own final *Eclogue*. Etymologically speaking, a pantomime "imitates everything"; this extremely popular but, for us, obscure ancient art form combined and transcended acting, dancing, and recitation or singing, sometimes (especially to disapproving eyes) with an erotic twist. The connection of ancient pantomime to a surviving text is precious evidence, and in this regard scholars have seen in Virgil's sixth *Eclogue* not the muffled literary sounds of translated and indirectly reported Greek voices but a script for virtuosic whole-body performance, replete with complex vocal hijinks. In other words, the voice's elusiveness in the text would have made its presence on the stage even more electrifying.

It is here that we meet the anecdote's other literary giant, for we are told that none other than Cicero himself was in the audience for this command performance—indeed, that it left him "stunned" (*stupefactus*) (Servius, on Virgil, *Eclogues* 6.11). This part of the story, preserved by an ancient commentator on Virgil's poetry, seems rather unlikely to be true, since Virgil's ancient biographers (who, admittedly, are also rather unreliable) place the beginning of his work on the *Eclogues* slightly after the orator's grisly death and their collected publication later still. Indeed, Cicero's presence certainly is reported and probably was invented precisely out of pious disbelief that Latin literature's two most important figures could have overlapped in Rome, however briefly, without coming into contact. That said, Cicero knew and several times mentions a pantomime named Cytheris, sometimes called Volumnia, who either could be the same one of the story or could have lent her name to it (Cicero, *Philippics* 2.58, 13.3; *Letters to His Friends* 9.26.2; *Letters to Atticus* 15.8.1). What makes the anecdote revealing is not its basis (or not) in truth but, rather, the plausibility that enabled it to circulate. Nowhere is this more striking than in the words it puts into the orator's mouth, which have him ask the name of the poet, whom he then calls "another hope of a great Rome"—another, that is to say, after himself. Cicero's self-serving pronouncement is no less arrogant than his question. "Whose is it?" asks one author of another, eliding the performance and the (female) body, voice, and shifting names of its performer, reduced to the incidental media of a fortuitous meeting of two great Roman minds. As reassuring as it is to know that the episode has probably been invented, it nevertheless provides us with a painfully telling emblem of the triumph of the authorial (and authoritative) voice over all others. The apotheosis of Cicero and Virgil as nothing less than vocal avatars of a personified Rome requires the sacrifice of Cytheris, or at least the forgetting of her, as well as that of count-less other voices that remain, of course, entirely unnamed. Her gender, to risk an under-statement, was no small factor in this silencing, but so too could the "soft and gentle" voice of a powerful, elite Roman man like Hortensius wind up on the cutting-room floor. The bottom line is that posthumous vocal fame largely depended on being able (and allowed) to craft a living voice in written form. This was not an option for most people in antiquity, including nearly all women—though it is worth noting that the surviving poetry of Sappho shows a persistent interest in sonic materiality.[17]

What, finally, can we conclude that the voice was, in antiquity? Vocabulary and phi-losophy have given us some answers. The noisy texts of Homer, Cicero, Virgil, and the rest have given us others, revealing a surprising world where vocal thinking could be as embedded in vocal media as our own. Other answers instead fell silent long ago—with the singers of epic, with Hortensius, with Cytheris. Perhaps, indeed, some even fell silent when Demosthenes and Cicero surrendered their living voices to written texts, no mat-ter how sophisticated those texts were in form and use. But in the end, what draws us to antiquity, like a Siren-song, may not lie so much in our search for its lost voices (or for a lost theory of the voice) as in the very mix of sound and silence that survives as antiqui-ty's legacy to us. For it is this hybridity that makes antiquity so like the voice itself: just when it seems most present, it again slips tantalizingly out of reach.

Suggestions for Further Reading

I explore several of this chapter's themes to greater depth in *The Ancient Phonograph* (Butler 2015); see also *Sound and the Ancient Senses* (Butler and Nooter 2019). Other bibliography is vast; the following suggestions, limited to works available in English, are meant only as points of departure. Though there has been much to be excited about in recent work on ancient music, the standard technical introduction remains Martin West (1992), which includes a brief chapter specifically on the voice (39–47). Among other ancient rhetorical manuals, the most revealing discussion of delivery, including but not limited to vocal delivery, is probably that of Quintilian's *The Orator's Education*, book 11, chapter 3, best consulted in the current Loeb Classical Library translation (with facing Latin; Quintilian 2001). This and other Latin sources are surveyed in Jon Hall (2007, 218–234), which features a usefully thorough dissection of the discussion of the voice in the anonymous *Rhetorica ad Herennium*. There are excellent explorations of the relationship between human and animal voices, including in Aristotelian thought, in Mark Payne (2010). On pantomime (which, however, was often mute), see Edith Hall and Rosie Wyles (2008), with a discussion of Virgil and Cytheris in the essay by Costas Panayotakis (185–197). The very fruitful subject of the voice in ancient tragedy has not been discussed here but is the theme of a chapter of *The Ancient Phonograph*; see also Nicole Loraux (2002), Nooter (2012), Nooter (2017). The voice is a frequent object of sophisticated contemplation in the work of James I. Porter (2009, 92–108; 2010); in particular, his 2010 book includes much ancient critical and philosophical material dissonant with the high canon (see its index, s.v. *voice*).

Notes

1. For, however, a fresh look at the evidence, with some cautions and revisions, see Graziosi (2002, 21–40), who suggests that rhapsodes exaggerated their similarity to the (earlier) composers of the texts they performed.
2. I am grateful to an anonymous reader of this chapter for this suggestion and for the quotation of Pierce in the next paragraph.
3. Peters compares the similar dreams of Charles Babbage.
4. Serious work on ancient music that remains accessible to the nonspecialist, including recorded reconstructions of what some of it may have sounded like, has been done by Armand D'Angour (Oxford), who conveniently collects his efforts at www.armand-dangour.com.
5. Suetonius, *Life of Vergil*, which praises Virgil's reading ability and borrows from Seneca the Elder a story that the young poet Julius Montanus declared that he would have plagiarized Virgil if, in so doing, he could have stolen too his "voice, expression, and delivery." For a brief introduction to the work of professional *lectores*, see Starr (1991, 337–343).
6. Repeated by Isidore, *Etymologies* 1.9.1.
7. On these roots see Watkins (2011, 7, 100).
8. Aristotle, *On the Soul* 2.8.420b. Translated by J. A. Smith, who provides the italics, in Barnes (1984).
9. Translated by d'A. W. Thompson in Barnes (1984). Aristotle's terms, it should be noted, somewhat differently obscure the question of voiced consonants than do the English equivalents given here. Similar distinctions are made by Galen; relevant passages are collected by Jeffrey L. Wollock (1997, 11–12).
10. On Lucretius on the origins of language, see Atherton (2005) and, more broadly, Reinhardt (2008),
11. "Aristotle's cough" is the point of departure of (and partial inspiration for) Connor (2014, 7–8). So too does the cough, including but not limited to Aristotle's, form the opening chapter of Appelbaum (1990, 1–13), who notes that "the entire history of soul-talk may be drowned out by a good cough" (5).
12. Nevertheless, the attention to anatomy that distinguishes Aristotle from, e.g., Plato repeatedly presents the voice as an embodied (and ensouled) *medium*, and this presentation can offer subtleties that rapid and synthetic readings miss. One example of this can be found in the very passage that Derrida uses as emblematic of the "phono-logocentrism" of the whole Western philosophical tradition; I discuss this further in *The Ancient Phonograph* (Butler 2015).
13. For an accessible discussion of this and related texts, see Sullivan (2004), Irvine (2006, 91–97), and Colish (1985, 321–327). On their impact on the theory and practice of music into the Middle Ages, see Dillon (2012, 36–43).
14. Cicero, *On the Orator* 3.213, where he goes on to explain that this reveals how much stock Aeschines placed in delivery, "since he thought the same speech would be different if the person delivering it were changed."

15. Cf. Plutarch, *Cicero* 3.

16. Along these lines, but moving simultaneously in other directions, see the superb reading of *Eclogue* 6 by Breed (2006, 74–94).

17. On Sappho see, most recently, Gurd (2016, 13–17; 19–22).

WORKS CITED

Appelbaum, David. 1990. *Voice*. Albany: State University of New York Press.

Atherton, Catherine. 2005. "Lucretius on What Language Is Not." In *Language and Learning: Philosophy of Language in the Hellenistic Age: Proceedings of the Ninth Symposium Hellenisticum*, edited by Dorothea Frede and Brad Inwood, 101–138. Cambridge: Cambridge University Press.

Barnes, Jonathan, ed. 1984. *The Complete Works of Aristotle: The Revised Oxford Translation*. Princeton, NJ: Princeton University Press.

Breed, Brian W. 2006. *Pastoral Inscriptions: Reading and Writing Virgil's* Eclogues. London: Duckworth.

Butler, Shane. 2015. *The Ancient Phonograph*. New York: Zone Books.

Butler, Shane and Sarah Nooter, editors. 2019. *Sound and the Ancient Senses*. London: Routledge.

Colish, Marcia L. 1985. *The Stoic Tradition from Antiquity to the Early Middle Ages*. Leiden: E. J. Brill.

Connor, Steven. 2014. *Beyond Words: Sobs, Hums, Stutters and Other Vocalizations*. London: Reaktion Books.

Derrida, Jacques. 1976. *Of Grammatology*, translated by Gayatri Chakravorty Spivak. Baltimore: Johns Hopkins University Press.

Dillon, Emma. 2012. *The Sense of Sound: Musical Meaning in France, 1260–1330*. New York: Oxford University Press.

Graziosi, Barbara, 2002. *Inventing Homer: The Early Reception of Epic*. Cambridge: Cambridge University Press.

Gurd, Sean Alexander. 2016. *Dissonance: Auditory Aesthetics in Ancient Greece*. New York: Fordham University Press.

Hall, Edith, and Rosie Wyles, editors. 2008. *New Directions in Ancient Pantomime*. Oxford: Oxford University Press.

Hall, Jon. 2007. "Oratorical Delivery and the Emotions: Theory and Practice." In *A Companion to Roman Rhetoric*, edited by William J. Dominik and Jon Hall, 218–234. Chichester: Wiley-Blackwell.

Irvine, Martin. 2006. *The Making of Textual Culture: "Grammatica" and Literary Theory, 350–1100*. Cambridge: Cambridge University Press.

Koestenbaum, Wayne. 1993. *The Queen's Throat: Opera, Homosexuality, and the Mystery of Desire*. New York: Poseidon.

Loraux, Nicole. 2002. *The Mourning Voice: An Essay on Greek Tragedy*. Ithaca, NY: Cornell University Press.

Nooter, Sarah. 2012. *When Heroes Sing: Sophocles and the Shifting Soundscape of Tragedy*. Cambridge: Cambridge University Press.

Nooter, Sarah. 2017. *The Mortal Voice in the Tragedies of Aeschylus*. Cambridge: Cambridge University Press.

Payne, Mark. 2010. *The Animal Part: Human and Other Animals in the Poetic Imagination.* Chicago: University Of Chicago Press.

Peters, John Durham. 2003. "Space, Time, and Communication Theory." *Canadian Journal of Communication* 28 (4): 397–411.

Porter, James I. 2009. "Rhetoric, Aesthetics, and the Voice." In *The Cambridge Companion to Ancient Rhetoric*, edited by Erik Gunderson, 92–108. Cambridge: Cambridge University Press.

Porter, James I. 2010. *The Origins of Aesthetic Thought in Ancient Greece: Matter, Sensation, and Experience.* Cambridge: Cambridge University Press.

Quintilian. 2001. *The Orator's Education*, Vol. 5, edited and translated by Donald A. Russell. Cambridge, MA: Harvard University Press.

Reinhardt, Tobias. 2008. "Epicurus and Lucretius on the Origins of Language." *The Classical Quarterly* 58 (1): 127–140.

Starr, Raymond J. 1991. "Reading Aloud: Lectores and Roman Reading." *The Classical Journal* 86 (4): 337–343.

Sullivan, Blair. 2004. "The Unwritable Sound of Music: The Origins and Implications of Isidore's Memorial Metaphor." In *The Echo of Music: Essays in Honor of Marie Louise Göllner*, edited by Blair Sullivan, 39–53. Warren, MI: Harmonie Park Press.

Watkins, Calvert. 2011. *The American Heritage Dictionary of Indo-European Roots*, 3rd ed. Boston: Houghton Mifflin.

West, Martin. 1992. *Ancient Greek Music.* Oxford: Oxford University Press.

Wollock, Jeffrey L. 1997. *The Noblest Animate Motion: Speech, Physiology, and Medicine in Pre-Cartesian Linguistic Thought.* Amsterdam: John Benjamins.

CHAPTER 2

OBJECT, PERSON, MACHINE, OR WHAT

Practical Ontologies of Voice

MATT RAHAIM

IT'S not just that voices *sound* different. Voices *are* different. And, as I'm going to argue, they are *differently*. A crowd of protesters becomes a "human microphone," amplifying the words of a single orator into a unified, public demand—while a nearby market buzzes with the sound of private negotiations in a dozen different languages. A child solemnly recites the Qur'an with immaculate clarity, unmodified by personal caprice—while a star singer on *Arabs Got Talent* closes her eyes as she sings, expressing what are, in principle, *her* personal feelings. A skilled hunter closes his eyes and aurally scans the chorus of forest animals around him for the voice of his prey—while a devout evangelical strives to discern the voice of God in her inner chorus. We get chills from an extended melisma on a single vowel; we marvel at the expressive silence of a heretic who refuses to recant; we laugh out loud at a convincing impersonation of a politician; we pick up a poetry anthology that promises to give voice to a heretofore silent constituency; we worry about the voice of the people revealed by polls; we hearken to the voices of birds, elephants, frogs, and whales; we allow ourselves to be guided by the inner voice of reason, of self-actualization, of conventional piety.

In English, it sounds perfectly reasonable to use the word *voice* for any of these practices, and the comforting unity of the term may lull us into thinking of them all as manifestations of a single essence: *the voice*. This sense is strengthened when we discover words in other languages with similar[1] semantic fields (*vox, avāz, moksori*), and even apparently cross-cultural vocal concepts (e.g., *vox populi/avāz-e avām/minjung ŭi moksori*—"the voice of the people.") This idea of a universal voiceliness is conceptually reified by the many convincing claims, in various languages, about *the* voice. To name a few: Galen's description of the voice as a kind of reed instrument (*aulos*) (Wollock 1997, 172); Sarangadev's yogic schema of the voice proceeding through desire, vital fire (*vahni*), and subtle breath (*prāṇa*) (1991 [ca. 1250], I.3.3–4); Amanda Weidman's wide-ranging model of the voice as a "a sonic and material phenomenon and a powerful metaphor" (2015, 232). In medicine and psychoanalysis, in the musicologies and vocal pedagogy, in moral philosophy and systems theory, we encounter claim after claim about the essential characteristics of "the voice": what it is, what it is made of, and what it does.

And yet the more we attend to screaming and singing, testimonials and silent protest, voices of prophecy and voices of the people, the harder it is to discern *the voice* as such. We are faced not only with a diversity of vocal sounds, but with a wide array of *things*: vocal processes, substances, and persons. Some *voice-s* are generated by a larynx, and some are not; some demand obedience, and some invite debate; some move through the air in waves, and some never do; some seem to be personal and expressive, and some are manifestly impersonal. Hindustani vocalists and opera singers alike speak of *losing their voice* when it comes out hoarse, but for a gathering of protesters chanting slogans in a public square, hoarseness is not by any means a loss of political voice. In a laryngologist's clinic, a hoarse voice is not the sign of a missing ("lost") larynx, but of a broken mechanism, very much *there* and in need of fixing. And for a singer-songwriter, hoarseness may even be the very mark of a *real* voice: one that is authentically hers.

There are, in other words, many perfectly ordinary ways in which a voice might be real. When we ask if that voice is *really* Nancy Ajram (or just a recording), whether we are *really* hearing the voice of our late uncle (or if the spirit medium is faking it), whether a mayor's sonorous Texan drawl is *real* (or consciously cultivated), whether voters are *really* demanding single-payer health care (or whether this is a statistical illusion), whether we *really* have a broken voice (or if it's *all in our head*), we are asking radically different questions in each case. Each requires a different kind of answer, produced through different practices: score study, laryngoscopy, polling, techniques of listening, acoustical analysis, and so on.

Vocal ontology asks after the relationship between a voice that shows up as real—as a sound might *show up* on a spectrogram, or a politician's accent might *show up* as authentically Texan to a discerning listener, or a significant political shift might *show up* in polling numbers—and the set of situated practices that make its reality available.[2] This chapter suggests ways in which particular ontological accounts of situated voices might work in a dialectic with general theories of voice. An ontological orientation to the voice should be distinguished from two close cousins that sometimes are casually called by the name "ontology": an *ontic* orientation (making claims about what the voice as such always and inherently *is*—political, material, semiotic, affective, physiological, etc.) and an *epistemological* orientation[3] (describing valid ways of knowing and representing a voice that is already ontically taken for granted: how to measure frequencies [in an acoustical world of vibrating matter], how to interpret spoken utterances [in a semiotic landscape of meaningful signs], how to locate prey [in a soundscape where sounds index other beings], etc.). Ontics and epistemology each have their place. But both begin from a voice that is already real, already *there*—a voice on which we take *perspectives* and *represent*. Reflection on *how* a particular voice *is* requires a different conceptual attitude.

To specify further: mapping out the situated practices from which voices emerge is a way of doing *practical ontology* (Jensen 2004; Gad et al. 2015). When we search the house for kindling and find a sheet of old newspaper, roll it up tightly, and arrange it carefully beneath dry wood, kindling not only *means* something different from the newspaper-for-reading we had in our hands earlier that week—nor, in practice, are we simply taking a different *perspective* on it—in a simple, practical sense, it *is* something different. The crackling voice of the NOAA weather service loop on a sailor's radio shows up as a voice-for-information on a sailboat in bad weather; a karate teacher's voice shows up for a student as an authoritative voice-for-obedience in the dojo. In the spirit of Annemarie Mol's now-classic account of how disease is *enacted* multiply through laboratory techniques and devices (2002), I turn here to what we might call *the voice multiple*, encountered through diverse practices and technologies of attunement, broadcasting, and reproduction. To reflect on this ontological multiplicity does not require a commitment to cosmic relativism. Just as we might speak both of physics in general and the specific physics of an airplane wing, we can speak of ontology in general (as an analytic orientation) and of a specific set of situated infrastructures and practices that disclose a coherent world of things—*an* ontology. Thus, to speak of *ontologies* in the plural is not to imply parallel universes, as though a prior, given, coherent vocal cosmos were suddenly shattered into numerous incommensurable fragments.

Though much of the controversy over the so-called "ontological turn" in the social sciences has centered around agency, multinaturalism, and world-incommensurability, practical ontology tends to remain agnostic about these metaphysical questions.[4] Rather than cloaking forms of unmarked ontic hegemony in a cosmic shroud (Thompson 2017), the goal is to foreground the practices of particular, situated listeners, holding them to account for what is disclosed. We need not predicate the prior existence of a thing called *the voice* in order to attend to any particular voice—indeed, a close attention to situated ontologies highlights ways in which the usual conceptual domain of *voice* bleeds into politics, acoustics, race, ethics, gender, music, and poetics. We need not posit the ontic existence of spirits to account for the practices that make their voices ontologically available for consultation; still less do we need to subsume them in a prior cosmic totality of economic forces, celestial hierarchies, or cultural life-worlds. As we will see, mapping ontologies onto discrete cultures is a particularly treacherous pitfall, landing us in the "cultural and cognitive essentialism which a generation of anthropologists … worked to discredit" (Hastrup in Gad et al. 2015, 69). Put positively, suspending our explanatory recourse to prior cultural essences (in favor of the fine details of situated vocal realness) allows us to consider the span of coherent ontological formations that operate between and beyond the commonsense borders of nations, cultures, and peoples. In many ways, this is easier to see with voices than with other classic anthropological topics that verge on the ontological (the body, nature, kinship, etc.). A broader consideration of these theoretical questions is deferred for a few more pages.

But first, in accordance with the general methodological thrust of this chapter, we turn to particulars. How many particulars? There is no limit in principle to how many vocal ontologies there may be, but we can only meaningfully consider a handful at once.

To begin from only two examples might give the impression of a dialectic resolvable in synthesis; to give three might give the impression of a closed taxonomy; to offer a world tour risks reversion to a cultural nationalist logic of vocal difference. Thus, still uncertain of what "the voice" *is*, we plunge in to five vocal situations: five geographically proximate but ontologically far-flung *voice*-s, each revealed as real in its own way by five different situated practices.

VOICE 1

We begin at a political demonstration in Mumbai.[5] In March of 2016, the head of an Indian Islamic political party had publicly refused to chant the nationalist slogan "*Bhārat mātā kī jai!*" ("Victory to Mother India!", widely performed as an affirmation of identity: nationally Indian, religiously Hindu, or both). In response, members of the Shiv Sena (a nationalist party that has long advocated for the congruence of Hindu and Indian identity) had publicly called for the cancellation of citizenship for anyone who refused to chant the slogan. There were many responses to this. One that played particularly well on TV was a gathering, on March 17, of several hundred Muslims at the Makhdoom Ali Mahimi shrine, near the Arabian Sea, to chant *Bhārat Mātā kī jai* in front of the gathered news teams.

The footage that aired that day (on several TV channels and Internet media outlets, for example *India News* and F3 news)[6] begins with a series of rapid establishing shots, both visible and audible. The Indian flag is raised, we hear a brass band playing the Indian national anthem, and the camera pans quickly across several legible indices of Islam: a minaret, green-and-white painted buildings, a crowd of men singing the national anthem with white caps and neatly-trimmed beards. Within seconds, it is clear just where we are and whose voices we are hearing. After the national anthem, the performance of the slogan begins. A solo voice calls out "*Bhārat Mātā kī*" and the crowd responds "*jai!*" They repeat this several times before moving on to other songs and slogans. In case there was any doubt left about what we are meant to be hearing, the title of the videos posted on YouTube, and the comments of the news anchors who comment on it, make it clear: "Muslims raised the slogan [*nāra lagāyā*] Bharat Mata ki jai at the Mahim shrine"; "Muslims will fly tricolour [flag], chant 'Bharat Mata ki Jai' in Mumbai dargah"; and so on.

If the voice of this crowd were simply a bearer of information, or a series of vibrations, or an instantiation of cultural conventions, this would not be a newsworthy event at all. Schoolchildren all over India recite *Bhārat Mātā kī jai* every day, and news crews do not roll up to broadcast it. But this event is not a tautological affirmation of identity ("we Indians are Indian"). It shows up as a performative *defiance* of a prior performance of not-chanting enjoined upon Indian Muslims. It becomes a newsworthy political event only to the degree that the voice shows up as the voice of a particular constituency, broadcast in the midst of a mass-mediated controversy about voicing citizenship, within a discursive field dominated by a Hindu-Muslim binary. Its performative work is not the sum of its innumerable phonetic or political or physiological or melodic features. Its power depends not just on what it *means*, but on a network of practices and sedimented infrastructures that make it what it *is* in the first place.

VOICE 2

Later, only a few hundred feet away, a smaller group of elite Sufis gather in the *khānqah* (lodge) of the same shrine complex for a very different kind of ritual, one which has been held regularly for centuries, in various places and political climates: a *mahfil-e samā*. In gatherings like this across South Asia, *qawwāls* sing poems for accomplished members of the Chisti Sufi brotherhood. But these qawwāls do not take center stage at a mahfil-e samā; often, there is no stage for them at all. Pride of place goes to a prominent spiritual authority, presiding over the occasion in silence, in the manner of a king observing a performance at court. Nor, for all of their technical skill and sensitivity, are the qawwāl-s the authors of the special, mystical content of the poems—they are merely the vehicles. When all goes well, the poems sung by the qawwāl may reach the heart of an initiated Sufi who has been prepared by his master for listening. For a listener whose heart is properly attuned to this inner content, the voice of the qawwāl delivers a secret message that leads them through successive stages of emotional intensity and finally into *wajd* or spiritual ecstasy (see Qureshi 2006 [1986], 118–122). But this is an extraordinary occurrence; most listeners, even those who are enthusiastic connoisseurs of mystical poetry, do not go into *wajd*. They may savor the poetry, they may even be deeply moved, but, for the moment at least, the inner content remains obscure.

Whether anyone goes into *wajd* or not, this voice *is* something other than a public performance of identity. It is not a source of information, or a performance of political identity, or an expression of the qawwāl's personal feelings. It is a voice-for-*samā*: a voice for disciplined listening that leads to ecstasy. Surely, uninitiated listeners hearing qawwāli at an outdoor gathering in a public area of the shrine may encounter the voice of a *qawwāl* as artistry for enjoyment, as melodic patterns for classification, or even (were one to drag the proper equipment along), as acoustic waveforms for analysis. But a closed, elite *mahfil-e samā* is directed toward spiritual elites for whom the voice in the room *is* something utterly different. No linguistic competence, no music theoretic insight, no amount of acoustic, grammatical or political analysis will reveal its content. Through proper comportment, through received Chisti techniques of listening, and above all through the mysteries of blessing passed through a spiritual lineage, the secret borne by this voice shows up to some but not to others.

VOICE 3

A few kilometers north, we encounter a radically different vocal ontology that, confusingly enough, is also called by the name "Sufi." An immaculately dressed super-star sings a classical poem of mystical devotion into a microphone on a brilliantly lit stage. This is a concert, not a ritual for the benefit of spiritual elites. This is a pop star, not a qawwāl, and he certainly is not trying to bring anyone into *wajd*. His voice is sweet and melodious, the kind that gives you chills. *Anyone* might be moved by such a beautiful voice, and this availability to "anyone" is part of what makes it what it is. It is a voice-for-appreciation, a voice-for-applauding, a voice-for-authenticity.

Even for those cheering in the front row, this voice is not the sort of thing that brings *wajd*. Just as an ornamental leather-bound book high up on a shelf in a den-tist's waiting room is not a book-for-studying, this is not a voice-for-*samā*. This is all about the singer; they are hearing *his* voice, cheering for *him*. Though the song has clear Muslim devotional lyrical references, this voice stands outside of the authorita-tive hierarchies of any Sufi brotherhood in particular. It is produced and heard as *his* voice, an expression of sincere, personal feelings freely revealed—in principle—to any listener.

VOICE 4

Just down the road at a recording studio, a playback singer has just finished recording the title song of a film, and the recording engineer turns to his computer and works his magic. He clicks and zooms in on her voice—a long purple rectangle framing a white waveform—making it so large that it takes up half of his computer monitor. He expertly trims away the sounds of inhalations between phrases, cuts and pastes particularly excellent parts over mistakes, and extends a long /a/ by clicking and dragging. Once the track is assembled, he painstakingly adjusts the EQ, compression, and reverb to give it the proper shine and texture.

Working on the voice in this way is like repairing and buffing a wrought-iron railing. As long as the engineer is working on a digital audio workstation, he is not dealing with the track as a digital file, consisting of 1s and 0s. But neither is he dealing with an organ of cartilage and muscle, nor with a ritual performative, nor with a carrier of an esoteric meaning, nor even an expression of the singer's personal subjectivity. The voice at hand in the course of mixing is a peculiar kind of object: durable, change-able, subject to trimming, cutting, pasting, extension, enhancement, and, crucially, reproduction.

VOICE 5

A bit further south, in a wealthy enclave near Shivaji Park, a voice clinic sees a steady stream of clients. The clinician here treats singers from nearly every public vocal world in India, from highly sought-after film singers to reciters of the Qur'ān. Her office is brightly lit by fluorescent lights and fragrant with disinfectant. Here, through the use of various techniques, instruments, and heuristics, the voice shows up vividly as a mechanism in the throat made of muscle, bone, and cartilage, subject to various states of health and disease. To one patient, she prescribes six daily glasses of water and a week of vocal rest; to another, she prescribes surgery to remove a nodule.

When the voice doctor tells a client how to take care of her voice, how to avoid wearing down the voice, how to repair damage to the voice, she is talking about a fleshy organ: a thing that swells, that develops nodules, that functions and malfunctions and can be repaired. Though like a "vocal track" this voice is in some sense an object, it is not a sound object to be shortened, lengthened, cut or pasted. It is alive, self-repairing, whole, subject to health and disease, hydration and dehydration, like the whole organic body of which it is a part. Just as important, this voice also shows up as the rare and special kind of thing for which a doctor bears a direct ethical responsibility.

PRACTICAL ONTOLOGIES OF VOICE

Here we are faced not only with five different-*sounding* voices, with different "traits," as they might appear if they were presented in quick succession in audio clips. Moving from situation to situation, in practice we are faced with five radically different sorts of *thing*. Just as a rock star yelling "I love you!" to a gathered crowd is an entirely different sort of *thing* than a lover whispering it to his beloved for the first time, so too is the amplified voice of a "Sufi" superstar in a music hall an entirely different thing than the voice of a qawwāl at a *mahfil-e samā*. This is not a matter of simply taking a *perspective* on an acoustic signal. Each of these voices already shows up to us as real through a specific constellation of interwoven practices and infrastructures.

For an isolated vocal track to show up for editing, we need a soundproof booth, we need headphones, we need microphone technique, we need the discipline to sing at the right moment and remain quiet at others. For a collective vocal performance of citizenship to show up, we need a set of legal-institutional formations that afford nationality, we need camera techniques, we need a leader to coordinate a crowd to chant in unison, we need a national public tuned into mass media and the cultural logic of nationalism. For laryngeal physiology to show up, we need to shine a bright light down into the dark cavern of the throat, we need a special camera, we need a screen to see the image, we need the imaginative faculty to map the image on to a normative anatomy. The diagnosis of a glottal closure disorder requires a very particular attunement: to equipment, to learned practices of measurement, and to an unambiguous, unreflective sense of physiological norms and aberrance. A skilled vocal diagnosis (like virtuosic teasing, like transcription, like a cultivated receptivity to opera) requires habits of discernment and imagination honed over years of practice. It is not that laryngologists hold out any hope about arriving at a fixed, complete "objective" totality (looking at an image of the larynx, we ignore the glare from stray flecks of mucus; the image is always a bit blurrier than we like; we do not know or care how *many* water molecules are in the vocal folds). Neither are we arbitrarily inventing "subjective" fantasies (we can certainly be verifiably right or wrong about a laryngeal nodule, tonal intervals, about phonetics, sincerity, and any number of other vocal realities). Unlike an arbitrary act of willful fantasy, working within a vocal reality includes the possibility of being surprised: a voice can show up quite differently than we *think* it should. But no "voice" shows up for us as real in the first place without the infrastructure, situation, habits, and practices that make it available.

Some of these attentional practices are so habitual that they become invisible. The work necessary to attend to a friend's utterance as a *request* is usually unconscious in one's mother tongue, but it becomes more obvious when contending with background noise; it can be downright exhausting when trying to have a conversation in an unfamiliar language. When transcribing a singing voice, an ontology of tones (in which every vocal utterance shows up as a sequence of discrete notes) seems perfectly natural. In the course of transcribing a vocal line, we may pick out a sequence of tones on the piano without ever doubting that the "voice" we thereby come to know is made of notes. Even speech, screaming, and weeping—which ordinarily do not show up as tones—can be analyzed as pitch sequences.[7] But anyone who has struggled their way through a course in ear training can attest to how much training it takes to hear a sung melody as a sequence of notes. These notes show up as vividly real to a specially disciplined and privileged few—but to most they do not show up at all.

Note that situations are not necessarily *contexts*.[8] At the moment we are calling out the name of a missing child, aurally scanning our surroundings for her voice, we would never say that we are "in the context of a search." Just so, singing *at* a mahfil, *for* attentive listeners is not the same as singing "in the context of listeners," much less "in the context of India"—a *context* is assigned after the fact, in reflection, by constituting a voice as a text for interpretation in a context. We certainly can find "contexts" for interpretation wherever we textualize performances—for example, transcribing a recording of a senate hearing, after the fact, trying to make sense of what someone's utterance might have *meant*. But to conceive of a voice "in a context" already entails an implicit ontological commitment to the voice as a text-for-interpretation, freely sliding in and among different contexts. Of the vocal ontologies sketched out earlier, only a vocal track, in the course of editing it, shows up as anything like an invariant text to be interpreted in various contexts; at times, tightly scripted speech or song may as well. But to foist this text-centered ontology indiscriminately onto all voices (to reduce *all* vocal situations to contexts) would be to foreclose crucial political, ethical, and conceptual possibilities: defiance, indeterminacy, noise, improvisation, performativity, spirit possession, imitation.

Vocal ontologies each offer something quite different in turn to a situated actor, but never all at once. There is no reason to expect that there will be a shared essence, or a lowest common denominator among these innumerable realnesses—not materiality, not vibration, not divinity, not individual personhood. This much is counterintuitive. It certainly seems natural to imagine that the voice has its origin in the physiology of the larynx. But even leaving aside physiological diversity (bird syrinxes, cricket elytra, dolphin bursae), not everything we call "voice" *has* a physiology in the first place. As Richard Wolf teaches us (2014), the "voice in the drum" disclosed so vividly to devout listeners has no larynx, lips, or tongue. Nor does the "voice of the people" that we discover through polls, ballots, and statistical analysis. Nor, even, in practice, does a vocal track. A related (but ontically distinct) commonsense approach holds that all voices are essentially made of vibrations. Again, this is true of some voices, but not all. Some Naqshbandi sufi-s, for example, counsel their disciples that the silent, inner repetition of devotional formulas is more effective than doing so audibly. The egalitarian stream of anti-caste politics inflected by the songs of Kabir is fueled by an ontology of voice in which an unconditioned, nonvibrational *shabd* (word) is equally at the heart of each human being, regardless of caste, in which the conditional hummings and babblings of singing and speaking, with beginnings, end, and media, are only secondary by-products. One who "hears voices" in his room at night cannot take readings of their pitch or formant patterns—but these are voices nonetheless. The voices that psychologists call "auditory vocal hallucinations" do not show up to those who hear them as neatly located in the head; for those who hear them, they are no more hearing hallucinations than a violinist is hearing nerve impulses when she plays. The maddening, prophetic power of such a voice lies precisely in its ontology: it does not show up as "inner speech" generated by the self, but as a voice out there in the world, with its own agency. Tanya Luhrmann's work demonstrates that these voices are neither acoustical nor purely fanciful; they are situated and coherent, made real through enculturated habits of attention and listening (Luhrmann et al. 2015). Nor do all voices communicate a message. Speech therapists and laryngologists work hard to systematically listen for a particular kind of pure voice free of semantic meaning, local belongings, or aesthetic standards. The now common practice of listening to a singer's voice (say, Fairuz or Fischer-Dieskau) as an object of wordless aesthetic pleasure reveals a voice as a "senseless play of sensuality" (Dolar 2006, 43). The power of glossolalia, the affective intensity of inchoate wailing, the numinous aura of chant in a liturgical language which one does not fully understand—these all depend on the presence of a voice that *is* something other than a message.

In search of a common vocal essence, we may even try to find metaphoric linkages between separate things called by the name "voice." We may, for example, speculate that having a "voice" in politics is an abstraction thinkable only by means of a concrete image: a person speaking publicly, vocally exerting power by rendering an individual will audible. But any such origin myth puts us right back where we started, generalizing a vocal function from a particular situation. Think of a ritual public abdication, or an enforced pledge of allegiance, or a national apology—the expression of individual will is by no means the essential political function of the voice. Conversely, think of a silent protest, or the determined refusal to chant *Bhārat Mātā kī jai*, or dropping a ballot in a box—not-speaking can be a powerful means of political voicing. This is why each politics of the voice turns out again and again to be *a* politics of voice. To insist on a single, ahistorical primal scene of vocal politics is not only conceptually misleading; it is politically impoverishing as well.

ANTHROPOLOGICAL ONTICS, ETHNOGRAPHIC ONTOLOGY

This focused attention to vocal particularities at the expense of a general theory of voice is admittedly a bit disorienting at first. But ethnography, like history, has always been a gadfly for supposedly universal anthropologies: of gender, of the gift, of ethics, of music—deferring the comfort of a totalizing ontic scheme by returning us to practices, reminding us that even the things that show up for us most vividly are disclosed by particular situations. All of us find ourselves from beginning to end in one situation or another: yelling across a schoolyard, listening closely to a staged performance, slowing down and playing back a section of a recording for transcription, singing along at a demonstration. Even a recording of a voice, no matter how detached it may seem in relation to an originary moment of voicing,[9] shows up *for* somebody, played through particular speakers, in a room of a particular size, for a particular occasion. Perhaps the listener really is bracketing its source and medium through some form of disciplined reduced listening.[10] But to the extent that it is shows up as a *voice*, it always shows up in a situation (though again of a rather different kind than "the voice of Etta James," or "the voice of Egypt" presented by a curatorial approach to a canon of recordings).

So is it enough to stop there, with a dizzying array of ethnographic particulars? Since there is always another situation around the corner, should we abandon the anthropological project of wide-ranging conceptual synthesis for the ethnographic project of finding exceptions? Is it enough to simply say that voices are irreducibly local and plural and walk away?

Of course not. We can't account ethnographically or historically for particular voices without *some* provisional ontic scaffolding—some sense of what is really there—any more than we can take fieldnotes without a language. But, just as we have learned to do with practices of writing, we can be mindful of the limits of ontic predication and tack back and forth between description and reflection. When we read that voice is "a phenomenon that lies at the intersection of music, sound, embodiment, subjectivity and collective identity" (Weidman 2011, 13) or that "it is always the body social that is enunciated in and through the voice" (Feld et al. 2004, 341), we need not latch onto either one as an ontic account of a vocal essence that transcends situations. But neither are these just arbitrary fantasies. Rather, well-constructed ontic formulations serve as practical rules of thumb, casting light on some situations and shadows on others, providing a schematic accounting of ontological types, explicating our own implicit analytic and theoretical choices, and even offering the possibility of provisionally tracing ontological formations that reach beyond particular places and times.

LOCATING VOCAL ONTOLOGIES

As we have seen in the five vocal ontologies sketched out earlier, there are very often incommensurable ontologies of voice in the same city, in the same room, even for the same person. But a fine-grained focus on the situated revelation of voices does not require a commitment to individualist subjectivism, or a fragmented relativism of incommensurable perspectives. Quite the opposite: stances and infrastructures that offer voices are always already relational, already shared, already social (Berger 2009, 97). Nor is this sociality freely relativistic. To be sure, as with the putative *cultures* of postwar anthropology, social scientists face the temptation to assign characteristic ontological worlds to nations and peoples.[11] But the groupist identification of voices with quasi-social totalities only obstructs our ontological view of these socialities.

To put it aphoristically: the horizon of an ontological formation is not the boundary of a nation. In the first place, vocal ontologies often stretch far beyond political boundaries. The vocal ontology of *samā* is available to elite sufis across the Islamicate cosmopolis, including speakers of Indic, Turkish, Persianate, and Arabic vernaculars, inflected by al-Ghazali's prescriptions for ethical listening, shaped by discourses of Qur'anic revelation, cultivated in a vast network of Sufi shrines and lodges. The cosmopolitan ontology of voice in which singing is to be savored in a dark and quiet concert hall, to be enjoyed as leisurely entertainment, as sensuously beautiful above all else, is part of what has made *dhrupad* available for the enjoyment of concertgoers in Europe. The transnational circulation of Bollywood movies, from the Indian Ocean to the Red Sea to the Mediterranean, has naturalized the vocal identity of playback singer and film actor, so that Lata Mangeshkar's voice shows up as embodied rather than acousmatic, blending seamlessly with the character on screen. The emergence of the popular, ubiquitous voices of recording stars in the 1920s and 1930s was scaffolded by transnational infrastructures, trade networks, and practices of listening (Denning 2015).

In the second place, nations (and cities and locales in general) are ontologically diverse. All five of the "voices" I cited earlier—and dozens more—are within a few kilometers of each other. In Bangkok, in Delhi, in Beirut, in a tiny Minnesotan farm town, a short walk reveals a range of competing vocal ontologies: a friend greets us and we respond, a vendor calls out to advertise his wares, grocery shoppers hum along with a love song, a news anchor on TV addresses a national public. Each of us moves fluidly among broad (if finite) repertoires of vocal ontologies.

Thus, were we to try to sketch them on a map, vocal ontologies would seem to be both bigger than nation-states (by virtue of their transnational span) and smaller than nation-states (by nature of the ontological diversity that obtains even in the same city). This apparent paradox is a consequence of trying to locate voices (which have widely various spatialities) on a master cartographic frame, a two-dimensional surface quilted with nation-state-shaped cultures (Gupta and Ferguson 1992). But starting from apparently small-scale, situated vocal ontologies may well reveal common *voice*-s that reach beyond commonsense racial, national, civilizational totalities. It opens up the neoliberal contours of a transnational Reality TV ontological formation that discloses a measureable substance called vocal *talent* distributed unpredictably among individuals; to hear something of the inimitable majesty that Qur'anic recitation has even for non-Arab Muslims and non-Muslim Arabs; to identify the contestations of authenticity within a widely dispersed sphere of hip hop vocal cosmopolitanism. All of this requires us to think beyond national borders for identifying ontological formations.

INDETERMINACY AND THE VOCAL POLITICS OF WHAT

Much of the foregoing has highlighted the stark differences between discrete vocal ontologies. This might lead us to think of a dazzlingly variegated museum of ontology, in which each voice is presented with perfect clarity in a glass display case, in which we can stroll seamlessly from real voice to real voice (here is a voice-for-*samā*, and here is a vocal mechanism, and here is a vocal track) serially assured of each in turn. But to think only in terms of ontological certainty would be misleading.

Think of how much time we spend in puzzlement about voices. Think of a bad phone connection, of an awkward conversation in a new language, of a failed ear-training exam, of ventriloquism, of a magisterial ethnographic voice that seems to put words in its subjects mouths, of jokes[12] that rely on ambiguity about what an utterance *is*. Laryngoscopic images and spectrograms are never as clear as we want them to be, and it is often hard to tell if we *really* see what we think we see at first try. Recording engineers know that fidelity is always finite, that every microphone introduces artifacts, and mix albums with their ears alive to the indeterminate edges of audibility. Evangelicals trying to hear the voice of God spend years training themselves to sort through many other inner voices, learning to discern a clear divine message (Luhrmann 2012, 131). Like any perceptual encounter, an indeterminate vocal haze "sets a kind of muddled problem for [the] body to solve," in which, through turning knobs, squinting, holding our breath, moving closer to a sound source, listening in particular way, or other situated practices of vocal discernment, we try to "find the attitude which will provide it with the means of becoming determinate, of showing up" (Merleau-Ponty 2002 [1945], 248–249).

Even when we do find an attitude that provisionally renders a voice determinate, we never quite arrive at a seamless world of vocal being once and for all. The totalizing certainty of an all-encompassing mode of being in which everything has a place is just one extreme pole of an ontological continuum. Our dance along this continuum, in which our ontic expectations are unpredictably undercut, is precisely what affords vocal rapport with an other (Levinas 1979 [1961], 201) that is never fully graspable.[13] This dance of ontological indeterminacy also opens up questions about vocal dynamics: how we shift from one voice to another, from one situation to another, from one voice-revealing infrastructure to another.

Further, attending to the friction between practical ontologies of voice opens up what Annemarie Mol calls a "politics of what" (2002, 172). It allows us to recognize and account for commonsense vocal-ontological formations, the practices that constitute them, the workings of power that make them seem obvious, and the contestations that pit them against each other. It is precisely this ontological indeterminacy that makes possible the emergence of a singer—say, Umm Kulthum, Lata Mangeshkar, Zeki Müren, Lee Greenwood—whose voice, through the magic of mass media, may show up convincingly as a voice-of-a-person, as a voice-of-a-nation, or even, binaurally, as both at once (cf. Danielson 1998; Srivasta 2004; Stokes 2010). A parallel ontological ambiguity between human and nonhuman voice seems likewise to have generated distinctive colonial forms of aurality in nineteenth-century Colombia (Ochoa Gautier 2014). None of these indeterminate *voice*-s resolves into to a single, monolithic cultural meaning; none balloons into the universal anything-and-everything of "the voice." The question of what a voice *is* is at the heart of the matter. Practical ontology thus offers a way into vocal politics without retreating into the soundscapic realism of a given acoustical world *or* into the individualist subjectivism where one hears whatsoever one wills. A voice may, after all, be palpably, publicly *real* without being inevitable.

NOTES

1. The semantic fields of these words are by no means identical. As Nicholas Harkness (2013, 11) points out, Korean phoneticists tend to use the word *ŭmsŏng* rather than *moksori*; Laura Kunreuther likewise points out that *avāz* has a rather different range of semantic possibilities than *vox*, including, for example, noise (2016).
2. As used here, "showing up" and "disclosure" are two sides of the same ontological coin. A set of situated practices *discloses* a world of real things; a thing in a world *shows up* as real (becomes available for editing or contemplation, registers as an intelligible utterance, gains personhood, authoritatively commands a listener) by virtue of these situated practices. This much follows Hubert Dreyfus's now-canonical English rendering of Heidegger's term *Begegnen* (1991, x; 1996[1927]). As we will see, however, Dreyfus's acceptance of Heidegger's assignment of basic ontological moods (*Grundstimmung*) to nations—by which Japanese babies are brought up in a consistently ontologically distinct way from American babies, for example (61), and thus live in a homogeneous, sealed-off cultural world—will not work for a rigorous, ethnographically grounded vocal ontology.

3. Steven Feld's catchy term "acoustemology," though glossed as "acoustic epistemology," often reaches deeper than ways of knowing a world that is simply given (Feld, 2015). Approaching a recording as raw "data" may indeed encourage an analysis grounded in an apparently given text, thus collapsing the ontological into the merely epistemological. But acoustemology may also verge on the ontological to the extent that it is concerned with world-disclosure rather than simply ways of knowing or representing a given world.

4. On agency see Kipnis (2015); on multinaturalism see Viveiros de Castro (2004); on world-disclosure and incommensurability see Kompridis (2006, 239).

5. Known officially as Bombay prior to 1995, and unofficially even now by many of the city's residents. There is no neutral way to cite this city's name, particularly when communal identity is at issue.

6. See also F3 News, Mumbai, March 17, 2016.

7. Cf. Diana Deutsch's "Sometimes Behave So Strangely," or Alvin Lucier's "I Am Sitting in a Room," both of which derive their uncanny power from the ontological gray area between hearing words and hearing tones.

8. There is, of course, a familiar tradition in the social sciences of calling situations "contexts," going back at least to Malinowski's "contexts of situations" (1946 [1923], 306).

9. For more on the apparent detachment of source and sound, and whether this is a pathological ("schizophonic,") or normative ("rhizophonic") condition, see Stanyek and Piekut (2010). I would add, however, that the acoustical propagation of vibrations (by virtue of which, as Piekut and Stanyek point out, sound-as-vibration is *always* heard at some physical distance from its source) is a rather different issue than the appearances of sound as ontologically distinct from a source—either through acousmatics or reduced listening.

10. For a thorough treatment of this listening practice stretching from Husserl through Pierre Schaeffer and Michael Chion, see Kane (2014).

11. This is one of the most disturbing sociological assumptions of Heidegger's Nazi-period ontology: that each civilization has a characteristic, consistent ontological mood (*Grundstimmung*) that persists on the scale of centuries (for a sympathetic summary, see Dreyfus [1991, 170]). For a summary of critiques of such ontological "worlds" congruent with peoples see Gad et al. (2015).

12. "To give two examples: the "*che bella voce!*" joke in Dolar (2006), in which a voice-as-command is conveniently taken to be a voice-as-aesthetic-object; and the oft-recycled "nobody here but us chickens!", which hinges on the absurd friction between what the utterance *claims* and what it evidently *is* (3). See also Gourard's "eerie" phonographic tricks in Kane (2014, 183–185).

13. See Rahaim (2017) for a reading of Levinas that treats vocal and musical action as a possible vehicle for rapport that preserves metaphysical alterity.

Works Cited

Berger, Harris. 2009. *Stance: Ideas about Emotion, Style, and Meaning for the Study of Expressive Culture.* Middletown, CT: Wesleyan University Press.

Cavarero, Adriana. 2005. *For More Than One Voice: Toward a Philosophy of Vocal Expression.* Redwood City, CA: Stanford University Press.

Danielson, Virginia. 1998. *The Voice of Egypt: Umm Kulthum, Arabic Song, and Egyptian Society in the Twentieth Century.* Chicago: University of Chicago Press.

Denning, Michael. 2015. *Noise Uprising: The Audiopolitics of a World Musical Revolution.* New York: Verso.

Dolar, Mladen. 2006. *A Voice and Nothing More*. Cambridge, MA: The MIT Press.

Dreyfus, Hubert. 1991. *Being-in-the-World: A Commentary on Heidegger's Being and Time, Division I*. Cambridge, MA: The MIT Press.

Feld, Steven. 2015. "Acoustemology." In *Keywords in Sound*, edited by David Novak and Matt Sakakeeney, 12–21. Durham, NC: Duke University Press.

Feld, Steven, A. Fox, T. Porcello, and D. Samuels. 2004. "Vocal Anthropology: From the Music of Language to the Language of Song." In *A Companion to Linguistic Anthropology*, edited by Alessandro Druanti, 321–346. Oxford: Blackwell.

Gad, Christopher, C. Jensen, and B. Winthereik. 2015. "Practical Ontology: Worlds in STS and Anthropology." *NatureCulture* (3): 67–86.

Gupta, Akhil, and James Ferguson. 1992. "Beyond 'Culture': Space, Identity, and the Politics of Difference." *Cultural Anthropology* 7 (1): 6–23.

Harkness, Nicholas. 2013. *Songs of Seoul: An Ethnography of Voice and Voicing in Christian South Korea*. Berkeley: University of California Press.

Heidegger, Martin. 1996 [1927]. *Being and Time*, translated by Joan Stambaugh. Albany: SUNY Press.

Jensen, C. B. 2004. "A Nonhumanist Disposition: On Performativity, Practical Ontology, and Intervention." *Configurations* 12 (2): 229–261.

Kane, Brian. 2014. *Sound Unseen: Acousmatic Sound in Theory and Practice*. New York: Oxford University Press.

Kipnis, Andrew. 2015. "Agency between Humanism and Posthumanism: Latour and His Opponents." *HAU: Journal of Ethnographic Theory* 5 (2): 43–58.

Kompridis, Nikolas. 2006. *Critique and Disclosure: Critical Theory between Past and Future*. Cambridge, MA: The MIT Press.

Kunreuther, Laura. 2016. "Sounding Democracy: Performance, Protest, and Political Subjectivity." Unpublished talk, Society for Ethnomusicology Annual Meeting, Washington, DC.

Levinas, Emmanuel. 1979 [1961]. *Totality and Infinity: An Essay on Exteriority*. The Hague: Martinus Nijhoff.

Luhrmann, Tanya. 2012. *When God Talks Back: Understanding the American Evangelical Relationship with God*. New York: Vintage Books.

Luhrmann, Tanya, R. Padmavati, H. Tharoor, and A. Osei. 2015. "Differences in Voice-Hearing Experiences of People with Psychosis in the USA, India, and Ghana: Interview-Based Study." *British Journal of Psychiatry* 206 (1): 41–44.

Malinowski, Bronislaw. 1946 [1923]. "The Problem of Meaning in Primitive Languages." In *The Meaning of Meaning: A Study of the Influence of Language upon Thought and of the Science of Symbolism*, edited by C. K. Ogden and I. A. Richards, 296–336. 8th ed. New York: Harcourt, Brace & World, Inc.

Merleau-Ponty, Maurice. 2002 [1945]. *The Phenomenology of Perception*. New York: Routledge.

Mol, Annemarie. 2002. *The Body Multiple: Ontology in Medical Practice*. Durham, NC: Duke University Press.

Ochoa Gautier, Ana María. 2014. *Aurality: Listening and Knowledge in Nineteenth-Century Colombia*. Durham, NC: Duke University Press.

Qureshi, Regula. 2006 [1986]. *Sufi Music of India and Pakistan: Sound, Context, and Meaning in Qawwali*. Karachi: Oxford University Press.

Rahaim, Matthew. 2017. "Otherwise than Participation: Unity and Alterity in Musical Encounters" In *Music and Empathy*. Farnham, Surrey: Ashgate.

Srivasta, Sanjay. 2004. "Voice, Gender, and Space in Time of Five-Year Plans: The Idea of Lata Mangeshkar." *Economic and Political Weekly* 39(20): 2019–2028.

Stanyek, Jason, and Benjamin Piekut. 2010. "Deadness: Technologies of the Intermundane." *The Drama Review* 54 (1): 14–38.

Stokes, Martin. 2010. *The Republic of Love: Cultural Intimacy in Turkish Popular Music.* Chicago, IL: University of Chicago Press.

Thompson, Marie. 2017. Whiteness and the Ontological Turn in Sound Studies. *Parallax* 23(3): 266–282.

Viveiros de Castro, Eduardo. 2004. "Perspectival Anthropology and the Method of Controlled Equivocation." *Tipití* 2 (1): 3–22.

Weidman, Amanda. 2011. "Anthropology and the Voice." *Anthropology News* 52 (1): 13.

Weidman, Amanda. 2015. "Voice." In *Keywords in Sound*, edited by David Novak and Matt Sakakeeny, 232–252. Durham, NC: Duke University Press.

Wolf, Richard. 2014. *The Voice in the Drum: Music, Language, and Emotion in Islamicate South Asia.* Urbana: University of Illinois Press.

Wollock, Jeffrey. 1997. *The Noblest Animate Motion: Speech, Physiology and Medicine in Pre-Cartesian Linguistic Thought.* Amsterdam: John Benjamins Publishing Company.

CHAPTER 3

···

SINGING HIGH

Black Countertenors and Gendered
Sound in Gospel Performance

···

ALISHA LOLA JONES

IN 2011, when Patrick Dailey sang the solo in Nathan Carter's arranged composition of "Some Day" at New Psalmist Baptist Church in Baltimore, it was the first time the The Word Network broadcast a countertenor performance.[1] Based on Rev. Charles A. Tindley's (1851–1933) beloved 1916 hymn "Beams of Heaven (Some Day)," Carter's 2003 version is set for SSAATTBB choir, solo, and organ.[2] The choir in Baltimore sang the first verse and refrain, after which a trio of female voices, as specified by Carter, sang the second verse and refrain. Finally, with "noble" posture comprising a lifted chest and arms held close to the body, Dailey sang the third verse and then ad libbed while the chorus repeated the refrain in the antiphonal or call and response manner that is central to gospel music styles. Notably, the third verse was set for a soloist, but Carter does not specify a gendered high-voice classification such as soprano or tenor.

While the absence of a soloist classification in the music is not remarkable, the arranger's preferences in performance practice are. Carter's omission of a specific vocal designation for the notated soloist part also suggests that the ideal soloist is anyone who can sing the part in a high *tessitura* (a comfortable singing range). The absence of a specific voice classification in the sheet music institutionalizes a gender inclusive and imaginative casting of the part. This casting flexibility overlaps African American vernacular practices that embrace extended vocal range techniques, fluidity between conventional vocal designations with the European-derived concert music composer's traditional prerogative and progressiveness in voicing rare singers. Further, to manage contentious cultural tensions surrounding men "singing high like a woman" (Jones 2016, 216), the voicing flexibility helps contextualize African American operatic countertenors who lead worship in gospel settings.

Noticing the attention that Patrick Dailey's performance garnered, I first interviewed the Tennessee native on November 11, 2011. Over the course of our many conversations and subsequent collaborations, we discussed his performance practice choices and the issues he faces as a countertenor who performs in African American gospel contexts. According to Dailey, when Carter conducted this composition in concerts with his Morgan State University choir, the countertenor Ernie Saunders, as well as various soprano soloists, were generally featured.[3] By programming high vocalists in a gender inclusive manner within a historically black collegiate context, Carter provided his pupils with language and codes of conduct to present rare vocal designations to new audiences in live venues and multimedia platforms such as New Psalmist Baptist Church and The Word Network.

Dailey admitted that even in a twenty-first-century context, African American countertenors are perceived as peculiar:

> The fact of the matter is that you are already gonna present something—even if it is in the classical audience—you are already gonna present something to them that might be foreign to them already. You don't wanna turn them off at the very beginning.
> (Interview, November 11, 2011)

As I considered Dailey's anxieties, the following questions emerged and form the foundation for this chapter: What assumptions about identity do gospel listeners bring to their encounters with high-singing male performances? What are the connections between the gospel audience's perceptions of a male singer's identity, body, vocal style, and range that make for positive reception of a countertenor's ministry? What are the interfaces in which the hegemonic perceptions of high-singing male soloists' identities are disputed or furthered as audiences decipher the countertenor's rare sound? And what are the techniques African American countertenors deploy to challenge or confirm those assumptions?

Drawing on a case study of African American countertenor Patrick Dailey and an ethnography of his live performance, this chapter is an ethnomusicological assessment of his social and theological navigation of the indistinguishable sexual and gendered vocal sound. African American gospel singing challenges the sonic gender binary framework that the American public expects of men as singing low and women as singing high. Public expectations can and do influence African American vocalities. I focus on Dailey's aforementioned performance practices in Carter's "Some Day" at New Baptist and at a symposium in Chicago, Illinois, as a means to highlight some of the complications that arise as sonically ambiguous presentations of gender intertwine and compete with longstanding heteronormative frameworks of gendered voice in gospel. I briefly review historical discourses on countertenors and gender expression as a way of framing my discussion on the ways in which audiences may assess their performance competence. African American gospel countertenors are situated in Western opera's visual gender-bending traditions such as *en travesti* production—a practice in which men dress in conventionally women's clothing. Absent the visual cues of gender-bending displayed in opera, their vocal sound is an aesthetic and worshipful interruption of gendered gospel vocal music performance. I then analyze my interviews with Dailey to glean the choices he makes to demonstrate performance competence in African American worship as a man who sings high. Dailey negotiates the tensions and intersections deftly between these dual processes of musical performance. He does so with an aspiration to deliver a presentation that is what he refers to as "anointed": music that is *from* and *for* God. Dailey's performance engages African American audiences' various types of cultural familiarity to portray competency as a worship leader and trained artist.

Black Countertenor Sound

African American countertenors with training as soloists in both Western art music and gospel music are unconventional, especially outside of historically black college and university (HBCU) contexts. Black vocalists are still underrepresented in predominantly white institutions (PWIs). While many countertenors are trained at HBCUs, the countertenor *fach* is often socioculturally perceived in broader African American contexts as queer, and the domain of nonblack musicians. Scholars have not yet explored the careers of African American countertenors, or such singers' approaches to participating in multiple cultural contexts such as gospel music settings. "Countertenor" is the vocal designation in Western classical music for men who are trained to "sing high," deploying a mature and comfortable vocal delivery such that uninitiated listeners are often unable to determine whether the sound is emanating from a male or female body. Their voices are designated as what Naomi André (2006) calls a "treble timbre," which means they perform music that matches the vocal range and quality of women contralti, mezzo-soprani, soprani, and boy soprani in the Western art music tradition.

Countertenors vocally transcend barriers of gender conformity, a phenomenon I understand as the musical ways that people consciously or subconsciously allow or adjust their vocalizations to fit society's expectations of how gendered bodies make sound. They are sometimes cast to sing women's operatic roles costumed in women's garments; however, they do not dress in women's attire while participating in church music ministry. The music ministers who employ countertenors also face challenges in choosing repertoire for them, particularly when those ministers do not have an established tradition or repertoire from which to draw.

At the Center for Black Music Research (CBMR) Symposium on Black Vocality in Chicago, Illinois (October 2013), Patrick Dailey performed after I presented research on his broadcast performance at New Psalmist Baptist Church before scholars, black music enthusiasts, and church musicians. I asked participants who remarked on our joint lecture-performance whether they had previously heard a countertenor. Some attendees, specifically those who were familiar with men who sing high in Western art music, likened Dailey to the historic castrato depicted in the 1994 blockbuster film

Farinelli. They drew a comparison in an effort to describe the similarity in Dailey's sound to Farinelli's portrayed sound. Participants were not sure why their ideas of countertenor and castrati sounds were similar to each other. Countertenors are not castrati, but they do share a similar vocal range and much of the same repertoire. The reference to Farinelli is a key sonic connection in that the castrato legacy exemplifies cultural and religious practices in which the Roman Catholic Church manipulated—and dare I say, violated—men's sexuality by castrating them for singing in service of the church (Feldman 2015). While extensive coverage of castrato scholarship is outside the scope of this chapter, I note the extent to which historical perceptions of castrati and the commoditization of gendered sound production in sacred music shed light on countertenors' reception today.

Uninitiated symposium participants conflated countertenors and castrati largely because these singers register as queer and unmanly to modern listeners.[4] This was evident in the remarks of participants at the CBMR symposium who said that they were unsure why countertenors and castrati sounded similar. I must note that while Farinelli, the Italian opera singer known as "the greatest castrato of all time," was played by an Italian actor in the 1994 film, his sound was a digitized high voice composite of an African American countertenor named Derek Lee Ragin and a Polish soprano Ewa Malas-Godlewska. The manufactured Farinelli voice is a symbolic approximation of a historic aural soundscape, "an apt metaphor for the historical castrati whose voices were altered via their surgery and then greatly manipulated in the six to twelve years of vocal training in conservatories" (André 2006, 18). In examining the manufactured voice as a metaphor, I submit that the movie director Gérard Corbiau's use of a "virtual voice" (20) may be interpreted in four important ways. First, it inadvertently reinscribes, perhaps in the service of mass media expectations of sonic or vocal perfection, "classical music industry" discourses of black voices as inadequate instruments for Western art music performance. Second, the artificiality of the digitalized voice corresponds to the procedures by which some Western art music pedagogues, producers, directors, and conductors perceive and have written about the countertenor voice as a gimmick and artificially produced. Third, the fact that some participants at the symposium confused a countertenor with a castrato, even one whose voice was digitally manipulated, suggests that many people are unaware or misinformed of what constitutes countertenor and castrato designations and styles. And finally, in a sonic patriarchal construct, the composite voice symbolically imbues the woman's voice with the perceived superior male vocal qualities. To produce the composite voice of Farinelli as sung in the movie, performance required a symbolic merging of vocal categories via the sonic castration and whitening of an African American countertenor and the "manning up" of a European soprano as they digitally combined the voices to design a mixed racial and gendered representation of sound. With regard to my research, that peculiar racial and gendered digitalized mixture evokes queries regarding the male high-singing voice as an embodied symbol of gendered sound throughout global vocal music discourse.

REPRESENTATIONS AND SYMBOLISM OF
MALE HIGH-SINGING IN MUSIC RESEARCH

Many societies around the world have male high-singing traditions. I trace African American countertenors' lineage to the overlap of two singing sociocultural heritages: African-derived oral and European-derived concert music. Within both singing heritages, musicians and listeners cultivate gendered perceptions of vocal styles, repertoire, range, and characterizations of vocal sound. However, sociocultural tensions emerge as African American countertenors venture into formal training and performance in Western art music performance, while also maintaining their musical roots in the worship traditions of black congregations. In historically African American Protestant congregations, countertenors manage congregations' anxieties about the performance of masculinity, while in Western art music they navigate the racial and gender biases of casting in the predominantly white opera industry.

From African religious rites to African American gospel music, black men have used a spectrum of vocal qualities in vocal music performances. According to historical accounts chronicled by Francis A. Kemble, white observers characterized men of African descent who worked in the antebellum rural South as singing with wide vocal range, with "rich, deep voices swelling out," and noted that the male voices seemed "oftener tenor than any other quality" (Kemble 1863, 106). Citing Kemble, musicologist Eileen Southern described some of the men's style as *falsetto* and their range as ascending to male soprano, as men's singing extended to what she called an "oftener tenor" quality and register (Southern 1997, 236).[5] With regard to gospel vocal ranges in particular, Southern observed a gendered traversing of vocal registers: "male singers often emphasize their falsetto tones; female singers, their lower register tones" (477). Southern's research suggests that there is a conventionally gendered range for male and female singers—ranges that twentieth- and twenty-first-century gospel artists have emotively expanded and varied. The lower vocal range has represented masculinity, virility, potency, hardness, and manliness—so much so that I found in my research with gospel baritones that their "low vocal designation is prized for its stimulating timbral qualities, suitable for setting the mood for worship in the sanctuary and sex in the bedchamber" (Jones 2018, 8). Alternatively, the higher vocal range has represented femininity, effeminacy, impotency, softness, and unmanliness. In some of my interviews with men examining the stereotype that all male choir directors or vocal worship leaders are gay, the men derided male vocalists who "sing high like a woman" (Jones 2016, 216). Should listeners subscribe to an imagined fixity of gendered vocal range boundaries, African American men who sing high or sing in a higher register during gospel performance may be perceived as socioculturally queer, trespassing into a vocal domain designated for women.

Male high-singing has been featured in sacred performance throughout Europe since the middle of the sixteenth century. The Western preferences for high-singing male voices soaring above choirs in sacred compositions stemmed from an aesthetic of a metaphoric angelic and gender nonconforming sound. Such preferences for high-male singing in European music overlaps with the aesthetics found in African-derived music styles in the United States such as rhythm and blues (R&B) and African American quartet music. In fact, black men have pursued careers in opera and concert performance throughout the world since the nineteenth century (Smith 1995; Cheatham 1997). However, the contributions of black high-singing male solo vocalists who have been trained in Western art music have not been explored extensively in ethnomusicological research.

The void in the literature is due in large part to racial and gendered biases to casting African American men in principal opera roles. Eileen Southern explained that historically, black "male singers generally found it more difficult to succeed in the concert world than did the prima donnas. For that reason, they were more likely to join ensembles, minstrel troupes in the nineteenth century, or touring concert companies" (Southern 1997, 249).[6] African American operatic tenor and vocal pedagogue George Shirley adds, "Black American singers of opera have always been relatively few in number for reasons external to the race as well as internal. We remain minorities in the profession numerically and racially, which should certainly come as no surprise in an art form that appeals only to a minority of the majority in America!" (Shirley 2014, 262). Even though there has been a disparity in casting African American men, they have made significant contributions to contemporary concert and opera performance through their musical style, sound quality, performance in diverse venues, and social navigation.[7]

Carter's compositions are an intervention for the dilemma of barriers to entry into the opera and concert industries, providing African American soloists with the space to represent the performance practices of gospel and concert music. He prompts them to do so in a manner that displays their multiple, musical consciousness in sacred music. Keeping in mind the melding of the African and European derived heritages, the sonic symbolism of male high-singing evoked in Carter's compositional choices is multivalent. Carter's voicing of the treble timbres (female trio and high vocalist) in the "Some Day" composition resembles the type of personnel who were traditionally chosen to embody symbolic transcendence in medieval to eighteenth-century Western church music repertoire. For the aristocracy of that time, treble timbre singers represented a sounded embodiment of divine power the heroic, the monarchy, the heavenly, the celestial, the otherworldly, and the "aesthetic of the marvelous" (André 2006, 3). Within medieval Western music traditions, high voices, regardless of gender, were privileged as sonic representations of culturally entrenched hierarchical values, dominance, and proximity to the heavenlies (Leonardi and Pope 1996, 28). In fact, the heavenlies were imagined as a location where celestial beings were eternally young. Their vocal dominance also sonically illustrated passion, eroticism, and ecstasy.

The historical countertenor personae and their sound have been characterized in disproportionately anatomical, gendered, and angelic language in comparison to other vocal classifications. Many writers have also signaled the complexity of conceptualizing gendered vocal sound quality by deploying anatomical metaphors with terms like "the Queen's Throat" (Koestenbaum 1993) and "the Diva's Mouth" (Leonardi and Pope 1996).

Even in the gendered characterizations throughout the literature of countertenor sound, spectators and listeners remarked upon bodily queering of their orifice and larynx that produced the high range they sang. Like the participants at the CBMR Black Vocality symposium, the aforementioned authors also compare countertenor vocal sound to castrato sound as they examine the applicability of the metaphors to countertenors. Perhaps the similarity in the countertenor, castrato, and contralto sound and personae registers with twenty-first-century listeners in the same manner that it registered to nineteenth-century aristocracy as "hearing the past while simultaneously creating something new from the past" (André 2006, 18). Throughout the rest of this chapter, I will compare discourses around these vocal designations to account for the fluidity of gender that is represented in what Naomi André calls an "aural genealogy" of "treble timbres" (12).

The countertenor designation is an embodied negotiation between feminine sound and masculine vocal power (Leonardi and Pope 1996, 25), a combination that has been characterized as "angelic" (François 1995), "The Heavenly Voice" (Pennacchi and Scillitani 2013), or "The Supernatural Voice" (Ravens 2014). "Denaturalized, denied access to manhood and maturity, the castrati were said to have access to the heavens; theirs were the voices of angels" (François 1995, 445). The angelic characterization signals a longstanding Christianized *discordia concors* discourse that was conveyed through visual and performing arts representations of various classifications historically conflated with androgyny: hermaphrodite, intersex, third sex, transvestite, transsexual, and effeminate. Gender studies scholar Piotr Scholz researches the cultural history of the links between castrati and eunuchs, both of which embody the musical and social performance of gender ambiguity. He asserts that androgyny is the embrace of both sexes as symbolically united in a being.[8] The castrato's high vocal sound was a signifier of androgyny and sexual impotency. Moreover, one's embodiment of the androgynous was a cosmic symbolism of one's polar opposites uniting, and thereby achieving, the highly desirable goal of resemblance to the omnipotent God. In the article "Homosexuality's Closet," gender studies theorist David Halperin considered men's negotiation of "an angelic sound" with regard to renowned countertenor David Daniels as embodying the woman's soul. "The secret, inchoate transgendered condition evidenced by his paradoxical combination of masculine and feminine attributes, patterns of feeling, and personae" (Halperin 2002, 29). Thus the sounded unification of polar opposites also conveys a potential autoeroticism in the male treble timbre sound, where there is a musical consummation between the feminine sound/soul that is enveloped by the masculine vocal power/body.

Despite the venerable tradition of men singing in a conventionally female register, skepticism around the countertenor vocal designation persists. I contend one must allow that any singer's exploration of his or her marketable sound is a process of selecting a comfortable vocal range and making choices for his or her vocal longevity. That subjective and collaborative selection process is both natural and relative to their vocal instrument and technique. For example, tenor and vocal pedagogue Richard Miller described in his early writings the countertenor voice classification as a baritone who chooses to sing in his falsetto register.[9] Falsetto was traditionally considered in the

Italianate school of thought as "una voce falsa" (a fake voice), a type of vocal trick. Miller wrote, "Countertenors do not require the same amount of laryngeal muscle activity as the fully registered male voice" (Miller 1993, 13). He framed countertenor singing as a style rather than a vocal designation.[10] Like Richard Miller, countertenor and vocal pedagogue Peter Giles (1982, 1994) observed that high male vocalists have been perceived as men who imitate the female voice, who perform a gimmick, or men whose singing is a vocal experiment. Miller later slightly adjusted his assessment in *The Structure of Singing: System and Art in Vocal Technique* (1996). He referred to countertenors as male falsettists in order to account for the similarities between the vocal designation and the style and over time dealt with the politics of his bias against countertenor vocalization. "A performance phenomenon that must be dealt with in any serious consideration of contemporary singing is the male falsettists. The solo countertenor is here to stay. It is unrealistic for teachers of singing to regard him as a nonlegitimate (sic) performer. The countertenor should be taught, and he should be taught seriously" (123). In briefly addressing the countertenor as "a performance phenomenon," he falls short and reified their vocal illegitimacy among vocal pedagogues by not expanding on technique appropriate for the voice type, in the same way he wrote a pedagogy for the other vocal classifications. Even though countertenors have not always been taken seriously throughout history, their vocal designation is still deployed throughout operatic, art song, and sacred vocal music performance.

As African American countertenors move between the worlds of Western opera and gospel music, what kinds of choices do they make to demonstrate their performance competence as male trained singers who "sound like women"? In what ways do they also navigate their audience's expectations about the parameters for men's vocal sound qualities? To examine Dailey's sociocultural strategies of gendered sound in gospel music settings, I asked him about his performance choices as a formally trained opera singer who leads worship in African American Protestant churches. I now turn to a discussion of some of the strategies that he deploys to navigate the social and theological tensions that manifest as he sings in gospel music circles.

SOCIAL AND THEOLOGICAL TENSIONS: MANLINESS AND PERFORMING SPIRITUAL COMPETENCE

New Psalmist Baptist Church, the venue where Patrick Dailey made his television debut, is one of the largest churches in the Washington, DC–Baltimore, Maryland area. The members of this predominantly African American congregation are socioeconomically diverse, ranging from working to upper-middle class, encompassing various education levels. Dailey's performance at New Baptist[11] was broadcast on cable television on The Word Network ("Some Day," n.d.), featuring primarily preaching and gospel music programming.[12] Such television shows are popular among many black preachers, musicians, and lay participants who regularly depend on television or streaming media to view worship services from around the world.[13]

At the beginning of the service, senior pastor Bishop Walter Thomas pointed out that Morgan State University is noted for training black musicians such as the featured soloist for that morning's service, Patrick Dailey. Many Morgan State students and alumni worship at New Psalmist. In fact, Bishop Thomas, the conductor Fernando Allen, and Dailey are all proud heirs of the Morgan State University musical legacy championed by the late composer-arranger Dr. Nathan Mitchell Carter Jr. (1936–2004).

Morgan State students and alumni like Dailey perform a variety of repertoire on the concert stage and in church, a repertoire that includes anthems and praise and worship songs. Dailey led what is classified as a sermonic selection, which is a song that both precedes and sets the tone for the sermon. "I have asked the choir to sing this melody to remind us that one day we will all get home," Bishop Thomas said in his introduction during the service. "Brother Patrick Dailey, a tremendous singer, who God has blessed and I believe will have a glorious future in music, will sing this song." By personally introducing the soloist Patrick Dailey, Thomas was an ally for the singer who performs what some visitors to the church and television viewers might have perceived as an unusual, even uncanny vocal performance. Thomas facilitated a pastoral and educational moment that guided uninitiated listeners unaccustomed to Dailey's countertenor vocal worship leadership.

When I interviewed Dailey, he expressed his anxieties about the aural-visual qualities of his transdenominational vocal worship leadership, how he vocally and verbally presents himself, as well as the manner with which he uses his body in church performances to signify a conventional masculinity or sexuality. His strategies revealed that historically black Protestant audiences' receptiveness to countertenors' vocal performance is closely linked to the ways their sound is embodied. As a seasoned countertenor, Dailey knows his comportment will be heavily scrutinized. Dailey offered both spiritual and performance practices to guide the audience's reception of his voice within African American gospel contexts.

The performance venue context is key for Dailey's preparation. Even though he was apprehensive about making the distinction, Dailey shared with me that the congregation's education level and cultural exposure are crucial factors in the positive reception of his performance. He assessed the congregation's competence before agreeing to minister by gauging their familiarity with his vocal sound. Likewise, Dailey maintained that it is important for countertenors to assess the experience of the congregation's music director in selecting repertoire for countertenors. Do they have a sense of the repertoire that is in his *fach*? In other words, do they know how to select music that is vocally comfortable and flattering for him? Are they willing to hire him to perform gospel selections that do not conflict with his vocal technique? Some music directors have requested, for example, that Dailey sing in a gospel tenor range, suggesting they perceived it to be in his "natural" or "fitting" (meaning manly) range.

"Can you sing *us*?" African American novices to Western art music often ask this of formally trained black singers who sing in gospel settings. Dailey shared that this type of query was put to him, and I was also asked a similar question by youths several years ago when I was a guest artist in the education department of the Washington National Opera. Certain patrons will inquire some variation of "Can you sing us?" to assess whether the black vocalist is culturally competent in and still connected to African American singing styles. The singer, congregation, and director mutually gauge each other's cultural competence. Dailey understood this as a request to demonstrate his cultural accessibility by signifying on various gospel vocal techniques such as singing melismas that sonically evoke styles perfected by contemporary gospel artists Kim Burrell or the Clark Sisters.[14]

Using his transferable musical skills in his performance of "Some Day" at New Psalmist Baptist Church, Dailey's melismas, or the stylistic approach referred to as "runs" in gospel music vernacular, during the reprise (a repeated passage of music) he provides an ideal illustration of the ways gospel and opera overlap. Both operatic and gospel performance traditions utilize stylized melisma within the performance of efficacious singing. Musicologist Martha Feldman explained that in eighteenth-century *opera seria*, for example, enchantment was achieved through various stylistic feats (Feldman 2007, 26). In the manner of a *prima donna* (the principal female singer in an opera) singing a signature *cadenza* (a sung ornamented passage that is either written or improvised) in an aria of the *bel canto* (translated as beautiful singing) tradition, he utilized ornamentation that alluded to traditional melisma, "runs" from the core gospel repertoire. Dailey also demonstrated that he is aware of gospel repertoire and vocal delivery when he used a reprise. In effect, he "sings us." For example, competent gospel performers can respond to or interact with the congregation's enthused participatory cues or request to repeat a particular phrase in real time consultation with the conductor or director and the accompanying instrumentalists. Since Dailey responded with that gospel performance competence, participants interpreted his reprise as a musical response to the Spirit manifesting in the presentation.

As I have written in the 2016 article "Are All the Choir Directors Gay?," I observed that Dailey evoked the "black Baptist man" persona when performing in church and gospel performance settings (222). He indicated that when he is a soloist in African American churches, he "presents like a good Baptist man" by lowering his voice slightly and verbalizing a traditional salutation before he sings in order to deflect any questions about whether or not he is a homosexual. Dailey said, "I will say it like a good Baptist man who loves the Lord. I don't get up and say (in a higher register), 'Hey y'all, he's so worthy, chile.'[15] Mmmhmmm. No" (interview, November 11, 2011). When I asked for clarification about his "good Baptist" persona, Dailey clarified that the persona description was a composite of heterosexist and patriarchal masculinity with whom he often interacted in traditional black church denominations and organizations.

To achieve this Baptist persona, Dailey also expressed that he performs "a neutrality" in his speaking register while he becomes acquainted with a congregation and their "competency" in terms of formal salutations. With new audiences, he speaks in a slightly lower register than his singing voice to establish an aural baseline, but not too low so as to avoid injury. When he demonstrated his adjustment to a lower range to me, I still detected an "oftener" soprano quality in his comfortable speaking register. Dailey often greets his audience with the salutation, "First giving honor to God who is the head of my life." He used this verbal cue to signify an ideal black masculinity with a traditional "black church" salutation to the congregation that is a composite of protocol. Protocol, as demonstrated through salutations, is a prized dimension of African American Christian communication, hospitality, and a performative means through which he obtains an "ideal" southern black Christian manhood.

> Often when I get up in front of a new audience, I am very neutral. Like, if I am at church and they want me to sing an aria, I will say, (in a slightly lower register) "Praise the Lord everybody. I am Patrick Dailey. We are not going to be before you long. We are gonna sing this one aria for you and we will get out of the way."
>
> (Interview, November 11, 2011)

His protocol competency is signified with a salutation that starts in the manner of "First, giving honor to God" or "Praise the Lord, everybody." Dailey's demonstration of salutation literacy and performance of social familiarity is intended to convey to the audience that he is an insider and a competent worship leader as he introduces new repertoire and the vocal technique associated with countertenor performance. He maintained that taking such measures to frame his masculinity are vital for engaging those female and male patrons whom he maintains find performances of "soft" masculinity offensive.

As Dailey ministers in worship, he is also conscious of a congregation's simultaneous attraction to and speculation about the embodied nature of his gift. Like most black countertenors with whom I have spoken, Dailey frequently received questions about his gender expression and his sexual orientation after singing for new audiences. Many listeners comment, "You sound like a woman," as either a compliment or in disbelief. It is a frequent remark to which he and many other countertenors have diverse reactions. This experience implies that considerations are still evoked about what his trained sound indicates about identity and his sexual preference. To ask it more bluntly: to whom is countertenor sound attractive?

Throughout history, enthusiasts attest that countertenor sound is attractive to both women and men—a parallel that resembles listeners' reception of castrati—especially those who are familiar with operatic roles that feature countertenors. As Halperin observed, although they are in the minority, there are certainly straight countertenors. However, there is something about the quality of sound and social meanings associated with the vocal facility that "seems to attract gay male singers—or to bring out a male singer's queer potential" (Halperin 2002, 27). Despite the countertenor's queer "potential" being brought out, as Halperin put it, countertenors may also aurally evoke both envy and desire in women. Female listeners may experience what I connote as the latent or overt aural homoeroticism of countertenor same-gendered sound. After hearing my research on African American countertenors at a University of California, Los Angeles (UCLA) voice studies conference, one woman confided in me that she is attracted to countertenors more than any other vocal designation: "If I could have that voice! Their voices are such a turn-on to me. If I could, I would only date countertenors. They are so hot" (personal communication, January 2015). She admitted that she was drawn to the countertenors' combination of the virtuosic, high voice, and the bravado they embodied on stage. Inextricable from his verbal cues before his performances are the ways in which he uses his body to speak and sing to signal a good Baptist man's gender expression.

EMBODIED COUNTERTENOR SOUND

In addition to sonically and verbally packaging his presentation so that African American audiences may be receptive to his performances, Dailey also uses his body to orient and manage their perceptions about his identity. He expressed particular anxiety about their search for feminine masculinity in his mannerisms. Many historically black Protestant congregations deplore "effeminacy" in black men, and become easily suspicious of mannerisms that fall outside of the heteronormative ideal. As the following interview excerpt suggests, there is a hegemonic gestural masculinity that Dailey believes he must perform in order to position himself for congregations' positive reception of his singing. Heterosexual-presenting men—regardless of their sexual preferences—are the ideal masculinity. He understood his conscious, gestural heteropresentation as a necessary device for him to be viewed as a competent and appropriate minister.[16] Patrick Dailey is also a formally trained dancer in ballet and modern genres. Dailey maintained that it was through dance training that he focused on his heroic, "masculine posture," comportment, and the ability to visually and musically partner with women in both dance and operatic performance.

> ALISHA JONES: What do you mean by "present like a man"?
> PATRICK DAILEY: There is Patrick and there is Patty. I guess Patty is the more fierce one but I am Patrick on that [audition] stage...For me, the presentation is masculine.[17] It is me being myself because not only are you a black man. You are also a gay black man. All of your life you have to deal with being a black man. There is enough that we have fought for as a people. You can't turn people off. I have seen people sing and they wear the tightest H&M pants, they have the forearm going on, different color eyes, you know the contacts, foundation and powder on their face too—and you're a baritone.   (Interview, November 11, 2011)

Dailey claimed that black men face professional hassles when they do not physically present themselves in a manner consistent with hegemonic perceptions of ideal masculinity. George Shirley remarked on the importance of a singer's professional ability to "look the part" and improve upon their stage deportment if it is wanting. He noted, "I will encourage acquisition of physical poise and grace of movement" (Shirley 2014, 274). Dailey's heteronormative performance of masculinity as signified by training to be a competent dance partner prepared him to perform an ideal masculinity consistent with black social values of respectability.[18] He expressed that his goal is not to be a distraction.

"Do not let your slip show," he said. In other words, do not use mannerisms that can be construed as "effeminate" or feminine masculinity. This statement illustrates that Dailey does not transfer the practice of performing *en travesti* (in women's attire) into gospel presentations.

Patrick Dailey's social and theological negotiation of his countertenor sound exemplified the various sonic and visual scripts that a singer might enact across African-derived and European-derived cultural contexts. He adjusted his speaking range to a lower register to cue familiar masculinity for African American audiences with whom he is becoming acquainted. Dailey pursued a great deal of agency as he vetted new congregations and clients by making decisions about whether or not they are compatible musically. Dailey asserted his authority in deciding which engagements to accept. He allowed for opportunities to demonstrate his versatile music approach that merges African American gospel with Western art music. While he exercised his musical discretion in selecting his engagements, Dailey also exhibited anxiety regarding his singing, gesturing, and speaking habits that might suggest queer potential in his identity.

While making a mark in sacred music history, Patrick Dailey's performance of Carter's arranged composition of "Some Day" reveals the subtle ways Western art music conventions of classifying vocalists are utilized and revised in the interpretation of cross-cultural performance in African American churches. The interpretations generated from the legacy of castrato performances furnish a point of reference for similar issues of the countertenor's vocal technique, sexuality, and gendered sound in historic Christian worship. And Dailey's work highlights the social and theological issues that countertenors may take into account in order to make choices in appropriate repertoire, vet receptive congregations, tailor their performance practice, and demonstrate their worship leader competency. Dailey adapted his musical performance of ideal masculine communication in order to demonstrate his competency as a transdenominational worship leader in African American churches. However, in examining Dailey's intersectionality, we find socioculturally diverse perceptions of what vocal range indicates about one's spirituality, sexual orientation, and attractiveness to their sonic and visual admirers. Undoubtedly, continued scholarly analysis of African American countertenors' contributions and experiences within multiple musical worlds will yield a well-rounded analysis of what it means for all African American musicians to finally find a home, *some day*, in music performance and research.

NOTES

1. The Word Network is an African American Christian television network based in Southfield, Michigan.
2. SSAATTBB is an acronym within choral arrangement that refers to the first and second soprano, first and second alto, first and second tenor, and first and second bass choral voicing.
3. Carter conducted the renowned Morgan State University Choir for thirty-four years, from 1970 until his passing in 2004.

4. "In their own time, the castrati voices were altered voices and would not occur without a type of surgery called orchiectomy" (André 2006, 18). Castration, orchiectomy, or gonadectomy are surgical, chemical, or any other procedure in which men lose their testicles and thus become sterile and greatly reduce the production of testosterone hormone.

5. As I consider the expression of "singing high," I draw a division between the countertenor vocal designation and the term *falsetto*. Both countertenor and falsetto are Western classical singing notions, but falsetto style is used in other musical styles as well. Among many vocal pedagogues, falsetto pertains to men's vocal style or affect that is perceived as beyond their normative vocal range. According to vocal pedagogue Richard Miller, "In the international language of singing, falsetto describes that imitative female sound that the male singer is capable of making on pitches that lie above normal male speaking range" (Miller 1996, 121). In African American music performance, in Anne-Lise François's research on falsetto use in gospel-influenced disco, she counters that the popular assessment of falsetto as a gimmick is a hegemonic perspective. She argues that the foundation for analysis of falsetto style is built upon "1) the falsetto voice's homelessness with respect to either gender, and 2) its legitimacy within what is itself a Diaspora-formed or exilic tradition" (François 1995, 443). The intangibility in the gender homelessness imagery captures the cost for men who sound castrated or androgynous without a physical condition to blame for their musical distinctiveness.

6. See also Story (1993) and Eidsheim (2008).

7. Anne-Lise François argues that one of the "nonconformist" ways in which black men have lifted their voice to higher heights, independent of and despite limited performance platforms, is through falsetto style in pop music such as disco and soul. François examines, for example, falsettist Curtis Mayfield's contribution that "In the same way, it might be said that he can't help but sing in falsetto; the haunting otherworldliness of his voice is forced and urgent. In a world where 'the price of meat is higher than the dope on the street,' there is no choice but to sing in the register of the other (world). Falsetto is the only way to make oneself heard in a world which is already a lie—the white-owned world which is also that of one's suffering community. To go 'back to the world' then is to be made to sing—to assume the voice of otherness—so as to express precisely that in one's self and one's vision which is denied fulfillment in this world. But to reclaim the world is also to urge the present with reiterative emphasis in the knowledge that one's inner ghosts have no other place to go" (François 1995, 444–45).

African American men's falsetto singing signifies a means through which men sound transcendence to cope with social injustices. They also vocally sound a wide range of topics that demonstrate their ability to feel and skillfully perform for listeners who are embedded in various cultural matrices (Jackson 2000, 13). Black male high voice soloists/falsettists have musically transcended in popular, gospel, and Western art music that merits in depth research and cannot be exhausted in this chapter. In Western art music, African American countertenors include Derek Lee Ragin, Ken Alston Jr., Victor Trent Cook, Tai Oney, Matthew Truss, Cortez Mitchell, and Patrick Dailey. In popular music, black male high-singing vocalists include Smokey Robinson, Philip Bailey, Claude Jeter (Swan Silverstones), Bryan McKnight, Maxwell, Prince, Curtis Mayfield, the Stylistics, Al Green, Ron Isley of the Isley Brothers, Little Richard, and El DeBarge. In gospel music black male high-singing vocalists include Richard Smallwood, John P. Kee, Rance Allen, Anthony Charles Williams (formerly known as TONEX), and many gospel quartet singers. This is by no means an exhaustive list of black men who sing high.

8. Scholz further defines androgyny as "the union of the physical characteristics of male and female in our being and the notion of asexuality, a characteristic of spiritual beings, especially angels" (1999, 7).
9. I would like to fully disclose that I worked for Richard Miller as a laboratory assistant (2000–2004) at the Otto B. Schoeplfe Vocal Arts Center (OBSVAC), Oberlin Conservatory in Oberlin, Ohio.
10. Richard Miller maintained that countertenors are more likely to achieve agile movement in rapid passages and embellishments. He writes further that such an approach allows for easy control of dynamics. Miller also clarifies that countertenors who sing in falsetto should not be confused with those who sing *voce piena in testa* (full head voice) (Miller 1993, 13).
11. The footage of Dailey's performance from the broadcast was posted on the New Psalmist Baptist Church YouTube channel on September 15, 2011 (see "'Some Day' The New Psalmist Baptist Church Mass Choir with Soloist: Patrick Dailey").
12. The Word Network's demographics and programming format is described on its website as follows:
    "The network has gained recognition as the network of choice for African American programming by featuring ministries, an informative Christian focused television lineup and gospel music…The Word network recognizes that music is a large part of the Christian experience, and offers line up of gospel artist, interviews, videos and musical specials featuring artists such as Marvin Sapp, Kirk Franklin, Mary Mary, Donnie McClurkin, Hezekiah Walker, J. Moss, Deitrick Haddon, Cece Winans, Byron Cage and newcomers such as Wess Morgan and VaShawn Mitchell, to name just a few" (The Word Network n.d.).
13. Dailey's debut via The Word Network exemplifies the mutual influence between black religiosity and multimedia engagement. In his book *Watch This!* (2009), Jonathan L. Walton describes the importance of considering participation in worship via multimedia outlets like televised services and live streaming as a part of modern religious practices. My inclusion of the television and Internet domains in my ethnomusicological research helps to account for the multiple narratives and media that are engrafted in globalized religious practice. In addition, the decision makers in these platforms expose listeners and spectators to versatile music ministers and equip them with tools to properly receive them.
14. Melisma is a group of notes sung on one syllable or vocable.
15. "Chile" is a vernacular form of "child," which is a term of endearment.
16. I deploy "minister" as a signifier of social peculiarity, as one who is set apart, and who demonstrates social and theological discipline to God and humankind in presentation, posture, and attitude.
17. In this context "fierce" is a queer vernacular characterization of one's striking performativity.
18. For more on respectability, consult Calvin Whites Jr.'s *The Rise of Respectability* (2012).

Works Cited

André, Naomi. 2006. *Voicing Gender: Castrati, Travesti and the Second Woman in Early-Nineteenth-Century Italian Opera*. Bloomington: Indiana University Press.
Cheatham, Wallace McClain, ed. 1997. *Dialogues on Opera and the African-American Experience*. Lanham, MD: Scarecrow Press.

Eidsheim, Nina. 2008. "Voice as a Technology of Selfhood: Towards an Analysis of Racialized Timbre and Vocal Performance." PhD diss., University of California, San Diego.

Feldman, Martha. 2007. *Opera and Sovereignty: Transforming Myths in Eighteenth-Century Italy*. Chicago: University of Chicago Press.

Feldman, Martha. 2015. *The Castrato: Reflections on Natures and Kinds*. Berkeley: University of California Press.

François, Anne-Lise. 1995. "Fakin' it/Makin' it: Falsetto's Bid for Transcendence in 1970s Disco Highs." *Perspectives of New Music* 33 (Issue 1/2, Winter – Summer): 442–57.

Giles, Peter. 1982. *The Counter Tenor*. London: Frederick Muller Limited.

Giles, Peter. 1994. *The History and Technique of the Counter-Tenor: A Study of the Male High Voice Family*. Aldershot: Scolar Press.

Halperin, David. 2002. "Homosexuality's Closet." *Michigan Quarterly Review* 41 (1, Winter): 21–54.

Jackson, Travis A. 2000. "Spooning Good Singing Gum: Meaning, Association, and Interpretation in Rock Music." *Current Musicology* 69 (Spring): 7–41.

Jones, Alisha Lola. 2016. "Are All The Choir Directors Gay?: Black Men's Sexuality and Identity in Gospel Performance." In *Issues in African American Music: Power, Race, Gender, and Representation*, edited by Portia K. Maultsby and Mellonee V. Burnim, 216–36. New York: Routledge.

Jones, Alisha Lola. 2018. " 'You Are My Dwelling Place': Experiencing Black Male Vocalists' Worship as Aural- and Autoeroticism in Gospel Performance." In *Women and Music Journal*, Vol. 22. Lincoln: University of Nebraska.

Kemble, Frances Anne. 1863. *Journal of a Residence on a Georgian Plantation*. New York: Cosimo, Inc.

Koestenbaum, Wayne. 1993. *The Queen's Throat: Opera, Homosexuality and the Mystery of Desire*. New York: Poseidon Press.

Leonardi, Susan J., and Rebecca A. Pope. 1996. *The Diva's Mouth: Body, Voice, and Prima Donna Politics*. New Brunswick, NJ: Rutgers University Press.

Miller, Richard. 1993. *Training the Tenor Voice*. New York: Schirmer Books.

Miller, Richard. 1996. *The Structure of Singing: System and Art in Vocal Technique*. New York: Schirmer Books.

New Psalmist Baptist Church. " 'Some Day': The New Psalmist Baptist Church Mass Choir with Soloist: Patrick Dailey." September 15, 2011. https://www.youtube.com/watch?v= GKjX7uBJktA.

Pennacchi, Gino, and Alessandro Scillitani. 2013. *The Heavenly Voices: Legacy of Farinelli*. Italy: Arthaus.

Ravens, Simon. 2014. *The Supernatural Voice: A History of High Male Singing*. London: Boydell Press.

Scholz, Piotr. 1999. *Eunuchs and Castrati: A Cultural History*. Princeton, NJ: Markus Wiener.

Shirley, George. 2014. "Il Rodolfo Nero, or The Masque of Blackness." In *Blackness in Opera*, edited by Naomi Andre, Karen M. Bryan, and Eric Saylor, 260–74. Urbana: University of Illinois Press.

Smith, Eric Ledell. 1995. *Blacks in Opera: An Encyclopedia of People and Companies, 1873–1993*. Jefferson, NC: McFarland & Company.

Southern, Eileen. 1997. *The Music of Black Americans: A History*. 3rd ed. New York: Norton.

Story, Rosalyn M. 1993. *And So I Sing: African-American Divas of Opera and Concert.* New York: Amistad.

Walton, Jonathan. 2009. *Watch This!: This Ethics and Aesthetics of Black Televangelism.* New York: New York University Press.

White, Calvin. 2012. *The Rise of Respectability: Race, Religion, and the Church of God in Christ.* Fayetteville: University of Arkansas Press.

The Word Network. n.d. http://www.thewordnetwork.org/about. Accessed February 14, 2014.

PART II

CHANGING VOICE

VOICE AS BAROMETER

CHAPTER 4

....

MEDICAL CARE
OF VOICE DISORDERS

....

ROBERT T. SATALOFF AND MARY J. HAWKSHAW

VOICE disorders are common and may be particularly troublesome for singers, actors, and other serious vocalists. Since the 1980s, the standard of medical care for patients with voice disorders has improved dramatically. Techniques of history-taking and physical examination have become much more sophisticated over the last few decades. The consequences of systemic disorders upon voice function has been recognized, and interdisciplinary voice teams have evolved to provide comprehensive voice care. This chapter provides an overview of state-of-the-art diagnosis and treatment.

INTRODUCTION: THE HISTORY

UNTIL the 1980s, most physicians caring for patients with voice disorders asked only a few basic questions such as: "How long have you been hoarse?" and "Do you smoke?" Since the early 1980s, the standard of care has improved dramatically.

Good medical diagnosis in all fields often depends on asking the right questions and then listening carefully to the answers. This process is known as "taking a history." Recently, medical care for voice problems has used a markedly expanded, comprehensive history, recognizing that there is more to the voice than simply the vocal folds (Sataloff 2017a). Virtually any body system may be responsible for voice complaints. In fact, problems outside the larynx often cause voice dysfunction in people whose vocal folds appear fairly normal and who would have received no effective medical care a few years ago.

PHYSICAL EXAMINATION

Physical examination of a patient with voice complaints involves a complete ear, nose, and throat assessment and examination of other body systems as appropriate (Sataloff 2017b). Subjective examination has been supplemented by technological aids that improve the ability to "see" the vocal mechanism and allow quantification of aspects of its function. During phonation at middle C, the vocal folds come together and separate approximately 250 times per second. Strobovideolaryngoscopy allows the examiner to assess the vocal folds in slow motion. This technology allows visualization of small masses, vibratory asymmetries, adynamic (nonvibrating) segments due to scar tissue or early cancer, and other abnormalities that were simply missed in vocal folds that looked normal under continuous light. The instruments contained in a well-equipped clinical voice laboratory assess six categories of vocal function: vibratory, aerodynamic, phonatory, acoustic, electromyographic, and psychoacoustic. State-of-the-art analysis of vocal function is extremely helpful in the diagnosis, therapy, and evaluation of progress during the treatment of voice disorders.

COMMON DIAGNOSES AND TREATMENTS

Following a thorough history, physical examination, and clinical voice laboratory analysis, it is usually possible to arrive at an accurate explanation for voice dysfunction. Of course, treatment depends on the cause. Fortunately, as technology has improved voice medicine, the need for laryngeal surgery has diminished. In many cases, voice disorders result from respiratory, neurological, gastrointestinal, psychological, endocrine, or some other medical cause that can be treated. Many conditions require prescription of drugs. However, medications must be used with caution because many of them have adverse side effects that may alter voice function. Consequently, close collaboration is required among all specialists involved in the patient's care to be certain that treatment of one causal condition does not produce a secondary dysfunction that is also deleterious to the voice. When the underlying problem is corrected properly the voice usually improves, but collaborative treatment by a team of specialists is most desirable to ensure general and vocal health and optimize voice function.

HOARSENESS

Most people with voice problems complain of "hoarseness" or "laryngitis." A more accurate description of the problem is often helpful in identifying the cause. Hoarseness is a coarse, scratchy sound most commonly caused by abnormalities on the vibratory margin of the vocal fold. These may include swelling, roughness from inflammation, growths, scarring, or anything that interferes with symmetric, periodic vocal fold vibration. Such abnormalities produce turbulence that is perceived as hoarseness. Breathiness is caused by lesions (abnormalities) that keep the vocal folds from closing completely, including paralysis, muscle weakness, cricoarytenoid joint injury or arthritis, vocal fold masses, or atrophy of the vocal fold tissues. These abnormalities permit air to escape when the vocal folds are supposed to be tightly closed. We hear this air leakage as breathiness.

Fatigue of the voice is inability to continue to phonate for extended periods without change in vocal quality. The voice may fatigue by becoming hoarse, losing range, changing timbre, breaking into different registers, or by other uncontrolled behavior. These problems are especially apparent in actors and singers. A well-trained singer should be able to sing for several hours without developing vocal fatigue. Fatigue is often caused by misuse of abdominal and neck musculature or overuse (singing or speaking too loudly for too long). Vocal fatigue may be a sign of general tiredness or of serious illnesses, such as myasthenia gravis.

Volume disturbance may present as an inability to speak or sing loudly, or an inability to phonate softly. Each voice has its own dynamic range. Professional voice users acquire greater loudness through increased vocal efficiency. They learn to speak and sing more softly through years of laborious practice that involves muscle control and development of the ability to use the supraglottic resonators effectively. Most volume problems are secondary to intrinsic limitations of the voice or technical errors in voice production, although hormonal changes, aging, and neurological disease are other causes. Superior laryngeal nerve paralysis will impair the ability to speak loudly. This is a frequently unrecognized consequence of herpes infections (such as cold sores) and may be precipitated by an upper respiratory tract infection.

Even nonsingers normally require only about 10 to 30 minutes to warm up the voice. Prolonged warm-up time, especially in the morning, is most often caused by reflux laryngitis, a condition in which stomach acid refluxes up the esophagus and ends up burning the throat. Tickling or choking during speech or singing is associated with laryngitis or voice abuse. Often a symptom of pathology of the vocal fold's leading edge, this symptom requires that voice use be avoided until vocal fold examination has been accomplished. Pain while vocalizing can indicate vocal fold lesions, laryngeal joint arthritis, infection, or gastric (stomach) acid irritation of the arytenoids, but it is much more commonly caused by voice abuse with excessive muscular activity in the neck rather than acute pathology on the leading edge of a vocal fold. It does not usually require immediate cessation of phonation pending medical examination.

AGE

Age affects the voice, especially during childhood and older age (Sataloff, Kost, and Linville 2017). Children's voices are particularly fragile. Voice abuse during childhood may lead to problems that persist throughout a lifetime. It is extremely important for children to learn good vocal habits and for them to avoid voice abuse. This is especially true for children who choose to participate in vocally taxing activities, such as singing, acting, and cheerleading. Many promising careers and vocal avocations have been ruined by enthusiastic but untrained voice use. For children with vocal interests, age-appropriate training should be started early. Any child with unexplained or prolonged hoarseness should undergo prompt, expert medical evaluation performed by a laryngologist (ear, nose, and throat doctor) specializing in voice care.

In geriatric patients, vocal unsteadiness, loss of range, and voice fatigue may be associated with typical physiological aging changes, such as vocal fold atrophy (wasting). In routine speech, such vocal changes allow a person to be identified as "old" even over the telephone. Among singers, they are typically associated with flat pitch and a "wobble" often heard in older, amateur choir singers. Recent evidence has shown that many of these acoustic phenomena are not caused by irreversible aging changes. Rather, they may be consequences of poor laryngeal, respiratory, and abdominal muscle condition, which undermines the power source of the voice. The medical history usually reveals minimal aerobic exercise and shortness of breath climbing stairs. With appropriate conditioning of the body and voice, many of the characteristics associated with vocal aging can be eliminated, and a youthful sound can be restored.

This topic is discussed in greater detail in other literature (Smith and Sataloff 2012).

HEARING LOSS

Hearing impairment can cause vocal strain, particularly if a person has sensorineural hearing loss (involving the nerve or inner ear) and is unaware of it. This condition may lead people to speak or sing more loudly than they realize. Hearing loss is an important consideration in singers and other musicians (Sataloff, Sataloff, and McGovern 2017).

EFFECTS OF VOICE USE AND TRAINING

The amount of voice use and training also affects voices. Inquiry into vocal habits frequently reveals correctable causes for voice difficulties. Extensive untrained speaking under adverse environmental circumstances is a common example. Such conditions occur, for example, among stock traders, salespeople, restaurant personnel, and people who speak on the telephone in noisy offices. The problems are aggravated by habits that impair the mechanics of voice production, such as sitting with poor posture and bending the neck to hold a telephone against a shoulder. Subconscious efforts to overcome these impediments often produce enough voice abuse to cause vocal fatigue, hoarseness, and even nodules (callous-like growths, usually on both vocal folds). Recognizing and eliminating the causal factors through voice therapy and training usually results in the nodules disappearing and voice improvement.

SINGERS, ACTORS, AND OTHER
VOICE PROFESSIONALS

It is essential for the physician to know the extent to which any patient uses his or her voice professionally. Professional singers, actors, announcers, politicians, and others put Olympic demands on their voices. Interest in the diagnosis and treatment of special problems of professional voice users is responsible for the evolution of voice care as a subspecialty of otolaryngology. These patients are often best managed by subspecialists familiar with the latest concepts in professional voice care.

SMOKE AND OTHER
SUBSTANCES IN THE AIR

Exposure to environmental irritants is a well-recognized cause of voice dysfunction (Del'Aria and Opperman 2017; Rossol 2017a, b; Sataloff 2017c). Smoke, dehydration, pollution, and allergens may produce hoarseness, frequent throat clearing, and voice fatigue. These problems generally can be eliminated by environmental modification, medication, or simply breathing through the nose rather than the mouth, as the nose warms, humidifies, and filters incoming air. The deleterious effects of tobacco smoke on the vocal folds have been known for many years. Smoking not only causes chronic irritation, but moreover, it can result in histologic (microscopic) alterations in the vocal fold epithelium. The epithelial cells change their appearance, becoming increasingly different from normal epithelial cells. Eventually, they begin to pile up on each other rather than lining up in an orderly fashion. Then they escape normal homeostatic controls, growing rapidly without restraint and invading surrounding tissues. This drastic change is called *squamous cell carcinoma*, or cancer of the larynx.

EFFECTS OF FOODS
AND DRUGS ON THE VOICE

The use of various foods and drugs may affect the voice as well. Some medications may even permanently ruin a voice, especially androgenic (male) hormones, such as those given to women with endometriosis or with postmenopausal sexual dysfunction. Similar problems occur with anabolic steroids (also male hormones) used illicitly by bodybuilders. More common drugs also have deleterious vocal effects, usually temporarily. Antihistamines cause dryness, increased throat clearing, and irritation and often aggravate hoarseness. Aspirin contributes to vocal fold hemorrhages because of the same anticoagulant properties that make it a good drug for patients with vascular disease. The propellant in inhalers used to treat asthma often produces laryngitis. Many neurological, psychological, and respiratory medications cause tremor that can be heard in the voice. Numerous other medications cause similar problems. Some foods may also be responsible for voice complaints in people with "normal" vocal folds. Milk products are particularly troublesome to some people because they increase and thicken mucosal secretions.

Voice Effects from Other Parts of the Body

The patient history must also assess the function of the respiratory (breathing), gastrointestinal (gut), endocrine (hormones), neurological, and psychological systems. Disturbances in any of these areas may be responsible for voice complaint.

Problems anywhere in the body must be discovered during the medical history. Because voice function relies on such complex brain and nervous system interactions, even slight neurological dysfunction may cause voice abnormalities. Voice impairment is sometimes the first symptom of serious diseases, such as myasthenia gravis, multiple sclerosis, and Parkinson's disease. Even a history of a sprained ankle may reveal the true cause of voice dysfunction, especially in a singer, actor, or speaker with great vocal demands. Proper posture is important to optimal function of the abdomen and chest. The imbalance created by standing with the weight over only one foot frequently impairs support enough to cause compensatory vocal strain, leading to hoarseness and voice fatigue. Similar imbalances may occur after other bodily injuries. These include not only injuries that involve support structures, but also problems in the head and neck, especially whiplash. Naturally, a history of laryngeal trauma or surgery predating voice dysfunction raises concerns about the anatomical integrity of the vocal fold, but a history of interference with the power source through abdominal or thoracic surgery may be just as important in understanding the cause and optimal treatment of vocal problems.

Gastrointestinal Disorders

Gastrointestinal disorders commonly cause voice complaints (Sataloff et al. 2013). The sphincter between the stomach and esophagus is notoriously weak. In gastroesophageal reflux laryngitis, stomach acid refluxes into the throat, allowing droplets of the irritating gastric juices to come in contact with the vocal folds and even to be aspirated into the lungs. Reflux may occur with or without a hiatal hernia. Common symptoms are hoarseness (especially in the morning), prolonged vocal warm-up time, bad breath, sensation of a lump in the throat, chronic sore throat, cough, and a dry or "coated" mouth. Typical heartburn is frequently absent. Over time, uncontrolled reflux may cause cancer of the esophagus and larynx. This condition should be treated conscientiously. Physical examination usually reveals a bright red, often slightly swollen appearance of the arytenoid mucosa, which helps establish the diagnosis. A barium esophagogram with water siphonage may provide additional information but is not needed routinely. In selected cases, 24-hour pH monitoring provides the best analysis and documentation of reflux. The mainstays of treatment are elevation of the head of the patient's bed (not just sleeping on pillows), use of antacids, and avoidance of food for three or four hours before sleep. Avoidance of alcohol and coffee is beneficial. Medications that block acid secretion are also useful, including cimetidine (Tagamet), ranitidine (Zantac), famotidine (Pepcid), nizatidine (Axid), omeprazole (Prilosec), lansoprazole (Prevacid), and others. In some cases, surgery to repair the lower esophageal sphincter and cure the reflux may be more appropriate than lifelong medical management. This option has become much more attractive since the development of laparoscopic surgery, which has drastically decreased the morbidity associated with this operation.

LUNG PROBLEMS

Respiratory problems are especially problematic to singers and other voice professionals, but they may cause voice problems in anyone. They also cause similar problems for wind instrumentalists. Support is essential to healthy voice production. The effects of severe respiratory infection are obvious and will not be enumerated. Restrictive lung disease, such as that associated with obesity, may impair support by decreasing lung volume and respiratory efficiency. However, obstructive pulmonary (lung) disease is the most common culprit. Even mild obstructive lung disease can impair support enough to cause increased neck and tongue muscle tension and abusive voice use capable of producing vocal nodules. This scenario occurs even with unrecognized asthma and may be difficult to diagnose unless suspected because many such cases of asthma are exercise induced. Vocal performance is a form of exercise, whether the performance involves singing, giving speeches, sales, or other forms of intense voice use. Patients with this problem will have normal pulmonary function clinically and may even have normal or nearly normal pulmonary function test findings at rest in the office. However, as the voice is used intensively, pulmonary function decreases, effectively impairing support and resulting in compensatory abusive technique. When suspected, this entity can be confirmed through a methacholine challenge test performed by a pulmonary specialist.

Treatment of underlying pulmonary disease to restore effective support is essential to resolving the vocal problem. Treating asthma is rendered more difficult in professional voice users because of the need in some patients to avoid not only inhalers but also drugs that produce even a mild tremor. The cooperation of a skilled pulmonologist specializing in asthma and sensitive to problems of performing artists is invaluable.

HORMONES

Endocrine problems also have marked vocal effects, primarily by causing accumulation of fluid in the superficial layer of the lamina propria, altering the vibratory characteristics. Mild hypothyroidism typically causes a muffled sound, slight loss of range, and vocal sluggishness. Similar findings may be seen in pregnancy, during use of oral contraceptives (in about 5 percent of women), for a few days prior to menses, and at the time of ovulation. Premenstrual loss of vocal efficiency, endurance, and range is also accompanied by a propensity for vocal fold hemorrhage, which may alter the voice permanently. The use of some medications with hormonal activity can also permanently injure a voice. This is particularly true of substances that contain androgens (male hormones), as discussed earlier.

ANXIETY

When the principal cause of vocal dysfunction is anxiety, the physician can often accomplish much by assuring the patient that no organic difficulty is present and by stating the diagnosis of anxiety reaction. The patient should be counseled that anxiety-related voice disturbances are common and that recognition of anxiety as the principal problem frequently allows the patient to overcome the problem. Tranquilizers and sedatives are rarely necessary and are undesirable because they may interfere with fine-motor control, affecting the voice adversely. Recently, beta-adrenergic blocking agents, such as propranolol hydrochloride (Inderal), have achieved some popularity in the treatment of preperformance anxiety in singers and instrumentalists. Beta-blockers should not be used routinely for voice disorders and preperformance anxiety. They have significant effects on the cardiovascular system and many potential complications, including hypotension, thrombocytopenia purpura, mental depression, agranulocytosis, laryngospasm with respiratory distress, and bronchospasm. In addition, their efficacy is controversial. If anxiety or other psychological factors are an important cause of a voice disorder, their treatment by a psychologist or psychiatrist with special interest and training in voice problems is extremely helpful. This therapy should occur in conjunction with voice therapy.

VOICE ABUSE

Voice abuse through technical dysfunction is an extremely common source of hoarseness, vocal weakness, pain, and other complaints. In some cases, voice abuse can even create structural problems, such as vocal nodules, cysts, and polyps. Now that the components of voice function are better understood, specialists have developed techniques to rehabilitate and train the voice in speech and singing. Such voice therapy improves breathing and abdominal support, decreases excess muscle activity in the larynx and neck, optimizes the mechanics of transglottal airflow, and maximizes the contributions of resonance cavities. It also teaches vocal hygiene, including techniques to eliminate voice strain and abuse, maintain hydration and mucosal function, mitigate the effects of smoke and other environmental irritants, and optimize vocal and general health. The voice therapy team includes an otolaryngologist (ear, nose, and throat doctor) specializing in voice, a speech-language pathologist specially trained in voice, a singing voice specialist with training in vocal injury and dysfunction, and, when needed, an arts medicine psychologist, psychiatrist, pulmonologist, neurologist, exercise physiologist, or other specialist. Progress is monitored not only by listening to the patient and observing the disappearance of laryngeal pathology when it is present, but also by quantitative measurement parameters in the clinical voice laboratory. In some cases, however, there are structural problems in the larynx that are correctable only with surgery.

TONSIL PROBLEMS

For most singers noninfected tonsils do not affect the voice, although it is possible for extremely large tonsils to alter voice and breathing function. In general, when tonsils cause trouble, they do so by becoming infected. Recurrent tonsillitis in singers is particularly problematic. On the one hand, no one is anxious to perform tonsil surgery on a singer. On the other, a singer—particularly a professional--cannot afford to be sick for a week five or six times a year. Tonsil problems can occasionally also cause other difficulties that affect one's performance activities, such as halitosis.

In general, singers should be managed using the same conservative approach employed for other patients with tonsil disorders. Every effort should be made to cure tonsil-related maladies through medical management, such as antibiotics and tonsil hygiene (as with a toothbrush or water pick). However, if these methods fail, tonsillectomy should be considered. It is essential that the surgeon remove only the tonsil, avoiding injury to the surrounding muscle and adjacent palate. It commonly takes singers three to four months to achieve voice stabilization following surgery, although they are usually able to begin vocalizing with supervision within two to three weeks postoperatively. Usually, tonsillectomy has very little effect on the voice, and sometimes it has a positive effect. However, voice problems can occur following tonsillectomy, especially if there is extensive scarring. As with any surgical procedure, the endotracheal tube used for anesthesia can also result in laryngeal injury.

VOCAL NODULES

Small, callous-like bumps on the vocal folds called nodules are caused by voice abuse (Sataloff 2017d) (Figure 4.1). Occasionally, laryngoscopy reveals asymptomatic vocal

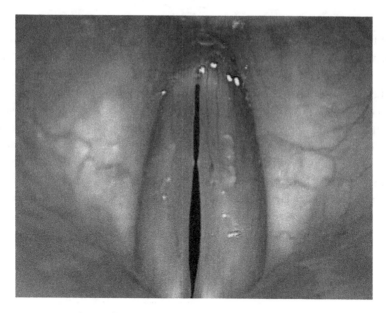

FIGURE 4.1 Typical appearance of vocal nodules.

nodules that do not appear to interfere with voice production; in such cases, the nodules need not be treated. Some famous and successful singers have had untreated vocal nodules. In most cases, however, nodules are associated with hoarseness, breathiness, loss of range, and vocal fatigue. They may be due to abuse of the voice during either speaking or singing. Voice therapy always should be tried as the initial therapeutic modality and will cure the vast majority of patients (Rose, Horman, Sataloff 2017). This is true even if the nodules look firm and have been present for many months or years. Even in those who eventually need surgical excision of the nodules, preoperative voice therapy is essential to prevent recurrence.

Caution must be exercised in diagnosing small nodules in patients who have been speaking or singing actively. In many people, bilateral, symmetrical soft swelling at the junction of the anterior and middle thirds of the vocal folds develop after heavy voice use. No evidence suggests that people with such physiologic swelling are predisposed to development of vocal nodules. At present, the condition is generally considered to be within normal limits. The physiologic swelling usually disappears within 24 to 48 hours of rest from heavy voice use.

CYSTS

Submucosal cysts of the vocal folds occur after traumatic lesions that produce blockage of a mucous gland duct, although they may also occur for other reasons and may even be present at birth. They often cause contact swelling on the opposite vocal fold and are usually initially misdiagnosed as nodules. Often, they can be differentiated from nodules by strobovideolaryngoscopy when the mass is obviously fluid filled. They may also be suspected when the nodule (contact swelling) on the other vocal fold resolves with voice therapy, but the mass on one vocal fold persists. Cysts may also be found unexpectedly on one side (Figures 4.2a and b) and occasionally both sides, when surgery is performed

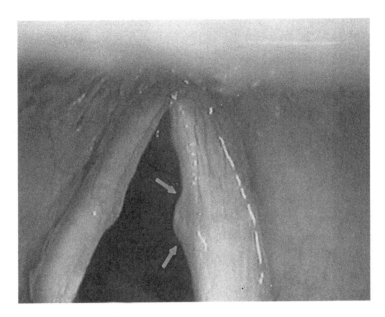

FIGURE 4.2A Right-side fluid-filled vocal fold cyst.

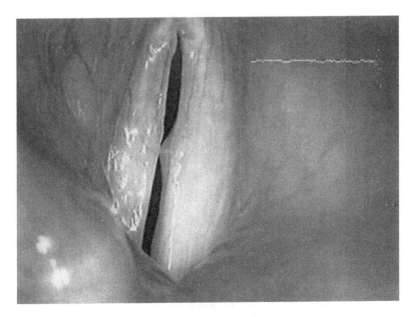

FIGURE 4.2B A left-side reactive nodule in abduction.

to remove apparent nodules. Unlike nodules, cysts often do require surgery and are not usually resolved with voice therapy alone. Surgery should be performed superficially and with minimal trauma, as discussed later.

POLYPS

Many other structural lesions may appear on the vocal folds. Of course, not all respond to nonsurgical therapy. Polyps are usually unilateral (on one side), and they often have a prominent feeding blood vessel coursing along the superior surface of the vocal fold and entering the base of the polyp (Figure 4.3). The pathogenesis of polyps cannot be proven in many cases, but the lesion is thought to be traumatic in many patients. At least some polyps start as vocal hemorrhages. In some cases, even sizable polyps resolve with relative voice rest and a few weeks of low-dose corticosteroid therapy, but many require surgical removal. If polyps are not treated, they may produce contact injury on the contralateral (opposite) vocal fold. Voice therapy should be used to ensure good relative voice rest and prevention of abusive behavior before and after surgery. When surgery is performed, care must be taken not to damage the leading edge of the vocal fold, especially if a laser is used.

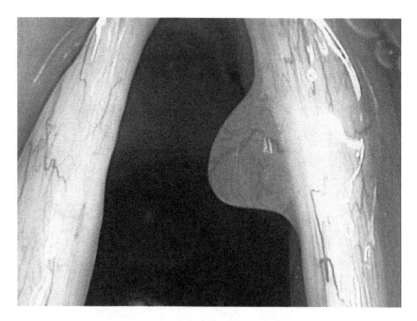

FIGURE 4.3 Typical appearance of a sessile, unilateral polyp of the right vocal fold.

ALLERGY AND POSTNASAL DRIP

Allergies and postnasal drip alter the viscosity (thickness) of secretions, the patency of nasal airways, and have other effects that impair voice use. Many of the medicines commonly used to treat allergies (such as antihistamines) have undesirable effects on the voice. When allergies are severe enough to cause persistent throat clearing, hoarseness, and other voice complaints, a comprehensive allergy evaluation and treatment by an allergy specialist is advisable. Postnasal drip and the sensation of excessive secretions may or may not be caused by allergy. Contrary to popular opinion, the condition usually involves secretions that are too thick, rather than too abundant. If postnasal drip is not caused by allergy, it is usually managed best through hydration, and mucolytic agents such as those discussed later. Reflux laryngitis can cause symptoms very similar to postnasal drip, and it should always be considered in people who have the sensation of throat secretions, a lump in the throat, and excessive throat clearing.

UPPER RESPIRATORY TRACT INFECTION WITHOUT LARYNGITIS

Although mucosal irritation usually is diffuse, patients sometimes have marked nasal obstruction with little or no sore throat and a "normal" voice. If the laryngeal examination shows no abnormality, a person with a head cold should be permitted to speak or sing. They should be advised not to try to duplicate their usual sound, but rather to accept the insurmountable alteration caused by the change in the supraglottic vocal tract. This is especially important in singers. The decision as to whether performing under such circumstances is professionally advisable rests with the singer and his or her musical associates. Throat clearing should be avoided, as this is traumatic. If a cough is present, medications should be used to suppress it, preferably nonnarcotic preparations.

LARYNGITIS WITH SERIOUS VOCAL FOLD INJURY

Hemorrhage in the vocal folds (as discussed later) and mucosal disruption (a tear) are contraindications to voice use. When these are observed, the therapeutic course includes strict voice rest in addition to correction of any underlying disease. Vocal fold hemorrhage is most common in premenstrual women who are using aspirin products. Severe hemorrhage or mucosal scarring may result in permanent alterations in vocal fold vibratory function. In rare instances, surgical intervention may be necessary. The potential gravity of these conditions must be stressed so that patients understand the importance of complying with voice restrictions.

Laryngitis Without Serious Vocal Fold Injury

Mild to moderate edema (swelling) and erythema (redness) of the vocal folds may result from infection or from noninfectious causes. In the absence of mucosal disruption or hemorrhage, they are not absolute contraindications to voice use. Noninfectious laryngitis commonly is associated with excessive voice use in preperformance rehearsals. It may also be caused by other forms of voice abuse and by mucosal irritation produced by allergy, smoke inhalation, and other causes. Mucous stranding between the anterior and middle thirds of the vocal folds often indicates voice abuse. Laryngitis sicca (dry voice) is associated with dehydration, dry atmosphere, mouth breathing, and antihistamine therapy. It may also be a symptom of diabetes and other medical problems.

Deficiency of lubrication causes irritation and coughing and results in mild inflammation. If no pressing professional need for voice use exists, inflammatory conditions of the larynx are best treated with relative voice rest in addition to other modalities. However, in some instances, speaking or singing may be permitted. The more good voice training a person has, the safer it will be to use the voice under adverse circumstances. The patient should be instructed to avoid all forms of irritation and to rest the voice at all times, except during warm-up and performance. Corticosteroids and other medications discussed later may be helpful. If mucosal secretions are excessive, low-dose antihistamine therapy may be beneficial, but it must be prescribed with caution and should generally be avoided. Copious, thin secretions are better than scant, thick secretions or excessive dryness. People with laryngitis must be kept well hydrated to maintain the desired character of mucosal lubrication. Psychological support may also be extremely valuable, especially in singers and professional speakers.

Infectious laryngitis may be caused by bacteria or viruses. Subglottic involvement frequently indicates a more severe infection, which may be difficult to control in a short period. Indiscriminate use of antibiotics must be prevented. However, when the physician is in doubt as to the cause and when a major voice commitment is imminent, vigorous antibiotic treatment is warranted. Steroids may also be helpful, as will be discussed later.

Voice Rest

Voice rest (absolute or relative) is an important therapeutic consideration in any case of laryngitis. When no professional commitments are pressing, a short course (up to a few days) of absolute voice rest may be considered, as it is the safest and most conservative therapeutic intervention. Absolute voice rest is necessary only for serious vocal fold injury, such as hemorrhage or mucosal disruption. Even then, it is virtually never indicated for more than seven to ten days; three days are often sufficient. In many instances of mild to moderate laryngitis, considerations of finances and reputation mitigate against a recommendation of voice rest in professional voice users. In advising performers to minimize vocal use, Dr. Norman Punt of London, England, used to counsel, "Don't say a single word for which you are not being paid." His admonition frequently guides the ailing voice user away from preperformance conversations and postperformance greetings. Patients with such vocal problems should also be instructed to speak softly, as infrequently as possible, often at a slightly higher pitch than usual, and with a slightly breathy voice. They should also avoid excessive telephone use and speak with the same abdominal support they would use in singing. This is relative voice rest, and it is helpful in most cases. An urgent session with a speech-language pathologist is extremely valuable in providing guidelines to prevent voice abuse. Nevertheless, the patient must be aware that some risk is associated with performing with laryngitis, even when voice use is possible. Inflammation of the vocal folds is associated with increased capillary fragility and increased risk of vocal fold injury or hemorrhage. Many factors must be considered in determining whether a given voice commitment is important to justify the potential consequences.

Other Treatments

Steam inhalations deliver moisture and heat to the vocal folds and tracheobronchial tree and are often useful. Some people use nasal irrigations, although these have little proven value. Gargling also has no proven efficacy, but it is probably harmful only if it involves loud, abusive vocalization as part of the gargling process. Ultrasonic treatments, local massage, psychotherapy, and biofeedback directed at relieving anxiety and decreasing muscle tension may be helpful adjuncts to a broader therapeutic program. Psychotherapy and biofeedback, in particular, must be supervised expertly if used.

What Else Can Be Done to Help a Person With Voice Problems?

Voice lessons given by an expert teacher are invaluable for singers and even many nonsingers with voice problems (Baroody, Sataloff, and Carroll 2017). When technical dysfunction is suspected or identified, the singer should be referred to a teacher. Even when an obvious organic abnormality is present, referral to a voice teacher is appropriate, especially for younger singers. Numerous "tricks of the trade" permit a singer to safely overcome some of the disabilities of mild illness. If a singer plans to proceed with a performance during an illness, he or she should not cancel voice lessons as part of the relative voice rest regimen; rather, a short lesson to ensure optimum technique is extremely useful. For nonsingers with voice problems, training with a knowledgeable singing teacher under medical supervision is often extremely helpful. In conjunction with therapy under the direction of a certified, licensed speech-language pathologist, appropriate singing lessons can provide the patient with many of the athletic skills and "tricks" used by performers to build and enhance the voice. Once singing skills are mastered even at a beginner level, the demands of routine speech become trivial by comparison.

Special skills can be refined even further with the help of an acting voice trainer who may also be part of a medical voice team (Freed, Raphael, and Sataloff 2017). Such training is invaluable for any public speaker, teacher, salesperson, or anyone else who cares to optimize his or her communication skills.

Vocal Fold Hemorrhage

Vocal fold hemorrhage is a potential vocal disaster. Hemorrhages resolve spontaneously in most cases with restoration of normal voice. However, in some instances, the hematoma (collection of blood under the vocal fold mucosa) organizes and fibroses, resulting in the formation of a mass, a scar, or both. This alters the vibratory pattern of the vocal fold and can result in permanent hoarseness. In specially selected cases, it may be best to avoid this problem through surgical incision and drainage of the hematoma. In all cases, vocal fold hemorrhage should be managed with absolute voice rest until the hemorrhage has resolved and normal vascular and mucosal integrity have been restored. This often takes six weeks and sometimes longer. Recurrent vocal fold hemorrhages are usually due to weakness in a specific blood vessel, which may require surgical treatment.

Laryngeal Trauma

The larynx can be injured easily during altercations and motor vehicle accidents. Steering wheel injuries are particularly common. Blunt anterior neck trauma may result in laryngeal fracture, dislocation of the arytenoid cartilages, hemorrhage, and airway obstruction. Late consequences, such as narrowing of the airway, may also occur.

Laryngeal injuries are frequently seen in association with other injuries, such as scalp lacerations, that may be bleeding and appear much more dramatic. The laryngeal problem is often overlooked initially, even though it may be the most serious or life-threatening injury. Hoarseness or other change in voice quality following neck trauma should call this possibility to mind. Prompt evaluation by visualization and radiological imaging should be obtained. In many cases, surgery is needed.

EFFECTS OF ABDOMINAL, SPINE, AND CHEST SURGERY ON THE VOICE

This topic is not discussed in detail in this book. However, any operation that impairs use of the support system for singing can affect the voice adversely. Incisions through abdominal muscles cause pain initially, and they may cause long-term weakness or asymmetry, which can alter effective support for singing. When support is not effective, people tend to compensate using neck and laryngeal muscles excessively. This can result in vocal nodules and other injuries. Injuries in surgery involving the spine or chest may have similar adverse consequences.

In addition, surgery often results in a period of postoperative bed rest. Bed rest can result in deconditioning of muscles. In order to resume singing safely after bed rest or a period of muscle rest (abdominal, chest, back, or extremity) following surgery, aerobic and muscular reconditioning should take place before unrestricted singing resumes. Surgery can also affect posture, balance, and stance for singing (seated or standing). Postural changes, whether caused by surgery, injury, aging, or other factors, alter the way in which muscles are used and the voice is supported. Such postural changes can result in singing dysfunction and even vocal injury.

VOCAL FOLD PARALYSIS

Paralysis may involve one or both vocal folds and one or both nerves to each vocal fold (Rubin and Sataloff 2017). When paralysis is limited to the superior laryngeal nerve, the patient loses his or her ability to control longitudinal tension (stretch) in the vocal fold. Although superior laryngeal nerve paralysis involves only one muscle (cricothyroid), the problem is difficult to overcome. The vocal fold sags at a lower level than normal, and the patient notices difficulty elevating pitch, controlling sustained tones, and projecting the voice. Superior laryngeal nerve paralysis is caused most commonly by viral infection, especially the herpes virus that causes cold sores. The recurrent laryngeal nerve controls all the other intrinsic laryngeal muscles. When it is injured the vocal fold cannot move toward or away from the midline, although longitudinal tension is preserved, and the vocal fold remains at its appropriate vertical level if the superior laryngeal nerve is not injured. If the opposite (normal) vocal fold is able to cross the midline to meet the paralyzed side, the vocal quality and loudness may be quite good. Compensation often occurs spontaneously during the first 6 to 12 months following paralysis, with the paralyzed vocal fold moving closer to the midline. Unilateral vocal fold paralysis may be idiopathic (of unknown cause), but it is also seen fairly commonly following surgical procedures of the neck, such as thyroidectomy, carotid endarterectomy, anterior cervical fusion, and some chest operations. Vocal fold paralysis should be treated initially with voice therapy. At least six months—preferably twelve months—of observation are needed unless it is absolutely certain that the nerve has been cut and destroyed, as spontaneous recovery of neuromuscular function is common. If voice therapy fails, vocal fold motion remains impaired, and voice quality or ability to cough is unsatisfactory to the patient, surgical treatments are generally quite satisfactory.

Spasmodic Dysphonia

Spasmodic (or "spastic") dysphonia is a diagnosis given to patients with specific kinds of voice interruptions (Jaworek, Deems, and Sataloff 2017). These patients may have a variety of diseases that produce the same vocal result, which is called a *laryngeal dystonia*. There are also many interruptions in vocal fluency that are diagnosed incorrectly as spasmodic dysphonia. It is important to avoid this error, because different types of dysphonia require different evaluations and treatments and carry different prognostic implications. Spasmodic dysphonia is subclassified into adductor, abductor, and mixed types. It may occur with or without tremor. Botulinum toxin and voice therapy are the mainstay of treatment.

Other Neurological Voice Disorders

Many neurological problems commonly cause voice abnormalities (Dahl et al. 2017). These include myasthenia gravis, Parkinson's disease, essential tremor, and numerous other disorders. In some cases, voice abnormalities are the first symptoms of the condition.

Cancer of the Vocal Folds

Cancers of the larynx are common and are usually associated with smoking, although cancers also occur occasionally in nonsmokers (Anderson and Sataloff 2017) (Figure 4.4). In many cases, the reason is unknown. However, it appears as if other conditions, such as chronic reflux laryngitis and laryngeal papillomas, may be important predisposing factors. Persistent hoarseness is one of the most common symptoms. Laryngeal cancers may also present with throat pain or referred ear pain. If diagnosed early, they respond

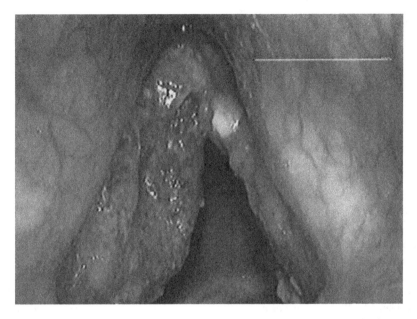

FIGURE 4.4 Squamous cell carcinoma involving both true vocal folds.

to therapy particularly well and are often curable. Treatment usually requires radiation, surgery, or a combination of the two modalities. It is usually possible to preserve or restore the voice, especially if the cancer is detected early.

DRUGS FOR VOCAL DYSFUNCTION

Detailed descriptions of drugs used for voice dysfunction are beyond the scope of this chapter and may be found in other literature (Sataloff et al. 2017). Many medications including antibiotics, antihistamines, steroids, diuretics, aspirin, ibuprofen, psychotropic drugs, chemotherapy, sprays, and other medications including alternative and complementary preparations sold over the counter may impact voice function.

VOICE SURGERY

Scar tissue occurs in response to trauma, including surgery. If scar tissue replaces the normal anatomic layers, the vocal fold becomes stiff and adynamic (nonvibrating). This results in asymmetric, irregular vibration with air turbulence that we hear as hoarseness, or microscopically incomplete vocal fold closure allowing air escape, which makes the voice sound breathy. Such a vocal fold may look normal on traditional examination but will be seen as abnormal under stroboscopic light. Conveniently, most benign pathology (eg, nodules, polyps, cysts) is superficial. Consequently, surgical techniques have been developed to permit removal of lesions from the epithelium or superficial layer of the lamina propria without disruption of the intermediate or deeper layers in most cases (Sataloff 2017e). These techniques minimize scarring and optimize voice results.

Works Cited

Anderson, T. D., and R. T. Sataloff. 2017. "Laryngeal Cancer." In *Professional Voice: The Science and Art of Clinical Care*, 4th ed., edited by R. T. Sataloff, 1695–716. San Diego, CA: Plural Publishing, Inc.

Baroody, M. M., R. T. Sataloff, and L. M. Carroll. 2017. "The Singing Voice Specialist." In *Professional Voice: The Science and Art of Clinical Care*, 4th ed., 1231–50. San Diego, CA: Plural Publishing Inc.

Dahl, L., J. W. Lim, S. Mandel, R. Gupta, and R. T. Sataloff. 2017. "Neurologic Disorders Affecting the Voice in Performance." In *Professional Voice: The Science and Art of Clinical Care*, 4th ed., 1031–58. San Diego, CA: Plural Publishing Inc.

Del'Aria, C., and D. A. Opperman. 2017. "Pyrotechnics in the Entertainment Industry: An Overview." In *Professional Voice: The Science and Art of Clinical Care*, 4th ed., edited by R. T. Sataloff, 791–802. San Diego, CA: Plural Publishing Inc.

Freed, S. L., B. N. Raphael, and R. T. Sataloff. 2017. "The Role of the Acting-Voice Trainer in Medical Care of Professional Voice Users." In *Professional Voice: The Science and Art of Clinical Care*, 4th ed., 1277–86. San Diego, CA: Plural Publishing Inc.

Jaworek, A. J., D. A. Deems, and R. T. Sataloff. 2017. "Spasmodic Dysphonia." In *Professional Voice: The Science and Art of Clinical Care*, 4th ed., 1077–100. San Diego, CA: Plural Publishing Inc.

Rose, B., M. Horman, and R. T. Sataloff. 2017. "Voice Therapy." In *Professional Voice: The Science and Art of Clinical Care*, 4th ed., 1171–94. San Diego, CA: Plural Publishing Inc.

Rossol, M. 2017a. "Artificial Fogs and Smokes." In *Professional Voice: The Science and Art of Clinical Care*, 4th ed., 809–16. San Diego, CA: Plural Publishing Inc.

Rossol, M. 2017b. "Pyrotechnics: Health Effects." In *Professional Voice: The Science and Art of Clinical Care*, 4th ed., edited by R. T. Sataloff, 803–08. San Diego, CA: Plural Publishing Inc.

Rubin, A. D., and R. T. Sataloff. 2017. "Vocal Fold Paresis and Paralysis." In *Professional Voice: The Science and Art of Clinical Care*, 4th ed., 1059–76. San Diego, CA: Plural Publishing Inc.

Sataloff, R. T. 2017a. "Patient History." In *Professional Voice: The Science and Art of Clinical Care*, 4th ed., 363–86. San Diego, CA: Plural Publishing Inc.

Sataloff, R. T. 2017b. "Physical Examination." In *Professional Voice: The Science and Art of Clinical Care*, 4th ed., 391–404. San Diego, CA: Plural Publishing Inc.

Sataloff, R. T. 2017c. "Pollution and Its Effect on the Voice." In *Professional Voice: The Science and Art of Clinical Care*, 4th ed., edited by R. T. Sataloff, 777–90. San Diego, CA: Plural Publishing Inc.

Sataloff, R. T. 2017d. "Structural Abnormalities of the Larynx." In *Professional Voice: The Science and Art of Clinical Care*, 4th ed., 1533–86. San Diego, CA: Plural Publishing Inc.

Sataloff, R. T. 2017e. "Voice Surgery." In *Professional Voice: The Science and Art of Clinical Care*, 4th ed., 1371–478. San Diego, CA: Plural Publishing Inc.

Sataloff, R. T., J. Sataloff, and B. McGovern. 2017. "Hearing Loss in Singers and Other Musicians." In *Professional Voice: The Science and Art of Clinical Care*, 4th ed., edited by R. T. Sataloff, 621–38. San Diego, CA: Plural Publishing Inc.

Sataloff, R. T., K.M. Kost, and Sue Ellen Linville. 2017. "The Effects of Age on the Voice." In *Professional Voice: The Science and Art of Clinical Care*, 4th ed., 585–604. San Diego, CA: Plural Publishing Inc.

Sataloff, R. T., M. J. Hawkshaw, J. Anticaglia, M. White, K. Meenan, and J. J. Romak. 2017. "Medications and the Voice." In *Professional Voice: The Science and Art of Clinical Care*, 4th ed., 1103–33. San Diego, CA: Plural Publishing Inc.

Sataloff, R. T., P. O. Katz, D. M. Sataloff, and M. J. Hawkshaw. 2013. *Reflux Laryngitis and Related Disorders*, 4th ed. San Diego, CA: Plural Publishing Inc.

Smith, B., and R. T. Sataloff. 2012. *Choral Pedagogy and the Older Singer*. San Diego, CA: Plural Publishing Inc.

CHAPTER 5

FLUID VOICES

Processes and Practices in Singing Impersonation

KATHERINE MEIZEL AND RONALD C. SCHERER

EVERY day, Las Vegas hosts numerous Elvises. And throughout Vegas arenas, theaters, casinos, nightclubs, and baseball fields, crowds might simultaneously applaud for Prince, Dean Martin, Frank Sinatra, or Marilyn Monroe—not ghosts of the stars, but impersonators who celebrate cultural history through performances of famous performances. Though many celebrity impersonators reach for precise imitations, others rely on the characteristics that most visibly set them apart from their models, so that they embody both the star and something that is *not*-the-star. As Freya Jarman-Ivens has argued in her discussion of Elvis impersonation, listeners may best understand who they believe an artist *is* through a recognition of what they believe he *isn't* (Jarman-Ivens 2006, 223). So rather than simply representing an outrageously obvious inauthenticity, the transgressive image of a female Elvis, or of a Chinese Elvis, or of a "Mini" Elvis might actually shape an audience member's imagination of an authentic original.[1]

The negotiation of authenticity concerns not only the impersonator's audience, but also the impersonator. Kirsten Hastrup, after Richard Schechner (1985) and Victor Turner (1982), positions theatrical performance as a ritual, and as "site of passage" for any who attend (Hastrup 1998, 29). But in the liminality of the stage, impersonators themselves also experience a related process. They become actors in multiple, simultaneous ways; as they perform the identities of others they are also doing the work of their own identities, and vocalizing it—either from their own throats, or lip-synching with a voice from someone else's. And those whose acts are rooted in their distinction from the stars they imitate, emphasizing rather than hiding incongruities between what audiences see and what they hear, reveal how the work of identity may be most clearly visible in the enactment of difference.

An impersonated voice is acousmatic—separated from its source—but is re-embodied in a new source different from the original. Though the audience is aware of this process, it is not quite transparent—a voice is hidden inside a person; as Mladen Dolar explained of ventriloquism, a voice implies a body, but more specifically "a bodily *interior*, an intimate partition of the body which cannot be disclosed—as if the voice were the very principle of division into interior and exterior" (Dolar 2006, 71, our emphasis). This internal mystery intensifies when the body is apparently dissimilar to the original source of the voice, particularly in terms of perceived racial or ethnic identity, size and shape, or gender. Likewise, it may be a voice that familiarly belongs to another, publicly recognizable body, the voice of a star. If the voice can be, in Dolar's words, "located at the juncture of the subject and the Other" (102), then it may also be located in their *dis*juncture.

This chapter investigates the experiences of a celebrity impersonator who capitalizes upon such disjunctures, harnessing them to negotiate her own voice by performing the voices of others. Her work illuminates singing impersonation as not simply mimesis, but as a sociovocal strategy of identity, and demonstrates the simultaneous reification and interdependence of the enclosed aural body and the disclosed visual body as products of multiple (inter-)subjectivities. For this project, the two authors have brought together their respective backgrounds in ethnomusicology (Meizel), voice science (Scherer), and vocal performance (both) to explore how celebrity singing impersonation works. Along the way, we have learned a great deal about their own disciplinary perspectives, balancing very different understandings of voice as a physical/physiological and metaphorical/metaphysical concept. To Scherer, for example, *voice* indicates the source of vocal sound, that is, the signal produced by the pulsatile airflow that exits the oscillating glottis. (This, heard without considering the sonic filter provided by the vocal tract above the larynx, will sound quite buzz-like.) Meizel, on the other hand, is accustomed to thinking about voice as the totality of a body's vocalization, including the filtered sound listeners perceive as timbre—and most significantly, as a metaphor for agency. To incorporate these differences, we approached the impersonated voice as holistically as possible, and to learn about the physical, physiological, and social processes that contribute to the phenomenon. Meizel conducted ethnographic interviews and recorded one impersonator's voice on-site in Las Vegas before a performance, and Scherer led the acoustic study of the recordings. We thus position our chapter as a preliminary experiment in collaborative voice research, and hope that it will encourage others to do the same.

Singing Impersonation

The performative continuum of singing impersonators generally includes imitative cover versions, tribute bands, and comedic parody. In *Play It Again: Cover Songs in Popular Music*, George Plasketes identifies these forms as part of a larger turn-of-the-millennium "cover complex," which, he proposes, "may be viewed as a postmodern manifestation of rampant recontextualization in music" (Plasketes 2010, 2). Katherine Meizel has written elsewhere about cover performance, observing that in a cover, an artist uses various musical and vocal changes in order to "make it their own," and to "reach a precarious balance between . . . the need to live up to the work of a song's original artist, and an originality that is seen as an innovative expression of individuality" (Meizel 2011, 63).

Because it is inside the body, a voice is always somewhat secret, and while impersonators might rely on visual techniques to mimic an artist's body language or superficial physical characteristics, they must also (re)invent a version of the artist's interior vocal spaces. The impersonator needs to be, as voice actor and impersonator Jeff McNeal terms it, "a good listener," paying attention to the artist's diction, inflection, and expressive phrasing, but also perceiving and imitating subtle adjustments in the internal shaping of the vocal tract—what Mr. McNeal calls "throat modeling" (interview, August 22, 2013). David Huron, a scholar at the forefront of music cognition, identifies a *kinesthetic* type of listening, "characterized by the auditor's compulsion to move." He explains that "feet may tap, hands may conduct, or the listener may feel the urge to dance. The experience is not so much one of 'listening' to the music, as the music 'permeating' the body... 'motivation' rather than 'contemplation' " (Huron 2002). Even when a performance does not involve dancing, the impersonator's experience of sound certainly permeates the body, producing a conscious, or even semiconscious, physiological response. We might think about singing impersonation as the result of a special sort of kinesthetic listening that translates the internal *and* external movements of one voice, one body, to another— not creating any kind of perfect mimesis, but highlighting the meanings made during the listening process.

VÉRONIC DiCAIRE'S *50 VOICES*

The authors of this chapter were introduced to its focus when Meizel traveled to Las Vegas on a brisk night in October of 2013, to conduct ethnographic research at a Bally's Casino show that offered its audience *50 Voices*. But none of those 50 stars whose voices filled the theater were present—instead, the voices of Tina Turner, Katy Perry, Adele, Shakira, Anita Baker, Whitney Houston, Taylor Swift, Donna Summer, and dozens of others all issued from the throat of one petite blonde French Canadian woman. Véronic DiCaire (her stage name is Véronic) started her career as a solo singer in Montréal, and also performed in musical theater, but because people noticed her remarkable facility for changing her voice, she was soon hired to imitate French and French Canadian singers, especially Céline Dion, for events and television appearances. She attracted attention when she opened for Dion on her world tour in 2008, impersonating her, and eventually became the superstar's protégé. She then expanded her repertoire from a handful of francophone singers' voices to dozens of transnationally known figures.

Véronic's multiple voices highlight the disjunctures in which certain ideas about identity are grounded—a person who looks like *this* should not sound like *that*—and raise significant questions about the contested boundaries between imitation and appropriation, about the ambiguous shades of essentialism, and about the role of voice as a sonic accoutrement of racial transvestism. Regarding her performance of Tina

Turner, for example, Véronic acknowledged the fraught implications suggested by a white performer imitating a Black performer, and noted that impersonation can walk a fine line between mimicry and mockery. This is one reason she has chosen to forego detailed costuming or wigs in her performances, instead embodying Tina Turner and others through movement and voice.

Véronic said that as she develops them, she locates each of her voices *in the body*, and works closely with her vocal coach on this process:

> Let's say for this voice you need to place your voice…in your legs, or, you know, in your shoulders, you need to think about that. And other times it is only a thought…for Céline [Dion], my thought was to be very in the nose. Well, [my teacher] would say, for example, okay, the nose is good, but…she also sings with *this* [elongates neck, using her hands] and the long neck, so *imagine* the long neck, and so that's how we are working with the voices.   (Interview, October 11, 2013)

When she was working on her Tina Turner impersonation, she said, thinking about the body became a crucial part of her vocal configuration. She indicated that:

> I couldn't get her voice…I couldn't get her. I was listening and listening, and it was obsessive…And then at one point I said, OK, Tina Turner, I'm gonna get you tonight…I went on YouTube, I went to watch her, and the thing that was missing was the high heels. So I went into my wardrobe, and got my highest heels, I put them on, I double-checked on YouTube, and she had her knees a bit bent, and her shoulders, and her neck…and I went like this and I hold my mic like her…and I was like, OK, that's it, that's it. This is my Tina Turner.   (Interview, October 11, 2013)

Because bodily appropriation has been fundamental to the history and continuation of racial oppression (and its intersection with misogyny) in the United States, the implications of a white woman's Vegas performance of a Black woman's posture, movements, and vocality are significant. Véronic talked about the problematic idea of "Black voice," and her perception—derived from a doggedly persistent colonial discourse—that it is based in structural physiological differences between racial groups. In her imitations of African American singers, she said, she focuses on adjusting her soft palate and the position of her jaw, and placing her voice "up front" in order to compensate for such differences. However, though she imagines any differences to lie in the structure of facial *bones*, she accomplishes her target sound by manipulating the *soft tissues* and spaces of the vocal tract. This actually contradicts her understanding and supports current scholarship disproving the notion that racialized biological difference could be a source for vocal diversity.

Especially because all of Véronic's voices are so heavily impacted by the body language, gesture, posture, and even dance moves of the artists she mimics, the space between tribute and disparaging caricature can be difficult to navigate. Part of the challenge, she admitted in an interview, is compressing the most iconic characteristics of an artist into the short time her show allows each of her voices (about a minute and thirty seconds), without resorting to exaggerated mockery. But some essentialism appears to be necessary to the act of impersonation. In a 2013 study of spoken impersonation, López et al. found that listeners better recognize the target speaker upon hearing broader caricatures, intended to emphasize particular aspects of the speaker's voice, than when they hear imitations attempting to sound as close as possible to it (López et al. 2013, 3).

THE IMPERSONATOR'S "OWN" VOICE

It becomes a challenge for Véronic to hold on to her "own voice" amid her sea of impressions. She views "her" voice as the basis for all of her imitations, and tries to keep it in mind even as she moves away from it.

> My voice is still there. It has to. Because it's the base of all of my other voices. When I started to work on my imitations, impressions, at one point I came back and I was like, where am I? I couldn't connect to the voices I had just worked on, and everything was lost, and my teacher said, "Véronic, I think you're lost. I think we should reconnect with Véronic['s] voice." ... So when I'm off, I sing as myself. I, when I have doubts, I sing as myself, to reconnect, Because I find that I don't want to be Celine Dion, I don't want to be Pink in my real life, in my day to day life, I'm not them, I'm Véronic...if I want to be strong for these voices I have to be strong for myself. I have to be Véronic. And that's why I don't dress up, because I don't want to transform *as*, I want the people to connect with the voice and let their imagination go where I want them to go. Come with me in this world, in this voice.   (Interview, October 1, 2013)

The singing voice she recognizes as her own, "*as* Véronic," sounds a bit like Sheryl Crow's voice. But one aspect of her voice that she feels to be unique involves an idiosyncrasy in her vocal physiology that she believes to be the source of her an unusual flexibility. In an interview she related a visit with famed French otolaryngologist Jean Abitbol, who, even before he knew she sang impersonations, told her that an especially "uneven" (her word) set of cartilages in her larynx would likely make her a good impressionist (interview, October 1, 2013). In *The Odyssey of the Voice*, Abitbol suggests that impersonators may have especially powerful muscle and cartilage structures in the larynx, which are uncommonly flexible. He further points to an observation he made with the use of a videofiberscope, identifying a "cross-eyed" larynx in which the arytenoid cartilages may permit one vocal fold to lengthen more than the other (as in Véronic's "uneven" cartilages), and may even allow the vocal folds to partially overlap (Abitbol 2006, 412). Abitbol writes that impersonators may also reshape their vocal tracts for an imitation and may "contort" the epiglottis and alter its position in the pharynx, or adjust their soft palates (413). Acoustically, Abitbol believes that an impersonator's own vocal "fingerprint" will remain identifiable regardless of imitative intent (414–415), and that those aforementioned physiological qualities that allow impersonation contribute to that fingerprint. Since she learned about her laryngeal structures during her meeting with Dr. Abitbol, Véronic has viewed her own voice and her own body as *meant for* the sounding of otherness; her declaration of self-identity might best be heard in the forms and formants of 50 other voices.

ACOUSTIC ANALYSIS

Those formants—the clusters of frequencies that resonate most strongly specific to the shaping of the vocal tract—can tell us something about how impersonations work, and about the body in the voice as it makes subtle, hidden changes in the reconstruction of sonic identities. A 2013 study published by López et al. proposed that in speech-based (nonsinging) impersonation, the perception of *similarity* among voices is associated with laryngeal voicing parameters, but that the accuracy of speaker *identification* is primarily linked to features of the vocal tract (López et al. 2013, 1). The phonetic (Zetterholm 2002; Kitamura 2008; Tanaka et al. 2010; Bin Amin et al. 2014 López et al. 2013) and sociological (Ferris 2011) research in vocal impersonation to date has purely addressed speech,[2] but we propose that *singing* impersonation, where often phonemes are elongated in a slower temporality, may also potentially contribute important—and unique—information. To this purpose, we acoustically analyzed a selection of Véronic's impressions to compare her performances with those of the original artists.

In Véronic's green room, she generously agreed to allow Meizel to record some examples in which she imitated pop stars Lady Gaga and Adele. First, she listened to an a cappella passage from "Born This Way," a version pop icon Lady Gaga had performed on her 2011 HBO special *Lady Gaga Presents The Monster Ball Tour: at Madison Square Garden* (https://www.youtube.com/watch?v=wPWnmnBHHoM). Then Véronic echoed the passage imitating Lady Gaga at the same pitch (the fundamental frequencies measure within 3 to 5 Hz of each other). The same process was used with a passage from British singer Adele's 2010 hit "Rolling in the Deep," sung for a CNN interview with Anderson Cooper in 2012 (February 12. CBS *60 Minutes Overtime*, https://www.youtube.com/watch?v=-PMomc_-QHE). Véronic also recorded singing passages from Joe Cocker's celebrated "You Are So Beautiful" and the Céline Dion hit "Je Ne Suis Qu'une Chanson."

Acoustic characteristics such as pitch contours, vibrato rates and extents, and formants were analyzed. It is important to note that the recording conditions—in Véronic's green room, rather than in a professional studio setting—provide less-than-ideal samples for empirical study, and that those short performances were contextually quite distinct from those in Véronic's show. Additionally, although passages were chosen from Adele's and Lady Gaga's performances based on Véronic's work with those particular songs in *50 Voices*, she pointed out that her own performances sometimes use keys different from the celebrity examples. When asked to try changing her voice several times repeating just one phrase, she noted that it is difficult for her to produce accurate impressions in songs for which she has not explicitly developed an impersonation. Nevertheless, despite these limitations, Véronic's gracious participation allowed for reasonable acoustic analyses that compare the work of the original artist and Véronic's imitations.

PITCH CONTOUR AND VIBRATO

In studies of spoken impersonation, one of the most significant questions is how closely the inflections—pitch, timing, and intensity—match between the impersonator and target voice. For singers, though the melody is prescribed, this is still an essential inquiry. In the examples of this study the pitch contours for the most part match, but there are some discrepancies between Véronic's performances and the original artists'. Figure 5.1 (a display using the software Praat) compares a passage from Lady Gaga's "Born This Way," including the lyrics "she rolled my hair and put my lipstick on/ in the glass of her boudoir," to Véronic's version. Much of the recordings' content shows close similarities between the two performances. However, following the timing, it is clear that Lady Gaga spends more time on the word "she" an octave below the pitch for "rolled," whereas in Véronic's passage, the vowel is so brief it is difficult to perceive, and so is that low pitch. Véronic also shortens the "-stick" in "lipstick," as well as the end of the first phrase ("on"), which she finishes in a downward glide that Lady Gaga does not use, and the end of Véronic's "boudoir" descends again rather than using a lower neighbor ornament like Lady Gaga's.

The comparison of pitch contours for this example also highlights similarities and differences in vibrato rate and extent. In Véronic's performance the vibrato is less consistently present than in Lady Gaga's, though it is most visible at the ends of phrases. Véronic's vibrato for the word "on" does not continue for as long as Lady Gaga's (there are fewer cycles visible), but the rate is precisely (and remarkably) the same at 5.88 Hz (cycles per second) each. However, the extent of the vibrato (measured as the peak-to-peak difference within the vibrato cycles) in the two examples differs considerably, with Lady Gaga at just over 3 semitones and Véronic with less extent at just over two. Analysis of another recorded passage in which Véronic used her own voice to sing the French word "soir" in "Je Ne Suis Qu'une Chanson" revealed that at only a slightly higher pitch, her vibrato rate was 5.55 Hz and her extent was just 1.6 semitones (Table 5.1). This may indicate that in her impersonation of Lady Gaga, Véronic accelerates her vibrato rate a little, and at least widens its extent toward that of Lady Gaga (which suggests unusual flexibility).

"She rolled my hair and put my lip-stick on,   in the glass of her bou-doir"

A side-by-side examination of examples by Adele and Véronic-as-Adele (Figure 5.2) shows similar results. These examples juxtapose the two versions of the lines, "There's a

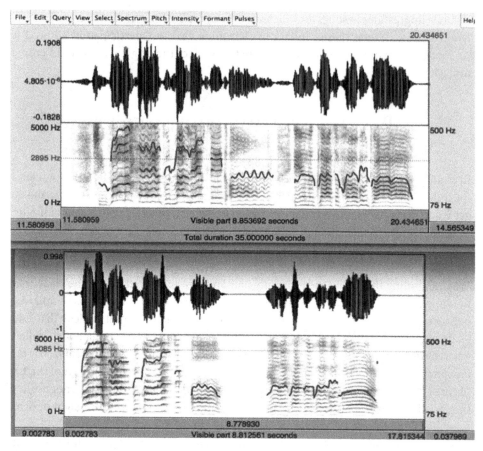

FIGURE 5.1 Lady Gaga (top) and Véronic, phrase from "Born this Way" (melodic contour is indicated on the spectrograms by blue lines).

Table 5.1. Comparison of vibrato rates at ends of phrases

Adele's "Rolling in the Deep" and Véronic's Impersonation

/ɑ/in "Heart" Adele	6.67 Hz
/ɑ/in "Heart" Véronic	6.67 Hz
/ɑ/in "Dark" Adele	5.88 Hz
/ɑ/in "Dark" Véronic	6.25 Hz

Lady Gaga's "Born This Way" and Véronic's Impersonation

/ɔː/in "on" Gaga	5.88 Hz
/ɔː/in "on" Véronic	5.88 Hz

Véronic, in "Je Ne Suis Qu'une Chanson," as herself

/a/in "soir" Véronic	5.55 Hz

fire starting in my heart/ reaching a fever pitch, and it's bringing me out the dark." The pitch contours are again close, and in many places the fundamental frequencies match precisely; however, the spectrograms illustrate some discrepancies in timing, as Véronic shortens the ends of all three phrases—though the time is made up for with slightly longer pauses between those phrases. Onstage, of course, the pauses reflect the pace of the backing track (Véronic does not use a live orchestra in Las Vegas), and this may produce timing nearer to that of Adele's original, bestselling recording. Both sets of examples show differences in the distribution of intensity; while Véronic's recordings exhibit a higher amplitude overall due to recording conditions, there are also differences in the intensity of particular syllables or words, including in "Rolling in the Deep" and the word "my." The intensity of certain formants varies as well, with significant differences in the first and second formants; for example, in the first vowel,/ɛ/, of the diphthong in "There's *a* fire," Adele's first formant is relatively stronger than Véronic's, and Véronic's second formant is stronger than Adele's. We also compared vibrato rates and extents at the ends of each phrase (the words "heart" and "dark"), and found that at the end of the first phrase, Véronic again perfectly matches Adele's vibrato rate at 6.67 Hz, though the extents again diverge at 1.9 semitones for Adele and one semitone for Véronic (Table 5.1). But at the end of the second phrase, if Véronic aimed for Adele's 5.88 Hz rate in "dark,"

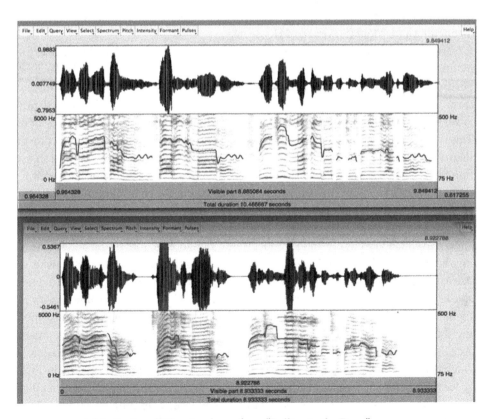

FIGURE 5.2 Adele (top) and Véronic, phrase from "Rolling in the Deep."

she overshot it to 6.25 Hz—though it is still a higher rate than her own Véronic-as-Véronic "soir" at 5.55 Hz. Extents are again dissimilar, Adele's at 2 semitones and Véronic's at nearly 2.8—perhaps an exaggeration of a familiar characteristic in Adele's singing? In both sets of samples, the passages from Adele's and Lady Gaga's songs, it is interesting to observe that Véronic's vibrato rates and/or extents are most clearly visible and most even at the ends of phrases, whereas the original voices maintain more pervasive vibrato throughout.

> There's a fire—starting in my heart, reaching a fever pitch and it's bringin' me out the dark

Spectral Features

Singing impersonation also involves acoustic features that lead to the perception of timbre and are most likely related to formant frequencies and their relative intensities. The way listeners perceive vowels is most affected by the first two formants (F1 and F2), the frequencies and relative intensities of which are related to the location along the vocal tract of the primary constriction(s), the size of the constriction, and dimensions of the lip opening and extent (Stevens and House 1955).

Véronic's impersonations of Adele are compared to Adele's productions relative to formants 1 and 2 for four segments from "Rolling in the Deep" seen in Figure 5.3 In the upper portion of the figure for the phrase "a fire," the article "a" was produced as a transition from an approximate /e/ to /i/. For /e/, Véronic uses a higher F2 (by 280 Hz) and a slightly lower F1 (by only 61 Hz) and then transitions to approximately identical F1, F2 values for /i/. This suggests that Véronic had a relatively higher tongue placement for the/e/portion. In Figure 5.3 there are two instances of /a/to/r/ in the words "dark" and "heart." The transition for "dark" is shown by the dashed lines. Here Véronic is nearly identical to Adele for F1 for both /a/and/r/, but decidedly higher in F2 for both (by an average of 359 Hz), suggesting that Véronic may have used a slightly greater mouth (lip) opening for both sounds. In contrast to this is the similar orthographic /a/ to /r/ transition for the word "heart" in which Véronic's F1 and F2 values were quite close for both the /a/ and /r/, meaning there was very little vowel change, basically lacking the transition to the /r/, whereas Adele made a definitive move from the /a/ position to a more typical /r/ position in F1, F2 space (refer to the lower solid lines in Figure 5.3). For /r/, Véronic's F1 value was 291 Hz higher than Adele's, and Véronic' F2 value was 336 Hz lower than Adele's, essentially missing the /r/ location in F1, F2 space. Thus, for the word "heart," Véronic did not match Adele's production well. The last illustrated comparison in Figure 5.3 is the isolated /a/ in "mah heart," for which the match was excellent and toward the extreme right of the F1, F2 space for /a/ even for speech (Peterson and Barney, 1952). The findings of Figure 5.3 illustrate the type of formant trajectories that may be employed to examine the similarities of the primary acoustic measures for vowels when studying imitation.

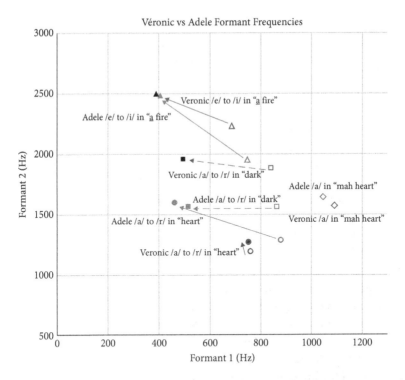

FIGURE 5.3 Comparison of formant values between Adele and Véronic imitating Adele for portions of "Rolling in the Deep." Arrows indicate F1, F2 trajectories between sounds.

Véronic also recorded singing "Jingle Bells" as *herself* and then as Christina Aguilera, Britney Spears, and Celine Dion. Another formant comparison was made among the recordings for /ɛ/ in "bell," /e/ in "way," and /ɔ/ in "all." Figure 5.4 shows the F1, F2 positions for the /ɛ/ in "bell" (upper figure). Figure 5.4 indicates that Véronic altered her acoustic structures to imitate the performers' vowel sounds. Véronic's imitation of Britney has the closest F1, F2 values to her own sound, whereas F2 was lower than for her imitation of Celine (by 141 Hz) and higher than for her imitation of Christina (by 296 Hz). It is noted that the F1 values for all four were quite close in value. The F2 control suggests that again Véronic may have made primarily a mouth opening (lip opening) variation for Celine (more opening) and Christina (less opening). Figure 5.4 also shows the F3 versus F4 comparisons, formants that are thought to be related more to the timbre of the sound than to the vowel identity per se. Here it is curious that the F3 and F4 values are the lowest for her own singing of /ɛ/, with the greatest difference created for the imitation of Britney (by 579 Hz for F3 and 794 Hz for F4). Her imitation of Britney (but not the others) was quite breathy, however, and thus the intensity of F3 and F4 was sufficiently low that they most likely had no perceptual consequence.

Figure 5.5 compares Véronic's production of /e/ in "way" against her imitations of the other three artists. In this case, her imitation of Celine Dion gives the closest match to her own F1, F2 values, with higher F1 values than the imitation of either

Britney (by 161 Hz) or Christina (by 108 Hz). The comparison for F2 differs: Véronic's production is lower than her imitation of Britney (by 657 Hz) but higher than for her imitation of Christina (by 291 Hz). We can surmise, then, that for her imitation of Britney, the lower F1 and higher F2 is most likely due to moving the constriction for the /e/ more forward in the oral cavity. In contrast, for her imitation of Christina, she may merely have produced the /e/ with a more closed mouth positioning to lower both F1 and F2 relative to her own production. For F3 and F4 (the lower figure in Figure 5.5), again Véronic has the lowest F3, F4 values compared to her imitations, with again Britney's /e/ having the largest difference for both F3 and F4 (also, though with a breathy voice production by Véronic).

In the final comparison, Véronic sings the /ɔ/ in "all" with formants shown in Figure 5.6. This time Véronic's production is closest to her imitation of Christina for F1 and F2. Her imitation of Britney places both F1 and F2 higher than her own (F1 by 164 Hz and F2 by 307 Hz). Véronic's F1, F2 values place her vowel more into the /ɑ/ location for speech (Peterson and Barney 1952), and the imitation of Britney places the F1, F2 values into the upper portion of the /ɑ/ space, close to /ʌ/ (Peterson and Barney 1952). Her imitation of Celine, however, places both F1 and F2 lower in the F1–F2 space, which moves the vowel closer to traditional values for /ɔ/ but still within the /ɑ/ space. In general, regarding F1 and F2, the vowel for the word "all" is more like /ɑ/ than /ɔ/, with most likely a larger mouth opening for the imitation of Britney, and a more closed mouth (perhaps with a little lip rounding) for the imitation of Celine. For this vowel and F3 and F4, Véronic's own production again has the lowest F3 value, but this time, as Figure 5.6 indicates, her imitations give higher F4 values compared with Christina and Celine, but lower F2 values than for Britney.

The exercise of comparing the artist's own productions with her imitations of others gives insight into how she must adjust from her own typical physiological set. The skill to make large as well as subtle changes should be visible in the alterations of the formant values, and elucidate both the accuracy and the discrimination skills of the imitator. The results show significant variability in terms of similarity to the target; they sometimes match Adele's nearly precisely, and sometimes they do not. They tend to be closer to Adele's F1 and F2 in high vowels, such as /i/, though one particular /a/ stands out. In the phrase "starting in my heart," Adele uses a pronunciation for "my" that has long been common in Anglophone popular music, and that is embedded in the appropriative history of rock, and its roots in Delta blues: the truncation of the diphthong in "my." The syllable in this articulation sounds like /mɑ/ ("mah") rather than /mɑːi/ ("mah-ee"). Upon examining this moment as sung by both Adele and Véronic, we discovered a very close match in formant positions for F1, and a fairly close match for F2 (Figure 5.3).

Significantly, F3 is quite different, at 3006 Hz and 2447 Hz for Adele and Véronic, respectively. Some scholars in voice science have identified the third formant, typically shaped by the parts of the vocal tract closer to the larynx (the pharynx and laryngeal space above the glottis), as key in the perception of speaker or singer-specific vocal timbre (Sundberg 1987). One question the authors began with asked whether in impersonation, one might expect that this third formant might vary more in the effort to

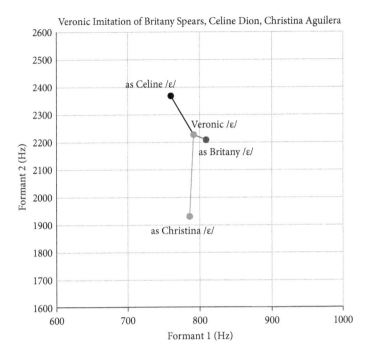

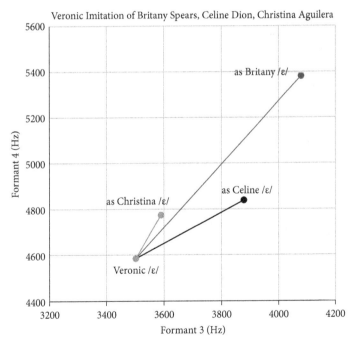

FIGURE 5.4 F1 versus F2 (upper figure) and F3 versus F4 (lower figure) for Véronic and her imitations of Christina Aguilera, Britney Spears, and Celine Dion for the/ɛ/vowel in "bell" while singing "Jingles Bells."

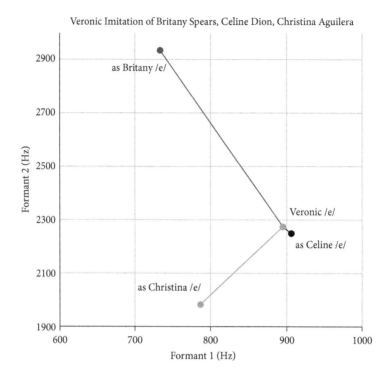

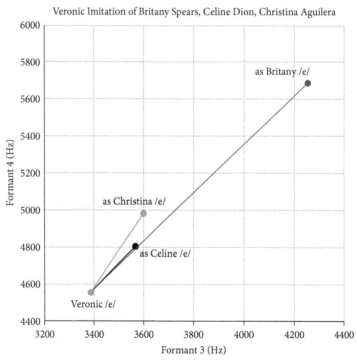

FIGURE 5.5 F1 versus F2 (upper figure) and F3 versus F4 (lower figure) for Véronic and her imitations of Christina Aguilera, Britney Spears, and Celine Dion for the /e/ vowel in "way" while singing "Jingles Bells."

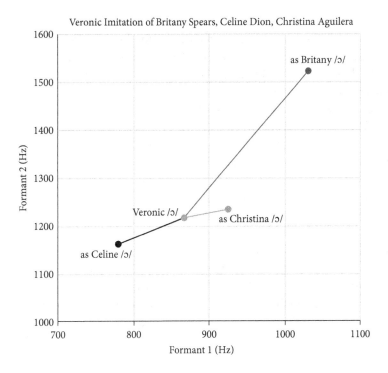

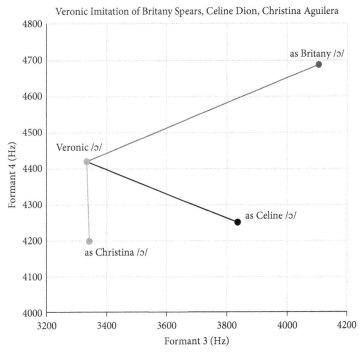

FIGURE 5.6 F1 versus F2 (upper figure) and F3 versus F4 (lower figure) for Véronic and her imitations of Christina Aguilera, Britney Spears, and Celine Dion for the/ɔ/vowel in "all" while singing "Jingles Bells."

match the target's, or stay similar to the impersonator's own acoustic signature. In Véronic's French example, singing as herself, her F$_3$ for the /a/ in "soir" is not far from the aforementioned measurement, this time at 2432 Hz. This appears to support the notion that the third formant may still remain close to the impersonator's own when attempting to match another's sound.

However, further investigation discussed earlier returned quite different results. Véronic was recorded singing one single phrase of text in her own voice as well as in those of Céline Dion, Britney Spears, and Christina Aguilera. After a great deal of deliberation, she chose these target voices as well as the phrase, the first line of the song "Jingle Bells." An examination of three vowels across these samples showed that Véronic's F3 varied by up to more than 1000 Hz (Figure 5.4 and 5.5), which would indicate that the formant shifted a great deal in the process of imitating different voices.

We compared, too, the formant transitions between sounds, such as Véronic's and Adele's transitions from /a/ to /r/ in "heart" and "dark," and from /e/ to /i/ in the word "a" (Figure 5.3). The latter matched closely, while the former tended toward a larger discrepancy. We posit that the larger number of similarities overall in /i/ and /e/ vowels may reflect the relative ease in the perception of these vowels compared to vowels such as /a/.

Finally, in our search for similar stylistic choices between Véronic's and Adele's "Rolling in the Deep," we found a moment of particular interest in the phrase "reaching a fever pitch." As the syllable "-ing" transitions to "a," both Adele and Véronic spend enough time on the "ng" phoneme to nearly make it a syllable with its own intent, and for both the transition shifts from one vocal register to another. This shift is demonstrated in the spectral slices (Figure 5.7) for "-ing" and "a" (/Iŋ/ and /ə/). In these images, it is clear that for /I/ in "-ing" the first harmonic (H1) has a much higher

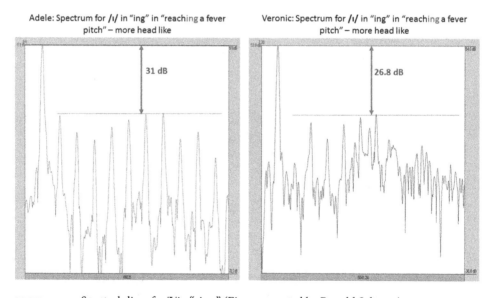

Adele: Spectrum for /ɪ/ in "ing" in "reaching a fever pitch" – more head like

31 dB

Veronic: Spectrum for /ɪ/ in "ing" in "reaching a fever pitch" – more head like

26.8 dB

FIGURE 5.7 Spectral slices for/I/in "-ing." (Figures created by Ronald Scherer.)

intensity in decibels than the next several harmonics. Additionally, for both, the spectral energy in the /I/ of "-ing" is concentrated in the fundamental frequency, consistent with a light mechanism.[3] The syllable "a" (/ə/), however, is executed by both singers in a heavier mechanism[4] where the harmonics are closer to each other in intensity (Figure 5.8 and 5.9).

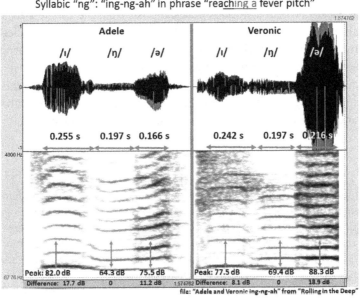

FIGURE 5.8 Comparison of phonemic timing in "-ing a" of "reaching a." (Figure created by Ronald Scherer.)

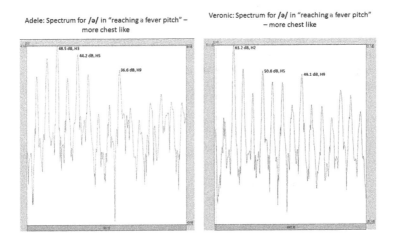

FIGURE 5.9 Spectral slices for /ə/ in "a." (Figure created by Ronald Scherer.)

SUMMARY

Though the samples and our analyses are limited, they do offer early indications that: 1) impersonators rely upon a great variety of productive adjustments specific to each target artist's voice; and 2) singing impersonators like Véronic are successful not due to a perfectly accurate imitation, but instead to the selective matching of particular moments in an original artist's recorded work—aural signposts that cue listeners to imagine the voice and the body originally associated with those sounds. This also implies that listeners can process identity clearly relying only on discrete moments of acoustic correspondence, which function as internally shaped sonic snapshots that, like more external bodily gestures, provide the information we need to *hear voices*. Perhaps this method of acoustic outlining highlights the disjuncture that Jarman-Ivens sees as central to impersonation, and serves as a crucial reminder of the careful work that defines it.

NOTES

1. Some of the concepts in this chapter also appear in Meizel's monograph *Multivocality: An Ethnography of Singing on the Borders of Identity* (Oxford University Press, forthcoming).
2. Fiberoptic observations of the supraglottal structures of voice impersonators (Feder 1988) suggest that the epiglottis, the pharyngeal walls, the opening to the piriform sinuses, the false vocal folds, and the aryepiglottic folds can all be adjusted to create special vocal effects.
3. Sometimes referred to as "head register" in Western classical pedagogy.
4. Sometimes referred to as "chest register" or "modal register" in Western classical pedagogy.

WORKS CITED

Abitbol, Jean. 2006. *Odyssey of the Voice*, translated by Patricia Crossley. San Diego, Oxford, and Brisbane: Plural Publishing.

Bin Amin, Talal, Pina Marziliano, and James Sneed German. 2014. "Glottal and Vocal Tract characteristics of Voice Impersonators." *IEEE Transactions on Multimedia (TMM)* 6 (3): 668–78. https://sites.google.com/site/talalbinamin/publications

Dolar, Mladen. 2006. *A Voice and Nothing More*. Cambridge, MA: The MIT Press.

Feder, R. 1988. *The Voice of the Impersonator*. Educational video. Available through The Voice Foundation, Philadelphia.

Ferris, Kerry O. 2011. "Building Characters: The Work of Celebrity Impersonators." *Journal of Popular Culture* 44 (6): 1192–208.

Hastrup, Kirsten. 1998. "Theatre as a Site of Passage: Some Reflections on the Magic of Acting." In *Ritual, Performance, Media*, edited by Felicia Hughes-Freeland, 29–46. London: Routledge.

Huron, David. 2002. "Listening Styles and Listening Strategies." Presentation handout, Society for Music Theory Conference, Columbus, Ohio, November 1. http://www.musiccog.ohio-state.edu/Huron/Talks/SMT.2002/handout.html.

Jarman-Ivens, Freya. 2006. "Breaking Voices: Voice, Subjectivity and Fragmentation in Popular Music." PhD diss., University of Newcastle.

Kitamura, Tatsuya. 2008. "Acoustic Analysis of Imitated Voice Produced by a Professional Impersonator." *International Speech Communication Association*, 9th Annual Conference, Brisbane Australia, Spetember 22–26: 813–16.

López, Sabrina, Pablo Riera, María Florencia Assaneo, Manuel Eguía, Mariano Sigman, and Marcos A. Trevisan. 2013. "Vocal Caricatures Reveal Signatures of Speaker Identity." *Scientific Reports* 3 (3407): 1–7.

Meizel, Katherine. 2011. *Idolized: Music, Media, and Identity in* American Idol. Bloomington: Indiana University Press.

Meizel, Katherine (forthcoming). *Multivocality: An Ethnography of Singing on the Borders of Identity*. Oxford and New York: Oxford University Press.

Peterson, G. E. and Barney, H.L. (1952). "Control Methods Used in the Study of Vowels," *Journal of the Acoustical Society of America*. 24(2): 175–84.

Plasketes, George. 2010. "Introduction: Like A Version." *Play It Again: Cover Songs in Popular Music*, edited by George Plasketes, 1–10. Burlington, VT: Ashgate Publishing.

Schechner, Richard. 1985. *Between Theater and Anthropology*. Philadelphia: University of Pennsylvania Press.

Stevens, Kenneth N., and Arthur S. House. 1955. "Development of a Quantitative Description of Vowel Articulation." *Journal of the Acoustical Society of America* 27 (3): 484–93.

Sundberg, J. 1987. *The Science of the Singing Voice*. DeKalb, IL: Northern Illinois University Press.

Tanaka, Mari, Hideki Kawahara, and Shigeo Morishima. 2010. "Acoustic Features Affecting Speaker Identification by Imitated Voice Analysis." *Proceedings of the 20th International Congress on Acoustics*. http://www.acoustics.asn.au/conference_proceedings/ICA2010/cdrom-%20ICA2010/papers/p842.pdf

Turner, Victor. 1982. *From Ritual to Theatre: The Human Seriousness of Play*. New York: Performing Arts Journal Publications.

Zetterholm, Elisabeth. 2002. "A Comparative Survey of Phonetic Features of Two Impersonators." *Proceedings of Fonetik* 44 (1): 129–32.

CHAPTER 6

··

THIS AMERICAN VOICE

The Odd Timbre of a New Standard in Public Radio

··

TOM McENANEY

WHEN National Public Radio (NPR) decided to replace Frank Tavares, who read the names and taglines of the corporation's underwriters until late in 2013, the network's vice president of programming, Eric Nuzum, described the kind of voice they were seeking. "The phrase I use is 'ambiguously genuine,'" Nuzum told *The New Yorker*'s Reeves Wiedeman (Wiedeman 2013, 23). "They sound like a real person, but they don't sound like a specific age, or as if they were from a specific region." NPR located this "ambiguously genuine" voice in Sabrina Fahri, who, as Wiedeman explains, was born in New York and "moved with her family to Singapore, Belgium, and Switzerland before eventually returning to Brooklyn to work as an actress, a journey that left her with an accent more or less from nowhere." The "genuine" voice in this instance means "a voice from nowhere," a voice that cannot be traced back, as Nuzum says, to a specific age or a specific region. To produce this voice without a trace of its time or place, Fahri, so the article suggests, had to move to a number of different places, and, one would think, learn a number of different languages, or speak a "global" English.[1] Circulating through polyglot international capitals of finance and diplomacy, Fahri's voice strangely loses rather than accumulates a sense of place and particularity: her accent neutralized, canceled out. Her "voice from nowhere," a voice that NPR prizes for its lack of specificity, has become, in Nuzum's estimation, an ideal vehicle to announce the names of financial sponsors supporting NPR.

The NPR corporation's selection of Fahri's voice—and Nuzum's explanation of the selection process—illustrates a number of issues key to the history of voice on the radio, in general, public radio, more specifically, and the complicated role any radio voice plays in relation to a public mission. In the following pages I will explore how these histories help situate particular innovations in public radio voice. Among the programs where one might identify such sonic transformation, I have chosen the radio program *This American Life* for its representative claim on an "American" life and voice, and what its producers, hosts, and critics often refer to as its "democratic" attitude. Moreover, since critics tend to agree that *This American Life* has been the single program most responsible for alterations in the sonic norms in US public radio broadcasting, and considering the program and its wildly popular offshoots—*Serial* (2014–) and *S-Town* (2017)—have broken podcasting download records, I hope to understand it as a sonic archive of changes in an "American" radio sound that help us question what it means to "sound American." In particular, the early and defining years of *This American Life* relied on a number of contributing voices—from Sarah Vowell to David Sedaris to the show's host Ira Glass—that broke from some explicit and implicit, written and unwritten norms of public radio broadcasting in the United States. These voices, in Vowell's words, "sound like they shouldn't be on the radio" (Belluck 1998). The decision to not only include such voices on the radio, but make them central to *This American Life*, indicates a shift in the sonic style and norms of public radio's "voice from nowhere," the publics those sounds hail, and the new forms of publics and counterpublics that arise as a consequence (Warner 2005).

Without falsely separating the sounds of these voices from the content of the stories they tell, I emphasize sound in the following pages to correct a remarkable inattention to vocal tone, pitch, cadence, and timbre in radio history, and aesthetic and political theory more generally.[2] The political value and weight of fairly minor sonic changes becomes audible only through close attention to the field of sounds against which what I call the "odd timbre" of *This American Life*'s early voices emerge. In some cases, hearing the meaning in these sounds also depends on the history of broadcast regulation, and the peculiar structure of radio broadcast itself. Radio, after all, burdens the voice—especially its sound—with the primary labor needed to reach an audience. Thus, in this chapter I will begin with the history of efforts to create the sound of a public radio voice in England and the United States, linking this twentieth-century struggle to a longer history of the *vox populi*, before turning to *This American Life*'s voices and the new role they play in helping develop a novel approach to the sound of the public radio voice.

A Voice From Nowhere

In order to make audible the standards against which *This American Life* defines itself, one first needs to understand something of the history of the "voice from nowhere" praised by Nuzum. Attention to Sabrina Fahri's voice, and the microhistory of its raison d'être at NPR, brings together a number of issues in radio and voice studies that have intrigued sound engineers, linguistic anthropologists, policymakers, and critical theorists over the course of radio's history. As early as 1928, the French radio producer Paul Deharme recommended that one speak on the radio with neutral "*grey diction*" to erase the particularity of the voice, and convert one's voice into "a kind of phonograph" (Deharme 1928, 408; emphasis in original). Eight years later, the German-born media critic Rudolf Arnheim advocated a "pure sound" in radio that would eliminate any sense of place. In radio broadcasting, Arnheim argued, spatial "resonance is eliminated, out of a very proper feeling that the existence of the studio is not essential to the transmission and therefore has no place in the listener's consciousness" (Arnheim 1936, 143).[3] Deharme and Arnheim's comments provided guidance to voice actors and broadcasters in "the art of radio"—as Arnheim titled his book—and their statements also archive trends in audio engineering and political oratory as radio consolidated standards in the 1930s.

According to sound historian Emily Thompson, by 1932 innovations in electrical engineering and acoustic design helped erase the sound of space at Radio City Music Hall, where the use of microphones, insulation, and speakers made the spectacle on the stage sound the same from every seat in the room (Thompson 2002, 234). Thompson names this elimination, erasure, or silencing of sounds that would call attention to the difference between the place of production and the various venues of reception "The New Acoustics," an electrification of the acoustic world she argues produced "the sound-scape of modernity" (5, 1). While Thompson does not engage radio production, the object of her study—Rockefeller Center—housed the Radio Corporation of America (RCA), where new technology, such as broadcast microphones, often supplied its sub-sidiary, the National Broadcasting Company (NBC). With such corporate synergy in mind, it is not surprising that the "erasure of space" Thompson uncovers in Radio City finds enthusiastic support in Arnheim's instructions for eliminating resonance on the radio. Both the technologies and the aesthetic guidelines participate in constructing a modern soundscape in which radio artists, engineers, and even politicians sought to make sound that seemed to come from nowhere.

In perhaps the most famous example of this innovative sonic ideology, the older media of nonelectrical devices worked together with the newly sophisticated electrical devices to drive transformations in political sound. When Franklin Delano Roosevelt issued his intimate "fireside chats" over the radio in the 1930s, the sensitive micro-phone he used required that he speak with a dental bridge to prevent his teeth from audibly whistling, and to erase any sonic marker that might amplify the actual distance between the president and the people.[4] Eliminating the sound of space enabled a new style of political oratory that shaped a nuanced democratic populism against the fanatic fascist models in continental Europe. Describing the latter, Theodor Adorno and Max Horkheimer argue that "The *Führer's* metaphysical charisma…turned out finally to be merely the omnipresence of his radio addresses, which demonically parodies that of the divine spirit. The gigantic fact that the speech penetrates everywhere replaces its con-tent" (Adorno and Horkheimer 2002 [1944], 129). Roosevelt took a different path to his listener's ear. He turned the volume down to reach the people, understanding that with the microphone he didn't need to scream in order for his voice to reach a massive audi-ence. His quieter speech helped create a sense that he spoke to his listeners in an inti-mate space, as a friend or neighbor, rather than a voice from on high.[5] In this way, the carefully designed sound of Roosevelt's voice broadcasted as the fireside chats erased the feeling of (geographical, political, and social) distance. Different tones, volumes, and pitches of voice, in these examples, both represented and helped create or consolidate specific political programs. Eventually, the mere sound of the voice could index an entire political system for listeners huddled around the radio.

As these examples help demonstrate, the innovations in audio engineering needed to be coupled with a belief and investment in the "neutral," "standard," and "placeless" voice. While new technology did not determine the political parameters of oratory, newly sensitive microphones and radio enabled new forms of audible speech deployed by different political actors through a variety of methods and techniques. Fascist and democratic orators had access to the same sonorous media, but shaped radio's "voice from nowhere" or "voice from everywhere" to their particular ends. While it would be mistaken to claim that a universal radio aesthetic has held sway since the emergence of broadcast in Argentina and the United States in 1920, the importance of an apparently placeless voice seems entwined with the development of the social uses of radio.[6] The importance of "the voice from nowhere" that NPR sought as recently as 2013 has remained a powerful ideal in public broadcasting, especially in the United States and England. And in order to understand the significance of a break from this standard, in order to understand what one hears when one hears a voice seemingly unfit for public radio—in other words, in order to understand the surprisingly original voices of *This American Life*—one requires a vocabulary and a series of histories to render legible these audible differences.

In the case of the political voices mentioned earlier, their transcendent or intimate qualities were taken as a nearly inevitable consequence of combining an individual voice's representative status as leader of a nation with broadcasting's new configuration of geographical distance and the experience of simultaneous listening. These voices came to their listeners already packaged as "national" voices. But how does public radio transfer this representative function to the voices of its broadcasters, who are not presidents, prime ministers, congresspeople, or parliamentarians? How does one construct the voice of public radio, and how do listeners identify such a voice? Can a voice's timbre alone index itself as linked to a specific community? How might a voice's sound entail, or participate in the creation of a new community? To return to my opening example, when Nuzum and Wiedeman hear Fahri's voice as a "voice from nowhere," as somehow placeless, we might wonder what kinds of audible markers it carries or mutes to produce such a voice. Or, remembering that the voice is not heard in a social vacuum, we might ask how the effect of a placeless voice is socially produced. What norms and standards help structure how Nuzum and Wiedeman hear Fahri's voice as placeless? In order to answer the more general aspects of these questions, without delving into a psychological analysis of these particular social actors, I will turn to the most widely recognized public radio voice in the twentieth century: the voice of the BBC.

BBC English and Received Pronunciation

The idea of speech without a place is often connected to a sound pattern that both popular and scholarly publications refer to as "BBC English" (Roach 2004). Now mainly known as "received pronunciation" (RP), in the jargon of linguistic anthropology this form of speech "is *a supra-local accent*; it is enregistered in public awareness as indexical of a speaker's class and level of education; it is *valued precisely for effacing the geographic origins of speaker*" (Agha 2003, 233; emphasis added). As Asif Agha explains here, although British listeners hear this accent as geographically "placeless," they recognize the voice as indicating a specific social class and level of education. This "enregisterment" or social understanding of BBC English or RP derives from a specific history. As Lynda Mugglestone has written, a rising interest in elocution and the publication of elocution manuals at the end of the eighteenth century helped transform British culture such that by the close of the nineteenth century "notions of a non-localized accent (and assimilation to it) had come to act as a dominant social symbol, the salient element in what the phonetician Henry Sweet defined as 'a class-dialect more than a local dialect'" (Mugglestone 1995, 5).[7] While the BBC apparently did not have an official policy or strict guidelines to delimit the tones or accents their broadcasters could use, RP's canonization at the BBC was a consequence of this accent's cultural capital within the English university system. The BBC hired graduates of Cambridge and Oxford, and these speakers dominated the BBC's national and international broadcasting.[8] Through the sheer number of listeners who heard that sound pattern, associated with a national-imperial (British) broadcasting corporation, the voices on the BBC transformed the sound of a voice associated with only 3 percent of the country's speakers, primarily located in only the elite classes in and around London, into the national-imperial standard or norm, "valued precisely for effacing the geographic origins of speaker" (Agha 2003, 234). This norm has so thoroughly permeated British society that citizens have actively protested when BBC broadcasters speak with marked or regional accents (John Honey cited in Agha 2003, 237). Recent ethnographic studies linked to these debates within the BBC about the increased use of accents not associated with the Southeastern corner of England from which RP derives, further acknowledge that the standard pronunciation on the BBC is RP (Revoir 2010). Thus, RP or BBC English demonstrates how radio can reinforce, disseminate, and thus largely produce norms and standards of voice across a large linguistic territory. What might sound like a voice without place owes its status to radio broadcasting's own fiction of placelessness, its own utopian image of voice.

As the voice scholar Anne Karpf has observed, RP has continued to spread throughout the British media system. Drawing on studies of elocutionary training for call center workers in India, Karpf notes that workers

> must first complete a spell of "accent training" or so-called "accent neutralization" (although there's nothing neutral, of course, about the accents that the workers are trained to use)... Excellence in Indian call centers is now almost synonymous with anglicising the voice... In a nice irony, the Indian call-centre workers are expected to use an accent, with its perfectly pronounced 't's and 'p's, that many of their non-Received Pronunciation (RP) British counterparts can't achieve.
>
> (Karpf 2006, 193)[9]

A linguistic standard, first propagated through broadcast radio, now demands changes in the voices of employees in order to train them to speak *not* just like the callers phoning for information, but rather like the media system itself. The history behind the utterance of these workers is the creation story of the "voice from nowhere."

But is there an equivalent "placeless" accent in the United States? How does Sabrina Fahri's voice produce a sound effect that Nuzum's professional radio ear hears as if it comes from nowhere? The sociolinguist William Labov's 2005 publication of *The Atlas of North American English: Phonetics, Phonology, and Sound Change* codifies the diversity of regional accents throughout the United States, and implicitly argues against any standard American accent, or what some call "general American" (Labov 2005, 190). In interviews and publications, Labov also rejects the idea that mass media have homogenized the sound of speech in the United States: "The opposite is true. Whatever the influence of the mass media are, it doesn't affect the way we speak everyday. And the regional dialects of this country are getting more and more different, so that people in Buffalo, St. Louis and Los Angeles are now speaking much more differently from each other than they ever did" (Siegel 2006). Instead of reducing the sound of social space, Labov argues that the sound of people's voices in the United States has become *the* means to differentiate them: "Most of the important changes in American speech are not happening at the level of grammar or language—which used to be the case—but at the level of sound itself" (Labov quoted in Seabrook 2005). With so much audible diversity it seems inaccurate, if not ridiculous, to describe a voice in the United States as geographically neutral. Perhaps this is why NPR's Nuzum had to find a voice whose informal training occurred through the accumulated practice of speaking and listening with voices primarily outside the United States. As Wiedeman suggests in the comments with which I began this chapter, Fahri's voice is the opposite of RP: it is from too many places, and hence from nowhere in particular.

However, as the critics here observe, "nowhere" does not only indicate a lack of geographic place. The social space a voice can inhabit, and the social markers embedded within pronunciation can depend on class as much as region. While FDR's dental bridge allowed him to speak closer to the microphone, and thus helped make him sound closer to his listeners, Labov has argued that when the former governor of New York dropped his "r"s "it sounded upper class. But after the Second World War... with the loss of Britain's imperial status 'r'-less British speech ceased to be regarded as 'prestige speech'...and the dropping of 'r's became exclusively working class" (Seabrook 2005). This class change encoded in language leads Labov to conclude that New York City's "dialect is much more indicative of one's social status than of one's neighborhood. 'Although no one wants to admit this...because we're supposed to live in a classless society'" (Seabrook 2005). As Labov emphasizes here, and as Nuzum and Wiedeman's silence about class implies, tuning our ears to the sound of place often substitutes for listening to class.[10]

Of course, even the ideology of the classless society encoded in sound can serve to index place. Writing in 1950, the novelist Raymond Chandler, who settled in Los Angeles after a childhood spent in both the Midwestern United States and England, claimed that the sound of speech in the United States lacks class:

> The tone quality of English speech is usually overlooked. This tone quality is infinitely variable and contributes infinite meaning. The American voice is flat, toneless, and tiresome. The English tone quality makes a thinner vocabulary and a more formalized use of language capable of infinite meanings…This makes good English a class language, and that is its fatal defect.   (Chandler 1995 [1950], 1014–1015)

While one might disagree with Chandler's characterization, it draws attention to the relative value attributed to overtly recognizing and associating social actors with a social class in traditional British society, versus the relative antagonism to such overt class markers in the United States.[11] NPR's Nuzum follows this insight: he listens for age and region, but not social class, which is not meant to enter the sonic contours of the US radio voice. After all, as Labov claims, to hear class as a listener in the United States stands in opposition to the norms of American listening. And yet Wiedeman hints at an interpretation of the voice from nowhere as itself the product of a certain class. We might hear his biographical summation of Fahri's voice—its travel through the global capitals of commerce and diplomacy—as not only the cosmopolitan burnishing of a global voice, but the journey of a voice produced through its accumulated circulation in those financial capitals. It could be that Nuzum hears Fahri's voice as the perfect fit for NPR's corporate underwriters because, in some sense, her voice is the sound effect of global commerce.

THE SOUND OF THE PUBLIC/THE VOICE OF AMERICA/VOX POPULI/VOX VITREUS

I have taken this somewhat circuitous route to the voices of *This American Life* in order to frame the specific field-changing qualities of these voices, and to make their originality legible as a particular innovation in representative speech. If Fahri's voice has acquired neutrality in Nuzum's ears, the voices of *This American Life* have just the opposite effect on most critics. And if Fahri's voice should sound like it comes from nowhere, the representative function of the voices on *This American Life* relies on these voices registering with listeners as a sonic image of pluralism, an America that corresponds to Labov's diverse atlas. Unique, casual, and demotic, as the program's title announces, these voices aim to depict a sonorous archive of everyday American life.

Despite the seemingly straightforward aim of this project, the national and cultural adjective "American," and the program's distribution by Public Radio International across many NPR stations return to and revise the problem of the broadcasting voice raised with RP or Farhri's voice.[12] Specifically, listening to *This American Life* raises the questions: how does a program represent a nation through the voice, and how does it define a public or publics?[13] Has NPR constructed its own version of a "standard American" tone, a US version of RP? If so, does *This American Life* share in that tone, or challenge it? And, perhaps most importantly for the present volume, what can we glean from the sound of the radio voice alone? What methodologies, technologies, and techniques of analysis and interpretation would best approach a study of the odd timbre of *This American Life*?

By focusing on the voices of host Ira Glass and a select group of contributors to *This American Life*, I am perhaps sidestepping the very difference that defines the show against other broadcast journalism: the sounds of *other* people's voices. Introducing a segment about the aftermath of Hurricane Katrina that was rebroadcast for the program's five-hundredth episode, Glass remarks,

> I remember when we put that show together. You know, we all knew there had already been lots of coverage of Katrina everywhere. And we thought the one thing that we could do was that... 'Til then, when you heard from people in New Orleans in the news it was mostly in tiny little sound bites. And we thought the one contribution we could make was just let people talk longer. You know, it's easier to connect emotionally when you hear more.   (Glass 2013a)

"Middle of Somewhere," the story to which Glass refers here, is just one example of how *This American Life* attempts to create a public voice and a public emotional connection by turning the microphone over to people other than its reporters. And yet, while I recognize that much of the show's storytelling depends on field reporting and interviews with a variety of different subjects from throughout the country, and sometimes beyond, I begin with the show's most famous voice—that of its host, Ira Glass—in order to approach these questions through the show's own logic, and the one voice heard in nearly every episode the program has broadcast.

Glass has foregrounded these questions of voice and public, and self-reflexively built them into the programming since the show first aired on Chicago's WBEZ on November 17, 1995 as *Your Radio Playhouse*. On that first episode, Joe Franklin, the legendary television and radio talk show host, tells Glass, "Your voice...I've heard so much about the sparkle, about the energy in your voice. The voice, on radio especially, is everything" (Glass 1995). "Sparkle" is not an adjective that has since been applied to Glass's voice by media critics and sound scholars. Later commentators have described his voice as imbued with a "precious, adenoidal charm" (Loviglio); "too nasal, muffled, verging on meek" (Rainey); "crackly and, at times, uncomfortably intimate" (Sela); and "casual" (Belluck). None of these characteristics of his voice match what one critic calls "the softly authoritative cadence that NPR so enjoys in its news readers" (Sela), or "the knowledgeable and comfortable anchorman who sounds as if he knows more than he says" (Looker, quoted in Vowell 1996, 66). The features that make, or at least at one time made Glass's voice unique on radio, and that have drawn him both praise and scorn, seem nearly opposite to the bright and shiny character in Franklin's adjective—"sparkle"—which more closely relates to Glass's name than the qualities of his voice. However, attention to the adjectives in Franklin's brief attempt to frame how we hear that voice might miss the point. One might argue that the primary function of Franklin's voice's presence on the show is to link his praise of Glass to a whole pantheon of talk show hosts—Johnny Carson, David Letterman, Jay Leno, Conan O'Brien—whom Franklin has coached throughout his career. Franklin's praise—the sound of his voice alone—implicitly inserts Ira Glass into this list of talk show royalty.

On the other hand, the transitive property of Franklin's voice—metonymically bestowing future success on Glass's voice through its past success with other hosts— might also miss the mark, insofar as it aims at a popular audience and a traditional format that Glass's show seems to eschew. Where Franklin values "sparkle," Glass's listeners have preferred what they consider "nasal" and "crackly," and in the negotiation of these adjectives different publics begin to form. However, before pursuing the implications of these differences further, it is worth noting how Franklin's later return to the show helps clarify these questions of sound, representation, and the creation of different publics. While Franklin insists that "the voice is everything" on *Your Radio Playhouse*'s first episode, when he is invited back on the show for the first episode of *This American Life* on March 21, 1996, he has changed his tune: "The name is everything," he tells Glass (Glass 1996). The latter mentions some alternative titles ("America Whatever," "Ira Glass and His Radio Cowboys," "Glass House," "Glasnost," "Radiolicious"), but when he comes to "This American Life" Franklin pauses, and then definitively tells him that it is the best he has heard. Why? "The name is everything. Look at Marilyn Monroe," Franklin says. "Marilyn Monroe told me that the important thing in a name is the vowel sound—the A-E-I-O or U... At least you've got one. You've got the sound 'I.' Life. Life. The name is everything." When Glass protests that there is an "i" in "this," Franklin replies, "not the A-I-O-U sound. It's gotta be... It's a soft, it's a soft, it's a soft 'i.' It's gotta' be a hard 'I,' like the word, like the noun 'I.' You know what I'm saying? It's gotta' be the sound of A-E-I-O or U." Thus, for Franklin, the *sound* of the name is everything. First, a series of phonemes, and only second, a semantic artifact, *This American Life* comes to us as a self-consciously constructed project about sound and naming, sound and identity, sound and representation. Franklin's reference to Marilyn Monroe only further emphasizes the program as the familiar construction of Americana: the celebrity who invents her name and identity because of its sound becomes another model for Glass's attempt to both represent and invent American life through sound.

Without overstating Franklin's folk wisdom, it should be noted that the vowel sounds he singles out have phonetic significance that link sound and name. What Franklin calls the hard "I" in "life" is, as he says, "the noun 'I,'" and the same "I" one hears in "Ira," or what the International Phonetic Alphabet identifies as the dipthong "aɪ." Vowels like /aɪ/ carry information about the vocal tract—as opposed to less information-rich consonants or fricatives—and provide some of the key signals to begin to help listeners— machine and human—distinguish one speaker from another (Trevisan et al. 2005).[14] Furthermore, vowel formants, the main resonating pockets that increase the intensity or volume of frequencies within the vocal tract, help create the vocal color or timbre that textures a voice. Franklin, with his acute ear for the broadcasting voice, hears how the specific vowel sound in *This American Life* will carry resonating force for the show's future audience, and link the host's name with the program's title.[15]

When Joe Franklin tells Ira Glass "the voice is everything," and then, six months later, "the name is everything," he does not contradict himself. Rather, he identifies the project of *This American Life*: to produce a representative *sonic* portrait of life in the United States. Changing the name to *This American Life* inserts the program in a familiar and fraught project to find a representative voice for the United States, or the more hubristic, imperial, and myopic "America." Naming the program *This American Life* ostensibly turns the show away from the theatrical overtones of *Your Radio Playhouse*, and towards the documentary impulse that primarily brings audiences stories from people's lives, rather than intended fictions or interviews with celebrity or political figures. At the same time, this impulse, and the invocation of "American" in the show's title, pulls the program into a long historical debate about political and cultural representation that has been attached to the democratic project in the United States since its inception.

The title *This American Life* raises questions about "lending" or "giving" a voice to the people, about the role of "representative" speech, and the inherent authority, and potential tyranny of the public-sponsored broadcast voice. Critics such as Jay Fliegelman, Jason Frank, Christopher Looby, and Nancy Ruttenburg, among others, have identified how seventeenth-, eighteenth-, and nineteenth-century public speech, political rhetoric, poetry, and narrative fiction in the United States worked through the potentially uncontainable expressive power of the *vox populi*, or what Ruttenburg calls the voice of "democratic personality" (Fliegelman 1993; Frank 2010; Looby 1996; Ruttenbburg 1998; Slauter 2009).[16] According to these studies, the idea of an American life and the American nation arises through the voice.[17] Unable to appeal to a common ethnic identity or a sense of inevitable nationality—what Looby calls the "blood loyalty or immemorial facticity" that bolstered concepts of European nationhood—the United States founders turned to the spoken word (Looby 1996, 4). The Declaration of Independence, Fliegelman reminds us, "was written to be read aloud. Part of its own agenda as a 'declaration' was to 'publish and declare' (with the former verb carrying the contemporary sense of 'to announce formally and publicly') that 'these colonies...are free'" (Fliegelman 1993, 25). Democracy inhered in the vocal utterance because the voice, unlike print, did not separate the literate from the illiterate. The *public* voice made itself available to a wide community of listeners, rather than segregating an audience into those who could gain access to a speech or a book because of class, "birth, office, or occupation," and those who were barred from hearing it on these same grounds (26). A voice in public, addressed to the people, also carried possible affiliation or contamination with the voice of the people, who were there to contest or join in with a speaker.

While it is beyond the scope of this chapter, one could trace the history of such public speech in the United States and its connection to the *vox populi* and the question of representative democracy from Jefferson to talk radio.[18] I invoke the history here in order to consider how "public radio" in the United States particularizes the idea and practice of the people's voice. For if the radical potential in the public voice as the people's voice first emerged in the seventeenth-century American colonies, public radio was only established relatively late in the history of US democracy and even US broadcasting. Public radio, in an approximation of its present form in the United States, was legislated into existence at the close of Lyndon Johnson's Great Society with the passage of the Public Broadcasting Act of 1967, and the 1971 debut of NPR's flagship program *All Things Considered*.[19] From its first broadcast, this public radio had a sound that emphasized the public. According to the radio historian Susan Douglas, *All Things Considered*

> revived the sort of eyewitness account pioneered by CBS in the late 1930s and exploited ambient sounds and on-the-spot interviews to create a you-are-there feel. The reportorial style demanded dimensional listening...The hallmark of *All Things Considered*, in addition to the length and depth of its news stories, was its inventive and playful use of sound. Ambient sound—of distant gunshots, of sirens, of crickets at night, of children at a playground—were standard features of all stories, evoking place and mood.   (Douglas 2004, 321–323)

Contrary to the "erasure of space" characteristic of much radio broadcasting, the program's emphasis on ambient sound, interviews with everyday people, and "dimensional listening" that required listeners to orient themselves in the sonic space of the broadcast made the sound of public space inherent to the mission of public radio. It is from this idea of public radio—as a sound and a structural encounter with the voice of the people—that *This American Life* emerges. Some of the apparent innovation of *This American Life*, in other words, pertains more to its return to NPR's founding moments than a dramatic break with public radio's history in the United States.

However, the structure of representing the voice of the people is only one aspect of the democratic project and its particular instantiation through public radio. For all of the interest in the voice of the people in political theory, there is very little attention in these studies to the sound of those voices. Despite Thomas Jefferson's affection for the "familiar style" in rhetoric, or John Durham Peters's recognition that styles of talk on US radio in the early 1930s included "a tonal shift toward snugger modes of address" (Peters 1999, 217), theorists rarely engage the importance of *sound* in shaping the significance of the *vox populi*.[20] While "voice" in most critical formulations still primarily means an identifiable, patterned, and thus repeatable verbal (written or spoken) token, which we might also call a "register," or a "style," I am interested in the sound of the voice, and the notoriously amorphous concept of "timbre": the tonal color that helps the ear distinguish between voices.[21] These apparently nonsemantic aspects of the voice—the contours of the sonic envelope rather than the *logos* within it—also participate in the formation of publics. I have already described how such a representative voice emerges as a standard in BBC English, and it could be noted how other forms of state-sponsored radio sought to regulate tone in order to produce a more limited spectrum of available pitches and speech patterns.[22] Conscious of such molds, the early years of *This American Life* paid particular attention to the voices of its commentators, and it is to the sonic quality—the pitch, tone, and timbre of Ira Glass and his most frequent early contributors—rather than the structural role of *the* voice, through which we can better understand how *This American Life* hails listeners and constructs a new vocal model for public radio in the United States.

Already in the first episode of *Your Radio Playhouse*, Glass's mother Shirley poses a similar question: "Who is your target audience?" (Glass 1995). Shirley Glass proceeds to voice her concern that her son's program is "in danger of appealing to a narrow range of listeners if it becomes uh, uh, a little too, um…I don't know what words to use." Glass offers "artsy," and his mother confirms: "Artsy. Yeah. [Laughs]." Shirley Glass's question, which uses the vocabulary of advertising and Nielsen ratings, identifies *Your Radio Playhouse* as sending signals that would narrow the broadcast audience. To pose her question in another discursive register, we might ask to which publics or counterpublics does this public radio program appeal? And, in striving to represent American life, do Ira Glass and the show's other frequent contributing voices make the vocal sound of *This American Life* into an imitable standard?

Given the program's early and ongoing self-reflexivity, it should not surprise us that in the January 11, 2013 episode Ira Glass seems to ask and think through these very questions (Glass 2013b). As with nearly every episode of *This American Life*, "Doppelgängers"—the week's theme—begins with Ira Glass's voice. Except that it doesn't. What the listening audience might hear as Glass's voice is actually that of the comedian Fred Armisen impersonating Glass. As the two dialogue, Glass trains Armisen to perfect his mimicry: "Do I sound that nasal?" Glass asks, and Armisen resignedly responds, "Maybe."[23] Implicitly, the two also train the listening audience to discern the nuanced differences that make up the Glass effect: what is perceived as the nasality, and the measured cadence and low volume delivery that characterize Glass's voice.[24]

Rendered in musical notation, Armisen's impersonation helps bring out the particulars of Glass's rhythm and tone.[25] In Figure 6.1, bars one and two in the first system show Armisen, followed by Glass in bar three, and Armisen's correction in bar four. Surprisingly, Glass's pitch is several notes lower than Armisen's initial impression. What Glass and Armisen call the "nasal" quality in Glass's voice—recognized by them both in row four—leads Armisen to imagine a higher pitch—an illusion shared by many critics—that he only retunes upon hearing Glass speak again. Armisen's eventual "pitch perfect" impression in bar four is impressive, but more remarkable is the still recognizable difference of his voice when it is heard. This residue beyond pitch marks the complex physiological and social difference inherent in the problem of timbre (Fales 2002).[26] Although Armisen can mimic tone and rhythm—those sonic elements that distinguish one voice from another, even when tuned to the same pitch—Glass's timbral individuality escapes both Armisen and the musical transcription. While other tools, such as spectrogram analysis, can help render legible nonmelodious aspects of the voice, what matters most at this moment is how Armisen transforms Ira Glass's voice into an identifiable character study.

Rather than allow his voice to serve as a conduit, a delivery device for content and meaning, Ira Glass turns his voice into an object in this exchange.[27] In addition, his dialogue with Armisen demonstrates that the show has recognized the genre of its voice, a

FIGURE 6.1 The musician David Steinberg's melodic transcription of Fred Armisen's impersonation of and conversation with Ira Glass on the January 11, 2013 episode of *This American Life*.

voice with its own rules of use that help identify it as impressionable, insofar as it makes
an impression on its audience—it is not merely any voice—and in the sense that one can
copy it by shaping one's own voice to its sonic contours.

But how far can that copy travel? To whom is it recognizable? And, again, to which
publics does it appeal? As Armisen, one of the stars on *Saturday Night Live* from 2002 to
2013 and the cocreator and star of the television show *Portlandia*, works on perfecting
his impression, he offers a possible answer. In his conversation with Glass, Armisen reveals
that he had pitched a parody about Glass and *This American Life* to *Saturday Night Live*'s
producers, but that it was ultimately rejected because its object, the voice of Ira Glass,
was not recognizable to enough viewers: it wasn't famous enough for the SNL audience to
recognize the parody. Armisen's revelation delimits the public reach of Glass's voice. Years
before the *This American Life* spinoff *Serial* podcast would become a *Saturday Night Live*
parody hit, Armisen's story makes clear that the "public" of public radio is distinct from
the general public of *Saturday Night Live*, and that Glass's voice falls outside a certain
threshold of popular culture in the United States.[28] However, including this story on *This
American Life* is not a merely self-effacing gesture. For the limited reach of Glass's voice,
the limitation of its public, is the very limit that helps create that voice's actual public. The
failure to be heard by one group only increases that voice's relevance to another group.

Shirley Glass, in the show's first episode, only worries about the limits, the too-narrow
confines of that voice. Borrowing the language of Pierre Bourdieu's sociology of culture,
one might say that she does not consider the *distinction* of such a voice, nor the *cultural*

capital it entails. In Bourdieu's terms, the *Saturday Night Live*' producers' rejection of Glass's voice produces that voice's "distinctive *value* from its negative relationship with the coexisting position-takings corresponding to the different positions" (Bourdieu 1993, 30).[29] Thus Glass's voice, along with the show's other early voices, such as those of Sarah Vowell and David Sedaris, who helped cement *This American Life*'s vocal sound, create and shape their particular public against already existing expectations of the mainstream, and against the norms of the public radio voice.[30] To return to a quote near the beginning of this chapter, Sarah Vowell says, "Most of the voices [on *This American Life*] sound like they shouldn't be on the radio" (Belluck 1998). This negative aesthetic, which Vowell carries in her own voice, self-described as that of a "snotty 6-year-old" (Belluck 1998), clarifies that the show's cultural capital derives from these misfit sounds adamantly inappropriate for the norms of public radio.[31]

Vowell, herself a keen critic of public radio and the voice, has helped formulate in her listening diary *Radio On* (1996) the sonic ground against which *This American Life* distinguishes itself. Just six months before the first episode of *Your Radio Playhouse*, in a long entry from May 1995, Vowell laments NPR's loss of a sound she defines as "play made audible," and "an un-newsy obsession with beauty" in exchange for "bare-voiced reportage" (Vowell 1996: 67–68). In her critique she reserves praise for Ira Glass, "one of NPR's most interesting commentator/producers," and "a tape of [David] Sedaris's Ira Glass-produced commentaries," which she finds conspicuously absent from an NPR "greatest-hits collection" (68). Listening to the tape, Vowell relishes the shift from the *Morning Edition* host to Sedaris, as "the move from familiar announcer to voice-out-of-nowhere" (70). Unlike the voice of presidential oratory, or Sabrina Fahri's apparent neutrality, Sedaris's voice comes from nowhere because of its uncanny strangeness. What Vowell identifies as his "boyish nasal timbre," Sedaris himself has called his "excitable tone and high, girlish pitch."[32] Other commentators have noted "his quiet, nasal voice" (Lyall 2008), "pleasingly strange" (Minor 2013), similar to "a woodsprite's airy tones" (Loviglio 2007), and "like no other human's," marked by an "odd pitch and slightly sing-songy quirkiness" that make it "hard to place the speaker as younger or older, male or female" (Haber 2013). Young, ageless, strange, mythical, inhuman, and ambiguously gendered, Sedaris's voice challenges classifications. Yet it is through listening to Sedaris that Vowell, thrilled by his odd timbre, helps define herself against a public who fails to hear how she hears:

> I was so surprised and delighted by the combination of deadpan delivery, sick humor, and childlike pathos, that when I got to work and that hour of *Morning Edition* rolled around again, I forced my museum coworkers to listen. They didn't laugh, though one woman managed to mutter, "Weird." I began questioning if the museum career was such a hot idea for me after all. Did I really want to spend the rest of my professional life working with people who didn't laugh at jokes about syphilis and torture spoken by a sarcastic but lovable apartment cleaner on vacation?   (69)

A totem and a taboo, Sedaris's voice makes clear to Vowell the type of voice and the kind of listening that she values. Her coworkers' rejection of that voice as simply "weird" confirms the negative aesthetic she will pursue on *This American Life*: a program for voices—Sedaris's among them—that "sound like they shouldn't be on the radio."

Vowell's commentary, in both her book and interviews, give a semantic shape to tone and timbre; her statements help us hear social meaning in sound. This discursive labeling provides one means to talk about the sound of a voice, and one way to think about how voices both represent and create publics through sound on *This American Life*. It also demonstrates how the specific sound of voices on the program might serve to help entail new forms of speech on public radio. At least implicitly, Vowell hears Sedaris, praises his voice, and then eventually goes to work on *This American Life* alongside him. Even within the context of the story in *Radio On*, sound and sense converge in Vowell's hearing of Sedaris, and their combination enables a change in the social field.

To borrow from the jargon of linguistic anthropology, we might think of the story Vowell tells about listening to Sedaris and trying to share that listening with her coworkers as a "metapragmatic" event.[33] Certain sonic markers in Sedaris's voice point to or index aspects of a social world, such as expected social roles, including gender and sexual identity, or norms in register, such as speaking with shock or disgust about syphilis and torture, rather than with "deadpan delivery." The pragmatic markers in the voice would be those changes in pitch or volume that would index the social space without changing the object of reference. The metapragmatics come into play when Vowell labels how changes in Sedaris's tone construct different communities, and explains how she uses the shared listening to that voice to define herself and her own hopeful community against the limits of another social world. "Weird," the linguistic token applied to Sedaris's voice by Vowell's coworker, clarifies the borders of these social spaces in stark and familiar terms: Vowell's story clarifies her affiliation with the "weird" against the museum workers' implicit "normal." While sounds might be heard differently by different listeners, the stories about these sounds and the eventual sedimentation of those stories into cultural norms reveals the process by which vocal timbre, pitch, and tone come to organize social space.[34]

The "weird" or "odd" sound of Sedaris's voice initiates Vowell into the nascent radio community that she will help define under the banner of *This American Life*. Perhaps the key to this community comes in the only description of Sedaris's voice that addresses its sound with any specificity: Vowell's approximation of the physical sound of his "boyish nasal timbre." Connecting such sound with a general trend in the evolving acoustics of NPR voices, Jason Loviglio remarks that Ira Glass has "found great success with a voice far higher in pitch than is typically found in broadcasting and with some of the same precious, adenoidal charm" as David Sedaris (Loviglio 2007, 71). To Loviglio's ear, both "sound as if they are speaking from their throats and through their noses, a gentle honking, rather than in the stentorian diaphragmatic speech typical of US male broadcasters, from Edward R. Murrow to Walter Cronkite and Dan Rather. These voices, in short, project a softer masculinity than is typical in American broadcast journalism" (71).[35] The sound of Sedaris and Glass's voices, in Loviglio's understanding, participate in a more general historical shift within public radio, wherein "low-pitched, monotone women's voices and high-pitched and pitch-variable men's voices" "function as crucial 'sound effects' for conveying the tricky cultural work of NPR," which "prides itself both on its inside-the-beltway access and its typically American populist fascination with the textured amateurism of the local, the real, the everyday" (Loviglio 2007, 73). The sound of the voice, in this case, marks an epochal shift in norms of gender and sexuality that both represents and actively negotiates the field of political ideology.

Loviglio might be correct about the changing sound of gender on NPR, and his investigation into these voices as "sound effects" of cultural change harmonizes with my own interest in reading the sound of *This American Life*'s voices as both symptom and effect of a changing public. However, his reference to "the rubber-duck-voiced Sarah Vowell" (Loviglio 2007, 76) reveals the limits of his conclusions. Vowell's inclusion in the *This American Life* cohort reminds us that alongside questions of gender, these voices—the "boyish nasal timbre" (Sedaris), "precious adenoidal charm" (Glass), and "snotty 6-year old" (Vowell)—share what folk discourses identify as a "nasal" and childlike quality Loviglio identifies as "pitch variable," but which we can also hear as returning the sound of "play made audible" Vowell recalls from NPR's early years. This "new nasal" sound—which phonetic experts tell us is not "nasal" in any technical sense, but which cultural critics, radio announcers, and "folk" theories continue to identify as "nasal"—is non-normative, rebellious, quirky, and anti-authoritarian.[36] It deflates the "stentorian," or loud and warrior-like sound of classic male broadcasting, or the engineered sound of presidential "authority and masculinity," which Jonathan Sterne has identified as "thick, deep, and sharp, but not too nasal" (Sterne 2008, 83). Within this cohort Glass's voice both participates in this new nasal sound and, with its casual cadence, inviting pauses, and lower volume delivery, links his own voice with another tradition of US oratory, from Jefferson to FDR, meant to create an "intimate public."[37] As the show's host, the sound of his voice serves as an auditory bridge between the older forms of oratory and the more extreme, and rarely intimate volumes of Sedaris or Vowell. These latter voices disturb and estrange the norms of public broadcasting, approaching a no-man's-land between what Sianne Ngai calls the "cute" or the "zany": simultaneously repulsive and attractive in their childlike pitch (Vowell has since voiced the animated superhero teen Violet Parr in the 2004 film *The Incredibles*), and sonically and socially precarious as their vocal sounds challenge norms of gender, sexuality, and even age (Ngai 2012).[38]

In their quirkiness—a term whose history conjures both an unexpected sound, witty remark, and a general oddity, eccentricity, or sharp and sudden twitch away from sonic-social normativity—these voices clear new ground or open new social-acoustic space for an American public unaligned with the traditional broadcast voice of authority.[39] They announce new ways to sound against the constraining definitions of speech pathologies, rhetorical manuals, and professional voice trainers. And yet alongside this cultural opening, their odd timbres also sonorously efface questions of region and class, thereby allowing them to fit into the democratic project of voice in the United States.[40]

CODA: NEW STANDARDS

The nasal, childlike, and sometimes childish character that the aforementioned listeners hear in some of *This American Life*'s contributing voices participates in a changing political culture that emphasizes inclusiveness, challenging the very categories of gender and sexuality without calling attention to the regional or class background of those voices. However, the ambition of this sound can sometimes conflict with the showrunner's statements. In Ira Glass's words, the show's appeal to an audience of over one million listeners derives from a new normal based on the class origins of its producers: "We don't try to guess what the audience will like. We simply put on what we like. We're all suburban kids. We feel we have the most normal tastes in the world. We think: If we like it, other people will like it" (Anstead 2006, 43). Statements like this, which normalize and universalize a class experience and perspective, threaten to undermine the democratic and pluralist ambitions of the program, and render an especially narrow vision of American life. The show's expansion and constriction of available social roles, and hence the available publics within public radio that Glass alludes to here, reveals some of the ongoing barriers connected to class and race in the shifting footing of *This American Life*'s imagining and construction of new publics through sound.

But does the "new nasality" actually contribute to reinforcing broader exclusions in public radio? Recent work in linguistic anthropology claims that nasality indexes "whiteness," implicitly—and with adamant "nonaggressiveness"—drawing racial boundaries through sound.[41] Additionally, NPR—often the outlet for, if not the distributor of *This American Life*—has faced increased criticism for its lack of racial diversity, leading its executives to strategize how "to bring in more diverse voices to reflect the rich diversity of this country," and its ombudsman, Edward Schumacher-Matos, to ask, "to 'sound like America,' does NPR need a staff that more closely mirrors the total demographic weight of each ethnic and minority group?" (Schumacher-Matos 2012). (His own answer was a qualified negative.)

The voices from the early contributors to *This American Life* cannot resolve these tensions, and, in many ways, their chief value has been that creative and critical function of unsettling and estranging any potentially normal encounter with the voice. (One need listen no further than David Sedaris's comic impersonation of Billie Holiday singing the Oscar Meyer theme song for a sonic event that troubles the borders of race, gender, and sexuality) (Glass 1998). Furthermore, any valuation of those voices should account for the impact they have had on other voices. For instance, Glynn Washington, the African American host of NPR's *Snap Judgment*, has said that Ira Glass's voice brought him into radio, and that the way to continue diversifying the public of public radio is to continue hiring diverse hosts to form and share new perspectives.[42] Regardless of the scholarly claims linking nasality and whiteness, Glass's voice, in this lived encounter, directly helped change the racial makeup of NPR and introduced new perspectives and voices to the public corporation's airwaves.

Similarly, Daniel Alarcón, the novelist and cofounder of Public Radio International's *Radio Ambulante*, describes that radio program as "*This American Life*, but in Spanish, and transnational" (Alarcón 2014a).[43] Alarcón, who has joked that he might "sound like a bad Latin version of Ira Glass," finds a particular significance in the sound of radio voices:

> I got into radio after my first novel came out, and I was asked to do a radio documentary. And I did all the interviews, and wrote a bunch of the script. It was edited without me. And I think the piece that came out is great. But one thing that bothered me was a lot of the Spanish voices were left out. What you lose in a voiceover sometimes is the nuance. You lose the energy in the, in the, in the accent. You lose the inventiveness in the actual word choice. You also lose the placement of silences, and the humor; you know? A lot of times you'll lose the humor. You start to really appreciate the beauty of all those different ways of speaking. I didn't want those Spanish-language voices to get cut.   (Alarcón 2014b)

While something of what Alarcón says here relates to general problems of translation—word choice and the nuance of language—much of it pertains to the sound of those voices alone. Alarcón helped establish *Radio Ambulante* to make sure those sounds are not lost, and to remind listeners how much information—emotion, humor, place—is contained in a voice's sound. Bringing the model of *This American Life* to the Americas—including the United States—archives and represents a new version of what it means to sound American. With *Radio Ambulante*, the new legacy of Glass, Sedaris, and Vowell's odd timbres might be to reimagine the very sonic cartography of American voices.

NOTES

1. For more on the phenomenon of "global English" see Raley (2012). See also McArthur (2001).
2. Ethnomusicology, linguistic anthropology, media theory, and especially the new interdisciplinary field of sound studies have all contributed to helping us understand the political and cultural importance of sound. Mladen Dolar's remarkable *A Voice and Nothing More*, however, is more representative of a long and hegemonic tradition of psychoanalytic theory—and poststructuralist theory in general—which has failed to account for the voice's sounds as something more than epiphenomena, or an abstract "surplus" that troubles the "logos" (Dolar 2006). A brief list of voice and radio theorists whose writing reflects an intense interest in the sound of the voice would include Alejandra Bronfman, Ashon Crawley, Susan Douglas, Christine Ehrick, Steven Feld, Nicholas Harkness, Michelle Hilmes, Charles Hirschkind, Jason Loviglio, Mara Mills, John Durham Peters, R. Murray Schaeffer, Jonathan Sterne, Jennifer Stoever, Thomas Streeter, and Neil Verma.
3. "The listener rather restricts himself to the reception of pure sound, which comes to him through the loudspeaker" (Arnheim 1936, 142).
4. According to Tom Lubin, Roosevelt used the Western Electric 618A dynamic microphone made in 1934 at Bell Labs (9). See Howard (2010). Jason Loviglio mentions FDR's dental bridge in *Radio's Intimate Public: Network Broadcasting and Mass-mediated Democracy* (2005). Hitler used a Neuman microphone. See Lyden (2008).

5. See Loviglio (2005, 4–7).
6. For more on the contest to claim responsibility for the first radio broadcast—as distinct from the first radio transmission of any kind—see Claxton (2007) and Matallana (2006).
7. "It is this creation of a set of nonlocalized and supra-regional norms, or of what can be seen as a set of 'standard pronunciation features' which provides a major focus of the late eighteenth and nineteenth centuries, as writers on the language endeavoured to supplant the heterogeneities of actual usage in terms of accent with the homogeneity of the 'correct' way to speak, regularly asserting the assumed values of the monolithic and the unlinear as they did so" (Mugglestone 1995, 5).
8. D. L. LeMahieu observes that Sir John Reith, the head of the BBC from 1922 to 1938, "deeply regretted not having a degree from Oxford or Cambridge, and hired a disproportionate number of his lieutenants from those institutions. Announcers were expected to speak with a proper accent, and in the early years of the BBC wore full evening dress while broadcasting" (LeMahieu 1988, 183).
9. For an earlier moment in radio history about the peculiar alignment of English and Indian sonic publics see Orwell (1968).
10. Michael North has noted how the standard language movement in the late nineteenth and early twentieth centuries in the United States sought to both regiment the class aspects of US social life, and to marginalize speech forms associated with specific ethnic and racial groups. See North (1998).
11. A 1972 National Opinion Poll in England asked, "'Which of the two of these would you say are most important in being able to tell which class a person is?' The largest group of respondents (33%) rated, 'The way they speak' as the most important factor. Other studies have focused on accent in particular…These experiments indicate that Britons view accents in terms of a stratified model of speaker rank" (Agha 2003, 240).
12. Since May 28, 2014, *This American Life* has distributed the show itself through PRX. In a message posted by Ira Glass on the show's blog, Glass emphasized this decision as a further democratization of the program: "What [PRX is] about is the democratization of public radio. Making it easy for you or any newcomer to get their work into the hands of program directors…When you get tired of being a listener and decide to make your own show, seriously, you should give them a look" (Glass 2014).
13. The valence of these terms here and throughout this chapter refer to both the notion of the "public" in "public radio," and the theoretical complexity of publics argued for by Warner (2005).
14. The limitations of voiceprint identification have been usefully critiqued by a number of scholars. See especially Sterne (2008).
15. I am indebted to Steven Rings for guiding me through some of these linguistic problems.
16. Charles Brockden Brown's *Wieland* (1798) has been taken up by several of these thinkers as a chosen site to work through the changing formation of representative speech and the popular voice in the early United States. For a reading of the text that situates it within a history of ventriloquism and media theory see Connor (2001).
17. Commenting on the voice's role in the foundation of the United States, Looby claims, "Precisely because the new nation's self-image was characterized by its difference from a traditional (quasi-natural) conception of the nation, indeed by the conscious recognition of its historical contingency that was produced by the abrupt performativity of its inception, vocal utterance has served, in telling instances, as a privileged figure for the making of the United States. This figuration has occasionally taken the odd form of an improbable

claim that the United States was actually 'spoken into being'…For the moment let me just say that I take this strange trope to register in a particularly condensed form the more widespread American sense of nation fabrication as an intentional act of linguistic creation, the belief that the nation was made out of words. The question of whether such a linguistically grounded nation is best figured as *written* or *spoken* is not, for many writers of the period, a foregone conclusion but, on the contrary, a live issue of some consequence. To anticipate a bit: since the new United States, by all accounts, manifestly lacked the kind of legitimacy and stability that might be expected of a nation that was grounded in blood loyalty or immemorial facticity—since its legitimacy was explicitly grounded in an appeal to rational interest, not visceral passion—*voice* embodied a certain legitimating charisma that print could not" (Looby 1996, 3–4).

In different terms, Jason Frank, like Ruttenburg, argues for the centrality of a theological and secular combination in early democratic politics: "Both democratic history and democratic theory demonstrate that the people are a political *claim*, an act of political subjectification, not a pre-given, unified, or naturally bounded empirical reality. In the United States the power of claims to speak in the people's name derives in part from a constitutive surplus inherited from the revolutionary era, from the fact that since the Revolution the people have been at once enacted through representation—how could it be otherwise?— and in excess of any particular representation. This dilemma illuminates the significance and theological resonance of popular voice: *vox populi, vox Dei*. The authority of vox populi derives from its continually reiterated but never fully realized reference to the sovereign people beyond representation, beyond the law, the spirit beyond the letter, the Word beyond words—the mystical foundations of authority. The postrevolutionary people are at once enacted through representational claims and forever escaping the political and legal boundaries inscribed by those claims" (Frank 2010, 3).

18. Nancy Ruttenburg's work already traces the influence of what she names "democratic personality" from the seventeenth century through the end of the nineteenth century. A radical theological utterance that joins *vox dei* and *vox populi* in the first and second Great Awakenings, Ruttenburg's "democratic personality" names the speech form in which disenfranchised subjects, such as women or slaves, claiming to serve as simple conduits for the voice of God, gained authority to publicly condemn the most powerful figures within a community (Ruttenburg 1998, 16 and 24). The history of eighteenth- and nineteenth-century literature in the United States, from Charles Brockden Brown's *Wieland* (1798) through Whitman's *Leaves of Grass* (1855–1892) and Melville's *Billy Budd* (1891 [1924]), is the taming of this form of speech and then its eventual reirruption in Melville's writing. We find these issues continuing with a difference with the development of radio technology. Radio broadcasting, with its ability to make private voices audible to a massive number of listeners, transformed that history, and made a voice "public" in a previously unthinkable manner. Early DXers, who built personal radio transmitters and receivers to communicate with strangers across tremendous distances, encountered their own voices and those of others in the newly public space of the ether. However, when governments across the globe intervened to regulate the crowded airwaves in order to reduce signal interference in the late 1920s, and the commercial radio format consolidated itself in the United States in the early 1930s, the DXers gave way to populist cultural and political figures including demagogues like Father Coughlin and Huey Long, for whom speaking *to* a massive number of people was often confused with speaking *for* or in the voice of the people. New versions of the popular voice arose in pirate broadcasting and resistance to commercial

networks, including extraordinary cases like Robert F. and Mabel Williams's "Radio Free Dixie" broadcasts from Havana, Cuba to the southern United States. Finally, call-in shows and "talk radio," however one-sided the format might be in practice, offered another iteration of the voice of the people. "In the very early years of radio, characterized by 'DXing' (ham radio code for distance signaling), when listeners tried to tune in stations from as far away as possible, people didn't have to imagine their compatriots several states away—they heard them, with all their differences and similarities, on the air" (Douglas 2004, 24–5). See also Brinkley (1983). On the consolidation of commercial radio in the United States see Streeter (1996), Tyson (2001), and Barker (2002).

19. For more on the early history of NPR see Looker quoted in Vowell (1996) and Douglas (2004).

20. Fliegelman, attentively reading the elocutionary texts of the period, observes Jefferson's affection for the "familiar style" of rhetoric against "the elevated" and "the middling," and notes that an influential text on rhetoric insisted that "'an affected artificial manner of speaking'...give way to one in which 'the tones of public speaking' were 'formed upon' the 'tones of sensible and animated conversation,' in which prepared texts should always appear extemporaneous, and in which the public realm, in ways that problematically blurred the distinction between them, should be modeled more and more on the private" (Fliegelman 1993, 27).

21. For more on the difficulties of defining timbre, see Fales (2002).

22. One notable case is Juan Domingo Perón's government in Argentina, which forbade specific tones during his first term as president. See Matallana (2006).

23. As I explain elsewhere in this chapter, Glass's voice is not "nasal" in any technical or medical sense. However, critics tend to use this term to define his voice, and, as we see in their conversation around Armisen's impersonation, Glass and Armisen hear what they call a "nasal" sound to be key to Glass's voice. (Glass, notably, challenges how "nasal" his voice might be.) One of the readers for this volume as well as one of the volume's editors suggested that calling Glass's voice "nasal," with a pejorative meaning, might be related to anti-Semitic discourse, conscious or not. Glass's own discussion of his voice emphasizes both a self-deprecating identification of ethnic heritage—"I'm just a whiny Jew" ("Distinctive")—and an everyday, casual delivery: "You should never say a sentence on the air that you couldn't say in a normal dinner conversation" (Glass 2010, 55). Nazi propaganda during the Third Reich often pointed to not only a physical stereotype of Jewish noses, but suggested that a Jew "talks through his nose" (this description can be found, for example, in a children's book by Julius Streicher titled *Der Giftpilz*, published in 1938). It's worth pointing out that the same adjective, "nasal," is frequently—and, again, technically incorrect—applied to the voices of David Sedaris and Sarah Vowell, neither of whom identify as ethnically or culturally Jewish. However, the pejorative racialized associations, deeply embedded in Western culture, may still be at work in the discourse about their voices.

24. As early interviews with Glass make clear, his cadence is the result of his own punctilious postproduction editing: "The casual cadence belies the excruciating care with which the show is produced. Mr. Glass spent years developing his style, and he writes out his words beforehand. In each story, he manipulates pauses so they underscore an arresting image" (Belluck 1998). An article in the parody newspaper *The Onion* renders Glass's cadence in print through an overabundance of commas to underscore these pauses: "When we finished, I have to tell you, I felt something I never expected: a profound

sense of contentment—maybe even relief," Glass said. "Afterwards, the other producers and I sat around for a long while, remarking on how interesting and strange it was to finally complete the study, and how perhaps it is, in some way, symbolic of life in general" ("'This American Life'"). Finally, the lower volume delivery that helps characterize Glass's voice has been interpreted by some critics as "'muffled'" (Rainey 2010) and others as "that sincere, in-the-same-room-as-you voice" (Coburn 2007).

25. I am indebted to David Steinberg for his extraordinary efforts in transcribing the voices of Armisen, Glass, Sedaris, and Vowell into musical notation.

26. See Fales (2002).

27. See Dolar (2006) for a psychoanalytic and poststructuralist approach to what he names, following Lacan, "the object voice."

28. Hosted by *This American Life* producer Sarah Koenig, who also coproduced the show with fellow *This American Life* producer Julie Snyder, *Serial* became the most downloaded podcast in that form's brief history. See Carr (2014).

   The *Saturday Night Live* parody is "Christmas Serial: Saturday Night Live," *YouTube*, December 21, 2014 (https://www.youtube.com/watch?v=ATXbJjuZqbc).

29. Bourdieu (1993). Bourdieu's writings have been applied to hipster subculture by Mark Grief (2010).

30. The epochal shift in tone norms has been the focus of a recent debate concerning female use of "vocal fry" and the standards of male NPR broadcasters. In response to an episode of *Slate's Lexicon Valley*, cohosted by Bob Garfield, who also cohosts the WNYC program *On the Media*, Amanda Hess writes, "I suspect that the spread of 'creaky voice' makes Garfield so mad because it represents the downfall of his own mode of communication, which is swiftly being replaced by the patterns and preferences of 11-year-old girls." She adds, "Of course, young women could work to flatten their speech patterns to conform to Garfield's own NPRish affectation, which one commenter describes as 'Richard Pryor making fun of WASPs'" (Hess 2013). Vocal fry stands in contrast to NPR and marks a change in generational sonic norms of speech. As Hess states, "A 2011 *Science* investigation into vocal fry confirms that the vocal creak is not a universally-reviled tic. *Science* cites a study conducted by speech scientist Nassima Abdelli-Beruh of Long Island University, who observed the creak in two-thirds of the college women she sampled. She also found that 'young students tend to use it when they get together,' with the speech pattern functioning as a 'social link between members of a group'...Garfield may be satisfied to learn that Abdelli-Beruh 'does not hear vocal fry on National Public Radio, which targets an older audience.'" I would only add that the so-called nasal tones of Glass, Sedaris, and Vowell performed an earlier modification and challenge to generational and corporate sonic norms on public radio in the United States (Hess 2013). I am indebted to Steven Rings for alerting me to Hess's response.

31. Vowell's negative approach, which often invokes Nirvana, the Velvet Underground, and other bands considered part of the proto or postpunk genealogy, occasionally places *This American Life* and her own thoughts on radio into a long line of negative aesthetics best encapsulated in the writings of Greil Marcus (1990) and Jon Savage (2005).

32. Sedaris's charming, funny, and sad recollection of speech therapy classes he was forced to attend as a fifth-grader reveals his early awareness of his voice as an object. He describes how the therapist alienates him from his voice and marks his voice as culturally and sexually non-normative: "'One of the s e day s I'm going to have to hang a s ign on that door,' Agent Samson used to say. She was probably thinking along the lines of SPEECH THERAPY

LAB, though a more appropriate marker would have read FUTURE HOMOSEXUALS OF AMERICA. We knocked ourselves out trying to fit in but were ultimately betrayed by our tongues…Thanks to Agent Samson's tape recorder, I, along with the others, now had a clear sense of what I actually sounded like. There was the lisp, of course, but more troubling was my voice itself, with its excitable tone and high, girlish pitch. I'd hear myself ordering lunch in the cafeteria, and the sound would turn my stomach. How could anyone stand to listen to me?" (Sedaris 2000).

33. Linguistic anthropologist Michael Silverstein has developed the language of metapragmatics across a number of articles. See Silverstein (1976). For the implications of Silverstein's work in literary theory see Lucey (2006).

34. For more on the pragmatic and metapragmatic uses of language see Lucey (2010).

35. For more on how "softness" can function as a sonic sensuousness that becomes a generalized cultural marker or "qualisign" for changing gender relationships, see Harkness (2013).

36. Jody Kreiman states, "I think what people usually hear when they say a voice is 'nasal' is that there is a difference in the shape of the voice source spectrum." According to Kreiman, what Sedaris and Vowell's voices share, especially in contrast to a speaker like Dan Rather, is that the former voices have "more energy in the higher harmonics." Similarly, what Glass and Armisen identify as "nasal" in Armisen's impersonation of Glass, Kreiman identifies as a change in the shape of the larynx, mouth and vocal tract, but nothing that phoneticians would identify as physiologically "nasal." Much of Kreiman's work has been dedicated to moving away from the inadequate and even confusing descriptive tradition for categorizing voices inherited from the Greeks and Romans, and constructing a means to quantify the sonic patterns of vocal speech. What I am calling the "new nasal" sound here identifies what nonscientific listeners categorize as "nasal" voices (Kreiman, personal communication, July 3, 2015). See also Kreiman et al. (2007).

37. See Fliegelman (1993), Durham Peters (1999), and Loviglio (2005) for more on this tradition. I borrow the term "intimate public" from Loviglio's *Radio's Intimate Public*.

38. The voices of Sedaris and Vowell, in particular, might also be identified as sharing something of a period style from the decades of the 1990s and early 2000s, the sonorous correlate for what James Wood has identified as "hysterical realism" in fiction (Wood 2000).

39. Nicholas Harkness has named this indelible connection of the physiological and cultural "the literal phonosonic voice—the 'voice voice'—that emerges from vibrations and resonance in the vocal tract," and the "tropic extension of the voice" (Harkness, 2014, 77). The first "is the site in which the phonic production and organization of sound intersect with the sonic uptake and categorization of sound in the world," and the second "describes an alignment to, or taking up of, a kind of perspective or moral stance in respect of semiotic text. It is the expression of an interest in relation to, or explicitly against other interests in the social world" (77). The various resonances of "quirkiness" or "quirk" can be found in the Oxford English Dictionary.

40. Nasality—the common trait popularly identified across these voices—poses particular difficulties for phonologists, and for those social linguists and linguistic anthropologists concerned with studying its possible social functions. Recent work in these fields has aligned nasality with the social type of the "nerd," and with "whiteness." Thus, these voices also might delimit the racial and social field of their potential publics through their very pitches (Bucholtz 2001; Podesva et al. 2013).

41. See Bucholtz (2001) and Podesva et al. (2013).

42. A recent profile on Washington begins as follows:

"I had a girlfriend," he continues, "and we kept fighting and breaking up." They were living in Michigan and had planned a relationship-saving trip to Canada. "And on the way out of Ann Arbor, this show comes on—it's this guy I had never heard before, a dude named Ira Glass. I was like, 'Whoa!' and she was like, 'Turn this noise off right away!'" That was the epiphany Washington needed. "I was like, 'Stop the car.' I knew right then the relationship was not going to work." That was 1997, when *This American Life*, Glass's public radio show, was just two years old, and people were beginning to suspect that his style of curated storytelling might be radio's next big thing. Now Washington, a proud student of Glass's, is the next big thing."

The profile closes with Washington's diagnosis of NPR's diversity: "At industry conferences, he is constantly asked how to bring 'diversity' to public-radio listenership. He's getting sick of this question. 'This is what you do,' he told me. 'You *hire* the people you're trying to reach'" (Openheimer 2013).

43. In an interview with Alarcón on WNYC's program *On the Media*, cohost Bob Garfield played clips of Ira Glass's introduction to *This American Life* alongside Alarcón's introduction to *Radio Ambulante*. In response, Alarcón said, "If I sound like a bad Latin version of Ira Glass, it's not because I'm trying to emulate him. It's because I feel very uncomfortable in front of the microphone. So, I'm working on that. And my apologies to Mr. Glass" (Alarcón 2014a).

Works Cited

Adorno, Theodor, and Max Horkheimer. 2002 [1944]. *Dialectic of Enlightenment*. Redwood City, CA: Stanford University Press.

Agha, Asif. 2003. "The Social Life of Cultural Value." *Language and Communication* 23 (3): 231–73.

Alarcón, Daniel. 2014a. "Es la hora: Hispanic Media in English." *On the Media*. NPR, New York: WNYC. http://www.wnyc.org/story/es-la-hora-hispanic-media.

Alarcón, Daniel. 2014b. "This Is Radio." *Vimeo*, March 30. http://vimeo.com/90498483.

Anstead, Alicia. 2006. "Q & A: Our Glass. Interview with Ira Glass by Alicia Anstead." *Inside Arts* (Nov./Dec.): 41–3.

Arnheim, Rudolf. 1936. *Radio*. London: Faber and Faber.

Barker, David C. 2002. *Rushed to Judgment: Talk Radio, Persuasion, and American Political Behavior*. New York: Columbia University Press.

Belluck, Pam. 1998. "Arts in America: A Visual Radio Show with Birds and Guilty Psychics." *New York Times*, March 19. http://www.nytimes.com/1998/03/19/arts/arts-in-america-a-visual-radio-show-with-birds-and-guilty-psychics.html.

Bourdieu, Pierre. 1993. *The Field of Cultural Production: Essays on Art and Literature*, translated by Randal Johnson. New York: Columbia University Press.

Brinkley, Alan. 1983. *Voices of Protest: Huey Long, Father Coughlin and the Great Depression*. New York: Vintage.

Bucholtz, Mary. 2001. "The Whiteness of Nerds: Superstandard English and Racial Markedness." *Journal of Linguistic Anthropology* 11 (1): 84–100.

Carr, David. 2014. "'Serial,' Podcasting's First Breakout Hit, Sets Stage for More." *New York Times*, November 23. http://www.nytimes.com/2014/11/24/business/media/serial-podcastings-first-breakout-hit-sets-stage-for-more.html?_r=0.

Chandler, Raymond. 1995 [1950]. "Notes (Very Brief, Please) on English and American Style." In *Later Novels and Other Writings*, 1012–15. New York: Library of America.

Claxton, Robert. 2007. *From Parsifal to Perón*. Gainesville: University of Florida Press.

Coburn, Marcia Froelke. 2007. "His American Life: A Look at Ira Glass." *Chicago Magazine*, June 25. http://www.chicagomag.com/Chicago-Magazine/March-2006/His-American-Life/.

Connor, Steven. 2001. *Dumbstruck: A Cultural History of Ventriloquism*. New York: Oxford University Press.

Deharme, Paul. 1928. "Proposition pour un art radiophonique." *La Nouvelle Revue Française*, XXX: 413–23. Reprinted and translated in Anke Birkenmaier, *Modernism/Modernity* 16 (2) (2009): 403–13.

Dolar, Mladen. 2006. *A Voice and Nothing More*. Cambridge, MA: The MIT Press.

Douglas, Susan. 2004. *Listening In: Radio and the American Imagination*. Minneapolis: University of Minnesota Press.

Fales, Cornelia. 2002. "The Paradox of Timbre," *Ethnomusicology* 46 (1): 56–95.

Fliegelman, Jay. 1993. *Declaring Independence*. Redwood City, CA: Stanford University Press.

Frank, Jason. 2010. *Constituent Moments: Enacting the People in Postrevolutionary America*. Durham, NC: Duke University Press.

Glass, Ira. 1995. "New Beginnings." *This American Life*, ep. 1. Chicago: WBEZ. November 17. http://www.thisamericanlife.org/radio-archives/episode/1/new-beginnings.

Glass, Ira. 1996. "Name Change / No Theme." *This American Life*, ep. 17. Chicago: WBEZ. March 21. http://www.thisamericanlife.org/radio-archives/episode/17/name-change-no-theme.

Glass, Ira. 1998. "Music Lessons." *This American Life*, ep. 104. Chicago: WBEZ. May 6. http://www.thisamericanlife.org/radio-archives/episode/104/music-lessons.

Glass, Ira. 2010. "Harnessing Luck as an Industrial Project." In *Reality Radio: Telling True Stories in Sound*, edited by John Biewen and Alexa Dilworth, 54–66. Chapel Hill: University of North Carolina Press.

Glass, Ira. 2013a. "500!" *This American Life* ep. 500. Chicago: WBEZ. July 12. http://www.thisamericanlife.org/radio-archives/episode/500/500.

Glass, Ira. 2013b. "Doppelgängers." *This American Life* ep. 484. Chicago: WBEZ. January 11. http://www.thisamericanlife.org/radio-archives/episode/484/doppelgangers.

Glass, Ira. 2014. "Radio Distribution Announcement." Chicago: WBEZ. May 28. http://www.thisamericanlife.org/blog/2014/05/radio-distribution-announcement.

Grief, Mark. 2010. "The Hipster in the Mirror." *New York* Times, November 12. http://www.nytimes.com/2010/11/14/books/review/Greif-t.html?pagewanted=all&_r=0.

Haber, Leigh. 2013. "David Sedaris: The Secret to Getting Along with Your Family." *Oprah*. April 22. http://www.oprah.com/relationships/David-Sedaris-Interview-Lets-Explore-Diabetes-With-Owls.

Harkness, Nicholas. 2013. "Softer Soju in South Korea." *Anthropology Theory* 13 (1/2): 12–30.

Harkness, Nicholas. 2014. *Songs of Seoul: An Ethnography of Voice and Voicing in Christian South Korea*. Berkeley: University of California Press.

Hess, Amanda. 2013. "Why Old Men Find Young Women's Voices So Annoying." *Slate*. January 7. http://www.slate.com/blogs/xx_factor/2013/01/07/vocal_fry_and_valley_girls_why_oldmen_find_young_women_s_voices_so_annoying.html.

Howard, Todd M. 2010. *Getting Great Sounds: The Microphone Book*. Boston: Course Technology PTR.

Karpf, Anne. 2006. *The Human Voice: How This Extraordinary Instrument Reveals Essential Clues About Who We Are*. New York: Bloomsbury.

Kreiman, Jody, Bruce R. Gerratt, and Norma Antoñanzas-Barroso. 2007. "Measures of the Glottal Source Spectrum." *Journal of Speech, Language, and Hearing Research* 50 (3): 595–610.

Labov, William. 2005. *The Atlas of North American English: Phonetics, Phonology, and Sound Change*. Berlin: Mouton de Gruyter.

LeMahieu, D. L. 1988. *A Culture for Democracy: Mass Communication and the Cultivated Mind in Britain*. Oxford: Oxford University Press.

Looby, Christopher. 1996. *Voicing America: Language, Literary Form, and the Origins of the United States*. Chicago: University of Chicago Press.

Loviglio, Jason. 2005. *Radio's Intimate Public: Network Broadcasting and Mass-Mediated Democracy*. Minneapolis: University of Minnesota Press.

Loviglio, Jason. 2007. "Sound Effects: Gender, Voice, and the Cultural Work of NPR." *The Radio Journal—International Studies in Broadcast and Audio Media* 5 (2–3): 67–81.

Lucey, Michael. 2006. *Never Say I: Sexuality and the First Person in Colette, Gide, and Proust*. Durham, NC: Duke University Press.

Lucey, Michael. 2010. "Simone de Beauvoir and Sexuality in the Third Person." *Representations* 109 (Winter): 95–121.

Lyall, Sarah. 2008. "David Sedaris Talks Funny: But Is It Real?" *New York Times*. June 6. http://www.nytimes.com/2008/06/08/arts/08iht-sedaris.1.13528384.html?pagewanted=all&_r=0>.

Lyden, Jacki. 2008. "Couples Custom Microphones Carry Colorful Past." *NPR*, April 20. http://www.npr.org/templates/story/story.php?storyId=89705610.

Marcus, Greil. 1990. *Lipstick Traces: A Secret History of the Twentieth Century*. Cambridge, MA: Harvard University Press.

Matallana, Andrea. 2006. *"Locos por la radio": Una historia social de la radiofonía en la Argentina, 1923–1947*. Buenos Aires: Prometeo.

McArthur, Tom. 2001. "World English and World Englishes: Trends, Tensions, Varieties, and Standards." *Language Teaching* 34 (1): 1–20.

Minor, Kyle. 2013. "David Sedaris Has a Pleasingly Strange Voice." *Salon*. April 25. http://www.salon.com/2013/04/25/david_sedaris_has_a_pleasingly_strange_voice/.

Mugglestone, Lynda. 1995. *"Talking Proper": The Rise of Accent as Social Symbol*. Oxford: Clarendon Press.

Ngai, Sianne. 2012. *Our Aesthetic Categories: Zany, Cute, Interesting*. Cambridge, MA: Harvard University Press.

North, Michael. 1998. *The Dialect of Modernism: Race, Language, and Twentieth Century Literature*. Oxford: Oxford University Press.

Openheimer, Mark. 2013. "NPR's Great Black Hope." *The Atlantic*, June 19. http://www.theatlantic.com/magazine/archive/2013/07/nprs-great-black-hope/309394/.

Orwell, George. 1968. "Poetry and the Microphone." In *My Country Right or Left, 1940–1943: Collected Essays, Journalism, and Letters of George Orwell, Volume 2*, edited by Sonia Orwell and Ian Angus, 329–36. New York: Harcourt, Brace and World.

Peters, John Durham. 1999. *Speaking Into the Air: A History of the Idea of Communication*. Chicago: University of Chicago Press.

Podesva, Robert J., Katherine Hilton, Kyuwoon Moon, and Anita Szakay. 2013. "Nasality as Enregistered Whiteness: An Articulatory Sociophonetic Study." Paper presented at New Wave of Analyzing Variation (NWAV) 42, Pittsburgh, PA, October 17–20.

Raley, Rita. 2012. "Another Kind of Global English." *Minnesota Review* 78: 104–12.

Rainey, Jim. 2010. "Ira Glass, Storyteller." *Los Angeles Times*, February 17.

Revoir, Paul. 2010. "Stuart Hall's English Lesson for the BBC: Plummy-Voiced Broadcaster Attacks Obsession with Regional Accents." *Daily Mail Online*, August 3. http://www.dailymail.co.uk/tvshowbiz/article-1299827/Stuart-Hall-attacks-BBC-obsession-regional-accents.html.

Roach, Peter. 2004. "British English: Received Pronunciation." *Journal of the International Phonetic Association* 34 (2): 239–45.

Ruttenburg, Nancy. 1998. *Democratic Personality*. Redwood City, CA: Stanford University Press.

Savage, Jon. 2005. *England's Dreaming: Sex Pistols and Punk Rock*. New York: Faber and Faber.

Schumacher-Matos, Edward. 2012. "Black, Latino, Asian, and White: Diversity at NPR." April 10. http://www.npr.org/blogs/ombudsman/2012/04/10/150367888/black-latino-asian-and-white-diversity-at-npr.

Seabrook, John. 2005. "Talking the Tawk." *The New Yorker*, November 14. http://www.newyorker.com/archive/2005/11/14/051114ta_talk_seabrook.

Sedaris, David. 2000. *Me Talk Pretty One Day*. Boston: Little, Brown.

Siegel, Robert. 2006. "American Accent Undergoing Great Vowel Shift." *All Things Considered*. February 16. http://www.npr.org/templates/story/story.php?storyId=5220090.

Silverstein, Michael. 1976. "Shifters, Linguistic Categories, and Cultural Description." In *Meaning in Anthropology*, edited by Keith H. Basso and Henry A. Selby, 11–55. Albuquerque: University of New Mexico Press.

Slauter, Eric. 2009. *The State as a Work of Art*. Chicago: University of Chicago Press.

Sterne, Jonathan. 2008. "The Enemy Voice." *Social Text* 96 (25): 79–100.

Streeter, Thomas. 1996. *Selling the Air: A Critique of the Policy of Commercial Broadcasting in the United States*. Chicago: University of Chicago Press.

Streicher, Julius. 1938 [1999]. *Der Giftpilz*, translated by Randall Bytwerk. http://research.calvin.edu/german-propaganda-archive/story3.htm.

"'This American Life' Completes Documentation of Liberal, Upper-Middle-Class Existence." 2007. *The Onion*, April 20. http://www.theonion.com/articles/this-american-life-completes-documentation-of-libe,2188/.

Thompson, Emily. 2002. *The Soundscape of Modernity*. Cambridge, MA: The MIT Press.

Trevisan, M. A., M. C. Eguia, and G. B. Mindlin, 2005. "Topological Voiceprints for Speaker Identification." *Physica D: Nonlinear Phenomena* 200, (1–2): 75–80.

Tyson, Timothy. 2001. *Radio Free Dixie: Robert F. Williams and the Roots of Black Power*. Raleigh: The University of North Carolina Press.

Vowell, Sarah. 1996. *Radio On*. New York: St. Martin's Griffin.

Warner, Michael. 2005. *Publics and Counterpublics*. New York: Zone Books.

Wiedeman, Reeves. 2013. "Voice Over Dept: 'Ambiguously Genuine.'" *The New Yorker*, November 18. http://www.newyorker.com/magazine/2013/11/18/ambiguously-genuine.

Wood, James. 2000. "Human, All Too Inhuman." *The New Republic*, July 24. http://www.newrepublic.com/article/books-and-arts/human-all-too-inhuman.

CHAPTER 7

....

THE VOICE OF FEELING

Liberal Subjects, Music, and the Cinematic Speech

....

DAN WANG

NEAR the end of the 2003 romantic comedy *Love Actually*, a man enters a restaurant in search of a woman. When Jamie (Colin Firth) sees Aurelia (Lúcia Moniz) standing behind a balustrade above him, he begins to confess his romantic feeling for her in a voice that cuts through the restaurant's chatter and turns all attention to him. She was his housekeeper in the weeks before, when they were alone at his cottage. But the speech includes the first words that are understood between them, because neither had been able to speak the other's language. Now, as he addresses her in a broken Portuguese that he has just cobbled together, the camera cuts between him on the restaurant's floor and her above as a love theme blooms under his stammered words. When the speech is over, she assents, and the theme swells in the underscore as the crowd cheers and the camera follows her down to the restaurant floor, finally drawing face-to-face with Jamie in the film's frame (see Figure 7.1).

In this scene, a social order coheres around the formation of a couple, whose two-as-one unity is captured in the symmetry of this final gaze. In theories of sentimentality and the scene of recognition, feeling often spreads across paths first paved by sight. James Chandler, for instance, describes sentiment as that which circulates through a relay of looks (Chandler 2013, 12), while Elizabeth A. Povinelli, writing about the significance of the romantic couple in liberal cultures, summarizes its transformative promise with the motto, "In your gaze I become a new person, as do you in mine" (Povinelli 2006, 188). Implicit in these accounts is a certain way of imagining the relation between sight and feeling: the gaze marks an event of contact between people, and this contact is the scaffolding through which feeling flows. The connection of sight serves as the structural condition of feeling's possibility—witness, in the endings of romantic comedy, the final portrait of the couple as a closed visual loop.

The bond between feeling's flow and an event of recognition and reciprocity is foundational to certain widespread modes of storytelling, such as melodrama, in which the exposure and recognition of a character's hidden virtue often produces the occasion for

FIGURE 7.1 Jamie and Aurelia at the end of *Love Actually*, their eyes locked on each other.

excessive affect (Williams 1998). The idea that feeling *should* accompany meaningful moments of interpersonal contact is also commonly found in political hope. Lauren Berlant, writing about the United States in particular, calls this national sentimentality: a "rhetoric of promise that a nation can be built across fields of social difference through channels of affective identification and empathy" (Berlant 1999, 53). At the heart of this form of political belief is a link binding reciprocity and feeling, since affect is a sign that channels between people are open, that feeling is flowing *somewhere*. This somewhere, in turn, quickly becomes the *there* of narrative, since to feel moved by someone else's suffering can feel like *moving in* the right direction, evidence that something politically productive has already begun to happen. Feeling, reciprocity, narrative: the promise of national sentimentality is the algorithm that connects these terms into a seamless sequence.

The scene that opens this chapter appears to model this seamlessness. Jamie exposes something private that Aurelia recognizes and reciprocates, bringing about a flow of feeling (rendered in the soundtrack that swells under cheers and applause) that ushers the couple together and the plot to a close—romantic comedy's cadence, perfect and authentic. Yet this analysis leaves some details unaccounted for. Does the fact that Jamie has only known Aurelia in the capacity of an employee have any bearing on the liberal story of love's equally shared feeling? Or on the way that Jamie, a British citizen, declares the feeling he cannot ignore to a roomful of Portuguese immigrants in the south of France, having abandoned everything to fly there under the aegis of love? These matters of plot only emphasize the way that the conventional heterosexual love story is already founded on discrepancies of freedom and power, even while its ending promises the beautiful symmetry of one soul's recognition by another. The sentimental model of feeling can only account for the end of the story, since it understands all people's feelings to be equally suitable for eliciting the empathy and recognition of others. How, then, might we model the scene in a way that accounts for its disparities of power, and not just its promise of symmetry? What aesthetic figure could capture not only the event of fusion, but also the exercise of power, in feeling's flow?

We might begin with the speech, instead of the gaze. Beginning an analysis with the gaze predisposes a reading of the scene that centers recognition—a contact of sight that stands for empathy or identification. The flow of feeling then serves as the affective accompaniment to an interpersonal event. But the speech relocates feeling in the scene: feeling is not just attached to a moment of contact between people, but is also mobilized *in the voice itself* that fills the room with the sound of its affection. As Jamie speaks, his voice floats over a love theme whose melody repeats and expands until it underscores the roar of the crowd's approval. Here, the voice is not just used to communicate something within the speaker, but also produces a rhythm and a tone in the room that magnetizes a collective's sense of itself as a unit. In other words, there is a relation between the concept of voice in a scene—on one hand, as simply a medium for the delivery of words, and on the other, as aural force—and the picture of social relation that results. To see how the voice produces a tone that transforms into the basis of collective affect, for instance, would be to recognize how a scene that is superficially about recognition by others may also involve the speaker's protection and continued hiddenness from the social, insofar as the transformation abrogates the time of the other's response.

This chapter addresses the nature of social worlds that coalesce around events of speech in two films from contemporary liberal culture: *Love Actually* and *The King's Speech* (2010). Though one centers on romantic union and the other on the union of nation, both films culminate in scenes whose formal outlines are nearly identical: a character played by Colin Firth must deliver a speech, though his ability to speak is in some way compromised, and the coherence of a social order hangs on his ability to make his voice flow. By locating the drama of intersubjectivity in the individual's capacity simply to produce a voice, these cases refer little to an idea of personhood delivered through the other's gaze. Instead, they resonate with theories of liberal subjectivity that emphasize the way in which speaking itself produces an efflorescence of personhood. By focusing on speech and not the gaze, these alternative accounts allow us to consider what images like the one above seem resolutely to foreclose: that the other may be structurally negligible in empathic and moving scenes of recognition. The common elements in the following examples of intimate and national resolution suggest a broad blueprint of liberal togetherness, one in which a certain concept of the voice sustains and unites an idea of individual expressiveness with the promise of a collectivity magnetized by feeling.

PRIVATE LANGUAGE, PUBLIC CONFESSION

Heartfelt speeches are legion in the endings of romantic comedy. Yet in *Love Actually*, a film composed of ten interrelated storylines that take place primarily around London, the plot that centers on Jamie and Aurelia makes speech and its impossibility central to its romantic intrigue. The story begins when Jamie discovers his brother in bed with his girlfriend. Distraught, he retreats to his holiday cottage, where he is introduced to Aurelia by the cottage's proprietor as a "perfect lady to clean the house." Jamie speaks no

Portuguese, and Aurelia little English, but from this point until its closing scenes the storyline will feature no other characters and no settings apart from the cottage and the car in which Jamie drives Aurelia home each night. Confined to them, the story adumbrates a world of language in which communication is not one of its uses. As it happens, Jamie and Aurelia both talk a lot, but apart from mimed gestures and the occasional cognate between Portuguese and English, this romance derives its comedy from language's failure to mean anything. The same goes for its pathos: in one scene, Jamie and Aurelia, face to face, confess their romantic feelings for each other in a symmetry that can only be grasped by the film's audience, who are assisted by subtitles. That the mutual confession of love does *not* produce a couple suggests what is still missing (and what the remainder of the plot must supply): not the capacity to put feelings into words, which they have, but the dimension of language that is social, that allows confession to have meaning for someone else.

After the holiday, the two leave the cottage, and a montage shows glimpses of Jamie learning Portuguese. Then, a few weeks before Christmas, Jamie arrives at a family gathering bearing gifts—only to drop them unceremoniously before dashing off to the airport. Running in romantic comedy is a sign that the last decision has been made, and all that's left is distance. If the story of romance ends in recognition and reciprocity, then the formal purpose of the run is to bridge the distance that separates the two protagonists, bringing them within hailing range of the voice. Yet *Love Actually* features no fewer than two other storylines in which a man, having decided to pursue his crush, hurtles through space while underscored by a triumphant orchestra.[1] These balletic displays through streets and airports, buffeted by horns and crashing cymbals, tie the moment of romantic resolve to a delight in physical freedom, a joy in sheer motion that almost makes it seem as though the character had formerly been shackled. These triumphant runs are not only in the service of covering a distance. Rather, they suggest that to possess desire, to be organized by its clarity, and to be able to transform intent into bodily action can be profoundly affirmative of one's subjectivity, regardless of what the other's response will be.

Alasdair MacIntyre has argued that desire becomes a material for subjectivity through the very terms of liberal political structure. While liberalism, a political perspective associated with the European Enlightenment, initially proposed only a social, legal, and economic framework in which people with "widely different and incompatible conceptions of the good life" could express and debate their preferences in a public arena (MacIntyre 1988, 336), it followed that individuals would have to know and express their preferences in order to become politically legible as persons in the first place. Under these conditions, desire becomes a fraught object of knowledge. The individual must ideally be on constant alert for the emergence of new desires, which can then be voiced in public as both the raw material of democratic world-making and as badge of personhood. But the possibility of incoherent or contradictory desire is always a threat to the coherence of the individual's subjectivity: desire is never only that when not knowing what you want is tantamount to not knowing who you are.

Just as saying "I want" in a liberal cultural order is also to announce that I am, the run in romantic comedy presents the clarity of desire as a freedom of the body. Hence the run does not bridge a distance so much as it inaugurates a new spatiality: it marks the point where the drama of desire shifts from the internal to the external, when the subject's anxious interior monitoring comes to an end and the newly clear desire propels the body through the world. The run is a sign that no contradiction or incoherence remains in the runner's psyche. Instead, the business of noticing and expressing preferences is simplified into the mere crossing of a gap, traversable by taxis and planes—as if the universe's physical extension, its existence as a field of nonidentical locations, could itself be a diagram of desire.

To describe the closing scene of recognition as a convergence of bodies and gazes in space, then, fails to consider how a concept of space and time is part of the scene's fantasy. Consider how the speech and the soundtrack generate the scene's closing representation of an affective public. When Jamie storms into the restaurant where Aurelia works (bringing with him a crowd of people who had gathered around him on the way), the triumphant cue that had underscored his journey there fades out and exposes the ordinary sounds of a restaurant: dispersed conversations, clinking silverware, and the sound of an in-house band. The camera cuts around the room, alighting on unfamiliar faces. Then Aurelia enters the frame. At this moment, the band stops playing, and a single, closely miked piano note over sustained strings saturates the sound mix. The entrance of this note replaces the restaurant's din with a warm aural focus that turns out, as it continues, to have been the beginning of a melody: the "Portuguese Love Theme," written by the film's composer Craig Armstrong, that had underscored all the couple's previous scenes together. Then, as Jamie begins to speak, the restaurant goes quiet and the camera pans around the room to reveal faces turned to him in rapt attention.

This moment marks the couple's first encounter outside the privacy of the cottage, but it is also the storyline's first representation of a public. The speech's function, then, is not just to communicate something between Jamie and Aurelia. It also cuts through the dispersed temporalities of a dozen private dinner conversations and replaces them with a collective sense of a beginning, in the beginning of the speech. When Jamie first entered the restaurant, the band music that washed around islands of differentiated conversation indicated what Henri Bergson calls a spatial concept of time: metrical, a click-track, free of contouring by specific human experience (Bergson 1950). When Jamie's voice replaces the band, however, the collective sense of temporality in the room shifts to what Bergson calls *duration*: as his voice cuts through the chatter and produces a collective absorption in the present as a shared experience, each moment is no longer simply "one point alongside another" but is rather enmeshed in the movement of an "organic whole, as happens when we recall the notes of a tune, melting, so to speak, into one another" (100). It is fitting that musical melody is the example that Bergson uses to illustrate the concept of duration, since Jamie's voice is joined with a melody in the underscore that continues through to the end of the speech. Yet the underscore does not accompany the scene of speech so much as it takes part in generating the scene's possibility: its sound is tied to the sound of the voice that breaks through the restaurant's scattered pockets of time, forming its diners into a collective by forming them as an audience.

That the feeling of togetherness can be taken as proof of actual togetherness is a basic feature of sentimentality. When politicians give speeches announcing a new day or a new beginning for the nation, this abstract claim feels credible in part because the speech itself enacts, for a dispersed audience, the experience of feeling a given moment in time as a collectively apprehended present. Yet this also suggests that a voice laden with feeling can produce the feeling of sociality in itself, and therefore bypass the need for the response and returned gaze of others. To see the confession itself (rather than the other's acceptance and recognition of the confession) as the central formal event of romantic closure makes it possible to read for inequalities in each person's role in producing the social, as the English subtitles translating Jamie's stammered Portuguese seem to suggest: "I know I seems crazy, but sometimes things are so transparency, they don't need evidential proof. And I can inhabit here, or you can inhabit with me in England." But the fact that Aurelia works in Marseille when she is not working at Jamie's cottage suggests that she may not be as free as he is to inhabit wherever she likes. Indeed, as Jamie delivers his plea to an audience of immigrants in the south of France, the desperation of his offer recalls that those with the least material and structural encumbrances can leave the most gorgeous sacrifices at the altar of love, and thereby most fully exemplify the liberal subject's obeisance to the decisiveness of desire.

And this is an analytical weakness of the model that takes feeling to circulate through a relay of looks: its location of feeling in the *relay* presumes the points along its path to be essentially contentless and identical. When what matters is the feeling that flows between people, or the reciprocity and symmetry of the gaze, there is no account of the ways that feeling's flow could be built on a ground of difference, as it is in the gendered story of heterosexual romance. Yet Jamie's speech seems to deliver a fantasy that the individual voice of desire can lead directly to an experience of the social, skipping (we might say formally) the other's response. Here, the voice itself inaugurates the drama of communication, though not in the sense that the other absorbs and responds to the claims it forwards. It is rather that the social is born with the voice, that Jamie's effort to speak through his limited Portuguese, to put into the world the thing he must say, *is* the culmination and the ground of the social. The exemplary figure, then, is not the gaze but the stutter—the sound of meaning struggling to escape the body, the tension and release of the voice as the locus of life itself.

The Voice of the People

Seven years after *Love Actually*, Colin Firth finds himself again faced with the task of delivering a speech at the end of a film. Though its concerns seem distant from those of holiday cottages and restaurant proposals, there are nevertheless continuities between

The King's Speech and the conventional story of romance. For instance, the later film also centers on a couple: the titular monarch (played by Firth) and his speech therapist Lionel Logue (Geoffrey Rush). Moreover, the structure of the film has been compared by Firth, in the DVD's special features, to that of romantic comedy ("boy meets therapist, boy loses therapist, boy gets therapist"); and one could also note that the director Tom Hooper's first choice for the King was, apparently, not Firth but Hugh Grant (Walker 2011), who is famous for using his stammer in romantic comedies as an instrument of charm.

But the stammer in this historical drama is not just a quirk—a repetitive detail used for character color. Rather, it underwrites the film's understanding of history, trauma, and the narrative aspiration to lyricism in the present. The film follows Bertie (as the King is known to intimates) as he ascends the throne and is faced with the task of delivering, over the radio, an address to the English empire at the outbreak of the Second World War. But Bertie has spoken with a stammer since childhood, a personal problem whose implications for public life are made visceral in the film's opening scene. The year is 1925, and Bertie, still a prince, must deliver his first live address over the radio at the closing ceremony of the British Royal Exhibition, staged at the cavernous Wembley Stadium. As Bertie ascends the stairs to a microphone placed squarely in the middle of the stands, the crowds all around him rise to face him (their wooden chairs scraping noisily), their bodies and expectant faces pressed close. Alexandre Desplat's minimalist underscore—which here floats a high, isolated piano melody over a sustained string pedal, the musical equivalent of a held breath—evaporates just as the flashing red light next to the microphone goes solid, abandoning Bertie to the silence of dead air. We see Bertie's face up close as his mouth works silently. Then, a sound, but not a human one—a horse neighs from the field, and the camera cuts away to track its source, already distracted from recording Bertie and the speech he is supposed to give. It is not just feedback from the human and animal bodies clustered around him that interrupt the voice's issuing in this opening scene, but also the way that the PA system turns his voice against itself, picking up the surplus frictions of Bertie's stammer and sending them echoing around the arena until their mechanical repetitions suffocate his faltering attempts to make sense.

What seems to unravel Bertie's speech, in other words, is its environment—the fact that it is delivered into a real space filled with real bodies. His voice is broadcast nationally, but it is also absorbed by the live crowd gathered around him in the arena, who breathe and produce sound into the same air that carries the sound of his voice, and whose faces register in real time a growing embarrassment as the speech falters. The overpresence of other bodies in the stadium, their sounds and expectant stares, unnerve the voice and its efficient delivery. This is how the film introduces the problem whose overcoming will occupy the remainder of the story, which largely centers on the therapeutic relationship between Bertie and Lionel. The two meet only after Bertie is unsuccessfully matched with a series of other speech therapists, who all offer him prosthetic solutions that range from cigarettes to a mouthful of marbles. What distinguishes Lionel is that he does not, at first, treat the problem as a mechanical one, instead asking Bertie about his earliest memories and his relationships with his family. His treatment of Bertie's "speech" problem with the procedures of psychotherapy suggests a belief that the voice cannot be healed until the whole self is healed.

The film's telling of a story about speech as a story of psychotherapy constitutes a claim that it makes about the voice. Bertie initially resists Lionel's questions because he does not think of his speech problem as a personal matter. But by the end, this romance will unite the voice's physical being with the imprint of personal history: the film's finale forwards the argument that the voice generating national solidarity cannot just be a voice, something transmissible through radio waves, but must also have a backstory, specifically one whose narrative begins in a scene of childhood trauma. The moment in the film that most explicitly presents this idea takes place immediately after the death of Bertie's father and current King, in the meeting between Lionel and Bertie that most resembles a session of psychotherapy. The mood on this occasion is more relaxed than usual: Bertie plays with a model airplane left behind by Lionel's sons, all while the therapist nudges him into recalling the various abuses to which he was subjected as a child. When he arrives at the story of the maid who deprived him of food for three years without his parents' knowing, however, his voice falters in the telling, and stops short of the essential detail. Lionel suggests that he try singing it, because, he says, "continuous sound will give you flow." What needs flow, here, is not just the voice but something in Bertie's relation to his past, which is not so much a repressed memory as a lump of unredeemed pain that prevents the present from becoming expressive. There is a stall in the narrative of his life, a knot that has never been smoothed over, and this knot becomes the knot in the throat that afflicts him in the present. Because the film's narrative drama depends on the improbable notion that all hope of English resistance to the Nazis rests on Bertie's ability to deliver a speech, the stutter is the mechanical hinge that unites personal and national history—or as Geoffrey Rush glosses the plot on the DVD commentary, "it's the journey toward becoming a King and becoming a human being."

In other words, to complete the narrative line from the failed speech that opens the movie to the successful one that ends it, the plot must first introduce another narrative line via the psychotherapy plot: that of autobiography. Bertie is compelled to narrate his life from his earliest memories, but the story stalls—and this stall turns out to be what keeps the other story, the film's plot, from reaching its end. In the notion that the English people will not be ready for war unless Bertie acknowledges his voice's history and confronts its origin in traumatic experience, we may detect the premises of Berlant's notion of national sentimentality, which forwards the belief that significant political change will come about when those who do not have a particular experience of being socially subordinated are exposed to poignant and moving evocations of the pain experienced by people who do. Under this model, an individual's pain is linked to a vision of a healed or whole social order through an act of testimony, a genre of speech that typically represents private experience as a narrative to make it available as social material.

Hence stuttering, in this film, is never represented as something that Bertie may learn—unevenly and imperfectly, perhaps—to live with, in an ongoing and ordinary way.[2] Instead, the film conceives of "life" as something strung out on a narrative trellis between trauma and transformation, and imagines the eventual release of the voice to be the sign that the self is no longer stuck in past trauma but has "moved on," fulfilling its life trajectory. The voice is like the superhero: an initial trauma wracks the body with both pain and promise, such that pain is never just itself but is also the beginning of something, an incipient moment that already contains the kernel of some future redemption. The same is true of pain in sentimental politics. If testimonies of pain are supposed to lead to healed and whole social orders, then it is as if the initial experience of pain retroactively becomes the birth of the social itself, which the suffering subject incubates painfully until it can be spoken into existence. It is significant for this point that the film's protagonist is the King who, as Bertie himself admits, has no purpose outside of the people's belief that "when I speak, I speak for them." Here we see how a political rhetoric is made into drama: if sentimental politics holds that it is through testimonies of pain that a nation is able, through the identification and empathy those testimonies generate, to renew and heal itself, the film selects as its protagonist the one person for whom an inability to speak *presents a national dilemma*. Thus the King, who is by definition not a subject, becomes in his very exceptionality the general model of a liberal political subjectivity.

Yet how does the conversion from private pain into a socially healed order actually happen? Berlant argues that the logic of sentimental politics rarely seems to work, in part because it fails to account for how specific experience of subordinate pain—to which only some people in a social order have access—can become a basis for universal identification and empathy (Berlant 1999, 72). The remainder of this chapter will focus on how the fantasy of this conversion takes place in the film's finale, when the King's voice finally issues forth, righting his own and also the world's history in the process. In the climactic scene, Bertie and Lionel are huddled in a small, sound-proofed recording booth, the receiver of a microphone bisecting their eyeline. When the speech is about to begin, Lionel delivers a sweeping conductor's gesture, and the *Allegretto* from Beethoven's Seventh Symphony cues on the soundtrack (an addition by the film's editor, Tariq Anwar). The movement begins with a single chord in the orchestra, but in the film, the chord is intoned twice—a kind of instrumental stutter. As Bertie begins to speak, however, the strings' dactylic rhythm chops up the mostly static string textures heard so far in Desplat's score, driving the texture forward as the cue expands in pitch range and instrumental thickness. The scene seems to recall Lionel's earlier advice to Bertie that the continuous sound of singing would give his voice flow. And flow is invoked here again, though in the metadiegetic register of the director's commentary. Until this point, Hooper says, the film's visual style has been dominated by static shots and the slight shakiness of a hand-held camera, but in the speech scene "the camera really starts to move for the first time," the earlier style giving way to the lyricism of the Steadicam. When the stutter in Bertie's throat releases into flow, the camera also begins to roam, cutting away from the little recording booth to reveal shots of ordinary people gathered in tableaus of absorbed listening around radios, which become the organizing centers of citizens' bodies in pubs, living rooms, factories, and battlefields across the land.[3] When the speech ends and the music stops, the camera ceases its roaming across the vast expanses of the British empire and returns to the confinement of the little recording booth.

What are the differences between this scene of successful speech and the failed one at the film's beginning? Their settings seem related in their extreme contrast: where Bertie was earlier flummoxed by the crowding of bodies around him and the sounds that ricocheted back to him in Wembley's cavernous arena, he now disappears into a tiny room draped with fabrics meant to absorb all extraneous sound, including the possibility that his own voice might return to him. The King can only speak when he removes himself from an environment populated by others, and when his voice is no longer pitched to and absorbed by bodies that breathe the same air and that can affect him in turn. To put it more bluntly: it is only when he recuses himself from *the scene of the social itself* that his voice, paradoxically, can generate an image of the social in the film's visual field. It is true that the speech is spoken to an intimate other, Lionel, who tells Bertie before he begins to "say it to me as a friend." And yet Lionel is not the speech's addressee. The ears it is meant for are out there, somewhere through the medium's relay. The fact that Lionel's conducting gestures seem to invoke the presence of music (even though the Beethoven symphony is nondiegetic) seems to indicate what is essential in the speech: less the sense of its words than, say, its musicality, the simple fact that it is expressive. Lionel's role in the booth is not to receive a communicative act, though his presence there makes the communication possible. His role is simply to keep the speech going, to draw it out of its speaker.

Taking these two films together casts Jamie's speech in *Love Actually* in a different light. That is, *The King's Speech* allows us to consider what it might mean if the speech's addressee in the Portuguese restaurant were not Aurelia but the crowd, and the intimate relay with Aurelia served only to generate the kind of voice through which the crowd could sense itself as a collective, held together by a shared affective contour, a rhythm of being-together opened by the voice of feeling. Here, the social is not what emerges after Aurelia absorbs Jamie's speech and, by responding, opens a *second* realm of desire that might force Jamie to compromise or abandon the shining futures he has imagined. Rather, Aurelia's assent is like the necessary cadence that rounds off a melody whose essential impression has already been made. The scene ends, it is true, with Aurelia and Jamie mirroring each other as they step into frame, their eyes locked in the classic two-shot of romantic comedy. Yet it is instructive to note that *The King's Speech* frames Lionel and Bertie in the same way, but bisects the gaze with a microphone that picks up the voice made possible by their intimacy (see Figure 7.2). Intimacy, here, is not the end, but rather the means by which Bertie comes to generate the voice of a king.

The shift in the voice's status from the intimate to the public also attends the music selected for the scene. Hooper justifies his use of Beethoven to underscore the speech (instead of music by Desplat) because of its recognizability, which, he says, "elevates the scene to the status of a public event." By contrast, Hooper describes music written specifically for a film as "internal" to the film. Thus the shift from Desplat to Beethoven in the speech scene amounts to a shift in how the audience is interpellated: no longer as the "private" audience of this film's score, but, in their recognition and prior knowledge of the Beethoven cue, as part of a larger publicity. Yet Hooper's attempts to describe exactly *who* is included in this larger public reveal the structural limitations of a climactic scene that is, in principle and by Hollywood convention, supposed to move any audience

FIGURE 7.2 Lionel and Bertie in *The King's Speech*, a microphone bisecting their eyeline.

member who has a heart. Hooper explains his choice of the symphony by saying that "we all have some memory, or most of us have some memory, of this music. Some of us know it very well." Who is this "we" that becomes "most of us" and then a "some of us" that he does not specify? The claim about the widespread familiarity of Beethoven's Seventh might be less plausible, for instance, if made by an American director on the DVD commentary of an American Best Picture winner peopled with an American cast. Note too that Hooper does not emphasize "our" collective familiarity with the music in the present but rather the fact that we have "some memory" of it, projecting a shared past of collective listening. Is Hooper, speaking in the first-person plural, thinking about growing up with the BBC's broadcasts of classical music, a cultural signifier that the BBC has long associated with itself and thereby with the nation's identity? Such a connection would be corroborated by the film's framing as a history of English broadcasting and by the delicate voice of the BBC presenter that opens the film.

We might notice, here, the circularity of romanticizing a major event of English broadcasting by using music whose belonging to what Hooper calls "public conscious-ness" presupposes an audience already formed by that history of broadcasting. On this point, Sara Ahmed has described the ways in which a sense of national coherence can arise through "loyalty to what has already been established as a national ideal" (Ahmed 2010, 122). The Beethoven cue, therefore, does not perform the suturing func-tion that the speech scene enacts, in which channels of sound and affect are working to lace together a fractured and dispersed population. Hooper's comments suggest instead that those he means to bind with the cue have, in a sense, already been bound, which complicates the scene's depiction of a structural event of *coming together*. Feeling's flow, here, is not proof that a wall has collapsed, nor that some new structural configuration has viscerally come into being. It is more like a leftover charge that surges through old wires.

Nor does the feeling with which Bertie intones the speech stand as proof of his true self or evidence of his interiority. Here, the film seems almost to offer a critique of the cliché that climactic speech comes in response to an experience of great feeling, since Bertie's speech is not written by him, but is instead handed to him as a script covered in expressive marks that are meant to guide his performance (see Figure 7.3). His speech does not reveal anything essential or meaningful about him as a person—which, in the model of the scene of recognition, would then be heard and understood by the national audience in a surge of feeling—but is closer to the performance of a score. The Beethoven cue does not primarily relate to the speech as an index of the feeling or core of person-hood it conveys; rather, what seems to bind the cue and the speech is simply the fact that they flow, that they are both instances of an expressiveness that is consciously per-formed. This is consistent with the way that feeling is conceptualized throughout the film. Over the course of his treatment with Lionel, Bertie has been told to sing, dance, and swear as strategies for relieving his vocal difficulties. But in Lionel's office, cursing is not an expression of anger, nor are singing or dancing external proofs of someone's feel-ing or artistic intent. They are rather part of a toolbox of tricks that are used to lubricate a flow of words that do not necessarily reveal anything about the speaker's inner life. In the spirit of William James's reversal of the common sense of feeling's causality, where, as he proposed, we do not cry because we are sad but are sad because we cry, we might say that Bertie's speech functions not as a medium for feeling, but rather that feeling func-tions as a medium for speech. The distinction between these formulations marks a dif-ference of emphasis within a generalized cultural anxiety. The first suggests the presence of an anxiety about feeling, and offers the assurance that we have interiors, that we can make our individuality known. The second suggests that the anxiety is rather about

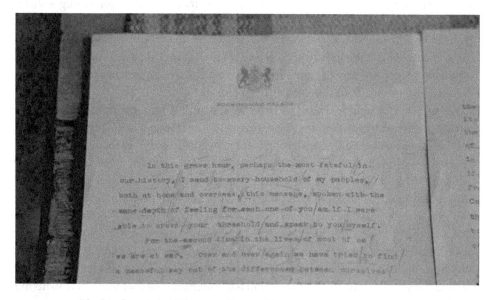

FIGURE 7.3   The king's speech, with expressive markings.

speech, and offers the assurance that the existence of feeling will make it possible for us to understand each other, that conversation between us is possible.

If the question the movie asks is whether a monarch can produce the coherence of an empire, and the answer takes the form of the King producing the empire as an audience, then we learn something about what audience means for this film, and how it conceives of the audience's relation to the heroic utterance. Unlike the audience in the Portuguese restaurant, whose collectivity, we might say, is guaranteed by the fact that they exist physically together in a room, the audience of the king's speech can only be counted as a collective through their mutual absorption in the speech. It is as if, in this film, there is no room or hall that could guarantee a priori the togetherness of a group of people—that this togetherness comes into existence only so long as the expressive utterance persists in producing them as an audience.

Thus, the status of the voice in *The King's Speech* introduces a variation, or further stipulation, of the fantasy in melodramatic narratives that the hero's moral or emotional truth will at some point be recognized, which is a fantasy that presumes the existence of an audience—let us say a society—that is present to witness and recognize this truth. This would be the fantasy, as in *Love Actually*, that there is an audience for a character's declarations, for whom their proofs of goodness or innocence will count; and this would be the comedy in romantic comedy, where the ending figures not just individual or even coupled happiness, but the happiness of the individual's or the couple's reintegration into society. But the question animating *The King's Speech* is not only whether someone can assert or expose their essential goodness (which is the Manichean concern of the nationalist war plot), but also whether there exists an audience at all to whom the proofs of goodness could be presented, who could either affirm or deny one's place in the world. That is, the melodrama of these films hinges not only on the question of goodness but also on the possibility of expressiveness, because only in the utterance's production of an audience will there be anyone to deliver the needed recognition. But if the only way to imagine a people is through the utterance that produces them as an audience, then the only people one could imagine would be a people in thrall. If the film makes it possible for us to empathize with the king, to feel ourselves, through the usual Hollywood magic, in his story of struggle and overcoming, it is also that the expressive utterance makes it possible to speak of an "us" in the first place, as if the possibility of togetherness were contained in the voice's ardent impress.

Both *Love Actually* and *The King's Speech* end with the ratification of social worlds. But what purchase does the social have when both films include sequences in which we see the protagonist in the process of learning to speak (which suggests that he cannot yet fully speak), and when the climax of each film centers not just on an act of speech, but with the sense that the protagonist has finally achieved speech—that he is, in a sense, speaking for the first time? To end a film with the birth of speech indicates the film's concept of, or interest in, speech. That is, it will not primarily be an instrument used to provoke, cajole, persuade, soothe, or otherwise affect another, where what the speech means—what effect it has within a negotiation of shared life—can only be found out once the other responds, after which the speaker may have to speak again, adjusting for what he has learned from the response. This would be a model in which the drama of speech takes place after the birth of speech. But these two films instead situate their interest in the period before the birth of speech, an event that is soon followed by the end of each film and thereby compresses the time of a shared life in language to a solitary gasp. It would seem that the power carried by speech in these endings is possible only by denying that recognition and identity for the hero may be granted not in the moment of speech itself but in the other's reception and return of speech, following the interval of listening and response. Here, we might conceive of the other's difference, formally, not as a spatial displacement (implied in the model of the returned gaze) but in the temporal lag of response. It is a lag that these films deny in order to produce the speech itself as culminating event, bringing up the credits almost as soon as the voice fades away.

The time of the lag of the other's response is elided, and in its place is the time of the plot. Could we not now tell the relation between feeling, music, and recognition in a different way? Conventionally, a movie unfolds a narrative in which actions take place. The flow of feeling, recognition's reward, will come at some point along the narrative, tied to some event within its sequence of action. Yet an alternate account might begin, rather than end, with feeling, with sheer vibration that impacts the body in the present. Then, at some point, fantasies of personhood are loaded onto affectivity, so that a suffused and sonorous being-in-the-body is imagined to be the proof and experience of subjectivity. It is when viscerality becomes attached to this intangible promise that feeling no longer operates only in the present, but projects backward the horizontal dimension of a narrative that culminates in the achievement of presence. Here, narrative itself is a vital component of the fantasy that the true self *emerges* at an incandescent point when what I say is also who I am, merging the voice's inner and outer halves to produce the sense that I exist in the fact that I speak. It is the story that I will become myself when I become completely communicative, an event always to come that turns the interest of the life before into simply its becoming.

Notes

I am grateful to Marcelle Pierson, Lauren Berlant, Martha Feldman, Berthold Hoeckner, Elizabeth Hopkins, Zachary Loeffler, Daniel Morgan, and Bradley Spiers for reading and commenting on versions of this chapter.

1. It is significant for the film's representation of gender and power that one of these men is the Prime Minister—symbolically, the most powerful man in Britain—whose summoning of resources as he pursues his former assistant, including a security detail and a full motorcade, provides the material expression of the momentum that his desire can produce in the world. The next section explores further the logic by which a head of state, in his very exceptionality, becomes the general model of a liberal political subjectivity.
2. Berlant proposes, in contrast to the trauma/reparation model of pain, the idea of subordinate pain as shocking but not surprising, ongoing, and everyday (Berlant 1999, 77–84).
3. Special thanks to Kiri Miller for pointing out that the voice produces absorption not only in the attentiveness of listening but also as a choreography, a bodily attunement and mimesis, as its audience turns and huddles around the source of the sound.

Works Cited

Ahmed, Sara. 2010. *The Promise of Happiness.* Durham, NC: Duke University Press.

Bergson, Henri. 1950 [1910]. *Time and Free Will: An Essay on the Immediate Data of Consciousness.* New York: Macmillan.

Berlant, Lauren. 1999. "The Subject of True Feeling: Pain, Privacy, and Politics." In *Cultural Pluralism, Identity Politics, and the Law,* edited by Austin Sarat and Thomas R. Kearns,. 49–84. Ann Arbor: University of Michigan Press.

Chandler, James. 2013. *An Archaeology of Sympathy: The Sentimental Mode in Literature and Cinema.* Chicago: University of Chicago Press.

The King's Speech. 2010. Produced by Iain Canning, Emile Sherman, and Gareth Unwin. United Kingdom: UK Film Council, See-Saw Films, Bedlam Productions.

Love Actually. 2003. Produced by Tim Bevan, Liza Chasin, Eric Fellner, Debra Hayward, and Duncan Kenworthy. Paris: StudioCanal; United Kingdom: Working Title Films, DNA Films.

MacIntyre, Alasdair. 1988. "Liberalism Turned into a Tradition." In *Whose Justice? Which Rationality?*, 326–48. Notre Dame: University of Notre Dame Press.

Povinelli, Elizabeth A. 2006. *The Empire of Love: Toward a Theory of Intimacy, Genealogy, and Carnality.* Durham, NC: Duke University Press.

Walker, Tim. 2011. "Colin Firth Was the Third Choice to Play George VI in *The King's Speech*." Telegraph.co.uk. January 20. http://www.telegraph.co.uk/news/celebritynews/8269816/ColinFirthwasthethirdchoicetoplayGeorgeVIinTheKingsSpeech.html.

Williams, Linda. 1998. "Melodrama Revised." In *Refiguring American Film Genres: History and Theory*, edited by Nick Browne, 42–88. Berkeley: University of California Press.

PART III

ACTIVE VOICE
VOICE AS POLITICS

....

CHAPTER 8

TRANS/FORMING
WHITE NOISE

Gender, Race, and Disability in
the Music of Joe Stevens

....

ELIAS KRELL

> I...yearn...for a community that is accountable rather than countable, that is big enough to hold all those we will encounter, from the marginal man, to the monster, from the ladyboy to the terrorist, and whom we are pressured to leave behind in order to become ascendant subjects... The...question may be: where do we want to go, and how do we get there without leaving so much and so many behind?
>
> —Jin Haritaworn, *The Biopolitics of Mixing: Thai Multiracialities and Haunted Ascendancies*

It is a chilly summer day in San Francisco in June 2009 and I am inside the El Rio nightclub along with about fifty others in anticipation of a transmasculine triple-header[1] featuring Joe Stevens, Lucas Silveira, and Alex Davis. Transgender social justice aims have not yet entered mainstream awareness, and our anticipation exists within a myopia of trans representation. It is rare to attend an event organized by and starring three trans people. However, I glance around often during the show, seeking other people of color or trans feminine persons, and encounter dis-ease around the lack of representation of those persons both on stage and in the audience. The feelings that accumulate in my body as I encounter particular absences are heightened by their dissonance with the feelings of celebration that permeate the space and bodies of the (largely white and female-assigned) persons present.

That evening marked a turning point in my research. I began to be interested in how affects of utopia themselves—ushered in by an emergent trans activism that produced any action claimed under the umbrella of trans "visibility" as laudable—sometimes discursively produce their own elisions through the very mechanisms of "utopia." [2] This chapter considers the recently increased visibility of white, middle-class, able-bodied trans men in the public sphere and, drawing from C. Riley Snorton and Jin Haritaworn (2013), among others, suggests that this visibility, however welcome in many respects, both is produced by and produces trans "Others" who are too Brown, Black, disabled, foreign, lower-class, or otherwise strange to fully "count" as trans.[3] This chapter is my partial answer to Haritaworn's epigraphical provocation. Haritaworn compels us to take seriously the project of discovering how we can get better at "trans liberation." Accounting for power should not be anathema to celebrating what *is* working in this transgender mo(ve)ment; this paradoxical view may in fact be requisite to avoid the exclusions of earlier gender and sexual "rights" movements (Rivera 2002; Krell 2015).

This chapter explores the cultural objects of singer-songwriter Joe Stevens and his music as metonyms for the recently increased visibility of white, middle-class, able-bodied trans men in the public sphere.[4] Specifically, I focus on the voice and mobilize an analytic of *vocal noise* to creatively and critically examine power as it emerges along intersectional vectors of gender, race, class, and ability, in our current historical and political trans "moment." As Hillel Schwartz observes, "Timeless and untimely, noise is the noisiest of concepts, abundantly self-contradictory."[5] It is precisely the messiness and unruliness of noise that makes it apropos of the obvious, and occluded aspects of trans social justice movements today. Following Alice Walker's (1983) assertion that progress is neither linear nor inevitable, noise is an epistemology that amplifies the resonances between power and privilege as they affect people's lives in contemporary trans activisms. A voice analytic brings the body to bear on noise studies, an aspect often overlooked in the literature.

My first section suggests that Stevens's music makes an affective and effective mess of dominant transgender narratives. Queering the binary of tragic/celebratory affects, Stevens's songs offer ambivalent and contradictory ones. He not only makes a mess of standard transgender narratives, he makes mess sound good. Voice is a central mechanism by which this is accomplished. A second section examines white privilege through the lens of vocal noise, extending whiteness studies into privilege as sound(ing). A third and final section refracts privilege through dis/abilities that complicate Stevens's claims to status and power. Throughout, I take a cue from vocal noise and endeavor to withhold easily won conclusions, allowing contradictory aspects to coexist.

My research methods are ethnographic and theoretical. My ethnographic data consist in interviews, live performances, and musical recordings. Through Stevens's and his band's generosity, I had the opportunity to tour with them briefly in 2011. Thus, the project brings a trans analytic to bear on ethnomusicological inroads into touring ethnography (Pruett 2007). In addition, Stevens and I hosted one another's bands six times between 2009 and 2014. I have seen him perform thirteen times. I engaged him in four hour-long formal interviews and many more informal conversations. My chapter engages scholarship in musicology, ethnomusicology, communication sciences, disability studies, critical race theory, queer and trans theory, and performance studies, as well as trans topics in the media. Philip Auslander's (2008) work on the interrelatedness of live and mediated performance, and Mark Butler's (2014) critical intervention on the performativity of musical recordings inspire my analysis of recordings and live performances. Without collapsing their differences, analyzing live and recorded performances highlights how each listening augurs a different encounter with the music.

At El Rio, Davis, the least established and the youngest of the three, opens the show. With bright-eyed demeanor, he says, "Are you excited to hear tonight's lineup?" A smattering of "yeah!" and "whoo!" percolate around the space. After saying how honored he is to be here, Davis plays a five-song set of original music. Four of the five songs highlight themes of being born in the wrong body and finding himself via medical transition. One song's refrain thanks his doctor for helping him find himself. The feeling of the space is somber and respectful.

I cannot help but think of Dean Spade's (2006) insistence that the status of surgery as the primary marker of transgenderism obscures the astronomical costs of these procedures and elides those who cannot afford to or do not wish to approximate this norm.[6] Queer and trans people of color (QTPOC), the working classes and the poor, disabled, and immigrants are less able to afford the doctors hailed in Davis's songs than are white, middle-class subjects. Moreover, Jonathan Sims, the doctor who developed sexology (the branch of science responsible for the techniques through which class- and race-privileged trans people medically transition), conducted much of his experimentation on the bodies of Black slave women (Washington 2006; Snorton 2017). The hyphens that link trans-as-medical are forged through and potentially continue to produce medical, economic, and political structures of racialized and class-based violence.

Stevens's and Silveira's sets follow. Usually performing in bands, Coyote Grace and the Cliks, respectively, Stevens and Silveira are well-known in white, mostly middle-class, and mostly female-assigned queer and trans communities in Canada and the United States. They have been performing for ten and fifteen years longer than Davis, respectively. Even still, each discusses their (trans)gender journeys much more explicitly than I have heard them in my two years researching them, and in the same terms as Davis. My ear catches the strangeness (as in unfamiliar) of this narrative in their mouths. Stevens often says, "you're never done transitioning...ever" and, rather than "finding himself" in medical transition, has told me "I still identify with my female self" (*Riot Acts*; interview, June 9, 2011). Before performing his song "Bullet in a Gun," Stevens says, "I wrote this song when I was a girl." He is joking, but there is a somewhat awkward pause that follows, almost as if he is trying to think of something to add and cannot.

After Stevens finishes, Silveira saunters onto the stage in his characteristically confident rock and roll style. He too offers a very brief statement and then says, "I think that's the most I've said about being trans on stage, ever" (performance, June 9, 2011). As with Stevens, there is an awkwardness to this moment that is audible in the silence and tension in the air as he makes this observation-cum-confession. I find it instructive that in the five years that Silveira lived and performed as a nonmedically transitioned trans man, when he would have *had* to verbalize his transgenderism in order to be visible, he never spoke of his gender on stage. And yet, two years after beginning hormone replacement therapy (HRT) and after becoming visible as masculine, he finally speaks about it.

There are many reasons why the singers may have spoken in the way they did: perhaps they felt more comfortable disclosing this information with an all-trans masculine line-up, or maybe they were distracted by changing their banter and clung awkwardly to this new topic. One reading we cannot rule out is that the affective and narratological links between transgenderism and medical transition are so powerful that once introduced into the space, they set the tone for the rest of the night.

Even stage banter, as I learned while touring with Stevens and Silveira, is rehearsed and repeated by artists from night to night. That night at El Rio, it was as if the arm of history—a history in which mostly middle- to upper-class white trans women learned to parrot a narrative from their psychiatrists in order to attain needed services (Stryker 2008; Meyerowitz 2002)—reached into the present and guided Stevens and Silveira into narrating in that mode. Reversing the hierarchy of opener-to-closer, Davis's set, buttressed by the financial and racial capital that medical transition carries, historically and at present, set the tone for the evening. It is just these kinds of resonances that the rubric of vocal noise is well-positioned to address.

The ways in which Stevens's and Silveira's complicated histories of and perspectives on medical transition were simplified that night is indicative of the power of this affective and narratological link. Vocal noise enables us to listen to power and potentially to revoice trans social justice. A vocal analytic amplifies the living breathing intersections of power and privilege that structure transgender celebratability in North America today. Ultimately, this chapter levies ethnomusicology and performance as ways of *doing* trans of color critique.

PERFORMING NOISE, METAPHORIZING GENDER

When I first hear Stevens's voice on a recording in 2009, I am struck by a quality as soothing as it is raspy (*Boxes*). It sounds as if there is a bit of air escaping his vocal cords, as if he is slightly hoarse, which the reader could emulate by making a breathy "ah" sound. Stevens's fans repeatedly cited this aspect of his voice as part of what they love about his music in interviews (November 18, 2013).

Taking my definition of breathiness as "vocal noise" from the communication sciences, I unpack the stakes of this term more thoroughly in the third section. I explore how Stevens's hoarseness disrupts the affective and narratological discourses that congeal around transgender identity. This standard narrative posits a person realizing at a very young age that their gender does not align with how others view them. This person then begins on the road to "transition" (sometimes left unspecified but often assumed to be medical), which allows them to come into full personhood. Representations of trans people in the media are often either positively or negatively valenced depending on success at reaching and inhabiting the end point of this trajectory.[7]

Rather than a gender transition that follows a linear A-to-B trajectory from premedical misery to postoperative joy, "Guy Named Joe," on the album *Boxes and Bags* (2006), constructs a far less straightforward path. The song begins with a C minor spinning-wheel articulation in the guitar, over which Stevens sings:

> The wind has come to take me down a notch
> A peg, or a level or two
> The swollen moon has got her sights set on me too
> The devil sun gonna take me higher
> Higher than I've ever been before
> I told my mom, no, I can't take no more
>
> ("Guy Named Joe")

On the word "higher" Stevens's voice emits an audible escape of breath, performing the "wind" that he sings about. This air can be heard as an indicator of the ways in which the threats that take marginalized people "down a notch" are internal(ized) as well as external, as Gloria Anzaldúa (2015 [1981]) observes. As per Anzaldúa, I suggest that, while never ceding the need for widespread systemic change, Stevens's vocal noise suggests that liberation also requires working in and on oneself. This labor includes navigating the lowering of the vocal range, relearning to sing after beginning HRT, and the inner work around identity that vocal changes beget, as I have theorized elsewhere (Krell 2013).

The chorus lyrically and sonically complicates a narrative that trans people find "home" in their medically-transition selves (Stone 2006; Crawford 2008):

> Who am I to change my life?
> Who am I to fuck with form?
> Who am I to weather a storm?
> But I go slow
> I said goodbye to everyone I know
> And in the morning I awoke
> And I was this guy named Joe.

Performing what Shana Goldin-Perschbacher (2007) frames as vocalizations of vulnerability and intimacy, Stevens sustains a common tone (a note that C minor and F major share) on the diphthong "I" of "who am I." Underneath, the guitar transitions from C minor to F major. For three beats the "I" transitions the song from verse to chorus, minor to major, and from the spinning wheel of the wind to a calmly plucked breeze. Stevens's "I" both remains constant and changes; we hear it transform because the soundscape underneath changes but the voice itself remains constant. In this way,

"Guy Named Joe" articulates new identities while sonicizing what remains constant (the sustained "I" in "who am I?"). Literally going "slow," Stevens's voice takes time to adjust to the idea of what being trans means and will mean for him and those close to him. In so doing, the song foregrounds trans as something that is as much a process of saying goodbye as it is a process of new beginnings, as well as the losses that accompany coming out to oneself and others.

The song "Ghost Boy" also complicates the assumption that trans people hate our premedical transition bodies and identities. After a sparse guitar introduction, the song begins a halting, percussive rhythm that persists throughout much of this song that recounts Stevens's experience at a ten-year reunion for his all-girls boarding high school in Arizona. This rhythm occurs at an *andante* tempo, as we might imagine Stevens's footsteps as he walks down the hallway:

> There was someone here, when I came she disappeared,
> I catch a glimpse in what people say.
> I am a self-made man,
> Born with my two hands
> I been waiting for so long to finally stand.
> But I have no history
> One day I just came to be
> I barely know who I am.
> And I walk down these halls,
> Nobody knows my name and,
> I know this place like it was mine too.
> She is everywhere,
> I turn a shade of blue and I didn't come back here to stay.
> I'm just a ghost boy walking through.

The song narrates how, upon his return, no one at the school recognized him, not even former teachers he had had for several years. The contrast between the percussive guitar rhythm and smooth legato voice echoes the chasm Stevens feels between his present body and his history at this institution. Rather than coming "home" to himself, medical transition augured an alt-homecoming, where he returns but in a body that renders him unrecognizable, turning him into a ghost in relation to halls and people only he can see. The strangeness and unfamiliarity with which people see him makes of him a stranger not only to his former classmates and teachers but also to himself.

The "she" in "Ghost Boy" refers to Stevens before his medical transition. Rather than taking advantage of the hypervisibility of (medically) transitioned selves, Stevens's "she" is everywhere—literally, whenever the chorus repeats.[8] Contra the dictum that all trans people want to escape their pretransition selves—a narrative that some might say is loaded with misogynistic potentialities when one is transitioning from a female to male identification—Stevens tells us, "I wish she hadn't left so soon." When I ask him in an interview what this line means, he offers, "I mean, I wasn't even answering to my own name yet. I had years of this identity as a female singer songwriter built up. Even though it wasn't who I was, it was an identity that I'd worked really hard for. And now nobody knew who I was" (interview, February 6, 2013).

The song and in our interview, suggest that extra-gender identities are affected by trans identity: Stevens's identity as a singer songwriter also had to transition. Countering the trans narrative we might expect in response to a school's ethos that girls grow up to be women, Stevens shows that the loss of a coerced identity is still a loss. Further, "Ghost Boy" amplifies the ways in which trans people themselves have to adjust to their name and pronoun changes. A confident stance is often required in order to assuage others' concerns. This emotional labor can belie a slower, inner process by which one comes to re/cognize oneself. When Stevens sings, "Words don't come to me, half as easily, as they did to her when she would sing," he sings of both the difficulty of pronouncing new identities and also of the potential in music to announce new selves.

While Stevens's music makes narratological messes of dominant narratives of transgenderism, it also replicates race, class, and gender systems. In "Ghost Boy" he sings that he is "nobody special now, I'm just another guy." Likewise, in "Guy Named Joe," Stevens wakes up, not unlike Kafka's anti-hero, to find himself transformed into a monstrosity of normalcy. In these songs, Stevens implicitly theorizes white and middle-class masculinity and risks universalizing whiteness in/as transmasculinity. When we consider that anonymity is not available in the same ways to Black or Latino trans men, nor to trans feminine persons of any race, it becomes clear that Stevens's theorization is both gendered and "surreptitiously racialized," to borrow a concept from Angela Davis (2015).

However, Stevens relates to this anonymity uncomfortably, an idea that is rich with subversive, anti-racist potential. In the film, *Riot Acts* (2011), the artist discusses being received with suspicion in many of the lesbian music spaces that were previously his community home. In an interview, he said, "they assume Ingrid is bisexual and that's why we're playing in this bar" (interview, February 6, 2013). The fact that Stevens is interpolated as straight is also racialized. That is (trans) men of color occupy a sphere of increased policing that draws upon legacies of hypersexualization, especially of Black and Native American men (Smith 2005, Johnson 2008). This racialized sexuality intersects with transsexuality to generate an intersectional risk of being interpolated as deviantly racialized and sexualized (Snorton 2014; Hernández 2008). Stevens's sexuality is always already potentially less scrupulously examined due to the normalcy his whiteness affords him.

Before HRT, he was used to "being the only one of whatever I was" as a masculine girl (interview, February 6, 2013). Considering that he came of age in a predominantly white, middle/upper-class neighborhood in Sacramento, California, reveals that Stevens's framing of being "the only one of whatever I was" is based primarily if not exclusively on gendered difference. Marlon B. Ross (2005) has written about how racialized and classed sameness are the vehicles through which gender and sexual variance emerge in white queer theory. Even the name "Joe" is a cypher for racialized and classed normalcy, of inhabiting the unmarked category in the nonwhite/white, working/middle-class dualities. Thus, while his songs potentially muss up standard transgender narratives, at times they also inadvertently reproduce trans normalcy through a universalized whiteness.

A performance analytic highlights the ways in which sound, affect, and emotionality are linked. Stevens's "Guy Named Joe" and "Ghost Boy" make an affective mess of dominant narratives of transgenderism while at the same time benefitting from all the ways in which messiness is coded as attractive when enacted by white middle-class able-bodied men. Privilege is potentially productive, I argue, if people imagine ways to interrupt that "normalcy" (by calling out sexism, transmisogyny, and racism, for example), and by understanding that discomfort is something most, if not all, POC, especially QTPOC, experience in relation to a white mainstream. In the next section I consider white privilege more extensively, through a rubric of vocal noise.

WHITE NOISE AND THE SONIC POLITICS OF PRIVILEGE

Vocal noise allows us to think of privilege not as a smooth space without frictions, tensions, and caverns, but as porous and in process. Bryant Keith Alexander's (2004) essay on the performativity of whiteness brings performance studies to bear on whiteness studies. Alexander observes that:

> Whiteness "itself" resists codifying. It is only noticeable in its performance ... [and] has to be acknowledged as something that is performative, something that does something in the world ... that is linked with access, the social construction of power, worth and value—that leads to the (dare I say it) practice of privilege.   (650)

Given Alexander's formulation, we might well ask, what is the "practice" of privilege that emerges in white middle-class trans masculine performance? I have already suggested that Stevens is permitted a degree of aural messiness because of his white masculine gender presentation. To extend this assertion, we might consider how the gravel of Stevens's voice, and the ways it is heard as desirable by his fans, are neither reducible to nor separable from a privileging of white masculinity over white femininity, and of whiteness over nonwhiteness in and beyond the US context. A white male performer with a husky voice can be read in a number of ways, but a white person read as female would likely be read as queer or unusual if they have a raspy voice. There is something about raspiness, it seems, that "sounds better" coming from masculine bodies. We can understand this as one aspect of the privileging of masculinity over femininity, as Julia Serano (2007; 2013) has theorized in her foundational formulation of transmisogyny. If Stevens were a trans feminine performer the sand-papery voice would be much less readily consumed as desirable by the audience, and with potentially high stakes for being heard and seen as masculine through that raspiness.

Furthermore, Black or Brown trans and cis female performers are at risk of racist discourses that render them "masculine," due to the historical construction of femininity as white and middle-class (Collins 2004).[9] Racialized transmisogyny, a term I offer here as an extension of Collins's "racialized sexism," makes the stakes much higher for trans women of color (TWOC) with voices akin to Stevens's because discourses of gender authenticity fall heavily on voice (Halberstam 2007 Bettcher 2006). The popularity of singers like Billie Holiday might seem to counteract this idea, but, as David Brackett (2000) makes clear, it was only after Holiday death, and after her fame was firmly established among Black audiences, that white music producers risked promoting her. The status of Holiday's voice as a "cult" phenomenon to white citybluesers, to riff off Fabian Holt (2007), only proves that Holiday's voice and Blackness were marginalized (and marginally fetishized) by the music industry. This marginality was recently gestured toward by white queer singer Taylor Mac, who joked at a cabaret performance that Holiday and other Black blues singers "didn't actually know how to sing."[10] This casual act of entertainment—meant for a dominantly white audience—shows how white, middle-class norms structure what counts as good "clean" singing, where cleanliness means not noisy (while somewhat self-servingly lifting Mac up as the arbiter of what counts as singing).[11]

While she does not discusses the title in her essay, Shannon Jackson's "White Noise" is instructive for thinking about white privilege in/as sound. The essay begins by critiquing white feminists's response to Ntozake Shange's *Spell #7*:

> "*cuz today i'm gonna be a white girl*"
>
> That phrase launches a notorious monologue in Ntozake Shange's *Spell #7* (1979), one that satirizes the behaviors and perceptions of whitegirlhood. It became particularly notorious among white feminists... *Is she a woman or is she black?* went the inane and therefore unannounced subtext of the discussion, posed by a faction of girls who thought of themselves as women but didn't think of themselves as white. "What's the first thing white girls think in the morning?" Shange's monologue asked this group who wasn't used to hearing themselves being generalized, "do they get up being glad they aint niggahs?" White liberal feminists were outraged by the suggestion—"Why, of course not!"—unaware that the capacity *not* to be either glad nor sad was a luxury of the oblivious. The fact that "such a thought would never enter their heads" was precisely, insidiously, the point.   (1998, 49; emphasis in original)

Throughout the essay, Jackson theorizes white privilege as a set of negatives—the capacity *not* to have a certain reaction, *not* to have to think of oneself as racialized, *not* to be aware of the experiences of those who are racialized. When she defines privilege positively, she recurs to the term "oblivion," suggesting that becoming aware of one's privilege involves a process of "retroactively waking up" after one already believes one is awake.

Colloquially, white noise often connotes a benign or palliative effect—a fan used to block out unwanted noise, from the street outside, for example. This type of white noise is designed to disappear as sound itself. The analogy of urbanity is apropos of noise as a racial performative. If we center people of color in a white majoritarian sphere, for example, white noise emerges with an insidious aspect, one that occludes POC voices while at the same time obscuring this performative effect(s). Its own disappearing act can be heard when whiteness denies its dominance "Why, of course not!"; an (ironic) act of voicing that defends whiteness as innocent benevolence.

An ethnographic example from my case study with Stevens is illustrative of some of the ways in which race operates for Stevens. The following is excerpted from my ethnographic notes while on tour with him:

> I am sitting across from Stevens at The Crane in Champaign-Urbana, IL, and he talks about going to a bar with a friend of his after the Sacramento Pride parade. Soon after entering, Stevens notices he is one of two white people in the crowded bar. Stevens turns to her, asking, "Are these people gay?" He is embarrassed but he can't tell. His friend looks at him incredulously, and said, "Are you kidding??? It's *Pride!!!*" When Stevens looks around he notices that the only other white guy in is, in his words, "acting like a douchebag," bobbing his head up and down to the music awkwardly and dancing alone. This makes Stevens mad, he says, half jokingly, half genuinely, thinking to himself, "You're making us [white folks] look bad!" Then he stops his story and says, pensively, "I wonder if it's hard for queer people of color . . . if they feel out of place in white queer spaces." His earnestness suggests he's never thought about this before. I respond that it has been rare that my Latin@ and queer identities have occupied the same spaces, but, feeling pressure not to paint QPOC lives as tragic, I add that there are queer spaces as well.   (Interview, November 18, 2011)

In a follow-up interview, I ask:

> EK: Can we talk about when you were dating X? You were talking about it being difficult to tell if people were gay.
> JS: Yeah, their clothing and social cues were different . . .

In this statement, Stevens demonstrates a lack of familiarity with cultural markers of Blackness generally, a lack of fluency that makes the patrons' queerness illegible to him. This example is also illustrative of the dominance of certain kinds of queer visibility over others by the mainstream media as well as queer institutions and organizations. As various scholars have articulated, racism in QT communities has long ensured that queer subjects are depicted as white and male (Johnson 2005; Ross 2005; Cohen 2005). In addition, white queer movements sometimes deploy anti-Black and Brown (in the United States) and anti-Islamic (in Europe) sentiments in order to move certain portions of the LGBT community forward at the cost of many others (Puar 2007; Haritaworn 2012; 2013). The result is that queerness becomes legible in and through whiteness and Black and Brown bodies are positioned as (heterosexual) threats to that queerness.

Johnson (2005) and Ross (2005) demonstrate that unlike white gay men who flock to white gayborhoods, Black queers leave and enter communities under a very different set of factors. QTPOC cannot simply commune under (the presumption of a) similar gender or sexuality, because people are just as racist inside gay communities as they are outside of it (Johnson 2011). As Jackson (1998) states, white people do experience racism—they are just usually on the other side of it (51). Queer and straight white communities are often oblivious to the ways in which QPOC need to seek out communities of color in order to fight racism outside *and* inside queer communities. Stevens's inability to tell whether the Pride patrons were queer is thus in line with a structural elision at the intersections of QT and POC. The example of a white trans man reading everyone as heterosexual on the gayest day of the year (at least enough to warrant the question) reflects the broader unintelligibility of queer Blackness in a white (queer and hetero) sphere. Black queerness is literally blocked out by the white noise with which Stevens walks into the space.

But the bar initiates an encounter with something else unfamiliar to Stevens, namely his own whiteness. Embarrassed by the other white man in the room, Stevens experiences the burden of representation that often inheres on racialized subjects in white spaces. Sonic epistemologies reveal the performativity of privilege in and as specific embodied contexts: it is when Stevens enters a space where his is not the dominant sound that he becomes aware of himself as being raced and of POC as potentially queer. A voice analytic offers us opportunities to listen to quotidian manifestations of privilege as well as moments where voices of color literally speak back to them. Stevens is awakened from his oblivion, per Jackson, through the sound of a voice of color speaking back to him ("are you *kidding*?").

While traveling with them briefly, I observed that Coyote Grace and their audiences performed privileges that at times produced abject others. While on tour in Indianapolis, Stevens's bandmate tells the audience members in the front row to sit "Indian style" in order to accommodate more persons. Brown bodies, and practices narrated as Brown and specifically indigenous, lent authenticity to the white bodies of this "roots" duo through a casual act of appropriation that literally made white bodies on the ground more comfortable. Another example, a band promotional email sent July 2009, suggested we all take our "pasty" winter limbs and expose them to the sun. This invitation was underscored by several American flags waving in the background. The fact that we do not all become "pasty" in the winter notwithstanding, the patriotic fervor of the missive comes close to if not succeeding in enacting a trans nationalism, following Jasbir Puar's "homonationalism" (2007). We might recall Puar's admonition that believing we are too oppressed to be capable of oppression can be a precondition for enacting violence. Elizabeth and Stevens have both said that all they need to do is "show up" and that is their activism.[12] A trans of color critique suggests that physically showing up may not be sufficient for enacting a critical and antiracist trans politic.[13]

Voicing Coping, Coping as Sound

When we drive together in 2011, Stevens plays me songs from his high school and early college years. I am speechless. Usually there are aspects of prosody or timbre that carry over postvocal drop, but, despite knowing him and his music for two years, I cannot recognize this voice. It is not that his range has dropped in pitch, which I had expected (testosterone HRT almost always has this effect), but the timbre itself has changed completely. When I tell him this, he smiles, seeming to be a bit embarrassed, and says that it was probably from drinking and smoking. He began both during his early teens, and shares that both increased until he came out to himself at age twenty-two. In this last section, I theorize transgenderism alongside disability through vocal noise.

Just prior to graduating from Cornish College, in 2003, Stevens walked into a random bookstore and saw Loren Cameron's *Body Alchemy: Transsexual Portraits* (1996). This book of photographs of and by trans masculine persons ushered in what Stevens calls his "light bulb" moment. "I finally figured out what was wrong with me" (interview, September 4, 2011). Stevens's embarrassment regarding his smoking and drinking habits can productively be placed in conversation with disability studies and communication science's understandings of vocal "health."

It is standard in communication sciences to define "noise," as Kent and Singh (2000) do, as "any unwanted sound; a sound that interferes with perception of another sound," or, as per Nicolosi et al., "1. a complex soundwave having...irregular vibrations to which no definite pitch can be assigned; 2. Generally considered as unpleasant or undesired sound; 3. Unwanted additions to a signal not arising at its source" (Nicolosi et al. 2004). Noise in the voice is defined as any sound, including breathiness, hoarseness, or other factor, that produces irregularity in pitch or volume or interfere with regular pitch and or intensity. The *MIT Encyclopedia of Communication Disorders* considers "breathiness" one aspect of "noise" in voice, where the vocal cords do not completely adduct, or close, such that air escapes:

> Too faint adduction...prevents the vocal folds from closing the glottis...during the vibratory cycle [i.e., phonation]. As a result, airflow escapes the glottis [the opening formed by the vocal cords] during the quasi-closed phase. This generates noise and produces a strong fundamental. This phonation mode is often referred to as breathy.
> (Kent 2004, 52)

Applying the definition of noise as "unwanted additions to a signal not arising at its source" to voice, we can understand the vocal cords to be considered the "source" of the sound. I find these theorizations useful for listening to transgender voices in part *because* of the evaluative assumptions that guide them. I am less interested in an ontology of noise than I am in discovering how scientific and scholarly conceptions of noise potentially fall most heavily on queer voices.[14]

The discovery of Stevens's teenage voice initially stumped me because I was not sure how to theorize Stevens's hoarseness within the context of his transgenderism. A shift in gender identity and morphology seemed to define transvocality—not smoking and drinking. But in conversation with my brother, he offered that this aspect of Stevens's vocal journey was indicative of the fact that trans voices do not exist in a bubble. I suggest that it is this literal grating of life upon the body that makes voice such a productive analytic for individual identities and social justice movements.

Stevens's voice is as much a negotiation between his life and his body as it is a marker of his transgenderism. Stevens identified as a lesbian until he was twenty-two in part because he had no referents for livable transgender life. Struggling with depression and dropping out of school, Stevens deployed smoking and drinking (both alcohol and caffeine) as coping mechanisms. I suggest this in part because he increased use of both until coming out. That he did not stop using after coming out does not discredit this point: bodies carry memories within them from this and others' lifetimes (for example, we know that alcoholism is hereditary). It is difficult to overemphasize the significance of the fact that Stevens lived for twenty-two years with no external representation of transmasculinity whatsoever. Suffice it to say that without that referent, the very possibility of being (a large part of) who he was, was withheld from him.

The characterization of noise as not emerging from the "source," as the literature states, implies an *a priori* voice unencumbered by noise. We might be tempted to say that the originary "source" of Stevens's voice was his voice before his coping mechanisms became full-fledged addictions. Indeed, *Hegde's PocketGuide to Communication Disorders* tells us that hoarseness is "a grating or husky voice quality . . . associated factors include vocal abuse and misuse" (2008 23). Without foreclosing the possibility that vocal therapies may be useful for some, I want to suggest that a definition of vocal noise as that which we do not want to hear is tautological. We might supplement the scientific literature by considering how systemic inequities produce contexts that necessitate coping mechanisms. A performance analytic illustrates how the construct of a true voice before anything has happened to it is simply that: a construction against which to compare and pathologize other sounds.

A sonic epistemology shows how the guiding presumption that there exist "generally undesirable" sounds itself produces voices that are un/desirable. That is, sound is the effect of a body in relation to sonic norms, and a marker of who "feels" those norms and who is not feeling it. Vocal noise as it is used in the communication sciences performatively produces sounds as un/natural and un/healthy. A trans analytic allows us to hear the sound of survival, where subjects feel the accumulated effects of not approximating a norm, and where they risk being heard as "unpleasant" in comparison to those who cope or just generally feel better. Comparison, as the novelist Octavia Butler insisted, is a slippery slope toward pathology (Butler 2000); vocal noise thus becomes a metonym for the "undecipherable" wavelength of subject positions who literally and figurally are not heard.

At the same time that Stevens benefits from the privileges that accrue to his white masculine body, his chronic additions trouble his access to status and power. In addition to his transexuality, Stevens's struggles with alcoholism situate him precariously within the standards of middle-class white masculinity (my research subject has shared this information with me and discussed his condition publicly). Unlike in rock or punk music, where noisy large spaces connote a rough masculine aesthetic, Stevens generally plays in quieter and cleaner concert halls or cafés, or daytime outdoor festivals. These spaces carry an affective prescription of cleanliness that runs through the musical *and* moral personas the artist is supposed to convey—one that runs counter to the messiness of addiction (and renders him a queer subject in the sense of being out of place, strange, and deviant).

In March 2013, I sit with Stevens backstage before a show in Chicago, and he tells me that his addiction impairs his ability to do anything beyond quotidian necessary tasks. He has been binge-drinking for a month following a full year of sobriety that he had been documenting and thus publicizing on social media. "I'm having a really hard time," he tells me, and I can see the exhaustion in his face. Then he tells me of a conversation he had with a woman in Sacramento who uses a wheelchair. Stevens asks this elder in the disability activist movement in Northern California if she thinks he could claim disability as an identity because of his alcoholism, and she says, "The thought amongst disabilities activists I know is the more the merrier." Stevens feels tentative about claiming this identity because he is visibly able-bodied; "I feel like I'm not sure I have a right to claim it."

> I know this is [a problematic] analogy, but last night, there was this dinner for all the performers, and everyone was talking at the table...and...the analogy I can think of, and I know it's not the best, I know it's...[problematic], but the way I can describe the feeling is that I felt like I was at the bottom of some stairs, in a wheelchair, watching everybody walk up and down them like it...like it's nothing for them.   (Interview, March 31, 2013)

Stevens is aware of the privileges his apparent visibly able body grants him, and is concerned that his claim to a disabled identity appropriates a subject position from disabled folks who do not deal with addiction. He is hesitant to claim the term, but, upon reconsidering, adds "well, it's definitely more helpful than thinking I'm an asshole."

Theorizing disability and transgenderism together reveals how addiction can manifest as a coping mechanism for living in a world that actively erases nonbinary identities through various means including gender segregated spaces, administrative documents, and more. For example, Stevens implicitly theorizes his transgenderism and addiction together when he says that "it takes so much energy to abstain from drinking when I'm not drinking, and then it takes even more energy to deal with life when I am drinking" and to deal with the shame involved. In his words, "It's just baffling to me that I can't control it when I'm in that space" (interview, March 31, 2013).

A survey of the literature reveals that addiction is an undertheorized but growing component of disability studies (Johnson 2007; Starr 2002; Henderson 1991). Addiction occupies a marginal position alongside other invisible disabilities. Reese Henderson writes, "Section 104 of the Americans with Disabilities Act of 1990 clarifies the coverage of addicts under disability discrimination law, but leaves unclear the status of alcoholics." Along the main current in critical disability studies, Johnson orients culpability for alcoholism to systemic failures within healthcare, employment, housing, and societal stigma:

> Alcoholism is a disability about which stereotypic assumptions are particularly problematic. Alcoholics in particular suffer from the "systematic prejudice, stereotypes

and neglect" that were the central concerns of the [American with Disabilities Act]. They are more likely to be discriminated against because they are often not perceived to be suffering from a "real" illness. Alcoholics have also historically been subjected to ridicule and contempt.   (Johnson 2007, 174–75)

This passage conveys a hierarchy of authenticity, wherein addictions are viewed as self-imposed liabilities. Johnson writes that "blame-the-victim" stigma elides the immense disparities in legal, health, and societal support for those dealing with addiction in the United States. In a different context, Fiona Campbell (2009) asserts that blame-the-victim strategies produce "able" bodies as *naturally* privileged. When the responsibility lies on the person with the addiction, employers, educators, and corporations do not have to adjust behavior or policies that are causes of dis/ability in the work or school place (Starr 2002). Thinking of Johnson, Starr, and Campbell together highlights how individualist approaches to vocal health risk producing the very binaries of health and illness that they seek to overcome. I suggest that Stevens's vocal noise was largely a result of his nicotine and alcohol addictions, and that these are inseparable from his experience as a young person in a world with no referents of trans life. He may be at greater risk of having his addictions attributed to personal failings *because* of his transgenderism where any deviation from the norm becomes a sticking point for ableism. Trans-ing gender, race, class, and ability reveals how whiteness grants him affects of sympathy and innocence that do not necessarily accompany people of color who struggle with addiction.[15]

Stevens's addictions productively trouble the binary of in/visible disabilities (Samuels 2003). Fieldwork revealed the slow and cumulative effects of addiction on the body: Whether from alcoholism, anxiety, or a combination thereof, Stevens's hands shake a bit more each time I see him and he tells me backstage of a show in 2013 that alcoholism deteriorates the nerves over time. Stevens is visibly able-bodied depending on how close you are standing to him, whether he is warming up on his Gibson in front of you, or performing high up on a stage at an outdoor festival. A performance-centered epistemology affirms the precarity of bodies that perform. His hand tremors are closely related in genesis to what he narrates as the causes of his vocal breathiness and yet are likely coded as less desirable to his fans.[16]

A theory of voice that takes disability seriously as a critical frame understands "noise" as constitutive of rather a pathology within Stevens's voice, and demonstrates how disability is a generative a rubric for transgender vocality. As both ontological object and processual practice, Stevens's vocal noise articulates the static between his trans identity/body and a transphobic world.

Stevens's addictions threaten his claims to "natural" white American masculinity: his shaking hands, exhausted body, and scratchy voice articulate a space between respectability and messiness, a gap within which white middle-class trans masculinity emerges and is also threatened. Stevens's fans relish his vocal breathiness, but voices are always heard in relation to the physical bodies from which they (are imagined to) emanate. Rather than "unwanted additions…not arising at the [vocal] source," Stevens's vocal noise is a metonym for the messiness inherent in navigating life in a society in which we were never meant to survive (Muñoz 1999, 98). Stevens's claims to power via race, gender, and class are challenged via his chronic addictions at the same time that they are buttressed by the messiness afforded him by his white middle-class masculinity.

CONCLUSIONS

A vocal analytic foregrounds the living, breathing intersections where subjects negotiate power. I have suggested that sound-based epistemologies open productive avenues along which to explore the ways in which racism, and anti-Black racism in particular, structure mainstream LGBTIQQ rights claims (Spade 2014). Soyini Madison and Judith Hamera (2006) write that performance potentially unmasks contingent, temporary, and risky possibilities for subverting historically sedimented power differentials. Supplementing this work, I suggest that performance and voice together highlight how trans visibilities are differentially produced along the lines of race, gender, class, and disability. I have cautioned that the rapid ascension of a few privileged trans persons, does little to change the realities of the most marginalized. Performance and music are key modes through which independent QTPOC artists fight for access to services and for the ability to inhabit complex personhoods, to borrow a term from Avery Gordon (2008).

If, as Colin Dayan reminds us (2002), slavery and colonialism are *living* legacies that have material effects on contemporary lives, it is imperative that we account for how the visibility of some trans people potentially circumscribes what counts as legitimately and/or fully trans. The point is, not to lay white and middle-class privileges at the feet of one person. Rather, it is to take seriously Haritaworn's question of how we enact "trans liberation" (a term coined by Les Feinberg, 1999) in a way that ties trans claims to other global anticolonial and anti-racist social justice efforts. If there is cause for optimism, it may be because decolonial work has never been primarily or exclusively carried out by white bodies.

NOTES

1. Featuring three female-to-male (FTM) transgender singers.
2. I have written about performance, utopia, and violence drawing upon the seminal work of José E. Muñoz (Krell 2015).
3. I aim to examine, rather than essentialize, "privilege." Indeed, I began the chapter with the trans masculine triple-header in order to demonstrate that white trans masculine privilege is hardly limited to the figure of Stevens.
4. My reference to the language of trans "visibility" in this introduction is somewhat fraught. Given the continued prevalence of anti-Black and anti-trans feminine violence in the United States, we should be suspicious of claims that "visibility" leads to justice for people

of color, trans or otherwise. I actively strive to queer the dominant trans narrative that visibility equals freedom by centering sound rather than visual-based epistemologies. Accounting for all of the reasons for a marked increase in visibility of class- and race-privileged trans people in recent years would necessitate an entire book; suffice it to say, that one reason is due to transmisogyny in feminist and queer spaces, and of the privileging of masculinity in and outside queer spaces as well. At the same time that I critique the rise in visibility of white middle-class able-bodied trans men, I do not want to fall into the temptation, popular at present, to denigrate trans men at the cost of intersectional analysis. Such claims are often performatives that constitute the speaker as in-the-know (as Alok Vaid-Menon offers, if every person who uses the phrase "trans women of color" donated $10 to a grassroots organization that employs and serves that community...), rather than offering anything meaningful about trans persons and our needs. Nonintersectional critiques of trans masculinity elide the multiple oppressions that poor, disabled, and men of color, trans and otherwise, face and also elide the violence Black men in particular face. Such an obviation, at a time in which movements such as #blacklivesmatter are trying to bring visibility to Black suffering across lines of gender, is white supremacist.

5. As cited in Hainge (2013, 6). Noise studies is broad interdisciplinary field and I do not have the space to parse it out here. See Hegarty (2007), Attali (1985), Hainge (2013), and Link (2001). I focus on communication sciences because this broad field is most concerned with how noise is produced in the body, for example via vocality and the concept of vocal health.

6. I would add, as Spade elsewhere observes, some trans people cannot medically transition for health reasons. I take seriously Namaste's (2000) critique of fetishizing nonbinary identities for their theoretical promise and obscuring the realities of people who need to transition to survive. Further, Francesca Royster offers a counter to Namaste, suggesting that we need to remember to lift up trans people of color as living beings rather than only always arbiters of precarious life and destined for death (personal communication, April 1, 2013).

7. My point is not to dismiss those who find these narratives helpful but rather to caution that their dominance mutes other realities of some of those in an already marginalized group.

8. Moreover, his songwriting is imbricated with this process: "When I wrote songs as a girl, I had so much more angst I was dealing with. They were very subconscious...now all of a sudden I had energy that needed to release, but all of a sudden I was like, how do I [write a song]?" (February 6, 2013).

9. A recent "scientific" study argued that Black women are "objectively" less attractive than women of other races. The data was revealed to consist of a survey taken by a small number of white men who were asked to rate a series of photographs. The "experiment" was resoundingly critiqued as proving only that Black women are discriminated against in a white majoritarian sphere (Solomon 2011). An underreported aspect of this study is its implicit transphobia: higher levels of testosterone were listed by the lead scientist as a "cause" of Black women's unattractiveness, suggesting that an ugly woman is a woman who looks like a man. This study and its construction (only) effectively demonstrated that transphobia, sexism, and anti-Black racism work in tandem to construct Black women as failed women—a stigma that falls most harshly on trans women of color (TWOC) and especially Black trans women.

10. Taylor (2013).

11. I suggest that Black female voices became the raw material through which Mac constructs white valuations of singing—rather self-servingly, since this constitutes Mac as one who knows good singing and can offer it to their audience. More specifically, Mac's white trans femininity became a vehicle for thinly veiled anti-Black racism: the queer white body is forgiven its off-color humor *because* of its gender transgression, a gender transgression that is produced through whiteness, demonstrating how queerness is always already imbricated in white-skin privilege. It is instructive that Holiday's legitimacy cannot be taken for granted even today, and these judgments around race, gender, and class emerge precisely because the aesthetic voice is not presumed to be political.

12. In *Riot Acts* (2007), at Urbana-Campaign (2011), and in personal interviews with Stevens and Ingrid (2009, 2011, 2012).

13. "Critical trans politics" is a phrase and theoretical concept I take from Dean Spade's *Normal Life*.

14. In this formulation, I take inspiration from Eve Sedgwick (2008), who demonstrates that an epistemology of the closet mobilizes certain figures, in her main example, duplicity, that fall most heavily upon queerness, with material consequences for queer people.

15. See Lamble's (2008) persuasive writing on how whiteness becomes a precondition for grieving the loss of transgender life, for example during Transgender Day of Remembrance.

16. Stevens has been public about these struggles and is beginning to consider taking a more active part in disability activisms for transgender persons (interview, March 31, 2013). Stevens spent years attending Alcoholics Anonymous (AA) meetings and has an encyclopedic knowledge of treatment programs. He critiques AA's Protestant Christian moralism that places the emphasis on individual behavior and ignores institutional practices that make life unlivable for QT/POC. Stevens speaks hopefully of starting to work with other queer and trans people struggling with addiction: "I've been to regional and national conferences for sober people and as far as I know there's no one doing work with queer people, addiction, and disability—I want to be that person" (interview, March 31, 2013).

WORKS CITED

Alexander, Bryant Keith. 2004. "Black Skin/White Masks: The Performative Sustainability of Whiteness." *Qualitative Inquiry* 10 (5): 647–72.

Anzaldúa, Gloria. 2015 [1981]. "La Prieta." In *This Bridge Called My Back: Radical Writings by Women of Color*, 4th ed., edited by Cherrie Moraga and Gloria Anzaldúa, 198–209. New York: SUNY Press.

Attali, Jacques. 1985. *Noise: The Political Economy of Music*. Minneapolis: University of Minnesota Press.

Auslander, Philip. 2008. *Liveness: Performance in a Mediatized Culture*. 2nd ed. New York: Routledge.

Bettcher, Talia Mae. 2006. "Understanding Transphobia: Authenticity and Sexual Abuse." In *Trans/Forming Feminisms: Trans/Feminist Voices Speak Out*, edited by Krista Scott-Dixon, 203–10. Toronto: Sumach Press.

Brackett, David. 2000. *Interpreting Popular Music*. Berkeley: University of California Press.

Butler, Mark. 2014. *Playing with Something that Runs: Technology, Improvisation, and Composition in DJ and Laptop Performance*. Oxford: Oxford University Press.

Butler, Octavia. 2000. *Lilith's Brood*. New York: Aspect/Warner Books.

Cameron, Loren. 1996. *Body Alchemy: Transsexual Portraits*. Berkeley: Cleis Press.

Campbell, Fiona. 2009. *The Contours of Ableism*. New York: Palgrave Macmillan.

Carter, Mandy. 2008. "Still No Freedom for Trans People of Color." *Colorlines*, January 7. http://www.colorlines.com/articles/still-no-freedom-rainbow-transgender-people-color.

Cohen, Cathy. 2005. "Punks, Bulldaggers, and Welfare Queens: The Radical Potential of Queer Politics." In *Black Queer Studies*, edited by E. Patrick Johnson and Mae Henderson, 21–51. Durham, NC: Duke University Press.

Collins, Patricia Hill. 2004. *Black Sexual Politics: African Americans, Gender, and the New Racism*. New York: Routledge.

Crawford, Lucas Cassidy. 2008. "Transgender without Organs? Mobilizing a Geo-Affective Theory of Gender Modification." *WSQ: Women's Studies Quarterly* 36 (3): 127–43.

Dayan, Colin. 2002. "Legal Slaves and Civil Bodies." In *Materializing Democracy: Toward a Revitalized Cultural Politics*, edited by R. Castronovo and D. D. Nelson, 53–94. Durham, NC: Duke University Press.

Davis, Angela. 2015. "Our Feminisms: From #Occupy to #Sayhername." Keynote Address, Vassar College Chapel, September 16.

Feinberg, Leslie. 1999. *Trans Liberation: Beyond Pink or Blue*. Boston: Beacon Press.

Goldin-Perschbacher, Shana. 2007. "'Not With You But of You': 'Unbearable Intimacy' and Jeff Buckley's Transgendered Vocality." In *Oh Boy! Masculinities and Popular Music*, edited by Freya Jarman-Ivens, 213–34. New York: Routledge.

Gordon, Avery. 2008. *Ghostly Matters: Haunting and the Sociological Imagination*. Minneapolis: University of Minnesota Press.

Hainge, Greg. 2013. *Noise Matters: Towards an Ontology of Noise*. London: Bloomsbury.

Halberstam, Judith. 2007. "Queer Voices and Musical Genders." In *Oh Boy! Masculinities and Popular Music*, edited by Freya Jarman-Ivens, 183–96. New York: Routledge.

Haritaworn, Jin. 2012. *The Biopolitics of Mixing: Thai Multiracialities and Haunted Ascendancies*. Aldershot: Ashgate.

Haritaworn, Jin. 2013. "Degenerate Landscapes: Performing Walking Death in Transnational and Transtemporal Berlin." Summer Institute on Performance, Technology, and Biopolitics. Center for Global Culture and Communication, Northwestern University, July 8–12.

Hegarty, Paul. 2007. *Noise/Music: A History*. New York: Continuum.

Hegde, M. N. 2008. *Hegde's PocketGuide to Communication Disorders* 3rd Edition. Clifton Park, NY: Delmar Learning.

Henderson, Reese John Jr. 1991. "Addiction as Disability: The Protection of Alcoholics and Drug Addicts under the Americans with Disabilities Act of 1990." *Vanderbilt Law Review* 44: 713.

Hernandez, Daisy. 2008. "Becoming a Black Man." *Colorlines*. https://www.colorlines.com/articles/becoming-black-man.

Holt, Fabian. 2007. *Genre in Popular Music*. Chicago: University of Chicago Press.

Jackson, Shannon. 1998. "White Noises: On Performing Whiteness, on Writing Performance." *Theater Drama Review* 42 (2): 49–65.

Johnson, Judith. 2007. "Rescue the Americans with Disabilities Act from Restrictive Interpretations: Alcoholism as an Illustration." *Northern Illinois University Law Review* 27 (2): 169–246.

Johnson, E. Patrick. 2005. "'Quare' Studies: Or (Almost) Everything I Know about Queer Studies I learned from my Grandmother." In *Black Queer Studies: A Critical Anthology*, edited by E. Patrick Johnson and Mae Henderson, 124–60. Durham, NC: Duke University Press.

Johnson, E. Patrick. 2011. *Sweet Tea: Black Gay Men of the South*. Chapel Hill: The University of North Carolina Press.

Kent, Raymond D.2004. *The MIT Encyclopedia of Communication Disorders*, edited by Raymond D. Kent. MIT Press.

Krell, Elías. 2013. "Contours through Covers: Voice and Affect in the Music of Lucas Silveira." *Trans/Queer*. Spec. issue of *Journal of Popular Music Studies* 25 (4): 476–503.

Krell, Elías. 2015. "Who's the Crackwhore at the End? Performance, Violence, and Sonic Borderlands in the Music of Yva las Vegass." *Text & Performance Quarterly* 35 (3): 5–41.

Lamble, Sarah. 2008. "Retelling Racialized Violence, Remaking White Innocence: The Politics of Interlocking Oppressions in Transgender Day of Remembrance." *Sexuality Research & Social Policy* 5 (1): 24–42.

Link, Stan. 2001. "The Work of Reproduction in the Mechanical Ageing of an Art: Listening to Noise." *Computer Music Journal* 25 (1): 34–47.

Madison, D. Soyini, and Judith Hamera. 2006. "Introduction: Performance at the Intersections." In *Sage Handbook of Performance Studies*, edited by D. Soyini Madison and Judith Hamera, xi–xxv. Thousand Oaks, CA: Sage Publications.

Meyerowitz, Joanne J. 2002. *How Sex Changed: A History of Transsexuality in the United States*. Cambridge, MA: Harvard University Press.

Muñoz, José Esteban. 1999. *Disidentifications: Queers of Color and the Performance of Politics*. Cultural Studies of the Americas Volume 2. Minneapolis: University of Minnesota Press.

Namaste, Viviane K. 2000. *Invisible Lives: The Erasure of Transsexual and Transgendered People*. Chicago: University of Chicago Press.

Nicolosi, L., Harryman, E. and Kresheck, J. 2004. *Terminology of Communication Disorders: Speech–Language–Hearing*. Lippincott Williams & Wilkins, Philadelphia, PA.

Pruett, David B. 2007. "MuzikMafia: Community, Identity, and Change from the Nashville Scene to the Popular Mainstream." PhD diss., Florida State University.

Puar, Jasbir K. 2007. *Terrorist Assemblages: Homonationalism in Queer Times*. Durham, NC: Duke University Press.

Rivera, Sylvia. 2002. "Queens in Exile: The Forgotten Ones." In *GenderQueer: Voices Beyond the Sexual Binary*, edited by Joan Nestle, Clare Howell, and Riki Wilchins, 67–85. Los Angeles: Alyson Books.

Ross, Marlon. 2005. "Beyond the Closet as Raceless Paradigm." In *Black Queer Studies: A Critical Anthology*, edited by E. Patrick Johnson and Mae G. Henderson. Durham, NC: Duke University Press, 161–89.

Royster, Francesca. Personal communication, April 1, 2013.

Samuels, Ellen. 2003. "My Body, My Closet: Invisible Disability and the Limits of Coming-Out Discourse." *Gay & Lesbian Studies Quarterly* 1 April; 9 (1–2): 233–255.

Sedgwick, Eve. 2008. *Epistemology of the Closet*. Berkeley: University of California Press.

Serano, Julia. 2007. *Whipping Girl: A Transsexual Woman on Sexism and the Scapegoating of Femininity*. Emeryville, CA: Seal Press.

Serano, Julia. 2013. *Excluded: Making Feminist and Queer Movements More Inclusive*. Berkeley: Seal Press.

Smith, Andrea. 2005. *Conquest: Sexual Violence and American Indian Genocide*. Cambridge, MA: South End Press.

Snorton, C. Riley. 2014. *Nobody Is Supposed to Know: Black Sexuality on the Down Low*. Minneapolis: University of Minnesota Press.

Snorton, C. Riley. 2017. *Black on Both Sides: Race and the Remaking of Trans History*. Minneapolis: University of Minnesota Press.

Snorton, C. Riley, and Jin Haritaworn. 2013. "Trans Necropolitics." *Transgender Studies Reader, Volume II*, edited by Aren Aizura and Susan Stryker, 66–76. New York: Routledge.

Solomon, Akiba. 2011. "The Pseudoscience of 'Black Women Are Less Attractive.'" *Colorlines*, May 17. http://www.colorlines.com/articles/pseudoscience-black-women-are-less-attractive.

Spade, Dean. 2006. "Compliance Is Gendered: Struggling for Gender Self-Determination in a Hostile Economy." In *Transgender Rights*, edited by Paisley Currah, Shannon Minter, and Richard Juang, 217–41. New York: Routledge.

Spade, Dean. 2015. Normal Life: Administrative Violence, Critical Trans Politics, and the Limits of Law. Durham: Duke UP.

Starr, Sonja B. 2002. "Simple Fairness: Ending Discrimination in Health Insurance Coverage of Addiction Treatment." *Yale Law Journal* 111 (8): 2321–65.

Stone, Sandy. 2006. "The Empire Strikes Back: A Posttranssexual Manifesto." In *The Transgender Studies Reader*, edited by Susan Stryker and Stephen Whittle, 221–35. New York: Routledge.

Stryker, Susan. 2008. *Transgender History*. Berkeley, CA: Seal Press.

Washington, H. A. (2006). *Medical Apartheid: The Dark History of Medical Experimentation on Black Americans from Colonial Times to the Present*. New York: Doubleday.

Walker, Alice. 1983. *In Search of Our Mothers' Gardens: Womanist Prose*. San Diego: Harcourt Brace Jovanovich.

Audiography/Filmography

Against a Trans Narrative. Dir. Jules Rosskam. MamSir Productions. 2008.

Coyote Grace. "Guy Named Joe." *Boxes and Bags*. Mile After Mile Music, 2006. CD.

Coyote Grace. "Ghost Boy." *Boxes and Bags*. Mile After Mile Music, 2006. CD.

Davis, Alex, Lucas Silveira, and Joe Stevens. Live Performance. *El Rio*. June 9, 2011.

Riot Acts. Dir. Madsen Minax. Outcast Films. 2011.

Stevens, Joe. Live Performance. Urbana. November 17, 2011.

Stevens, Joe. Live Performance. Bloomington. November 18, 2011.

Taylor, Mac. "An Abridged Concert of the History of Political Popular Music." Performance. Museum of Contemporary Art. Chicago. September 27, 2013.

CHAPTER 9

VOICE IN CHARISMATIC LEADERSHIP

ROSARIO SIGNORELLO

VOICE is one of the most reliable and efficient behaviors that leaders use to display their charisma, conveying personality traits and arousing emotional states, in order to influence followers. The acoustics of charismatic leaders' voices is the result of evolved modes of vocalization filtered through language and culture-specific strategies to manipulate voice quality. These manipulations cause different vocal patterns, resulting in the perception of leaders' different traits and types of charisma, emotional triggering, and social attractiveness. This chapter first illustrates a theoretical approach to describing the phenomenon of charisma in leadership, and illustrates how charisma is semantically represented and measured in different languages and cultures. It also addresses several questions regarding the role of voice in charismatic political spoken communication in different communication contexts (directly addressed to followers, other leaders, or diffused through digital media): 1) what are the biological versus language and culture-specific functions of charismatic voice in political speech? 2) How does voice quality convey charismatic leadership? 3) How does voice quality influence the interaction between leaders and followers, as well as leaders' attractiveness? and 4) How is the charismatic voice perceived in different languages and cultures? With a background in phonetic sciences and social psychology, the methodologies I use and the definitions with which I operate reflect these fields' affordances and limits.

WHERE DOES THE CHARISMATIC VOICE COME FROM?

The majority of human and animal species that are organized in social groups have a leader. Individuals come into competition with other individuals, often within their own species and social group, in order to gain access to resources like food, and access to mating in order preserve their own genetic inheritance (Raymond 2008). In order to do this, individuals must win the competition, impose themselves, and become leaders. Throughout the evolutionary process, human and other animals have developed morphological traits in terms of size, stature, and so on that allow them to impose themselves upon other individuals of their own and other species. They utilize these traits in order to vanquish competition, dominate, and become leaders (Raymond 2008). Thus, the relationship between leaders (of any type: political, economic, philosophical, etc.) and other individuals in a social group can be described as a social exchange that aims for mutual profit, in which there are advantages for both parties (Hollander and Julian 1970). The leader of the group directly influences the quality of life of the other group members, and the ability to choose a good leader is therefore fundamental to individuals' survival and reproduction.

Human individuals aspiring to become leaders of their social group not only need a biological predisposition in order to do so, but also have to learn strategies for utilizing this predisposition to express their leadership. These strategies are regulated by the leaders' and listeners' language and culture and are implemented through verbal and nonverbal communication. This is why leader prototypes share morphological and behavioral universalities (Signorello 2014a) and also develop specific communicational skills in different cultures (Bass 1990; Hofstede 1993). As Den Hartog et al. explains, "leadership can be recognized based on the fit between an observed person's characteristics with the perceiver's implicit ideas of what 'leaders' are" (Hartog et al. 1999, 225). In the quest for leadership, biological predispositions and learned strategies of communication enable an individual to emerge as a leader. They constitute the leader's charisma.

The phenomenon of charisma has been described in several ways. In the fifth century C.E., Socrates considered charisma to be the ability that leaders demonstrate when they are able to combine vision with mental and physical skills to preside over others. For Max Weber (1920), charisma is the extraordinary quality of a person who is believed to be endowed with superhuman properties that make him or her stand out as a leader. Social psychological theories consider charisma as a socially constructed phenomenon wherein leaders act as the entrepreneurs of their identity in order to establish a relationship with the other individual of the social group (Haslam et al. 2011).

Formal investigation of charismatic leadership can be traced back to the study of rhetoric and persuasion in ancient Greece. Modern research on charisma emphasizes two elements that have emerged. First, both the biological and culture-specific characteristics of leadership must be accounted for. Human history presents us with mythic figures of leaders who are considered iconic and capable of enacting revolution (in Mongolian, "Genghis-Khan" means universal sovereign; "Caesar" in English (and in Italian) is occasionally used for describing a person who wields great power over others—that is, a leader). Even though revolution may be the act of powerful individuals in mythology, research into social psychology (e.g., Riggio et al. 2008; Reicher et al. 2005; Haslam et al. 2011) shows that it is in fact a collective act. At the basis of this social characterization of leadership, natural selection may favor the ability of followers to choose their leadership (e.g., Darwin 1871; Tigue et al. 2012).

Second, the introduction of behavioral measurement of the charismatic voice has led to a better understanding of many components that charismatic leaders use to influence their listeners. The first modern approaches to the study of leadership are Tuppen's "Dimensions of Communicator Credibility" (1974) and Boss's "Essential Attributes of Charisma" (1976). They pioneered analytic studies of charismatic leaders' perceivable behaviors that express the personality and the emotions of the leader that have the goal to convey charismatic leadership.

The expression of charismatic leadership occurs through perceivable behaviors such as vocal practice, perhaps the most reliable and efficient behavior—one that reflects the speaker's morphological apparatus (that of a female versus male, adult versus child) and psychological attributes (Kreiman and Sidtis 2011). Voice evolved in order to signal traits of social and physical dominance to others, (Ohala 1982; 1983; 1984; 1994; 1996) and it plays an important role in individuals' ability to perceive good and reliable leadership (Tigue et al. 2012). Anatomical differences (biological factors), combined with culturally acquired habits of voice production (language and cultural factors), provoke different voice quality patterns (Kreiman and Sidtis 2011) and are at the origin of the perception of the speaker-leader's charisma (Signorello 2014a).

Leaders use voice for persuading and accomplishing the goal of persuasion by communicating their types of charisma (for example, a caring or an authoritarian leader) and charismatic traits (for example, *active, dynamic, charming, wise, intelligent, dominant, resolute*), as well as arousing emotional states in listeners (*happiness, anxiety, rage*). The speaker-leader uses charismatic voice behavior based on biological functions as well as language and culture-specific functions (Signorello 2014a). The "biological" function (i.e., equal across genders, languages, and cultures) consists of manipulating changes in vocal pitch in order to convey dominance characteristics. The "language and culture-specific" function, learned and dependent upon the language spoken and the culture that one belongs to, manipulates vocal quality to convey different traits and types of charisma to persuade the audience.

The speaker-leader strategically utilizes an adapted vocal behavior for various communication contexts to express a specific type of charismatic leadership that is consistent with a specific audience in a given language and culture. This leads to the development of several psychological models of charisma within the same leader and among different leaders. For example, cultures that tolerate strong leadership may require a greater authoritarian and strong expression of it than cultures where a more consultative or considerate leadership is expected (Hartog et al. 1999). If authoritarian charismatic leadership is required in a different social group or communication context, or even just in a particular moment of the communication, the leader must not appear sensitive or empathetic, and must not arouse positive emotions like *happiness*. If listeners expect a *placid* style of leadership, a vocal behavior that reflects *aggression* may be seen as an indication of a noncharismatic leader.

In the study of the charismatic voice, it is important to understand that the act of communicating and perceiving distinct leadership traits depends on the communication context between the leader and the other individuals. As Lewin (1952) observed, leaders' behavior and their forms of expression result from the interaction they have with the environment, and leadership results from the interaction between leaders and their followers in a given culture.

A MODEL OF THE CHARISMA PHENOMENON

Charisma is a set of leadership characteristics, such as vision, emotions, dominance, and personality traits, that are displayed through either the "charisma of the mind" (leaders' verbal behaviors and written texts that convey the strength of idea and vision through verbal behavior), the "charisma of the body" (the leader's nonverbal behaviors such as voice, facial expression, gesture, posture), or both. Charisma of the mind and charisma of the body are perceived in specific contexts of communication and are responsible for distinguishing the leader from other individuals in social groups. For example, the words from a text of one of Gandhi's speeches represent his charisma of the mind, and his facial expressions and postures are elements of the expression of his charisma of the body. This framework constitutes the model of charisma developed by Signorello and Poggi (Signorello et al. 2011; 2012a; 2012b; D'Errico et al. 2013; Signorello 2014a), all of which was developed from Poggi's theory of persuasion (2005).

A Charisma of the Mind

Charisma of the mind is one of the two elements of the expression of internal qualities of charismatic leadership that communicates thought, a leader's actions, and the role of a visionary to reach the masses. In order to communicate visionary traits, the leader can use written and spoken language, the *logos*, in Aristotle's sense (Aristotle 1991). In the process of persuasion, the leader uses charisma of the mind that uses discourse, logic, and reason. Shamir et al. (1993; 1998) emphasize the importance of symbolic language, labels, and metaphors for leaders' speeches. Rhetoric and the use and effect of metaphor are among the typical ways in which charisma of the mind expresses leaders' internal traits.

Literature about the charisma of the mind utilizes Gandhi's leadership as an explicit example of the expression of internal charismatic traits through charisma of the mind. In the literature his leadership is defined as "rhetoric" in a declamatory sense (Bligh and Robinson 2010), and Gandhi as a person has been described as a fundamentally shy individual who did not possess the typical qualities of an orator (Rudolph and Rudolph 1983). These results theoretically demonstrate the independence of the two charismas: a leader can be gifted with only charisma of the mind and still be perceived as charismatic.

Charisma of the Body

Even if the semantic content of Gandhi's message was a fundamental component of the impact of his leadership among the masses, and therefore in the leader-follower relationship, the case of Gandhi's charisma cannot be simplified as if it were suffering from the absence of physical qualities or personality in the message's manner of delivery, as stated by Bligh and Robinson (2010) and by Rudolph and Rudolph (1983). Gandhi's charisma would probably have a major component in his charisma of the mind but the perceived charisma from his use of nonverbal behavior would constitute what we define the charisma of the body.

Charisma of the body is the other element of expression of internal qualities of charismatic leaders and is communicated through nonverbal behaviors: vocalizations, facial expressions, gesture, head movements, gaze, posture. Leaders use these behaviors for shaping, expressing, and sharing their message and emotions during their speeches. In *De Oratore* (1967), Cicero wrote that the persuasive orator must arouse emotions from the audience because many people may not be persuaded by rational speech, such as occurs in political oratory. Boss (1976) recognized the crucial importance of nonverbal behavior in the process of the perception of charisma, explaining that the "charismatic leader" is someone who possesses extraordinary skills in expression.

For the charisma of the body, the specific characteristics of the charismatic leader are divided into *pathos* and *ethos*. The *pathos* is the orator's use of emotive values in relation to the audience (Aristotle 1991). Charismatic leaders are gifted with a great degree of emotional intelligence, meaning that they have the ability to feel emotions, transmit them, and be empathetic to the emotions of others. In the process of persuasion, orators manipulate the audience's emotions to persuade them to adhere to their goals.

Ethos communicates the orator's authority (Aristotle 1991). Persuasion in political discourse also occurs by leading followers to share certain beliefs. In order to do so, the source of the belief—that is, the charismatic leader—must be considered as a reliable source (Castelfranchi and Falcone 2000). From the followers' point of view, the leader must have at least three characteristics in a political rhetoric situation. These are the three subdivisions of *ethos*: *benevolence*, a tendency to act in the public's best interest; *competence*, the ability to plan and predict; and *dominance*, the ability to impose oneself against competition (Poggi 2005; Poggi et al. 2011). In political rhetoric, leader A is perceived as a source of benevolence (*ethos benevolence*) when followers B think that A's goal is to adopt and accomplish the B's goals, without competing against them (Poggi 2005). Leader A is perceived as a competent source (*ethos competence*) when followers B believe that A has the power necessary for accomplishing his or her goals, which include the B's goals (Poggi 2005). Leader A is perceived as a dominant source (*ethos dominance*) when transmitting a dominant personality through strong motivation as well as character, strength, and persistence (Poggi 2005).

The Description of the Charismatic Leader's Traits

A leader's type of charisma is constituted by the combination of psychological traits that distinguish their charisma of the mind and charisma of the body. Leadership traits may be specific to a certain culture or universal among several cultures. According to Den Hartog et al. (1999), at least nine traits perceived in charismatic leadership are universally endorsed (*motive arouser, foresight, encouraging, communicative, trustworthy, dynamic, positive, confidence builder, motivational*) and at least ten traits are culture-specific (*enthusiastic, risk-tasking, ambitious, self-effacing, unique, self-sacrificial, sincere, sensitive, compassionate, willful*). Den Hartog et al. (1999) also argue that universally underlying internal traits can take on a different expression from one culture to another. If traits and types of charisma fit listeners' prototypes of good and reliable leadership, the leader will be recognized as the group's leader (see also Offermann et al. 1994; Foti and Luch 1992).

The MASCharP: Multidimensional Adjective-Based Scale of Others' Charisma Perception

Through an empirical and nonbiased approach, Signorello and collaborators (Signorello et al. 2012b; D'Errico et al. 2013; Signorello 2014a; Dastur 2016; Vessalinova and Signorello, 2017) collected positive and negative traits of charisma in several languages to develop the Multidimensional Adjective-based Scale of others' Charisma Perception (MASCharP), a perceptual tool to be used in research on the perception of charismatic traits from individuals' perceivable behaviors, such as vocalizations in political speech. This approach entailed three experimental phases.

Phase 1
The first phase involved the collection of lexical and semantic descriptions of charismatic traits communicated through an individual's perceivable behaviors, from speakers of the studied languages. This collection included adjectives that describe charismatic as well as noncharismatic prototypes of leadership.

Hundreds of adjectives used for describing a charismatic leader were identified in these investigations. The languages of this study were American English, American Spanish, European Spanish, French, Italian, Brazilian Portuguese, Japanese, Swedish, Korean, Mandarin Chinese, and Bulgarian. This study involved several cultures from countries in close geographic proximity (France, Italy, Spain, Sweden, and Bulgaria) and countries at larger geographical distance (Brazil, America, Japan, China, and South Korean).

Phase 2

The second phase involved dimensions of theoretical classification of the adjectives gathered. As in Di Blas and Forzi (1998), the adjectives were selected by their frequency of usage. Only the most frequently used terms that are representative and descriptive of charismatic traits in the participants' language were retained. In the first stage of organization, adjectives with a frequency greater than one were retained, indicating a cognitive commonality between at least two individuals who agree on a semantic-representational connection that designates the adjective as a trait of charisma.

The adjectives used most frequently to describe charisma were then categorized in dimensions that were deduced from aspects of the persuasive process discussed earlier. The data were then organized according to semantic proximity, as in the case of Saucier (2009) and Di Blas and Forzi (1998), corresponding to the dimensions of Poggi's theory of persuasion (Poggi 2005).

This selection was designed to evaluate whether cultural distance provokes a different attribution of charismatic traits. The results show that speakers' spoken language and culture act as filters in the attribution of a leader's traits. The selection of adjectives and dimensional classification constitute the MASCharP. Two examples of the MASCharP for American English (Table 9.1) and French (Table 9.2) are presented here.

Phase 3

The third phase involved the use of MASCharP to create a psychometric tool for measuring the perception of charisma. Each adjective from MASCharP can be evaluated with a Likert scale (Likert 1932). This tool can be used in research on the perception of the traits of charismatic leaders through all perceivable human behaviors and has been already used in several studies to measure the type and degree of charisma conveyed by voice (Signorello et al. 2012a; 2012b; D'Errico et al. 2012; D'Errico et al. 2013; Signorello 2014a).

Biological Functions
of the Charismatic Voice

The key to understanding the biological function of the charismatic voice is studying the status of the vocal pitch (fo; the acoustic measure related to the rate of vocal fold vibration that determines the perceived pitch of the voice; Kreiman and Sidtis 2011). fo is a prominent acoustic parameter in the perception of biological information about the speaker. Human and nonhuman vocalizers utilize fo to signal size and potential threat to the receiver (Ohala 1982; 1983; 1984; 1994; 1996).

Listeners associate perceived vocal pitch with primary and secondary meanings (Ohala 1982; 1983; 1984; 1994; 1996). Low fo and vocal tract resonances convey a primary impression of a relatively large body size and a secondary impression of a dominant

Table 9.1 MASCharP American English

Dimension	Positive Charisma	Negative Charisma
Pathos	caring, passionate, kind, enthusiastic, understanding	rude, mean, cold, unkind, egotistical
Ethos Benevolence	extroverted, optimistic, trustworthy, outspoken, friendly, genuine, sociable	introverted, pessimistic, dishonest, selfish, hostile, aloof
Ethos Competence	intelligent, witty, humble, brave, determined, bold, respectful, assertive, well-spoken	ignorant, stubborn, closed-minded, arrogant, reserved
Ethos Dominance	dynamic, confident, energetic, strong, leader, engaging, persuasive	aggressive, angry, apathetic, shy, weak, overbearing, dull, obnoxious, intimidating
Effects of emotional induction	charming, funny, attractive, humorous, interesting, relatable, personable	boring, annoying, uninteresting, depressing

Positive and negative traits of charisma. American English participants.

Table 9.2 MASCharP French

Dimension	Positive Charisma	Negative Charisma
Pathos	passionné, empathique, enthousiasmant, rassurant	froid, indifférent
Ethos Benevolence	extraverti, positif, spontané, fiable, honnête, juste, sociable, accommodant, fait sentir l'autre important	non fiable, malhonnête, égocentrique, individualiste, introverti
Ethos Competence	visionnaire, intelligent, perspicace, organisé, créatif, sage, déterminé, résolu, entreprenant, expansif, sincère, clair, communicatif, séducteur, compétent, innovateur	incompétent, désorganisé, incertain, faux, incompréhen-sible, menaçant, prudent
Ethos Dominance	dynamique, vif, courageux, sûr de soi, fort, énergique, leader, autoritaire, captivant, persuasif, convaincant	calme, apathique, faible, conformiste, non influent, inquiétant
Effects of emotional induction	charmant, attrayant, sympathique, séduisant, envoûtant, éloquent, influent	ennuyant

Positive and negative traits of charisma. French participants.

Source: Signorello (2014a, 107).

and threatening vocalizer with an aggressive behavior. High fo and resonances convey a primary impression of a smaller body size with a secondary meaning of a subordinate, nonthreatening vocalizer seeking cooperation from the receiver. For example, individuals who characterize their vocal behavior by lower fo, low resonance, tightly spaced formant value and narrower pitch range are perceived as a physically and socially dominant individuals.

Vocal pitch therefore significantly influences the selection of a group leader. Male and female political leaders with low-pitched voices are more likely to be selected as leaders and be more successful in obtaining positions of leadership (Klofstad et al. 2012). Speaker-leaders who wish to communicate dominant traits must also modify their fo based on the listeners' dominance (Puts et al. 2007) as well as on the more generally based on the social status of the listeners (Signorello 2014a). When a male speaker interacts with a male listener, an adjustment of fo according to the perception of the listener's social status is made: if the male speaker is considered dominant, he will tend to lower his fo when addressing a listener whom he considers physically and socially submissive (Puts et al. 2007).

This data show that female and male speakers use lower pitched voices during the communication context of a formal conference addressed to other leaders (CON) (see Table 9.3). Formal conferences could be described as risky for the leadership. Even if the leader status has already been acquired, speaker-leaders need to be perceived as

Table 9.3 Average fundamental frequency (fO) values of charismatic voices in different communication contexts.

| Speaker | Gender | Language | Average fO (Hertz) | | | |
			MON	CON	INT	Kruskal–Wallis
Clinton	F		218	188	175	$H(2)=196.69$, p<.001
Fiorina	F		206	186	148	$H(2)=169.23$, p<.001
Obama	M	American English	217	182	112	$H(2)=317.88$, p<.001
de Magistris	M	Italian	182	147	130	$H(2)=531.81$, p<.001
Veltroni	M		199	166	110	$H(2)=855.29$, p<.001
Hollande	M	French	183	142	111	$H(2)=373.54$, p<.001
Sarkozy	M		190	184	125	$H(2)=229.47$, p<.001
da Silva	M	Brazilian Portuguese	176	141	100	$H(2)=700.26$, p<.001
Serra	M		165	114	122	$H(2)=1053$, p<.001
Across speakers Average fO			193	164	127	

MON (monologue addressed to the followers), CON (monologue addressed to other politicians), INT (interview addressed to an interviewer). All speakers. fO estimated in Hertz. Kruskal–Wallis nonparametric tests H tests (Kruskal and Wallis, 1952)

charismatic and persuade peers in helping them achieve further goals. So, the audience in the COM communication context does fundamentally contribute to the effectiveness of leadership. During CON, leaders use a lower fo because of the social status and gender of the audience: the audience members are mostly male leaders from other social groups or subgroups.

The Vocis Variatio Delectat Strategy

Signorello and collaborators (Signorello and Demolin 2013; Signorello 2014b; Signorello and Rhee 2016; Rhee and Signorello 2016) studied the adaptation of voice fundamental frequency (fo) and voice intensity (intensity; the acoustic measure of the sound power of voice that determines the perceived loudness of the voice; Kreiman and Sidtis 2011) by speaker-leaders in different communication contexts during which they convey their charisma types and traits. This vocal strategy is called *vocis variatio delectat*, in which speakers-leaders use a range of fo and intensity in their speech that is proportional to the communication context (language used, culture, diversity of the audience, audience's social status) in order to convey charisma and persuade a majority of their listeners. Using voice range profiles, which help in mapping voice acoustical range and dynamics of speakers' fo and intensity during speech, we studied the vocal behavior of charismatic leaders from several cultures and languages, throughout different communication contexts (intrasubjects) and among different speakers (intersubjects). Previously, the use of voice range profiles has been restricted to nonspontaneous recordings of pathological voice (e.g., Baken and Orlikoff 2000), singing voice (e.g., Lamarche et al. 2009), or acting voice (e.g., Emerich et al. 2005).

As shown in the voice range profiles illustrated in Figures 9.1a, 9.2a, 9.3a, 9.4a, 9.5a, 9.6a, 9.7a, 9.8a, and 9.9a, speaker-leaders of both genders, speaking different languages (American English, French, Italian, and Brazilian Portuguese), used a wide range of fo and intensity in their formal monologues addressed to potential followers (MON). This type of formal monologue is very risky for leadership status because listeners participating in the communication have the power to elect or refuse the leader, at least in democratic groups. In this context, emotional states and persuasive strategies used by the speaker-leader to convey beliefs and achieve goals have a high psychological activation. The wide vocal range used by these speaker-leaders is an expression of social attractiveness and dominance, used to fit different expectations of how leaders sound. Therefore, leaders use greater fo range to reach a diverse audience (based on gender, age, social status, ethnicity, education). Lower fo is used to convey dominance and attractiveness (as also shown by Collins 2000; Feinberg et al. 2006) to both sexes (e.g., Collins 2000) and to species (e.g., Ohala 1984). Higher fo is used to convey competence, reassurance, calmness, benevolence (Signorello 2014a), and submission (Ohala 1983; 1984; 1994; 1996).

The voice range profiles represented in Figures 9.1b, 9.2b, 9.3b, 9.4b, 9.5b, 9.6b, 9.7b, 9.8b, and 9.9b show the voice acoustic behavior during the communication context of a formal

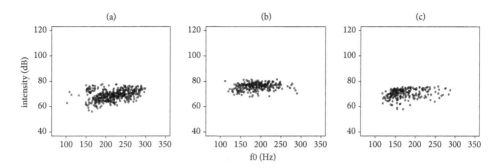

FIGURE 9.1 Voice range profile of the American English speaker Hillary Clinton. Contexts of communication: a) MON, b) CON, and c) INT. X-axis: voice fundamental frequency (fo) in Hertz (Hz). Y-axis: voice intensity (intensity) in decibels (dB). Acoustic measurement from /a/ vowels.

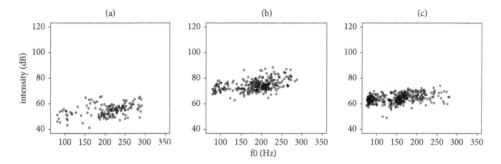

FIGURE 9.2 Voice range profile of the American English speaker Carly Fiorina. Contexts of communication: a) MON, b) CON, and c) INT. X-axis: voice fundamental frequency (fo) in Hertz (Hz). Y-axis: voice intensity (intensity) in decibels (dB). Acoustic measurement from/a/vowels.

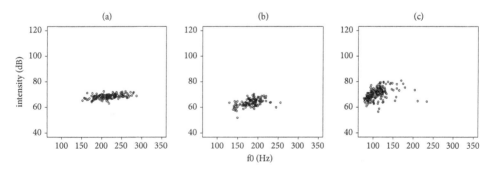

FIGURE 9.3 Voice range profile of the American English speaker Barack Obama. Contexts of communication: a) MON, b) CON, and c) INT. X-axis: voice fundamental frequency (fo) in Hertz (Hz). Y-axis: voice intensity (intensity) in decibels (dB). Acoustic measurement from/a/ vowels.

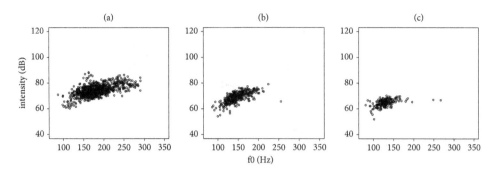

FIGURE 9.4 Voice range profile of the Italian speaker Luigi de Magistris. Contexts of communication: a) MON, b) CON, and c) INT. X-axis: voice fundamental frequency (fo) in Hertz (Hz). Y-axis: voice intensity (intensity) in decibels (dB). Acoustic measurement from/a/vowels.

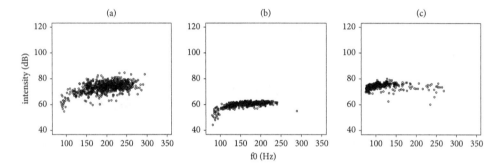

FIGURE 9.5 Voice range profile of the Italian speaker Walter Veltroni. Contexts of communication: a) MON, b) CON, and c) INT. X-axis: voice fundamental frequency (fo) in Hertz (Hz). Y-axis: voice intensity (intensity) in decibels (dB). Acoustic measurement from/a/vowels.

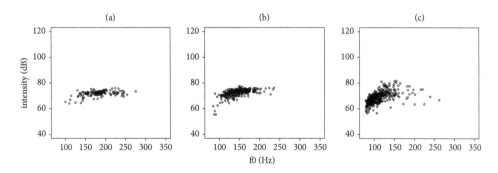

FIGURE 9.6 Voice range profile of the French speaker François Hollande. Contexts of communication: a) MON, b) CON, and c) INT. X-axis: voice fundamental frequency (fo) in Hertz (Hz). Y-axis: voice intensity (intensity) in decibels (dB). Acoustic measurement from/a/vowels.

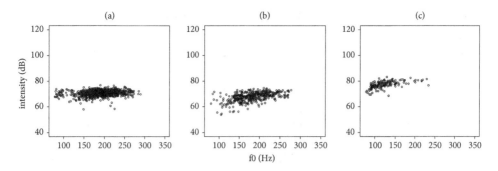

FIGURE 9.7 Voice range profile of the French speaker Nicolas Sarkozy. Contexts of communication: a) MON, b) CON, and c) INT. X-axis: voice fundamental frequency (fo) in Hertz (Hz). Y-axis: voice intensity (intensity) in decibels (dB). Acoustic measurement from/a/vowels.

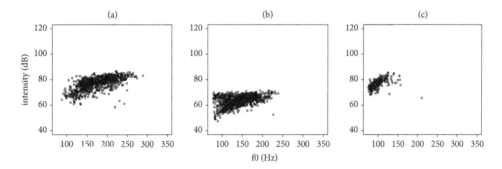

FIGURE 9.8 Voice range profile of the Brazilian Portuguese speaker Luiz Inácio Lula da Silva. Contexts of communication: a) MON, b) CON, and c) INT. X-axis: voice fundamental frequency (fo) in Hertz (Hz). Y-axis: voice intensity (intensity) in decibels (dB). Acoustic measurement from/a/vowels.

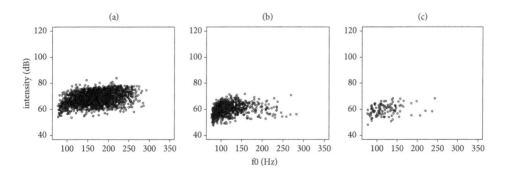

FIGURE 9.9 Voice range profile of the Brazilian Portuguese speaker José Serra. Contexts of communication: a) MON, b) CON, and c) INT. X-axis: voice fundamental frequency (fo) in Hertz (Hz). Y-axis: voice intensity (intensity) in decibels (dB). Acoustic measurement from/a/vowels.

conference addressed to other leaders (CON) wherein speaker-leaders use a significantly reduced vocal range of fo and intensity, compared to the previous communication context. As shown in Table 9.3, another important difference of this communication context from the MON communication context is the average fo. As stated earlier, speaker-leaders who wish to convey traits of dominance must also modulate their fo according to the listener (Puts et al. 2007) and more generally according to the social status of the listeners who make up the audience. In order to be more dominant during this communication context the speaker-leaders must lower their vocal pitch.

Finally, the voice range profiles illustrated in Figures 9.1c, 9.2c, 9.3c, 9.4c, 9.5c, 9.6c, 9.7c, 9.8c, and 9.9c show the vocal extension of voice in informal nonpolitical speech. All speaker-leaders use a significantly narrower range of fo and intensity during the communication context of an informal interview addressed to an interviewer (INT). The informal interview was used as a control condition because the persuasive strategies are significantly different from those used in the contexts illustrated earlier. By not having to strain their voice for persuasive purposes or arouse emotional states in listeners (as well as to avoid vocal fatigue), the speaker-leaders use their normal fo and intensity frequencies and ranges.

The statistical comparative analysis of speaker-leaders' voice range profiles in different communication contexts combined with the qualitative analysis of the voice range profiles demonstrates that the speakers' vocal range is significantly different from one context to another. Intersubject, cross-cultural similarity in vocal behavior confirms the biological functions of the use and perception of vocal fo and therefore the cross-cultural nature of the *vocis variatio delectat* strategy. Speaker-leaders use a vocal profile adapted to the communication context and to their persuasion goals, in order to dominate and please listeners.

The Influence of Vocal Pitch on the Perception of Charismatic Traits

In several studies, vocal pitch (the perceptual correlate of vocal fundamental frequency; Kreiman and Sidtis 2011) has emerged as a vocal feature that serves as an important biological cue that signals social and physical dominance (e.g., Ohala 1982; 1983; 1984; 1994; 1996; Puts et al. 2007), conveys leadership (Klofstad et al. 2012; Anderson and Klofstad 2012), and that influences the choice of a leader (Tigue et al. 2012). Signorello and collaborators (Signorello et al. 2012b; D'Errico et al. 2013; Signorello 2014a) studied the influence of the average vocal pitch as well as the modulation of vocal pitch in the perception of more or less dominant leadership. These studies are characterized by their cross-cultural approach to the perception of vocal pitch, testing its biological validity.

In the first study (Signorello et al. 2012b), the voice stimuli of an Italian speaker-leader (politician Umberto Bossi) were manipulated according to their frequency and delexicalized by low-pass filtering to render the words unintelligible, while preserving vocal pitch contour and sentence prosody. French and Italian subjects then listened to these stimuli to evaluate the speaker's traits of charismatic leadership conveyed by the voice. The results show a significant negative correlation between the perception of the *authoritarian-threatening* type of charisma (the more dominant type of charismatic leadership) and the average vocal pitch ($r = -.19$, $p < .05$), a wider vocal pitch range ($r = -.18$, $p < .05$), and a higher maximum vocal pitch ($r = -.18$, $p < .05$) (Signorello 2014a, 168). This means that low frequencies of vocal pitch and a narrow pitch range achieve the perception of one of the more dominant charismatic leaders. Meanwhile, the *benevolent-competent* type of leadership (a less dominant type of charismatic leadership) is significantly and positively correlated to an increase of the average vocal pitch ($r = .52$, $p < .01$), the minimum vocal pitch ($r = .49$, $p < .01$), the maximum vocal pitch ($r = .55$, $p < .01$), and the vocal pitch range ($r = .53$, $p < .01$). This implies that a high average vocal pitch and a wide vocal pitch range condition a listener to hear such voices as attributes of a less dominant charismatic leader.

This study was repeated (D'Errico et al. 2013; Signorello 2014a) with two other speaker-leaders (François Hollande, French, and Luigi de Magistris, Italian). French and Italian listeners perceived less dominant charismatic leadership (benevolent-competent) when the leaders had a high vocal pitch (averages: 200 Hz for French listeners; 212 Hz for Italians listeners) and a wide vocal pitch range (16 semitones for French listeners; 12 semitones for Italian listeners). In this second study on the process of choosing a leader, Italian participants chose an authoritarian-threatening type of charisma as the greatest influence on their voting preference ($r = .61$, $p < .0001$), whereas French participants chose the proactive-attractive ($r = .46$, $p < .001$) and benevolent-competent ($r = .41$, $p = .004$) (less dominant) types of charisma. This could be explained by the pitch range the leaders used. The modulation of vocal pitch through a wide versus narrow vocal pitch range conveyed not only dominance and attractiveness (which are based on lower vocal pitch frequency), but also competence.

LANGUAGE AND CULTURAL FUNCTIONS OF THE CHARISMATIC VOICE

The Vocis Climax Strategy

In rhetoric, speech arguments are often sequentially organized by the orator in propositions of growing importance, from the beginning of the speech to the end. This rhetorical figure of *climax* consists of delivering words, sentences, and arguments in increasing order of duration or importance, with the peak of importance at the end (Reboul 1998). Signorello (2014a) studied the vocal strategy *vocis climax* to describe the progression and culmination of vocal *climax* between charismatic leaders. The strategy allows speakers to amplify the emotional atmosphere between them and the audience with the aim of arousing emotional states to persuade.

Table 9.4 Vocis climax strategy

Speaker	fO			Intensity		
	MON	CON	INT	MON	CON	INT
Clinton	↘*	ns	↘***	ns	ns	↗***
Fiorina	↘*	ns	ns	ns	ns	↗***
Obama	ns	↘*	ns	↗**	↘***	↗***
de Magistris	↗***	↗***	↗**	↘***	↗***	↘***
Veltroni	↗***	↗***	↗**	↘***	ns	ns
Hollande	↘***	ns	ns	↘**	↘***	ns
Sarkozy	↘*	ns	ns	ns	↘*	ns
da Silva	↗***	↗***	↘**	↗***	ns	ns
Serra	ns	↗***	ns	ns	↗***	ns

↗ time-related increasing of the average value of the acoustic parameter. ↘ time-related decreasing of the average value of the acoustic parameter. Formal monologue addressed to followers (MON); Formal conference addressed to other politicians (CON); Informal interview addressed to the interviewer (INT). ns = not significant ($p > .05$); **$p < .01$; ***$p < .001$.

A comparison of speaker-leaders' use of the *vocis climax* demonstrates different strategies among different languages, cultures, and communication contexts. Results illustrated in Table 9.4 show specific cultural and individual-based strategies used by the speakers to adjust fO and intensity frequencies over time. The *vocis climax* strategy is purely dependent on how leaders "learn" how to lead the audience in their own culture. For instance, all speakers besides speakers Serra and Obama significantly adjust the average fO and intensity over time, from the beginning to the end of the speech, in the MON communication context; both Italian speakers (de Magistris and Veltroni) and Brazilian Portuguese speaker da Silva increase it; meanwhile both French speakers (Hollande and Sarkozy) and both American English female speakers (Clinton and Fiorina) decrease it. During communication context CON, all Italian and Brazilian speakers significantly increase fO and intensity over time.

Language-based strategies mostly affect formal speech contexts (MON and CON). The Italian speakers increase their fO over time during every communication context and significantly decrease intensity during MON. The French speakers decrease their fO over time during every communication context and significantly decrease intensity during CON. The Brazilian Portuguese speakers increase their fO over time during every communication context and significantly decrease intensity during MON.

There is a specific distinction in the manipulation of fO and intensity related to speakers' genders from an intralinguistic perspective. Results illustrate that the female American English speakers significantly decrease fO over time during MON, while the male American English speaker Obama shows no significant strategy in this communication context. Inversely, speaker Obama significantly decreases fO during CON, while speakers Clinton and Fiorina show no significant strategy in this communication context.

However, all three American English speakers significantly increase intensity during INT (the control condition).

Perception of Charisma Traits and Types Through Overall Vocal Quality

Along with vocal pitch and loudness, there are several other vocal characteristics that speaker-leaders manipulate in order to persuade listeners. Phonation types (modes of vocal fold vibration), temporal characteristics (phrase length, pausing), and prosodic factors (pitch contour) constitute the overall vocal quality that contributes to the communication of specific leaders' charismatic types and traits and to the emotional arousing in the audience. As stated earlier, the manipulation of these vocal characteristics also belongs to language and culturally specific strategies of charismatic voice manipulation.

Literature on the relationship between vocal characteristics and the perception of charisma shows that speaker-leaders' vocal behavior varies depending on context and time. Touati (1993) found that the voice of France's former president Jacques Chirac was characterized by increased pitch contour and range during the pre-election period, compared to a flatter pitch contour and reduced range in his postelection voice. Rosenberg and Hirschberg (2009) studied the correlation between the perception of charisma through vocal stimuli extracted from both male and female American politicians' monologues. Their results showed that the pitch contour was correlated to the perception of charisma. Similar studies (Biadsy et al. 2007; 2008; Strangert and Gustafson 2008) used the same monologues from American politicians that Rosenberg and Hirschberg (2009) used and asked Swedish, Palestinian Arabic, and American listeners to evaluate charismatic traits from the speech stimuli. These intercultural studies showed that prosodic charismatic correlates of voice can either be shared among cultures or be specific to a single culture. One of the experiments (Biadsy et al. 2007) demonstrated how listeners perceive charismatic traits through voice without their understanding the language of the speaker-leader.[1]

Signorello and collaborators (Signorello et al. 2012a; 2012b; D'Errico et al. 2013; Signorello 2014a) also investigated the influence of vocal quality on perception of charisma to create comprehensive voice quality profiles for several types of charismatic voices by correlating acoustic and perceptual measures of vocal quality to better understand the overall type and specific traits of charisma, the emotional states aroused, and the choice of leader. These profiles take into account the language and culture of the speakers-leaders and listeners to avoid bias.

The results from these studies are illustrated in Tables 9.5–9.7, which present profiles of the *positif-charmant* (positive-charming), *fiable-prudent* (trustable-careful), and *attrayant-passionné* (attractive-passionate) types of charismatic leadership for French listeners. These tables show that a specific vocal pattern can convey different traits and types of a leader's charisma and that two patterns can influence the perception of the same type of characteristic leadership when perceived by different individuals or social

Table 9.5 Charismatic voice profile of the *positif-charmant* (positive-charming) leader

Vocal quality pattern	Type of Charisma	Charismatic traits	Emotional state aroused	Choice of Leader
Average f0 225 Hz, min f0 107 Hz, max f0 270 Hz Wide pitch range (16 ST) Abrupt increasing and decreasing pitch contour movements Loudness relative range 27 dB	Positif	*positif* *enthousiasmant* *juste* *communicatif* *honnête*	ns	French listeners would most likely vote for this type of charismatic leadership (r = 0.77)
Phonation types: Modal voice; Harsh-high (middle-range) parts (f0 250 Hz, HNR 7 dB†); Harsh-low final vowels at the end of sentences (Low f0, HNR 2.9–3.7 dB†) Length ∼ 4 s	Charmant	*charmant* *captivant* *creatif*	ns	French listeners would probably vote for this type of charismatic leadership (r = 0.39)

Vocal quality pattern, type of charisma perceived, principal traits of charisma elicited, emotional state aroused, and listeners' choice of a leader. Charismatic traits are translated in English from French for illustration purposes. Charisma type and traits resulting from a principal component analysis (PCA) conducted on the 9 adjectives with orthogonal rotation (varimax). The Kayser-Meyer-Olkin measure verified the sampling adequacy for the analysis KMO = 0.77 ('good' according to Kaiser, 1974), and all KMO values for individual items were > 0.60, which is well above the acceptable limit of 0.5. Bartlett's test of sphericity, (x^2(136) = 36, p<.0001), indicated that correlations between items were sufficiently large for PCA. The items that cluster on the same components suggest that the first component, Positif charisma explained the 46% of the variance; Charmant charisma (or Factor 2), explained the 27% of the variance. Positif charisma, subscale of the overall charisma database, had high reliabilities, Cronbach's α = 0.91. Charmant charisma, subscale of the overall charisma database, had medium reliabilities, Cronbach's α = 0.76. However, the adjectives *charmant* (α = 0.57) and *captivant* (α = 0.58) had relatively low reliability. †Value calculated on /a/ vowels; ns = not significant.

groups. These charisma types are a structured composition of several traits of charisma from the dimensions composing the MASCharP (see Tables 9.1 and 9.2).

Tables 9.5 shows that voices characterized by a wide pitch range, from very low to very high frequencies, abrupt pitch contour movements, harsh or modal phonation,[2] and sentence-final vowels in creaky phonation carry a positive-charming type of charisma. This pattern of vocal quality is more attractive, that is, it influences more French listeners choice, if it is the positive dimension, composed by adjectives like *positif, enthousiasmant, juste, communicative*, and *honnête*, that is perceived (see Table 9.5).

A vocal pattern characterized by a narrow pitch range that spans from low to high frequencies (but not as high as the two vocal patterns described in Tables 9.5), smooth pitch contour movements, harsh-low, harsh-mid, or modal phonation types,[2] and a medium duration communicates the trustable-careful type of charismatic leadership

Table 9.6 Charismatic voice profile of the *fiable-prudent* (trustable-careful) leader

Vocal quality pattern	Type of Charisma	Charismatic traits	Emotional state aroused	Choice of Leader
Average f0 152 Hz, min f0 95 Hz, max f0 210 Hz Medium pitch range (13 ST) Moderate falling pitch contour movement Loudness relative range 26 dB	Fiable	*juste* *captivant* *sage* *fiable*$ *non égocentrique*$	ns	French listeners would most likely vote for this type of charismatic leadership (r = 0.64)
Phonation types: Modal voice, phrase-final harsh-high (middle-range) vowel with low hoarseness (HNR 9.49 dB†) Length ~ 3 s, Long interwords pauses (~1 s)	Prudent	*prudent* *envoutant* *comprehensible*$	ns	French listeners would probably vote for this type of charismatic leadership (r = 0.43)

Vocal pattern, listener language-culture, type of charisma perceived, principal traits of charisma elicited, emotional state aroused, and listeners' choice of leader. Charismatic traits are translated in English from French for illustration purposes. Charisma type and traits resulting from a principal component analysis (PCA) conducted on the adjectives with orthogonal rotation (varimax). The Kayser-Meyer-Olkin measure verified the sampling adequacy for the analysis KMO = 0.74 ('good' according to Kaiser, 1974), and all KMO values for individual items were > 0.59, which is well above the acceptable limit of 0.5. Bartlett's test of sphericity, ($\chi^2(67) = 28$, p<.0001), indicated that correlations between items were sufficiently large for PCA. The items that cluster on the same components suggest that the first component, Fiable charisma explained the 36% of the variance; Prudent charisma, explained the 27% of the variance. Fiable charisma, subscale of the overall charisma database, had medium reliabilities (Cronbach's α = 0.77). However, the adjectives *non fiable and égocentrique* had relatively low reliability (both Cronbach's α = 0.60). Prudent charisma, subscale of the overall charisma database, all had medium reliabilities (Cronbach's α = 0.75). $Fiable, non égocentrique, and comprehensible are reverse items (original rated adjective are *non fiable, égocentrique,* and *non comprehensible*). †Value calculated on /a/ vowels; ns = not significant.

(Table 9.6), which reflects the image of a leader described by the participants through adjectives such as *juste, captivant, sage, fiable,* and *non egocentrique.* This type of leadership communicates appearance of a leader enough to share to access to vital resources with other individuals. This pattern of vocal quality is more attractive if it is the *fiable* dimension that is perceived (see Table 9.6).

Finally, whenever political leaders use voice of the quality patterns featuring lower average vocal pitch, narrower pitch range, increasing and suddenly falling pitch contour movements, modal phonation types,[2] and a short duration of the speech unit, communicates the attractive-passionate type of charismatic leadership (Table 9.7), which reflects the image of a leader described by the participants through adjectives such as *attrayant, sympathique, enthousiasmant, accommodant* and also *passionné, communicatif, intelligent,*

Table 9.7 Charismatic voice profile of the *attrayant-passionné* (attractive-passionate) leader

Vocal quality pattern	Type of Charisma	Charismatic traits	Emotional state aroused	Choice of Leader
Average f0 138 Hz, min f0 96 Hz, f0 189 Hz Medium-low pitch range (11 ST) Increasing pitch contour at the beginning of the tonal unit and falling pitch contour at the end	Attrayant	*attrayant sympathique enthousiasmant accommodant sincere*	ns	French listeners would most likely vote for this type of charismatic leadership (r = 0.90)
Loudness relative range 27 dB Phonation type: Modal voice Length ~ 2 s	Passionné	*passionné communicatif intelligent clair*	ns	French listeners would probably vote for this type of charismatic leadership (r = 0.48)

Vocal quality pattern, type of charisma perceived, principal traits of charisma elicited, emotional state aroused, and listeners' choice of a leader. Charismatic traits are translated in English from French for illustration purposes. Charisma type and traits resulting from a principal component analysis (PCA) conducted on the 9 adjectives with orthogonal rotation (varimax). The Kayser-Meyer-Olkin measure verified the sampling adequacy for the analysis KMO = 0.89 ('great' according to Kaiser, 1974), and all KMO values for individual items were > 0.80, which is well above the acceptable limit of 0.5. Bartlett's test of sphericity, $(\chi^2(140) = 36, p<.0001)$, indicated that correlations between items were sufficiently large for PCA. The items that cluster on the same components suggest that the first component, Attrayant charisma explained the 42% of the variance; Passionné Charisma explained the 35% of the variance. Attrayant charisma, subscale of the overall charisma database, had high reliabilities (Cronbach's $\alpha = 0.90$). Passionné charisma, subscale of the overall charisma database, had medium reliabilities (Cronbach's $\alpha = 0.71$). †Value calculated on /a/ vowels. ns = not significant.

clair, and *sincere*. This type of leadership communicates the appearance of a leader attractive enough to excite the follower while effectively communicating his intelligence through eloquence in speech. This pattern of vocal quality is most attractive whenever the *attrayant* dimension is perceived (see Table 9.7).

CONCLUSIONS

Individuals' desire to become a social group's leader is dictated by two factors: the primary need to have easy access to resources (for example, food and mating) and, in human social groups, the cultural need to access leadership status and have social power to be distinguishable from other individuals. Leaders express their charismatic leadership through vocalizations, whose acoustic features and perceptual responses originate from both biological predisposition and cultural strategies of expression and communication.

Understanding the phenomenon of charisma (the set of leadership characteristics, such as vision, emotions, dominance and personality) as well as its expression (through the charisma of the mind and the charisma of the body) means taking into account the biological needs of the aspiring leaders and how they adapt their perceivable behaviors to the cultural expectations in which charisma is manifested.

Political leaders manipulate the sound of their voices to convey types and specific traits of charisma to arouse emotional states in listeners, make them share beliefs, and persuade them in their choice of leader. Listeners use speakers' perceived voice characteristics to assess leadership quality and to choose which leader to follow. Acoustic characteristics of leaders' voices are revealed to have two different functions in the perception of charisma: the modulation of vocal pitch reflects individuals' biological needs to become leaders, and aspiring charismatic leaders shape their vocal quality and style according to specific cultural expectations.

Vocal pitch has been found to be a potential cross-cultural signal of charisma that leaders use to convey their leadership status, and listeners exploit to assess good and reliable leadership. Speaker-leaders adapt vocal pitch to communication contexts: the more diverse the audience (in terms of gender, age, social status, educational background, etc.), the more variation in vocal pitch average and range. Lower vocal pitch and narrow vocal pitch range are used by the speaker-leaders when addressing an audience of similar social status as them. Certain vocal quality patterns are also used by the speaker-leaders to fit listener expectations about the vocal style that best conveys charisma in a given language and culture. Authoritarian-threatening and proactive-attractive charisma can be conveyed by the same vocal pattern but are perceptually distinguished in different languages and cultures (see Tables 9.5 and 9.6). Competent-benevolent charismatic leadership can be conveyed by several vocal quality patterns (see Table 9.7). In this way, language and cultural expectations influence the choice of the leader.

Future research about charismatic voice will include more studies investigating voices of women in leadership to understand how female speaker-leaders manipulate their voices in order to find a cultural balance between being perceived as more or less dominant. Furthermore, how do women manipulate vocal quality to persuade and to fit cultural expectations of a female leader's vocal behaviors? Research will also focus on vocalizations in nonhuman primate leaders to study the biological function of the voice of leaders from a cross-species perspective. For example, do nonhuman primates manipulate fo to convey leadership status and dominate other individuals in a way similar to that of humans? And also, does their vocal behavior change from the period before, during, and finally after being a group's leader?

ACKNOWLEDGMENTS

I am deeply thankful to Jody Kreiman (University of California, Los Angeles), Didier Demolin (Université Sorbonne Nouvelle and CNRS), Bruce R. Gerratt (University of California, Los Angeles), Isabella Poggi (Università degli Studi Roma Tre), Nathalie Henrich (Université de Grenoble Alpes and CNRS), Zhaoyan Zhang (University of California, Los Angeles), Francesca

D'Errico (Università Telematica Internazionale Uninettuno, Italy), and Paolo Mairano (Università degli Studi di Torino, Italy). I also would like to thank the editors of the present handbook, Nina Eidsheim (Université de Lille) and Katherine Meizel (Bowling Green State University).

NOTES

1. A portion of the listeners was also a speaker of English as second language and they were asked to rate American speakers. This procedure may have led to biased scores because of the listeners' comprehension of the semantic message.
2. See Esling (2006) for the phonetic description of specific phonation types.

WORKS CITED

Anderson, R. C., and C. A. Klofstad. 2012. "Preference for Leaders with Masculine Voices Holds in the Case of Feminine Leadership Roles." *PLoS ONE* 7 (12): e51216. http://doi.org/10.1371/journal.pone.0051216.

Aristotle. 1991. *Rhetoric*, translated by George A. Kennedy. Chicago, IL: University of Chicago Press, Acheron Press, Kindle ed.

Baken, R., and R. Orlikoff. 2000. *Clinical Measurement of Speech and Voice*, 2nd rev. ed. San Diego: Singular Publishing Group.

Bass, B. M. 1990. *Bass and Stogdill's Handbook of Leadership: Theory, Research, and Managerial Applications*, 3rd ed. New York: Free Press.

Biadsy, F., J. Hirschberg, A. Rosenberg, and W. Dakka. 2007. "Comparing American and Palestinian Perceptions of Charisma Using Acoustic-Prosodic and Lexical Analysis." In *Proceedings of Interspeech 2007 8th Annual Conference of the International Speech Communication Association*, Antwerp, Belgium, August 27–31, 2007, ISSN 1990-9772, ISCA Archive.

Biadsy, F., A. Rosenberg, R. Carlson, J. Hirschberg, and E. Strangert. 2008. "A Cross-Cultural Comparison of American, Palestinian, and Swedish Perception of Charismatic Speech." In *Proceedings of the 4th Conference on Speech Prosody*, 579–82. Campinas, Brazil. https://www.researchgate.net/publication/251695316_A_Cross-Cultural_Comparison_of_American_Palestinian_and_Swedish_Perception_of_Charismatic_Speech

Bligh, M. C., and J. L. Robinson. 2010. "Was Gandhi 'Charismatic'? Exploring the Rhetorical Leadership of Mahatma Gandhi." *The Leadership Quarterly* 21 (5): 844–55.

Boss, P. 1976. "Essential Attributes of Charisma." *Southern Speech Communication Journal* 41 (3): 300–13.

Castelfranchi, C., and R. Falcone. 2000. "Trust is Much More Than Subjective Probability: Mental Components and Sources of Trust." In *32nd Hawaii International Conference on System Sciences—Mini Track on Software Agents*, 1–10. Maui: Institute of Electrical and Electronics Engineers Press.

Cicero. 1967. *De Oratore*, translated by E. W. Sutton. Cambridge, MA: Harvard University Press.

Collins, S. A. 2000. "Men's Voices and Women's Choices." *Animal Behavior* 60 (6): 773–80.

Darwin, C. 1871. *The Descent of Man, and Selection in Relation to Sex*. London: John Murray.

Dastur, Y. 2016. "Charisma Perception in the Japanese Language." Master's thesis, University of Southern California.

Den Hartog, D. N., R. J. House, P. J. Hanges, S. A. Ruiz-Quintanilla, and P. W. Dorfman. 1999. "Culture Specific and Cross-culturally Generalizable Implicit Leadership Theories: Are Attributes of Charismatic/Transformational Leadership Universally Endorsed?" *The Leadership Quarterly* 10 (2): 219–56.

D'Errico, F., R. Signorello, D. Demolin, and I. Poggi. 2013. "The Perception of Charisma from Voice: A Cross-Cultural Study." In *Proceedings of the 2013 Humaine Association Conference on Affective Computing and Intelligent Interaction*, edited by IEEE Computer Society, 552–7.

D'Errico, F., R. Signorello, and I. Poggi. 2012. "Le Dimensioni del Carisma." In *IX Convegno Annuale dell'Associazione Italiana di Scienze Cognitive—AISC*, edited by M. Cruciani and F. Cecconi, 245–52. Rome: Università di Trento.

Di Blas, L., and M. Forzi. 1998. "The Circumplex Model for Interpersonal Trait Adjectives in Italian." *Personality and Individual Differences* 24 (1): 47–57.

Emerich, K. A., I. R. Titze, J. G. Švec, P. S. Popolo, and G. Logan. 2005. "Vocal Range and Intensity in Actors: A Studio Versus Stage Comparison." *Journal of Voice* 19 (1): 78–83.

Esling, J. 2006. "Voice Quality." In *The Encyclopedia of Language and Linguistics*, 2nd ed., edited by K. Brown, 470–4. Oxford: Elsevier.

Feinberg, D. R., B. C. Jones, M. J. Law Smith, F. R. Moore, L. M. DeBruine, R. E. Cornwell, S. G. Hillier, and D. I. Perrett. 2006. "Menstrual Cycle, Trait Estrogen Level, and Masculinity Preferences in the Human Voice." *Hormones and behavior* 49 (2): 215–22.

Foti, R. J., and C. H. Luch. 1992. "The Influence of Individual Differences on the Perception and Categorization of Leaders." *Leadership Quarterly* 3(1, Spring): 55–66.

Haslam, S. A., S. D. Reicher, and M. J. Platow. 2011. *The New Psychology of Leadership*. Hove, UK: Psychology Press.

Hofstede, G. 1993. "Cultural Constraints in Management Theories." *Academy of Management Executive* 7 (1): 81–94.

Hollander, Edwin P., and James W. Julian. 1970. "Studies in Leader Legitimacy, Influence, and Innovation." *Advances in Experimental Social Psychology* 5(1970): 33–69.

Kaiser, H. F. 1974. "An Index of Factorial Simplicity." *Psychometrika* 39(1): 31–6.

Klofstad, C. A., R. C. Anderson, and S. Peters. 2012. "Sounds Like a Winner: Voice Pitch Influences Perception of Leadership Capacity in Both Men and Women." *Proceedings of the Royal Society B: Biological Sciences* 279 (1738): 2698–704.

Kreiman, J., and D. Sidtis. 2011. *Foundations of Voice Studies: An Interdisciplinary Approach to Voice Production and Perception*. Oxford: Wiley-Blackwell.

Kruskal, W. H., and W. A. Wallis. 1952. "Use of Ranks in One-criterion Variance Analysis." *Journal of the American Statistical Association* 47 (260): 583–621.

Lamarche, A., S. Ternström, and S. Hertegård. 2009. "Not Just Sound: Supplementing the Voice Range Profile with the Singer's Own Perceptions of Vocal Challenges." *Logopedics, Phoniatrics, Vocology* 34 (1): 3–10.

Lewin, K. 1952. *Field Theory in Social Science: Selected Theoretical Papers*. London: Tavistock.

Likert, R. 1932. "A Technique for the Measurement of Attitudes." *Archives of Psychology* 22(140): 1–55.

Offermann, L. R., J. K. Kennedy, and P. W. Wirtz. 1994. "Implicit Leadership Theories: Content Structure, and Generalizability." *Leadership Quarterly* 5 (1): 43–55.

Ohala, J. J. 1982. "The Voice of Dominance." *Journal of the Acoustical Society of America* 72 (S1): S66–S66.

Ohala, J. J. 1983. "Cross-Language Use of Pitch: An Ethological View." *Phonetica* 40 (1): 1–18.

Ohala, J. J. 1984. "An Ethological Perspective on Common Cross-Language Utilization of F0 of Voice." *Phonetica* 41 (1): 1–16.

Ohala, J. J. 1994. "The Frequency Code Underlies the Sound-Symbolic Use of Voice Pitch." In *Sound Symbolism*, edited by Leanne Hinton, Johanna Nichols, and John J. Ohala, 325–47. Cambridge: Cambridge University Press.

Ohala, J. J. 1996. "Ethological Theory and the Expression of Emotion in the Voice." In *Proceedings of the 4th International Conference on Spoken Language Processing* 96 (3): 1812–15.

Poggi, I. 2005. "The Goals of Persuasion." *Pragmatics & Cognition* 13 (2): 297–336.

Poggi, I., F. D'Errico, and L. Vincze. 2011. "Discrediting Moves in Political Debate." In *Proceedings of the Second International Workshop on User Models for Motivational Systems: The affective and the rational routes to persuasion (UMMS 2011) July 11, 2011, Girona, Spain*, edited by P. Ricci-Bitti, 84–99. Heidelberg: Springer.

Puts, D. A., C. R. Hodges, R. A. Cárdenas, and S. J. C. Gaulin. 2007. "Men's Voices as Dominance Signals: Vocal Fundamental and Formant Frequencies Influence Dominance Attributions Among Men." *Evolution and Human Behavior* 28 (5): 340–44.

Raymond, M. 2008. *Cro-magnon toi-même! Petit Guide Darwinien de la vie Quotidienne*. Paris: Seuil.

Reboul, O. 1998. *Introduction à la Rhétorique*. 3rd ed. Paris: Presses Universitaires de France.

Reicher, S., S. A. Haslam, and N. Hopkins. 2005. "Social Identity and the Dynamics of Leadership: Leaders and Followers as Collaborative Agents in the Transformation of Social Reality." *The Leadership Quarterly* 16 (4): 547–68.

Rhee, N., and R. Signorello. 2016. "The Acoustics of Charismatic Voices in Korean Political Speech: A Cross-Gender Study." *Journal of the Acoustical Society of America* 139 (4): 2123–3.

Riggio, R. E., I. Chaleff, and J. Lipman-Blumen. 2008. *The Art of Followership: How Great Followers Create Great Leaders and Organizations*. San Francisco: Jossey-Bass.

Rosenberg, A., and J. Hirschberg. 2009. "Charisma Perception from Text and Speech." *Speech Communication* 51 (7): 640–55.

Rudolph, S. H., and L. I. and Rudolph. 1983. *Gandhi: The Traditional Roots of Charisma*. Chicago: University of Chicago Press.

Saucier, G. 2009. "Semantic and Linguistic Aspects of Personality." In *The Cambridge Handbook of Personality Psychology*, edited by P. J. Corr and G. Matthews, 379–99. Cambridge: Cambridge University Press.

Scherer, K. R. 2010. "Voice Appeal and its Role in Political Persuasion." In *International Workshop on Political Speech*, Rome. http://www.klewel.com/conferences/sspnet-roma-political-2010/.

Shamir, B., R. J. House, and M. B. Arthur. 1993. "The Motivational Effects of Charismatic Leadership: A Self-concept Based Theory." *Organization Science, A Journal of the Institute of Management Sciences* 4 (4): 577.

Shamir, B., E. Zakay, E. Breinin, and M. Popper. 1998. "Correlates of Charismatic Leader Behavior in Military Units: Subordinates' Attitudes, Unit Characteristics, and Superiors' Appraisals of Leader Performance." *Academy of Management Journal* 41 (4): 387–409.

Signorello, R. 2014a. "La Voix Charismatique: Aspects Psychologiques et Caractéristiques Acoustiques." PhD diss., Université de Grenoble, France and Università degli Studi Roma Tre, Italy.

Signorello, R. 2014b. "The Biological Function of Fundamental Frequency in Leaders' Charismatic Voices." *Journal of the Acoustical Society of America* 136,(4): 2295–5.

Signorello, R., and D. Demolin. 2013. "The Physiological Use of the Charismatic Voice in Political Speech." In *Proceedings of the 14th Annual Conference of the International Speech Communication Association (Interspeech)*: 987–91.

Signorello, R., F. D'Errico, I. Poggi, D. Demolin, and P. Mairano. 2012a. "Charisma Perception in Political Speech: A Case Study." In *Proceedings of the VIIth GSCP International Conference: Speech and Corpora*, edited by H. Mello, M. Pettorino, and T. Raso, 343–8. Firenze: Firenze University Press.

Signorello, R., F. D'Errico, I. Poggi, and D. Demolin. 2012b. "How Charisma is Perceived from Speech: A Multidimensional Approach." In *ASE/IEEE International Conference on Social Computing*: 435–40.

Signorello, R., I. Poggi, D. Demolin, and F. D'Errico. 2011. "Il Carisma del Corpo: Caratteristiche Acustiche della Voce Carismatica." In *X Giornate della Ricerca*, Universita degli Studi Roma Tre.

Signorello, R., and N. Rhee. 2016. "The Voice Acoustics of the 2016 United States Presidential Election Candidates: A Cross-Gender Study." *Journal of the Acoustical Society of America* 139 (4): 2123–3.

Strangert, E., and J. Gustafson. 2008. "What Makes a Good Speaker? Subject Ratings, Acoustic Measurements and Perceptual Evaluations." In *Proceedings of the 9th Annual Conference of the International Speech Communication Association (Interspeech 2008)*: 1688–91.

Tigue, C. C., D. J. Borak, J. J. M. O'Connor, C. Schandl, and D. R. Feinberg. 2012. "Voice Pitch Influences Voting Behavior." *Evolution and Human Behavior* 33 (3): 210–16.

Touati, P. 1993. "Prosodic Aspects of Political Rhetoric." In *ESCA Workshop on Prosody*, Lund, Sweden, September 27–29, edited by David House and Paul Touati, ISCA Archive 168–71. University of Lund.

Tuppen, C. 1974. "Dimensions of Communicator Credibility: An Oblique Solution." *Speech Monographs* 41 (3): 253–60.

Vessalinova, N., and Signorello, R. 2017. "A Semantic Comparison of Bulgarian and American English Descriptors of Leaders' Charisma." In *26th Annual Linguistics Symposium at California State University*, Fullerton, CA.

Weber, M. 1920. *The Theory of Social and Economic Organization*. New York: Oxford University Press.

CHAPTER 10

CHALLENGING VOICES

*Relistening to Marshallese Histories
of the Present*

JESSICA A. SCHWARTZ AND APRIL L. BROWN

INTRODUCTION

THE Marshallese Educational Initiative, an Arkansas-based nonprofit founded by the authors of this chapter in 2013, has focused on intercultural pedagogy and outreach with projects such as the Marshallese Oral History Project and Digital Music Collection (MOHP), Nuclear Remembrance Day, and collaborative work with Marshallese college student members of the Manit Club (Culture Club) that emphasize creative "pathways of connection" within their complex diaspora.[1] Such work has necessitated attention to Marshallese voices as central to indigenous epistemologies and as a powerful diagnostic of Marshallese communal health in the transcorporeal sense.[2] As anthropologists of the senses such as Sara Pink, Nadia Seremetakis, and Paul Stoller have noted, a consideration of culturally specific sensorial orientations is important in the communication and representation of knowledge (Pink 2015; Seremetakis 1994; Stoller 1997). The throat, in Marshallese sensorial approach, is the metaphorical seat of the emotions that prompt a feelingful care for others, human and nonhuman. Western acculturated individuals might say that they are "of the same heart or mind" if they feel a certain kindred spirit to someone or our community, but Marshallese have an ideal of being of "one throat" (*burō wōt juon*). Marshallese prize the throat and its resonance in voice as both timbre and a sonorous mediator of their language that vivifies relations of land and lineage, which are connected to their shared cosmological heritage. According to our interlocutors and collaborators, Marshallese voices—shared by Marshallese living in internal and external diaspora in the Republic of the Marshall Islands (RMI), an archipelago of twenty-nine low-lying coral atolls in the central Pacific, or in Springdale, Arkansas, a land-locked state that sits at the crossroads of the Midwestern and Southern United States—make, and in many respects are, the Marshallese story, and forge "pathways of connection" necessary for its continuation.

Contributing to collaborative studies that focus on music in participatory research, such as Samuel Araújo and Vincenzo Cambria's work in the *favelas* of Rio de Janeiro, we work with students to assess the ways in which we can orient our listening practices to Marshallese voices as they sound the challenges of everyday life in a diaspora compelled and sanctioned by centuries of colonial and imperial interventions (Araújo and Cambria 2013; Freire 2010). We consider the vocal mechanism (throat/voice) and how it comes to mark and complicate the political, ecological, and cultural divisions upheld in modernity. The fight to maintain customary practices in response to external domination and control has demanded that Marshallese often nest their customs in a larger cultural dynamic. The voice, being adaptable and flexible, we argue, is one tool Marshallese utilize to innovatively preserve their values and archive their experiences of struggle and success. Voice and the honing of vocally directed listening practices prove to be powerful tools in hearing the Marshallese representational resources that combat the paralytic experiences of disenfranchisement and fear of "culture loss."

We situate the project within the vocal movements of the Marshallese diaspora and present our theoretical orientation that draws from Nina Eidsheim's *voice challenge* activity as a tool in critical voice studies, paired with postcolonial studies focused primarily on the Pacific. Such discourses offer a robust frame for our collaborative work with the Manit Club students, which took shape as a series of conversations and exercises exploring the often messy systemic overlays of the voice, politics, culture, and outreach. These discussions continue, and our initial reflections offer insight into questions about values and violences that, embodied and emplaced, shape everyday life for many Marshallese, and mark their culture (*mantin majel*) as distinct from American culture (*mantin pālle*).[3] Tracing the contemporary moment and development of *mantin majel* through a series of encounters—and modes of countering social, cultural, and historical "nonlistenings" of great consequence—we explore the ways in which these students rethink oral and vocal traditions as historical archives, and listen as they consider the many contingencies that inform the production and reception of Marshallese voices, stories, and their communicative potentialities (Pilzer 2012, 11). Marshallese hear history and culture in the communicative dimensions of the voice. Taking aspects of Marshallese intergenerational knowledge transmission into consideration, we share how the students as well as nuclear survivors participate in the voice challenge by stressing their voices as impacted by historical and cultural conditions that necessitate and afford particular vocal emergences.

THE VOICE THROUGH CONTEMPORARY MUSIC

The song "Mour ilo Springdale" ("Life in Springdale"), released in 2014, paints a picture of the precious and quotidian occurrences in the Marshallese diaspora for residents of Springdale, Arkansas. Life is relatively good, we hear, and there are employment

The Voice Through Contemporary Music

Intro.

Ah, iakwe, iakwe eok ijo, brother. Hello!	Hey, hello, hello there, brother. Hello!
Hello, hello, iakwe, ejet mour?	Hello, hello, hello, how is life?
Emṃan, emṃan, emṃan.	Good, good, good.
Ejjej, eokwe kaṃṃoolol Irooj.	Wow, well give thanks to God.
Aet, aet!	Yes, yes!
Laiō ebwe an lōñ ri-Ṃajeḷ la.	Man there's a lot of Marshallese.
Ebwe an lōñ ri-Ṃajeḷ, ebwe an lōñ.	There's a lot of Marshallese, there's a lot.

Verse I

Mour ilo Springdale elap an emṃan;	Life in Springdale is so much better;
bwe ewor Tyson, George's im Cargill;	Because there is Tyson, George's and Cargill;
Kōkappok jerbal rainin ilju kō–hire;	You look for a job today tomorrow you're hired;
Kōdeḷọñ Walmart, kōlo ri-Ṃajeḷ im	You walk in Walmart, you see Marshallese and
kōba iakwe.	you tell them hello;
Kaṃṃoolol Anij bwe ejjeḷọk jikin emṃan	Give thanks to God for there is no better place
ḷọk jen Springdale in. (repeat)	much better than Springdale. (repeat)

Chorus

Ejjeḷọk jikin emṃan jen	There is no other place much better than in
Springdale;	Springdale;
Mour eo iē emṃan im epidodo;	The life is good and easy;
Eloñ price ko rejjab kanooj in lap;	The prices aren't that expensive;
Jādede otōmjej rej komṃan keemem.	Every Saturday there's always keemem.
Kaṃṃoolol Anij bwe ejjeḷọk jikin emṃan	Give thanks to God for there is no better place
jen Springdale in. (repeat)	than Springdale. (repeat)

"Mour ilo Springdale" ("Life in Springdale") (excerpt)
Music and Lyrics by Michael Bellu[7]

FIGURE 10.1 "Mour ilo Springdale" ("Life in Springdale"), excerpts. Music and Lyrics by Michael Bellu (n.d.).

opportunities at poultry plants, such as Tyson Foods and Georges, unlike in the RMI where the employment rate is consistently over 30 percent (Asian Development Bank 2006, 68; RMI Census 2011).[4] This US mainland city tucked in the corner of northwest Arkansas, where Walmart is headquartered, makes the region a surprisingly cosmopolitan place to live. Walmart is not only stocked with many goods that Marshallese wait for in their homeland, but it serves as a casual meeting place for Marshallese. On the weekends, *keemems* (customary first birthday gatherings) and church bring the close-knit community together in celebration and for worship. These communal spaces are filled with songs that, like "Mour ilo Springdale," challenge any notion of Marshallese cultural stasis. Vocal movements of the diasporic community share lyrics that connect Pacific Island and Southern-Midwest cultures. The musical spaces are equally as capacious, with a Marshallese delivery of words shaping melodic lines over musical accompaniment that resounds a laid-back Pacific-meets-country-western slide guitar twang. Navigating their contemporary moment, Marshallese utilize communication technologies, such as the Internet (SoundCloud and YouTube), to chart the new territories that are increasingly becoming their homes (see Figure 10.1).[5]

In *Routes and Roots: Navigating Caribbean and Pacific Island Literatures*, Elizabeth M. DeLoughrey offers a "tidalectic between sea and land," which emphasizes the interconnections between places rather than their boundaries, a dialectical way of envisioning land/sea, roots/routes (DeLoughrey 2007, 3). DeLoughrey shares with readers the importance of navigation perspectives and charting in Micronesian epistemologies of space and time that counter western notions of oceanic empty space and insularity used to justify colonial and imperial conquest:

> Pacific models of ocean navigation differ from western paradigms because they do not flatten and stabilize space through the bird's eye view of nautical charts. Instead, Pacific navigators have developed a complex system of charting a vessel's movement through space where the voyaging canoe is perceived as stable while the island and the cosmos move toward the traveler (3).

"Mour ilo Springdale" is one song that shares how Marshallese are bounded not by land or culture, but rather by specific constraints located in American ideology that puts money before all else. Anthropologist Peter Rudiak-Gould has explored the ways in which *mantin majel̦* emerged through colonial contacts that necessitated the definition of a Marshallese way of life or, what is often reduced to as "culture," in contrast to the German, Japanese, or American way of life (Rudiak-Gould 2013, 21). He identifies three main interrelated categories of *mantin majel̦*: subsistence ("free of charge" as shown with gifts of food and relating back to the precolonial economy), conviviality (togetherness and sharing), and respect for chiefs and land (23). Interestingly, this unified identity of *mantin majel̦* sits in contrast to *mantin pālle* (American way of life), which is the foreign way—often considered the cause for the denigration of the esteemed *mantin majel̦*. *Manit* is never criticized, and even the Constitution reads tradition as "a sacred heritage, which we pledge ourselves to maintain" (Constitution 1979). The sounds of the Marshallese produced by Marshallese voices come from the part of the body that connects the three categories of *mantin majel̦*: the throat, which like the Western metaphorical conceptualization of the heart, has a deeply ethical function. It takes in the sustenance afforded by subsistence. It provides the mechanism through which the voice is sounded, literally sounding the experience of conviviality. And, through the transmission of knowledge and lineage through oral history, the chiefs and lands are maintained and revered. In sum, the loss of language and voice—a composite orality at the level of the individual—becomes a synecdoche for the social body, a population in decline.

Rehearing what might be thought of as a "tidalectics" of vocal movements, where throat/voice afford a complex visceral charting and navigation of roots/routes in diaspora, we hear two English words marked and nested in each of the two verses padded by the singers' flow: "hire" (verse I) and "price" (verse II), which are used instead of the Marshallese words, etymologically related, that translate to "price, hired and cost" (*wōn̦ea-* and *wōn̦āān*). The words "hire" and "price" are understood in Marshallese through context, but Bellu chooses to use the English words that both sound different and relate to different, albeit connected, activities in Springdale. First you are hired at a poultry plant, and then you are able to afford goods because the prices are low and you have a job. These words are audible markers of such routine activities centered around money and the capitalist economy that forms the center of life in Springdale, forcefully distinguishing this life from what Marshallese pride as their subsistence-based culture. Listening to this song, then, a resource emerges to hear a different way of life in a place that is not one's homeland, specifically in terms of life in the United States when compared with the Marshall Islands. While the song welcomes Marshallese to a good life in Springdale, it maintains that living in Springdale is decidedly *not* the same as living in the Marshall Islands. The juxtaposition is heard in terms of *mantin majeḷ*. Marshallese ancestral connections to their homeland are evidence of the hundreds, and even thousands, of years of labor and care invested in the land. This is not the case in the United States, and as such, things are not free in Springdale, even if the Marshallese make it home through their communal gatherings, practices that respect the *iroij*, or chief, and *Anij* or God, and through preservation of elements of culture, such as the language as exemplified through the lyrics of the song. By emphasizing the terse words "hire" and "price," we are attuned to their out-of-place feeling and the hospitality of the Marshallese language or voice conveying the feeling as such.

Voice as the connective resonant mechanism par excellence helps us work through and understand the Marshallese in diaspora, their methods of maintaining cultural continuity and global connections, and the breadth of imperial violence that is often reduced to "the idiosyncrasies of individuals, psychology, and culture," necessitating the politicization of culture and individuals as representatives of that culture (Petryna 2013, xviii). Where these voices mediate broader ideological tensions and social issues, they teach about agential possibilities as a Foucaultian "history of the present," which is crucial to the learning objectives of the Manit Club (Foucault 1972; 1977). These students are taking great strides in critically assessing the role of the senses, specifically the throat and voice as central to the making and unmaking of culture: that is, hearing a mediation, feedback, or dialectic between notions of culture as dynamic and custom as fixed for political ends.

In Marshallese performances, the vocal complex as a material experience of cultural sensibilities is politicized and outsiders have politicized the vocal complex. Such relatedness between culture and politics is nuanced, yet culture is sometimes politically bound as fixed, which alters intergenerational utilization of cultural roots and political routes.[6] As Susan Wright explains, anthropologists previously held that culture was static, a position used by dominant powers to go about "measuring, categorizing, describing, representing and thereby supposedly 'knowing' others" so that these "objects of that knowledge were made the subjects of new forms of power and control (Wright 1998, 8)."[7] During the sociopolitical rights movements of the late 1960s and 1970s led by First Nations, the disenfranchised began to publically embrace their indigeneity, and as Alberto Gomes writes, use their indigeneity as "a significant political strategy in the counter-hegemonic ... movements against exploitative, oppressive and repressive regimes" (Gomes 2013; Niezen 2003; Cohen 1998; Bodley 2008).[8] Indigenous groups embraced the idea of culture as fixed to secure political gains against the dominant colonial powers and in the process, politicized their indigeneity by showcasing selected colorful traditions (dance, art, music) to validate and distinguish themselves at the cultural level (Wright 1998).[9]

The politicization of indigeneity and of culture continues to manifest itself in the Pacific in various ways. In Pacific scholarship, the politicization of culture and indigeneity was highlighted through a public anthropological debate between Jocelyn Linnekin and Haunani-Kay Trask, when Native Hawaiians took issue with the US Navy's bombardment of what they considered sacred lands (Tobin 1995). Linnekin, writing on culture and custom as symbolically coconstitutive, asserts the Native Hawaiians' characterization of the lands as traditionally sacred was a recent invention. Trask, however, challenged the concept of invented tradition by arguing that Hawaiians assert a "'traditional' relationship to the land not for political ends…but because they continue to believe in the cultural value of caring for the land" (Trask 1990, 15–16; 1991). For the Marshallese, legal redress has been sought through claims to culture loss due to damages to lands and to people, but these claims are often denied recourse based on western ways of objectifying land and defining it materially in terms of monetary value relative to western constructions of such value (Kirsch 2001).

Questions of value and violence echo in Marshallese sound archives that contain voiced traces of damaged, disregarded lands, peoples, and epistemologies. While Marshallese value of land is thus not unique in the Pacific, and neither is understanding of the voice as indexing or speaking to the status of the land, Marshallese sensorial orientation reminds us of an important aspect of this embodied environmental knowledge all but discarded in the conceptualization of the body in Western modernity.[10] As late as the nineteenth century and throughout westward expansion, Americans measured the health of the land through their bodily responses. Relistening to Marshallese voices as sounding the pathways, or routes, laid by the throats as the emotional anchor or roots of this Micronesian population bounded by a culture defined in many ways by encounters, we are challenged to hear past the violence and biopolitical controls to transcorporeal resistance and representation.

THE VOICE CHALLENGE IN PARTICIPATORY RESEARCH

We needed a poignant, intelligible pedagogical tool in our participatory research with the Manit Club that would enable students to experiment with abstract thought via hands-on exercises. The voice challenge, conceptualized by musicologist Nina Eidsheim as a participatory activity using social media meant to encourage participants to think through various sensorial experiences, quickly became that tool (interview, June 11, 2015).[11] Participants were invited via Facebook to post responses to the questions: 1) This is my voice in: _____? and 2) I use my voice to: _____?

Eidsheim, as her critical work on the sensing properties of the material voice suggests, was interested in providing an interactive space for unconventional ways of performing and listening, and through such an activity people could learn about "the incredible range of the voice ... not just in terms of pitch, but [for example] timbrally ... the infinite expressive range" (Eidsheim 2011; 2015). Eidsheim's approach to exploring vocal range is adventurously experimental, and it has sociocultural as well as political implications. In a world of sounds, our conversational voice in its many incarnations might represent a box, Eidsheim said in a personal interview, and the task is to open the box and understand its constitutive and illustrative possibilities. "I think we can talk about family, we can talk about friends ... school ... nations, peer groups, any kind of social and cultural sphere we are part of, sort of map how we musically are very fluidly vocal coders, or part of different vocal communities," Eidsheim stressed (2015). She offered an example of how someone in pain might not have the words but use their tone to convey a need to be left alone and acknowledged at the same time. She added, "we all have the capacity to pick up on subtle vocal messages when somebody is less than inviting and rejects further conversation, not with their words, but with their tone of voice" (June 11, 2015).

In exploring our ability to understand less inviting voices, we can begin to understand how vocality and its boxed constraints or expansive ranges become heard, listened to, and marked as, for example, "inviting." The voice challenge proved to be an important mechanism in highlighting the interplay of innovation, experimentation, tradition, and preservation; it also demonstrated how voices carry custom through culture. Eidsheim, in response to a question of how she might work with the Manit Club, noted that she would begin a vocal exercise with an exploration of range. Thinking through range, we heard the possibilities of spatial (diasporic networks) and temporal (historical) ranges evoked as students vocalized their participation in various vocal communities that speak to the dialectical approach to the roots/routes of culture. In the first meeting of the series, "the Sounds of Marshallese," this range can be heard amidst its historical coordinates that aim to confine Marshallese voices and culture but are ultimately unsuccessful.

SERIES 1: SOUNDS OF MARSHALLESE

The purpose of the various voice workshops with the Manit Club is not to teach Marshallese students their culture, but rather to teach how to think critically, begin to deconstruct colonial constraints on movements of Marshallese culture, and utilize the voice to understand their own culture and determine how to share it with others. One of our initial conversations centered upon describing sounds of *manin majel* in the RMI and Arkansas (see Figure 10.2).

The students described *manit* as "loud," as exemplified specifically through Marshallese talking or singing. One student, Chris Nashion, described how Marshallese sing "at the top of our lungs," and how Marshallese singing in church "don't follow the notes, we just sing."[12] Benetick Kabua Maddison added, "Back when we didn't have notes, people just sang; singing may have come from *roros* and usually chanting was loud and it was ... used during things like wars and tattooing."[13] The "loudness" of the Marshallese language had one exception, however. "Americanized Marshallese" spoken in public

FIGURE 10.2 Manit Club during a workshop.

was described as "soft." Thus Marshallese language as a sound of *manit* is loud, whereas its Americanized counterpart, which is a debased or silenced version of Marshallese culture, is not.

The cultural production of this dynamic tension extends back to the mid-nineteenth century when Marshallese had to vigorously defend their collectively honed practices as they were attacked by each colonial power that occupied their islands. First, missionaries with the American Board of Commissioners on Foreign Missions, who upon their arrival in 1857 introduced Christian practices and expressions such as hymns, allied with the German political authority in the late nineteenth century and effectively banned interatoll warfare and with it land negotiation, worship practices, and population control. They also forbade certain aspects of indigenous expressive culture, such as *roros*—low, rhythmic chants used in ceremonial activities and to build up strength and encourage the completion of tasks—that archived communal experiences.[14] As RMI Commisioner Alfred Capelle noted, missionaries listened "with foreign ears"; unaccustomed to Marshallese phonology, they were unable to represent the complexity of Marshallese sounds when constructing a written version for the pages of Bibles and hymnals, and thus reduced and reshaped Marshallese sounds, and laid claim to words, throats, and lands.

The missionary version of Marshallese is still written and until recently, taught in Marshallese schools. In 1976 a Marshallese-English Dictionary was published that utilized diacritical markings. It opens with a pronunciation guide that more accurately reflects the rich meanings of Marshallese words through sound (Abo et al. 1976). For example, the word "ailin" was written by the missionaries to represent the English version of "island," while the dictionary version of the word is spelled, "aelōñ," which translates to "above the currents" and conveys the deeper meaning of everything above the water.

The dictionary was also written as a political intervention to reclaim Marshallese language and, with a focus on the "sounds of Marshallese" and land names, Marshallese vocal agility and claims to land. While printed Marshallese dictionaries exist, the lack of Marshallese accented voices delivering loaded words indexes loss, as does the lack of understanding of "ancient words" used by the elders.

The students shared how Marshallese elders openly lament that knowledge of traditional Marshallese ways are in decline and that the young people in Arkansas *jaje manit* or don't know their culture, which means that they don't know, and therefore can't respect, their customs.[15] The theme of cultural loss pervades many meetings of the Manit Club and voice is central to this discussion. The students all located language and its proper voicings as central to the maintenance of culture and generational cohesion. What became clear during our conversations was the immense pressure these young Marshallese students are under. Having lived the majority of their lives outside of the RMI, they are committed to upholding Marshallese cultural values and traditions and teaching younger Marshallese about *manit*, yet simultaneously many are embarrassed that they do not speak Marshallese and are unaware of the specifics of Marshallese history, including that of nuclear testing.

Series 2: Filtering Accents and the Voice Challenge

Another conversation in the series of voice challenge talks centered on accents and the role they played in identifying one's culture. Nashion, a native English speaker who has never lived in the Marshall Islands, identified his parents' home atolls. As a response was being posed about how accents are heard, he interrupted the question by asking if his sounded "whitewashed," unaware that he had spoken the words with a distinct Marshallese accent.[16] Several students, particularly those who want to enter the medical field, are eager to learn Marshallese so that they can converse with their elders, but fear they lack the resources. The embarrassment and anxiety of many of the students speaks to the embodiment of the colonial mentality and larger systemic violence that often serves as a crucial limitation in diasporic subject formation when access to knowledge is deemed a failure of the individual and in turn a failure of the subjugated culture.

In preparation for the voice challenge, we explained its format, shared the Facebook page, and asked them to work through the prompt—extending their vocal positionality and range—"This is my voice_____(fill in the blank)." The students were reluctant to participate. Given the shyness of Marshallese students, which is based more in the fear of providing an inaccurate answer than fear of speaking, the students were left alone with a voice recorder to record their responses, which the students performed in a variety of ways. Some were playful, some thoughtful, all were sincere, and all showed semiresistance to the staged performance.

This is my voice when I'm high.
This is my voice cause I'm hungry.
This is my voice when I don't understand Marshallese.
This is my voice when I'm eating.
This is the voice when I'm whispering?
This is my voice when I'm on the phone. Hello?
This is my voice when I just came out of the bathroom.
This is my voice when I'm tired.
This is my voice when... [laughing, indecipherable].
This is my voice when I'm done [turns recorder off].[17]

The audio and video recordings of the challenge provided a chronology of events. After a minute of quiet conversation in English in which they discussed what was expected of them, one student started up the performance with playful, rapid-fire responses that registered both laughs and a few words of disapproval. After a two-minute pause, interrupted by conversations in a mix of English and Marshallese and the chastisement of one student who said, "you guys, it's already been like two minutes," the remaining responses were given over another three-minute span. Each response resounded the malleability and flexibility of the students' voices, but it also spoke to the various constraints within which they are asked to perform as part of their "vocal communities" on a day-to-day basis and how they feel about these performances, specifically within the content of grasping their everyday lives as part of Marshallese diasporic culture and the less audible *mantin majeḷ* they either strove to hear or buried in jest.

Mailieann Beasha, whose response to the challenge was "whispering," was asked to give an impromptu performance the following week while at work at Walmart. The largest of the big box stores, Walmart frames itself as a salt of the earth, small-town company where people matter and whose purpose is to help each person "save money, live better" (Moreton 2009). The implication of this simple motto is that one must spend money to live, a far cry from the traditional subsistence living of the Marshallese. Mailieann is only one of a few Marshallese who work part-time at Walmart and her performance was conducted alone, her shyness demonstrated through the camera.

Working in the electronics section, Mailieann goes by the Americanized shorthand version of her name, "Miley," as indicated on her blue and white nametag. She stands in front of a row of flat screen televisions, each playing the same smartphone commercial. Networked communication, it seems, is the theme of the day, and Miley takes a second to prime for her voice challenge performance. She bends her elbows, extends her forearms with palms facing upwards and, with a gesture that registers, at first consideration, an embarrassed exasperation with the performance, says, "this is my voice when I'm working at Walmart" (see Figure 10.3).

Stitched into her vest are the words "Proud Walmart Associate," but pride is not the affect that comes through in mannerism or tone. Throughout Miley's elocution, she avoids looking into the cellphone camera. Her words shift from the sing-songy, "this is my voice when I'm," to the more direct and staccato, "working at Walmart." Miley's vocal mutability and accent shifts afford her the resources to participate in many vocal

FIGURE 10.3 Miley performing the voice challenge in Walmart.

communities. Understanding the performance of her voice as it is challenged to play communicative roles amidst the various technologies of communication in the stores, all with a price, inspired further contemplation of how vocal "plays" can be heard as new pathways to many knowledges, each knowledge with its own filter to protect it from being unnecessarily debased. Vocal play and filters, then, protect the archive of the throat: the feelings of those who are often tasked as speaking for a vocal community silenced for decades and dispersed across the RMI and the US. Digging into this archive, the students learn about their own throats that get choked up as emotional ties to their global community. They hear their embodied reactions not as incorrect but rather as protective mechanisms or points of departure from which they can navigate other uncomfortable encounters with audiences who may never fully understand the importance of hearing *aelōñ* as such.

SERIES 3: WORLD WAR II AND TRANSMISSION

Hearing their own voices—not as limitations but as resources and routes to their roots—prompted rich discussions among students on *mantin majeļ* and technologies of transmission, such as the importance of *bwebwenato*, or talking stories, which continues to be a means of intergenerational communication for Marshallese in diaspora.

The use of social media to converse and share videos, particularly Facebook, and to share music, particularly on YouTube and SoundCloud, are new means of communication embraced by many Marshallese. As he was preparing to present sounds of Marshallese at a history conference with the authors on a panel about MOHP in Sacramento, Maddison shared a song he had heard on SoundCloud. Much like "Mour ilo Springdale," this upbeat tune also employs a synthesized country music sound. Recently recorded, the song, "Ejjab Kiki Jela Eo" loosely translates as "It Cannot Rest."[18] The lyrics recount how the Marshallese were caught in the middle between Japanese and US military forces as they battled each other for possession of Marshallese lands during World War II.

The Japanese occupied the Marshall Islands after World War I and taught Marshallese that they were working together as part of a larger imperial project.[19] The Marshallese describe being shocked when Japanese civil administration turned into military rule and Marshallese internal displacement fractured families as fortifications were constructed during the Asia–Pacific wars of the 1930s–1940s. The Marshallese population was subjected to forced labor, sexual violence, starvation, and forced separation to prevent potential sabotage through communication.[20] Marshallese describe the musical motives used to throw Japanese off as silly twists of voice, trivial sounding to the Japanese but coded with information vital for their fellow Marshallese to live. Strings of words that pointed to food stores and safe spaces sung in a tuneful manner fell deaf on Japanese ears (Schwartz 2012b). These forms of martial "nonlistening" and resistant revoicing became crucial in preserving and defending notions of *mantin majel* as Marshallese lives.

Though all the lyrics to "Ejjab Kiki Jela Eo" were not clear to Maddison—because of the use of ancient words—what was clear was the conveyance of *mantin majel*. Maddison explains:

> The song is about our rulers and their people during World War II and the fact that they were going through so much; the Japanese were chasing them with swords and the Americans were dropping bombs on the islands to kill the Japanese. While the Marshallese were trying to run for their lives, the ground was shaking and they heard loud explosions and saw flames in the sky. However, the Marshallese chiefs and their people living during those tough times never gave up on their islands. The knowledge or history of what they went through is not dead. It's still alive to this day.
> (Personal communication, August 4, 2015)[21]

The meanings behind the sounds are powerful, yet Maddison does not have full access to this song that archives Marshallese history because his language has been made foreign to him. Part of what is understandable, "boom"—the guns, "boom"—the bombs, are sounds that mark territory being fought over by two imperial powers. This example shares the changing and shaping of listening orientations and Marshallese vocal practices.

After pushing out the Japanese, the US military claimed Marshallese lands and proclaimed that nuclear testing would commence on Bikini Atoll in 1946 for the "good of mankind." Instead of ceding the land in an acquiescent manner, Bikinian King Juda met US Commodore Ben Wyatt's request with an equivocal refrain, "Men Otemjej Rej Ilo Bein Anij" (Everything is in God's Hands). While Commodore Wyatt was frustrated, his militaristic nonlistening to the rhythmically powerful, almost chant-like verse of Juda's cautionary elocution has demanded voluminous revoicings since the 1946 exodus. The words "Men Otemjej Rej Ilo Bein Anij" circulate today as a reminder in speech and songs, resounding American Protestant hymns that promise freedom with deeply expressive gestures that deny the realization of freedom, exemplary of a revoicing that amplifies the cultural nonlistening.

"Ejjab Kiki Jela Eo" is Marshallese synthesized country music, which we can hear within this history of cultural encounter. US soldiers, mostly from southern and western states, introduced country music to the Marshallese, which served as a mechanism for an affective alliance with the Americans.[22] Country music's ties to gospel and evocation of "God and country" appeal to Marshallese religious and moral sensibilities that were, in part, cultivated through American-Marshallese cultural and political interactions. Country western songs were taught to Marshallese to encourage patriotic loyalty to the United States. Today, Marshallese use these sounds to reflect on their historical positionality and contemporary displacement, away from their land, and through their emplacement in the rural American South and an imagined West. Like Juda's vocal protest that continues to circulate, Marshallese historical songs draw on sound symbolism to mark, and perhaps negotiate, unrequited suffering and struggle in the collective memory. Sound, much like diaspora, speaks to the disenfranchisement and displacement of people, and their ever-present connection.

SERIES 4: US NUCLEAR TESTING AND THE POLITICIZATION OF THE VOICE

With the visceral memory of encounters, wars, and their ecological ramifications that continue to be heard in a range of Marshallese vocal practices, Marshallese cannot rest. One mode of political outreach has been in commemorative ceremonies such as Nuclear Victims' and Survivors' Remembrance Day, a national holiday in the Marshall Islands to commemorate the aftermath of the Castle Bravo nuclear detonation conducted on March 1, 1954. The fallout from Bravo, which at 15 megatons was the largest nuclear bomb exploded by the United States, sent irradiated coral dust throughout the Marshall Islands.[23] Women and children, who were particularly susceptible, suffered from thyroid abnormalities (e.g., nodules, lesions) that required surgery, many of which were repeated, and resulted in laryngeal neuropathy (roaring, hoarseness, vocal/glottal fry when singing). These physiological disruptions have, for Marshallese, created social stigmas and affected the way they carried out their customary roles, such as singing the soprano parts in hymns and harmonizing. Women survivors sing of their sorrows as they moved to unfamiliar lands, stayed on their contaminated land with poisonous foods, birthed unformed babies, and couldn't speak or sing from fear to physiological distress.[24] Voice, as it connects to land, resounds a listening silence endemic to radiation poisoning; a revoicing of the land is a necessary reminder of the actual inability to listen and of the experiences of nuclear survivors to teach us how to listen to land in peril.

On the sixtieth anniversary of Bravo, MEI used the platform to host an educational outreach event, Nuclear Remembrance Day 2014: Reflect. Honor. Educate. (NRD), and invited survivors, diplomats, and scholars to speak to the shared legacies of nuclear test-ing and climate change. Neisen Laukon, a Rongelapese survivor who returned to the contaminated atoll at the age of four with her family in 1957, spoke and recalled the psy-chological and physiological damage to her body and other Marshallese as a result of exposure (Laukon 2014) (see Figure 10.4).

Moving between Marshallese and English, Laukon described how her mouth and lips blistered after she consumed foods from the island, and how she and family members suffer from mysterious, undiagnosable illnesses. She also related how her cousin Jonitha, whom she brought on stage with her, "had her throat cut too" (thyroid surgery). Laukon repeated how she "didn't know" what happened and that "no one ever told us what was happening." While most of her presentation was measured and soft, her voice raised in

FIGURE 10.4 Neisen Laukon speaking at Nuclear Remembrance Day.

tone and volume as she said, "we were treated like guinea pigs." As her voice lilted downward and softened again, she followed, "it's sad to hear, but it's true."

After Laukon spoke, women from Rongelap, some of whom were unable to sing due to surgeries, performed "177," a song titled after section 177 in the Compact of Free Association, an agreement signed between the US and RMI that references Marshallese effected by fallout. The song speaks to the plight of the women, left "irradiated," "weak," and "abandoned" (Schwartz 2012a; Barker 2004; Johnston and Barker 2008). By emphasizing their vocal timbres and inability to harmonize and sing, or to communicate through togetherness (crucial to *ṃantin ṃajeḷ*), the Rongelapese women and others direct our attention to their poignant resistance of biopolitical controls, fractured modernities, and devalued indigenous epistemologies. The voice is one of the most salient reminders of a throat healthy or in peril and thus an environment healthy or in peril. The politicization of this cultural mechanism can be read as central to Marshallese politics of belonging and of hospitality, which are, of course, part of the larger issues of diaspora. When we conceive of them critically and to the larger issues to which they speak, these tools of politicization can be framed as pedagogical exercises that asks Marshallese students to listen and hear themselves.

Series 5: Cultural Relistening

Voices do not stay still, nor do they stay quiet. They talk back, and most of us have been unwilling to listen, preferring instead the silence of still images, which we can more easily invest with our own thoughts and agendas. We can ignore the survivors altogether and focus our outrage on the historical injustices, or we can use them as symbols to help us do so. Or, we can comfortably continue to ask, with some paternalistic good nature, what we as individuals or as different kinds of social groups (nations, students, genders) can *do for* the survivors, rather than what they have done, and what they can teach us.

—Joshua D. Pilzer, *Hearts of Pine* (11)

Marshallese have a problem with having a big voice in reality. We are not viewed as significant and because of that we are tuned out in history. One voice isn't going to change our fate but WE as Marshallese NEED to be heard. It's our duty to revive our history and culture in order to never let our legacy die out. To listen for the fragility of the Marshallese voice is to hear our history, where it all began. The bombings of our islands and the scar it left behind. To really understand the hardships people went through and are still going through and will eventually go through is to really hear the fragility. We are put down and cast aside but we will never forget our suffering all for the "better of mankind."

—JociAnna Chong Gum, Marshallese Ṃanit Club[25]

Taken together, these quotes offer an imperative for us to listen to survivors' voices against premature closure and a tuning out of agency. Ethnomusicologist Joshua Pilzer, writing on Korean survivors of the comfort women system in *Hearts of Pine* (2011), offers an implicit challenge in his introduction. He provides the injunction to listen to voices for their initial incommensurability, inability to be immediately appropriated, and their subjective positions that unfold over time (Pilzer 2012; Brodzinsky and Schoening 2012; Lemere and West 2011; Field 2012; Cave and Sloan 2014). The survivors, Pilzer writes, can *teach* us something through an engagement by listening to both their intimate and public voices as a means to self-heal and inform. Premed student JociAnna Chong Gum offers a similar injunction in her response to listening to the irradiated voices of Marshallese survivors of nuclear weaponry. Listening beyond what might be considered a dysfunctional affect, Chong Gum asks us to listen, ultimately, to the material fragility of Marshallese voices to hear their strength. She also echoes the promise made by the US government to the population of Bikini Atoll—namely, that the atomic bombs that eventually contaminated their homeland for the foreseeable future were for the "good of mankind" and to bring world peace (Niedenthal 2001).

Where these voices mediate broader ideological tensions and social issues, they teach about agential possibilities in the historical present that form the foundation of larger networks in which these survivors, despite their vulnerability, would rather be known for "creating new pathways" via their expressivity, than as victims of modernity, so that their culture might not only endure but also shape the global systems in which it is engaged (Clifford 2013, 7; Kunreuther 2014).[26] Their strength lies not on the side of capitulation but rather of mediation centered in the body itself—flesh, political, social, and their abilities to teach how, when one is forced into vocal communities with certain expectations, you may use your voice in other ways to share knowledge and maintain *mantin majel*.

The students listened to a song by Lijon Eknilang, a well-known Rongelapese musician and activist, whose voice was damaged due to surgery for thyroid abnormalities caused by radiation exposure, the "177" song performed at NRD, and an excerpt of Neisen Laukon's NRD speech. The Manit Club students were asked to listen to the songs, and without knowing the context of their performance, to describe the sounds of their voices. Though a few of the students recognized some of the 177 singers, most were unfamiliar with the performers, songs, and details of US nuclear testing and its impact. The history of US nuclear testing is seldom taught in US schools, where most of the Manit Club students have attended since they were children, and there are no Marshallese history books in use.[27] Additionally, those most affected by nuclear testing seldom share their experiences due to shame and stigmatization they suffered while living in the islands and because most still lack a full understanding of what happened to them and why. After students were provided with a brief history and information that many of the performers' voices were damaged by thyroid surgeries, students were asked to relisten and note if they heard the voices differently. Students were then asked to listen to Laukon and provide impressions.

In the first excerpt, Eknilang plays the guitar as she sings a song about the Bravo detonation.[28] She struggles to maintain rhythm and pitch and the vocal timbre is strained and raspy. Chong Gum's initial analysis was based on rhythm, which she described as "broken" and "cracked".[29] Other students described the sound in affective terms, "sad" and "tired." Knowing the story behind Eknilang, the descriptions became more intimate and animated. Chong Gum wrote that she heard her voice as "fragile" and "inspiring." "Her voice isn't underwhelming," she wrote, "it's now overwhelming—beautiful."[30] Students were visibly frustrated and confused as to why they had never learned the details of the nuclear testing and its impact. "This is our peoples' history," Chong Gum said, "but we don't know it."[31] Chong Gum's words reflect voice as history, intergenerational education, and culture. As such, Eknilang offers her voice to the voice challenge by stressing, "This is my voice affected by radiation." "This is my throat after multiple thyroid surgeries." "This is my voice on medications for my thyroid." And, "This is my voice as I struggle to share my family's questions about these medications we are on that make us sick." Eknilang's voice, in line with Marshallese culture, contains the history and culture, and that is how the students learn about this crucial, often untold part of their culture, and one of the main reasons they live in the United States. Eknilang's voice offers the historical struggle that subtends the Marshallese students' lack of information. "This is my voice working against imperial violence of erasure."

Marshallese increasingly feel that these stories need to be told. Neisen Abon, after listening to Laukon's speech, wrote, "I think it is important that she tells her story. Not many people know who we are, where we come from and why. Our voice matters and that's why it's important. It's to let others know what kind of struggles the US put/gave the Marshall Island[s]. And what people back then had to witness and go through."[32] Chong Gum added that the survivors articulate their "hardship and pain and it shows through [their] voice[s]."[33] She describes the survivors as conquerors and, despite criticism, how each wants to share the "rich neglected story behind her voice. Beauty isn't always defined by correct pitches and angelic tones, but a deep/big meaning behind a broken, small voice is even more beautiful in my opinion."

Marshallese voices are not small, but Chong Gum's statement maintains a lineage with the values of collectivity that are central to *mantin majel*. To use a "big voice" might resound an inauthentic throat. In appeals for nuclear redress, it is important for Marshallese survivors to strike the balance between sharing their voices as reverent and powerful. As Marshallese survivors of nuclear testing reach out, these reserved, deeply meaningful appeals are made to God and to the United States. The chiefs are not the recipients of the appeals, and this silence might be read as a convivial rupture. It might also be heard as a generative silence that echoes the need for societal reconfiguration that addresses *mantin majel*. Voice resounds in these stories of how it is almost impossible, under colonial violence, to maintain *mantin majel*, which makes it imperative to remember. Thus the survivors are teaching adaptation, struggle, and resilience as a matter of the throat and the emotional transcorporeal materiality that connects us humans to each other and to nonhumans.

In the case of relistening to the voices of the survivors, hearing their words as sounds and listening to the content not only in terms of the symbolically intelligible words, but also as the material play between recomposition and dissolution of the body as psyche or throat as heart, it might prove useful to think of this pedagogical moment on a temporal register. For example, Rob Nixon has delineated a type of violence that works overtime at structural integrities of land and its people (Nixon 2011). This "slow violence" is, according to Nixon, less recognizable than the spectacular displays of floods consuming islands or bombs exploding. It is more apt to consider the patient decay embedded into imperial violence—nuclear testing and, moreover, anthropogenic climate change—that can be heard *as* temporal procedures.

Relistening to voices that reshape the forms of songs can serve as a metaphor for the people who had to reshape their modes of communication and societal structures following nuclear weapons testing. Their dynamic expressivity continues to be crucial to their survival given that nuclear issues persist and are complicated by sea levels rise. Cultivating a practice of relistening to Marshallese survivors, with a cultural knowledge of the senses and the history of the present, becomes a crucial way for Marshallese in diaspora to embody and emplace their culture. The survivors share their vocal flexibility within the violent constraints that shape all lives, and, especially the Marshallese in diaspora given their unique political, social, and cultural contingencies and heritages. Loss is one of these heritages; it is colonial in the making. The voice shares a loss as such and it shares the gain of political intelligibility within Marshallese epistemologies and negotiations of time. Loss, then, is not all we hear. We hear an intercultural gain in communication and in education. We hear the maintenance of sensorial knowledge and cultural transmission or preservation through vocal innovation and politicization.

Conclusion: Climate Change and Invitations

In the wake of rising sea levels due to climate change, the vulnerable, low-lying atolls of the RMI are threatened, as are the Marshallese people. Much akin to the impact of nuclear testing, which resulted in loss of land due to contamination and forced relocations, climate change similarly threatens the lands and thus puts pressure on *mantin majel̦*. Marshallese poet Kathy Jetnil-Kijiner has emerged as a champion fighting against climate change through her voice as she recites slam poetry. Her performance and style is reminiscent of *roros* with its rhythmic consistency and urgency to move people to action. Another, more expansive politics of indigeneity of the Pacific has arisen through the voices of the Pacific Climate Warriors, almost exclusively male groups of traditionally clad Pacific Islanders from various nations who recite war chants in their native languages, then end their performance in English with the mantra, "We are not drowning, we are fighting" (The Pacific Climate Warriors n.d.).

Marshallese are challenging the world to listen to their voices on multiple levels. First Nations peoples and indigenous populations around the world are joining the Marshallese and other Pacific Islanders in the forefront of climate change activism, using their specific environmental knowledge of the land and characterizing themselves as traditional caretakers of it to shape political climate debates (Doolittle 2010). Thinking through the different ways in which the politics of indigeneity is constructed through voice, our next series of workshops with the Manit Club will focus on climate change utilizing political realities and educational resources at hand. As we contribute our voices to the voice challenge on Facebook, we invite you, the readers of the *Oxford Handbook of Voice Studies*, to join us by participating in the voice challenge and by relistening to Marshallese voices in diaspora.

NOTES

1. James Clifford (2013) discusses how indigenous people, despite complete societal disruption, are "creating new pathways in a complex modernity." For more information about MEI, visit the organization's website at http://www.mei.ngo.
2. Stacy Alaimo (2010) presents a theoretical intervention in understanding the body as part of a larger "transcorporeal" complex of movements between material bodies human and nonhuman, forming a larger sense in our minds of what "community" and thus vocal community means.
3. The term *manit* is the singular form of the plural *mantin majel̗*.
4. In the RMI Census of 2011, the unemployment rate was cited as 4.7% because of the addition to the census of "home production." Without this category, the rate would stand at 39% in 2011.
5. Approximately one-third of the Marshallese population lives in the United States.
6. During the 1980s when debates over multiculturalism and pluralism were at their height, scholars settled on the notion that culture was dynamic. James Clifford viewed culture as "contested, temporal, and emergent," while historian Eric Hobsbawn argued that "traditions which appear or claim to be old are often quite recent in origin and sometimes invented." See James Clifford (1986, 19) and Hobsbawn (1983, 1).
7. Jocelyn Linnekin (1990) describes this objectification as part of a greater "ideological conquest that began with missionization and continues in the arena of international politics" (153).
8. We use James Clifford's definition of indigenous as referring to societies that are "relatively small-scale, people who sustain deep connections with a place" and who share "comparable experiences of invasion, dispossession, resistance, and survival" (Clifford 2013, 15).
9. Some scholars and indigenous groups take issue with notions of the invention of culture, however.
10. Linda Nash (2006) speaks to this phenomenon in which health was once framed externally and contextualized through the environment. "People experience their bodies differently in different historical moments, according to the languages and practices available to them," Nash writes (11).
11. Nina Eidsheim, interview with the authors, June 11, 2015, Los Angeles, CA. The ALS (amyotrophic lateral sclerosis) ice bucket challenge was a recent social media phenomenon in which millions of participants filmed dropping a bucket of ice water on their heads, uploaded it to Facebook, then challenged friends and family to do the same, all to raise awareness and financial support for ALS. The voice challenge also served as a lead up to The Voice Studies Now! Conference that brought together authors featured in this *Handbook*.

While the initial idea for the voice challenge was Eidsheim's, the questions were formulated through a month-long conversation with Katherine Meizel, Michael D'Errico, and Jillian Rogers.

12. Chris Nashion, Manit Club meeting, April 4, 2015, Springdale, AR.

13. Benetick Kabua Maddison, Manit Club meeting, April 4, 2015, Springdale, AR.

14. *Roros*, used during food gathering, warfare, and divining the supernatural, were performed alone, but most were used in group activities and utilized call and response techniques. See Tobin (2001).

15. As the primary translator for MOHP and founder of the Manit Club, Maddison encountered firsthand the difficulty in understanding "ancient words," which he describes as words spoken by elders who are in their sixties and older and who are more familiar with the language used by their ancestors prior to missionary influence. Without access to the land, and the tasks and ways of being and doing associated with it, much of that terminology is not being transmitted.

16. Nashion, Manit Club meeting, April 17, 2015, Springdale, AR.

17. Manit Club students performing the voice challenge, recording, April 17, 2015, Springdale, AR.

18. Anta James, "Ejjab Kiki Jela Eo," Hawai'i, SoundCloud, https://soundcloud.com/james-anta.

19. The Japanese acquired the Marshall Islands in 1920 as part of the Mandate System of the League of Nations following World War I.

20. Shaine Benkim, interview by Albious Latior, July 16, 2014, translation, and Ajlok Beasha, interview by April Brown, trans. Albious Latior, May 26, 2013, translation, Marshallese Oral History Project, Marshallese Educational Initiative, Springdale, AR.

21. Benetick Kabua Maddison, text correspondence with the authors, August 14, 2015.

22. Aaron Fox in *Real Country* (2004), points to how country music, or *al in kaubowe* (cowboy songs), relates "notions and principles of memory, emotion, sociability, narrativity, and especially the materiality of the speaking and singing voice, which is the very meeting point for words and embodiment" (155).

23. The populations on Rongelap and Utrōk Atolls, most directly affected by Bravo's fallout, were subjected to decades of top secret US testing on human populations exposed to radiation, termed Project 4.1. The US government remains silent and the unwitting participants remain unaware of the extent and purpose of the testings. See Barker (2004) and Johnston and Barker (2008).

24. Communication technologies greatly shaped Marshallese lives. The radio was connective on the main island and brought some of these "radiation songs" that archived nuclear experiences to the masses on other atolls. Some would attempt to help and circulate the songs, contributing their voices to the chorus in protest of those silenced by nuclear violence. See Schwartz (2012a).

25. JociAnna Chong Gum, email correspondence with Brown, May 20, 2015. Chong Gum was explaining how she would teach others by helping them think through the Marshallese voice.

26. The terms "survivor" and "victim" are labels that carry implications of value and agency. "Survivor" often is meant to denote strength and coping ability, while "victim" implies weakness. Additionally, usage of both labels has been criticized as objectifying and hegemonic.

27. Anthropologist Julie Walsh (2012) with the Center for Pacific Islands Studies, University of Hawai'i at Manoa, authored a Marshallese textbook, *Etto nan Raan Kein: A Marshall*

Islands History with Hilda Heine, Carmen Milne Bigler, and Mark Stege, but it was never adopted for classroom use.

28. Lijon McDonald, field recording by Jessica A. Schwartz, 2009.
29. JociAnna Chong Gum, written response to listening exercise, administered by Brown, May 13, 2015, Springdale, AR.
30. Chong Gum, listening exercise (underlining in original).
31. JociAnna Chong Gum, conversation with Brown, May 13, 2015, Springdale, AR.
32. Neisen Abon, written responses to listening exercise, administered by Brown, June 20, 2015, Springdale, AR.
33. Chong Gum, listening exercise.

WORKS CITED

350Pacific, "Warrior Videos." https://350pacific.org/warrior-videos.

Abo, Takaji, Byron Bender, Alfred W. Capelle, and Tony De Brum, eds. 1976. *Marshallese-English Dictionary*. Pali Language Texts, Micronesia Series. Honolulu: University of Hawai'i Press.

Alaimo, Stacy. 2010. *Bodily Natures: Science Environment, and the Material Self*. Bloomington: Indiana University Press.

Araújo, Samuel, and Vincenzo Cambria. 2013. "Sound Praxis, Poverty, and Social Participation: Perspectives from a Collaborative Study in Rio de Janeiro." *Yearbook for Traditional Music* 45: 28–42.

Asian Development Bank. 2006. *Juumemmej: Republic of the Marshall Islands Social and Economic Report 2005*. Manila, Philippines: Asian Development Bank.

Barker, Holly. 2004. *Bravo for the Marshallese: Regaining Control in a Post-Nuclear, Post Colonial World*. Belmont, CA: Wadsworth Publishing.

Bellu, Michael. n.d. "Mour ilo Springdale." Translated by Benetick Kabua Maddison. SoundCloud, https://soundcloud.com/gnahz-nowkrat/mour-ilo-springdale.

Bodley, John H. 2008. *Victims of Progress*. Lanham, MD: Altamira Press.

Brodzinsky, Sibylla, and Max Schoening, editors. 2012. *Throwing Stones at the Moon: Narratives from Colombians Displaced by Violence*. San Francisco: McSweeney's Books.

Cave, Mark, and Stephen M. Sloan, eds. 2014. *Listening on the Edge: Oral History in the Aftermath of Crisis*. New York: Oxford University Press.

Clifford, James. 1986. "Introduction: Partial Truths." In *Writing Culture: The Poetics and Politics of Ethnography*, edited by James Clifford and George E. Marcus, 1–26. Berkeley: University of California Press.

Clifford, James. 2013. *Returns: Becoming Indigenous in the Twenty-First Century*. Cambridge, MA: Harvard University Press.

Cohen, Cynthia P. 1998. *The Human Rights of Indigenous Peoples*. Ardsley, NY: Transnational Publishers.

Constitution of the Republic of the Marshall Islands. 1979. RMI Embassy website. http://rmiembassyus.org/images/pdf/government/Constitution.pdf.

DeLoughrey, Elizabeth M. 2007. *Routes and Roots: Navigating Caribbean and Pacific Island Literatures*. Honolulu: University of Hawai'i Press.

Doolittle, Amity A. 2010. "The Politics of Indigeneity: Indigenous Strategies for Inclusion in Climate Change Negotiations." *Conservation & Society* 8 (4): 286–91.

Eidsheim, Nina S. 2011. "Sensing Voice: Materiality and the Lived Body in Singing and Listening." *The Senses and Society* 6 (2): 133–55.

Field, Sean. 2012. *Oral History, Community, and Displacement: Imagining Memories in PostApartheid South Africa*. Palgrave Studies in Oral History. New York: Palgrave MacMillan.

Foucault, Michel. 1972. *The Order of Things: An Archeology of the Human Sciences*. New York: Pantheon.

Foucault, Michel. 1977. *Discipline and Punish: The Birth of the Prison*, translated by Alan Sheridan. New York: Pantheon.

Foucault, Michael. 1997. *Society Must Be Defended: Lectures at the College de France, 1975–1976*. Translated by David Macey. New York: Picador.

Fox, Aaron. 2004. *Real Country: Music and Language in Working-Class Culture*. Durham, NC: Duke University Press.

Freire, Paulo. 2010. *Pedagogy of the Oppressed*. Translated by Myra Bergman Ramos. 30th Anniversary Edition. New York: Bloomsbury.

Gomes, Alberto. 2013. "Anthropology and the Politics of Indigeneity." *Anthropological Forum* 23 (1): 5–15.

Hobsbawn, Eric. 1983. *The Invention of Tradition*. Edited by Eric Hobsbawn and Terrence Ranger. Cambridge: Cambridge University Press.

James, Anta. "Ejjab Kiki Jela Eo," SoundCloud. https://soundcloud.com/james-anta.

Johnston, Barbara R., and Holly Barker. 2008. *Consequential Damages of Nuclear War: The Rongelap Report*. Walnut Creek, CA: Left Coast Press.

Kirsch, Stuart. 2001. "Lost Worlds: Environmental Disaster, 'Culture Loss,' and the Law." *Current Anthropology* 42 (2): 167–98.

Kunreuther, Laura. 2014. *Voicing Subjects: Public Intimacy and Mediation in Kathmandu*. Los Angeles: University of California Press.

Laukon, Neison. 2014. Untitled presentation. Nuclear Remembrance Day 2014: Reflect. Honor. Educate. February 28. Little Rock, AR: Clinton Presidential Center.

Lemere, Maggie, and Zoe West, eds. 2011. *Nowhere to Be Home: Narratives from Survivors of Burma's Military Regime*. San Francisco: McSweeney's Books.

Linnekin, Jocelyn. 1990. "The Politics of Culture in the Pacific." In *Cultural Identity and Ethnicity in the Pacific*, edited by Joceylyn Linnekin and Lin Poyer, 149–74. Honolulu: University of Hawai'i Press.

Moreton, Bethany. 2009. *To Serve God and Wal-Mart: The Making of Christian Free Enterprise*. Cambridge, MA: Harvard University Press.

Nash, Linda. 2006. *Inescapable Ecologies: A History of Environment, Disease, and Knowledge*. Berkeley: University of California Press.

Neidenthal, Jack. 2001. *For the Good of Mankind: A History of the People of Bikini and Their Islands*. Majuro: Micronitor/Bravo Press.

Niezen, Ronald. 2003. *The Origins of Indigenism: Human Rights and the Politics of Identity*. Berkeley: University of California Press.

Nixon, Rob. 2011. *Slow Violence and the Environmentalism of the Poor*. Cambridge, MA: Harvard University Press.

Petryna, Adriana. 2013. *Life Exposed: Biological Citizens after Chernobyl*, 2nd ed. Princeton, NJ: Princeton University Press.

Pilzer, Joshua D. 2012. *Hearts of Pine: Songs in the Lives of Three Korean Survivors of the Japanese "Comfort Women."* New York: Oxford University Press.

Pink, Sarah. 2015. *Doing Sensory Ethnography*, 2nd ed. Los Angeles: Sage Publishers.

Republic of the Marshall Islands. 2011. Census of Population and Housing, 2011. https://www. doi.gov/sites/doi.gov/files/migrated/oia/reports/upload/RMI-2011-Census-Summary-Report- on-Population-and-Housing.pdf.

Rudiak-Gould, Peter. 2013. *Climate Change and Tradition in a Small Island State: The Rising Tide*. New York: Routledge.

Schwartz, Jessica A. 2012a. "'A Voice to Sing': Rongelapese Musical Activism and the Production of Nuclear Knowledge." *Music & Politics* 6 (1): 1–21.

Schwartz, Jessica A. 2012b. "'Between Death and Life': Mobility, War, and Marshallese Women's Songs of Survival." *Women and Music: A Journal of Gender and Culture* 16: 23–56. doi:10.1353/wam.2012.0023

Seremetakis, Nadia C. 1994. *The Senses Still: Perception and Memory as Material Culture in Modernity*. Boulder, CO: Westview.

Stoller, Paul. 1997. *Sensuous Scholarship*. Philadelphia: University of Pennsylvania Press.

Tobin, Jack. 2001. *Stories from the Marshall Islands: Bwebwenato Jan Aelon Kein*. Honolulu: University of Hawai'i Press.

Tobin, Jeffrey. 1995. "Cultural Construction and Native Nationalism: Report from the Hawaiian Front." In *Asia Pacific as Space of Cultural Production*, edited by Rob Wilson and Arif Dirlik, 147–69. Durham, NC: Duke University Press.

Trask, Haunani-Kay. 1990. "Politics in the Pacific Islands: Imperialism and Native Self Determination." *Amerasia* 16 (1): 1–19.

Trask, Haunani-Kay. 1991. "Natives and Anthropologists: The Colonial Struggle." *Contemporary Pacific* 3 (1): 159–67.

Walsh, Julie, with Hilda Heine, Carmen Milne Bigler, and Mark Stege. 2012. *Etto ñan Raan Kein: A Marshall Islands History*. Honolulu: Bess Press.

Wright, Susan. 1998. "The Politicization of 'Culture.'" *Anthropology Today* 14 (1): 7–15.

CHAPTER 11

....

VOICE DIPPED IN BLACK

The Louisville Project and the Birth of Black
Radical Argument in College Policy Debate

....

SHANARA R. REID-BRINKLEY

The truth is you don't want Black folks...
You're just looking for yourself with a little bit of color.
— Elizabeth "Liz" Jones, in *Cross-X*

MORE than a decade ago, the University of Louisville's Malcolm X Debate Program, a mostly Black student group, founded a small grassroots movement in competitive college debate. Spearheaded by one of the few Black directors of a national college policy debate team, Dr. Ede Warner and the Louisville team committed their organizational and competitive practices toward increasing Black participation in debate. Despite their efforts in recruiting,[1] Warner began questioning the effectiveness of outreach work designed to create accessibility without a fundamental questioning of the racial structures and social dynamics that discourage Black students' participation in national college debate. He coached his students to directly engage the stylistic practices and norms of argumentation, making issues such as white privilege, universality, objectivity, and neutrality central concerns in discussions of public policy and debate participation.

Louisville battled a resistant majority white academic community for years. For example, note the following comment from the former director of the Mercer debate team (one of Louisville's major competitors), Joseph Zompetti: "I still feel strongly that arguing these things in debate rounds does more harm than good. I think you're correct to say that the community won't change voluntarily. I do think that discussions and structural changes from the AFA [American Forensics Association] or the NDT committee [National Debate Tournament] or CEDA [Cross Examination Debate Association] can help" (Zompetti 2004b). Despite the considerable controversy, Louisville's debate team would break through racialized barriers and become one of the most competitively successful debate teams in the country. During their winning 2003–2004 season, the team transformed into what became commonly referred to as the Louisville Project. The development of an acclaimed Louisville Method of Debate would have significant reverberations through both the college and high school debate communities more than fifteen years later. Troubling the assumption of neutrality, Louisville's performance and argumentation highlight the hypocrisy of traditional debate performance, its relationship to anti-Blackness, and the normative performance of whiteness as the marker of achievement. The Louisville team delves into the neoliberal ordering of American democracy, making visible the hypocrisy of white liberalism and its attendant antagonism—subtle and overt—toward Blackness.

The story of the Louisville debate team could quite easily be a celebratory one of how a group of Black students reshaped the discussions of race in a majority white community. And yet I am not persuaded by the ease of that narrative. For future directions in voice studies, I encourage readers and writers to consider how the embodiment of Blackness critically affects the reading of voice. Voice studies should address this important question: Does the Black, particularly the Black that performs Blackness, have voice in a civil society constituted by anti-Blackness? This reading of the Louisville Project hopes to complicate voice studies through an engagement with this central question. In the following sections I ground my discussion in theoretical work of anti-Blackness in relation to rhetoric and voice, how the Black body moves in the space of debate competition, and the development of the Louisville Project and its argumentative practices.

THEORETICAL CONSIDERATIONS

Rhetoric scholar Eric Watts considers the nature of rhetorical voice to be a "happening," rather than something that an individual *has* (Watts 2001, 185). Voice is not a noun, nor a possession; instead it operates as a verb, as a process, created in and through "relational" negotiations within rhetorical moments (180). Voice is a happening, a brief moment of recognition that allows the Black to enter the rhetorical moment. The Black cannot *have* voice because the Black cannot have speech. The Black is always already not recognizable as a speaking subject, thus for Watts the Black may temporarily account for this lack of speaking positionality by creating the "happening" of voice.

For Black people, Watts's interpretation of voice is a critical examination of the power of rhetoric in the context of racial politics, and yet there are theoretical blind spots in his analysis. While Watts's work attempts to speak to the problem of raced rhetorical moments, his lack of engagement with the notion of anti-Blackness produces conceptual limits for his interpretation of voice and the capacity of the Black to produce moments of voice. Watts's understanding of voice requires negotiation among speakers and audiences marked by "obligations and anxieties" and produced by the "ethical and emotional dimensions of discourse." In other words, to make voice a "happening" requires a *recognition by* those engaged in the rhetorical moment. Yet the politics of recognition for the

Black body are necessarily tied to the social and political narratives attached to the Black body as a speaking body. The Black body represents dirt or a stain, or to use symbolic anthropologist Mary Douglas's language, a "pollutant," on and in the social body, one that must be controlled and contained (Douglas 2002). That bodies of color remain present despite the fact that they are supposed to be absent "is exactly what maintains white privilege" (Warren 2003, 47). The *soundingness* of Blackness only achieves recognition in a sociopolitical context where the very fact of Blackness holds significant meaning. In other words, the acoustic markers of Blackness are not just about differentiating the vocal utterings and tonal inclinations of particular cultures. It is about the announcement of the Black body into acoustic space where the utterance by the Black is inhabited simultaneously by the marker of not white, and thus not proper. Black utterance enters acoustic space as improper sound even in moments where the Black vocally attempts to mimic sound propriety as marked by normative whiteness. I am attempting to think through that which allows anti-Blackness to continue to cohere the American political landscape. It is the dynamics of the preutterance, that is, at the level of the flesh, that Blackness precedes the *heardness* or sonorousness of sound. By filling in the cracks between voice, the Black body and forces of anti-Blackness, I hope to contribute to Watts's discussion of voice as a rhetorical happening and to voice studies' engagement with theories of anti-Blackness.

If the Black body can never be rendered fully invisible, then that body must somehow be contained, its excesses subdued to produce a form of the Black body that can become recognizable within the space of whiteness. Society tames Blackness by requiring those marked by Blackness to demonstrate their commitment to the norms of whiteness through the performance of the body; generally a mimicking of whiteness. If whiteness is normative, then in order for the speaking Black body to be heard, or come to voice, it must perform in a manner consistent with that norm. For example, the stylistic norms of the college debate community are inextricably tied to the social performance of identity attached to racialized bodies. Style includes bodily performance, how our bodies signify as part of rhetorical practice. In other words, body performance is integral to communal practices in debate that produce a social and competitive environment hostile to Blackness. If the image of the nationally successful debater is a white, male, and economically privileged body, then the stylistic practices of those bodies become the standard by which all other bodies are evaluated. Their practices, their behaviors, their identities become the models or thrones upon which others must sacrifice their identities in the pursuit of "the ballot," or the win.

Racially different bodies must perform that difference according to the cultural norms of the debate community. For Black students it can often mean changing their appearance, standardizing language practices, and eschewing their cultural practices. In essence, in order to have an opportunity for achieving in debate competitions Black students must performatively whiten. "Acting Black" is problematic because those performative identities are not recognizable in the normative frame of debate practice. In fact, Blackness signifies a difference, an opposite; a negative differential. It is not that the debate community explicitly operates to exclude people based on race; rather it competitively rejects Black presence, or non-normative nonwhite performance. It is the combination of cultural values, behavioral practices, and the significance of Black flesh that produce barriers to meaningful inclusion.

For Afro-pessimists, the group of Black scholars who have popularized the study of anti-Blackness, the Black is juxtaposed against what it means to be master, human, citizen, and subject in a manner that is constitutive of US civil society.[2] The United States is built upon a notion of freedom and liberty that necessitated the negative dialectic of the Slave to define the parameters of the nation-state. This foundational relationship has sutured together US civil society and continues to do so. For theorist Frank Wilderson, the grammar of Black/Slave suffering is marked by accumulation and fungibility (Wilderson 2010, 55–57), a relation "of being owned and traded" (Kelsie 2014, 6). The human's (white) grammar of suffering is marked by alienation and exploitation. The grammar of Black (Slave) suffering is not recognizable within the frame of human (white) suffering, it can only be misrecognized as alienation and exploitation.

For the study of rhetoric, an understanding of the political ontology of the Black as one that is necessarily defined by *its* status as Slave/object requires that we engage the question of whether or not the Black has the capacity for recognition in the construction of the moment of voice. Watts would agree that the Black does not have speech; that is why the production of voice is only a momentary process, a happening, by which Blacks can seek recognition. For the Black, the body announces itself prior to speech. So it follows that the Black lacks capacity for speech because they approach the speaking moment as a nonrecognizable subject and "positioned as incapacity" by the "modalities" of accumulation and fungibility.[3] For the Afro-pessimists, capacity is made coherent in civil society by a necessary relationship to Black incapacity. Wilderson notes that "white(Human) capacity, in advance of the event of discrimination or oppression, is parasitic on Black incapacity: without the Negro, capacity itself is incoherent, uncertain at best" (Wilderson 2010, 45). Not only does the Black lack the *same* capacity as the white in first approaching the speaking situation, she or he enters the situation *as* incapacity. The Black must battle with its political ontological condition as a precursor to the process of speaking and let alone the production of voice.

If the "happening" of voice depends on a relationality that produces "a public acknowledgment of the ethics of speaking and the emotions of others," the Black is always already relegated to the position of the unethical speaker that must defend and prove itself by seeking recognition from the Human/Subject in civil society (Watts 2001, 185). Further, it necessitates that the Black performatively and argumentatively approach the moment of voice with only the pretense of subjecthood and capacity. That the Black must construct the *pretense* of being an ethical speaker, while having no subject positioning to do so, requires an *in*authentic performance of the Black *object* as white *subject*. If rhetorical situations require pretense and *in*authenticity then they make unethical speaking the sine qua non of public speech. The Black must mimic the performance of human (white) capacity and becomes bound by the grammar of alienation and exploitation to achieve recognition. In other words, the Black must justify its Blackness or perform itself in a manner consistent with white civil society to even engage in a relational negotiation to produce the moment of voice. Such a practice supersedes and constitutes the ability of the white audience to recognize the Black as an ethical speaker. As rhetoric theorist Amber Kelsie notes, "From an Afro-Pessimist perspective, the problem is not that the Black is 'voiceless,' so much as it is that the voice/speech/body of the Black does not resonate. The Slave is always already being attended to by the white Other, but such recognition itself obliterates any possibility of social life for the Slave" (Kelsie 2014, 13). Full recognition of the Black is not really possible in the rhetorical situation, for the Black is the incoherence that constitutes the coherence of the Human/Subject. In other words, the Black cannot speak about Black suffering without their appeals being read through the frame of alienation and exploitation. The grammar of Black suffering remains unrecognizable and thus *un*acknowledgeable even in the moments where the Black has produced the voiced moment.

Given these considerable obstacles, how did the Louisville Project become successful and produce moments of recognition? Considering the team's transformation from one with a persistent losing record to one of the most successful Black debate teams in the history of national policy debate, it is clear this achievement could not have been possible without a communal recognition of Louisville's ethics and affect. Yet in the moments where those negotiations waver or break down, anti-Blackness as a structural antagonism produces insurmountable obstacles for engaging racialized conflict through discussion and deliberation.

The Development of the Louisville Collective

Amidst concern about the future of Black participation in college policy debate, the Louisville team began asking hard questions about the argumentative and performative choices Black students would need to make in order to be competitively successful. Warner became increasingly and publicly critical of the Urban Debate League (a nonprofit institution designed to increase the race, class, and gender diversity of competitive high school debate practice in the US) as a diversity model for debate. He argued that the Urban Debate League (UDL) project was a farce, that it was not designed to give poor Black students a shot at the highest levels of competition. The lack of successful UDL debaters in national competition at both the high school and college level demonstrated that access to debate alone would not resolve policy debate's diversity problem. "Why? Not because of anything they do, but because the game is rigged against them, who they are, and what the community asks them to become to achieve 'success'" (Warner 2005). Warner moved away from his previous support for and work with UDLs, taking a different path of engaging structural racism in competitive debate. In addition to an aggressive mass recruitment of UDL students and Black students from within the university, the debate team was reconstructed with a redefined purpose for continued participation in competitive policy debate.

Louisville questioned competitive debate's exclusive focus on government policy and its limited solutions to sociopolitical problems, developing alternative forms or styles through which to make argument. Debate is generally an oral, heavily evidence-based contest (in terms of number of average quotations from academic sources used in a debate), where people speak quickly in order to make as many arguments as possible. Moving beyond the conventional form by engaging in storytelling, the use of poetry, video footage, video games, music, hip-hop, and theater, Louisville began experimenting with the performative elements of debate speechmaking to supplement the traditional use of speed and hyper-technical argumentation. They introduced new ways of making arguments about public policy and public deliberation around the central political and social issues of our times.

As the project developed, the debate community was largely unsupportive of Louisville's experimentation with debate norms. Louisville's teams found it difficult to persuade many judges to vote for them, resulting in persistent losses at national tournaments. Their attempts at innovation resulted in angry verbal confrontations, broken friendships, and group segregations within the policy debate community. Accusations including "Klan member," "Plantation owner," and "Uncle Toms" on one side and "anti-intellectuals," "playing the race card," and "irrational" on the other seem to indicate that the controversy surrounding the Louisville Project reached a boiling point (Hoe 2005). For many in the policy debate community, Louisville's confrontational rhetoric and the dialectical nature of debate competition hurt attempts to build coalitions between the Louisville Project and others in the debate community (Blair 2004). As former director of forensics at Illinois State University, Joseph Zompetti, notes, the Louisville style of debating has resulted in "frustrations, anxiety, resistance, and backlash" (2004a). Allan Louden, former Director of Debate at Wake Forest University, refers to the conflict as a "schism" (2004). Jeff Parcher, former debate coach at Georgetown University, argues that this "schism" makes the future of debate "pessimistic." Parcher notes further that while "alliances" in debate have always existed, they have reached a new level of "intensity" one that he has never seen before in the debate community (Parcher 2004, 89–91).

In the summer of 2003, after three years of facing public censure and competitive failure, with the addition of Assistant Coach Darryl Burch, the Louisville team developed a foundational theme to encompass their criticism of traditional debate practice: "you can't change the state, but you can change the state of debate" (interview, July 4, 2012). The team began to work in earnest to develop the parameters of what would later be called the Louisville Project, and one team unit—comprised of members Elizabeth "Liz" Jones and LaTonia "Tonia" Green—were poised for what would become an unexpectedly successful year. They determined that debate participation should have a purpose and theirs would be to increase meaningful Black participation in debate.

Anti-Blackness and the Body: Defying Performative Form

Rather than taking on white debate norms, the Louisville debaters resist attempts to capture and purify their colored bodies, instead choosing to (re)mark their visibility.

For the Black body in the speech situation, it need not necessarily be *doing* anything for it to signify. The Black body is already marked, made visible and meaningful in public spaces. Yet simultaneously, the Louisville debaters *perform* Blackness *doing* something to *draw* attention to the body. It is in the *doing* of Blackness that the reading of the Black body as threatening and criminal is exacerbated from potential to probable threat. In contemporary America, the Blacks who overtly perform Blackness are the "uppity niggers" that must be feared because they neither kowtow fearfully in the face of whiteness nor are they willing to limit the performance of their Blackness for white people/audiences' comfort. Louisville performs Blackness in white spaces, rejecting integrationist or assimilationist performances, as a necessary means of renegotiating the ethical space of tournament competition dominated by anti-Blackness and white privilege.

During their speeches, Jones and Green often turn to speak accusatorily at their opponents, which involved neck rolling, a pushing forward of the body in the direction of the opponent, using staccato hand gestures, and eye-rolling—all behaviors that are often identified as "Black women's attitude." It is important to note that nationally competitive debaters often display aggressive personality traits in verbal competition as a marker of success. Such aggressiveness can be delivered in speeches through choices in vocabulary, tone, emphasis on words, speech volume, body movement, and ad hominem attacks. However, as noted, when debating with a non-normative body, norms are applied differently. Even if aggressive speech is normative in debate, when Jones and Green exhibit such typical debating style, they are stereotyped as loud and aggressive.

Green provides an excellent example of this performative "attitude" in an elimination round against Wake Forest University at the 2004 CEDA Nationals championship tournament. During the cross-examination period following Green's speech, the opponent attempted to concisely define a particular argument Green made during the speech in order to ask a question. He interrupted Green's explanation, although she pushed past his attempt to stop her from speaking. Her opponent succeeded in stemming the flow of words, wanting to move on to some other question. Green conceded, but note the following exchange as captured on video:

> Green: "Well, I'm trying to explain to you so that you can..." [Opponent indicates with a statement that he has a different question that he would like to ask.][4]
>
> Green: "Okay, well, go ahead. 'Cuz it seems like you not getting it anyway. So, ask me something..." [Opponent concedes that he may not understand, but his tone implies that this is more Green's fault than his own.]
>
> Green: "You're not, so ask me something else." [Unintelligible response from the opponent as Green continues to interrupt him.]
>
> Green: "Ask me something else." (Green 2004b)

Green is standing at a podium. The podium is table length and above waist high. She leans on one elbow tilting her body away from her opponent, slightly facing him, mindful of the judges and the audience seated in front of them. Green's hands move in a dismissive manner, indicated by quick shakes of the hand, simultaneous with a twisting of the wrist and periodic dropping of her hand on the table in frustration or irritation. She is exasperated with her opponent's mischaracterization of her arguments. She is giving him attitude, without being rude, although clearly bordering on it. Her dismissal of him is comedic to the large representation of people of color in the audience who were watching this historic debate. Her clipped, brusque tone clearly indicates frustration, but also the sense arises that she finds him somehow unworthy. Green looks away from him during most of the interaction, occasionally giving him the side-eye, sometimes accompanied by eye-rolling and sighs of disapproval. She willingly allows him to mischaracterize her argument without correcting it, and her tone indicates that he is deserving of such inconsideration. Green revises the normative debate practice of rhetorically dominating one's opponent with Black girl style, a rhetorical and bodily performance designed to turn hostile white places into Black girl spaces. Such overt *presencing* of Black femininity in the cold and austere spaces of competition in college classrooms is an act of disrupting the sonorous normality of both policy debate and civil society. That this interchange is occurring between a young Black woman and a young white man (from a prominent, private university), adds to the comedic strength of Green's rhetorical strategy in the cross-examination. Because it contrasts the stereotypical dynamic, Green's dismissiveness of a debater whose privilege normally protected him from such interaction is read as amusing, as evidenced by the laughter from the audience.

Cross-examination, one of the few times debaters directly address each other, provides an opportunity to clarify and gain information that can be used to strengthen one's position during the following speeches. After each of the constructive speeches the opposing team is given three minutes to question the last speaker. It is particularly within these periods that debaters can be most aggressive. Cross-examination can often be a hostile process, with each participant attempting to gain as much important information as possible while avoiding disclosures that might hurt their argument. Hostility in cross-examination can be a strategic tool of intimidation and dismissal. In each of the Louisville debates that I analyzed for this chapter, cross-examination became a unique space through which the Louisville debaters signified on common performative practices in debate.

Jones's and Green's behavior, while disconcerting to majority white audiences out-side of debate, is still representative of the aggressive behavior the community has engaged in for years. A speaker's aggression and assertiveness, in traditional debate, are effective appeals to white authority. Yet the performance of such behavior, by Black women, is often stereotyped as inappropriate. Their behavior, as defined by the common practices of the policy debate community, should be recognizable and thus acceptable to the majority white and male audience. Yet it is clear that those who encountered this team often seemed to exhibit a level of fear or discomfort with Jones's and Green's performance as opposed to admiration and respect, had they presented as a normative white male.

Despite Jones's and Green's repetition of some traditional styles of competition, their Blackened version of normative debate style is often read as disruptive. In as much as Jones and Green perform Black girl attitude, as read by their majority white audience, the more difficult it becomes to build an ethical relationship to the politics of recognition. The problem for Louisville is appeal to Black authority in a space built on appeals to white authority. Using performative Black femininity is a tactic that can elevate anxiety and become an obstacle in building ethical relations. These are forced interactions through competition, Louisville's tactic of making structural racism a part of the discourse of competition rather than appealing to formal, institutional channels produces a demand for recognition. Indeed, as the following sections detail, the Louisville Project disrupted normative debate practice in an effort to expose anti-Blackness as constitutive of the tradition of debate itself.

Destabilizing Normative Knowledge Production: Defying Content

The Louisville debaters seek to augment or supplement what counts as evidence in competition with other forms of knowledge produced outside of academia. Warner believed the overreliance on multiple quotations (or cards as they are referred to by debaters) produced the hyper speed and technique used by students to create a competitive advantage by overwhelming their opponents with the quantity of their evidentiary support, if not with the quality. Reliance on so-called expert evidence also contributed to disparity between those teams who had the coaching resources to complete extensive research and those who did not.

While Louisville saw the benefits of academic research, they were also critically aware of the normative practices that exclude racial and ethnic minorities from policy-oriented discussions because of their lack of training and expertise. Such exclusions prevent radical solutions to the material circumstance of anti-Black racism, classism, sexism, homophobia and transphobia. They are not at all rejecting the use of evidence. Instead, they question the community definition and standard of expert evidence. As Green notes in the double-octo-finals at CEDA Nationals in 2004, "Knowledge surrounds me in the streets, through my peers, through personal experiences, and everyday wars that I fight with my mind" (Green 2004a). The three-tier methodology—personal experience, organic intellectuals, and traditional evidence—became Louisville's process of argumentation tapping into diverse forms of knowledge-making practices.[5] With the Louisville method, personal experience and organic intellectuals are placed on par with traditional forms of evidence.

In the following example Jones offers a critique of traditional debate practice's sole reliance on expert evidence while offering an affirmation of personal experience, social location, and the theorization of material oppression:

> And do they know about the cards we hold
> Like stories of homes heated with stoves
> Unequal education, no healthcare, empty stomachs
> Past due rent bills and pockets filled with lint

> Mothers are cryin' as their children's tears hit concrete floors
> And clocks tick away at childhood.   (Jones 2004b)

Jones's interpretation of "cards" implies self and communal ownership over the knowledge produced by experience. This ownership is implied by the traditional use of debate evidence as well. Cards are not just resources; they are strategic tools in attacking the argumentative positions of a given opponent. Those who hold the *best* evidence or cards, as defined by community standards, have a greater control over the judgment of their argumentative efforts. In other words, traditional cards grant institutional authority to the debaters using them. Those debaters who forego these acceptable forms of evidentiary claims can be characterized as anti-intellectual. Note the following examples from debate coach Steve Woods, arguing that the Louisville Project is not only anti-educational but may also "chill discourse":

> The elimination of the line between the game and the real obliterates the possibility of evaluation along any other means than subjective and personal...In such a condition debate becomes ideological evangelism. It removes the option of conditional endorsement for the purposes of investigation and testing. The critical turn requires that one abandon contestant status but always assume a publicly accountable identity subject to the scrutiny of others. Such a climate is anti-educational in that it prevents the ability to approach issues from an educational standpoint that allows for experimentation and representation of ideas that are not internalizations of the person advancing them. Debate is no longer a free speech or experimental speech space. Instead, it becomes a moral judgment ground likely to chill discourse and silence exploration of a variety of voices.   (2003)

Note the following statement from coach Josh Hoe: "I, in no way, want to discredit the majority of the Louisville approach to debate. I disagree with portions of it which I find to embrace certain tendencies of other historical revolutions toward group think, scapegoating, and anti-intellectualism" (2004).

Jones argues that those who suffer the most in a society hold the real cards, the hard evidence. In other words, those who are subjugated in a social community are often uniquely situated to comment upon the normative social and political practices engaged in by dominant group members that maintain that subjugation (Solorzano and Yosso 2001, 473). However, Jones does not simply create a dialectical opposition between debate "cards" and the "stories" told by the subjugated. Instead, she reconfigures the meaning of "cards," signifying on its traditional meaning in the debate community. In Jones's performance, "stories" become "cards." The meaning of "cards" is not simply reversed, resulting in the replacement of traditional evidence as the measure of expertise; instead, Jones revises our understanding of what counts as knowledge and evidence.

Also, the use of hip-hop by the Louisville debaters in delivering the evidence signifies on this normative construction of expertise. Hip-hop and rap artists are hardly considered "academic" intellectuals. And yet, the Louisville debaters dub hip-hop practitioners "organic intellectuals." A term Louisville takes from Mari Matsuda, the use of "organic intellectuals" as a basis for evidentiary claims repeats the traditional practice of using warranted evidence, but revises by making Black cultural artists experts on race and racism in America. In Green's first speech in the double-octo-final round against an Emory team ranked in the top sixteen teams in the nation, she argues: "Mari Matsuda, a Hawaiian American, discusses her connections and parallels to the African American community and concluded that when we approach change, she felt that listening and opening up space for organic intellectuals are key ways in which we can begin to construct knowledge in a different way" (Green 2004a). According to Matsuda and the Louisville debaters, it is the intermingling of alternative knowledge practices with current practices that can lead to different methods of knowledge construction. For them, the introduction of "organic intellectuals" into the normative processes of knowledge production is a critical tool in developing new methodologies. Green notes further: "Not only do you open up space but you listen to them and follow some of their approaches, follow some of their methods. They have the power to construct a counter-hegemonic discourse to challenge power relations that is not through academia that is just as powerful at dismantling walls of institutional racism through their dissemination of subversive ideas" (Green 2004a). Green makes a crucial discursive choice when she distinguishes between opening up space for organic intellectuals and actually listening to and following their methods when formulating policy. Within debate rounds that are oriented toward critical interrogations of policy, debaters often argue for the importance of "opening up space" for those whose speech is excluded from policy discussions. However, simply opening space for those individuals to participate is often a maneuver by which structural racism maintains itself. In other words, you can open up space within a dominant discourse for those who have been excluded, but such an action does not necessitate structural change.

A Metaphorical Interpretation: Defying Form

During competition a team is either assigned to be affirmative in a debate, and thus must defend the resolutional statement, or is assigned the negative position and negates the affirmative. When a team is assigned to debate on the affirmative side they traditionally use the topic as a lens from which to offer a specific policy action that is consistent with the intent of the resolution. Thus an affirmative team need not defend all aspects of the resolution, just their specific example of the resolution (the affirmative plan). The debate resolution for the 2003–2004 school year read: "Resolved: That the U.S. Federal Government should enact one or more of the following: Withdrawal of its WTO complaint against the EU's restrictions on GM Foods; Increase economic or conflict prevention aid to Greece &/or Turkey; Withdrawal from NATO; Remove barriers to

EU/NATO participation in Peacekeeping and Reconstruction of Iraq; Remove TNWs
from Europe; Harmonize DNA intellectual property law with EU; Rescission of 2002
Farm Bill Subsidies" ("Tournament Topics 1946–2012" n.d.).

Rather than a literal interpretation of the resolution that calls for the affirmative to take
on the role of the US federal government, Louisville expands the traditional interpretation of the resolution and the prima facie burden of affirmative teams in competition.
Specifically, the Louisville debaters engage in a metaphorical interpretation of the resolution. Louisville's strategy is to engage the traditional methods of competitive debate
practice. They argue that the resolution should serve as a metaphor, an alternative to the
strict interpretation of the resolution that leads to a hyper focus on the cost-benefit
analysis of policy considerations. The metaphorical interpretation changes the frame for
the debate. The debate is taken out of the cost-benefit analysis frame where teams argue
over the relative merits of a policy as if it were actually going to be enacted in legislation
after the debate. Normally a debate about US withdrawal from the North Atlantic Treaty
Organization (NATO) would center on the implications to US leadership and the potential
for destabilizing China, Russia, and the Middle East. The debate would quickly degenerate to a comparison of body counts on both the affirmative and negative sides, with each
team arguing that the other team's position will result in a measurable and hence comparable risk of numerous conventional and nuclear wars. Pre-Louisville debate was often
parasitic, discussing bodies as objects, not subjects in policy-making. In debate competition, the race to identify a war or extinction impact as central to one's major arguments,
regardless of their potential probability, has resulted in limiting the significance of more
certain and existing structural impacts like anti-Black racism and economic oppression.
In the following examples, the Louisville debaters uses the foreign policy language of
"withdrawal" from NATO to talk about the "exporting" of US social and political practices abroad. They will then use "withdrawal" and "exporting" as the metaphorical basis
for discussing domestic US anti-Black racism.

Jones and Green defend that the US federal government should withdraw from NATO.
Thus, Louisville does make concessions to normal debate practice as a means of negotiating with the community to achieve common ground for competition. They play with the
neoliberal vocabulary of cost-benefit analysis, signifying on traditional debate practice to
turn the conversation toward structural racism. In the following passage taken from a
speech during a national competition, Jones identifies the consequences of continued US
participation in NATO and argues that these consequences require a withdrawal of the
United States from NATO, in keeping with one of the options in that year's resolution:

> The USFG (United States Federal Government) should withdraw from the North
> Atlantic Treaty Organization because the racism embedded in our institutional norms
> and procedures is exported to other lands. Huey P. Newton drew connections and
> parallels between police forces occupying the Black community and military forces
> stationed abroad in countries of color such as Iraq, Haiti, and Afghanistan. NATO
> began bombing in Kosovo in 1999 and set off the ethnic cleansing of three hundred
> thousand Roma people. The Romani people represent Europe's largest ethnic minority,
> a group of people also held captive in slavery during the 1300s. The United States is

the most powerful country in the world, economically, politically, and militarily. America has the greatest of voting representation in the World Bank and IMF. These global economic institutions provide loans to countries provided that they cut social spending for people and use that money to promote capitalism. America has the power to veto any United Nations decision because of our seat on the UN Security council. In 94 President Clinton was able to block intervention into the Rwandan genocide that ultimately displaced or killed 75% of the African country's population. Iran in 1953 and Iraq in 2003 are just two examples of the military power our country possesses to invade another state and overthrow its government.   (Jones 2004b)

In keeping with the resolution, in this section of the speech the Louisville team advocates a change in US foreign policy. Although clearly critical of the United States as a good faith actor in the international context, they still argue in support of US action. They argue for a negative state action, in which the United States would withdraw from NATO because the United States cannot be trusted as a good faith actor. Earlier in this speech, Jones discusses the effects of institutional racism on African Americans. She draws on statistics that provide striking evidence of the social and economic consequences of being young, Black, poor, and uneducated in the United States. She argues that these statistics are but one clear indication that institutional racism still plagues our society. Jones uses this section to draw a connection between Blacks in the United States and the Romani people in Eastern Europe. Yet even more specifically, Louisville argues that the institutional racism embedded within US society becomes "exported" to other nations by the very nature of its interaction in the international community. Jones argues that the United States engages in institutionally racist practices within the international community and she lists a number of examples in US foreign policy history to support her claim.

Although Louisville provides a clear justification for their policy statement (i.e., their support for a full withdrawal of the United States from NATO) this advocacy is not really the central tenet of their argument. US withdrawal from NATO is a rich metaphor for Louisville's critique of the normative practices and procedures of the debate community. Louisville argues that a metaphorical interpretation of the resolution allows debaters to shift their focus to issues they have the agency to change. Coach Burch, integral to the development of Louisville's practices, notes: "Instead of focusing our agency on the hypothetical situation of what the United States Federal Government should do, we should focus it on how we can utilize the space of debate to bring in more diverse voices" (interview, July 4, 2012). In the following excerpt, Jones explains the metaphor:

But you see, I'm really just trying to change the halls of Congress; that meets on the capital hill of debate tournament tabrooms where pieces of legislation or ballots signed by judges enact the policies of our community. My words right here, right now can't change the State, but they can change the state of debate. The University of Louisville enacts a full withdrawal from the traditional norms and procedures of this debate activity; because this institution, like every other institution in society, has also grown from the roots of racism. Seemingly neutral practices and policies have exclusionary effects on different groups for different reasons. These practices have a long and perpetuating history.   (2004b)

Signifying on American democratic institutional symbols, Jones points to the parallels in power structures between the federal government and the debate communities decision-making processes. The "halls of Congress" represent the halls of debate tournaments. "Capitol Hill," where laws are enacted, is a metaphor for debate tournament tabrooms where opponents and judges are assigned and wins and losses recorded. Ballots, or "pieces of legislation," represent the assigned judge's vote for one team over the other. In fact, debaters often argue that the "impacts" they identify or the solvency for their plan happens "once the judge signs the ballot," as if assigning a winner or loser actually results in the passage of a governmental policy. Jones argues that it is the ballot that is the most significant tool in influencing the practices and procedures of the community. In other words, the competitive nature of debate guarantees that teams and coaches remain responsive to trends among the judging pool.

Ultimately, debate competition is a run to capture or win the judges' ballot. The ballot "enact[s] the policies" of the debate "community," making the space of competition an immanent plane of community change. Before Louisville, the debate community had dealt with issues of diversity and inclusion within itself *outside* of tournament competition. Directors, coaches, assistants, and debaters engaged in outreach and recruitment practices designed to diversify the debate community did so in collaborative adult-driven institutions versus competitive settings where stakeholders were encouraged to dialogue without concern for winners or losers. Green's argument during tournament competition violates the tradition of discussing issues of inclusion in the community's institutional halls, and decidedly outside of competitive debate rounds:

> Racism is one of the leading exports of the United States Federal Government and it exports it on to other countries. It doesn't acknowledge its problems at home and the debate community replicates those values by playing in this fantasy world that we cannot change. By sitting silent, by not acknowledging, or addressing the problems within this community. It is easy for us to say that there are problems, racism and sexism, but the problem comes when we recognize those systemic issues and do nothing to change our methods of how we challenge those problems.
>
> (Green 2004b)

Green holds the community accountable for its failure to significantly increase diversity and inclusion. In doing so, she also holds teams accountable for their methodological choices, forcing other teams and judges to consider whether or not the traditional ways of engaging in competition results in an environment hostile to those debate bodies marked by race, gender, class, and sexual difference. That Louisville chooses to engage the issue of structural racism during competition was particularly discomforting even for those who support diversity efforts in debate. At the beginning of this chapter, I quoted Joseph Zompetti arguing that the debate round is an inappropriate space for the discussion, and that they might more beneficially take place along with structural change in the AFA, NDT, or CEDA (Zompetti 2004b).

Recall Green's argument that the US "exports" American racism to other nations. They radically posit that the debate community, like the federal government, exports its institutional racism to the UDLs. Instead of whitening to strive for success within previous standards, Green points to her difference and the structural power differentials through which all debaters marked by Blackness must compete:

> And, I gave an example of the Urban Debate Leagues, how people don't recognize how they export these type of oppressions onto Urban Debate Leagues, when they assume that they are ignorant and have nothing to contribute to this activity. So they teach them how to debate, never realize that they know how to debate in the first place. This is the example, these are the ways in which we have to change the social structures and the power relations that affect our world.   (Jones 2004a)

This critique of the UDL, along with director Warner's metaphorical likening of debate to a plantation, makes this rhetorical choice confrontational to a group with whom Louisville might have attempted to build coalitions (i.e., the liberal white moderates who help to sustain efforts to diversify debate through programs like the UDL).[6] Debate coach Roger Solt argues that the personalization of debate and the "scorn" for those who work with the UDL may force people out of debate:

> Those forced to debate against these highly personal kritiks are likely to be cast in the role of the villain, as active or at least complicit agents of racism, for example.[7] And even those who have invested years of effort in the pursuit of racial inclusiveness in debate, for example, through work with Urban Debate Leagues, are likely to find their exertions scorned. This is to say the least, unpleasant, and at some point, I fear, it will begin to drive people from the activity.   (2004, 59)

Despite having remained committed and active to diversifying competitive debate, community members responded to Louisville's criticism by framing their project as radical, and thus irrational and unreasonable. For the more centrist and conservative elements within the community, the harsh nature of Louisville's confrontational rhetoric toward the moderates and the liberals provided the impetus for a strategic dismissal of the Louisville Method. In other words, the more conservative or traditional teams simply engage in justifications of why traditional debate practice is good and why Louisville's method harms debate and its members.

We see where the kind of negotiation of the ethical parameters for coming to voice begin to break down. The frustration exemplified by the white liberal dilemma is characterized by a misunderstanding of the fundamental antagonism of anti-Blackness that defines Black suffering as accumulation and fungibility. The Black suffering that produces the exclusion of Black people from debate can only be understood within the white liberal dilemma as alienation and exploitation. Defining Black exclusion as alienation produces diversity initiatives as the response. The burden of the white liberal dilemma can then be released by the gift of access and opportunity. And yet the Louisville debaters peel away the diversity mask and confront the white liberal dilemma with the dirty little secret that it keeps well hidden. That *dark*, dirty little secret. The roots of debate training are irrevocably tied to the very foundation of US civil society and as such it too is sutured together by anti-Blackness. In other words, the style and practice of traditional debate develops in opposition to the rhetorical practices, cadences, rhythms, values, and meanings of Black speech. The very notion of civility, decorum, logical argument, and public deliberation are defined by their relationship to *not* Black modes of speaking, a relationship to Black incapacity.

Conclusions

The debate community's public response to Louisville and the development of Black debate practice is complex. Members of the community do not always engage in a simple rejection of Louisville's method. In fact, the community tends to generally agree with Louisville's goal of increasing meaningful Black participation in policy debate (at least in theory), while disagreeing with the means of achieving that goal. For example, Jeron Jackson, in a post to the debate listserv, wrote: "I think your purpose is wonderful, but the way you do it has some faults" (2004). The faults that have characterized the Louisville Method have tended to focus on the confrontational tone and antagonistic rhetoric targeted at a majority white community that considers itself a bastion of liberal academic thought. These are exemplars of much of the criticism levied against the project. They do not indicate a direct rejection of Louisville's goal of increasing "meaningful Black participation" or of the criticisms of exclusion and lack of diversity in the debate community.

By not avoiding, but rather pointing to Blackness, Louisville's argumentative and performative attacks on traditional debate practice forces the community to turn its analytical tools on the racialization of debate itself. White discomfort in policy debate, in reaction to Louisville's strategy and performance, has run the gamut of denial, anger, frustration, sympathy, engagement, and rejection. Even those whose social and political beliefs lean toward anti-racism have sometimes found Louisville's competitive strategies and rhetorical tactics distasteful. For the majority of the traditional debate community the experience of Black suffering could not possibly justify the disruptions of normative debate practice and social norms of civility and decorum.

I began this chapter with a quote from Liz Jones: "The truth is you don't want Black folks... You're just looking for yourself with a little bit of color" (Miller 2006, 326). The debate community wants Black people, but not *Blackness*. They want "a little bit of color" because a little Blackness is desirable. But the fullness of Blackness as attached to Black bodies is an excess that can only be read as threatening without a grammar of Black suffering. Inasmuch as difference destabilizes the traditional values and practices of the community, it must be treated as potentially dangerous and thus always already under suspicion. True recognition—the kind that would produce a real moment of voice—is not possible in this interracial space. The nature of anti-Blackness cannot be made intelligible because it cannot register as rational argument. To achieve intelligibility would require a questioning of the very rubrics by which civil society functions. Truth, rationality, democracy, liberty, freedom, history, and knowledge would all be called into question. Thus the white liberal dilemma in the debate community can only recognize alienation; it cannot comprehend or actively refuses a macabre dance with anti-Blackness, not realizing that the very nature of Human (white) existence is a dance with Black death.

That Louisville was able to garner wins during the 2003–2004 competition season might seem to indicate that despite the confrontational nature of their strategy they were able to come to voice, bringing structural racism to the forefront of community conversation. And yet more than a decade later, Black debate practice is still a controversial alternative style that has prompted overt acts of discrimination against Black teams, development of austerity policies designed to constrain Black debate practice, wide-scale exclusion of Black judges from adjudicating competition rounds, and threats of white flight from policy debate in response to the ever-growing success of Black debaters and alternative Black debate practices. The debate community is at an impasse, one that has been beneficial for the successful participation of Black students engaged in a critical interrogation of structural racism in debate. Many in the debate community have developed greater knowledge over the past decade, fostering a more accepting segment of the judging pool necessary to sustain competitive success. And yet simultaneous to the growth of this middle minority of tolerant judges, there is a hardening of the more conservative traditionalists and their rejection of the legitimacy of contemporary Black debate practice.

Theorizing voice as a happening, as a verb, as rhetorical movement in response to rhetorical moments, allows us to theorize about the constitutive nature of anti-Blackness to the politics of recognition attached to the captive Black body. The confrontational nature of the Louisville style of debate forces the machinations of anti-Blackness to reveal themselves in white spaces. In other words, Black radical debate practice has been persistently successful because it forces individual white people and white institutions to react to the immediacy of the competition space. Coming to voice as a temporal, momentary happening for the Black may not be about persuasion toward an instrumental goal. Instead, it might be a diversionary tactic designed not to breed recognition by (white) humanity, but to chip away at the façade of coherence that hides the disordering Blackness at the center of modern human subjectivity.

Notes

1. For further discussion of the Louisville Method and the significance of Black rhetorical practice in contemporary policy debate, see Reid-Brinkley (2008), Peterson (2008), and Dillard-Knox (2014).
2. Like any other academic label, some scholars are included under the catch phrase of "Afro-pessimism" who would not necessarily identify as such. However, the following authors' scholarly writings have been integral to the development of what has become a significant interdisciplinary area of the study of Blackness. For further reading, see Spillers (2000), Sexton (2010), Wilderson (2010), Hartman (1997), and Moten (2008). Foundational to the development of Afro-pessimism is the work of Frantz Fanon.

3. I would like to thank Amber Kelsie, whose unpublished work on the capacity of the Black to speak has been critical to the development of my thoughts on this matter.

4. The opponent in the debate requested to remain unidentified.

5. The three-tier methodology is a Louisville innovation to contemporary debate practice. Its tenets have become foundational to the development of Black debate practice over the past fifteen years.

6. Using the term "plantation" to describe the situation, Warner has pointed out that numerous college programs likely increased or sustained university support by touting the debate team's commitment to diversity through outreach and recruitment, providing a built in affirmative defense against claims of racial discrimination. So while the UDL granted access to debate to thousands of inner city students of color, particularly Black students, we would be remiss in assuming that the debate community's participation in the growth of the UDL is completely altruistic.

7. In the mid-1990s when critical arguments first began to appear in debate competition they heralded a new argument form that loosely became referred to by the policy debate community as Kritiks. William Shanahan, the reported originator of Kritik arguments, coined the German translation of "critique" to refer to the new argument form.

Works Cited

Dillard-Knox, Tiffany. 2014. "Against the Grain: The Challenges of Black Discourse within Intercollegiate Policy Debate." Master's thesis, University of Louisville.

Douglas, Mary. 2002. *Purity and Danger: An Analysis of Concepts of Pollution and Taboo.* London: Routledge.

Green, Tonia. 2004a. "Emory University Vs. University of Louisville, Double-Octo-Final Round CEDA Nationals: First Negative Constructive." Louisville, KY: Malcolm X Debate Program.

Green,Tonia. 2004b. "University of Louisville Vs. Wake Forest University, Octa-Final Round CEDA Nationals: First Affirmative Constructive." In *Instructional Videos*, edited by Tiffany Y. Dillard, University of Louisville Malcolm X Debate Program.

Hartman, Saidiya. 1997. *Scenes of Subjection: Terror, Slavery, and Self-Making in Nineteenth Century America.* New York: Oxford University Press.

Hoe, Josh. 2004. "Re: The Evil 'Traditional Debate' Machine - Not!" eDebate Archives. April 6. http://www.ndtceda.com/archives/200404/0406.html.

Hoe, Josh. 2005. "Fwd: Re: Nigga's Go Home." eDebate Archives. November 6. http://www.ndtceda.com/pipermail/edebate/2005-November/064386.html.

Jackson, Jeron Anthony. 2004. "So Tired of This." eDebate Archives. February 17.http://www.ndtceda.com/archives/200404/0341.html.

Jones, Elizabeth. 2004a. "Emory University vs. University of Louisville, Double-Octa-finals CEDA Nationals: Second Negative Constructive." Malcolm X Debate Program Archives, Louisville, KY.

Jones, Elizabeth. 2004b. "University of Louisville Vs. Wake Forest University, Octa-Final Round CEDA Nationals: First Affirmative Constructive." In *Instructional Videos*, edited by Tiffany Y. Dillard, University of Louisville Malcolm X Debate Program.

Kelsie, Amber. 2014. "The Speaking Slave: Reconceptualizing Rhetorical Contingency." Unpublished manuscript.

Louden, Allen. 2004. "Debating Dogma and Division." *Contemporary Argumentation and Debate* 25: 40–2.

Miller, Joe. 2006. *Cross-X: The Amazing True Story of How the Most Unlikely Team from the Most Unlikely of Places Overcame Staggering Obstacles at Home and at School to Challenge the Debate Community on Race, Power, and Education.* New York: FSG.

Moten, Fred. 2008. "The Case of Blackness." *Criticism* 50 (2): 177–218.

Parcher, Jeff. 2004. "Factions in Policy Debate: Some Observations." *Contemporary Argumentation and Debate* 25: 89–94.

Peterson, David. 2008. "Debating Race, Race-ing Debate: An Extended Ethnographic Case Study of Black Intellectual Insurgency in U.S. Intercollegiate Debate." PhD diss., University of California, Irvine.

Reid-Brinkley, Shanara. 2008. "The Harsh Realities of 'Acting Black:' How African-American Policy Debaters Negotiate Representation Through Racial Performance and Style." PhD diss., University of Georgia.

Sexton, Jared. 2010. "People-of-Color- Blindness: Notes on the Afterlife of Slavery." *Social Text* 28 (2): 31–56.

Solorzano, Daniel G., and Tara J. Yosso. 2001. "Critical Race and LatCrit Theory and Method: Counter-storytelling." *International Journal of Qualitative Studies in Education* 14 (4): 471–95.

Solt, Roger E. 2004. "Debate's Culture of Narcissism." *Contemporary Argumentation and Debate* 25: 43–65.

Spillers, Hortense J. 2000. "Mama's Baby, Papa's Maybe: An American Grammar Book." In *The Black Feminist Reader*, edited by Joy James and T. Denean Sharpley-Whiting, 57–87. Malden, MA: Blackwell.

"Tournament Topics 1946–2012". n.d. Cross Examination and Debate Association. http://groups.wfu.edu/NDT/HistoricalLists/topics.html.

Warner, Ede. 2005. "Plantations and Coalition-Building." *eDebate Archives* (2005).February 13. http://www.nctceda.com/archives/200511/0213.html.

Warren, John T. 2003. *Performing Purity: Whiteness, Pedagogy, and the Reconstitution of Power, Vol. 6: Critical Intercultural Communication Studies.* New York: Peter Lang.

Watts, Eric K. 2001. "'Voice' and 'Voicelessness' in Rhetorical Studies." *Quarterly Journal of Speech* 87 (2): 179–96.

Wilderson, Frank. 2010. *Red, White, and Black: Cinema and the Structure of U.S. Antagonisms* Durham, NC: Duke University Press.

Woods, Steve. 2003. "Changing the Game? Embracing the Advocacy Standard." *Contemporary Argumentation and Debate* 24: 85–99.

Zompetti, Joseph P. 2004a. "Personalizing Debating: Diversity and Tolerance in the Debate Community." *Contemporary Argumentation and Debate* 25: 26–39.

Zompetti, Joseph P. 2004b. "Re: Speaking to Transgress." eDebate Archives. April 15. http://www.ndtceda.com/archives/200404/0432.html.

PART IV

....

SENSING VOICE

VOICE AS (MULTI)SENSORY PHENOMENON

....

CHAPTER 12

....

VOICENESS IN MUSICAL
INSTRUMENTS

....

CORNELIA FALES

HALFWAY through the novel *The Voice of the Violin*, Inspector Montalbano joins his elderly friend Clementina for the weekly recital performed privately for her by the renowned but retired Maestro Barbera.

> At nine-thirty sharp, Maestro Barbera struck up the first notes. And before he'd been listening even five minutes, the inspector began to get a strange, disturbing feeling. It seemed to him as if the violin had suddenly become a voice, a woman's voice that was begging to be heard and understood. Slowly but surely the notes turned into syllables, or rather into phonemes, and yet they expressed a kind of lament, a song of ancient suffering that at moments reached searing, mysteriously tragic heights. And the stirring female voice told of a terrible secret that could only be understood by someone capable of abandoning himself entirely to the sound, the waves of sound. He closed his eyes, profoundly shaken and troubled. But deep down he was also astonished. How could this violin have so changed in timbre since the last time he'd heard it? With eyes still closed, he let himself be guided by the voice.
>
> (Camilleri 2004, 21–22)

Montalbano is the Sicilian protagonist of the Inspector Montalbano Mystery Series, and loyal readers know him to be intuitive and dedicated, but also gruff and intolerant of distraction; he has little capacity for self-reflection and, as he tells us several times, no musical sense whatsoever.

So what is it in the sound of the violin that slows the detective's normally frenetic mind, demanding that he focus on the music and its effects? This passage is remarkable in several respects, and we will return to Inspector Montalbano later. For now, it is enough to note his observations on the sounds he hears around him: first he hears the violin metamorphose in real time into a somewhat disturbing voice; second, he recognizes the source of that voice to be female; and third, he hears words in the sounds flowing by him, discerns the emotion with which they are pronounced, but cannot grasp their meaning.

By itself, Montalbano's claim to hear voiceness in a violin sound is far from unusual. Listeners in many, many cultures associate musical instruments with the human voice. In some cultures, the association of instrumental and vocal sound is so ubiquitous that it loses its metaphoric character and is incorporated into the literal terminology that describes musical instruments and their sounds.[1] Furthermore, there is some suggestion that the inclination to hear voices in nonvocal instruments is reflected in the neural networks of our minds. The search for "voiceness"—like the search for "faceness"—has become a priority in laboratories specializing in dedicated perceptual modules of the brain.

Three years after Nancy Kanwisher and her lab (1997) famously discovered face-selective regions of the cortex called the fusiform face area (FFA), Pascal Belin and his colleagues (2000) identified the location of bilateral voice-selective regions called temporal voice areas (TVA) in the superior temporal cortex.[2] Both discoveries were momentous, if only in suggesting that the perception of faces and voices is significant enough to human survival and social equilibrium to warrant dedicated processing mechanisms. But the mystery of "voiceness"—like "faceness"—emerges from the fact that both the voice- and face-selective centers in the brain appear to respond "preferentially" or "selectively," *but not exclusively*, to their respective stimuli. That is, both areas respond to nonpreferential stimuli (e.g., environmental sounds in the TVA and random objects in the FFA), but their responses to their respective preferred stimuli (voices and faces) is stronger and sometimes faster by comparison.[3]

This characteristic of both regions has inspired massive research as to what vocal or facial features each region selects for, and what degree of specificity it requires for preferential processing. Ideally, studies in auditory and visual systems will ultimately amass a collection of principles that outline what exactly the brain thinks a voice or a face is, or at least whether there exist any abstract conditions for "voiceness" or "faceness" that satisfy the brain's selective criteria. This research will be of special interest to us in our investigation of instrumental voiceness.

BACKGROUND: FINDING VOICENESS

One apparent difference between voice and face perception—at least as indicated by neuronal response in their respective stimuli-preferential areas—is that face selective areas appear to be more broadly flexible in the range of face-like features it accepts. Human viewers are primed to identify faces in all kinds of nonface-like contexts, a tendency that has been labeled "pareidolia." While a live human face or a colored photograph of a human face elicits the strongest response from the fusiform region, the same region will also accept a black and white photograph of a face, a schematic line drawing, or even pictures of everyday objects that incite pareidolic faces. Unlike fusiform research, studies of voiceness have returned incongruous findings. One of the few studies aimed specifically at voiceness (Bélizaire et al. 2007) presented listeners with continua of morphed vocal and instrumental sounds. Whereas the researchers expected a linear correlation of response in voice-preferential regions to tokens approaching the voice end of the continua, instead they found a correlation between the activation of listeners' right temporal lobes and degree of "naturalness" for each step along the continuum: one of the brain's requirements for voiceness, it seems, is evidence of a human speaker.[4]

Ironically, some of the general observations and experimental strategies in the search for "faceness" will be more relevant to the discussion here than the strategies used to uncover vocal features. For example, a scan of the literature and self-reflective viewing of face-like figures will yield both empirically verified and anecdotal observations as to the features that the fusiform region prefers to recognize in a face. In particular, a few broader principles will be especially useful to our investigation:

- First, the larger the number of figures inspected for faceness, or the longer the duration of inspection of a single figure, the more likely faceness will appear in a broad selection of unlikely figures. That is, the effort to identify a face in a figure or a session of interpreting multiple figures as faces seems to prime the FFA until it begins to react to figures that might not have excited it initially. This makes testing for absolute faceness challenging.
- Second, simplicity is conducive to faceness: the presence of one or two iconic features is more conducive to cortical response than a multitude of less iconic details. In particular, the presence of a few strongly face-appropriate features allows the visual system to ignore a number of conflicting details.
- Third, faceness occurs with various degrees of abstraction and from different points of view (e.g., in profile versus frontal stance).

I will suggest that these three broad principles have a correlate in the examples of instrumental voiceness to follow, and that an extension of the analogy of voice to face may offer a starting point for our search. This is perhaps not surprising. One might hypothesize that the evolution of instruments capable of voiceness was guided by generations of musicians and listeners who intuitively knew voiceness when they heard it, even if they could not articulate the features that provoked their response.[5]

INSTRUMENTAL VOICENESS

By instrumental voiceness I mean instrumental sound that, in performance, gives rise to a sense of voiceness in listeners. I specify *in performance* because the voiceness at issue here focuses primarily on features of the singing voice, which may or may not be evident in speech. It is in identifying and locating the acoustic source of these features that the broad principles characteristic of the search for faceness and voiceness are relevant.

We will see that sometimes an instrument's basic timbre is similar to the voice, with formants so well-defined that one could almost identify articulated vowels. At other times, an instrument communicates its voiceness in the small details of its attack or in its ability to distinguish itself from other instruments that typically surround it. At times an instrument is credited with voiceness because it "sings" in some undefined fashion that seems related to its pitch range, or to its tendency to swell in intensity or vary its timbre in a way reminiscent of the voice. Occasionally, there are instruments whose attribution of voiceness seems to have developed through listener consensus artificially, by long habit or convention. In other words, since voiceness exists in the mind rather than in the entity where it is found, it can be discovered in large structures and tiny details, perceptually or conceptually, specifically or abstractly. It can even occur because the music culture to which an instrument is indigenous wills it to have a voice that may be inaudible to outsiders.

Since arguably the most persuasive evidence of voiceness in an instrument is its ability to produce voice-like timbral formants, some general observations on the acoustics and perception of formants will be useful. Historically use of the term "formant" when applied to instruments has been controversial,[6] so I will specify that in this chapter, I use "formant" to refer to a spectral prominence in a specific frequency range that contributes to a particularly vocal quality in an instrument's timbre. In order to produce that quality, instrumental formants should have a relatively wide bandwidth, ideally with smooth slopes and a deep valley between them. In a chapter called "Formant Peaks and Spectral Valleys," Perry Cook claims categorically that "if more or fewer than three formants exist in the region between 250 and 3000 Hz, the sound is not perceived as speechlike" (1999, 136). I will not be quite so exacting here, in part because the quality we are looking for is not "speechlike," but "voicelike." Whether speechlike or voicelike, an instrument's timbre is the result of the interaction between the sourcewave produced by its resonating device and the filtering action of the resonator through which the sourcewave travels.

Generally speaking, the softer the material used to construct an instrument's resonator, the broader the spectral peaks of the sound that results. Obviously, the softest resonating material in acoustic instruments is the flesh and cartilage that comprise the human vocal tract, which is why the voice is the quintessential formanted sound. Many instruments besides the voice do in fact make use of the performer's mouth and some part of the vocal tract as resonators, either alone as in the case of the jaw harp and some plucked/struck bows, or coupled to the main resonator of the instrument as in the case of the harmonica or the didgeridoo. While it is risky to posit a rationale for aspects of performance practice, we might observe that the result of joining the performer's mouth to some part of an instrument is useful in part for the production of formants, but also because as resonator, the mouth is supremely supple, capable of reshaping itself, and thus the timbre of any sound that passes through it.

Instruments with resonators made from softer species of wood like spruce or cedar will also produce a more formanted sound than similar instruments with resonators of harder wood.[7] Furthermore, replacing some part of the hard surface of a resonator with animal skins, thus providing a softer surface to dampen sharper resonances, also enhances formants.[8] Yet another technique for raising formants in less well-endowed sounds is with the addition of noisy elements that function to shape formants around harmonics that would otherwise pierce through a sound's spectrum. The production of supplementary noise that is sufficiently dense to create formants capable of projecting voiceness usually requires the use of auxiliary devices. These include mirlitons embedded into the resonators of various instruments,[9] and "obstructors" lying between the strings and bridge of many chordophones.[10] In order to augment a timbre's voiceness, however, the supplementary noise must fuse with, rather than layer over,[11] the primary tone of the instrument (Fales and McAdams 1994).[12] We will return to the subject of supplementary noise later in this chapter.

While the presence of formants contributes in a large way to the perception of voiceness in instrumental sound, by themselves, they are not enough to convey voiceness to listeners; this is because the perceptual salience of nonvocal formants only emerges by contrast or motion. For a steady-state instrumental tone, in fact, an audience may not be able to tell whether it has formants or not,[13] since listeners do not ordinarily hear spectral shapes. Just as they do not, by default, "hear out" the individually pitched harmonics that perceptually fuse together into the sensation of timbre, so also are listeners unable to identify the coherent subgroups of harmonics that comprise formants—unless, that is, the spectral context of the formant changes, revealing the coherence that defines it. Without some defining motion, the formant simply fuses into the rest of the sound's timbre where it is essentially inaudible. Since pitch and timbre are the two frequency parameters of sound, the change of one through time sharpens the salience of the other.

Thus, the perceptual discovery of an instrumental formant can happen in three ways: either the formant moves, while the frequencies that comprise it remain stationary, or the formant remains stationary while the frequencies that comprise it move, or both formant and frequencies move, but independently of each other. Any of these three changes to the spectral context serves to put the formant into relief by emphasizing its contours as a perceived unit.

That it is difficult to imagine the inaudibility of an uncontrasted instrumental formant illustrates the complexity of the subject of this chapter. The nonlexical "voiceness" that we are looking for in instruments does not actually exist per se in vocal sound; there is no real analogue to an inaudible formant in speech. One of the differences between vocal and instrumental timbre is that the features of vocal timbre are perceptually interpreted with reference to an external system—that is, the sounds of speech. Even if a singer produces a melodic phrase on a single nonlexical tone, listeners will hear it as a melismatically prolonged vowel, an "ah," for example. Features of instrumental timbre, on the other hand, can only be interpreted relative to other features that coincide with it over time. In speech, listeners do not need contrast to perceive the formants that define the vowel [i]. And when formants move in vocal sound, the result is a series of phones that resolve into phonemes, the constituents of words. Phonetic features have an absolute value when they are heard phonemically as the raw material of spoken language, the ultimate significance of which is, finally, meaning. The significance of individual features of instrumental timbre is only ever relatively accessible.[14]

Other features we will encounter are visible in Figures 12.1a–d. Figure 12.1a depicts a tenor voice singing a popular French song from the 1960s, accompanied by an orchestra; 12.1b shows a piano introduction to a song with the voice entering at 7 seconds and 13 seconds; 12.1c is a single line of an Irish melody played on a bowed fiddle; and 12.1d consists of lines from a traditional song sung a cappella (vertical stripes are the singer's clapping during and between verses).

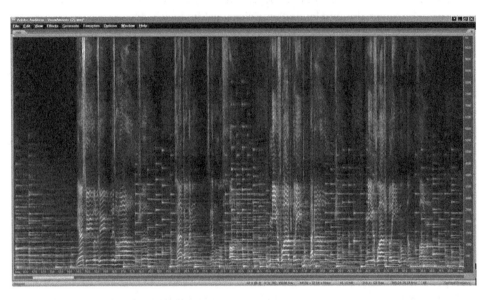

FIGURE 12.1A Voice accompanied by orchestra, Jacques Brel: "Les Vieux Amants."

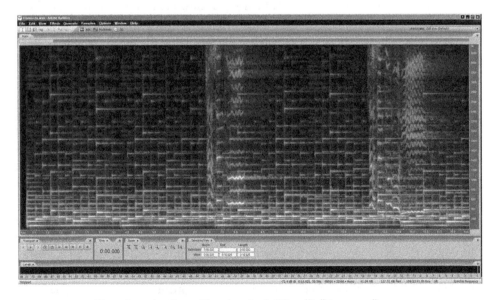

FIGURE 12.1B Piano introduction with voice, André Bocelli: "Romanza."

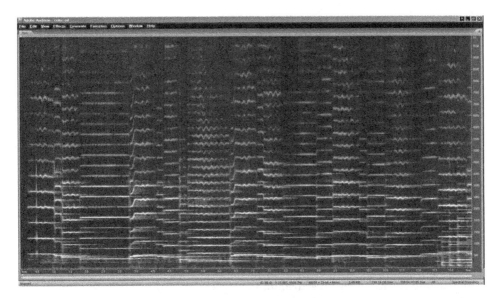

FIGURE 12.1C A single melodic line on a bowed fiddle.

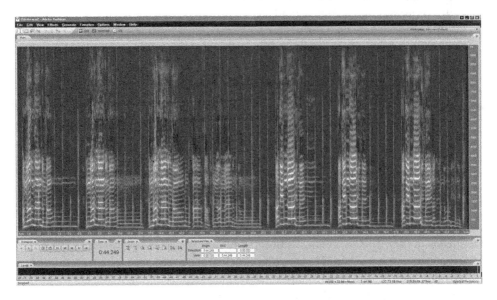

FIGURE 12.1D Stanzas from a song sung a capella with clapping, Odetta: "Another Man Done Gone."

The first two Figures (12.1a and b) demonstrate what I call the "voice visibility" rule in spectrographic analysis, which with some notable exceptions applies to most genres of vocal music across most cultures. Very simply, the rule states that in a composite spectrogram—that is, a spectrogram of sounds from multiple concurrent sources—of which one component is a human voice, the voice will usually be the most visible and trackable over the length of the spectrogram.[15] The voices in 12.1a and b are visually distinct from the instrumental sounds that surround them as a result of a collection of vocal idiosyncrasies that may individually occur in one or another instrument, but that rarely occur as a group in any acoustic sound but the voice. First, notice in 12.1a and b that the spectral spread of the voice is considerably broader than that of the other instruments; its audible harmonics remain robust and extend far higher in frequency than the other sounds.[16] Figure 12.1c, an unaccompanied violin, demonstrates that a violin, at least, is capable of projecting its sound into the high frequency ranges. Perhaps we need to concede that at least some of the discrepancy in spectral spread between the sounds is performative, rather than inherent to the instruments. That is, performers are playing their instruments with deliberately constricted spectra in order to allow the single voice in each figure to stand out in all its glory.

Other vocal characteristics that set the voice apart from other instrument in a complex spectrogram are most visible in a comparison of the solo fiddle in Figure 12.1c with the a cappella voice in 12.1d. First, notice the relatively straight trajectory of the violin tones compared to the irregular movement of the voice; this is also evident in Figures 12.1a and b, where the instrumental sounds continue with all their harmonics traveling in parallel along their trajectories at regular intervals while the voice curves around and over the other sounds. In Figure 12.1d, even when the singer means to sustain a tone in the first phrase of her song for a duration comparable to that of the violin, and even when she attempts to do so with little or no vibrato, her voice wavers in pitch; it glides from note to note, it descends from its pitch at the ends of phrases, and generally moves with visibly less "precision." By contrast, even when the violin in Figure 12.1c plays with a vibrato, it maintains a comparatively straight course compared to the vocal vibratos in Figures 12.1a and b, which appear to follow the curve of harmonics.

It is worth pointing out that a spectrogram shows many small details of which listeners are often not conscious, but that are nevertheless important to the overall sound they hear; in most cases, a listener does not hear the movement of a singing voice as "less precise" than that of other instruments (given a certain level of competence on the part of the singer). Another difference between the voice and other instruments that listeners may not register is visible in Figures 12.1b and c. Here, the spectrogram demonstrates the tendency of certain instruments, chordophones in particular, to produce tones whose components extend into and beyond the attack of the tone following. Each tone of the solo violin in 12.1c shows harmonics overlapping with the tone following to such an extent—sometimes for almost half a second—that if one were to play just the overlapping portion, one would hear a clear interval of two simultaneous notes. Yet within the context of the entire melodic segment in 12.1c, the brief polyphony of the overlapping tones is not audible—one hears only the monophonic notes of the melody. The sensation of a single line of melody, note following note, is an auditory illusion, as is absence of the overlapping intervals from a listener's listening awareness, most likely the result of top-down auditory processing that privileges the horizontal movement of the melody over the vertical configuration of simultaneous notes.[17]

Since there seems to be no established terminology designating the overlapping portion of one tone into the next, I will provisionally label this phenomenon "ringing," thus distinguishing it from reverberation by specifying that ringing issues from the instrument itself, rather than from some surface that reflects sound back to its origin.[18] Though most listeners understand tonal ringing as part of the timbral complexity of the next tone, the actual perception of ringing is not the same as simply hearing the next tone augmented by a few supplementary harmonics. Rather, ongoing rung sound may brighten the timbre or strengthen the fundamental of a subsequent tone, or it may contribute subtle affective features to a musical line.[19]

In a natural environment, ringing originates either in a vibrating column that maintains its oscillations after direct excitation has ceased, or from a continuation of the standing wave propagated in the resonator by the original source vibrations.[20] Either way, the important point here is that under normal circumstances, *the voice is incapable of producing natural ringing*. If rung sound originates in the vibrating column, then any instrument—like the human voice—with only a single vibrating source must continually alter its rate of oscillation with each new pitch, thus preventing sustained vibration. If, on the other hand, rung sound originates with the standing wave in the resonator, then the voice is handicapped by the significant damping capacity of the vocal tract, which is likely to quash the standing wave as soon as ongoing stimulation terminates. But for instruments capable of sustained ringing, a performer who deliberately suppresses the rung sound at particular points in a performance contributes significantly to the voiceness of instrument's sound.

Two other features of the voice that contribute to spectrographic voice visibility are neither inevitable nor unique to vocal sound, since they can be produced by certain other instruments. The first is the tendency of vocal music to progress by phrases as compared to the much longer expanses of sound produced by instruments not limited to air capacity. As a musical instrument, the singer's physiology lacks inorganic implements as well as organic technique that allow for continuous sound: imagine the result in vocal quality of a singer who managed to perform some sort of circular breathing.

The second feature common to vocal sound, in Western *bel canto* style especially, is the ability of artists to vary spectral range and complexity while maintaining a constant amplitude—in short, the ability to change the concentration of timbral energy without altering the volume. For many nonvocal instruments, by contrast, the primary way to create a sound whose very high frequency components contribute audibly to its timbral quality is to amplify the sound as a whole until previously inaudible elements cross the threshold of hearing. Singers trained in the Western classical tradition, on the other hand, are able to control both the glottal sourcewave and the filtering action of the resonator independently, and depending on the context of performance, they can expand or compress the spectral spread of their voice as necessary—all without changing the loudness of the sound. In addition to controlling the spectral magnitude of their sound, singers can also manipulate smaller portions of the spectrum for expressive purposes. They may use some of the affective cues used in speech prosody, emphasize the naturally noisy consonants of the text they are singing for a rough attack, or vary the intensity of their sound to imitate the effect of emotion on the vocal apparatus (Patel 2008).

Whenever an instrument can imitate one or several of these features of vocal sound—especially if the imitation contrasts suddenly with previous sounds created by the instrument—a sense of voiceness is produced. To the extent that the imitation is successful, it is clear that even listeners with no theoretical or practical experience with vocal sound are nevertheless possessed of an understanding—call it an expectation—of characteristics of the voice.

VOCAL INSTRUMENTS

The discussion of vocal instruments that follows is divided into three categories. The first category contains instruments whose tones show little movement in frequency—only two or three pitches at most—while producing substantial movement in formant position (i.e., with quasi-stable pitch and changing timbre). The second category contains instrumental sound that shows either consistent formant position and significant frequential movement, or both changing formant position and independent frequential movement (i.e., with either constant timbre and changing pitch, or with timbre and pitch changing independently). The third category consists of sounds that lack formants altogether, or whose formants contribute little to the sensation of voiceness, but that achieve voiceness by other means: either they use other features they share with the voice to project a sense of vocal movement, or they alternate or concur with vocal sound in such a way that the two both imitate and provide a model for the other. Though each of these three categories contains only a few instruments, in most cases the examples should be understood to represent a larger class of instruments with similar mechanisms of voiceness.[21]

Moving Formants, (Quasi-)stable Fundamental Frequency

While many musical instruments are capable of producing a range of pitched tones with characteristic timbre, the instruments in this category typically produce only one or a few pitches, often acting as a drone beneath prominent and shifting timbres. In order to generate such fluently changing timbre, these instruments must be equipped with moveable resonators. The greatest proportion of these are—as noted earlier—instruments whose resonator is the performer's vocal tract—specifically the mouth—or instruments with coupled resonators of which one is the performer's mouth. While this is true of two of the instruments in this category—the didgeridoo and the Philippino bamboo *kubing*—I focus here on the Bengali *gopiyantra*, whose vocal timbre does not depend on the musician's mouth, but rather on a moveable resonator. The longer version of this chapter at the *Oxford Handbook of Voice Studies* website compares the *gopiyantra* with the didgeridoo and the Philippino bamboo *kubing*, both of which produce the wide formants that distinguish speech and communicate voiceness in a manner typical of mouth resonated instruments.

Bengali Gopiyantra

The Bengali *gopiyantra* is one of the unusual instruments in this category, because it is an impulsive instrument and because it is one of the few instruments capable of regular and significant timbre change without resorting to the flexibility of the performer's mouth as resonator. Rather, the *gopiyantra*, pictured in Figure 12.2a, is one of the hybrid instruments described earlier that use animal skin as part of its resonator. Sometimes described as a plucked drum with both chordophonic and membranophonic qualities, the *gopiyantra's* resonator consists of a plain gourd open on both ends, the bottom of which is covered with animal skin. Through the skin, the gopyantra's single string stretches to a peg at the apex of a triangle formed by two slats attached to either side of the gourd resonator. In performance, the musician compresses or releases the two slats, a process that changes both the tension of the string and and the shape of the gourd resonator at the same time. The *gopiyantra* is a timbrally ingenuous instrument, but it is also a simple one, capable of only harmonicized pitches (it has no neck for stopping the string) and a limited range of timbres.

However simple the instrument, the sample of *gopiyantra* music shown in the spectrogram of Figure 12.2b is spectrally complex, and I encourage readers to listen to the

FIGURE 12.2A A *gopiyantra*.

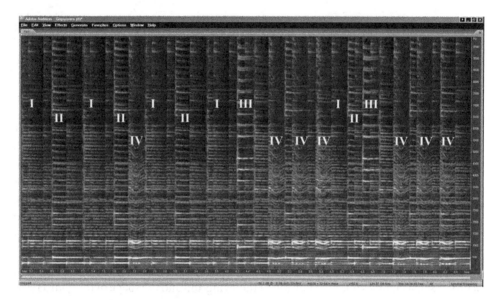

FIGURE 12.2B A line of a *gopiyantra* piece with roman numerals marking four characteristic timbres.

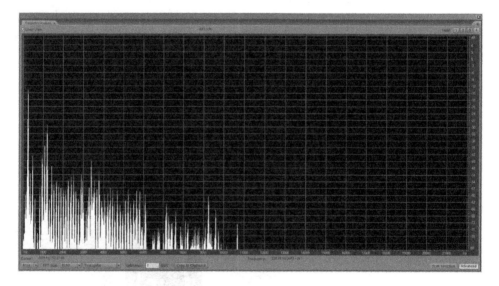

FIGURE 12.2C Timbre I: default and drone pitch 236 Hz, A#3.

sample on the website associated with this article. The *gopiyantra* is one of the few instruments that demonstrates voiceness by contrast—that is, it produces regular but sporadic voicelike segments, surrounded by the very nonvocal segments one might expect of an impulsive instrument. The spectrogram in Figure 12.2b shows the *gopiyantra*'s four different timbres, marked I through IV, which repeat over and over again throughout the piece. Timbres I, II, and III represent instrumental segments, while

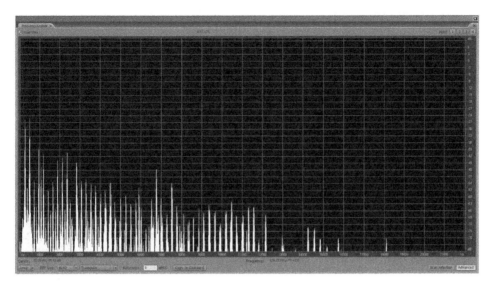

FIGURE 12.2D Timbre II: first octave 472 Hz, A#4.

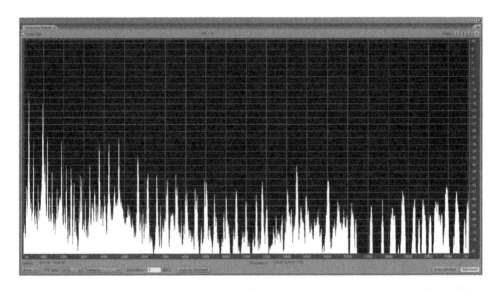

FIGURE 12.2E Timbre III: second octave, 943 Hz, A#5.

timbre IV represents voicelike segments. Each of the three instrumental segments occur on different pitches: timbre I occurs on the lowest drone pitch that continues throughout, while timbre II occurs on an octave higher and timbre III two octaves higher than the drone (timbre I). The voicelike segments (timbre IV) also occur on the drone pitch. These pitch differences corresponding to the different timbres account for the difference in the spacing of harmonics in the spectrogram (12.2b) and less clearly in the spectra (12.2c–f).[22]

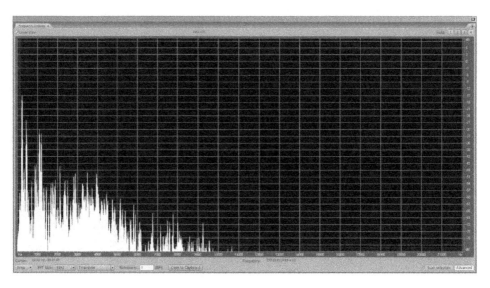

FIGURE 12.2F Timbre IV: vocal timbre, 465 Hz (A#4) to 434 Hz (A4) to 466 Hz (A#).

On first listening, the drone note (timbre I) sets up a rhythm of repeated timbre I notes, alternating regularly with timbre II, then in the second half of the sample with timbre III, each at their respective pitch levels. The drone of the *gopiyantra* sample "disappears" perceptually at first with each of the octave tones, the new pitch distracting the listener from the default drone. Then the drone "reappears" as the listener realizes that, of course, it was there all along underlying the pitched tones. In fact, the instrument only has one string responsible for all the pitch activity, both octaves and drone. A look at the spectrogram confirms that both octave pitches are indeed produced by harmonics of the default drone tone, but that it continues to sound its fundamental at the same time, while also changing the tone timbrally with each pitch change.

For our purposes, the interesting tone is the one I have labeled "vocal timbre" in Figure 12.2f and as IV on the spectrogram (12.2b). It supports my claim earlier that formants become salient only with motion. Perceptually, all the notes the gopyantra produces are potentially vocal: the spectra show fairly coherent formants, and the ongoing drone softens the impulsiveness of the sounds. But on the spectrogram, the frequencies comprising timbres I, II, and III—that is, all except the vocal timbre—remain horizontally flat over time, without movement. They each appear with a new attack, and the tempo is rapid enough that there is little audible decay before the next attack; thus, each tone sounds only a single pitch in a flat steady state from attack to attack. The result is that even with acoustic formants, timbres I, II, and III are completely lacking in voiceness due to the absence of pitch movement. The vocal timbre IV, on the other hand, has a fundamental that slides with all its components in parallel over the course of its duration from ~466 to 434 and back again to 466 Hz (from about A# to Ab to A#); with this movement, the tone suddenly takes on a striking vocalness, projecting with clarity what sounds to be the vowel [u], complete with transients into and out of the vowel core. In sequence, then, timbres I, II, and III seem to form the ground of the music, over which the vocal-timbre tones constitute an audible figure.

Though it is difficult to see in the small, black and white spectrogram here, the larger version of the same spectrogram on the website associated with this chapter provides visual evidence that when the timbre designated as vocal takes its turn in the rotation of timbres, it briefly demonstrates the voice visibility rule; in the midst of frequentially straight instrumental tones, the vocal timbre with its "swoop" stands out as clearly as any voice. Close inspection of the spectrogram in 12.2b also reveals that by default, the first octave and second octave instrumental timbres all feature notes that ring out strikingly, overlapping with the note following. Only strings producing the vocal timbre are deliberately dampened, stopping abruptly with the onset of a new timbre. From a perceptual point of view, the lack of ring in timbre IV contributes significantly to its voiceness— almost as much as its swooping movement. Note that these two regularities—voice visibility and ringing—work together to enhance the figure-ground configuration of the *gopiyantra* sample, both visually and aurally. Both the first and second octave timbres visibly ring through the vocal timbre as though to maintain the ground behind the figure of the vocal timbre layered on top of the others.

A final observation on the *gopiyantra*: unlike many instruments described in this chapter, the *gopiyantra* demonstrates its voiceness only in certain sections of its music. It is an impulsive instrument—generally less conducive to voiceness than sustained instruments—and in the majority of its music, it shows most of the characteristics that define an impulsively excited stringed instrument. Then suddenly with only a few changes, it becomes articulate, enunciating a vowel with such clarity that one almost imagines a singer joining the performance. It is a fascinating transformation, if only in demonstrating the importance of small instrumental details—ringing versus damping, the precision of instrumental pitch sustain versus a momentarily vocal swerving of pitch. In this, the *gopiyantra* demonstrates the second principle of faceness for vision: the ability of a few carefully chosen, iconic features of voiceness to counteract a host of instrumental characteristics.

(Quasi-)Stable or Moving Formants and Fundamental Frequencies

Compared to the first category, this category has rather less restrictive conditions for membership—indeed, for acousticians who insist that *all* musical sounds have formants, a majority of the world's instruments might claim eligibility. While, as noted in footnote 6, I disagree that all instruments produce formants, it is fair to observe that one of the differences between the two categories is this: many of the instruments represented by those discussed in the first category are indigenously acknowledged and sometimes deliberately produced as voicelike; they may have a particularly vocal role in their respective cultures or even substitute for the voice on special occasions. Some number of instruments in the second category, on the other hand—particularly ones representing the Western tradition in which pitch has always been the most important parameter— seem to satisfy the requirements for membership subtly, almost accidentally. That is, they may exhibit all the characteristics necessary for voiceness without being necessarily acknowledged or even perceived as vocal. In the end, of course, the act of hearing voiceness in instrumental sound requires some degree of auditory flexibility and willingness to hear the flow of timbre with the same attention normally applied to pitch.

The Mongolian Morin Khuur

The *morin khuur* is a bowed chordophone. (Please note that, as a class, bowed chordophones are treated in the third category, since I claim that they do not exhibit true formants as defined in this chapter.) The *morin khuur* is treated here, however, to represent the group of bowed chordophones whose resonators consist in part of animal hides, which, as noted earlier, typically (though not always) provides the soft material conducive to pronounced formants. The traditional *morin khuur* is a two-stringed, bowed spike fiddle with a trapezoidal resonator, a narrow neck, and strings made from a horse's tail. A carved horsehead sits at the top of the neck above the tuning pegs that hold the strings. Traditionally and still now in many regions, the *morin khuur* featured a resonator composed of animal skin attached to a wooden frame. As part of the Cultural Revolution in Mongolia, however, the skins were replaced with wood, along with other changes to the instrument in construction, tuning, and performance technique. Herein lies a mystery that we will return to presently.

The bow of the khuur is loosely strung with horsehair; in performance, the instrument is bowed underhand, so that two or three fingers on the bowing hand can alter the tension of the bow, and thus the timbre of the tone. The effect of the changing bow tension can be seen in the spectrogram of Figure 12.3a at about 4.5 seconds and again at 23 seconds into the sample where swooping formants occur in tones at a steady-state pitch. Notice also the careful distribution of overlapping ringing—where it is present, and where restrained. Part of the lack of ringing may be the result of the fact that the instrument has only two strings, but careful listening to the sound file from which Figure 12.3a is taken suggests that aesthetic expression is also part of the performer's choice of placement.[23] The spectrum in Figure 12.3b, sliced from 12.3a, indicates that the timbre of the *morin khuur* consists of several formants, each with distinct peaks and valleys between them. It is the clarity of the khuur's formant structure that separates this instrument from other bowed chordophones, which I have put into the third category. The *morin khuur* is typical of instruments with both moving formants and moving pitch, which make them more explicitly and naturally analogous to the human voice than the instruments in either the first or third category.

The mystery—for which I have found no answers—of the changes to the *morin khuur* that converted it into a national instrument consistent with "cultural enlightenment" is this: before the transition, the animal skin resonator produced "soft, muted sounds, suitable for playing inside the tent" (Pegg 2011). Research on other bowed chordophones with skin resonators[24] shows that for the most part they are exquisitely vocal, often

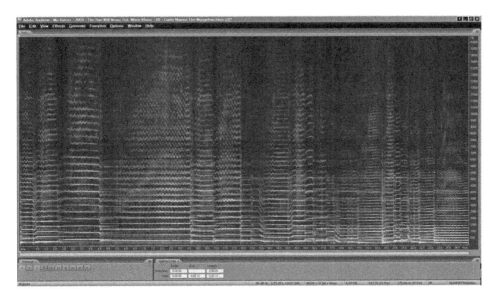

FIGURE 12.3A *Morin khuur*: "The Sun Will Never Set."

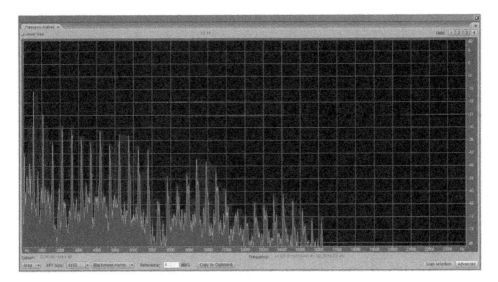

FIGURE 12.3B *Morin khuur*: "The Sun Will Never Set."

incorporating significant noise elements, with spectral envelops dominated by soft, blunt formants. Thus one would expect that the replacement of the skin resonator with a wooden box would almost certainly have increased the volume of the *morin khuur* and would probably have eliminated some or all of its noisy components, while also homogenizing its sounds and sharpening its formants. Since I have never heard the *morin khuur* in its original, softer form I cannot comment on the modern instrument's relative loudness, but I can hear that it is still thoroughly vocal and we have seen that its sound

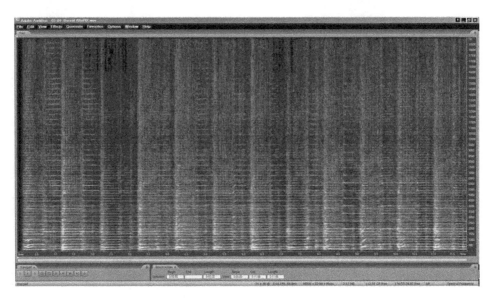

FIGURE 12.3C *Morin khuur*: "Booral Alta" with strong attacks.

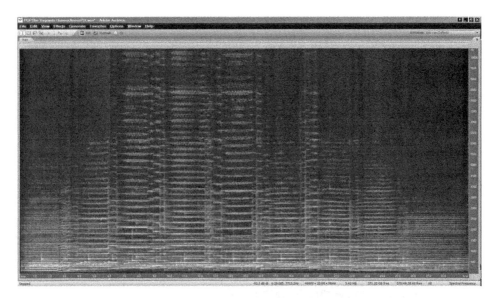

FIGURE 12.3D *Morin khuur* with orchestra: Popular Version of "The Vagrant's Homesickness" with orchestra, showing spectral spread to stand out.

still possesses well-shaped formants—both of which accounts for my decision to separate it from other chordophones as a member of the second category. I do not know how
the *morin khuur* has achieved such superior vocality. Deprived of its softer-than-any-
wood skin resonator, the instrument has nevertheless retained much of what I imagine
its original character to have been. More research on the construction and performance of the *morin khuur* might offer insights as to how it has retained its formant

structure and judicious use of noise, endowing it with a voice, by turns gruff, merry, bold, and world-weary.

One feature of all bowed chordophones (including those in the third category) important to the production of voiceness is the variability of their attack transients—the portion of the sound that precedes the steady state harmonics of a sustained tone. Both Western classical and traditional bowing of chordophones often emphasize the noisy features of the initial contact of the bow with the strings. The resulting sounds may range from harsh and buzzy to scratchy, depending on the performer's bowing technique. Empirical research long ago demonstrated that the onset of an instrument or speech sound—the attack—is often the most important element for listener identification of the source.[25] And studies in the phonetics of vocal discourse have identified the manipulation of initial consonants by speakers as an important means of communicating paralinguistic information. A skillfully wielded bow fills the same function as noise-enhanced consonants, shaping an attack for the steady-state vowels that follow. Figure 12.3c shows that the *morin khuur*, like almost all bowed chordophones, also makes use of its attack transients for paramusical purposes; here the roughness of the attack serves both a metrical and we might suppose an expressive function.

Probably the most prominent acoustic characteristic that instruments like the *morin khuur* (and the other bowed chordophones to be discussed in the third category) share with the voice sets both apart from many other pitched instruments: unlike most aerophones and some pitched idiophones, both the voice and most chordophones constitute vibrating systems in which the source vibrating device is loosely coupled to the resonator with minimal interaction between them. In part, the physical composition of both instruments is responsible for their loose coupling, since the vibrating device in each—the vocal folds and instrumental strings, respectively—is connected to its resonator in a way that allows only one-way movement in the transfer of energy between them. For the most part, in other words, the source vibration in the strings or the glottis is physically separate from the standing wave propagated in the body of the violin or the vocal tract.

In the tightly coupled systems most typical of aerophones, on the other hand, the source vibration occurs at one end of the standing wave of the vibrating column. Thus, once the source vibration (lips, reeds, etc.) introduces an oscillating airflow into the resonator, the standing wave that results feeds back onto the subsequent action of the initial source device.[26] From a musical point of view, then, one difference between loosely and tightly coupled systems is the relative independence of pitch and timbre in the first and the mutual dependence of pitch and timbre in the second.[27] Trueman notes that one effect of their loose coupling is that "both the violin body and the vocal tract have frequency responses with 'fine structure'—subtle yet substantial variations, particularly above about 1000 Hz" (1999, 44). The effect of the fine structure is that a skillful performer can use very small change in intonation—either in a vibrato or in the approach to a new tone—to invoke a radical change in timbre. This is, perhaps, most clearly audible in the sustained tone at 4.5 seconds into the *morin khuur* piece in Figure 12.3a, where the duration of the note gives the performer time to set up his vibrato and, in effect, move into the timbre of the sound.

While Figures 12.3a and b are taken from a traditional performance of the piece *morin khuur*, Figure 12.3d represents a popular rendition of a Mongolian folksong called "The Vagrants' Homesickness." The piece features the *morin khuur* playing the melody of the song surrounded by a lush orchestra and piano, with lots of reverb. The segment represented in the spectrogram of Figure 12.3d demonstrates that the ability of the voice described earlier to expand and contract the spectral spread of its tone independent of changes in amplitude is a feature shared by the bowed chordophones. The phrase begins with the *morin khuur* playing a sustained bass note while the other instruments ripple above it. About 3.5 seconds into the segment the *morin khuur* starts to ascend in pitch, while increasing its spectral spread and vibrato, until at about 60 seconds it plays in full spectrum, setting itself off from the other instruments. Like the voice discussed earlier, the Mongolian fiddle moves from a reduced to expanded spectrum with minimal perceived increase in amplitude.[28] Even at full spectrum, which lasts about 9.5 seconds (from 7 seconds to about 16 seconds), the intensity of the *morin khuur* waxes and wanes with the music. Even without hearing the music, the voicelike quality of this ability on the part of the *morin khuur* is evident in its apparent compliance with the "voice visibility rule."[29]

Unformanted Instruments; Voice and Instrument Model Each Other

We will look at only three instruments in this category, though there are many possible examples in different musical traditions.

Bowed Chordophones

Readers will recall that the bowed *morin khuur* was discussed in the second category because of its pronounced formants. As we will see presently, the more general class of bowed chordophones is relegated to the third category, because they most often lack voicelike formants as defined in this chapter. Nevertheless, we will also see that they do share a great many other features with the *morin khuur*.

Bowed chordophones are important across many of the world's cultures, where they are frequently esteemed for their vocalness. In the Western classical tradition, for example, the violin and the cello of all instruments are probably the most frequently cited as voicelike. The four violins[30] used as examples here share the productive and acoustic features proper to the violin family of instruments, but they also vary in size, timbre, and cultural origin. Instead of looking closely at the idiosyncrasies of each example, we will focus on their similarities and differences in regard to the voice. What we will find, finally, is that the vocalness so often attributed to bowed stringed instruments emerges from very different acoustic features than those demonstrated by instruments in the first two categories.

In Figures 12.4a–d, notice first of all that like the *morin khuur*, all of the chordophone pictured in these spectra show the fundamental frequency as most prominent, with the

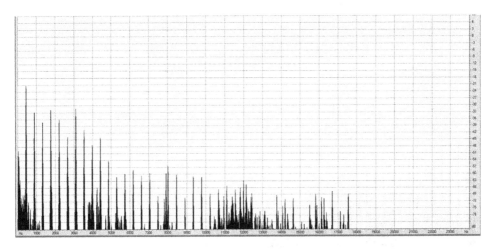

FIGURE 12.4A Bach Violin Sonata 3 BWV 1005, Largo, A4, 441 Hz.

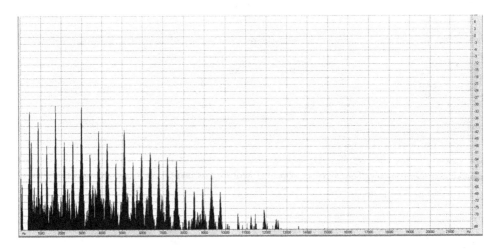

FIGURE 12.4B Ecuador: Iluman tiyu, Sanjuan, Quichua ensemble, G#4, 424 Hz.

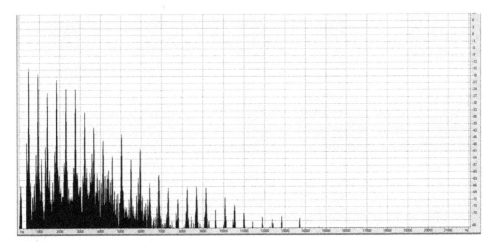

FIGURE 12.4C Bach Cello Suite 6 BWV 1012, Gigue, A4, 443 Hz.

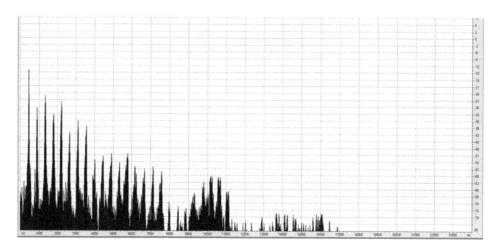

FIGURE 12.4D Mongolia: Gada Mairen for Solo *Morin Khuur*, A4, 443 Hz.

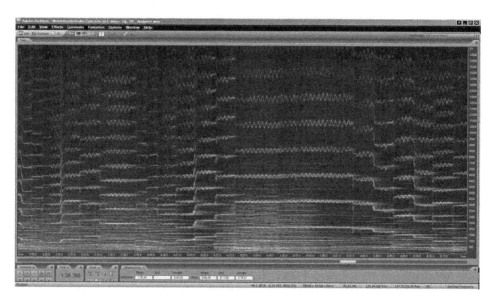

FIGURE 12.4E Mendelssohn Violin Concerto, Op. 64: Andante movement.

largest concentration of energy in the lower frequencies. The details of the spectrum representing a particular violin sound will vary depending on the pressure and action of the bow and its contact point relative to the bridge of the violin, the pitch of the tone, whether the tone is produced on a open or stopped string, and countless other variables in the conformation of the instrument or performance technique of the performer. Nevertheless, these spectra are typical of fiddles, due to the strong, low-frequency, natural resonances of the violin resonator (Benade 1990, 531–549). With some exceptions, the prominence of the violin's fundamental frequency is not matched in any systematic way by the voices of untrained singers. In these voices, the strength of the fundamental depends primarily on its relationship to the first formant of the vowel the singer enunciates. If the fundamental falls somewhere near the peak of the first formant, it may well be the strongest of the harmonics. For some male singers, if the second harmonic of the tones they produce falls within the bandwidth of the first vowel formant, it will be stronger than the fundamental; nevertheless, the perceived quality of the tone is very similar to that of a tone with a prominent fundamental. For female singers, the fundamental is likely to dominate when they sing near the top of or slightly above their comfortable range, when their sound swells to peak intensity, or when they use a strong chest voice.

In trained singers, on the other hand, at least in the *bel canto* tradition, vocal timbre has a bit of the same regularity as the violin timbre. First, singers who practice the technique of formant matching[31] produce by definition a persistent fundamental-dominated sound due to the combined energy of the fundamental and first formant peak. For both trained and untrained voices, though the spectra of vocal sound generally show a roll-off in frequency, with the first formant as the strongest, there is a greater energy balance between low and high frequency regions across voice spectra than is typical of the violin family. And like the violin, when the voice swells in intensity, the slope of the roll-off flattens. For trained tenors, sometimes altos and basses as well, the production of a singer's formant—an extra formant centered around 3000 Hz that increases the audibility of the voice over concurrent sounds—also works to soften spectral roll-off.

But the real difference in the timbres of the violin and the voice is that a vowel is defined both acoustically and perceptually by three or four very prominent formants. The body of a violin-type chordophone, on the other hand, produces a great many sharp-peaked resonances, so close in frequency that they may occur between consecutive harmonics of a tone. But natural harmonics rarely arrange themselves to fall precisely and symmetrically around these resonances; thus even otherwise formant-like spectral configurations may not consist of the gradually increasing and decreasing harmonics of speech formants, with smooth slopes and single peaks. Instead, the multiple resonances of the violin-type chordophones may result in a spectrum like the one pictured in Figure 12.4b, whose harmonics are so jagged that it would be difficult to determine the location of formants, if any. In comparing the transfer function of a violin resonator with the human vocal tract, Askenfelt (1991) points out:

> The large difference in the number of resonances in the filter [of the violin] means that for the strings there are always several "unused" resonances between two partials, while for the voice there are several partials within each formant, the high pitches excluded.   (n.p.)

But what Askenfelt does not mention is perhaps more important perceptually: that though many natural resonances of the violin resonator may be "unused" to create spectral peaks in the emitted tone, their influence is still evident in the *lack* of significant valleys between the formant peaks that do exist. Vocal formants are usually blunt and wide, but discrete and well-defined, each exerting its influence over a bandwidth of overtones at normal speaking pitch. And because the vocal tract produces sound with so few formants, they are most often sufficiently distant in frequency[32] to allow profound spectral valleys between them.

Both acoustically and perceptually the chordophones appear to show relatively few of the timbral features identified as vocal so far in this chapter. What, then, might be the source of their reputation as the most voice-like of instruments? We have already looked at several characteristics shared by the violins and the voice in discussing the *morin khuur* in the second category. Those included the expressive importance of the attack, the loose coupling between the source vibrating device and the resonator, the control of the fine spectral structure, and the tendency of performers to use phrasal articulation. A related characteristic shared by the chordophones and voice is their greater control over the tone quality of their sounds by regulating the number of harmonics and the balance between high and low partials.

The voice, of course, alters its timbre with each change in vowel. The violin is somewhat less precise in its timbral changes, but it shares the spectral flexibility described earlier for the voice: both instruments are able to contain or narrow the spectral spread of their sounds independently of amplitude; both are able to restrain the spectral magnitude of their sounds at higher amplitudes, as well as open up the spread of harmonics at lower intensities. In Western music, in fact, a violin or cello will regularly use its control over the spectral spread of its sound to stand out from the rest of the orchestra when it is the soloist in a concerto. Figure 12.4e, for example, shows a segment of the andante movement of Mendelssohn's violin concerto in E minor. Here, the spectral spread of the solo violin exceeds that of any of the orchestral instruments, so that it stands out even when its part demands soft and expressive playing. That the solo violin is able to be "heard out" clearly, even when some portion of the orchestral strings are playing the same pitch, indicates that the primary difference between the solo and tutti strings is timbral.

A final similarity in the sounds of the voice and strings—a feature not visible in the spectrogram due to the limitations of the graphics used here—is a phenomenon called jitter,[33] or somewhat less ambiguously, micromodulation (Bregman 1990; McAdams 1989). The source of these modulations is the natural tremor inherent in human movement, transferred to an instrument and its sound through performer contact. Like the voice, the violin is also subject to a greater magnitude of micromodulation as a vibrating system than many other instruments. If the intensity of micromodulation depends on the degree of contact between instrument and performer, then the voice is subject to greater than normal jitter, since its instrument is the body itself, while bowed chordophones are subject to greater than normal jitter since they are cradled or embraced by different parts of the body; the nature of the contact between bow and string particularly emphasizes the transfer of tremor from the performer's body to the instrument, with stopped strings showing more pronounced jitter than open strings (Askenfelt 1991). Experiments in timbre perception have found that some degree of frequency modulation is necessary both for the separation of sources (McAdams 1989) and for the perceptual fusion of harmonic components into a single sound (Chowning 1999, 264).[34]

Of the chordophone-voice similarities mentioned here, many are acoustic, and as noted earlier, produce subtle perceptual effects that may not be consciously identifiable by ordinary listeners. Listeners are unlikely to be aware of the loose coupling of the strings to the body of the violin, for example, or of the degree of micromodulation in both instruments. They will hear the result of both those characteristics, of course, but how do they know to associate the warmth and liveness that micromodulation contributes to a violin tone to the qualities jitter produces in the voice? The point I want to make here is that the acclaimed voiceness of the bowed chordophones relies on a less explicit conception of voiceness than we have encountered thus far. In his work on the historical evolution of the violin, Trueman (1999) looks to the musical repertoire of the violin as it both reflected and drove the changing capabilities of the instrument. In particular, he shows the historical movement of the violin away from the deliberate modeling of the violin on the voice to a repertoire in which the violin is an instrument in itself, producing sounds only it can make. Of Corelli's Sonata #3, Op. V, written at the turn of the century, Trueman says:

> Singing these lines is natural, and doing so reveals some of the essential qualities that we associated with the voice. Perhaps most obvious is the capability for *expressive sustain*. A good singer would do something with the opening sustained C: she might crescendo slightly and gradually add vibrato. Other features include *linearity* and *phrasing*. Stepwise motion predominantes and leaps are, for the most part, handled carefully. Lines are broken up into phrases which can be easily sung with a single breath. (12)

Ten years later, Corelli published a new edition of the sonata that collapsed two parts into one, and featured double stops and leaps in melodic phrasing that would be difficult for the voice to produce quickly and accurately. From this point on, says Trueman, Corelli was formative in the development of the violin as his concerti "gradually abstracted" (19) the concept of lyrical voiceness that had been the model for violin music to that point. The baroque violin that Corelli wrote for "opened up new territory for articulation" (9); it was no less vocally lyrical, but it was balanced with music idiomatic to the violin. In a more general sense, the quality of vocalness in the bowed chordophone family requires weighing features a violin shares with the voice against those features that are explicitly instrumental.[35] Later in his history of the violin, Trueman concludes that the modern violin is a *metaphor* for the human voice, but like most metaphors, it also goes beyond the voice in its potential (23). After all, if a composer wanted a sound that replicated the voice exactly, she or he would simply find a singer.

It is interesting that in commenting on the vocalism exploited by the violin, Trueman lists primarily melodic and articulatory rather than timbral features. Unlike the formants of the first category instruments, then, the qualities that contribute to the violin's voiceness are pitch- and motion-oriented. It's not that the violin *sounds* like a voice necessarily; rather it *behaves* like a voice. The voiceness of the violin lies as much in what it can do, as in how it sounds. In a single, continuous tone, both a bowed chordophone and the human voice can alter all the parameters of sound: it can swell in amplitude, glide from pitch to pitch, and exchange a dark for a joyous timbre. Both can emerge from a cloud of other sounds—as the voice does in Figure 12.1a, as the *morin khuur* does in Figure 12.3d, and as the violin does in Figure 12.4e, taken from the Mendelssohn violin concerto—with little apparent effort, sustaining themselves above a chaos of moving instruments. Both the fiddle and the voice have continuous pitch systems; thus, both can linger for a fraction of a second on a tone slightly flatter than the tone they are moving toward, the tone the audience expects, only to arrive at that tone with absolute precision. Many other instruments have one or a few of the same capabilities, but only a bowed chordophone can use them all to shape its sound with the same expressivity as the voice.

Conclusion: Hearing Voiceness

What does it mean to hear human vocal sound emanating from a distinctly nonhuman source? Is the voiceness perceived in instrumental sounds comparable to the faceness that excites the fusiform areas of the visual cortex? If the novel that supplied the quote at the beginning of this chapter had not been not a work of fiction, one might have cited it as evidence that in fact, voiceness is the same as the pareidolic faceness perceived in a configuration of rocks or clouds. And yet compared to the actual experience of voiceness, the description of Montalbano's response to the music he hears is unconvincing.

For most people, the perception of voiceness is idiosyncratic: they may hear it in different ways, with more or less intensity, with more or less pleasure, and sometimes not at all—a predictable disparity, given that voiceness occurs in the minds of listeners rather than in the external world. On the other hand, perceived voiceness also has certain common characteristics that seem to distinguish it from the perception of an actual voice, characteristics that are notably absent from the experience described in the Montalbano quote. For example, the sensation of voiceness colors, but does not replace, the sensation of the instrument. One typically hears voiceness *in* a violin, not *instead of* a violin. And except for instruments featuring the performer's mouth as resonator, the production of voiceness does not endow the instrument with the ability to convey lexical meaning. Still less does it give the instrument the kind of agency implied in Montalbano's description of a voice with a plaintive agenda containing important information accessible only to appropriate listeners.

In spite of scientific claims for congruity between the fusiform and voice-selective regions of the brain, and in spite of the considerable commonalities between the operations of the two areas, I contend that the concepts of faceness and voiceness as used in this chapter are not analogous. As noted earlier, the FFA responds to a far broader range of stimuli—including the faces produced by pareidolic perception—than the does TAA. Though this is not the place to explore the processing of facial pareidolia, research on the subject has uncovered characteristics of the phenomenon that are not apparent in the ordinary experience of voiceness. But if voiceness belies the strict congruity between the FFA and TAA, if it is not an example of auditory pareidolia, how do we hear voiceness?

I suggest that for ordinary listeners, finding voiceness in nonvocal instruments is an activity of interpretative imagination. As though to compensate for its parsimonious definition of preferred voice stimuli, the auditory system is a willing collaborator in a listener's imaginative forays. In the case of voiceness, it supplies the necessary raw materials in the form of the acoustic features discussed in this chapter, and it adapts easily to the individual or consensual contexts of its listeners. The difference between pareidolia and imagination, in other words, is that pareidolia is an act of perception, albeit illusory, while imagination is an augmentation or interpretation of a perceived stimulus. Whereas the results of facial pareidolia are taken by the perceiver, if only temporarily, to be an actual representation of external reality, the results of the auditory imagination are knowingly created by the perceiver to diverge from or extend external reality in some way that is pleasing or useful. In the case of voiceness, the auditory imagination allows listeners to fabricate an extra resonance of humanness that may be powerfully experienced, even while understood as entirely fictional.

NOTES

1. In many Bantu languages, for example, there is no way to refer to the sound of a specific instrument other than to use the same term that designates the human voice.
2. See Pisanski and Bryant chapter in this volume for more on this literature.
3. In other words, neither region remains unaware of nonvocal sounds or nonfacial objects, but the special mechanisms that define the TVA and the FFA become active only in the presence of the preferred percepts they are specialized to process.
4. Before measuring the activation level of voice-preferential regions to the voice-instrument continua, Bélizaire and his colleagues elicited behavioral judgments from subjects as to the degree of voiceness and the degree of naturalness of their experimental stimuli. From these judgments, they constructed the continua against which they could measure cortical response (Bélizaire et al. 2007).
5. This study has two limitations and should probably be labeled a pilot study rather than a true exploration of music performed in different cultures. The first of these is that my choice of sounds in this chapter is based on popular acknowledgment, the consensus of students working in my lab, or in some cases, my own subjective evaluation of voiceness; for instruments typical of the Western classical tradition, one can take these evaluations as representing a relatively "indigenous" point of view. However, for the non-Western instruments included here, an ideal version of this project would use sounds that are heard as voicelike to the music culture in which they originate. Instead, I have chosen sounds that are representative of the diversity of vocal instruments, or that present interesting issues in the study of acoustic generalities. The second weakness is that I have taken samples from recorded media without any knowledge as to the technological means of capturing the sounds, whether or not the recording entailed any post production, etc. By default, I am assuming that the recordings used here contain sounds as produced, with no editing or special effects added. Finally, for the sake of economy, I am limiting my examples to acoustic instruments, though electronically altered or created sounds reveal truly intriguing aspects of the relationship between voiceness and human listeners.

6. For a long time, the designation of formants in instrumental timbre was plagued with ambiguity. The notion of formants, of course, derived from phonetics and other disciplines concerned with speech and hearing. These fields traditionally focused on two features of formants: 1) the role of their bandwidth, shape, and spectral location in determining vowel quality; and 2) their stability across vocal register, allowing the independence of pitch and timbre so important to speech. In the early days of timbre exploration, acousticians focused primarily on the second of these features in their efforts to account for listener recognition of instrumental sound. Because their goal was to find spectral regularities across the pitch range of an instrument, they paid little attention to the divergent nature of those regularities, classifying them all as formants no matter how narrow a bandwidth they occupied or how perceptually insignificant they might be.

   Only certain classes of instruments are capable of producing the same timbre at all pitch levels—that is, with the same spectral shape and formant location regardless of fundamental frequency. Thus, acousticians no longer look for stable formants as definitive of an instrument's timbre in the same way that vowel formants define phonemes. They remain, however, a bit inconsistent in the spectral configurations they label "formant," a term by which they often designate any spectral resonance of whatever width, whether it resides in a instrument's resonator or the spectrum of its sound; occasionally it is even used as a term to describe the acoustic response of a room or auditorium relative to a performance locus.

7. For instruments constructed of some sort of metal, the question of whether tone quality depends on the type of metal or the exact ingredients of the alloy the instrument is made of remains controversial. Though there is more consensus about the construction of the bell and mouthpiece of an aerophone in effecting regularities in its timbre, the larger question of the bore is still unresolved.

8. Though normally such instruments are categorized according to their primary mode of vibration—most often chordophones—technically speaking they should be considered hybrid instruments to reflect the membranophone nature of the skin surface.

9. E.g., the Ghanaian balophone and the Burundi sanza.

10. E.g., leather strips placed between the strings of the Ethiopian lyre, the *begena*, and the wooden "buzzing bridge" or the *chien* attached to the French hurdy-gurdy, the *vielle*.

11. The difference between layered and fused noise is the following: acoustically, noise is *layered* over a tone when it is created, for example, by attaching cowry shells to the resonator of an aerophone, so that every time the musician moves his or her instrument, the shells clatter against the body of the instrument; the perceptual result is that the listener hears two sounds, the primary tone of the aerophone and the clattering of its attached shells; acoustically, noise *fuses* with a tone when it is created by a device such as a mirleton that is excited by the same vibrations as the primary tone; here the perceptual result is the sensation of a single, noisy or buzzy tone. In a more abstract sense, the perceptual difference between layered and fused noise is demonstrated by the sound of a radio announcer speaking through the noise of a badly tuned station (layered noise) vs. the sound of the same announcer speaking with a hoarse voice (fused noise).

12. Though impulsively excited instruments are not extensively discussed in this chapter, it is worth noting noise can also work to undo the nonvocal effects of impulsive sound by evening out the decaying waveform until it seems sustained. More generally, noise is useful for blurring or blending boundaries between pitches, or between pitch and timbre effects. Elsewhere I have referred to instrumental noise as a "perceptual sponge" because of its ability to encourage the fusion of disparate acoustic elements and to absorb the sounds around it.

13. I first realized this aspect of formant construction when a student of mine—an expert didgeridoo player—was demonstrating the existence of formants in the sound of his instrument. He played a long, sustained tone; he knew that the tone contained a formant, because he was familiar with the configuration of his vocal tract necessary for a prominently formanted tone. But to us who were listening, the formant was simply a static part of the timbre, fused into the rest of the timbre, without any perceptual salience at all; there was nothing in the sound he was making that indicated the existence of a high-resonance peak standing out from the hazy spectrum of the tone. It was not until he moved the formant— until he altered the cavity of his mouth so that the formant alternated between the low and high harmonics of the tone's steady fundamental frequency—that it became available to his listeners' perceptual awareness.

14. The profundity of this difference becomes clear in alternative interpretations of the same sound first as instrumental and then vocal sound. One well-known demonstration of this is called sine tone speech, developed at Haskins Laboratory. Sine tone speech is created graphically by painting the center frequency of the first three formants as they occur in a spoken phrase. When this image is converted into sound, the result is perceived as a series of quasi-instrumental hums and chirps by listeners who are unaware that what they hear actually delineates the sounds of speech. As soon as they are made aware that the hums and chirps can be heard as speech, they fall incontrovertibly into "speech mode," with the same mental all-or-nothing "click" that characterizes the perceptual experience of switching between ambiguous figures in the same image. Suddenly, they hear words where before there were only sine tones. Normally, listeners find it impossible to switch back into the default mode of hearing hums and chirps, once they discover the speech that lies behind the sounds.

15. Again, this is difficult to see in the figure as visible here; I suggest as always that readers refer to the same spectrogram in color on the publisher's website.

16. The spectral spread of the voice in Figures 12.4a and b is typical for vocal production for most genres in most parts of the world. A significant exception to this commonality occurs in trained *bel canto* performance practice where singers learn to restrain the acoustic spread of their voices to a frequency region below about 3500 Hz. Even for singers in the *bel canto* tradition, however, the production of certain phonemes—fricatives in particular—requires high frequency energy that punctuate the ordinarily even spectral spread of their voices.

17. Like most elements of a sound that listeners are unconscious of hearing, the overlapping sound is more obvious in its absence than in its presence. If one filters out the overlapping part of each harmonic from the tone following—that is, if one changes the acoustics to match a listener's perception—the difference is stark.

18. It is somewhat surprising that writings on the acoustics and perception of timbre rarely discuss the tendency of an undamped sound to continue beyond the direct excitation of its vibrating column. D. Cabrera (1997) calls the phenomenon "resonance," but that term most often refers to aspects of the filtering action of a resonator on a source wave. He tries to distinguish "resonance" as he defines it from "reverberation" by noting that the former is the result of "standing waves, vibrating within a solid body, or in an enclosed space" (109), while the latter is an effect of the acoustic conditions of the environment in which the sound is emitted. In truth, the acoustic difference between ringing and reverb may be simply a matter of degree. Generally speaking, in cases of significant or artificial reverb the perceived difference between instrumental ringing and reflection of sound is a factor of time and source location: ringing is relatively short in duration, and is an extension of

the source sound, whereas reverb may reflect a sound as much as 45 seconds following the excitation of the sound source and is clearly perceived as separate from the original sound and those that follow.

19. Cabrera points out that ringing sound acts to link one tone to the next and to disguise the attacks that signal a change in pitch; instead, the tones swell and decay gradually, and the complicated sounds that result perceptually privilege timbre over pitch (109–11). Cabrera is talking here about effects provoked by particularly strong ringing. But they are still natural, without electronic augmentation.

20. If the first explanation of ringing tones is correct (i.e., that it results from a vibrating column that continues to vibrate after the stimulus that initiated the vibration has stopped), then the overlap of tones would normally require an instrument with multiple, individually excitable vibrating columns (VC). This is because the VC will remain free to continue vibrating only as long as subsequent notes are produced via other VCs whose oscillations will not interfere with the ringing tone. That is, if an instrument has only one vibrating element on which all tones are produced, then the wave it generates must be disrupted to allow for a new fundamental frequency.

21. Please note that the printed version of this article only contains one case study under each category; a longer version of the chapter with additional case studies is available on the companion website. Moreover, all of the sounds discussed and color-enhanced legibility of the black and white figures presented here may be accessed at the same site. Listeners are strongly encouraged to listen to the sounds and inspect the colored spectrograms.

22. These spectra are less clear in terms of harmonic spacing because each spectrum actually includes more than the single timbre with which it is labeled.

23. The sound file also reveals what seems to be a fair amount of mechanical reverb, which the performer can only have reduced with deliberate damping.

24. For example, the Amharic *begena* and the Burundais *indigiti*, among others.

25. See, for example, Thayer (1974) and Risset and Matthews (1969).

26. This difference depends on the match (or lack of) between the impedance characteristic of the vibrating media of the source and resonator. In a tightly coupled system the impedance of source and resonator is approximately equal, whereas in a loosely coupled system, there is almost total mismatch.

27. In the voice or a chordophone, pitch is controlled by changes in the vibrating device, whereas in many aerophones, pitch is controlled largely by changing the resonator, thus manipulating its resonant frequencies; an aerophone with no mechanism for changing the length of the resonator is limited in pitch to the strongest natural resonance of the instrument and its harmonics. In nonmusical contexts, the loose coupling of the voice is essential for the production of speech, which often relies on the individual parameters of pitch and timbre to convey separate streams of information.

28. While it is impossible to separate the sound of the *morin khuur* from the orchestra, the softest segment registers an average RMS power of -13.41 dB; the loudest, at the peak of the morin khuur's ascent, is -11.56 dB RMS (where 0 dB RMS marks the maximum level of a signal without clipping). Even assuming that the accompanying instruments maintain a constant amplitude (which in fact they do not—to this listener, they swell a bit as the solo reaches its peak), the *morin khuur* manages a great deal of increased sound without increased loudness.

29. For additional case studies, including bassoon, French horn, Japanese shakuhachi, and African panpipe, please see the accompanying website.

30. Unless otherwise specified, I use the terms "violin" and "fiddle" interchangeably and generically to refer to all hourglass-shaped bowed chordophones, regardless of size, tuning, or other idiosyncrasies.

31. Formant matching (Sundberg, 1975) is a method of increasing the intensity and resonance of a singer's voice by shifting a vowel formant to coincide with the fundamental frequency of the pitch the vowel is sung on; the result is more or less distorted vowel quality, but increased amplitude to the vocal sound as a whole with no metabolic cost to the singer.

32. An exception to this occurs in sounds like the low back vowels in which (depending on the pitch of the voice) the first and second formants may be merged.

33. Note that jitter here refers to natural acoustic jitter as opposed to the artificial deviations from periodicity (also called "jitter") introduced to an audio signal by means of some sort of electronic processing.

34. Many attempts to synthesize natural sound have concluded that without the perturbations of micromodulation, all fidelity to the target sound is lost. Indeed, the fact that in Western classical tradition the voice and all the chordophones are rarely played without some degree of vibrato has been taken as evidence for vibrato as an effort to regularize the natural and irreducible tendency toward jitter.

35. This is the strategy taken by Daniel Trueman (1999) in his exploration of violin development and the music it made possible. For example, he frequently points out small differences in Bartok's violin and pre-Corelli violins, which were formerly effects that could be imitated by the voice, but that become "essential articulations" (33) with certain small changes that make them purely violinistic.

WORKS CITED

Askenfelt, A. 1991. "Voices and Strings: Close Cousins or Not?" In *Music, Language, Speech and Brain*, Proceedings of an International Symposium at the Wenner-Gren Center, Stockholm, edited by Johann Sundberg, Lennart Nord, and Rolf Carlson, 5–8. Houndmills: Macmillan. 243–256.

Belin, Pascal, Robert J. Zatorre, Philippe Lafaille, Pierr Ahad, and Bruce Pike. 2000. "Voice-Selective Areas in Human Auditory Cortex." *Nature* 403 (6767): 309–12.

Bélizaire, Guylaine, Sarah Fillion-Bilodeau, Jean-Pierre Chartrand, Caroline Bertrand-Gauvin, and Pascal Belin. 2007. "Cerebral Response to 'Voiceness': A Functional Magnetic Resonance Imaging Study." *Auditory and Vestibular Systems, Neuroreport* 18 (1): 29–33.

Benade, Arthur H. 1990. *Fundamentals of Musical Acoustics*, 2nd rev. ed. Mineola, NY: Dover Publications.

Bregman, Albert. 1990. *Auditory Scene Analysis: The Perceptual Organization of Sound.* Cambridge, MA: The MIT Press.

Cabrera, Densil. 1997. "Resonating Sound Art and the Aesthetics of Room Resonance." *Convergence: The International Journal of Research into New Media Technologies* 3 (4): 108.

Camilleri, Andrea. 2004. *Voice of the Violin.* New York: Penguin.

Chowning, John. 1999. "Perceptual Fusion and Auditory Perspective." In *Music, Cognition, and Computerized Sound*, edited by Perry Cook, 261–76. Cambridge, MA: The MIT Press.

Cook, Perry. 1999. *Music, Cognition, and Computerized Sound.* Cambridge, MA: The MIT Press.

Fales, Cornelia, and Stephen McAdams. 1994. "The Fusion and Layering of Noise and Tone: Implications for Timbre in African Instruments." *Leonardo Music Journal* 4: 69–77.

Kanwisher, Nancy, Josh McDermott, and Marvin M. Chun. 1997. "The Fusiform Face a: A Module in Human Extrastriate Cortex Specialized for Face Perception." *Journal of Neuroscience* 17 (11): 4302–11.

McAdams, Stephen. 1989. "Segration of Concurrent Sounds I: Effects of Frequency Modulation Coherence." *Journal of the Acoustical Society of America* 86 (6) (December): 2146–59.

Patel, Aniruddh D. 2008. *Music, Language, and the Brain*. New York: Oxford University Press.

Pegg, Carole. 2011. "Huur." *Oxford Music Online*. http://www.oxfordmusiconline.com/grovemusic/view/10.1093/gmo/9781561592630.001.0001/omo-9781561592630-e-0000049726.

Risset, Jean-Claude, and Max Matthews. 1969. "Analysis of Musical Instrument Tones." *Physics Today* 22 (2): 23–30.

Sundberg, Johan. 1975. "Formant Technique in a Professional Female Singer." *Acustica* 32 (2): 89–96.

Thayer, Ralph. 1974. "The Effect of the Attack Transient on Aural Recognition of Instrumental Timbres." *Psychology of Music* 2 (1): 39–52.

Trueman, Daniel. 1999. "Reinventing the Violin." PhD diss., Princeton University.

CHAPTER 13

....

THE EVOLUTION OF VOICE PERCEPTION

....

KATARZYNA PISANSKI AND
GREGORY A. BRYANT

INTRODUCTION

....

THE human voice is a rich source of information and an important means of interpersonal communication. Beginning with Darwin (1872), vocal communication has long interested evolutionary scientists, and in the last quarter century empirical research on voice production and perception from an evolutionary perspective has increased dramatically. One reason for this surge of interest is that behavioral ecologists and evolutionary psychologists have taken advantage of recent technological improvements in acoustic analysis software as well as sound recording and reproduction devices. More importantly, many voice researchers have recognized that the extraction of biologically relevant information from the vocal channel constitutes a set of adaptive problems widely shared across many species. Evolutionary scientists studying human vocal behavior therefore have a rich theoretical framework and an established comparative basis for developing specific research questions.

For any vocal species, we should expect perceptual adaptations designed to process acoustic features of the vocal sounds of conspecifics (e.g., other individuals of the same species). Humans are no exception—there is strong evidence that dedicated areas of the human brain, including the middle superior temporal sulcus (STS), are specialized for human voice perception (Belin et al. 2000; Pernet et al. 2015). The human STS is analogous to the vocal perception brain areas in several other species, such as macaques (Petkov et al. 2008). Much like how we learn to process faces and develop face-specific regions in our brains (Kanwisher, McDermott, and Chun 1997), voice-selective areas in humans reliably develop within seven months of birth (Grossmann et al. 2010), and perceptual biases toward speech sounds over similar nonspeech sounds appear as early as an infant's first day of life (Vouloumanos and Werker 2004).

The comparison of human voice processing to face processing is more than superficial. Belin, Fecteau, and Bedard (2004) suggested that low-level sound features are extracted in the primary auditory cortex and then encoded in the STS for other, functionally distinct tasks, such as extracting speech information, detecting emotions, and identifying the speaker. (See Cornelia Fales's chapter for discussion of timbre's analogy to face processing, where she draws on the same body of scholarship.) The cognitive architecture of face processing follows a similar strategy, with low-level processors feeding into systems solving social identification, affective and related perceptual tasks. It is also not surprising that face and voice processing highly interact, though the details of this multimodal interaction are not well understood (Campanella and Belin 2007). An evolutionary approach provides a framework for specifying the nature of these adaptive perceptual problems. In this chapter, we will describe recent work focusing on voice perception from an evolutionary perspective and will provide examples of the value of this approach for gaining a full understanding of this fundamental aspect of human behavior.

Levels of Analysis in the Evolutionary Study of Behavior

Tinbergen (1952, 1963) proposed that to understand any animal's behavior, we must answer empirical questions at different levels of analysis. Proximate questions focus on identifying specific causal processes that underlie a behavior. These causal processes often involve physical mechanisms and can include hormonal, neural, and other physiological systems in the body, as well as the vast array of developmental systems that contribute to adult phenotypes. Researchers in various disciplines typically define behavior as the product of numerous mechanisms, but these proximate analyses are often considered in the absence of an evolutionary approach (Barkow, Cosmides, and Tooby 1992). Tinbergen emphasized that ultimate questions, which instead focus on identifying the potential fitness consequences of a trait or behavior, must also be asked in order to fully understand a behavior.

The evolutionary analysis of any animal behavior involves the consideration of relevant adaptations underlying a given behavioral trait, as well as the phylogenetic history linking that trait across multiple species over time. Adaptations are evolved solutions to recurrent ecological problems faced by an organism: they are functionally organized, contribute positively to an organism's fitness, and are typically analyzed in terms of design features tailored to specific criteria. In a phylogenetic analysis, the evolutionary history of a given trait is reconstructed through cross-species comparative analysis. Functional and phylogenetic analyses together provide the ultimate explanation for a given behavioral or morphological characteristic.

Form and Function in Signal Design

Evolutionary behavioral scientists studying human and nonhuman vocal behavior must make a distinction between communicative *signals* and informative *cues* (Maynard

Smith and Harper 2003). Signals are defined as adaptive behaviors or structures shaped by selection to influence the behavior of others in a way that is beneficial to the sender (e.g., a vocalizer), and often coevolve with the adaptive responses of the receiver of that signal (e.g., a listener). Typically, signal production must benefit both senders and receivers to be evolutionarily stable. Cues, on the other hand, are any predictive behaviors or structures that influence receivers but were not designed to do so. Receivers might have evolved sensitivities to the predictive information, but the cues did not evolve to have that effect. Although many researchers studying communication have ignored this distinction, focusing instead on proximate levels of analysis involving the physical properties and mechanisms of communicative acts, the role of context in their perception, as well as cultural and developmental factors, both proximate and ultimate levels of analysis are important when seeking a complete understanding of any behavior.

Determining whether a communicative act regularly produced by an organism is a signal or a cue is sometimes difficult. Behaviors often have systematic effects on audiences, some by design and some not. The physical form of a signal can provide important clues regarding its function, and hence a form-fit analysis is often a good place to start when asking whether a trait or behavior evolved for a particular reason (Owren and Rendall 2001). Form-fit analysis investigates whether structural features of a trait show evidence of special design for solving specific adaptive problems (Lauder 1981; Williams 1966). Consider the case of human crying: signal or cue? Crying behavior in infants is clearly related phylogenetically to a variety of mammalian infant vocalizations designed to elicit parental care (for a review see Newman 2007). In humans, crying has particular acoustic features that exploit human audition, and has been shaped by coevolutionary processes reflective of the conflict of interest between senders (e.g., infants) and receivers (e.g., caretakers). Crying elicits investment of targeted listeners in the sender by motivating listeners to stop the signal, explaining a great deal of its aversive sound characteristics. Crying is clearly a signal in that it evolved to influence caretaker behavior in a manner that benefits both sender and receiver. In order for it to be effective (and affective) and to fulfill its function, crying requires a sound profile that is displeasing to listeners. While there is some evidence that the acoustic characteristics of a cry can communicate information about the particular conditions that triggered the crying (Soltis 2004; Zeifman 2001), it could also be the case that very little information about specific conditions is encoded in the cry signal itself and instead, listeners can infer with some reliability what the infant's needs are based on contextual information alone. Arousal and emotional valence can vary dramatically across cries, which may help in this judgment.

In addition to qualifying as a signal, crying also has byproduct cue value.[1] For example, in ancestral environments, a wailing infant could inform predators about its location and this could have negative fitness consequences not only for the crying infant, but for siblings and parents as well. This heavy potential cost likely figures into the evolutionary dynamics contributing to its effectiveness. A listener wants the crying to stop, not only because it is (proximately) annoying to listen to, but also because in ancestral environments it could be dangerous to broadcast. Cries also potentially reveal information to caretakers (or others) about the crier that is not provided by design. For instance, crying can reveal the infant's health condition that could affect investment decisions by parents. Some researchers have proposed that signaling health information, or vigor, could be one function of crying (Furlow 1997; Lummaa et al. 1998; Soltis 2004), but direct evidence for this proposal is weak. Nevertheless, some basic information is not given by the acoustic structure of cries. For example, cries from infant boys and girls do not systematically differ acoustically, yet listeners will attribute higher-pitched cries to girls and lower-pitched cries to boys. This assumption can affect men's judgments of discomfort (but not women's), as low pitched cries from presumed boys result in greater ratings of discomfort by adult men, revealing sex-stereotype biases in judgment patterns (Reby, Levréro, Gustafsson, and Mathevon 2016).

The example of crying illustrates the complexity of separating byproduct effects of vocal signals from adaptive effects that have been shaped by selection to benefit senders and receivers. In the following section, we will describe research examining the perception of body size and strength through vocal cues. We use the term cue when describing this work because it is not clear that the extracted information (e.g., assessed size or strength) is provided by design, or instead perceivable incidentally as a consequence of source-filter dynamics in vocal production machinery. That said, humans and other animals might advertise or exaggerate their size in various ways by exploiting the relationships between their bodies and their vocal apparatus, and if so, such behaviors should be considered signals in that they are adaptations for sending that specific information.

CAN WE JUDGE BODY SIZE AND STRENGTH FROM THE VOICE?

Like most terrestrial mammals, human vocalizations are generally produced by pushing air from the lungs up through the closed glottis, vibrating the vocal folds within the larynx, and generating phonation that is subsequently filtered by the supralaryngeal vocal tract. The human supralaryngeal vocal tract (henceforth vocal tract) is comprised of the pharyngeal, oral, and nasal cavities situated above the larynx. This two-stage mode of vocal production produces the two most salient nonverbal characteristics of the human voice: the fundamental frequency (denoted as F_0), that together with its harmonics we perceive as voice pitch, and formant frequencies or formants, that are resonances of the vocal tract and affect our perception of voice timbre (Titze 1994). The source-filter theory of speech production (Chiba and Kajiyama 1958; Fant 1960) was key in our understanding that fundamental and formant frequencies are largely independent of one another, and the theory has been central to recent advances in bioacoustics, including research examining vocal communication of body size and threat.

For several decades researchers have been interested in whether the human voice can provide reliable indexical information about the person speaking, in particular, the size of that person's body, their age, and sex (Kreiman and Sidtis 2011). Researchers have also attempted to understand whether the human voice was shaped by selection to advertise these various traits. Indeed, the ability to accurately gauge another individual's body size and strength could be advantageous in many social contexts for the sender or the receiver, or both.

Physical size and strength are key predictors of men's fighting ability. Both traits greatly influence women's mate preferences across diverse cultures, and both have a large impact on an individual's health and life history (Frederick and Haselton 2007; Gallup, White, and Gallup Jr. 2007; Peters 1986; Pisanski and Feinberg 2013). Among humans, body size estimation may also be a necessary precursor for speaker normalization, allowing listeners to recognize speech sounds (e.g., the difference between the vowel sounds "a" and "e") independent of the size of the vocalizer (Patterson, Smith, van Dinther, and Walters 2008). In this section, we will review studies that together suggest that reliable indicators of size and strength are in fact present not only in the visual modality, but also in the acoustic modality, and that listeners are able to estimate size and strength from the human voice alone with some degree of accuracy.

Perception of Body Size from the Voice

The mammalian larynx and vocal tract typically grow larger along with the rest of the body as an individual develops and matures. More massive vocal folds within a larger larynx will vibrate at a slower rate than will smaller vocal folds, producing a relatively lower voice pitch; however, the length and tension of the vocal folds also affect pitch (Hollien 2014; Titze 2011).[2] Independently of vocal fold dynamics, formant frequencies are inversely related to the length of the vocal tract such that taller people typically have longer vocal tracts and lower formants than do shorter people (Fitch and Giedd 1999; Titze 1994). As a consequence, both fundamental frequency (perceived as voice pitch) and formant frequencies (formants, affecting perception of voice timbre) independently track differences in body size between adults and juveniles. Voice pitch and formants are also sexually dimorphic (lower in males than females) and therefore also track differences in body size between the sexes in a range of mammalian species, including humans (Fitch and Hauser 2003; Rendall, Kollias, Ney, and Lloyd 2005).

In a meta-analysis, Pisanski, Fraccaro, Tigue, O'Connor, Röder, Andrews, and Fink et al. (2014) showed that within same-sex groups of adult men and women, formants provide more reliable cues to body size than does voice pitch. This is most likely due to relatively greater anatomical constraints on the development of the vocal tract (which is constrained by skull size) than on the development of the vocal folds, resulting in relatively stronger relationships between formants and body size than between pitch and body size (Fitch 1994; 1997). Indeed, this prediction is also supported by work on several other species whose vocal production follows the source-filter model (for reviews see Ey, Pfefferle, and Fischer 2007; Fitch and Hauser 2003; Taylor, Charlton, and Reby, 2016; Taylor and Reby 2010). In women, formants further explain a good deal of variation in body shape (e.g., waist-to-hip ratio; Pisanski, Jones, Fink, O'Connor, DeBruine, Röder, and Feinberg 2016).

The dissociation between voice pitch and actual body size among men and women may be tied to a number of factors. For instance, male vocal fold size and subsequent voice pitch are more heavily determined by exposure to testosterone than by body growth (Harries et al. 1998). In fact, individual differences in men's voice pitch in adulthood are predicted by their voice pitch in childhood, and voice pitch in childhood is predicted by voice pitch in infancy (Levrero, Mathevon, Pisanski, Gustafsson & Reby, 2018), suggesting that men's voice pitch could be tied the androgen levels in their mother's uterus (Fouquet et al. 2016). Humans are also capable of voluntarily altering their voice pitch, which is common during regular speech production or singing as well as during everyday social interaction, and may potentially disguise or exaggerate cues to size (Pisanski, Cartei, McGettigan, Raine, and Reby 2016). Indeed, men and women from diverse cultures have been shown to volitionally and spontaneously lower their fundamental frequency (and formant frequencies) when instructed to sound physically larger, and to raise both vocal frequencies when instructed to sound physically smaller (Pisanski, Mora, Pisanski, Reby, Sorokowski, Frackowiak, and Feinberg 2016).

Ignoring for a moment the obvious next question of just how accurately listeners can gauge size from the voice, a large body of work provides compelling evidence of strong systematic perceptual biases on size judgments from the voice. Studies consistently report that listeners from various cultures associate both low voice pitch as well as low formants with large body size between and within sexes (reviewed in Pisanski, Fraccaro, Tigue, O'Connor, and Feinberg 2014). These perceptual associations are only partially grounded in reality because voice pitch is in fact a very weak predictor of body size within sexes. For this reason, some researchers have suggested that the perceived association between low voice frequencies and large body size represents a deep-rooted and very general perceptual bias linking any low-frequency sound to largeness (Morton 1977; Ohala 1984; Rendall, Vokey, and Nemeth 2007).[3]

Despite the often erroneous perceptual bias linking low voice pitch to large size, several studies suggest that listeners can gauge body size from the voice with accuracy above chance. However, listener's performance is variable and generally modest. Reanalysis of early work by Lass and colleagues indicated that 14 percent of listeners' size estimates correlated with the absolute height or weight of the vocalizers in those studies (González 2003; 2006). When listeners were asked to report absolute height or weight, van Dommelen and Moxness (1995) found that estimated height predicted actual height only for men's and not for women's voices, and that men were more accurate than were women at assessing men's size. Collins (2000) and Bruckert et al. (2006) found that women were able to estimate men's weights but not men's heights, but that men's actual weight explained only 22 percent (Collins 2000) and 16 percent (Bruckert et al. 2006) of the variance in women's estimates.

Forced-choice tasks that involve simply indicating which of two vocalizers is taller elicit comparatively greater accuracy in size estimation than do absolute size estimates. On average, both men and women can correctly identify the taller of two men around 60 percent to 90 percent of the time, depending on the size difference between the men (Oliver and González 2004; Pisanski, Fraccaro, Tigue, O'Connor, and Feinberg 2014; Rendall et al. 2007). Accuracy in size judgments is comparable (Oliver and González 2004) or slightly lower (Rendall et al. 2007) for assessments of women's compared to men's body size.

Even blind persons can assess relative differences in men's (Pisanski, Oleszkiewicz, and Sorokowska 2016) and women's (Pisanski et al. 2017) heights from speech, suggesting that visual experience is not necessary for this capacity. This is further supported by empirical evidence that infants as young as three months of age use vocal cues to gauge body size (Pietraszewski et al. 2017). Importantly, despite a lack of visual experience linking the size of people's bodies with their voices, congenitally blind and late blind adults use the same perceptual rules when assessing body size as do sighted individuals (i.e., associating both low pitch and low formants with largeness even though low pitch does not predict size within-sexes; Pisanski et al. 2017). This provides further support for the hypothesis that body size estimation is based on a deep-rooted and general perceptual bias wherein low frequencies are judged as emanating from large sound sources.

Recent work has employed modern voice synthesis and analysis techniques to highlight the important interplay between fundamental and formant frequencies in the perception of body size from the voice. For example, experiments using natural (Pisanski, Fraccaro, Tigue, O'Connor, and Feinberg 2014) as well as synthetic (Irino et al. 2012) whispered speech (which is largely devoid of pitch information, as whispering involves very little vibration of the vocal folds) indicate that voice pitch is not essential for body size perception. However, studies by Charlton, Taylor, and Reby (2013) and Pisanski, Fraccaro, Tigue, O'Connor, and Feinberg (2014) suggest that voice pitch does play a facilitating role in size estimation by providing a dense harmonic spectrum and carrier signal for formants.[4] The fact that harmonics are more densely spaced in men's compared to women's voices may help to explain why size estimates are more accurate with men's than women's voices (see, e.g., Rendall et al. 2007).

As neither fundamental nor formant frequencies account for very much of the variation in body size and shape among same-sex groups of adults (Pisanski, Fraccaro, Tigue, O'Connor, Röder, Andrews, and Fink et al. 2014; Pisanski, Jones, Fink, O'Connor, DeBruine, Röder, and Feinberg 2016), and listeners are only moderately successful in accurately estimating body size from the voice, it appears that vocal indicators of size in humans are weak. Thus, empirical evidence to date suggests that variation in fundamental and formant frequencies is not likely due to strong selection for *honest* vocal indicators of body size and that listeners may not have evolved mechanisms to reliably assess size. Rather, selection may have acted on the human voice in ways that exaggerate actual body size, as appears to be the case in several other mammalian species (Charlton and Reby 2016; Fitch and Hauser 2003). Fundamental and formant frequencies in humans may also function to provide reliable information about other traits that are related to body size and that may be used as proxies of size, such as attractiveness and masculinity or femininity (Pisanski, Mishra, and Rendall 2012; Puts et al. 2016), or, as reviewed in the next section, physical strength.

Perception of Physical Strength from the Voice

Throughout our evolutionary history, physical strength is likely to have reliably predicted men's ability to accrue resources and gain access to mates, as continues to be the case in many modern populations (Frederick and Haselton 2007; Gallup et al. 2007; Sell, Hone, and Pound 2012). There was probably strong selection pressure on men to advertise their physical strength, potentially through the vocal modality. Strength, although positively related to an individual's body size, is arguably more difficult to assess visually than is size,[5] and predicts fighting ability better than does height or weight (Sell et al. 2009). It follows that listeners may have been selected to rely more heavily on vocal indicators of strength compared to size; however, relatively few studies have examined the vocal communication of strength. A small but growing body of empirical work, reviewed in this section, suggests that the human voice may provide information about physical strength above and beyond information about body size that listeners are able to gauge.

Handgrip strength, upper-body strength, and flexed bicep circumference are common measures of physical strength in empirical studies. Upper-body strength is particularly sexually dimorphic and has been found to predict men's self-reported fighting ability, aggression, and sexual behavior (Gallup et al. 2007; Lassek and Gaulin 2009; Sell et al. 2009; 2010). Sell et al. (2010) showed that listeners could judge men's upper-body strength from the voice alone with above-chance accuracy. Strength estimates were made with voices obtained from four distinct cultures, and were unaffected by language. Although listeners were able to estimate strength from the voice, the authors were not able to identify which acoustic features were used to make this judgment, as neither fundamental nor formant frequencies predicted the actual physical strength of vocalizers in that study. Recent evidence indicates that listeners can also assess strength from nonverbal vocalizations (i.e., human roars), and that roars may function to maximize impressions of strength compared to speech (Raine, Pisanski, Oleszkiewicz, Simner & Reby, 2018).

Examining potential vocal correlates of strength, Puts, Apicella, and Cardenas (2012) reported a negative relationship between voice pitch and arm strength (a standardized average of hand-grip strength and upper-arm circumference) in a sample of Tanzanian Hadza men. The authors also reported a negative relationship between formant frequencies and arm strength in a sample of Californian men. Hodges-Simeon, Gurven, Puts, and Gaulin (2014) later examined vocal correlates of strength in a peripubertal sample of Tsimane horticulturalists, predicting that vocal indices of size and strength could be more salient in the years spanning puberty (when physical growth and sexual maturation is most rapid) compared to adulthood. In their study, arm strength reliably predicted the fundamental and formant frequencies of males (aged eight to 23) but not of females when controlling for age and body size. Height, adiposity (i.e., fat), and strength together explained most of the variance in men's vocal frequencies (and considerably less of the variance in women's vocal frequencies). Voice pitch predicted variation in men's physical strength above and beyond that which could be explained by body size.

While very few studies have focused directly on vocal communication of physical strength in humans, other work demonstrates that strength-related information (i.e., covariates or proxies of strength) are indeed present in the voice. For example, listeners across many diverse cultures judge individuals with voices of relatively low pitch or low formants as more physically and socially dominant, masculine, and physically larger than individuals with voices of relatively high pitch or formants. In turn, several studies indicate that low pitch or low formants are related to higher facial masculinity, body muscularity, self-reported and other-reported dominance, and levels of circulating testosterone (for reviews, see Pisanski and Feinberg 2013; Puts, Doll, and Hill 2014; Puts et al. 2016). Taken together, the human voice clearly conveys a myriad of useable information related to formidability and threat potential that is likely to have been shaped by sexual selection. The ways in which listeners disentangle or integrate various vocal cues of size, strength, and dominance are less clear.

Vocal Attractiveness

Researchers have been studying vocal attractiveness for several decades, and the results of this work have broad theoretical as well as practical implications. Studies of voice preferences provide insight into how selection has shaped the human voice, but also inform researchers and the public about perceptual biases, and help to uncover the potential socioeconomic and political implications of vocal stereotyping. For instance, like people with attractive bodies or faces, vocally attractive individuals are often accredited, unduly or not, with positive personality attributes including being perceived as relatively powerful, confident, emotionally stable, intelligent, kind, and socially competent (Kreiman and Sidtis 2011). This association between vocal attractiveness and other positive traits has been deemed the vocal attractiveness stereotype (Hughes and Miller 2015; Zuckerman, Hodgins, and Miyake 1990) and stems more broadly from the classical halo effect (Nisbett and Wilson 1977).

Research has focused largely on the relative contributions of fundamental and formant frequencies to voice attractiveness, and for good reason. Voice pitch and formants are sexually dimorphic and reliably predict a host of mate-relevant traits and preferences across mammalian species, including humans, suggesting that these voice features have been most strongly affected by sexual selection. Notably, a growing body of work has begun to highlight the contribution of various other vocal and multimodal traits in the perception of vocal attractiveness, as well as constraints on modulating (i.e., faking) vocal attractiveness.

Preferences for Sexual Dimorphism in the Voice

The human voice is sexually dimorphic. Men's voice pitch (F_0) is on average 120 Hz whereas women's F_0 is almost double that, averaging 210 Hz. Formant frequencies are also typically lower and more closely spaced among men than women (Pisanski, Fraccaro, Tigue, O'Connor, Röder, Andrews, and Fink et al. 2014). What this means, perceptually, is that men's voices sound much "deeper" (lower pitched and more resonant) than do women's. As an example, consider the deep and masculine voice of actor James Earl Jones (the voice of Star Wars's Darth Vader) compared to the much higher and feminine voice of cast member Carrie Fisher (who played Princess Leia). Differential exposure to androgens during puberty in addition to sexual dimorphism in the size of the vocal anatomy can account for some of the sexual dimorphism in fundamental and formant frequencies;[6] however, the sexual dimorphism in F_0 or voice pitch far surpasses what we might expect given the differences in body size and vocal fold mass and length between men and women.

As a general rule, men and women are attracted to sexual dimorphism in opposite-sex voices. Cross-culturally,[7] women prefer lower pitch and formants compared to average or higher pitch and formants in men's voices (i.e., masculine voices), whereas men often (but not always) prefer higher pitch and formants compared to average or lower pitch and formants in women's voices (i.e., feminine voices; for reviews, see Feinberg 2008; Pisanski and Feinberg 2013).[8] Preferences for sexual dimorphism in opposite-sex voices appear to develop during adolescence around the age at which mate preferences become relevant (Saxton, DeBruine, Jones, Little, and Roberts 2009) and are typically weaker within sexes than between sexes (Babel, McGuire, and King 2014; Jones et al. 2010; Pisanski and Rendall 2011).

Men's preferences for femininity in women's voices and women's preferences for masculinity in men's voices likely evolved under sexual selection as a means of identifying high-quality mates. Higher voice pitch in a woman's voice may be a fairly good indicator that she has relatively high levels of estrogens (Abitbol et al. 1999), which typically indicate fecundity and therefore reproductive value or fitness (Sherman and Korenman 1975; Venners et al. 2006). Women's voice pitch appears to increase during ovulation (Bryant and Haselton 2009) in conjunction with cyclical changes in estradiol and progesterone levels (Puts et al. 2013), and women's voices are judged by men as most attractive around the time of ovulation (Pipitone and Gallup Jr. 2008) and least attractive around the time of menstruation (Pipitone and Gallup 2012; see also Haselton and Gildersleeve 2011). In addition to often (but not always) being perceived as attractive, high voice pitch in women is closely associated with perceptions of femininity (Feinberg, DeBruine, Jones, and Perrett, 2008; Pisanski and Rendall 2011), youthfulness (Collins and Missing 2003), flirtatiousness (Puts et al. 2011), and sexual interest (Jones et al. 2008). Women's voice pitch can also predict the number of sexual partners they report having had (Hughes, Dispenza, and Gallup Jr. 2004) It should be noted that men sometimes show a preference for relatively lower pitch in women's voices, possibly because low pitch can communicate intimacy, maturity, or confidence.

Among men, relatively low voice pitch or formants generally indicate that a man has higher levels of circulating testosterone compared to a man with a higher-frequency voice (Bruckert et al. 2006; Cartei, Bond, and Reby 2014; Dabbs and Mallinger 1999; Evans et al. 2008). Higher levels of testosterone in men are in turn positively associated with a host of mate-relevant characteristics, including dominance, physical strength and body size, and immune responsiveness (Puts, Doll, and Hill 2014; Rantala et al. 2012; Skrinda et al. 2014). Of course, androgen-dependent physical traits in men such as strength and size are also relevant in male–male competition, and thus men's voice pitch and formants have likely evolved both under intersexual selection (mate choice) and intrasexual selection (competition between same-sex individuals) (Puts, Doll, and

Hill 2014).[9] Like women, men's voice pitch predicts reproductive success, although in the case of men the relationship is negative (Apicella, Feinberg, and Marlowe 2007; Puts, Gaulin, and Verdolini 2006).

At the same time, high levels of testosterone in men have been linked to higher levels of infidelity, divorce, aggression, and lower levels of parental and resource investment (Booth and Dabbs 1993; Eisenegger, Haushofer, and Fehr 2011; Mazur and Booth 1998), and women judge men with lower voice pitch as more likely to cheat and less likely to invest in them and their offspring compared to men with higher voice pitch (O'Connor, Re, and Feinberg 2011; O'Connor 2012). As a consequence, high levels of testosterone and low voice pitch or formants in a man's voice may present a trade-off in the context of mate choice for women, wherein women who choose such masculine men as mates may benefit in some ways, but also pay a cost in other ways.

Many researchers have predicted that women's preferences for masculinity in men's traits and behaviors, including men's voices (e.g., low voice pitch or formants), will vary so as to maximize the benefits and minimize the costs of choosing a masculine mate. There is a good deal of empirical evidence to support this prediction. Women's preferences for relatively low voice pitch or low formants are stronger when women judge the vocal attractiveness of a hypothetical short-term versus long-term relationship partner (Feinberg et al. 2012; Puts 2005), particularly among women who attribute low trustworthiness and dominance to masculine men (Vukovic et al. 2011). Women with high-pitched voices (Vukovic et al. 2010) and those who rate themselves high on attractiveness (Feinberg et al. 2012; Vukovic et al. 2008) also show relatively stronger preferences for low voice pitch than do other women. Multiple studies examining women's preferences for facial, body, and vocal masculinity further show evidence for cyclic shifts, namely, stronger masculinity preferences during the most fertile phase of the menstrual cycle when ovulation risk is highest (for meta-analysis see Gildersleeve, Haselton, and Fales 2014; but see also Wood, Kressel, Joshi, and Louie 2014).[10] These results support the prediction that masculinity preferences may function to increase offspring health (Gangestad and Thornhill 2008; Jones et al. 2013).

In addition to cyclic variation, women's vocal masculinity preferences have been linked directly to changes in women's hormone levels (Feinberg et al. 2006; Pisanski, Hahn, Fisher, DeBruine, Feinberg, and Jones 2014; Puts 2006). Women's vocal masculinity preferences may indeed serve to protect women and their offspring from exposure to pathogens, as masculine men may have stronger immune systems compared to feminine men (Rantala et al. 2012; Skrinda et al. 2014). Studies confirm that higher levels of pathogen disgust sensitivity predict women's preferences for masculinity in men's faces, bodies, and voices (Jones et al. 2013). Women's facial masculinity preferences also correlate positively with population-level pathogen prevalence across nations (DeBruine et al. 2010).[11]

Although vocal femininity is attractive in women's voices and vocal masculinity is attractive in men's voices, it should be noted that extreme sexual dimorphism is unlikely to be attractive. Re et al. (2012) and Saxton, Mackey, McCarty, and Neave (2015) found that women did not prefer relatively lower-pitched men's voices at the extreme lower end of the spectrum (i.e., below 96 Hz). Re et al. noted that extreme low pitch can be indicative of vocal pathology and may therefore be perceived as unattractive. As discussed earlier, low voice pitch among men is also associated with various negative attributes that may be particularly salient in extremely low-pitched voices, such as aggression and infidelity. Although Re et al. (2012) found that men preferred relatively higher-pitched women's voices above the normal range of female voice pitch (i.e., up to 300 Hz, the highest frequency tested), Borkowska and Pawlowski (2011) found that men did not prefer relatively higher pitch in women's voices above a 280 Hz threshold. Men may not prefer voice pitches that fall into the range of adolescent voice pitch (i.e., above 300 Hz), because such voices indicate sexual immaturity. Several studies show that listeners also associate extremely high voice pitch with behavioral immaturity, babyishness, submissiveness, and incompetence (reviewed in Kreiman and Sidtis 2011).

Other Factors Affecting Vocal Attractiveness

We have thus far highlighted studies of voice attractiveness that have focused largely on sexually dimorphic features of the voice—fundamental and formant frequencies (pitch and formants)—that reliably indicate many evolutionarily relevant traits and behaviors. This large literature provides compelling evidence that pitch and formants have undergone sexual selection and play a meaningful role in mate choice and mate competition across mammalian species, including humans. In addition, judgments of vocal attractiveness hold relevance outside of a sexual context. Vocal attractiveness can, for example, affect perceptions of a vocalizer's personality (Zuckerman, Hodgins, and Miyake 1990), competitiveness for a job opening (Anderson et al. 2014), and political leadership capacity (Anderson and Klofstad 2012; Tigue, Borak, O'Connor, Schandl, and Feinberg 2012). Recent studies have begun to explore vocal attractiveness in a broader social context and suggest that multiple features of the voice play a role.

Babel et al. (2014) examined the relative contributions of harmonics-to-noise ratio, spectral tilt, jitter and shimmer, and speech duration in addition to fundamental and formant frequencies on attractiveness judgments of men and women's voices. Harmonics-to-noise ratio, spectral tilt, and jitter and shimmer are measures of vocal quality that affect perceptions of breathiness, creakiness, and smoothness in the voice and that at some level can be suggestive of vocal pathology, illness, smoking, or alcoholism (Kreiman and Sidtis 2011). The researchers found that breathiness was an attractive quality of women's voices, and one that may be associated with intimacy, whereas male voices with shorter durations of speech were judged as relatively more attractive than those with longer durations. Because men typically speak with shorter durations than do women (Simpson 2009), the authors suggested that this latter finding may in fact represent a preference for sexually dimorphic patterns in opposite sex voices.

Research indicates that men and women with attractive voices are also likely to have attractive faces (Abend et al. 2015; Collins and Missing 2003; Feinberg, DeBruine, Jones, and Little, 2008; Hughes and Miller 2015; Little et al. 2011; O'Connor et al. 2013; Puts et al. 2013; Saxton, Burriss, Murray, Rowland, and Roberts 2009; Skrinda et al. 2014;

Wheatley et al. 2014). This finding suggests that faces and voices may develop via similar mechanisms, and therefore provide similar information about an individual's mate quality (Feinberg 2008). It also hints at the possibility that information from one modality may interact with information gathered from another modality such that perceptions of vocal attractiveness may differ in the presence or absence of visual information from the face or body. Indeed, using videos to examine the interaction between vocal and facial indicators of attractiveness, O'Connor et al. (2013) found that men's judgments of women's vocal attractiveness were higher when voices were presented in conjunction with a relatively more feminine face. Men's judgments of women's facial attractiveness were also amplified by the addition of a feminine, high-pitched voice.[12] Little et al. (2013) showed that adaptation to sex-typicality or atypicality in voices affected perceptions of normalcy in faces, and vice versa. Although not yet tested, olfactory information is also likely to amplify or dampen judgments of vocal or facial attractiveness. Given that multiple modalities interact in everyday perception (for review see Spence 2011), multimodal signaling of attractiveness constitutes an important avenue for future work.

Future studies may further investigate the role of voice modulation in vocal attractiveness. There are inherent anatomical constraints on vocal production, such as vocal fold mass and vocal tract length, but manipulation of voice pitch and formants is possible within a limited range (see, e.g., Cartei, Cowles, and Reby 2012; Hughes, Mogilski, and Harrison 2014; Puts, Gaulin, and Verdolini 2006). Several studies report that men and women modulate their pitch and other aspects of their voices in response to attractive conversational partners (Anolli and Ciceri 2002; Fraccaro et al. 2011; Hughes, Farley, and Rhodes 2010; Leongómez et al. 2014; Pisanski, Oleszkiewicz, Plachetka, Gmiterek & Reby, 2018); however, evidence as to whether vocal modulation effectively alters perceptions of the vocalizer's attractiveness remains equivocal (Anolli and Ciceri 2002; Fraccaro et al. 2011; Hughes, Farley, and Rhodes 2010; Leongómez et al. 2014; Pisanski et al., 2018).

Vocal Communication of Affect and Intention

While some aspects of the voice are unavoidably informative, such as formant information revealing body size or honest indicators of one's hormonal profile such as fundamental frequency signaling mate quality, human vocal communication involves many complexities of voice control that interact with language and sociality. One major aspect of communicative behavior in social species, including humans, is the signaling of intention. We define intentional action as planned, goal-directed behavior to achieve a desired future state of affairs. A dog that bares his teeth at another dog is signaling his intention to bite and providing information regarding his investment in something usually obvious in the environment, such as a food source or protection of kin. The baring teeth signal likely evolved from the nonsignaling behavior of moving the lip out of the way of the teeth to prevent injury. The cue of lip movement prior to a bite is predictive and through a ritualization process it may have evolved into a signal, complete with the exaggerated features characteristic of acts shaped in contexts with a substantial conflict of interest between signalers (Krebs and Dawkins 1984).

Whenever there is a signal of one's intention, the prospect of deception exists, and a receiver's judgment of the honesty of a given signal must incorporate this possibility. Many theoretical models have been proposed to explain the evolutionary dynamics in the maintenance of signal reliability, and some things are clear. First, signals may not need to be costly to be reliable (Lachmann, Szamado, and Bergstrom 2001), but cost is one way to ensure reliability (Grafen 1990). Second, there are circumstances where some degree of deception can be evolutionarily stable if the benefits of repeated interaction are high enough (Johnstone and Grafen 1993). These aspects of animal signaling have profound implications for our understanding of human vocal behavior, especially as it relates to the role of different vocal systems that play a major part in our vocal repertoire.

Mammalian vocal production is implemented in relatively simple neural and motor circuits that have been conserved across many species (Ackermann, Hage, and Ziegler 2014; Jurgens 2002). In humans, vocal behaviors such as crying, laughter, fear screams, and copulation calls are driven by this emotional vocal system. Our perception of these vocal signals has been shaped by millions of years of evolution where the vocal production machinery is consistent and predictable. Yet humans, unlike any other species, have developed the capacity for language and speech, which has resulted in the development of specialized production mechanisms involving fine-grained control over vocal articulators, breathing, and laryngeal musculature (Ghazanfar and Rendall 2008). The volitional control over our vocal speech production, which interfaces in complicated and poorly understood ways with other cognitive systems involved with language in a broad sense, allows us to now produce cries, screams, roars, laughs, and other sounds without the necessary emotional triggers once required of our hominin ancestors, or our primate relatives today.

Researchers examining laughter have explored the implications of the dual pathway model of vocal production in the perception of different kinds of laughs. Informed by work on smiling (e.g., Ekman, Davidson, and Friesen 1990), theorists have proposed that laughter can come in at least two forms that correspond to spontaneous versus volitional control. Different names have been used for these two laugh types, such as voluntary versus involuntary (Ruch and Ekman 2001) and Duchenne versus non-Duchenne (Gervais and Wilson 2005). Bryant and Aktipis (2014) found that judges can distinguish between these laugh types, and there are predictable acoustic differences between them as well, mostly attributable to the role of arousal in the emotional triggering of spontaneous laughter, but also due to the differential role of breath control. McGettigan et al. (2014) have also shown that different brain areas are activated both when producing different types of laughter and when listening to them. Prefrontal areas associated with deliberate control of behavior are implicated in these laughter production mechanisms, as well as the neural system underlying the detection of others' mental states. Laughter is a prime example of how a phylogenetically ancient behavior has been shaped by recent selection in the context of language communication, and now operates at multiple levels in complex human social interaction.

Emotional Vocal Signals

Intentions can be signaled in any number of ways, including, quite predominantly, through a vocal channel. Researchers examining vocal behavior in humans and nonhumans have often focused on the communication of emotion. Here we define emotions as cognitive programs designed to motivate context-specific, adaptive behavior. Emotional programs include, as part of their design, communicative mechanisms in all modalities, but vocal control is intricately connected to central nervous system structures through the vagus nerve and voice parameters are profoundly affected by changes in emotional motivations (Porges 2001).

Consider a fear scream: in the context of danger, say for example the presence of a predator, emotional systems in the body prepare for rapid action. The body needs glucose for energy as well as increased oxygen intake and the emotion of fear is the program that coordinates the body's needs in this setting. Vocalizations produced under these conditions will often have a sound of urgency. For example, the calls may often be extremely loud, may contain nonlinear acoustic features associated with overblowing the vocal tract constraints (Fitch, Neubauer, and Herzel 2002), and may be characterized by raised pitch and faster temporal properties that together will reveal distress (Banse and Scherer 1996). The acoustic correlates of fearful vocalizations have a structural form that facilitates the communicative function of signaling urgency and danger (Owren and Rendall 2001). In the nonhuman animal literature, debates continue as to what animal signals mean and whether the notion of functional reference is necessary in our understanding of these signals (e.g., Rendall, Owren, and Ryan 2009). Among humans, however, we can say without a doubt that form-function relationships coexist with linguistic aspects of vocal production that are serving varying functions. These vocal channels co-occur for listeners, and audience members must distinguish between vocal emotional information and other prosodic features helping serve linguistic functions. In our example of a fear vocalization, which can play a role in behaviors such as alarm calls, pain shrieks, and threat displays, we can see how the acoustic form of the call relates to its signaling function. Emotional vocalizations can all be analyzed in this way, and the regularities predict and explain a good deal of universality in how people express themselves vocally. We see the same types of emotional sounds in music across cultures (Juslin and Laukka 2003) as well as in the ways mothers speak to babies (often referred to as infant-directed speech or motherese; Broesch and Bryant 2015; Bryant and Barrett 2007; Fernald 1992).

There has been a long tradition of considering emotional expressions as reflecting internal states that audience members can infer, essentially treating emotional expressions as cues (e.g., Ekman 1997), but this approach makes little sense evolutionarily. Animals, including humans, may pay a large price for giving away internal information for free, as this could provide a means of manipulation for receivers without any benefit for the sender. Signals only evolve in contexts where senders benefit (and typically receivers too; Maynard Smith and Harper 2003), and there is no reason to believe emotional expressions are an exception. Thus, we should consider emotional expressions to be signals, and to be produced strategically with adaptive benefits for senders. One quick point of diversion about the term "strategic." By this we do not mean volitional, deliberate, or necessarily conscious. Instead, we mean that the behavior is due to selection on the production mechanism that is shaped by a particular and typically beneficial outcome. Vocal emotions are designed to influence listeners in a specific way: they may often be associated with a particular subjective phenomenology; they may be under some conscious control or not; and they are probabilistically suboptimal in any particular circumstance. The strategy of the production of vocal emotions is built into their design.

Voice pitch plays a fundamental role in the sound profiles of many vocal emotional signals. As explained earlier, pitch is the perceptual correlate of F_0 and is determined primarily by the vibration rate of the vocal folds in the larynx (Titze 1994). This vibration rate is determined by both subglottal air pressure as well as laryngeal muscle activity. Because of the inherent relationship between emotional programs and physical arousal in an organism, structural correlates of arousal in communicative signals play a crucial role in their effectiveness. The positivity or negativity of emotions (i.e., valence) is another important dimension that is also signaled through physical features of emotional signals including the acoustic properties of vocalizations. Together, arousal and valence constitute a dimensional model of emotion (Russell 1980) that helps researchers make sense of various parameters of different emotional expressions, including vocal signals.

As described earlier, the emotion of fear is designed to motivate a rapid response in an animal (e.g., fight or flight). Emotional programs organize bodily systems in preparation for action. Specifically, fear activates energetic stores making glucose readily available for muscle systems. Respiration capacity is increased, perceptual systems are sharpened, and the animal enters a state that facilitates adaptive fleeing or fighting activity. This suite of preparedness has consequences for physical signals such as vocal expressions. Increased musculature tension results in increased F_0 as well as greater amplitude. Scared animals tend to scream more loudly and faster than they would typically vocalize, with additional nonlinear features (e.g., deterministic chaos, subharmonics) often present in the scream call as a result of excessive airflow pushing through the vocal tract (Fitch et al. 2002). The resulting sound is highly detectable in noisy environments for warning conspecifics of a common threat, such as a predator, but also serves as a warning to enemies for any number of reasons. Highly aroused animals are dangerous, and fear-related vocal signals can help communicate this danger to potential rivals.

In the case of fear, we should expect perceivers to be highly sensitive to relevant acoustic features that can help them predict something important about the environmental context. These sound features end up doing most of the communicative work in rich contexts—a perfect example of the "form follows function" principle in biology (Rendall and Owren 2001). Human sensitivity to fear vocalizations is clearly homologous to other mammals in this regard, and as such, can even affect judgments of very human-specific phenomena such as music. Blumstein et al. (2012) found that acoustic nonlinearities such as deterministic chaos (simulated through music distortion) in musical compositions was associated with greater arousal and negative valence in listeners relative to control versions of the compositions without these nonlinear features. This research was motivated by comparative work showing the incredible similarity in the sound profiles of different species and emotion categories revealing the important role that evolutionary processes have played in shaping human and nonhuman emotion signaling systems (Briefer 2012). Cultural evolutionary processes can result in sound features such as distortion in music being utilized as a compositional tool because it exploits our evolved sensitivity that we share with many mammalian species (Bryant 2013).

Cross-Cultural Perception of Emotion

There is overwhelming evidence showing that people across diverse cultures can accurately detect emotional signals in faces, and to a lesser extent, voices (Elfenbein and Ambady 2002). People are quite good at identifying vocal emotions, but as in faces, research reveals a within-culture advantage. While some work has examined the cross-cultural perception of emotions in voices in western, and generally industrialized, nations (e.g., Pell et al. 2009; Scherer, Banse, and Wallbott 2001; Thompson and Balkwill 2006), only recently have researchers studied emotional vocal perception in highly disparate, traditional societies. Bryant and Barrett (2008) found that Shuar hunter-horticulturalists could reliably identify basic vocal emotions in spoken English sentences. In this experiment, participants listened to spoken sentences that were produced while the speaker was looking at an emotional facial expression, and participants then judged which of two facial expressions the speaker was looking at during the recording of the sentence. Accuracy across different emotion categories varied, with recognition of happiness highest (71 percent) and recognition of disgust at chance. English speaking participants in the United States judged the same English sentences in a content-filtered condition. Results were fairly similar overall, though with some interesting cultural differences across emotional categories. For example, Shuar listeners often judged happy vocalizations as fearful, but did not judge fearful vocalizations as sounding happy. If acoustic similarities between happiness and fear were responsible for these errors, we should expect symmetry in the error pattern. Instead, the apparent bias might be due to different pragmatic display rules across cultures. In Shuar culture, expressions of happiness between strangers might reveal that a speaker is scared or nervous relatively more than in the United States. Within-culture advantages in detecting emotional expressions are often likely due to culture-specific belief patterns that will drive certain biases in listeners' judgments.

Sauter, Eisner, Ekman, and Scott (2010) found that the Himba—a seminomadic group of pastoralists in northern Namibia—were able to reliably recognize nonverbal vocal emotions both within and between cultures. English listeners were also able to recognize vocal emotions produced by Himba speakers. The researchers used a task in which short, read vignettes were followed by pairs of vocal recordings, and listeners reported which vocalization was appropriately tied to the story. Results showed bi-directional recognition for a subset of the emotion categories, most considered "basic" emotions (i.e., anger, disgust, fear, sadness, surprise, and amusement). However, the Himba participants did not choose the appropriate vocalization for most of the positive emotions, such as triumph and sensual pleasure, even though these emotions were recognized within-culture. The authors suggested that affiliative social signals might be subject to culturally specific display rules, and are therefore not as easily transmitted across cultures as are other types of social signals.

More recently, Gendron et al. (2014), using the same task in the same population, found a somewhat different pattern of results that they interpreted as evidence against the cultural universality of emotional expressions. The authors found that when participants judged valence-matched vocal alternatives after hearing a vignette, they did not correctly choose the intended emotion, but when the alternatives were arousal-matched (and therefore differed only in valence), participants correctly choose the intended category better than chance. Gendron et al. suggested possible universality in sensitivity to valence, but not in the recognition of specific emotions. Sauter, Eisner, Ekman, and Scott (2015) reanalyzed their own original data (from Sauter, Eisner, Ekman, and Scott 2010), focusing only on emotion categories in which judges were better than chance by removing some positive emotion trials from their analyses. The pattern of results obtained in both studies was similar regardless whether the distractor matched the target in valence or not. Moreover, the authors pointed out that Gendron et al.'s judges failed to answer correctly in a condition where the emotion alternatives were different in arousal and valence, which affords discrimination based on valence, and additionally suggested that Gendron et al.'s participants might not have fully understood the stories.[13]

The debate described here is important because it demonstrates particular difficulties in conducting cross-cultural research. At what point does the explanation of a research procedure teach participants something new about the phenomenon that they otherwise would not know, and does subsequent success in such tasks reveal underlying similarity or acquired knowledge? There is little question that to gather meaningful data in the field, researchers need to ensure participants properly understand the study task. These studies with the Himba provide a great illustration of how tasks requiring subjective interpretation are likely to elicit high variation, and are especially vulnerable to experimenter demand effects and other potential biases.

Recognizing Speaker Intention from the Voice

Much of what people intend to communicate by their speech acts is not contained in the language itself, but must be inferred by listeners based on multiple sources of information (Sperber and Wilson 1995). One central source of information is the nonverbal elements of the voice, and researchers across a variety of disciplines (e.g., psychology, linguistics, computer science, neuroscience, and biology) have explored the ways in which vocal signals are processed by listeners in communicative interactions. Humans seem to be unique in our particular sensitivity to recognizing ostensive intentions to communicate (Scott-Phillips 2014). That is, we can recognize informative intentions (i.e., the content of what one intends to convey), as well as communicative intentions (i.e., the intention to convey anything at all). From a listener's perspective, the perception of intention in the voice requires the separation of vocal signals of emotion from related linguistic and pragmatic prosodic signals (i.e., pitch, loudness, rhythm, and spectral information). It is not currently understood how all of these sources of vocal information interact to convey intention.

Prosodic signals in the voice are intricately tied to the affective and intentional goals of the speaker (Bryant and Fox Tree 2002; Cosmides 1983). Prosody assists listeners in making many distinctions, ranging from focus in lexical items (e.g., using pitch to emphasize meaning), to syntactic disambiguation, all the way up to discourse structure and conversational turns (for a review see Cutler, Dahan, and van Donselaar 1997; Kreiman and Sidtis 2011). General attitudinal information is recognizable fairly quickly in the voice, even without words or pragmatic context. For example, Swerts and Hirschberg (2010) found that listeners could detect whether upcoming speech content would be positive or negative before the linguistic information made it clear. The perception of upcoming "bad" news was most likely driven by a restricted pitch range and a fast speech rate. Speakers use a variety of vocal signaling strategies during discourse, and these vocal patterns often work independently of contextual and linguistic features.

Research on indirect speech such as verbal irony has explored the role of prosody in communicating intention, and many theorists adhere to the notion that voice properties uniquely convey types of verbal irony such as sarcasm. Much of the research in this area has relied on vocal recordings of actors (e.g., Anolli, Ciceri, and Infantino 2000; Cheang and Pell 2008). These studies have revealed that speakers tend to lower their voice pitch and produce noisier vocalizations when speaking sarcastically relative to typical speech. Analyses of spontaneous verbal irony are not nearly so consistent, and instead suggest that speakers are highly variable when producing ironic speech (Bryant 2010; Bryant and Fox Tree 2002). Judges also tend to conflate irony with many other affective and intentional categories such as anger, inquisitiveness, and authority even when listening to content-filtered speech in which the words are not available (Bryant and Fox Tree 2005).

Imagine listening to a conversation through a wall. The sound is muffled and words are difficult to understand. The wall essentially acts as a low-pass filter, meaning that frequencies above a certain threshold important for speech are removed. Nevertheless, listeners are typically able to gather a good deal of information about attitudes and intentions from a highly impoverished speech signal that contains little more than F_0. Theorists have long noticed that many similarities exist across languages and cultures in how speakers use nonverbal voice information, such as pitch, to convey different kinds of meaning (e.g., Ohala 1984). An important use of pitch in everyday speech involves changes at specific moments. These prosodic contrasts play a communicative role in a variety of signals, including in verbal irony (Bryant 2010), conversational turn-taking (Cutler and Pearson 1986), and even nonhuman animal communication (Blumstein et al. 2008; Morton 1977). The nature of detecting affect from prosodic information is a dynamic phenomenon in which moment-to-moment processing can alter many aspects of judgments (Roche, Peters, and Dale 2015). By using new techniques to monitor decision-making processes, such as mouse-tracking and eye movements, researchers can explore the complex dynamics of how listeners interpret prosodic contrasts and other aspects of human's communicative repertoire that are in motion.

Few studies have examined how people can recognize intent across different cultures, but work on infant-directed speech has shown that people are quite good at detecting intentions, especially in speech designed to make intentional information salient to listeners without access to other sources of linguistic information such as words and syntax (Bryant and Barrett 2007; Bryant et al. 2012). In these cross-cultural studies of infant-directed speech, listeners were presented with pairs of recordings of mothers acting out different intentions (e.g., prohibitives, approvals) in a language they do not speak, and then identified, in a forced-choice task, what the correct intention was in the vocalization. Accuracy in this task was well above chance, and listeners could identify whether speakers were intending to talk to a baby or another adult. Participants in these studies were also able to identify intentional information in adult-directed speech, a mode of speech that contains fewer nonverbal signals of intention than infant-directed speech. These results can be interpreted as evidence that intentional information in the voice contains some universal properties, and while we believe this is certainly true to a great extent, important variation also exists in people's ability to judge different categories of spoken language.

Conclusions

An evolutionary approach to voice perception focuses not only on mechanistic descriptions of vocal communication, but also on phylogenetic and functional explanations of why animals (including humans) attend to and process particular features of the vocal signal. When considering underlying adaptations in both the production and perception side of communicative interactions, it becomes necessary to consider the meaningful distinction between signals and cues. As we have described, many aspects of the voice may serve as cues to various features of the vocalizing animal (e.g., body size), while other aspects of the voice have been shaped by selection to affect or manipulate target listeners in particular ways (e.g., emotional signals). Attending to vocal cues can be highly informative and beneficial; hence, listeners have perceptual specializations that guide this adaptive behavior.

As the study of voice production and perception continues to grow in popularity and to unite seemingly disparate disciplines, some recent developing trends will help the field continue to move forward. In particular, improvements in voice analysis technology have facilitated greater numbers of researchers to use these tools. Perhaps more critically, improvements in the past decade in broadband Internet services and information storage have made large-scale cross-cultural studies much easier to implement (e.g., Bryant et al. 2016). It is now possible to readily and effectively develop and maintain international collaborations that allow researchers worldwide to share stimuli and data efficiently online, including via open-source databases. As in most areas in the behavioral sciences, voice researchers stand to benefit tremendously by implementing cross-cultural analyses. Most research on human behavior, and a good deal of what we think we understand, is rooted in research in industrialized societies on 18- to 23-year-old college students. Henrich, Heine, and Norenzayan (2010) deemed the typical participants in most behavioral research WEIRD (i.e., Western, Educated, Industrialized, Rich, Democratic). These authors make a good case for the notion that WEIRD subjects fall on the extreme end of the spectrum for many measured traits long considered universal, highlighting that more representative participants from around the globe will provide a better understanding of psychological phenomena. Investigations involving traditional, sustenance-based, small-scale societies reveal complexities in cultural variability previously downplayed or simply unnoticed. Voice researchers stand to gain a great deal from conducting their experiments across disparate cultures—the need is there, and the technology is available.

In this chapter we have attempted to present the latest empirical research on the evolution of voice perception, emphasizing how comparative work on nonhuman animals incorporating evolutionary principles can inform efforts to properly characterize human vocal communication, and specifically voice perception. Of course, much work remains. While research exploiting vocal production and processing is currently being conducted at each level of analysis, from low-level physiology to high-level abstract perception, we have a particular interest in examining how vocal communication manifests in naturally occurring contexts. To properly understand the nature of vocal communication, researchers should make every attempt to measure vocal communication outside of the lab (e.g., Pisanski et al., 2018) and with the advent of new technologies for recording and data storage, great strides could be made in the upcoming years. It is now possible to get accurate hormone measures, high-quality voice recordings and images, GPS-assisted location data, time-stamped contextual information, and many other kinds of measures for massive multivariate analyses in which complicated interactions between various sources of influence on vocal production and perception can be examined together. The future is bright for voice research in the evolutionary behavioral sciences.

NOTES

1. It is worth noting here that all signals have potential cue value in that they might inform intended and unintended perceivers in ways that are not part of the evolved design (Maynard Smith and Harper 2003).
2. Larger vocal folds vibrate at a slower rate than do smaller vocal folds, resulting in a relatively lower fundamental frequency and perceived pitch; however, regardless of mass, fundamental frequency increases when the vocal folds are stretched and become tenser.
3. Low pitch is perceptually associated with large physical size and high pitch with small size regardless whether the sounds are pure or complex tones, musical passages, or vocalizations (see, e.g., Bien, ten Oever, Goebel, and Sack 2012; Evans and Treisman 2010).
4. Harmonic density facilitates more accurate speech recognition via the same mechanism (Ryalls and Lieberman 1982).

5. There is, nevertheless, evidence that people are able to accurately assess strength from photographs of faces and bodies (Sell et al. 2009) and even from videos of avatars synthesized from male dancers (Hufschmidt et al. 2015).

6. During puberty, an increase in testosterone among males increases the mass of the vocal folds and causes a drop in voice pitch (Harries et al. 1998; Lieberman, McCarthy, Hiiemae, and Palmer 2001) that is much greater than the pubertal drop in pitch among females (Abitbol, Abitbol, and Abitbol 1999). The male larynx also descends slightly during puberty, elongating the male vocal tract relative to the female vocal tract thereby lowering formants (Fitch and Giedd 1999; Lieberman et al. 2001).

7. Although preferences for sexual dimorphism in the voice have been documented in many cultures, the degree to which listeners prefer sexual dimorphism in potential mates has been shown to vary cross-culturally as a function of various evolutionary relevant factors, such as pathogen prevalence (see Pisanski and Feinberg 2013).

8. Although the just-noticeable differences or discrimination thresholds in voice pitch and formant perception are approximately 5 percent for vowel sounds (Pisanski and Rendall 2011), studies that manipulate the voice using computer software indicate that larger differences, in the order of 10 percent from baseline or greater, are typically required to affect judgments of vocal attractiveness (Feinberg, Jones, Little, Burt, and Perrett 2005; Pisanski and Rendall 2011) as supported by psychoacoustic research (Re, O'Connor, Bennett, and Feinberg 2012).

9. See also Borkowska and Pawlowski (2011) and Puts et al. (2011) for empirical evidence in support of intrasexual competition in women.

10. Women taking hormonal contraceptives may not show systematic variation in their vocal masculinity preferences and are typically excluded from studies examining cyclic shifts in women's preferences (Gildersleeve et al. 2014).

11. Men's facial femininity preferences in women appear to correlate positively, rather than negatively, with the health of a given nation (Marcinkowska et al. 2014). The potential ultimate function of this relationship is unclear.

12. In another study, O'Connor, Fraccaro and Feinberg (2014) showed that women's perceptions of men's vocal attractiveness interacted with sociolinguistic cues to men's socioeconomic status.

13. Unlike Gendron et al., Sauter, Eisner, Ekman, and Scott (2010) tested participants for their comprehension of vignettes by asking participants to explain the stories, and only included those individuals who demonstrated full understanding. Gendron, Roberson, and Barrett (2015) responded by claiming that confirmation of vignette understanding with repeated explanation amounts to category learning, and thus undermines attempts at measuring actual universals.

WORKS CITED

Abend, P., Pflüger, L. S., Koppensteiner, M., Coquerelle, M., and Grammer, K. 2015. "The Sound of Female Shape: A Redundant Signal of Vocal and Facial Attractiveness." *Evolution and Human Behavior* 36 (3): 174–81.

Abitbol, J., Abitbol, P., and Abitbol, B. 1999. "Sex Hormones and the Female Voice." *Journal of Voice* 13 (3): 424–46.

Ackermann, H., Hage, S. R., and Ziegler, W. 2014. "Brain Mechanisms of Acoustic Communication in Humans and Nonhuman Primates: An Evolutionary Perspective." *Behavioral and Brain Sciences* 37 (6): 529–46.

Anderson, R. C., and Klofstad, C. A. 2012. "Preference for Leaders with Masculine Voices Holds in the Case of Feminine Leadership Roles." *PloS one* 7 (12): e51216.

Anderson, R. C., Klofstad, C. A., Mayew, W. J., and Venkatachalam, M. 2014. "Vocal Fry May Undermine the Success of Young Women in the Labor Market." *PloS one* 9 (5): e97506.

Anolli, L., and Ciceri, R. 2002. "Analysis of the Vocal Profiles of Male Seduction: From Exhibition to Self-Disclosure." *Journal of General Psychology* 129 (2): 149–69.

Anolli, L., Ciceri, R., and Infantino, M. G. 2000. "Irony as a Game of Implicitness: Acoustic Profiles of Ironic Communication." *Journal of Psycholinguistic Research* 29 (3): 275–311.

Apicella, C. L., Feinberg, D. R., and Marlowe, F. W. 2007. "Voice Pitch Predicts Reproductive Success in Male Hunter-Gatherers." *Biology Letters* 3 (6): 682–4.

Babel, M., McGuire, G., and King, J. 2014. "Towards a More Nuanced View of Vocal Attractiveness." *PloS one* 9 (2): e88616.

Banse, R., and Scherer, K. R. (1996). "Acoustic Profiles in Vocal Emotion Expression." *Journal of Personality and Social Psychology* 70 (3): 614–36.

Barkow, J. H., Cosmides, L., and Tooby, J., eds. 1992. *The Adapted Mind: Evolutionary Psychology and the Generation of Culture*. New York: Oxford University Press.

Belin, P., Fecteau, S., and Bedard, C. 2004. "Thinking the Voice: Neural Correlates of Voice Perception." *Trends in Cognitive Sciences* 8 (3): 129–35.

Belin, P., Zatorre, R. J., Lafaille, P., Ahad, P., and Pike, B. 2000. "Voice-Selective Areas in Human Auditory Cortex." *Nature* 403 (6767): 309–12.

Blumstein, D. T., Bryant, G. A., & Kaye, P. 2012. "The sound of arousal in music is context-dependent." Biology Letters, 8(5), 744–47.

Blumstein, D. T., Richardson, D. T., Cooley, L., Winternitz, J., and Daniel, J. C. 2008. "The Structure, Meaning and Function of Yellow-bellied Marmot Pup Screams." *Animal Behaviour* 76 (3): 1055–64.

Booth, A., and Dabbs, J. M. 1993. "Testosterone and Men's Marriages." *Social Forces* 72 (2): 463–77.

Borkowska, B., and Pawlowski, B. 2011. "Female Voice Frequency in the Context of Dominance and Attractiveness Perception." *Animal Behaviour* 82 (1): 55–9.

Briefer, E. F. 2012. "Vocal Expression of Emotions in Mammals: Mechanisms of Production and Evidence." *Journal of Zoology* 288 (1): 1–20.

Broesch, T., and Bryant, G. A. 2015. "Prosody in Infant-Directed Speech Is Similar Across Western and Traditional Cultures." *Journal of Cognition and Development* 16 (1): 31–43.

Bruckert, L., Liénard, J. S., Lacroix, A., Kreutzer, M., and Leboucher, G. 2006. "Women Use Voice Parameters to Assess Men's Characteristics." *Proceedings of the Royal Society Biological Sciences Series B* 273 (1582): 83–9.

Bryant, G. A. 2010. "Prosodic Contrasts in Ironic Speech." *Discourse Processes* 47 (7): 545–66.

Bryant, G. A. 2013. "Animal Signals and Emotion in Music: Coordinating Affect Across Groups." *Frontiers in Psychology* 4 (990): 1–13.

Bryant, G. A., and Aktipis, C. A. 2014. "The Animal Nature of Spontaneous Human Laughter." *Evolution and Human Behavior* 35 (4): 327–35.

Bryant, G. A., and Barrett, H. C. 2007. "Recognizing Intentions in Infant-Directed Speech: Evidence for Universals." *Psychological Science* 18 (8): 746–51.

Bryant, G. A., and Barrett, H. C. 2008. "Vocal Emotion Recognition Across Disparate Cultures." *Journal of Cognition and Culture* 8 (1–2): 135–48.

Bryant, G. A., Fessler, D. M. T., Fusaroli, R., Clint, E., Aorøe, E., Apicella, C., et al. 2016. "Detecting Affiliation in Colaughter Across 24 Societies." *Proceedings of the National Academy of Sciences* 113 (17): 4682–7.

Bryant, G. A., and Fox Tree, J. E. 2002. "Recognizing Verbal Irony in Spontaneous Speech." *Metaphor and Symbol* 17 (2): 99–117.

Bryant, G. A., and Fox Tree, J. E. 2005. "Is There an Ironic Tone of Voice?" *Language and Speech* 48 (3): 257–77.

Bryant, G. A., and Haselton, M. G. 2009. "Vocal Cues of Ovulation in Human Females." *Biology Letters* 5 (1): 12–15.

Bryant, G. A., Liénard, P., and Barrett, H. C. 2012. "Recognizing Infant-Directed Speech Across Distant Cultures: Evidence from Africa." *Journal of Evolutionary Psychology* 10 (2): 147–59.

Campanella, S., and Belin, P. 2007. "Integrating Face and Voice in Person Perception." *Trends in Cognitive Sciences* 11 (12): 535–43.

Cartei, V., Bond, R., and Reby, D. 2014. "What Makes a Voice Masculine: Physiological and Acoustical Correlates of Women's Ratings of Men's Vocal Masculinity." *Hormones and Behavior* 66 (4): 569–76.

Cartei, V., Cowles, H. W., and Reby, D. 2012. "Spontaneous Voice ender Imitation Abilities in Adult Speakers." *PloS one* 7 (2): e31353.

Charlton, B. D., and Reby, D. 2016. "The Evolution of Acoustic Size Exaggeration in Terrestrial Mammals." *Nature Communications* 7: 12739.

Charlton, B. D., Taylor, A. M., and Reby, D. 2013. "Are Men Better than Women at Acoustic Size Judgements?" *Biology Letters* 9 (4): 20130270.

Cheang, H. S., and Pell, M. D. 2008. "The Sound of Sarcasm." *Speech Communication* 50 (5): 366–81.

Chiba, T., and Kajiyama, M. 1958. *The Vowel: Its Nature and Structure*. Tokyo: Phonetic Society of Japan.

Collins, S. A. 2000. "Men's Voices and Women's Choices." *Animal Behaviour* 60 (6): 773–80.

Collins, S. A., and Missing, C. 2003. "Vocal and Visual Attractiveness Are Related in Women." *Animal Behaviour* 65 (5): 997–1004.

Cosmides, L. 1983. "Invariances in the Acoustic Expression of Emotion during Speech." *Journal of Experimental Psychology: Human Perception and Performance* 9 (6): 864–81.

Cutler, A., Dahan, D., and Van Donselaar, W. 1997. "Prosody in the Comprehension of Spoken Language: A Literature Review." *Language and Speech* 40 (2): 141–201.

Cutler, A., and Pearson, M. 1986. "On the Analysis of Prosodic Turn-taking Cues." *Intonation in Discourse*, edited by Catherine Johns-Lewis, 139–55. London: Croom Helm.

Dabbs, J. M., and Mallinger, A. 1999. "High Testosterone Levels Predict Low Voice Pitch among Men." *Personality and Individual Differences* 27 (4): 801–4.

Darwin, C. 1872. *The Expression of the Emotions in Man and Animals*. London: John Murray.

DeBruine, L. M., Jones, B. C., Crawford, J. R., Welling, L. L., and Little, A. C. 2010. "The Health of a Nation Predicts Their Mate Preferences: Cross-cultural Variation in Women's Preferences for Masculinized Male Faces." *Proceedings of the Royal Society B: Biological Sciences* 277 (1692): 2405–10.

Eisenegger, C., Haushofer, J., and Fehr, E. 2011. "The Role of Testosterone in Social Interaction." *Trends in Cognitive Sciences* 15 (6): 263–71.

Ekman, P. 1997. "Should We Call It Expression or Communication?" *Innovation: The European Journal of Social Science Research* 10 (4): 333–44.

Ekman, P., Davidson, R. J., and Friesen, W. V. 1990. "The Duchenne Smile: Emotional Expression and Brain Physiology II." *Journal of Personality and Social Psychology* 58 (2): 342–53.

Elfenbein, H. A., and Ambady, N. 2002. "On the Universality and Cultural Specificity of Emotion Recognition: A Meta-Analysis." *Psychological Bulletin* 128 (2): 208–35.

Evans, S., Neave, N., Wakelin, D., and Hamilton, C. 2008. "The Relationship Between Testosterone and Vocal Rrequencies in Human Males." *Physiology and Behavior* 93 (4–5): 783–8.

Ey, E., Pfefferle, D., and Fischer, J. 2007. "Do Age- and Sex-Related Variations Reliably Reflect Body Size in Non-Human Primate Vocalizations? A Review." *Primates* 48 (4): 253–67.

Fant, F. 1960. *Acoustic Theory of Speech Production.* The Hague: Mouton.

Feinberg, D., DeBruine, L., Jones, B., Little, A., O'Connor, J., and Tigue, C. 2012. "Women's Self-perceived Health and Attractiveness Predict their Male Vocal Masculinity Preferences in Different Directions across Short- and Long-Term Relationship Contexts." *Behavioral Ecology and Sociobiology* 66 (3): 413–18.

Feinberg, D. R. 2008. "Are Human Faces and Voices Ornaments Signaling Common Underlying Cues to Mate Value?" *Evolutionary Anthropology* 17 (2): 112–18.

Feinberg, D. R., DeBruine, L. M., Jones, B. C., and Little, A. C. 2008. "Correlated Preferences for Men's Facial and Vocal Masculinity." *Evolution and Human Behavior* 29 (4): 233–41.

Feinberg, D. R., DeBruine, L. M., Jones, B. C., and Perrett, D. I. 2008. "The Role of Femininity and Averageness of Voice Pitch in Aesthetic Judgments of Women's Voices." *Perception* 37 (4): 615–23.

Feinberg, D. R., Jones, B. C., Law-Smith, M. J., Moore, F. R., DeBruine, L. M., Cornwell, R. E., et al. 2006. "Menstrual Cycle, Trait Estrogen Level, and Masculinity Preferences in the Human Voice." *Hormones and Behavior* 49 (2): 215–22.

Feinberg, D. R., Jones, B. C., Little, A. C., Burt, D. M., and Perrett, D. I. 2005. "Manipulations of Fundamental and Formant Frequencies Influence the Attractiveness of Human Male Voices." *Animal Behaviour* 69 (3): 561–8.

Fitch, W. T. 1994. "Vocal Tract Length Perception and the Evolution of Language." PhD diss., Brown University.

Fitch, W. T. 1997. "Vocal Tract Length and Formant Frequency Dispersion Correlate with Body Size in Rhesus Macaques." *Journal of the Acoustical Society of America* 102 (2 Pt 1): 1213–22.

Fitch, W. T. 2000. "The Evolution of Speech: A Comparative Review." *Trends in Cognitive Sciences* 4 (7) 258–67.

Fitch, W. T., and Giedd, J. 1999. "Morphology and Development of the Human Vocal Tract: A Study Using Magnetic Resonance Imaging." *Journal of the Acoustical Society of America* 106 (3): 1511–22.

Fitch, W. T., and Hauser, M. 2003. "Unpacking 'Honesty': Vertebrate Vocal Production and the Evolution of Acoustic Signals." In *Acoustic Communication*, 65–137. New York: Springer.

Fitch, W. T., Neubauer, J., and Herzel, H. 2002. "Calls Out of Chaos: The Adaptive Significance of Nonlinear Phenomena in Mammalian Vocal Production." *Animal Behaviour* 63 (3): 407–18.

Fouquet, M., Pisanski, K., Mathevon, M., and Reby, D. 2016. "Seven and Up: Individual Differences in Male Voice Fundamental Frequency Emerge before Puberty and Remain Stable Throughout Adulthood." *Royal Society Open Science* 3 (10): 160395.

Fraccaro, P. J., Jones, B. C., Vukovic, J., Smith, F. G., Watkins, C. D., Feinberg, D. R., et al. 2011. "Experimental Evidence that Women Speak in a Higher Voice Pitch to Men They Find Attractive." *Journal of Evolutionary Psychology* 9 (1): 57–67.

Frederick, D. A., and Haselton, M. G. 2007. "Why Is Muscularity Sexy? Tests of the Fitness Indicator Hypothesis." *Personality and Social Psychology Bulletin* 33 (8): 1167–83.

Furlow, B. F. 1997. "Human Neonatal Cry Quality as an Honest Signal of Fitness." *Evolution and Human Behavior* 18 (3): 175–93.

Gallup, A. C., White, D. D., and Gallup Jr., G. G. 2007. "Handgrip Strength Predicts Sexual Behavior, Body mMorphology, and Aggression in Male College Students." *Evolution and Human Behavior* 28 (6): 423–9.

Gangestad, S. W., and Thornhill, R. 2008. "Human Oestrus." *Proceedings of the Royal Society B-Biological Sciences* 275 (1638): 991–1000.

Gendron, M., Roberson, D., and Barrett, L. F. 2015. "Cultural Variation in Emotion Perception Is real: A Response to Sauter, Eisner, Ekman, and Scott (2015)." *Psychological Science* 26 (3): 357–9.

Gendron, M., Roberson, D., van der Vyver, J. M., and Barrett, L. F. 2014. "Cultural Relativity in Perceiving Emotion from Vocalizations." *Psychological Science* 25 (4): 911–20.

Gervais, M., and Wilson, D. S. 2005. "The Evolution and Functions of Laughter and Humor: A Synthetic Approach." *Quarterly Review of Biology* 80 (4): 395–430.

Ghazanfar, A. A., and Rendall, D. 2008. "Evolution of Human Vocal Production." *Current Biology* 18 (11): R457–60.

Gildersleeve, K., Haselton, M. G., and Fales, M. R. 2014. "Do Women's Mate Preferences Change Across the Ovulatory Cycle? A Meta-Analytic Review." *Psychological Bulletin* 140 (5): 1205–59.

González, J. 2003. "Estimation of Speakers' Weight and Height from Speech: a Re-analysis of Data from Multiple Studies by Lass and Colleagues." *Perceptual and Motor Skills* 96 (1): 297–304.

González, J. 2006. "Research in Acoustics of Human Speech Sounds: Correlates and Perception of Speaker Body Size." *Recent Research Development in Applied Physics* 9: 1–15.

Grafen, A. 1990. "Biological Signals as Handicaps." *Journal of Theoretical Biology* 144 (4): 517–46.

Grossmann, T., Oberecker, R., Koch, S. P., and Friederici, A. D. 2010. "The Developmental Origins of Voice Processing in the Human Brain." *Neuron* 65 (6): 852–8.

Harries, M., Hawkins, S., Hacking, J., and Hughes, I. 1998. "Changes in the Male Voice at Puberty. Vocal Fold Length and Its Relationship to the Fundamental Frequency of the Voice." *Journal of Laryngology and Otology* 112 (5): 451–4.

Haselton, M. G., and Gildersleeve, K. 2011. "Can Men Detect Ovulation?" *Current Directions in Psychological Science* 20 (2): 87–92.

Henrich, J., Heine, S. J., and Norenzayan, A. 2010. "The Weirdest People in the World?" *Behavioral and Brain Sciences* 33 (2–3): 61–83.

Hodges-Simeon, C. R., Gurven, M., Puts, D. A., and Gaulin, S. J. 2014. "Vocal Fundamental and Formant Frequencies are Honest Signals of Threat Potential in Peripubertal Males." *Behavioral Ecology* 25 (4): 984–8.

Hollien, H. 2014. "Vocal Fold Dynamics for Frequency Change." *Journal of Voice* 28 (4): 395–405.

Hufschmidt, C., Weege, B., Röder, S., Pisanski, K., Neave, N., and Fink, B. 2015. "Physical Strength and Gender Identification from Dance Movements." *Personality and Individual Differences* 76: 13–17.

Hughes, S. M., Dispenza, F., and Gallup Jr., G. G. 2004. "Ratings of Voice Attractiveness Predict Sexual Behavior and Body Configuration." *Evolution and Human Behavior* 25 (5): 295–304.

Hughes, S. M., Farley, S. D., and Rhodes, B. C. 2010. "Vocal and Physiological Changes in Response to the Physical Attractiveness of Conversational Partners." *Journal of Nonverbal Behavior* 34 (3): 155–67.

Hughes, S. M., and Miller, N. E. 2015. "What Sounds Beautiful Looks Beautiful Stereotype: The Matching of Attractiveness of Voices and Faces." *Journal of Social and Personal Relationships* 33 (7): 984–96.

Hughes, S. M., Mogilski, J. K., and Harrison, M. A. 2014. "The Perception and Parameters of Intentional Voice Manipulation." *Journal of Nonverbal Behavior* 38 (1): 107–27.

Irino, T., Aoki, Y., Kawahara, H., and Patterson, R. D. 2012. "Comparison of Performance with Voiced and Whispered Speech in Word Recognition and Mean-Formant-Frequency Discrimination." *Speech Communication* 54 (9): 998–1013.

Johnstone, R. A., and Grafen, A. 1993. "Dishonesty and the Handicap Principle." *Animal Behaviour* 46 (4): 759–64.

Jones, B. C., Boothroyd, L., Feinberg, D. R., and DeBruine, L. M. 2010. "Age at Menarche Predicts Individual Differences in Women's Preferences for Masculinized Male Voices in Adulthood." *Personality and Individual Differences* 48 (7): 860–3.

Jones, B. C., Feinberg, D. R., DeBruine, L. M., Little, A. C., and Vukovic, J. 2008. "Integrating Cues of Social Interest and Voice Pitch in Men's Preferences for Women's Voices." *Biology Letters* 4 (2): 192–4.

Jones, B. C., Feinberg, D. R., Watkins, C. D., Fincher, C. L., Little, A. C., and DeBruine, L. M. 2013. "Pathogen Disgust Predicts Women's Preferences for Masculinity in Men's Voices, Faces, and Bodies." *Behavioral Ecology* 24 (2): 373–9.

Jurgens, U. 2002. "Neural Pathways Underlying Vocal Control." *Neuroscience and Biobehavioral Reviews* 26 (2): 235–8.

Juslin, P. N., and Laukka, P. 2003. "Communication of Emotions in Vocal Expression and Music Performance: Different Channels, Same Code?" *Psychological Bulletin* 129 (5): 770.

Kanwisher, N., McDermott, J., and Chun, M. M. 1997. "The Fusiform Face Area: A Module in Human Extrastriate Fortex Specialized for Face Perception." *Journal of Neuroscience* 17 (11): 4302–11.

Krebs, J. R., and Dawkins, R. 1984. "Animal Signals: Mind-Reading and Manipulation." In *Behavioral Ecology: An Evolutionary Approach*, edited by J. R. Krebs and N. B. Davies, 380–402. Oxford: Blackwell.

Kreiman, J., and Sidtis, D. 2011. *Foundations of Voice Studies: An Interdisciplinary Approach to Voice Production and Perception*. Hoboken, NJ: John Wiley and Sons.

Lachmann, M., Szamado, S., and Bergstrom, C. T. 2001. "Cost and Conflict in Animal Signals and Human Language." *Proceedings of the National Academy of Sciences* 98 (23): 13189–94.

Lassek, W. D., and Gaulin, S. J. 2009. "Costs and Benefits of Fat-Free Muscle Mass in Men: Relationship to Mating Success, Dietary Requirements, and Native Immunity." *Evolution and Human Behavior* 30 (5): 322–8.

Lauder, G. V. 1981. "Form and Function: Structural Analysis in Evolutionary Morphology." *Paleobiology* 7 (4): 430–42.

Leongómez, J. D., Binter, J., Kubicová, L., Stolařová, P., Klapilová, K., Havlíček, J., et al. 2014. "Vocal Modulation during Courtship Increases Proceptivity even in Naive Listeners." *Evolution and Human Behavior* 35 (6): 489–96.

Levrero, F., Mathevon, N., Pisanski, K., Gustafsson, E., and Reby, D. 2018. "The pitch of babies' cries predicts their voice pitch at age 5." *Biology Letters* 14 (7): 20180065.

Lieberman, D., McCarthy, R., Hiiemae, K., and Palmer, J. 2001. "Ontogeny of Postnatal Hyoid and Larynx Descent in Humans." *Archives of Oral Biology* 46 (2): 117–28.

Little, A. C., Connely, J., Feinberg, D. R., Jones, B. C., and Roberts, S. C. 2011. "Human Preference for Masculinity Differs According to Context in Faces, Bodies, Voices, and Smell." *Behavioral Ecology* 22 (4): 862–8.

Little, A. C., Feinberg, D. R., DeBruine, L. M., and Jones, B. C. 2013. "Adaptation to Faces and Voices: Unimodal, Cross-Modal, and Sex-Specific Effects." *Psychological Science* 24 (11): 2297–305.

Lummaa, V., Vuorisalo, T., Barr, R. G. and Lehtonen, L. 1998. "Why Cry? Adaptive Significance of Intensive Crying in Human Infants." *Evolution and Human Behavior* 19 (3): 193–202.

Marcinkowska, U. M., Kozlov, M. V., Cai, H., Contreras-Garduño, J., Dixson, B. J., Oana, G. A., et al. 2014. "Cross-Cultural Variation in Men's Preference for Sexual Dimorphism in Women's Faces." *Biology Letters* 10 (4): 20130850.

Mazur, A., and Booth, A. 1998. "Testosterone and Dominance in Men." *Behavioral and Brain Sciences* 21 (03): 353–63.

Maynard Smith, J., and Harper, D. 2003. *Animal Signals*. Oxford: Oxford University Press.

Morton, E. S. 1977. "On the Occurrence and Significance of Motivation-Structural Rules in Some Bird and Mammal Sounds." *American Naturalist* 111 (981): 855–69.

Newman, J. D. 2007. "Neural Circuits Underlying Crying and Cry Responding in Mammals." *Behavioural Brain Research* 182 (2): 155–65.

Nisbett, R. E., and Wilson, T. D. 1977. "The Halo Effect: Evidence for Unconscious Alteration of Judgment." *Journal of Personality and Social Psychology* 34 (4): 250–6.

O'Connor, J. J. M., Fraccaro, P. J., Pisanski, K., Tigue, C. C., and Feinberg, D. R. 2013. "Men's Preferences for Women's Femininity in Dynamic Cross-Modal Stimuli." *PloS one* 8 (7): e69531.

O'Connor, J. J. M., Fraccaro, P. J., Pisanski, K., Tigue, C. C., O'Donnell, T. J., and Feinberg, D. R. 2014. "Social Dialect and Men's Voice Pitch Influence Women's Mate Preferences." *Evolution and Human Behavior* 35 (5): 368–75.

O'Connor, J. J. M., Re, D. E., and Feinberg, D. R. 2011. "Voice Pitch Influences Perceptions of Sexual Infidelity." *Evolutionary Psychology* 9 (1): 64–78.

O'Connor, J. J. M., Fraccaro, P. J., and Feinberg, D. R. 2012. "The Influence of Male Voice Pitch on Women's Perceptions of Relationship Investment." *Journal of Evolutionary Psychology* 10 (1): 1–13.

Ohala, J. J. 1984. "An Ethological Perspective on Common Cross-language Utilization of Fo of Voice." *Phonetica* 41 (1): 1–16.

Oliver, J. C., and González, J. 2004. "Percepción a través de la Voz de las Características Físicas del Hablante: Identificación de la Estatura a partir de una Frase o una Vocal." *Revista de Psicología General y Aplicada* 57 (1): 21–34.

Owren, M. J., and Rendall, D. 2001. "Sound on the Rebound: Bringing Form and Function Back to the Forefront in Understanding Nonhuman Primate Vocal Signaling." *Evolutionary Anthropology: Issues, News, and Reviews* 10 (2): 58–71.

Patterson, R. D., Smith, D. R., van Dinther, R., and Walters, T. C. 2008. "Size Information in the Production and Perception of Communication Sounds." In *Auditory Perception of Sound Sources*, edited by W. A. Yost, A. N. Popper, and R. R. Fay, 43–75. New York: Springer.

Pell, M. D., Monetta, L., Paulmann, S., and Kotz, S. A. 2009. "Recognizing Emotions in a Foreign Language." *Journal of Nonverbal Behavior* 33 (2): 107–20.

Pernet, C. R., McAleer, P., Latinus, M., Gorgolewski, K. J., Charest, I., Bestelmeyer, P. E., and Belin, P. 2015. "The Human Voice Areas: Spatial Organization and Inter-individual Variability in Temporal and Extra-temporal Cortices." *NeuroImage* 119: 164–74.

Peters, R. H. 1986. *The Ecological Implications of Body Size*, Volume 2. Cambridge: Cambridge University Press.

Petkov, C. I., Kayser, C., Steudel, T., Whittingstall, K., Augath, M., and Logothetis, N. K. 2008. "A Voice Region in the Monkey Brain." *Nature Neuroscience* 11 (3): 367–74.

Pietraszewski, D., Wertz, A. E., Bryant, G. A., and Wynn, K. 2017. "Three-Month-Old Human Infants Use Vocal Cues of Body Size." *Proceedings of the Royal Society Biological Sciences Series B* 284 (1856): 20170656.

Pipitone, R. N., and Gallup Jr., G. G. 2008. "Women's Voice Attractiveness Varies Across the Menstrual Cycle." *Evolution and Human Behavior* 29 (4): 268–74.

Pipitone, N. R., and Gallup, G. G. 2012. "The Unique Impact of Menstruation on the Female Voice: Implications for the Evolution of Menstrual Cycle Cues." *Ethology* 118 (3): 281–91.

Pisanski, K., Cartei, V., McGettigan, C., Raine, J., and Reby, D. 2016. "Voice Modulation: A Window into the Origins of Human Vocal Control?" *Trends in Cognitive Sciences* 20 (4): 304–18.

Pisanski, K., and Feinberg, D. R. 2013. "Cross-Cultural Variation in Mate Preferences for Averageness, Symmetry, Body Size, and Masculinity." *Cross-Cultural Research* 47 (2): 162–97.

Pisanski, K., Feinberg, D., Oleszkiewicz, A., and Sorokowska, A. 2017. "Voice Cues Are Used in a Similar Way by Blind and Sighted Adults When Assessing Women's Body Size." *Scientific Reports* 7 (1): 10329.

Pisanski, K., Fraccaro, P. J., Tigue, C. C., O'Connor, J. J. M., and Feinberg, D. R. 2014. "Return to Oz: Voice Pitch Facilitates Assessments of Men's Body Size." *Journal of Experimental Psychology: Human Perception and Performance* 40 (4): 1316–31.

Pisanski, K., Fraccaro, P. J., Tigue, C. C., O'Connor, J. J., Röder, S., Andrews, P., Fink, B., et al. 2014. "Vocal Indicators of Body Size in Men and Women: A Meta-Analysis." *Animal Behaviour* 95: 89–99.

Pisanski, K., Hahn, A. C., Fisher, C. I., DeBruine, L. M., Feinberg, D. R., and Jones, B. C. 2014. "Changes in Salivary Estradiol Predict Changes in Women's Preferences for Vocal Masculinity." *Hormones and Behavior* 66 (3): 493–7.

Pisanski, K., Jones, B. C., Fink, B., O'Connor, J. J., DeBruine, L. M., Röder, S., and Feinberg, D. R. 2016. "Voice Parameters Predict Sex-specific Body Morphology in Men and Women." *Animal Behaviour* 112: 13–22.

Pisanski, K., Mishra, S., and Rendall, D. 2012. "The Evolved Psychology of Voice: Evaluating Interrelationships in Listeners' Assessments of the Size, Masculinity, and Attractiveness of Unseen Speakers." *Evolution and Human Behavior* 33 (5): 509–19.

Pisanski, K., Mora, E. C., Pisanski, A., Reby, D., Sorokowski, P., Frackowiak, T., and Feinberg, D. R. 2016. "Volitional Exaggeration of Body Size through Fundamental and Formant Frequency Modulation in Humans." *Scientific Reports* 6: 34389.

Pisanski, K., Oleszkiewicz, A., Plachetka, J. Gmiterek, M., and Reby, D. 2018. "Voice pitch modulation in human mate choice." *Proceedings of the Royal Society B: Biological Sciences* 285 (1893): 20181634.

Pisanski, K., Oleszkiewicz, A., and Sorokowska, A. 2016. "Can Blind Persons Accurately Assess Body Size from the Voice?" *Biology Letters* 12 (4): 20160063.

Pisanski, K., and Rendall, D. 2011. "The Prioritization of Voice Fundamental Frequency or Formants in Listeners' Assessments of Speaker Size, Masculinity, and Attractiveness." *Journal of the Acoustical Society of America* 129 (4): 2201–12.

Porges, S. W. 2001. "The Polyvagal Theory: Phylogenetic Substrates of a Social Nervous System." *International Journal of Psychophysiology* 42 (2): 123–46.

Puts, D. A. 2005. "Mating Context and Menstrual Phase Affect Women's Preferences for Male Voice Pitch." *Evolution and Human Behavior* 26 (5): 388–97.

Puts, D. A. 2006. "Cyclic Variation in Women's Preferences for Masculine Traits—Potential Hormonal Causes." *Human Nature* 17 (1): 114–27.

Puts, D. A., Apicella, C. L., and Cardenas, R. A. 2012. "Masculine Voices Signal Men's Threat Potential in Forager and Industrial Societies." *Proceedings of the Royal Society Biological Sciences Series B* 279 (1728): 601–9.

Puts, D. A., Bailey, D. H., Cárdenas, R. A., Burriss, R. P., Welling, L. L., Wheatley, J. R., et al. 2013. "Women's Attractiveness Changes with Estradiol and Progesterone across the Ovulatory Cycle." *Hormones and Behavior* 63 (1): 13–19.

Puts, D. A., Barndt, J. L., Welling, L. L., Dawood, K., and Burriss, R. P. 2011. "Intrasexual Competition among Women: Vocal Femininity Affects Perceptions of Attractiveness and Flirtatiousness." *Personality and Individual Differences* 50 (1): 111–15.

Puts, D. A., Doll, L. M., and Hill, A. K. 2014. "Sexual Selection on Human Voices." In *Evolutionary Perspectives on Human Sexual Psychology and Behavior*, edited by Viviana A. Weekes-Shackelford and Todd K. Shackelford, 69–86. New York: Springer.

Puts, D. A., Gaulin, S. J., and Verdolini, K. 2006. "Dominance and the Evolution of Sexual Dimorphism in Human Voice Pitch." *Evolution and Human Behavior* 27 (4): 283–96.

Puts, D. A., Hill, A. K., Bailey, D. H., Walker, R. S., Rendall, D., Wheatley, J. R., and Jablonski, N. G. 2016. "Sexual Selection on Male Vocal Fundamental Frequency in Humans and Other Anthropoids." *Proceedings of the Royal Society Biological Sciences Series B* 283 (1829): 20152830.

Raine, J., Pisanski, K., Oleszkiewicz, A., Simner, J., and Reby, D. 2018. "Human listeners can accurately judge strength and height relative to self from aggressive roars and speech." iScience 4: 273–280.

Rantala, M. J., Moore, F. R., Skrinda, I., Krama, T., Kivleniece, I., Kecko, S., et al. 2012. "Evidence for the Stress-Linked Immunocompetence Handicap Hypothesis in Humans." *Nature Communications* 3: 694.

Re, D. E., O'Connor, J. J. M., Bennett, P. J., and Feinberg, D. R. 2012. "Preferences for Very Low and Very High Voice Pitch in Humans." *PloS one* 7 (3): e32719.

Reby, D., Levréro, F., Gustafsson, E., and Mathevon, N. 2016. "Sex Stereotypes Influence Adults' Perception of Babies' Cries." *BMC Psychology* 4 (19): 1–12.

Rendall, D., Kollias, S., Ney, C., and Lloyd, P. 2005. "Pitch (F_0) and Formant Profiles of Human Vowels and Vowel-like Baboon Grunts: The Role of Vocalizer Body Size and Voice-acoustic Allometry." *Journal of the Acoustical Society of America* 117 (2): 944–55.

Rendall, D., Owren, M. J., and Ryan, M. J. 2009. "What Do Animal Signals Mean?" *Animal Behaviour* 78 (2): 233–40.

Rendall, D., Vokey, J. R., and Nemeth, C. 2007. "Lifting the Curtain on the Wizard of Oz: Biased Voice-based Impressions of Speaker Size." *Journal of Experimental Psychology: Human Perception and Performance* 33 (5): 1208–19.

Roche, J. M., Peters, B., and Dale, R. 2015. "'Your Tone Says It All': The Processing and Interpretation of Affective Language." *Speech Communication* 66: 47–64.

Ruch, W., and Ekman, P. 2001. "The Expressive Pattern of Laughter." In *Emotion, Qualia, and Consciousness*, edited by A. Kaszniak, 426–43. Tokyo: Word Scientific.

Russell, J. A. 1980. "A Circumplex Model of Affect." *Journal of Personality and Social Psychology* 39: 1161–78.

Ryalls, J. H., and Lieberman, P. 1982. "Fundamental Frequency and Vowel Perception." *Journal of the Acoustical Society of America* 72 (5): 1631–4.

Sauter, D. A., Eisner, F., Calder, A. J., and Scott, S. K. 2010. "Perceptual Cues in Nonverbal Vocal Expressions of Emotion." *Quarterly Journal of Experimental Psychology* 63 (11): 2251–72.

Sauter, D. A., Eisner, F., Ekman, P., and Scott, S. K. 2010. "Cross-Cultural Recognition of Basic Emotions through Nonverbal Emotional Vocalizations." *Proceedings of the National Academy of Sciences* 107 (6): 2408–12.

Sauter, D. A., Eisner, F., Ekman, P., and Scott, S. K. 2015. "Emotional Vocalizations are Recognized across Cultures Regardless of the Valence of Distractors." *Psychological Science* 26 (3): 354–6.

Saxton, T. K., Burriss, R. P., Murray, L. K., Rowland, H. M., and Roberts, S. C. 2009. "Face, Body, and Speech Cues Independently Predict Judgments of Attractiveness." *Journal of Evolutionary Psychology* 7 (1): 23–35.

Saxton, T. K., DeBruine, L. M., Jones, B. C., Little, A. C., and Roberts, S. C. 2009. "Face and Voice Attractiveness Judgments Change during Adolescence." *Evolution and Human Behavior* 30 (6): 398–408.

Saxton, T. K., Mackey, L. L., McCarty, K., and Neave, N. 2015. "A Lover or a Fighter? Opposing Sexual Selection Pressures on Men's Vocal Pitch and Facial Hair." *Behavioral Ecology* 27 (2): 512–9.

Scherer, K. R., Banse, R., and Wallbott, H. 2001. "Emotion Inferences from Vocal Expression Correlate across Languages and Cultures." *Journal of Cross-Cultural Psychology* 32 (1): 76–92.

Scott-Phillips, T. 2014. *Speaking Our Minds: Why Human Communication is Different, and How Language Evolved to Make it Special.* London: Palgrave MacMillan.

Sell, A., Bryant, G. A., Cosmides, L., Tooby, J., Sznycer, D., von Rueden, C., Krauss, A., and Gurven, M. 2010. "Adaptations in Humans for Assessing Physical Strength from the Voice." *Proceedings of the Royal Society Biological Sciences Series B* 277 (1699): 3509–18.

Sell, A., Cosmides, L., Tooby, J., Sznycer, D., von Rueden, C., and Gurven, M. 2009. "Human Adaptations for the Visual Assessment of Strength and Fighting Ability from the Body and Face." *Proceedings of the Royal Society B: Biological Sciences* 276 (1656): 575–84.

Sell, A., Hone, L. S., and Pound, N. 2012. "The Importance of Physical Strength to Human Males." *Human Nature* 23 (1): 30–44.

Sherman, B. M., and Korenman, S. G. 1975. "Hormonal Characteristics of the Human Menstrual Cycle throughout Reproductive Life." *Journal of Clinical Investigation* 55 (4): 699–706.

Simpson, A. P. 2009. "Phonetic Differences Between Male and Female Speech." *Language and Linguistics Compass* 3 (2): 621–40.

Skrinda, I., Krama, T., Kecko, S., Moore, F. R., Kaasik, A., Meija, L., et al. 2014. "Body Height, Immunity, Facial and Vocal Attractiveness in Young Men." *Naturwissenschaften* 101 (12): 1017–25.

Soltis, J. 2004. "The Signal Functions of Early Infant Crying." *Behavioral and Brain Sciences* 27 (4): 443–58.

Spence, C. 2011. "Crossmodal Correspondences: A Tutorial Review." *Attention, Perception, and Psychophysics* 73 (4): 971–95.

Sperber, D., and Wilson, D. 1995. *Relevance: Communication and Cognition.* Cambridge, MA: Harvard University Press.

Swerts, M., and Hirschberg, J. 2010. "Prosodic Predictors of Upcoming Positive or Negative Content in Spoken Messages." *Journal of the Acoustical Society of America* 128 (3): 1337–45.

Taylor, A. M., Charlton, B. D., and Reby, D. 2016. "Vocal Production by Terrestrial Mammals: Source, Filter, and Function." In *Vertebrate Sound Production and Acoustic Communication*, edited by R. A. Suthers, W. T. Fitch, R. R. Fay, and A. N. Popper, 229–59. Heidelberg: Springer.

Taylor, A. M., and Reby, D. 2010. "The Contribution of Source-Filter Theory to Mammal Vocal Communication Research." *Journal of Zoology* 280 (3): 221–36.

Thompson, W., and Balkwill, L. L. 2006. "Decoding Speech Prosody in Five Languages." *Semiotica* 158 (1/4): 407–24.

Tigue, C. C., Borak, D. J., O'Connor, J. J., Schandl, C., and Feinberg, D. R. 2012. "Voice Pitch Influences Voting Behavior." *Evolution and Human Behavior* 33 (3): 210–6.

Tinbergen, N. 1952. "Derived Activities: Their Causation, Biological Significance, Origin and Emancipation during Evolution." *Quarterly Review of Biology* 27 (1): 1–32.

Tinbergen, N. 1963. "On Aims and Methods of Ethology." *Zeitschrift für Tierpsychologie* 20 (4): 410–33.

Titze, I. R. 1994. *Principles of Voice Production.* Englewood Cliffs, NJ: Prentice Hall.

Titze, I. R. 2011. "Vocal Fold Mass Is Not a Useful Quantity for Describing Fo in Vocalization." *Journal of Speech, Language and Hearing Research* 54 (2): 520–2.

van Dommelen, W. A., and Moxness, B. H. 1995. "Acoustic Parameters in Speaker Height and Weight Identification: Sex-Specific Behaviour." *Language and Speech* 38 (3): 267–87.

Vouloumanos, A., and Werker, J. F. 2007. "Listening to Language at Birth: Evidence for a Bias for Speech in Neonates." *Developmental Science* 10 (2): 159–64.

Vukovic, J., Feinberg, D. R., Jones, B. C., DeBruine, L. M., Welling, L. L. M., Little, A. C., et al. 2008. "Self-Rated Attractiveness Predicts Individual Differences in Women's Preferences for Masculine Men's Voices." *Personality and Individual Differences* 45 (6): 451–6.

Vukovic, J., Jones, B. C., DeBruine, L., Feinberg, D. R., Smith, F. G., Little, A. C., et al. 2010. "Women's Own Voice Pitch Predicts their Preferences for Masculinity in Men's Voices." *Behavioral Ecology* 21 (4): 767–72.

Vukovic, J., Jones, B. C., Feinberg, D. R., DeBruine, L. M., Smith, F. G., Welling, L. L., et al. 2011. "Variation in Perceptions of Physical Dominance and Trustworthiness Predicts Individual Differences in the Effect of Relationship Context on Women's Preferences for Masculine Pitch in Men's Voices." *British Journal of Psychology* 102 (1): 37–48.

Wheatley, J. R., Apicella, C. A., Burriss, R. P., Cárdenas, R. A., Bailey, D. H., Welling, L. L. M., and Puts, D. A. 2014. "Women's Faces and Voices are Cues to Reproductive Potential in Industrial and Forager Societies." *Evolution and Human Behavior* 35 (4): 264–71.

Williams, G. C. 1966. *Adaptation and Natural Selection.* Princeton, NJ: Princeton University Press.

Wood, W., Kressel, L., Joshi, P. D., and Louie, B. 2014. "Meta-Analysis of Menstrual Cycle Effects on Women's Mate Preferences." *Emotion Review* 6 (3): 229–49.

Zeifman D. M. 2001. "An Ethological Analysis of Human Infant Crying: Answering Tinbergen's Four Questions." *Developmental Psychobiology* 39 (4): 265–85.

Zuckerman, M., Hodgins, H., and Miyake, K. 1990. "The Vocal Attractiveness Stereotype: Replication and Elaboration." *Journal of Nonverbal Behavior* 14 (2): 97–112.

CHAPTER 14

ACOUSTIC SLITS AND VOCAL INCONGRUENCES IN LOS ANGELES UNION STATION

NINA SUN EIDSHEIM

INTRODUCTION

SINCE the last decades of the twentieth century, independent artists and dedicated opera companies have produced site-specific operas.[1] There are various reasons for doing so, including artistic vision, making use of the only available or affordable space, or a desire to eject opera from the opera house. In 2012 a new opera company entered the Los Angeles new music and opera scene. This organization, The Industry, seeks to bring opera out of the two-dimensional proscenium frame. Its debut production took place in a repurposed warehouse called Atwater Crossing, which now serves as an art space. In this space the audience was seated in the round, while the performers were positioned at various "stations" in the midst of and in close proximity to the audience, as well as offstage. The opera, *Crescent City* by composer Anne Lebaron and librettist Douglas Kearney, was also projected onto a screen and through speakers.

There were many practical and performance-related challenges associated with this production. For example, the repurposed warehouse setting was acoustically challenging, as the dimensions of the space were not originally intended for the presentation of live acoustic music. And filling most of the space with the set, surrounded by the audience, as well as placing the orchestra on a mezzanine at the side, invisible to both singers and audience, made the visual coordination of cuing between the conductor, orchestra, and singers difficult. Despite these considerable challenges, the venue was fully dedicated to the production, and uninterrupted time in the space was a major advantage. It meant that the rehearsal schedule could be set freely, and that equipment could remain in the space throughout the opera's run. However, uninterrupted rehearsal time and space was not the scenario for The Industry's second production, *Invisible Cities*, which was set in Union Station.

Built in 1939 and hailed as the country's last grand train station, Union Station is a working environment and is open twenty-four hours a day. Seventy-five thousand people pass through the complex daily (according to the Union Station Fact Sheet). By producing the opera at one of Los Angeles' busiest connection points, The Industry took an additional step away from the proscenium. On the face of it, this choice would seem to indicate a more aesthetically open and egalitarian production, in that audiences and onlookers could choose their physical relation to the piece rather than being at the mercy of the controlled and exclusive sphere of the proscenium space. Also, the choice of such a setting would seem to be an effort toward free and inclusive access. Indeed, the production was described as a "wandering opera" (Hertzog 2013). Instead of the limited access created by a prize-point area of town that might feel out of reach for many, this opera was indeed delivered among the people of Los Angeles.

However, while Union Station seems like an egalitarian place to offer an opera, the ways in which access and opportunity manifest differently are thrown into sharp relief by the production's acoustic schema. A more disturbing change was illustrated by the way in which people who occupied the same physical space could inhabit completely different experiential spheres. This acoustical curation by *Invisible Cities* illustrates the (invisible) barriers between people that nonetheless constitute the force multipliers in how people are invited or disinvited to move through life. My very basic argument is that, even if unintentionally, *Invisible Cities* curates and organizes the acoustic sphere through its music and sound design. These aspects of the production separate people in similar ways that are sometimes hard to quantify—because they look "the same"—but create the structures for every layer of life in the United States. I posit that *Invisible Cities'* design mirrors the ways in which racial privilege creates separation within what otherwise seems like an equal-opportunity space.

Making use of voice studies' methodological and analytical possibilities, this chapter is also about the way in which certain aspects of an event present themselves (or don't) as objects of interest for analysis. Scholars and audiences mine a vocal artwork for data and meaning. If we consider *Invisible Cities* in terms of dimensions such as libretto, pitch and melodic material, harmony, form, and instrumentation, we will produce certain types of questions and answers. And if, as I do in this chapter, we consider *Invisible Cities* through the lens of voice and the reverberation envelope within which voice is heard, we realize that it curates and organizes the acoustic sphere through its music and sound design, both responding and contributing to a transformation of the atmospheric, and hinting at another thread within the inquiry into "air politics."

I use the term "atmospheric" as an attempt to capture in words that which is actualized with and through what is more broadly conceived as air. For example, to anthropologist Tim Choy, the term "air politics" denotes phenomena such as the "practices of atmospheric and chemical monitoring by individuals, organizations, and government bodies; controversies concerning trans-border pollution and trans-specific contagion;

the politicization of asthma; the emergence of carbon economies; and the roles of air and notions of nuisance in environmental law" (Choy 2011). And to geographer Ben Anderson, "atmospheres are singular affective qualities that emanate from but exceed the assembling of bodies" (Anderson 2009, 77).

As such, "to attend to affective atmospheres is to learn to be affected by the ambiguities of affect/emotion, by that which is determinate and indeterminate, present and absent, singular and vague" (Anderson 2009, 77). To these lists I add that listening to the acoustic realization of sounds and the reverberation of distinct spaces can offer evidence of broader and deeper shifts, not only in the spaces' value, but in the ways spaces offer differentiated access to people. Both of these aspects are challenging to discern. When we investigate *Invisible Cities* through the analytical lens of voice, we move from opera analysis toward consideration of air and the acoustic presentation of voices. Thus, while this volume asks, broadly, *What is voice?*, in this chapter I develop the question slightly, asking *What kinds of insight does voice afford us?* If we shift our mapping of the voice from what it does (sound) to how it sounded what kind of knowledge can it offer us?

What we see, then, is that an inquiry into voice does not supply only answers limited to voice. But because vocal practices—of both production and perception—are inherently cultural, collective, and political, voice is a repository for a given culture's values. Thus, listening to voice can be viewed as a heuristic of those values, and studying voice can offer a portal to the broader values within which voice and listening have been formed. By opening up the possibilities of vocal inquiry to areas beyond voice per se, and applying our findings transdisciplinarily, what we learn is that division and discrimination take place in the acoustic realm. And setting an opera in a public space brings this division into stronger relief. Through analyzing the acoustics of the voices in a production of *Invisible Cities* at Los Angeles' Union Station, we witness the divide of populations within the acoustic realm. However, if the opera were only considered in terms of the shared physical space, access would have seemed equal.

INVISIBLE CITIES AT UNION STATION

Opening on October 19, 2013, the production of *Invisible Cities* was advertised as "an invisible opera for wireless headphones." I concentrate here on the *production* of the piece rather than the content and music of the opera, *Invisible Cities* (based on its namesake, Italo Calvino's 1972 novel), composed by Christopher Cerrone. The opera company The Industry and dance company the LA Dance Project, both located in Los Angeles, together mounted the production.

During an interview with KCET, a Los Angeles television station that did an hour-long documentary on the production, director Yuval Sharon shared that its concept resulted from a challenge by sound designer E. Martin Gimenez, who dared Sharon to consider an "opera for headphones."[2] Sharon took on Gimenez's challenge. On first thought, such setting and mediation of the piece share characteristics with silent disco and the Metropolitan Opera's high-definition video transmission, *Live in HD*. Similarly to "silent disco" events, the audience would inhabit two spaces: the physical space and the space provided by the sound emitted from the headphones. However, unlike some silent disco gatherings where people bring their own music and the primary sharing takes place through listening and dancing together (to different music), *Invisible Cities'* audiences shared not only the same music, as in the Metropolitan Opera's HD video simulcast, but also a live performed music, albeit primarily experienced via headphones.[3]

For Gimenez, whose original challenge to Sharon initiated the opera-for-headphones endeavor, "Sound design is as much a character as the music" (Gimenez 2014). Studying the libretto, Gimenez designs the sound to communicate the drama, just as the director and lighting or costume designer does. To him, the "sound design is going to be as much of a character in the piece as the text, as the singers, as the dancers" (Gimenez 2014). For the sound design for *Invisible Cities*, Gimenez was thinking in cinematic terms. In the documentary about *Invisible Cities*, he explains his thinking process around the sound design for the opening: "Kublai Khan [is] alone in this Palace." The libretto begins: "There is a time of emptiness that comes over everything."[4] Taking on the challenge of conveying the character of "emptiness" in this scene, Gimenez asked himself: "How can I create [the camera's] close-up to a very wide angle" in sonorous terms (Gimenez 2014)?

The solution was to render the voice "bone-dry for that first line.... And then sonically, over the first line, over a minute," Gimenez explains. He continues, "We kind of sonically pan out, and this cathedral reverb slowly fades in and you kind of realize 'Oh, wait. He's all alone in this vast space.'" Acknowledging that because traditional "opera is based on hearing things unamplified in a beautiful room," while *Invisible Cities* goes "to the extreme opposite," Gimenez reflects that under his design, "each movement, each line kind of has a sonic character to it." He asks rhetorically, "How do we achieve that sonic character?," and answers his own question: "Using ambient mics. Using a lot of fake reverb within our console. That will help us to determine, dramaturgically, the goal within each scene" (Gimenez 2014). What you gain within a digitally controlled situation, in Gimenez's opinion, is dynamic range in the lower end (e.g., the ability to communicate in a whisper) and the ability to change the reverb and sound placement, and hence imbue these parameters with meaning.

My description of the 2013 production of *Invisible Cities*, which follows, is based on my own two attendances (the first time with headphones and the second without them), and on engagements with performance recordings and video documentation footage, interviews with the producers from a television documentary about the opera, and press and media coverage.

On the evening of the performance, audience members enter the station like other commuters: by train or metro, car or bus, on foot or bike. After they finally make their way through the walkways that lead from parking garages and train tracks, or from one of the two main entrances, to the main waiting hall, nothing looks or feels different from any other evening at the station. Even for those who are intimately familiar with the space, it looks the same as always. The only minor change is that the historic ticket lobby, which is normally closed to the public, is open for those with tickets, who pick up a set of headphones at one of the original ticket counters. While activity within this area of the complex is not part of the station's daily life, commuters are already familiar with its popularity as a special events and film location. Therefore, on a surface level, the station remains the same as on any other day, and the performance that is drawing nearer is not visible.

As curtain time approaches, ushers in everyday clothes, wearing small pin buttons marking their affiliation with the event, direct audience members to the Harvey House Restaurant, an iconic venue that has not been operated on a consistent basis since 1967. On the restaurant's main floor, which has been cleared of tables, the chamber orchestra is installed. People crowd around the edges and into the former restaurant booths along the walls. Sharon welcomes the audience and offers basic instructions, mostly precautions regarding cohabitation with the station's life. The event starts when the orchestra begins the overture.[5] (See Figure 14.1.)

Audience members stay for a while, watching and listening to the orchestra, before leaving the space of their own accord. After parting ways on exiting the restaurant, where the orchestra was both heard and seen and the sound with or without headphones was fairly similar, each audience member's experience of the opera takes a unique path. That is, for each person the opera unfolds according to his or her specific sonic, visual, and spatial experience. Accordingly, I will now adopt a first-person narrative, reflecting one iteration of the opera as it took place from a single perspective.

Leaving the Harvey House Restaurant, I am led directly into the enclosed South Patio. I see some people with headphones forming and moving around within clusters, while

FIGURE 14.1 The overture of Christopher Cerrone's *Invisible Cities* played in the Harvey House Restaurant, Union Station, Los Angeles (photo courtesy of The Industry).

others move singly. At first there is only orchestral music coming from the headphones, with the vague hum and bustle of the station pressing in, and sirens filtering in from a distance. As soon as I hear a voice in the headphones, my inclination is to go and find its source. It is when I hear sounds I do not see, and cannot tell immediately where or even from which general direction they come, that I begin to sense the gap between the acoustic and sonic world surrounding me and the omni-sonorous sound world offered through the headphones.[6] Since the acoustic cues conveyed by the mixed music do not reflect its placement within the physical space and acoustic character of the station, I find myself relying on visual cues, such as gatherings of small crowds, to seek out singers' locations. I assume other audience members have gathered around such activity.

The first performers I see are dancers on the South Patio, dancing in spotlights lighting up the garden. Since everyone who had been in the Harvey House Restaurant during the overture has to move through this area, it is so crowded that I move into the main waiting hall, and from there into the tunnels that lead to the gates and tracks. But before I even make it there, two friendly people whose pin buttons identify them as ushers emerge to let me know that the performance space ends at the edge of the waiting area. From that point until the finale, I move between the North Patio, the main waiting hall, and the area near the main entrance (on the Alameda Street side). In this way, audiences are subtly directed through and dispersed throughout the space, drawn to particular areas by an activity or steered away from others by the ushers.

The overall concept of an invisible opera emerges not only from the performers' engagement in the everyday activities of the hall, such as cleaning the floors or sitting down in the waiting area and reading a paper, but also because the performers are situated among the travelers. It is only when they break into operatic-style song that the singers distinguish themselves. Because it is difficult to identify the singers when they are not singing, this ambiguity turns nearly every person in the station into a potential professional singer. (See Figure 14.2.)

For patrons of Union Station, only the singers' acoustic voices are audible. The singers wear tiny lavalier microphones and in-ear earphones. The orchestra and vocal sounds are mixed live and returned to both performers and audience. While the orchestral musicians can see the conductor at all times, for the singers the earpiece carries their only cue. As alluded to earlier, audience members wearing headsets are exposed predominantly to the designed mix of operatic voices and orchestra. While volume can be adjusted individually, the headsets also function by default as light sound mufflers, generally limiting the sounds of the station's activity to those that pierce through during train departure loudspeaker announcements.[7] Wearing the headphones also visually distinguishes audience members from the station's everyday patrons, whether travelers or those who use the building for shelter. In contrast, the singers are indistinguishable in terms of appearance.

I also observe that this operatic performance within a public space carries with it an invisible separation between audience and performers, and between audience members and station patrons. The audience keeps a respectful physical distance from the performers, yet observes them in a very different manner than would, say, a station

FIGURE 14.2 Performance of Christopher Cerrone's *Invisible Cities*, main hall of Union Station, Los Angeles (photo courtesy of The Industry).

patron. In this way, while both groups inhabit a public place, they are there for different reasons, and hence interact differently with the surrounding space and people. At the same time, their common reference point—the opera—contributes to partially eroding the barrier that often exists between strangers in a public space. Whether a given person is at the station as a member of the opera audience or simply for transit reasons, the opera can constitute a shared aspect of experience. Perhaps for that reason, I overhear more conversations and interactions between strangers than on an average day at Union Station or another public space.

However, while the production of the piece encourages the audience to engage with the acoustic world offered through sound design, *Invisible Cities* cannot fully offer an alternative acoustics through its sound design-treated voice and orchestra, nor can it offer a clear sense of the acoustics of the hall.[8] Recall that for patrons of Union Station, only the singers' acoustic voices are audible, while opera attendees hear the sound designed voices through the headset, a contraption that also omits much of the station sound. Hence, *Invisible Cities* makes tangible the tension between two simultaneous acoustic worlds, and suggests a further tension between a renewal at the structural level and a more surface-level renewal based on gentrified acoustics. That is, the audience is separated from the Union Station patrons through privileged access to a refined and curated acoustic space. If we were to simply look at the multiplicity of people within the station during a performance, they would seem to inhabit the same space. However, the acoustic experience of a given person defines the division between the two populations.

In listening to the acoustics of the voices, we find that the separation that has existed all along is spatialized and materialized—or, perhaps, in the language of gentrification scholars, what takes place is "the physical renovation of acoustics," a renovation in which only certain listeners are to enjoy.[9] As some people are afforded loans to purchase homes in gentrifying areas, others are refused reasonable credit and terms. These people are thereby denied the benefits of the area's renewal, which commonly include a safer environment, green spaces, avoidance of various forms of pollution, and better schools. Similarly, while Union Station's patrons and *Invisible Cities'* audience members have intermingled within the same physical space, they have consumed, and have been consumed within, different acoustic spaces. Station patrons hear only the singing voices that happened to be within earshot inside the hall, while audience members hear all the voices and the orchestra set within the acoustic envelope of the careful and costly sound design.

This split in experience generally, and in access to "renovated" acoustic spaces specifically (as represented by Union Station and the setting of *Invisible Cities*), has come about as part of a general transformation of downtown Los Angeles. However, while we typically think of everything from small-scale renovation to full-scale gentrification as involving the construction of structures and surfaces—that is, involving shifts in the spatial-visual dimension—it is important to note that these changes also affect *the air between the structures* and the ways that surfaces reflect sounds. By following the lead of the voice, we can see how spaces, or dimensions of spaces, that seem to be shared are actually divided through what I think of as the gentrification of acoustics. In terms of vocal acoustics, this gentrification can take the form of building new structures, and hence new reverberant spaces, and new surfaces with higher or lower rates of sound reflection. It can also take the form of digital transformation of the acoustics of a structure, as in *Invisible Cities*.

THE INVISIBLE SEPARATION WITHIN AIR AND REVERBERATION

Typically, in researching the physical changes resulting from gentrification, we have looked to changes in physical structures and institutionally organized cultural activities, and to the influx of new demographics. To Marina Peterson's (2006) list of ways to understand the process of gentrification through music, we may add listening to the city through the multiplicity of "states" exemplified by the voice. Thus, by bringing listening modes suggested by the voice into our listening to music set within downtown Los Angeles, we can begin to sense how we may sharpen methods of tracking and understanding processes of urban renewal and gentrification.

I want to suggest that by listening with and through the voice, we are able to grasp dimensions that are not apparent within listening that favors one mode while suppressing incongruences. For example, in one way of listening to *Invisible Cities*, we might regard only the sound-designed presentation of the opera, taking it as the "correct" version and conceiving of the nonsound-designed voices as incomplete versions. In another mode, we could condemn the sound-designed version for suppressing the acoustic version and failing to regard the sonic reality of the space. However, the voice models multimodal, multisensory listening, and insists that listening can yield simultaneous noncongruent experiences. Through this modeling, voice shows that there is not only one mode to which we must preserve fidelity. Voice encourages us to stick with the complexity—and often the incongruity—that attends multiplicity. In taking listening to the voice as a model for listening to an opera set within a changing urban setting, this mode of listening taught me to maintain multiple acoustic realities simultaneously—rather than to determine fidelity to one and suppress the others—and to pursue what that multiplicity could tell me (in this case about a particular phase of gentrification in downtown Los Angeles).

Beyond music specifically, listening to voice taught me to consider what we might think about as *negative space*. By negative space I refer to the areas that are not filled with structures; I refer to the element that is mainly referred to as sound reverberating through, rather than the designed architectural structure or performed music more traditionally considered. I mean that while the list of changes typically contains the areas listed earlier, these physical modifications in the urban environment also cause alteration in the mass or "body" of empty space—which is typically filled with air. And it is that body of air that is animated by sound. The quality of that body of air is also marked by the types of surfaces that together make up its boundaries, its *skin*. In other words, air is a body with specific "surfaces" or edges determined, for example, by building materials. And sound is realized by its transmission through that body of air. Furthermore, sound is given its quality based on that body of air and the specific quality of its outer boundaries. In *Invisible Cities'* production, a digital, virtual space is animated—but it is only available to select listeners. So in a roundabout way, listening in to sound's acoustics or a space's resonances, in the multisensorial and multimodular manner that the voice suggests, is both one of the most encompassing and one of the most direct ways of gaining access to a multiplicity of elements.

In listening through voice, that which we take for granted—voice's and sound's acoustic envelope, acoustic and digitized—becomes animated and available for consideration. Following voice's lead brought out a story about social and economic relations in Los Angeles, as such differences were forwarded during *Invisible Cities'* run at Union Station. Thus, listening through multiplicity, as voice instructs, yields insights into stories of urban life. Specifically, this operatic production materialized the stark division between people in an otherwise seemingly equal-access space. Whether intentionally or not, listening closely to this production allows us to awaken from the anesthetic lie of social sameness and equal opportunity.

Considering the question of opportunity, writer Eula Biss reflects on race in the United States, comparing whiteness and privilege to racial debt. The privilege of whiteness, Biss writes, is due to a debt that cannot be repaid, as the nation has not made amends for its original sins of colonization and slavery. In the same way that she tends to forget about her financial debt on a daily basis and thus can identify the house on which she still has a bank loan as "mine," Biss notices that her daily racial privilege also carries a huge unpaid debt. "The comfort of living in a house that is truly owned by the bank, but feeling it is mine, is akin to the 'conundrum of whiteness'" (Biss 2015). As we are entirely comfortable in our mortgaged houses, we are comfortable with the ways in which what we might view as equal availability and opportunity—in air, public school, education, and economic prosperity—are not equal at all.

It is that privilege that anesthetizes us to differences, and allows us to lull ourselves into "believ[ing] wholeheartedly in the power of his own hard work and deservedness." The dilemma is summarized by Biss. "For me," she writes, "whiteness is not an identity but a moral problem." She looks to the German language and learns from Nietzsche that "the moral concept of *Schuld* ('guilt')...descends from the very material concept of *Schulden* ('debts')." In other words, "material debt predates moral debt." Nietzsche, Biss observes, "has the kind of disdain for guilt that many people now reserve for 'white guilt' in particular. We seem to believe that the crime is not investing in whiteness but feeling badly about it" (Biss 2015). As Biss concludes, "Whiteness is not a kinship or a culture. White people are no more closely related to one another, genetically, than we are to black people. American definitions of race allow for a white woman to give birth to black children, which should serve as a reminder that white people are not a family. What binds us is that we share a system of social advantages that can be traced back to the advent of slavery in the colonies that became the United States" (Biss 2015). As our guilt binds us together, our investment in a fantasy about equality unites us. Thus, while the comparison may seem glib, my thoughts wander to Union Station at the time of *Invisible Cities*. In the production of this piece, both realities are borne out.

The conceit behind the staging of *Invisible Cities*, and more generally behind the opera company The Industry, is that opera is elitist when it is presented on the proscenium stage, and that moving opera outside the confines of the proscenium constitutes an effort to be nonelitist. And when we look at all the people walking around Union Station during the performance, it seems at first to be an equal situation. However, if we consider the timbral and acoustic aspects of the voices and performance, we note that access is not equally distributed. Certain kinds of access to the voices sounded in that public space are split. Thus, The Industry highlights yet another dimension in which opportunity is unequal: namely, acoustic space.

The very invisibility and the seemingly fleeting nature of air, acoustics, and negative space (the open space *between* structures)—which we may notice as part of the opera when listening to voices' acoustics, rather than just to the notes they are instructed to sing or the timbres that mark the voices as operatic—seemed to me a poignant metaphor for voices more generally. The split in access to aspects of these voices mirrors a broader split in access to ways of vocalizing (or, to the ways in which the world wants a certain person to vocalize), and to the ways in which a person is entrained to hear his or her voice within the sociocultural and economic voicescape. Thus, *Invisible Cities'* sound design not only materializes differentiation of access, but also mirrors the ways in which racial privilege creates separation within a space which, without modes of thought suggested by listening closely to vocal acoustics, would otherwise seem to offer equal access.

Notes

1. While opera has for centuries been composed specifically for the conditions of the opera house, the term "site-specific," which originated in relation to artworks, was first applied to theatrical works in the 1980s. Fiona Wilkie notes the Welsh-based Birth Gof as an early example (Wilkie 2004). In the area of opera, what we think of as site-specific work might first be seen in GAle GAtes's *wine-blue-open-water* (1997), set in a Wall Street office building and called a "site-specific version of *The Odyssey*…a panoramic visual installation inhabited by performers" (*Playbill* 1997).

2. This is the advertisement tagline. The reference to technology is especially interesting given the (conspiracy) theories around specific singers and their alleged microphone use, which is thought to weaken their voice and art (Harada 2001). However, perhaps the high definition (HD) live streaming of the Metropolitan's operas has led us to conceptualize a viable connection between skilled operatic voices and mic'd live performances, as we have accepted recorded operatic voices mediated through microphones for decades.

   A 2013 *New York Times* article was devoted to the anxiety of some opera audiences over the presence of a microphone on the opera singer's body. Antony Tommasini writes, "As someone who cherishes classical music as an art form that glories in natural sound (while fully appreciating that many contemporary composers have used amplification in sonically alluring ways) I get nervous hearing Mr. Gelb [the Metropolitan Opera's general manager] talk of camouflaging wires on singer's bodies. And the Met has certainly kept this practice secret." In the same article, Jay David Saks, the sound designer for the Met's live broadcasts, responds to this perceived anxiety over keeping it natural, saying he prefers to "avoid wiring singers. 'For one thing, I don't get calls from people wanting to know why we do this sort of thing,' he said. 'It would be a lot easier without them. It ratchets up the complexity of my job.'" Towards the close of the article, Tommasini reports, "But Mr. Saks strongly rejected the idea that body microphones represent a more intrusive kind of amplification. 'I would bet everything I own that from listening to the broadcasts you could not tell which singers and which productions used body microphones,' he said. 'This story,' he said, referring to my pursuit of the matter, 'started from something someone saw, not from something someone heard'" (Tommasini 2013).

   While the acoustic operatic voice is fetishized, the recorded operatic voice is not vilified in the same way that a possibility mic'd "live" opera singer is. And, indeed, one of the first commercially viable record companies, the Victor Talking Machine Company, forged a strong connection with Enrico Caruso as the company's exclusive "spokesperson" (Leppert 2014).

3. Mark Swed (2014) has written about *Invisible Cities* in the context of site-specific work, comparing it to sound installation artist Janet Cardiff and her collaborator George Bures Miller's piece *Alter Banhof Video Walk*, at dOCUMENTA 13, June 9–September 12, 2012, Kassel, Germany.

4. The text is: "There is a sense of emptiness that comes over us at evening" (Calvino 1972).

5. It is beyond the scope of the book's overarching argument to discuss the music in detail. I tackle this topic in an article in progress. For more detail on the music, consult the essay, including sound excerpts, by the composer Christopher Cerrone (n.d.).

6. The headphones are omni-sonorous in that you can hear the same sound wherever you move within the wireless signal's range.

7. See Altman (1992).

8. Ihde (1976) has pointed out that we can gauge the size of a physical space through sight and sound, but that sometimes contradictions (such as, for example, mirrors or an anechoic chamber) makes this a challenging task. In this production, if listening only to the acoustics presented through the headphones, the listener is given a fictional mapping that bears no indicators as to the physical placement and relationships between singers and in regards to singers' relationship to the physical space of the station.

9. Fundamental to my emerging understanding of sound and music in relation to Los Angeles' gentrification process is Marina Peterson's work (2006; 2010). As an anthropologist of Los Angeles' urban development, Peterson understands cultural organizations and offerings as intimately tied to, and as direct results of, the neoliberal interests of the creators of Los Angeles' downtown. Several aspects of Peterson's study of music-related events in downtown Los Angeles are useful to note: the types of spaces where music-cultural events are typically held; the types of sounds which feature at these events, and their permitted decibel levels; and the types of bodies and physical behaviors permitted vs. turned away. Specifically, Peterson and other scholars of downtown Los Angeles are concerned with the privatization of public space regulates land use, sounds, and the public's use and behavior.

WORKS CITED

Altman, Rick. 1992. *Sound Theory, Sound Practice*. New York: Routledge.

Anderson, Ben. 2009. "Affective Atmospheres." *Emotion, Space and Society* 2 (2): 77–81.

"Artbound Special Episode 'Invisible Cities.'" 2013. Directed by Juan Devis. December 13, KCET. http://www.kcet.org/arts/artbound/counties/los-angeles/artbound-special-episode-invisible-cities.html.

Biss, Eula. 2015. "White Debt." *The New York Times Magazine*, December 2. https://www.nytimes.com/2015/12/06/magazine/white-debt.html.

Calvino, Italo. 1972. *Invisible Cities*, trans. William Weaver. Orlando, FL: Harcourt Brace & Company.

Cerrone, Christopher. n.d. "Invisible Cities: Composing an Opera for Headphones." http://www.kcet.org/arts/artbound/counties/los-angeles/invisible-cities-opera-composer-christopher-cerrone-union-station-music.html.

Choy, Tim. n.d. "Air's Substantiations," for Berkeley Environmental Politics Colloquium, unpublished.

Harada, Kai. 2001. "Opera's Dirty Little Secret." *Studio Live Design*. http://livedesignonline.com/mag/operas-dirty-little-secret.

Hertzog, Christian. 2013. "*Invisible Cities*, the Wandering Opera Through Union Station, Is A Welcome Adventure," *LA Weekly*, October 29. http://www.laweekly.com/arts/invisible-cities-the-wandering-opera-through-union-station-is-a-welcome-adventure-4184603.

Ihde, Don. 1976. *Listening and Voice: A Phenomenology of Sound*. Athens: Ohio University Press.

Leppert, Richard. 2014. "Phonography and Operatic Fidelities (Regimes of Musical Listening, 1904–1929)." Paper presented at the University of Chicago Music Department's Colloquium Series, May 2.

Peterson, Marina. 2006. "Patrolling the Plaza: Privatized Public Space and the Neoliberal State." *Downtown Los Angeles Urban Anthropology and Studies of Cultural Systems and World Economic Development* 35 (4): 355–86.

Peterson, Marina. 2010. *Sound, Space, and the City: Civic Performance in Downtown Los Angeles*. Philadelphia: University of Pennsylvania Press.

Swed, Mark. 2014. "Moving Sound to Anywhere but the Concert Hall." *Los Angeles Times*, March27.http://www.latimes.com/entertainment/arts/culture/la-et-cm-sound-art-notebook-20131229-story.html#page=1.

Tommasini, Antony. 2013. "Wearing a Wire at the Opera, Secretly, of Course." *New York Times*, June 28. http://www.nytimes.com/2013/06/30/arts/music/wearing-a-wire-at-the-opera-secretly-of-course.html?pagewanted=all&_r=0.

"Union Station Fact Sheet." n.d. http://www.unionstationla.com/user/pages/10.press-room/Union-Station-Los-Angeles-Fact-Sheet.pdf.

Union Station Map. Los Angeles County Metropolitan Transportation Authority, http://media.metro.net/projects_studies/union_station/images/131039_map_unionsta_brochure_v7_rb.pdf.

Wilkie, Fiona. 2004. "Out of Place: The Negotiation of Space in Site-Specific Performance." PhD diss., School of the Arts, University of Surrey.

"Wine-Blue Odyssey Opens March 19—In Wall Street Office." Playbill, March 18. http://www.playbill.com/article/wine-blue-odyssey-opens-march-19-in-wall-street-office-com-69834.

CHAPTER 15

....

TUNING A THROAT SONG
IN INNER ASIA

On the Nature of Vocal Gifts with
People's Xöömeizhi *of the Tyva Republic*
Valeriy Mongush (b. 1953)

....

ROBERT O. BEAHRS

THE sounds and smells of spring were in the air on the morning of March 31, 2017, when I ran into my teacher, Valeriy Kechilovich Mongush, in the central square of the remote town of Xandagaity in the Tyva Republic.[1] In front of us stood the House of Culture for the Övür district, or *kozhuun*, a place where Valeriy worked in his youth as a folk musician, when Tyva was part of the Soviet Union. In the distance, I could see the Russian Federation's present-day border with Mongolia (Uvs Aimag). To our left stood the *kozhuun* government building where Valeriy presently serves as a member of the House of Representatives. Behind us were the snow-covered Tannu-Ola Mountains that separate Övür from the rest of Tyva. Each of these markers had a long history and complicated provenance in this corner of Inner Asia, a place Valeriy has called home since his birth in 1953 (see Figures 15.1a and 15.1b).

Earlier that day, Valeriy had come down from his winter encampment in the foothills of Mount Ak-Bedik where he herds livestock (sheep, goats, and cows) with his family.[2] Valeriy had received a text message summoning him to Kyzyl, Tyva's capital city a half-day's drive away, for a Republic-wide gathering of musicians who call themselves *xöömeizhi*. *Xöömeizhi* means "those who do *xöömei*"—literally, "rasping," "buzzing," or "melodizing."[3] As it turned out, I was also headed to Kyzyl along with my colleague and research collaborator Victoria (Vika) Soyan Peemot and our friend and driver Vladislav (Vlad) Kan-ool.[4] We three had just finished a week of fieldwork with yak herders and singers affiliated with the municipal farm enterprise Adargan in nearby Sagly. We offered to give Valeriy a ride to Kyzyl, which he accepted. Along the way, we discussed the vocal practices to which Valeriy had devoted his life as a musician, multi-instrumentalist, composer, and culture worker, and for which he had earned the national honor of People's *Xöömeizhi* of the Tyva Republic in 1995 (see Figures 15.2a and 15.2b).[5] In Russian, Valeriy referred to these vocal practices as *gorlovoe penie* (literally, "throat-singing"), the term that non-Tyvan-speakers most commonly use to define the vocal practices of Valeriy's nomadic ancestors in the Sayan-Altai Mountains. However, when describing and conceptualizing these vocal practices in Tyvan, a Turkic language with Mongolian influences that Valeriy calls his mother tongue, he used the words *xöömei, kargyraa,* and *sygyt*.[6] As will become clear, disentangling Tyvan and Russian ways of understanding these vocal practices is critical for understanding the poetics and politics of voicing throat song in this remote region of Inner Asia.

In the car that day, Valeriy explained throat-singing to us like this: "The *xöömeizhi* has a gift (*chayalga*) from nature (*boidus*).[7] *Xöömei, kargyraa,* and *sygyt* are the three main techniques (*üsh kol xevir*).[8] Not everybody can *kargyraa* and *sygyt*; it is a gift born from nature!" (March 31, 2017).[9] To emphasize and explain the significance of this gift, Valeriy told us about an unexplained sickness that he had growing up in Solchur, a small village in Övür that we had just passed through on our road trip. In their search for a cure, Valeriy's family invited a Buddhist lama to come and diagnose the malady. According to the lama's assessment, the young Valeriy had a gift of *sygyt* (literally, "whistling") given to him by nature. Without knowing it, Valeriy was carrying the weight of this gift as a burden, which, left unexpressed, made him sick. Naturally, the cure for such a sickness was to *do sygyt* and, even more, to *become a sygytchy* (one who does *sygyt*). Though Valeriy did not say this, the diagnosis and cure likely came as no surprise to his family, since Valeriy's father, uncles, and older brothers were also gifted—some in *sygyt* but others in the two related techniques of *xöömei* (rasping, buzzing, or melodizing) and *kargyraa* (wheezing or snorting). Taking the lama's advice, Valeriy cultivated and practiced his gift of *sygyt* throughout his childhood and adolescence, with his family, community, and nature serving as his teachers. He also learned to do *xöömei, kargyraa,* and many other techniques during his life. According to Valeriy, this is how he became a *xöömeizhi*, a master of the arts of voiced rasping/buzzing/melodizing, wheezing/snorting, and whistling songs.

As we drove through the snow-covered countryside of Övür on our half-day road trip from Xandagaity to Kyzyl, Valeriy told us more stories about *xöömei, kargyraa,* and *sygyt*—where these gifts come from, what they are intended for, and what kinds of responsibilities they have required of him and of his fellow Tyvan-speaking brothers and sisters, uncles and aunts, fathers and mothers, and their fathers and mothers before them. In this chapter, I seek to convey and make sense of some of these stories about Valeriy's vocal and musical gifts as a member of the distinguished Övür school of throat-singers—stories about how Valeriy has used and continues to use his gifts to define and redefine his music, identity, traditions, and culture in Tyva during the last decades of the Soviet Union and into the post-Soviet era.

As an ethnomusicologist who has studied in Tyva since 2005, I also attempt to untangle Valeriy's vocal gifts of *xöömei, kargyraa,* and *sygyt* from the so-called throat-singing or

FIGURE 15.1A The House of Culture for the Övür District (founded in 1941) in Xandagaity, named after People's *Xöömeizhi* of the Tyva Republic Gennadi Tumat (1964–1996), a famous musician from Övür. Photo by the author (2016).

FIGURE 15.1B View of Xandagaity and Tannu-Ola Mountains from the town's central square. Photo by the author (2017).

overtone singing practices that have circulated internationally (especially since the fall of the Soviet Union in 1991) and have become dissociated from local meanings and values in Tyva. In particular, I am concerned that these practices' global awareness and circulation have focused on the "acoustic facts" of voice production to the exclusion of the histories and responsibilities that these gifts carry—that is, the knowledge of where these practices originate, what they mean, how their history reflects a changing and sometimes repressive political landscape, the intentionality of voicing as action, and the aesthetic and ethical dimensions of voicing song as a social practice. In short, I ask what Valeriy is doing—both real and imagined—when he is doing *xöömei*, *kargyraa*, or *sygyt*. What stories does he tell himself and others? How do his vocal practices reflect a changing political landscape? And what, in Valeriy's estimation, should practitioners like myself (and others who are eager to learn) do in order to understand these "three main techniques" (*üsh kol xevir*) or vocal gifts, and use them with a sense of purpose, care, and respect for local traditions? I posed these questions, and Valeriy answered with more stories, told, as he repeatedly reminded me, from his own perspective.

FIGURE 15.2A   Valeriy Mongush (b. 1953) in 1995 when he was honored with the title of People's *Xöömeizhi* by the Ministry of Culture of the Tyva Republic.

FIGURE 15.2B Valeriy Mongush with the author at Aldyn-Bulak, Tyva Republic in 2016.

NATURE'S GIFTS: A STORY OF
ORIGINS AND PURPOSE

We begin with a particular story that Valeriy told me on our road trip: "Earlier, Sat Manchakai [a famous *sygytchy*], who was my father's younger-brother-in-law (*churzhu*), explained it to me like this: '*Xöömei*, *sygyt*, and *kargyraa* come from three techniques (*üsh xevir*), from three different sources (*üsh anggy uktan*), my son.'"[10] Valeriy continued:

> First: "The origin of *xöömei* is in the lullaby (*öpei*) of a woman for her child, whom she brought into this world. According to my teacher, people do *xöömei* (*xöömei-leer*) from the woman's caressing (*ergeledirinden*) lullaby '*Öpei, oglum!*' ('Be calm, my son!')."[11]

> Second: "*Kargyraa* is an animal-pleasing song (*taalal yry*); these songs please (*taaladyr*) the livestock animals (*kadat maly*). The *kargyraa* song pleases (*taaladyr*) sheep, cows/yaks, and others, so that they will graze well."[12]

Third: "*Sygyt* is tuned together (*ünneshtir kady*) with the voice (*ün*) of the male red deer (*syyn*) when herders herd horses on the tops of the mountains (*syn kyry*). Notice that [*sygyt*] comes from wild animals (*cherlik ang*) and not from domesticated livestock (*azyral mal*); it is the song (*yry*) of the horse herder (*chylgychy*) who does *sygyt* like the voice of the red deer (*syyn ünü yshkash*) and herds horses."[13]

From this story, we learn that people receive special vocal gifts from nature, and that not everyone is gifted in one or more of the three main techniques of throat song. Those who do have a vocal gift can use it to carry out particular actions, in appropriate spaces, with desired outcomes for herding families, their domestic animals, and the wild animals living nearby. Vocal gifts are techniques for doing things within an imagined order of nomadic life that is naturalized to tradition, even when nomadic ways of living have mostly been abandoned by present-day Tyvans. Within this imagined order, as transmitted to Valeriy, *xöömei* is a lullaby—a caressing song of a mother for her baby with the desired outcome being to soothe that baby to sleep. People learned to do *xöömei* from a woman's caressing song for her son.[14] *Kargyraa*, meanwhile, is a song that the livestock herder uses to please domesticated livestock so that the animals (sheep, goats, cows/yaks) will graze calmly and produce better quality meat, milk, and wool. And while *sygyt* is also a song, in this case it is the song of the horse herder, not the livestock herder, who tunes his voice together with the voices of the wild Siberian red deer (also called maral) on the mountain tops where he herds horses (see Figure 15.3 and Table 15.1). However, the *sygyt*

FIGURE 15.3 A livestock herder near Solchur in Övür District, Tyva Republic, where Valeriy was born and raised. Photo taken by Victoria Soyan Peemot (2017).

Table 15.1 The author's schematic interpretation of the three main techniques from three different sources, as transmitted by Valeriy Mongush on March 31, 2017

Three Main Techniques	From Three Different Sources	Voicing as Action	Actors Configured in Voicing	Desired Outcome
xöömei	Lullaby	Caressing, calming	Woman, baby	A baby is soothed (and sleeps)
kargyraa	Livestock herding song	Pleasing, pleasuring	Livestock herder, domesticated livestock	Animals graze calmly and produce better quality meat, milk, wool, etc.
sygyt	Horse herding song	Tuned together (in relation to another's voice), making tender	Horse herder, horse herd, wild animals (male red deer), also wind and nonhuman entities	Horses graze peacefully and harmoniously with wild animals and nonhuman entities

song, as we shall learn, is in fact somewhat "out of tune" with respect to both the collective memories of Tyvan people's ancestors and the worldview that many were forced to abandon in pursuit of modernization during the first half of the twentieth century. As the next section explains, these three techniques form the foundation of an imagined order that allows us to study the aesthetic and ethical dimensions of voicing song as a social practice in Tyva.

THE IMAGINED ORDER: NOMADISM AS COLLECTIVE MEMORY

The tripartite typology for throat song, as explained by Valeriy, suggests an imagined order for nomadic life that configures vocal gifts in relation to gender, human–animal relations, and space. *Xöömei*, considered by many to be the most fundamental of the three techniques, is configured within this imagined order as a song that men learn from women to calm babies. The song is used within the domestic family space of the yurt (round felt tent), a place where usually only humans are allowed. *Kargyraa* is configured as a song used for pleasing domesticated livestock, here implied as the song of the live-stock herder, a role played by both men and women. These animals are typically herded in the valleys and semiwild spaces within the vicinity of the yurt. Finally, *sygyt* is config-ured as a song of the horse herder, a special kind of herder who is almost always a man. Horses are the most valued animal for herders (and Tyvans generally). *Sygyt* is used to herd these horses and is tuned to the male red deer, a wild animal, on mountain tops—untamed places far away from the domestic space of the yurt.

While this imagined order is simply another story that Valeriy and his fellow *xöömeizhi* tell about the ways that nomadic life worked in older times, it functions as a poetic author-ization for creativity among contemporary *xöömei, kargyraa,* and *sygyt* performers—what I call a "sonic-musical sensibility" of voicing that links aesthetics with ethics in an emer-gent form of singing as sociality.[15] This imagined order of *xöömei, kargyraa,* and *sygyt* within nomadic life also functions as a justification for prohibiting certain activities as taboo and endorsing others as natural and therefore good.[16] In this sense, nomadism becomes naturalized to tradition. The collective memories of throat songs that Valeriy and others continually make and remake in relation to nomadism also become naturalized to tradition. And this naturalization produces new forms of sonic-musical sensibility, identity, community, and culture in post-Soviet Tyva. More than anything, the imag-ined order of nomadism functions as a tool for Tyvans to grapple with the historic gains and losses from the rapid reforms of settling and modernizing nomadic communities during the period of independence when the country was called the Tuvan People's Republic or "Tannu Tuva" (1921–1944), the economic and cultural reorganization of society into collective farms during the Soviet Union (1944–1991), and the present-day political landscape as part of the Russian Federation (1991–present) engaging in a market-based economy.

AMBIVALENCE AS HISTORIC CONSCIOUSNESS

When Valeriy speaks in Russian about his vocal gifts, he often uses the phrase "to sing throat-singing" (*pet' gorlovoe penie*) as an umbrella term. This term dates from the time in Tyva's history when the Sayan-Altai Mountains were part of the borderlands of the Russian and Manchurian Empires, which coincided with the period during which cultural specialists and folklorists (mostly from Russia) began to collect, study, and codify the vocal techniques of Valeriy's ancestors as "double-voiced singing" (*dvuxgolosnoe penie*), a "solo duet" (*solnyi duet*), or a "song without words" (*pesnya bez slov*).[17]

However, when Valeriy speaks of his vocal gifts in his native Tyvan, he prefers the more specific terms *xöömei, kargyraa,* and *sygyt.* During our road-trip conversation in Tyvan, he never used the Tyvan verb *yrlaar* ("to sing") to describe *xoomei, kargyraa,* or *sygyt.* Rather, he uses *yry-* noun forms, which translate as "song" for *kargyraa* and *sygyt* and "lullaby" for *xöömei.* Valeriy also uses *xöömei, kargyraa,* and *sygyt* as verbs, which I have translated as acts of sound-making with the human voice similar to playing on a musical instrument (see Table 15.2). This distinction suggests that "singing" is an inappro-priate term for conceptually describing the performative actions that comprise *xöömei, kargyraa,* and *sygyt.* Rather than "throat-singing," "vocal-instrumental melodizing" may be a more appropriate description given the hypothesized etymological connections between the term *xöömei* and rasping (from Mongolian, referring to the throat of a

Table 15.2 Song voicing terminology in Tyvan language used by Valeriy Mongush. English translations by Victoria Soyan Peemot

Tyvan (Cyrillic)	Tyvan (Latin Transliteration)	English Translation (Approximate)
хөөн	xöön	Mood, tune
хөөмей	xöömei	Rasping, buzzing, melodizing (voiced like sheep, goats)
хөөмейлээр	xöömeileer	To xöömei
хөөмейжи	xöömeizhi	A person who does xöömei
каргыраа	kargyraa	Wheezing, snorting (voiced like cows/yaks, camels, bears)
каргыраалаар	kargyraalaar	To kargyraa
каргыраалавас	kargyraalavas	Not to kargyraa
сыгыт	sygyt	Whistling (voiced or unvoiced, like male red deer, wild animals, wind)
сыгыртыр	sygyrtyr	To whistle (usually voiced)
сыгырар	sygyrar	To whistle (usually not voiced)
сыгыртпас	sygyrtpas	Not to whistle
сыгытчы	sygytchy	A person who does sygyt

fur-bearing animal), buzzing (from the Tyvan word *xööleer*), or tuning of a musical instrument (from the Tyvan word *xöön*), and between the term *kargyraa* and wheezing or snorting (also likely from mixed Tyvan and Mongolian linguistic origins).[18] Thus, *xöömei* and *kargyraa* are less about *gorlovoe penie* (throat-singing) and more about "playing the throat" as a musical instrument, an idea better encapsulated by many of the Tyvan expressions for "giving voice" discussed in this chapter.

Sygyt provides an even starker example. Understood by Valeriy as a whistle, either voiced (*sygyrtyr*) or unvoiced (*sygyrar*), *sygyt* seems to be linked less with the throat and more with the nonhuman agency of the wind. As Valeriy describes:

A person uses (*azhyglaptar*) the wind with his lips. You use it and make it as *sygyt*. When I sit on a small hill and the wind blows on the top of that higher place in the taiga, if it makes a whistling sound like *syyg-syyg*, I can let out my *sygyt* (*sygydymny ... salyp bolur men*) together with it also in a relaxed, slow manner.[19]

It would be easy to dismiss the ambivalence in Russian and Tyvan terminology for *sygyt* as a mistranslation, but in fact it reflects Valeriy's own ambivalence in how he understands *sygyt* to be tuned together with voices not only of wild animals but also with the wind and other nonhuman entities (or spirit-masters) who inhabit the land. That is, even for Valeriy, *sygyt* does not have a fixed role within the imagined order of nomadism, an observation I discuss more in the next section. Yet as with *xöömei* and *kargyraa*, *sygyt*'s etymological origins and connections in Tyvan suggest an indigenous cosmology that includes human and nonhuman agents of sound-making not encompassed by the term "throat-singing." Re-examining Russian and Soviet-era terminology reveals a deeper, more complex social role for voicing song in Tyva.

TUNING *SYGYT* WITH THE MASTERS
OF THE TAIGA

Back in the car, as we continued on our road trip across Övür, we passed by the occasional flock of sheep and snow-covered mountains. I asked Valeriy to describe how he understands processes of sonic-musical creativity to unfold over time in relation to his surroundings and activities—whether real or imagined—when he uses his *sygyt* gifts to make music. Valeriy responded:

> In the way I understand it, the connection of the *sygytchy* and nature becomes unified. For instance, [*sygyt*] is different when you round up your herd on the top of the mountains than when you go down into the valley. In the valley, you release (*salyr*) your free, spacious *sygyt* in a relaxed manner and it makes tender (*uyaradyr*) the herded animals so they are pleased and graze well. When you arrive at the narrow place, such as a riverside, your *sygyt* reflects the taiga landscape surrounding you. When you come to places like Bichii-Chalaaty, which we crossed earlier [near Xandagaity], *sygyt* is thin and sonorous (*ötküt*). The masterful person (*master kizhi*) would adjust it to the lyrics of the song.[20]

Thus, in Valeriy's conceptualization, *sygyt* songs are tuned by the horse herder (*chylgychy*) for different purposes at different times. The tuning depends on real and imagined places where the herder is herding his horses and is always made in relation to the particularities of those places and the wild animals that inhabit them. On the tops of mountains, for example, *sygytchy* tune their songs to the voices of red deer and wild animals, but in the valley they tune their songs to "make tender" (*uyaradyr*) the animals so that they graze well (similar to how livestock herders use *kargyraa* to calm sheep, goats, and cows/yaks). We learn that the masterful *sygytchy* is one who has a place-based sensibility in his song, whether it involves, for example, reflecting the taiga landscape or crossing a particular stream. Furthermore, this masterful person tunes and adjusts the song, including the lyrics, to that place.

But while *xöömei* and *kargyraa* are clearly linked with actions of pleasing and calming, Valeriy is less clear about the voicing action of *sygyt*. Why does *sygyt* require a different kind of attunement to nature than *xöömei* or *kargyraa*? And why does Valeriy, as a *sygytchy* and herder himself, express reservations in ascribing meaning to the voicing actions with *sygyt*? The answers seem to be in *sygyt*'s ambiguous relationship with shamanism and the power of *sygyt* to summon and dismiss not only wild animals but also nonhuman beings, or what Valeriy refers to as the " 'Masters of the Taiga' (*taiga eezi*)." Valeriy continued:

> In old times some spirits (*dux*), Masters of the Taiga, were called (*kyigyrarda*) with whistling (*sygyryp*) and a conch shell (*tung*)…Different spirits arrive depending on what you use for calling them and what brings pleasure (*taalal*) to the Master of the Land. For instance, the female Master of the Land (*cher eezi*) takes great pleasure in *sygyt*. Or the seashell calls for the Master of the Land and all other spirits. Some spirits (*xei chüveler*) will run away when they hear whistling (*sygyrgan*), which echoes in the ears of those spirits. Those kinds of things also exist. Some of the evil spirits (*diirengner*) come to the yurt encampment (*aal*) with cruel intentions, but they run away when they hear a tender voice (*uyan ün*).[21]

The ability to summon and dismiss nonhuman beings with *sygyt* seems to be part of the gift from nature that Valeriy (like others in older times) was given in childhood. This ability exists regardless of whether the *sygyt* is voiced or unvoiced, and it often employs instruments such as the conch shell, which was adapted from Tibetan Buddhist rituals. But this gift was also a burden that, according to a Buddhist lama, manifested itself as a sickness in Valeriy's childhood—a sickness that was rectified by accepting his gift and becoming a *sygytchy*. And the gift of doing *sygyt* shares a kinship with the gift of summoning and dismissing spirits—one that Tyvan shamans also receive from nature (see Table 15.3).[22] As the next section explains, the "sickness" that Valeriy experienced in his youth from the burden of his unexpressed *sygyt* gift appears to share a kinship with

Table 15.3 Activities related to voicing songs; terminology in Tyvan language used by Valeriy Mongush. English translations by Victoria Soyan Peemot

Tyvan (Cyrillic)	Tyvan (Latin Transliteration)	English Translation (Approximate)	Usage by Valeriy Mongush
таалаар, тааладыр	*taalaar, taaladyr*	To enjoy, to feel pleasure, to please	Pleasing livestock animals with *kargyraa*
укталыр	*uktalyr*	To be rooted in, to come from, to have origin in	*Xöömei* has its origin in a woman's lullaby
үннештирер	*ünneshtirer*	To tune, to sound, to voice	Tuning *sygyt* together with the voice of the male red deer
кыйгырар	*kyigyrar*	To call	Calling spirits with *sygyt*
уярадыр	*uyaradyr*	To ease, to make tender	Using *sygyt* to calm horses while grazing
эргеледир	*ergeledir*	To caress	To caress a baby while doing *xöömei*
салыр	*salyr*	To release	Releasing one's *sygyt* into the valley

the trauma experienced by the nomadic ancestors of modern-day Tyvans, a trauma that stemmed from the perception by Soviet/Russian and certain Tyvan countrymen that Tyvans had unclean souls in need of purification.

Unclean Voices: A Historic Consciousness Out of Tune

As we descended out of the Tannu-Ola Mountains and entered into Chöön-Xemchik *kozhuun*, we passed through the town of Chadaana and the nearby Buddhist monastery called Üstüü-Xüree. The monastery was destroyed in 1937 during a period of Soviet repression of traditional beliefs, and was later rebuilt in the post-Soviet era through funds raised by a music festival with the same name.[23] During the 1930s, virtually all lamas and shamans were exiled, killed, or disappeared. This trauma is still felt today by Valeriy and by many of my friends and colleagues in Tyva who lost family members during this period. Looking out the window of the car, I was reminded of a conversation with Valeriy from a 2016 voice lesson (see Figure 15.4). Speaking in Russian, Valeriy had explained his understanding of the 1930s in Tyva's history to me like this:

> At the start of the Soviet times, we [my relatives] were told that it was forbidden to sing throat-singing (*pet' gorlovoe penie*). It was said that [these songs] caused pain and sickness—that if a person with the flu performs, his breath would transmit the sickness to others. There were times when it was forbidden. . . . Doctors were forbidding us from doing it. . . . Also, many people learned that if you drink alcohol and treat your body poorly, you lose your health and with it your *sygyt*.   (August 16, 2016)[24]

For Valeriy, the power of *sygyt* reveals an ambivalence around the historical trauma of his people as nomads being forcibly settled and brought into modernized collective farms and systems of culture during the twentieth century.[25] In this sense *sygyt* was both a blessing and a curse, not only for Valeriy as an individual singer but also for Tyvan people more generally, as the Sayan-Altai Mountain region was brought into "modernized" political systems in the world. On the one hand, a vocal gift like *sygyt*—similar to the gift of shamanic powers—was believed to cause sickness if left pent up inside the body, and so the lama's remedy was to release the *sygyt*, as Valeriy did in his youth. On the other hand, the gift of *sygyt*, as recalled by Valeriy through his and others' collective memory of the political and religious repressions carried out by ideologues in the 1930s, was not a gift at all. Rather, like other so-called backwards nomad practices, it was understood to be a sickness by the doctors and cultural ideologues who, according to Valeriy, forbade people from vocal-instrumental melodizing for fear of spreading disease.

This conceptualization and these actions, from Valeriy's account, had the result of repressing the vocal gifts and lodging the sickness even deeper into the collective bodies and consciousness of Tyvan people's ancestors. Many herders were forced to abandon

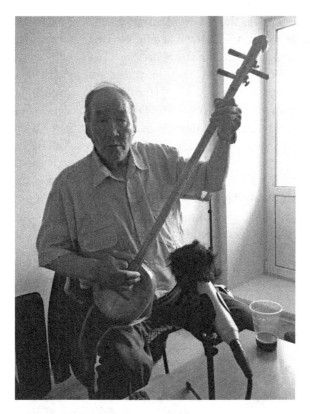

FIGURE 15.4 Valeriy Mongush with *doshpuluur* (three-string plucked lute) during our voice lesson in Kyzyl, Tyva Republic. Photo by the author (2016).

nomadic ways of life, settle in towns, collectivize livestock, and leave behind "backwards" practices, which were configured by the authorities as unclean and in need of purification.[26] Thus, Valeriy's comments about *sygyt* and sickness, through a lens of collective memory, suggests a politics of voicing throat song.[27] This politics sheds new light on Valeriy's individual life story and cultural work as a musician who devoted his life to building and developing traditions within state-sponsored institutions, even when similar institutions had worked to desacralize these traditions one generation earlier.

GIFTS AND RESPONSIBILITIES IN POST-SOVIET TYVA

Throughout my conversations and voice lessons with Valeriy, I learned that some vocal gifts come from nature and come with responsibilities that are configured within an imagined order of nomadism. When expressed correctly, these gifts are healthy and their responsibilities met; when repressed, their responsibilities remain unfulfilled, and they become burdens that can lead, in some cases, to sickness and trauma. But I learned another lesson from Valeriy: that gifts also come from people, bearing different responsibilities from gifts that come from nature.

Valeriy's uncle, Sat Manchakai (1918–1965), the gifted *sygytchy* who recounted the provenance of *xöömei*, *kargyraa*, and *sygyt* to Valeriy as a youth, was among the first generation of Tyvans to take the vocal gift of the horse herder (*chylgychy*) and use it for something other than herding horses: for making *sygyt* not on a mountaintop but on the stage.[28] Sat Manchakai's knowledge was transmitted to Valeriy as a young child participating in the regional culture clubs and amateur arts activities (*samodeyatel'nost'*). There he taught Valeriy to perform *sygyt* while also playing on the *doshpuluur* (in earlier times, a two-string plucked lute; now it has three strings) (see Figures 15.5a and 15.5b). Of course, Sat Manchakai was not the only person from whom Valeriy learned to sing and play music; Valeriy was gifted in many different techniques, including *kargyraa* and *xöömei*, courtesy of many of his fellow Tyvan brothers and sisters. Valeriy also understands these vocal transactions to be gifts, not from nature but from the kinship circles and community of *xöömeizhi* living and working in institutions of culture in Tyva

FIGURE 15.5A Sat Manchakai (1918–1965) playing a *doshpuluur*. While the instrument appears to be a Russian *balalaika*, it was considered a *doshpuluur* by the Tyvan musicians who played it. Photo courtesy of the Övür House of Culture, Xandagaity, Tyva Republic.

FIGURE 15.5B Valeriy Mongush playing a contemporary *doshpuluur*. Photo by Vasilii Maksimovich Balchyi-ool courtesy of the Övür House of Culture, Xandagaity, Tyva Republic.

and also herding his own livestock animals in the countryside. The work of Valeriy's life—helping to build *xöömei*, *kagyraa*, and *sygyt* from ancestral gifts into a nationally and internationally recognized music tradition that is practiced widely in Tyva today—can be understood as a refashioning of Tyvan culture and identity, something of which Valeriy is extremely proud.

Consistent with his own history, my teacher, Valeriy, transmitted the story of the origins and purposes of, and methods for doing, *xöömei*, *kargyraa*, and *sygyt* to me as a kind of gift. This gift includes his life stories as a musician and culture-worker in Tyva with the title of People's *Xöömeizhi*.[29] Valeriy's teachings are acquired from neither nature nor kinship; rather, they are the product of an intersubjective exchange between teacher and a student who traveled thousands of miles from the United States to study and learn the wisdom of *xöömei*, *kargyraa* , and *sygyt* from him (and others).[30] Valeriy's teachings began when I first met him in 2013 at the Sixth International Symposium entitled "*Xöömei* (Throat-Singing)—A Cultural Phenomenon of the Peoples of Inner Asia" in Kyzyl and continued over the next five years as his sometime student at the Center for the Development of Tyvan Traditional Culture and Crafts. From my voice lessons with Valeriy, I have learned that I should treat Valeriy's transmitted knowledge with respect and use it in the ways it is intended to be used—that is, to respect Tyvan traditions, nature, humans, animals, and other nonhuman entities. Valeriy shares his gifts freely and with pleasure, but they carry a responsibility for me to do the same. As Valeriy explained during a voice lesson (in Russian):

> Our throat-singing (*gorlovoe penie*) is inherited (*potomstvennoe*)...If you sing first for yourself, then others will get to listen to it as well. So that's why I close my eyes when I am singing. It's not because I'm afraid of someone or shy. When I perform with my eyes closed, I sing to nature or to my mother and father. I imagine that I am sitting in front of them even though they have been gone for a long time. But it does not matter—it feels like I am sitting in the yurt and performing tales (*tool*) with them. [My family] has given me such a valuable treasure, and [I imagine that] I am singing tenderly for them. It is always so, when I close my eyes, I am in the place which I am singing about. I forget that you, Robert, are sitting here, I close my eyes—and there is my mother, my father; my relatives are sitting with me, or my livestock is grazing.
>
> (August 16, 2016)[31]

Transmitting Vocal Gifts: Postcolonial Ethics in Humanistic Research

I had come to Tyva and to this study armed with theories and analytical practices for examining throat-singing as a set of "non-Western" singing techniques. My early interest in Tyvan music began, like many foreigners, with the seemingly superhuman abilities of *xöömeizhi* to isolate two or three overtone melodies while simultaneously singing a guttural drone using just one voice.[32] Certainly, I thought, *xöömei* must come with different singing techniques that would challenge the assumptions in my training in classical European *bel canto* singing in terms of voice placement, breathing, intonation, and articulation. Throughout my training in ethnomusicology, I had done exhaustive studies of the "acoustic facts" of throat-singing from different recordings, made transcriptions using sonograms and alternative notation methods, practiced, cultivated a toolkit of "inner choreographies" using my own vocal apparatus, and composed some of my own throat songs, too.[33] I even had my vocal folds examined with a laryngoscope while doing *xöömei*.

It has taken twelve years of closely studying voice and song in Tyva to see that *xöömei*, *kargyraa*, and *sygyt* are not merely techniques of singing. Indeed, as we learn from Valeriy, they are not really considered "singing" at all. Rather, they are means of playing the throat like a musical instrument and voicing song as a social practice with ethical and political consequences. Above all, they are vocal ontologies and stories of inherited wisdom in Tyvan language that many of my teachers possessed, especially those over age sixty and from rural areas like Xandagaity, where Valeriy is from.[34]

Over these twelve years, I have come to see that most of my teachers understand *xöömei*, *kargyraa*, and *sygyt* as techniques for doing things in the world. Their voicing was gifted to them by nature and by other *xöömeizhi* and is tuned for particular activities like herding sheep or performing on a stage. Furthermore, the activities of vocal-instrumental melodizing—really, of *giving voice*—are often, even usually, linked conceptually with taking care of others, both humans and nonhumans. This link applies just as much to a nomadic herder's gift of calming his sheep or a mother's lullaby as it does to cultural transmission between generations and among musicians from different regions, as well as to the development of *xöömei* into national folk music, much of which occurred during Valeriy's lifetime. Understanding these interactions as gifts—with their attendant trust, mutual respect, and reciprocity—helps us comprehend their complex history, ethics, and role in Tyvan culture. This framing has had many implications for how I move through my research, analysis, and theorization of these practices, and how I transmit my thoughts through conference presentations, lectures, publications, audiovisual media, and voice workshops.[35]

According to Valeriy, indigenous perspectives on voicing in the Tannu-Ola Mountains of Inner Asia imply a natural order that configures care-taking responsibilities on humans in relation to animals and spirit-masters in order to maintain balance in the world and produce desired outcomes. Russian (Orthodox Christian-inflected) colonialism in Siberia and Inner Asia sought to "purify" the "unclean" souls—that is, the inferiority—of nomadic peoples and separate culture from nature. As a result, the care-taking responsibilities of humans in relation to wild and domestic animals and spirit-masters, a central feature of nomadic life, became disaggregated over time. This disaggregation led to trauma on individual and collective levels, and we see it clearly in the aesthetic and ethical evaluations of interior "sickness" that Valeriy and his nomadic ancestors experienced as they were forced to settle into imposed social orders beginning in the 1930s. For Valeriy, "giving voice" to his own *xöömei*, *kargyraa*, and *sygyt* is good and healthy if expressed and expressed correctly. That is, voicing *xöömei*, *kargyraa*, and *sygyt* is part of asserting the value and pride of Valeriy's cultural heritage as a Tyvan person and comes with an *additional* responsibility. This additional responsibility, according to Valeriy, is about building culture within the institutions that worked to promote the music traditions of Tyvan people and transmitting them to others as an official ambassador—"People's *Xöömeizhi* of the Tyva Republic." Valeriy understands that his responsibility is primarily to his people and community, but also to others beyond Tyva.

Valeriy's perspective, like my research in Tyva more generally, has prompted me to radically revisit my own enculturation in what voice is, can do, and means. For one, Valeriy's attention to the origins of his musical gifts in nature and in human–animal interactions has challenged some of the fundamental tenants of liberal humanism that form the basis of my training as an ethnomusicologist in the United States. While *the voice* may appear to be a universal human concept, a deeper understanding of particular *voices* requires including perspectives that may not be shared by all cultures and sciences.[36] This distinction matters because voices are fundamental to and privileged in human experience. In the instance of Tyvan *xöömei* and related vocal practices, Inner Asian perspectives on what voices are, how they work, who can have them, and what they can and cannot do are critical for developing more nuanced theories of voicing and music-making. This reconceptualization allows us both to expand our current understandings about what it means to "give voice" and challenge our assumptions about what it means to be human. For example, based on my research, I now believe that voices do not work the same way for all people in all times and all places, particularly because "having a voice" extends beyond the human to animals and, as we learn from herders and hunters in Tyva, even to nonhuman beings, such as the Masters of the Taiga.

Furthermore, the caretaking of one's gifts—that is, using gifts wisely and with under-standing of and respect for their purpose—comes with responsibilities that change based on *who* the storyteller is, *what* story he, she, or it is telling, and *when* it is being told. The fact that mobile pastoralists living in the Sayan-Altai Mountains were consid-ered by Russians and many foreigners (including researchers) across the world to be "backwards" and "unclean" with a "sickness" in their voices shows that voicing is political, and that, in the case of Tyva, not all humans at all times have been treated as worthy of a voice, or at least not *their* voice.[37] The "sickness" lodged in the voices of nomadic peoples in Inner Asia was not inherent in their bodies, but rather was a perception invented by more "modern" people in order to impose a particular social order. When Valeriy devotes his life to the cultural work of building the gifts of his ancestors into the pride of Tyvan people, he is also implicated in and part of a kind of historiography and storytelling, one that is centered around the collective *caretaking* of his ancestors' gifts. This caretaking lies at the center of Tyva's proud traditions and national music, albeit one that maintains its local flavors across Tyva and nearby regions in Inner Asia through its diversity of origin stories, microlocal histories, and social negotiation at family gatherings, perfor-mances, and competitions.

My shifting understanding of the meaning and value of voicing throat song in Inner Asia has forced me to refashion my research questions in order to understand the knowledge that my teachers cultivate and transmit through their voicing and song-based practices. Indeed, in learning how Valeriy takes responsibility for his inherited knowledge, I have come to reflect on my own obligations as an ethnomusicologist. My interactions with Valeriy, alongside my Tyvan colleague and research collaborator Victoria Soyan Peemot, come with the obligation to respect Valeriy's role as an individual storyteller who trans-mits knowledge and ethics to us as a kind of gift. Our collaborative research process has been designed around the duty to safeguard Valeriy's ideas and vocal-musical gifts as a form of knowledge that he and his fellow countrymen own, manage, and have shared with us. Our efforts to take care of Valeriy's vocal gifts have prompted me to do the fol-lowing in this chapter: make clear that the ideas are transmitted to me primarily by one person; take care to include all of the original Tyvan and Russian text spoken by Valeriy in the endnotes; seek consent and permission to conduct research with Valeriy, transmit his stories, and include a vocal-musical sample made by Valeriy himself; be self-reflexive and take responsibility for the exchanges that occurred throughout the process of con-ducting, analyzing, and publishing this research with Oxford University Press, as well as consider their foreseeable uses in the future. The procedures we have put in place to

Table 15.4 A listening guide for the included audio excerpt titled *Kozhangnar* ("Joyful Songs"), written, arranged, and performed by Valeriy Kechilovich Mongush for *doshpuluur* and voice. The table includes lyrics and approximate time markings for the three main techniques of *xöömei*, *kargyraa*, and *sygyt* discussed in this chapter (the techniques of *ezengileer* and *borbangnadyr* are beyond the scope of this chapter). Used by permission from the composer.

Stanza	Voicing Technique	Lyrics in Tyvan	Lyrics in English
First 0:36–1:26	*Xöömei* 00:36–00:47 *Sygyt* 00:56–01:01 1:10–1:25	Авай, авай, авайымны Ааттынган кавайымны, Кавайымдан арта берген Кайгамчыктыг сыгыдымны.	Mother, mother, my mother My cradle where I was rocked, Even better than my cradle is my wonderful *sygyt*.
Second 1:33–2:13	*Xöömei* 1:40–1:47 *Sygyt* 1:56–2:13	Өпейлиимден өзүп келген Өөмейни, чадырымны. Өөмейден чаңгыланган, Өткүт үннүг сыгыдымны.	My yurt, my shelter where I have grown up since childhood. My *sygyt* with a sonorous voice Has echoed out from my yurt.
Third 2:41–3:26	*Sygyt* 2:57–3:27	Сынга-хемге чаңгыланган Сыынактың өткүт үнүн. Чыылганны уяраткан Сыгыдымның хоюг үнү, аялгазы.	The sonorous voice of the young stag Has echoed in the mountain range and the river. The smooth voice and melody of my *sygyt* has soothed the people gathered.
Fourth 3:33–4:28	*Sygyt* 4:15–4:28	Сырын хаттыг Солчурлардан Сырын-на эстеп турарын көр. Чылгычылап өскен оглу Сыгыт-ла салып орарын көр.	Take a look at the breeze that blows From the light-breezed Solchurs. Take a look at the son who gives *sygyt*; He has grown up as a horseman.
Fifth 4:35–5:23	*Xöömei* 4:37–4:48 5:08–21	Хөртүк харлыг Ак-Бедиктен Көрүп, харап турганымны, Көшкүн оглу төрээн болгаш Хөөмейлеп органымны.	I have watched and observed from The White Heights with snowdrifts, I have sat and done *xöömei* because I was born the son of nomads.
Sixth 5:26–5:59	*kargyraa* 5:31–5:40 5:49–5:59	Кадыр кашпал хана даглар Харап, көрүп турарын көр. Кадарчылап өскен оглу Каргыраалап орарын көр.	Take a look at the steep ravine and the wall mountains; They watch and observe. Take a look at the son who sits and does *kargyraa*; He has grown up as a herder.

acknowledge and safeguard the origins and nature of Valery's gifts are as important as the gifts themselves.

As we completed our road trip and arrived in Kyzyl, I mentioned to Valeriy that I had gotten the idea to write a chapter for the *Oxford Handbook of Voice Studies* about our chance meeting in Xandagaity earlier that day, and about our conversations, voice lessons, and vocal gift exchanges over the past few years studying *xöömei*, *sygyt*, and *kargyraa*. He replied in Tyvan:

> If there is an interest aimed to promote our Tyvan *xöömei* culture (*kul'turany*) in the world, everyday people like myself would say: "Oh, Bogda, let others come to understand all of Tyvan people's culture!" and work hard to transmit (*damchydyp beerin*) it further. If other Tyvans come, one does the same; one cannot say—"No, I do not know!" and then walk away. So, I am very happy for this research that Robert does.[38]

With this, Valeriy handed me a copy of his new CD and suggested that I might share the seventh track, entitled *Kozhangnar* ("Joyful Songs"), with my colleagues and students (listen to audio 15.1 on the companion website).[39] I include here the text to the song as an epilogue to this chapter (see Table 15.4); I hope that you, gentle reader, will listen to and accept Valeriy's vocal gifts with care.

ACKNOWLEDGMENTS

I would like to acknowledge a number of people and organizations without whose support (and gifts) this chapter could not have been written: Valeriy Mongush, Victoria Soyan Peemot, Valentina Süzükei, Choduraa Tumat, Nina Sun Eidsheim, Katherine Meizel, Gabriella Safran, Serena Le, Matthew Rahaim, Nick Harkness, Ted Levin, Benjamin Brinner, Steve Feld, Jocelyne Guilbault, Bonnie Wade, Katherine Hagedorn, Todoriki Masahiko, Matthew Sanders, Vladislav and Lyudmila Kan-ool, Aylana Irgit, Margaret and Randy Beahrs, the VoxTAP: Voice in Theory, Art, and Practice Townsend Center Working Group at U.C. Berkeley, the U.C. Multicampus Research Group: "Keys to Voice Studies: Terminology, Methodology, and Questions across Disciplines" (2012–2014), the Social Sciences Research Council (SSRC) Transregional Research Fellowship: "InterAsian Contexts and Connections" (2016–2017), the Department of Music and Center for Russian and East European Studies at the University of Pittsburgh, the Department of Music at Stanford University, the House of Culture for the Övür District, the Tuvan Institute of Humanitarian and Applied Socioeconomic Research, and the University of Helsinki.

NOTES

1. Tyva people are the titular ethnic majority living in the Tyva Republic, an administrative unit of the Russian Federation. There are approximately 280,000 speakers of Tyvan language living in multiple communities across the Circa-Altai Mountain region of Inner Asia in present-day Russia, Mongolia, and China. This chapter concerns the Tangdy-Tyva people, a reference to those people whose homelands surround the Tannu-Ula Mountains in the Tyva Republic. I have chosen to employ the post-Soviet indigenous name Tyva and the

adjectival form Tyvan, despite the fact that its adjectival use is debated among linguists. Tyva (pronounced tuh-VAH) is a transliteration of Тыва. Other commonly used terms are derived from Russian/Soviet variants of the regions name, Tuva, Tuvin, and Tuvinian, or Mongolian names for various Oirat clans who share historic relations.

2. The winter place is a fixed structure like a house with a shelter for animals, whereas spring/summer and autumn places are usually mobile encampments comprised of yurts (round felt tents) and animal corrals. Valeriy also has a permanent Russian-style house in the village of Solchur where he and his relatives share responsibilities managing livestock in addition to other agricultural activities, cultural duties, and government work.

3. *Xöömei* is pronounced in Tyvan like "HER-mey," but with a British accent. *Xöömeizhi* is pronounced like "HER-mey-zhee." *Kargyraa* is pronounced "kar-guh-RAH," and *sygyt* is pronounced "suh-GUHT." Related vocal traditions have been practiced by people across the greater Altai Mountain region of Inner Asia, including the Republics of Altai and Khakassia (also in Russia), where epic storytelling is called *kai* or *xai*, Mongolia, in particular, Ulaanbaatar (the capitol) and the Western Oirat-dominated regions of Xovd, Uvs, Zavkhan, and Bayan-Ölgii, where practices of *xöömii* and epic storytelling are also practiced, and the Altai Region of Xinjiang and Inner Mongolia in China. This chapter is concerned mainly with *xöömei*, *kargyraa*, and *sygyt* among Tyvan-speaking peoples.

4. This chapter is based on ongoing fieldwork conducted in Tyva in 2005, 2010–2013, and 2015–2018. My research has been enriched by meaningful collaborations with both Vladislav Kan-ool and Victoria Soyan Peemot, who have been guides for me in navigating language (Russian, Tyvan), cultural customs, and travel through rural areas of Tyva. In particular, I am grateful for Vika's incredible thoughtful and patient work as interlocutor in Tyvan between me and Valeriy during our road trip in 2017. The translations and endnotes in this chapter reflect our mutual attempt to understand Valeriy's words and translate them, with flaws, into English. Since 2015, Vika and I have engaged in a collaborative fieldwork research project across the Circa-Altai Mountain region, and we are currently in the process of producing joint publications, a series of films, exhibitions, and cultural heritage resources that have emerged as a result of this project.

5. Valeriy Mongush is known in particular for his instrumental skills on the *doshpuluur*, a three-string plucked lute used by Tyvans, and on the *bayan*, a chromatic button accordion used across Russia. As a composer and performer, Valeriy's music is known widely in Tyva and outside of Russia, where he has performed in England, Japan, Taiwan, and Mongolia.

6. Tyvan language is a branch of the Northern Turkic language family. Closely related languages are Altaian, Khakas, and Sakha, and more distantly related languages are Kazakh, Kyrgyz, and Uyghur. Tyvan also shares much of its lexicon with Mongolian, although, unlike Mongolian, it uses a Turkic grammar.

7. In Tyvan: "*Хөөмейжи дөмей-ле бойдус чаялгалыг кижи шээй.*" Similarly, Valeriy described that shamans receive their gifts from nature. Music (*xögzhüm*) also comes from nature.

8. In Tyvan: "*Хөөмей, сыгыт, каргыраа үш кол хевири ол.*" We have chosen to translate *xevir* as "technique," but it also means style, kind, or manner. Related voicing techniques such as *borbangnadyr* and *ezengileer* are not discussed in this chapter because, according to Valeriy, they are not understood to be the "three main techniques."

9. In Tyvan: "*Кижи болганы каргыраалавас, кижи болганы сыгыртпас, база бойдус чаялгазы болуп турары ол.*" Unless otherwise noted, all quotations attributed to Valeriy Mongush are in Tyvan from an interview conducted by the author in collaboration with Victoria Soyan Peemot on March 31, 2017 in the Tyva Republic, Russian Federation.

10. In Tyvan: "*Ооӊ мурнунда ачамныӊ чуржузу Сат Манчакайныӊ чугаалаары болза мындыг аан: 'Хөөмей, сыгыт, каргыраа деп үш хевир үш аӊгы уктан келген боор чүве диин, оглум'—ден аан.*" *Churzhu* is the younger brother of your wife; in this case, the younger brother of his father's wife (mother), making him an uncle. Sat Manchakai (1918–1965), from the Chöön-Xemchik district of Tyva, was among the first generation of Tyvans to build *xöömei*, *kargyraa*, and *sygyt* inside the cultural productions of Soviet Tyva's music and folklore clubs, institutions, and networks. In 1948, Manchakai famously performed *sygyt* with *doshpuluur* for an audience that included General Secretary of the Soviet Union Joseph Stalin, who reportedly gave three standing ovations in appreciation of the performance. See Süzükei and Tumat (2015).

11. In Tyvan: "*Ынчап кээрге хөөмей дээрге херээжен кижиниӊ чырык черге чаяап каан төлүн, ону эки хөөнүн киирип, ол кижини өпейлеп бээри өпейинден укталган хөөмей аан. Кыс кижиниӊ эргеледиинден, 'Өпей, оглум!'—деп турганындан улузуӊ хөөмейлеп алгаш чоруй барган деп тайылбырлап турар ол башкы болза.*" Valeriy explains that reciting the lullaby vocables "uvai, uvai, uvai" is one of the most basic ways to begin learning to voice *xöömei*.

12. In Tyvan: "*Каргыраа дээрге таалал ыры-дыр; кадат малыныӊ таалал ырызы. Каргыраа дээрге кадарчы кижиниӊ ол мал тааладыр, таалап оъттаар, хой-даа болза, сарлык-даа болза, кадат малы малдаар кижиниӊ ырызы каргыраа боор.*" Among Tyvan-speaking communities, *mal* refers to domesticated livestock, which includes sheep, goats, cows, yaks, camels, and horses. A distinction is drawn between the livestock of the encampment (*kodan maly*), which includes sheep, goats, cows, and the livestock of the wilderness (*cher maly*), which includes horses and sometimes yaks. *Taalal* is a noun; the verbs are *taaladyr* and *taalaar*. Vika describes their difference in meaning in Tyvan as follows: *taaladyr* is inflicted/caused by some external source, whereas *taalaar* is used to describe someone's feeling of pleasure. For example, "I am having pleasure" is "*Men taalap tur men*," or "I am singing to the baby so he will receive pleasure" is "*Men öpeiany taaladyr yrlap tur men*." See Table 15.3 for more terminology on activities related to voicing song.

13. In Tyvan: "*Ам сыгыт дээрге-ле ол ам сыннар кыры үнүп, бедиктерге дуу чылгы хавырып чорааш, сыын биле үннештир кады. Ол черлик аӊ апаар, көрүӊер даан, азырал мал эвес аан, сыын үнү ышкаш кылдыр сыгыдын салып, чылгызын кадарып чорааш, сыгыртып чораан дээрге-ле чылгычы кижиниӊ ыры-дыр.*" *Syyn*, or red deer, is also called maral. *Ünneshtir* means "voice-to-voice" or "similar with another's voice," and *kady* means "together." We are translating this as "tuned together." See Table 15.3 for more terminology on activities related to voicing song.

14. Valeriy also explained that many men do *xöömei* as a lullaby for their male and female babies. Valeriy's understanding of *xöömei* as a domestic lullaby that originates with women is debated by scholars and *xöömeizhi* at present. Its origins as a lullaby are less debated. A cultural taboo against women performing *xöömei* is still widely held in Tyva. Despite this taboo, many women have performed *xöömei* in public and continue to do so. Further research on the subject of women and *xöömei* is sorely needed, but institutional and ideological barriers prevent much of this research from moving forward at present. See Levin and Süzükei (2006) and Beahrs (2014).

15. For a discussion of "sonic-musical sensibility" in post-Soviet Tyva's traditional music scenes, see Beahrs (2014 and 2017).

16. For example, men are configured as the primary vocal actors, whereas women are configured in an ambiguous role with respect to *xöömei*. According to Valeriy's story, women are

the original practitioners of the *xöömei* lullaby, and men have actually learned to use this gift from them. Another one of the uses of the *xöömeizhi*'s vocal gifts appears to be to assist women with delivering babies using *sygyt* and *kargyraa*. Valeriy explained it like this: "In old times, *xöömeizhi* (men) were invited to help women who had troubles with delivering a baby. My mother was a midwife (*tudugzhu*), so my uncles from the mother side do *sygyt* and do *kargyraa*. When this kind of woman is in labor and then somebody does *sygyt* next to her, she copies how the man pushes out the air during *sygyt*, this helps the woman to adjust and make easier the way she pushes the baby out." This kind of story naturalizes the *xöömeizhi*'s vocal gift as efficacious in that it helps women with delivering babies. Valeriy's story also seems to suggest that there was and still continues to be a role for women to use *xöömei*, *kargyraa*, and *sygyt*. And even if Valeriy himself does not subscribe to this belief, the imagined order is also used to support a widespread cultural taboo in Tyva against women performing *xöömei*, *kargyraa*, and *sygyt* on the grounds that it is unbecoming, might cause reproductive health problems, and may put a curse on male family members. Despite the cultural taboo, many women have done *xöömei*, *kagyraa*, and *sygyt* in public throughout history and continue to do so with increasing acceptance. See Levin and Süzükei (2006) and Beahrs (2014).

17. See, for example, Yakovlev (1900), Ostrovskikh (1927), and Anokhin ([1903–1910] 2005). This work was expanded upon by Grumm-Grzhimailo (1926), Aksenov (1964), Maslov and Chernov (1979–1980), and Vainshtein (1979–1980). See also Kyrgys (2002), Levin and Süzükei (2006), Süzükei (2007), and Beahrs (2014).

18. As Turkologist Boris Tatarinsev writes, "by its form, *khöömei* is indisputably a mongolism, but in its meaning it has undergone considerable changes. *Khöömei* as a musical term developed within a mixed Tuvan-Mongolian environment, most likely among bilingual Tuvans who used the Mongolian names for the speech organs for the purposes of naming a phenomenon of musical culture. In all likelihood, *khöömei* was used not by coincidence. In its semasiological representation, and in addition, by its sound association with other already existing Tuvan words, specifically, with onomatopoetic words and verbs formed from them, such as *khööle*—'to buzz, to produce a buzzing sound (for example, a bee)'... A part of the Tuvan-speaking population, specifically the performers of throat-singing associate the word *khöömei* with this verb. Some suggest that the term *khöömei* comes from Tuvan *khöön* 'mood, wish, mode, tuning (of musical instrument)'...Having become a Tuvan word it was, in turn able to influence the semantics of the Mongolian word *khöömii* 'throat-singing' *khöömiilökh*, *khöömiidekh* 1. 'to perform throat-singing' 2. 'throat-singing'" (1998: 65–66). See also van Tongeren (1995), Kyrgys (2002), Levin and Süzükei (2006, 2018), Beahrs (2014), and Masahiko (2017). For more information on Mongolian *xöömii*, see Zemp and Hai (1991), Pegg (1992, 2001), Curtet 2013, and Colwell (2018).

19. In Tyvan: "*Ынчан кижи хатты ажыглаптар аан бодунуң эрни-биле; ажыглапкаш сыгыртан ышкаш кылдыр кылыптар чүве. Бо мен бо хире безерек черге орур турумда, дуу тайганың кырында хат хадыырга, ында сыгыртан ышкаш сыыг-сыыг кылып каап турар болза, мен база ооң-биле кады база сыгыдымны оожуум тааар база ынчаар салып болур мен аан.*" *Syyg-syyg* is used here to describe the sound of a specific wind.

20. In Tyvan: "*Ол ам мен бодап турарымга, ол сыгытчы кижи-биле бойдустуң харылзаазы чаңгыс ай апаар аан. Чижээлээрге чылгы хавырып чоруп тургаштың, бедик тайгалар кыры-биле чоруп турганың-биле шынаа черге чоруп турганың база бир аңгы апаар. Шынаа черге чоруп тургаш, делгем хостуг сыгыдың салып орар сен,*"

таваар, уярадыр салып орар сен, база-ла демги малың таалап оъттап чоруп турар. Ам кызаа, хем уну черлерге чедип келген үелерде, база даглыг черлиг кижиниң биле хемниг черниң кижизиниң аңгы дээн ышкаш, орта кээриңге сыгыдың ол-бо талазында тайга-туйга кызырт болган ышкаш апаар, Бичии-Чалаатыны кешкен черлерде ышкаш чиңге-чиңге азы ындыг өткүт-өткүт болу бээр. Ырының сөзүн канчаан ап аар сен, ол сөске дүүштүрер дээш мастер кижи ынчаар кылыр турган." The Tyvan word *ötküt* can be translated as "sonorous," "resonant," or "especially clear." For example, *ötküt ün* means "an especially clear voice," and this phrase appears in the second and third stanzas of Valeriy's song *Kozhangnar*. Valeriy sings lyrics before or after vocal-instrumental melodizing, but not usually at the same time (see Table 15.4 and Audio 15.1).

21. In Tyvan: *"Чамдык духтар хамык чүвелерни, бо тайга-туйга ээзи чүвелерни кыйгырарда шаанда, ам бо шагда сыгырып-сагырып, туң-таң тыртып тургаш ол…Ол чоокта туруп турар чер, сугнуң, ол тайгаларның ээлериниң кайы чүүге кыйгырыптарга чедип кээри аан. Чер ээзиниң таалалы кайызында туруп турары ол. Чижээлээрге ам сыгырты бээр болза, ам кыс чер ээзи кижи болза, муңгаранчыг таалаар дээн чижектиг. Азы туң, туң дээрге позывной хевирлиг чүве-дир ийин ам, колдуу кыйгырар, чер ээзи, хамык чүүлер кыйгырар. Ол кижиниң ынчангаш хей-хай ышкаш ындыг чүвелерни, чамдык чүвелер сыгырган ышкаш ындыг чүвелерден кулаккалаа чаңгылангаш, шыдавайн чоруй баар чүвелер бар. Ындыг чүвелер база бар боор аан. Ам чамдыызы болза, аалга каржыланып чедип келген диирең нер, ындыг чүвелер болза, уян үннү дыңнапкаш база чоруй баар аан."* Sometimes Valeriy uses Russian words when he speaks in Tyvan. Here, for example, he uses the Russian word *dux* to refer to "spirits." We have chosen to translate the Tyvan words *eezi* as "master" and *xei chüveler* and *diirengner* as "spirit," but the entities to which Valeriy refers may be better understood in English as "nonhuman beings" who inhabit the land.

22. The connection of *sygyt* to shamanism and spirit-masters has been a recurring topic of debate at the International *Xöömei* Symposia, which have occurred semiregularly in Kyzyl since 1992. While figures such as Mongush Kenin-Lopsan and Zoya Kyrgyz have drawn connections between *sygyt* and shamanism, many other scholars and musicians in the *xöömeizhi* community are ambivalent about the validity or importance of these connections at present.

23. The Üstüü-Xüree Festival of Live Music and Faith was founded in 1999, and has continued annually up to the present. The outdoor festival has been at the center of Tyva's post-Soviet renaissance of spirituality and local traditions and helped to raise funds for the reconstruction of the Üstüü-Xüree Buddhist temple. The festival attracts a mixture of local and international musicians, artists, fans, students, and religious practitioners. See Beahrs (2014).

24. In Russian: *"В начале советских времен, вот, нам говорили, что запрещали петь горловое пение. Это вызывает, ну, боль, туда-сюда, человек заболеет. Когда он сыгыт поет, если он немножко гриппом заболел и сыгыт поет, по его дыханию, тут болезни распространятся, туда-сюда. Запрещенные тоже были времена….Врачи запрещали….Если сам себя правильно вести не можешь, каждый раз выпиваешь, туда-сюда, здоровье потеряешь. И вместе с ним и сыгыт потеряешь."* Voice lesson in Russian with the author, Kyzyl, Tyva Republic, August 16, 2016.

25. The Soviet collective farming system reconfigured nomadic life in Tyva, but it also supported new forms of cultural expression and state-sponsored patronage for the arts through regional Houses of Culture. For a more detailed discussion on this topic in Tyva, see Süzükei (2007) and Beahrs (2014).

26. The cultivation of "folk music" from the vocal-instrumental techniques of Valeriy's ancestors constituted one such purification. See Beahrs (2014).

27. For Tyvan people, the animal "backwardness," exemplified in the ethnographic accounts of "wild" nomadic and shamanic voices, was separated from the human through a "zoo-politics of voice," a concept I adopt from Anna María Ochoa Gautier (2014; 2015). In connection with her insightful account of the politics of sounds, voices, and writing in late and postcolonial Colombia, Ochoa (drawing on Fabián Ludueña) distinguishes *zoé*, a less-than-human life away from the city, from *bíos*, a "qualified life" of humanly organized politics in the context of colonialism (2015, 20). As Ochoa Gautier writes, "one of the problems of the voice in the history of Western philosophy since Aristotle is that [the voice] has the potential of manifesting the animal in the human animal. Thus, one can think of the history of the voice in the West as one of trying to elucidate which vocal elements manifest between human and other animals as part of the history of the relation between voice, reason, and sentience" (Ochoa 2015, 16). But, as Ochoa points out, what if the goal of animal voicing for South American indigenous peoples (in her case, the Boga workers in riverine transport networks of nineteenth-century Colombia) was not to imitate animals, but rather to envoice the multiplicities of relationships that link humans with a broader ecology of being and doing in the world? Certainly, the separation of humans from nature—or even the separation of voice from soul—should not be seen as making these people less able to partake in the political world of human societies. And yet colonization achieved that very effect for indigenous peoples living throughout the world.

28. For biographical information on Sat Manchakai, see Süzükei and Tumat (2015).

29. For more information on Valeriy's biography, see Süzükei and Tumat (2015).

30. I would like to express my gratitude to other teachers who have taught me about *xöömei*, *kargyraa*, and *sygyt* in Tyva including: Evgeniy Saryglar, Sergei Ondar, Andrei Opei, Evgeniy Oyun, Kaigal-ool Khovalyg, Aldar Tamdyn, Kongar-ool Ondar, Choduraa Tumat, Aylangma Damyrang, Andrei Mongush, Igor Koshkendey, Ensemble Tyva, Tyva Kyzy, and Ensemble Alash.

31. In Russian: "*У нас горловое пение это потомственное... Про себя поешь горловое пение, а другим тоже это достается. Ну, я, например, когда начинаю петь, закрываю глаза. Это у меня привычка такая. Не оттого, что я кого-то боюсь, кого-то стесняюсь, а это, когда я исполняю, закрыв глаза, пою той природе или тому маме, папе. Представляешь, что перед ними сидишь. Ну их давно нету. Но все равно как в юрте перед ними сидишь и исполняешь тоол. Они тебе подарили такую ценность, а ты им нежно поешь. Я вот так все время, если глаза закрываю, на том месте нахожусь, о чем я пою. Забываю, что тут Robert сидит, глаза закрываю—а там мама, папа, родственники сидят или там скот пасется.*" Voice lesson in Russian with the author, Kyzyl, Tyva Republic, August 16, 2016.

32. My first encounter with the "Throat Singers from Tuva" was in an ethnomusicology class at Pomona College taught by my mentor Katherine Hegedorn in 2004. See, for example, the album *Tuva: Voices from the Center of Asia* (1990), produced by Ted Levin along with Zoya Zyrgyz and Eduard Alekseev. See also Levin and Edgerton (1999) and Levin and Süzükei (2006).

33. I adopt the term "inner choreographies" from my voice studies mentor (and coeditor of this volume) Nina Sun Eidsheim, who uses it to refer to the "movements that create internal physical configurations that give rise to a timbral identity" of a person's voice. See Eidsheim (2009 and 2015).

34. See Matthew Rahaim's chapter on vocal ontologies in this volume. See also Rahaim (2012). I am also indebted to Rahaim for his insightful attention to "God gifts" in relation to singers of Hindustani classical music in North India.

35. See, for example, Peemot (2017).

36. The term "voice," whether used with articles "the" or "a," whether referred to as "voice" or as "voices" in the English language facilitates a number of elisions that are often left uncritically explored in scholarship. For me as an ethnomusicologist and practitioner of *xöömei*, I seek to acknowledge the texture of multiple kinds of voices that I encounter during my fieldwork and explore their meanings, values, and roles in shaping society and making worlds. In the *Critical Handbook of Voice Studies* (2015), editors Thomaidis and MacPherson argue for a move away from totalizing (the) *voice* and towards *voices* conceived in the plural. I, too, share in this conviction for acknowledging multiple vocal ontologies and seek to contribute to this gap in the scholarship in voice studies through my ongoing research in Inner Asia. Moreover, I claim that voice studies productively challenges many of the Western European underpinnings of art and music; this allows us to move towards a more expansive and inclusive understanding of the diversity of forms of human and nonhuman expression that shape our world.

37. In conceiving of a politics of voice, I am most indebted to the work of anthropologist Amanda Weidman (2006). See also Feld (1996), Harkness (2014), Ochoa Gautier (2014), and Butler (2015).

38. In Tyvan: "*Бир эвес бистиҥ Тыва хөөмей культураны делегейге чырыдар дээш, сонуургап турган болганда, мен ышкаш мындыг ам бөдүүн улузуҥ: 'Ии, аа богда, Тывавыстыҥ хамык культуразын чон билзин!'—дээш ынаар дамчыдып бээрин кызар аан. Ам тывалар кээр болза, кижи дөмей-ле: 'Чок, мен билбес мен!'—дээш кыштап чоруй баар эвес. Ам шуут амыраар кижи диин мен Роберттиҥ кылып турар ажылынга.*" *Bogda* refers to a nature-God concept that is likely rooted in a syncretism of shamanism and Buddhism.

39. Valeriy Mongush's CD titled "Övürümnü" (2017) is available for purchase at the gift shop in the Center for the Development of Tyvan Traditional Culture and Crafts in Kyzyl. Voice lessons for students visiting Tyva can also be arranged through the Center.

Works Cited

Aksenov, Aleksei N. 1964. *Tuvinskaia narodnaia muzyka [Tuvan Folk Music]*. Moscow: Muzyka.

Anokhin, A. V. 2005. *Narodnaya muzyka tyurkov i mongolov [Folk Music of the Turks and Mongols]*. Edited by I. I. Belekov. Gorno-Altaisk: Ministry of Culture and Film of the Republic of Altai.

Beahrs, Robert O. 2014. "Post-Soviet Tuvan Throat-Singing (*Xöömei*) and the Circulation of Nomadic Sensibility." PhD diss., University of California at Berkeley.

Beahrs, Robert O. 2017. "Nomads in the Global Soundscape: Negotiating Aesthetics in Post-Soviet Tuva's Traditional Music Productions." *The New Research of Tuva* 2 (June 2017): 59–110.

Butler, Shane. 2015. *The Ancient Phonograph*. Brooklyn, NY: Zone Books.

Colwell, Andrew Hamilton. 2018. "Sounding Original: Nature, Indigeneity, and Globalization in Mongolia (and Southern Germany)." PhD Diss., Wesleyan University.

Curtet, Johanni, 2013. "La transmission du *höömij*, un art du timbre vocal: ethnomusicologie et histoire du chant diphonique mongol." PhD Diss., European University of Brittany.

Eidsheim, Nina. 2009. "Synthesizing Race: Towards an Analysis of the Performativity of Vocal Timbre." *TRANS: Revista Transcultural de Música* 13. https://www.sibetrans.com/trans/article/57/synthesizing-race-towards-an-analysis-of-the-performativity-of-vocal-timbre

Eidsheim, Nina Sun. 2015. *Sensing Sound: Singing & Listening as Vibrational Practice*. Durham, NC: Duke University Press.

Feld, Steven. 1996. "Waterfalls of Song: An Acoustemology of Place Resounding in Bosavi, Papua New Guinea." In *Senses of Place*, edited by Steven Feld and Keith H. Basso, 91–135. Santa FE, NM: School of American Research Press.

Grumm-Grzhimailo, G.E. 1926. *Zapadnaya Mongoliya i Uryanxaiskii Krai [Western Mongolia and the Uriankhai Country]*. Vol. III, Pt. 1. Leningrad: Russian State Geographical Society.

Harkness, Nicholas. 2014. *Songs of Seoul: An Ethnography of Voice and Voicing in Christian South Korea*. Berkeley: University of California Press.

Kyrgys, Zoya. 2002. *Tuvinskoe gorlovoe penie [Tuvan Thoat-Singing]*. Novosibirsk: Nauka.

Levin, Theodore, and Michael Edgerton. 1999. "The Throat Singers of Tuva." *Scientific American* 281 (3): 80–7.

Levin, Theodore, and Valentina Süzükei. 2006. *Where Rivers and Mountains Sing: Sound, Music, and Nomadism in Tuva and Beyond*. Bloomington: Indiana University Press.

Levin, Theodore, and Valentina Süzükei. 2018. "Timbre-Centered Listening in the Soundscape of Tuva." In *The Oxford Handbook of Timbre*, edited by Emily Dolan and Alexander Rehding. New York: Oxford University Press. doi:10.1093/oxfordhb/9780190637224.013.15

Masahiko, Todoriki. 2017. "Archaic Oirat Substratum of the 'Circa-Altai Musical Kulturkreis' in Tuva." *The New Research of Tuva* 3 (August 2017): 147–208.

Maslov, V. T., and B. P. Chernov. 1979–1980. "The Secret of a 'Solo Duet.'" *Soviet Anthropology and Archaeology* XVIII (3): 82–8.

Ochoa, Ana María. 2015. "On the Zoopolitics of the Voice and the Distinction Between Nature and Culture." In *The Routledge Companion to Art and Politics*, edited by Randy Martin, 16–24. New York: Routledge.

Ochoa Gautier, Ana María. 2014. *Aurality: Listening and Knowledge in Nineteenth-Century Colombia*. Durham, NC: Duke University Press.

Ostrovskikh, P.E. 1927. "Olennye tuvintsy [The Reindeer Tuvans]." *Severnaya Aziya obshchest-venno-nauchnyi zhurnal [Northern Asia Journal of Social Sciences]* 5–6:79–94.

Peemot, Victoria Soyan. 2017. "We Eat Whom We Love: Hippophagy among Tyvan Herders." *Inner Asia* 19 (1): 133–56.

Pegg, Carole. 1992. "Mongolian Conceptualizations of Overtone Singing (*xöömii*)." *British Journal of Ethnomusicology* 1 (1): 31–54.

Pegg, Carole. 2001. *Mongolian Music, Dance, & Oral Narrative: Performing Diverse Identities*. Seattle: University of Washington Press.

Rahaim, Matthew. 2012. *Musicking Bodies: Gesture and Voice in Hindustani Music*. Middletown, CT: Wesleyan University Press.

Süzükei, Valentina. 2007. *Muzykal'naia kul'tura Tuvy v dvadtsatom stoletii [The Musical Culture of Tuva in the Twentieth Century]*. Moscow: Izdatel'skii Dom "Kompozitor."

Süzükei, V. Yu., and Ch. S. Tumat. 2015. *Xöömeizhi Respubliki Tyva [Xöömeizhi of the Tyva Republic]*. Kyzyl: Minnisterstvo Kul'tury Respubliki Tyva [Ministry of Culture of the Tyva Republic]; Tsentr Razvitiya Tuvinskoi Traditsionnoi Kul'tury i Remesel [Center for the Development of Tuvan Traditional Culture and Handicrafts].

Tatarintsev, Boris. 1998. *Tuvinskoe gorlovoe penie. Problemy proiskhozhdeniya/Problems of the Origin of Tuvan Throat-Singing (bilingual edition)*. Kyzyl: International Scientific Center "Khöömei."

Thomaidis, Konstantinos, and Ben Macpherson, eds. 2015. *Voice Studies: Critical Approaches to Process, Performance and* Experience. New York: Routledge.

Vainshtein, Sevyan Izraelevich. 1979–1980. "A Phenomenon of Musical Art Born in the Steppes." *Soviet Anthropology and Archaeology* 18 (3): 68–81.

van Tongeren, Mark C. 1995. "A Tuvan Perspective on Throat Singing." In *Oideion: The Performing Arts Worldwide*, edited by Marjolijn van Roon Wim van Zanten, 293–312. University of Leiden: Centre of Non-Western Studies.

Weidman, Amanda J. 2006. *Singing the Classical, Voicing the Modern: The Postcolonial Politics of Music in South India.* Durham, NC: Duke University Press.

Yakovlev, E.K. 1900. *Etnograficheskii obzor inorodcheskago naseleniya doliny Yuzhnago Eniseya [Ethnographic survey of the non-Russian population of the southern Yenisei valley].* Minusinsk: Minusink Museum.

Zemp, Hugo, and Trân Quang Hai. 1991. "Recherches expérimentales sur le chant diphonique." *Cahiers de Musiques Traditionnelles* 4 (1991): 27–68.

Discography

1990. *Tuva: Voices from the Center of Asia.* Washington, DC: Smithsonian Folkways Records. SFW 40017 (CD).

Mongush, Valeriy. 2017. "Övürümnü." Kyzyl, Tyva Republic: Center for the Development of Tyvan Traditional Culture and Crafts, CD.

PART V

PRODUCING VOICE
VOCAL MODALITIES

CHAPTER 16

THE ECHOING PALIMPSEST

Singing and the Experience of Time at the Ecumenical Patriarchate of Constantinople

ALEXANDER K. KHALIL

INTRODUCTION: STYLIANOS FLOIKOS

ON December 24, 2016, Stylianos Floikos was given the title of "Lampadarios of the Great Church of Christ" by His All-Holiness, Ecumenical Patriarch Bartholomew, during the vespers service for Christmas at St. George Cathedral in Istanbul, Turkey. Stylianos Floikos, called Stelios, is what one might call a living legend in the city of Istanbul. Known for his huge voice, rumors of his exploits as a vocalist abound. Floikos's new office designates him as the second ranked *psaltis*,[1] or cantor, in the Orthodox Church worldwide, but, more significantly, he now holds a position that has been held by many of the most well-known Orthodox Christian *psaltes* in history, quite a few of whom are referred to by the title rather than their surname (e.g., "Petros Lampadarios" or "Stephan Lampadarios").

Stelios was born on the island of Imvros, probably the last large enclave of *Rum*, or ethnic Greek speakers—descendants of the Romans—in Turkey. His family moved to the rapidly dwindling *Rum*, Greek Orthodox quarter of Istanbul, so Stelios could be educated at the Patriarchal school in the Phanar neighborhood, once the cultural center of the Rum. At the age of ten Stelios's exceptional vocal talent was recognized by Basileos Nikolaides, then *"protopsaltis,"* or "first *psaltis,"* and he was made a *kanonarch* (an apprentice *psaltis*) at the Patriarchal Church. He has served there ever since. As Stelios grew as a *psaltis*, his community continued to shrink. As people left Istanbul for Greece (Koglin 2017, 95), the population dropped from 7,900 in 1978 to a mere 1,650 in 2004.[2]

Stelios attended theological school in Thessaloniki where he received advanced degrees in chant, studying theory under the late Dimitrios Sourlantzis. During a period in Vienna, he studied and performed opera as a dramatic tenor during what he describes as his brief "love affair with opera."

I had come to know Stelios almost a decade before he was made *lampadarios*, when I went to the Ecumenical Patriarchate in Istanbul to conduct research.[3] At that time, there were three *"archon" psaltes* at the Patriarchate: Leonidas Asteris, the *protopsaltis*, or head psaltis; Ioannis Chariatidis, the *lampadarios*,[4] who is ranked second; and Stelios, who held the title of second *domestikos*.[5] Today, with both Asteris and Chariatidis retired, and Panagiotis Neochoritis installed as *protopsaltis*, Stelios is the last remaining *archon psaltis* at the Patriarchal church to have grown up in the Greek Orthodox quarter of Istanbul and started his career in that church as a *kanonarch*.

Inside the Ecumenical Patriarchate's St. George Cathedral, *psaltes* gather at two *analogia*,[6] or lecterns, facing each other from opposite sides of the church directly in front of the *templo*, or *iconostas*, a large wooden edifice that separates the sanctuary from the rest of the church. While these two groups are referred to as "choirs," the music they sing is monophonic. The majority of the *psaltes* in each choir sing in unison with the leader of their side, while one or two *psaltes* may sing "*ison*," a type of vocal drone that holds the tonic quietly below the melody. The two choirs, right and left, are led by the *protopsaltis*, or head chanter, and the *lampadarios*, respectively. The choirs sing antiphonally, taking turns according to a set of rules (Figure 16.1 features the chanters of the right choir before Stylianos became the leader of the left choir).

The *psaltes* often read from musical scores written in an emic system of neumes (for an example of these neumes, see Figure 16.2). That has gone through an evolution from roughly the eighth century to the present day. The neumes, which are similar in level of descriptivity regarding pitch and rhythm to Western staff notation, guide the singer by indicating movement along a set of microtonal scales from which the eight church modes, or ochtoechos, are derived. Aside from melodic direction, neumes exist for rhythm, expression, ornamentation, and phrasing.

There is nothing particularly unusual about the organization and chanting described here: it could apply to chanting at almost any Greek or Levantine Orthodox Christian church. However, for several centuries St. George Cathedral has been one of the crucibles in which this tradition has developed. The Patriarchal *psaltes*, like *psaltes* in many regions, have a characteristic sound. When, in 2004, I first stood in the Patriarchal church and listened to them, I was deeply moved. I could best describe my impression with a word that is often applied to their chanting: *megaloprepia* (grandeur). This grandeur is not achieved through extensive melisma, ornamentation, or vocal acrobatics. The Patriarchal *psaltes* chant in a way that relative to many other *psaltes*, is more direct and concise. This highlights their sense of timing (*chronos*). The effect on me was that their chanting exuded a sense of awe. However, it seemed to me that they were not trying impart a sense of awe but were themselves in awe, and this was communicated through their relatively reserved interpretations. This reserved and concise sound, with its

FIGURE 16.1 Chanters of the right choir inside St. George Cathedral. From left: Stelios Floikos, Leonidas Asteris, and Stelios Berberis. (Photo by Christina Chan.)

precise rhythms and tempi, is also the sound of a community at work: His All-Holiness, Patriarch Bartholomew, works tirelessly not only at the affairs of the Orthodox church worldwide but also speaking out on global issues, in particular, the environment and the safety and well-being of children in war zones. Almost everyone present at a given service (save for the tour groups who pour through the Cathedral periodically every day) is a member of the clergy and the Patriarchal staff. They are direct and expeditious in manner and not likely to embellish anything nearly as much as can be found in many churches whose clergy are under less pressure. However, this makes any embellishment stand out more clearly.

I, too, am a *psaltis*. A student of John Mestakides, former *protopsaltis* of Jerusalem, I have served as a *psaltis* in several Greek and Antiochian parishes over the past three decades. As a *psaltis* in this tradition, I had long known of the Patriarchal *psaltes* and the unique heritage they bear. Practically every discussion in which I have participated or observed among *psaltes* about style or lineages of transmission—and there are many styles and lineages around Greece, Eastern Europe, and the Middle East today—would eventually touch on, if not begin and end on, the subject of the Patriarchal *psaltes* and a phenomenon known as *yphos* (ύφος).

YPHOS

The Patriarchate has been a center of the chant tradition for centuries. *Psaltes* would travel from across the Byzantine Empire, and later the Ottoman Empire, to join the musical culture of the city (formerly known as Constantinople and later as Istanbul), and some even to join the ranks of the *psaltes* at the Patriarchal Cathedral. While their diverse voices and styles certainly must have enriched the musical culture of the city, their voices were also transformed by it. Around the time of the Greek revolution (1821–1832), this movement began to slow and eventually change direction. The Rum community in Istanbul fell under intense pressure and was no longer a place that people flocked to from across the Ottoman Empire. As the situation in the city deteriorated, particularly in the early twentieth century, *psaltes* began a long and slow departure from the city, many having been forced out by pogroms against the *Rum* (Törne 2015) or economic hardship, dispersing the voice of its musical culture into diaspora. Aware of this decline, the Patriarchate began to assert its continued centrality and relevance in ecclesiastical music by claiming a more intangible aspect of Patriarchal chant: *yphos* (Erol 2015, 82).

Yphos, which translates roughly to English as "style," was first mentioned in notated hymnals that were described as bearing the "Patriarchal *yphos*" in their melodies (Erol 2015, 82). It was never made clear how or where *yphos* exists in these scores, or even exactly what it is, and so *yphos* remained intangible, and inaccessible to outsiders. This allowed the Patriarchate to position itself as arbiter of the tradition. A similar strategy was later adopted by Konstantinos Psachos, a nineteenth-century *psaltis* and chant scholar in his defense of the continuity of chant tradition (Psachos 1906) against scholars from Western Europe who posited that contemporary chant had become inextricably mixed with Ottoman styles of music (Lingas 2003). *Yphos* has continued into the vocabulary of today's practicing *psaltes*. The current conception of *yphos* is centered on the voice itself.

While it is believed that many different *yphi* (ύφη: pl of *yphos*) exist associated with various regional[7] and even personal traditions, the *yphos* of the Patriarchal *psaltes* is the most hotly debated *yphos* among *psaltes* today.[8] The twentieth century saw a succession of Patriarchal *psaltes*: Iakovos Naupliotis, Konstantinos Pringgos, Thrasyvolos Stantitsas, Basieleos Emmanualidis, Nikolaos Danielidis, Basileos Nikolaides, Ioannis Chariatidis, Eleftherios Georgiadis, Demosthenes Paikopoulos, Andreas Petrohelios, and Leonidas Asteris, each of whom had very distinctive voices and styles while having been said to maintain the Patriarchal *yphos*. Different *psaltes* (or perhaps armchair enthusiasts) often claim that one or another of these *psaltes* was the last bearer of the true Patriarchal *yphos*, citing differences in, as my teacher put it, "the sound of the voice." Many *psaltes* claim lineage to one of these master *psaltes* and so seek to connect themselves to the Patriarchal *yphos*. While these issues are discussed and debated by *psaltes* worldwide, who argue about minutiae of recordings from the Patriarchal Cathedral posted on YouTube, or details of various commercial recordings of the Patriarchal *psaltes*, the Patriarchal *psaltes* themselves are rarely ever brought into these discussions. They are not asked about their understanding of *yphos*. This is a particularly urgent issue today as Stelios is the last Patriarchal *psaltis* to have been raised in the Greek quarter of the city and to have served as a *kanonarch* from an early age. Stelios's voice reflects the sound of a community that no longer exists: a Greek-speaking quarter in Istanbul. While other voices will certainly follow his in fulfilling the duties of Lampadarios at the Patriarchal See, none will have the sound of this community etched into it. But how, and where, does one find this sound, especially considering how differently other Patriarchal *psaltes* sounded from each other? Further, how and where is the sound of a community or culture reflected in the voice?

My interest in Stelios, therefore, was not in assessing or asserting his authenticity as a Patriarchal *psaltis*, nor in collecting or preserving details of singing from the last remaining member of a branch of this tradition, but in understanding his voice. What aspects of voice or of singing were most expressive for him, most under his control? What aspects of voice did he associate with the long and weighty history of his position and people? How does he negotiate this through singing? The purpose of this chapter, then, is not to define *yphos* in some way. Rather, *yphos* served as a productive topic of discussion for many of my questions. I approached this as a participant observer over of a period of four years during which I spent time as an assistant *psaltis* in the Patriarchal church, and conducted many unstructured interviews with Stelios and other *psaltes*, clergy, and musicians in the area.

Stelios and I have discussed his perspective on *yphos* and what it encompasses for him throughout our interactions as colleagues and friends. To my surprise, when I brought up the topic during our first meeting, he immediately offered to demonstrate by singing from a notated score with and without *yphos*. He picked up a copy of the *Anastasimatarion* (Resurrectional Hymnal), and at random opened to the third mode *Ainoi* (Praises) by Petros Lampadarios (Vallindras 1998, 137). First, he chanted it without *yphos* and then again with *yphos*. It was difficult for me to imagine that either version lacked *yphos*. Neither version was lacking in ornamentation or any of the nuances of vocal movement that are part of the tradition. In Stelios's voice, the sound of the Patriarchal church is deeply etched. Every note he sang seemed to be, as my friend and colleague Constantine Kokenes put it, "dripping with *yphos*." It is impossible for someone who is part of this culture to hear anything that Stelios sings and not immediately identify the Patriarchal *yphos*. In spite of this completeness, the without-*yphos* version was indeed lacking in one very specific way: there were no deviations from the notated melody. Aside from performing some standard ornaments that are usually not written out, Stelios sang that melody in exactly the form in which it was written. As can be seen in Figure 16.2, Stelios's with-*yphos* version diverged more, albeit slightly, from the written melody. Through this exercise—which was to become an important part of the methodology we ended up using—Stelios was able to demonstrate that for him *yphos* was related to melodic interpretation, a process referred to by *psaltes* as *ektelesis* (lit. "execution"). Stelios seemed to be demonstrating that *yphos* is manifest through these variations.

FIGURE 16.2 The top line is the written melody in neumes. Below that is a transcription of only the information contained in the neumes. The third line is Stelios's without-*yphos* realization and the bottom line is Stelios's "with-*yphos*" realization.

There was nothing particularly surprising about the "with-*yphos*" realization: *psaltes*, myself included, commonly "analyze" a melody down to its underlying "*thésis*" or "melodic formula," and then choose from a variety of different possible *ekteleses* in realization. However, it was significant that Stelios located *yphos* in this process as it is an aspect of the voice over which chanters have control in real time. Through this demonstration, Stelios was able to indicate that *yphos* was something that afforded him a significant amount of agency while staying within the confines of the tradition. This led us to examine the space between the written melody and its realization in chant, a space negotiated by Stelios every time he chants.

To accomplish this, Stelios and I developed a simple methodology: we would, at different times, record him chanting at least two "without-*yphos*" versions of a large number of hymns chanted from selected scores. Then, over a period that spanned three years (2005–2008), we would record as many "with-*yphos*" realizations of these same scores as possible. After collecting several "with-*yphos*" realizations of a given score, I would transcribe the various renditions and discuss them with Stelios.

Of the very many recordings we made and discussed, one melody in particular afforded insight into Stelios's experience. It was the opening line of the *Ainoi* (Praises) in mode II in Petros Ephesios's *Anastasimatarion* (Ephesios 1820). Stelios chanted this melody multiple times, as transcribed in Figure 16.3. His first five opening phrases basically followed the melodic contour of the *thésis* on the page.

The last realization, however, features a phrase that is striking in its opposition to the direction of the written *thésis*, starting a fifth higher and then descending to the *vasis*.[9] While it was not unusual for him to chant *ekteleses* featuring material obliquely related to the notated line, it seemed significant that he would chant a melodic line that directly

FIGURE 16.3 Six ekteleses of a formula from Ephesios's book. At the top are the original neumes with their transcription immediately below.

opposed it. When I asked him why he had chanted that particular *ektelesis*, Stelios initially answered that he felt it was "dramatic." He went on to describe a recording of Konstantinos Pringgos, a well-known Patriarchal chanter from the early to mid-twentieth century, in which he also opposed this melodic line in a similar way and created a kind of tension "against [the] echoes" of the many realizations that naturally would have followed the contour of the line (Floikos, interview 2006). He was not merely repeating Pringgos's *ektelesis*; rather, it came to mind along with many other *ekteleses* as he was chanting so that while his chanted line in that instance was parallel or congruent with Pringgos's, it was at the same time in tension with or opposed to other lines he remembered.

After having been afforded this glimpse into Stelios's experience of chanting, further discussion ensued that enabled us to explore this process more deeply. From this, it emerged that although Stelios may be chanting alone, as a soloist, his experience of voice is richly polyphonic. This sense of polyphony arises as every time he chants remembered iterations of that same chant or that same *thésis* come to mind, creating an affect. This affect is caused by the juxtaposition between what he remembers, hearing, so to speak, in his mind's ear, and what he is currently singing. Being aware of this juxtaposition, Stelios then can negotiate it, essentially singing a counterpoint to it. Significantly, both the melodies that Stelios "hears" and the melodies he chants are not merely paradigmatic examples, a sort of catalogue of motivic building blocks from which to choose. He experiences them associated with particular people, places, or events. Stelios is not merely remembering and manipulating a repertoire of melodic material. Rather, he is in a sense joining an ongoing dialogue with other *psaltes*. This, in turn, causes him to experience a sense of presence that stems from an experience of time that is not linear so much as cumulative: all layers with which his voice interacts exude a sense of presence directly affecting his present realization. While this is centered on the voice, it is similar to the experience of reading texts that have accumulated on the same page over time, intersecting each other. Stelios experiences voice—both his own and that of other *psaltes*—as a palimpsest.

Palimpsestic Vocal Tradition: Disparate Voices Interact Across Time

A palimpsest is a manuscript that has been reused, having had its original text only partially erased and appearing on the page together with the later text. The word comes from Greek: *palin* ("again") and *psao* ("to write"). Parchment has often been expensive and difficult to obtain. Scribes recycled parchments by scraping the ink from inscribed parchments with a blade or stone and then writing new inscriptions. This was never a complete process, however. After an initial cleaning the paper would look clear, but as time passed the older text, through a variety of natural chemical processes, often became visible again on the page as a layer beneath the new text (Dillon 2007, 15–19). This process was often repeated more than once, eventually resulting in a richly multilayered text. Once the palimpsestic layers have emerged they join in a somewhat paradoxical relationship of simultaneous intimacy and separation; intimacy by the fact that they coexist in the same two-dimensional space, and separation because the various layers of text are usually quite distant in content, language, and time. Introduced by Sarah Dillon, the term "palimpsestuous" speaks to the experience of the palimpsest, the "simultaneous relation of intimacy and separation" that is experienced by the reader (2007, 4–6). Thus, the term "palimpsestic" (the adjective of "palimpsest" according to *Webster*) refers to the process of layering that produces a palimpsest, whereas "palimpsestuous" refers to the result of that process and the reappearance of the underlying script.

The visceral experience of chanting is, for Stelios, clearly palimpsestuous. That is, the memories that arise through the act of singing carry with them not only technical information, what notes, rhythms, intonations, and so on were sung but also sensation; how it felt physically to be singing those notes or rhythms. This extends beyond the limits of the singer's own body as he or she remembers his or her physical impression of how another person's body might have felt when they were singing.

Naturally, a palimpsest by definition features to an accumulation of layers of text. In order to accumulate, these layers must be bound by a single contextual point, a palimpsestic anchor. The classic anchor is, of course, the parchment or papyrus on which multiple layers of text were inscribed. In Stelios's art, however, these layers, consisting of remembered vocalizations, are inscribed on his voice itself.

The central effect of the palimpsestuous experience arises through the juxtaposition of real-time realization against multifarious remembered realizations experienced as layers anchored by the voice. In this way, as a voice creates resonance in an acoustic space, which in turn reflects and shapes it, resonance is also created in an internal space, which exists both in singer and listener. This internal space is experienced not as an individual space but as a social and cultural space because the voice creates resonances with the remembered voices of others, accumulated through long participation in the tradition.

This is not to claim that this internal cultural space—or felt resonance—is in some way shared: the particular resonances that the *psaltis* experiences cannot be directly communicated to a listener by chanting. The fact of this disjunct in communication between *psaltis* and the listener precludes the possibility that his memories of musical formulae can be arranged as a type of subtext, or signification. If not some form of signification, by which Stelios might make a nuanced and contextually relevant set of cultural references that an informed listener might catch, what is the affect of the resonances he creates, both for himself and listener?

Whether singing with or against the echoes of other *psaltes* (i.e., memories of their voices), the counterpuntal tension against their echoes allows for a sense of presence. It is this experience that is shared, if independently, by both *psaltis* and listener. I call this experience "past-in-present" because it is not fully an experience of the past, nor is it an artificial present experience dressed as past. Rather, in the experience of past-in-present, some part of the past is manifest experientially into the present.[10]

Stelios often described chanting in terms of being in dialogue. Metaphorically, the idea of a dialogue implies a dynamic interaction with someone who is experienced as present. How does Stelios enter a dialogue with voices from the past? If the material is neither seen nor heard, how does Stelios, in real time, manifest it in order to interact with it? This question seems to suggest disingenuousness on Stelios's part. Is he actually engaged in a presentation that consists of musical quotations, in concert with his own innovations, and that seeks to place him among a canon of historical *psaltes* with whom he wishes to identify? No. Having lived almost his entire life right there, zealously learning chant from *psaltes* who chanted with the Patriarchal style, standing by their side as they interpreted neumatic scores, carrying with them the memories of past *psaltes*, his ear is full[11] of their sound and Stelios chants within a generational chain, across centuries. The chanters, both known and unknown, canonized and un-canonized, come unbidden and inexorably to his consciousness by the simple act of his chanting. When Stelios chants, therefore, the many remembered melodies arise with seeming spontaneity, like a previously erased text on a classic palimpsest, to form a paradoxically tacit yet viscerally tangible counterpoint to his melody. These other melodic layers, and the associations they imply, occupy the same real-time space as Stelios's chant and thus are experienced as intimately associated with it by the fact of their simultaneity, while remaining separate by the fact of their acoustic silence. It is interaction with this silent, spontaneously manifest sense of presence, experienced both by Stelios and experientially-informed listeners, that is for him at once the center of his creativity and the body of the tradition that is transmitted through him. It is important to note that Stelios's "new" interpretations are only new in the sense that they are being chanted in the present moment. With exception of very small details of inflection and execution that may be peculiar to Stelios's voice—which Stelios emphatically explained to me has nothing to do with *yphos*—his interpretations are well within the stylistic bounds of his tradition.

The vocal palimpsest contributed to by Stelios extends well beyond the technical details of chanting melodic patterns and into his full life within the city of Istanbul. What are the larger implications of the experience of past-in-present that connect Stelios's voice with that of historical time? I propose that not only his fashioning and experience of the melodic line, but his sense of living within historical time is different from the linear way human beings often conceptualize time or represent it to each other. Stelios overall sense of historical time can best be described as palimpsestic. Thus, rather than linear progression, with its necessary gulf between past and present experience, Stelios experiences historical time as an accumulation that is manifest through and around the act of singing.

Istanbul is a city of palimpsestuousness. Even the name "Istanbul" is palimpsestuous. The Turks named the city after the Greek casual appellation for Constantinople: "*eis tin poli*" or "in the city." For Greek language speakers, "Istanbul" simultaneously points to its past and present, an oscillation between Turkish pronunciation, which represents the present nation, and a Greek meaning, which represents a past that has only been partially erased. Aside from place names—Kadikoy, for Kalchidoni (Chalcedon), or Fener for Phanar (the old center of the *Rum* milet)—palimpsests of many kinds can be found in practically every corner of this city in which more than one thousand years of architecture is stacked in seemingly haphazard juxtaposition.[12]

The Patriarchate, and especially the Patriarchal cathedral of St. George, while part of the larger palimpsest of the city, is literally a part of the past that has refused to be completely erased and stubbornly asserts and reasserts its presence, and can also be considered as a palimpsestic anchor in its own rite. For citizens of Istanbul, the existence of the Patriarchate, or "Rum Patrikanesi," simultaneously represents the presence of the empire of Byzantium and its absence. This is made more clear by Stelios's own description of his experience of singing, and of palimpsestic time in this place.

One cold December day, Stelios and I were called to accompany His All Holiness for the feast day of St. Spyridon to a church dedicated to this saint on the island of Halki,[13] several hours of travel by boat and horse carriage away.[14] I greeted a surprisingly animated Stelios at the door of St. George Cathedral to prepare for the trip in the bracing early morning cold. "Come inside, quickly," he urged, "there is something important I want to show you." We hastily entered the church, which was dark save for the steady and warm light of a couple of oil lamps.

I walked with Stelios up to the left-hand *analogion*, or lectern. In the echoing darkness, we stood still, waiting, apparently. After some moments, Stelios grabbed my wrist. He had an air of tense expectancy. "There," he pronounced, eyes wide with intensity, "can you feel it?" I stood still in the darkness with him for another moment, ears and eyes straining. "This is the source of our *yphos*," whispered Stelios as he gestured towards the rest of the church, towards nothing in particular. "Here," he said. He seemed to be referring to something that would require a sixth sense to feel, some ineffable, intangible, and perhaps spiritual phenomenon.

"When I first opened my mouth to chant [alone] here, I could feel this feeling," he said, again gesturing towards the darkness around us. "It was heavy. It pressed down on me, pressed on my mouth, and my body, and I almost could not chant. We [the Patriarchal chanters] can never forget it. It is always here. It is a kind of fear, or maybe awe. This is why our *yphos* is very sober." Again, he asked me, "Can you feel it too?" To my surprise, I could feel it. I could personally feel...something. I found myself at first unable to identify this fleeting glimpse of the ineffable. As my mind's eye became accustomed to the darkness, I began to recognize the feeling more clearly. It was as if a number of memories, appearing simultaneously and unceremoniously, with little regard for my chronological sensibilities, curled ephemerally in the air like incense around us. Some of these memories were of my own experience: my first time entering that very church at eleven years old, en route with my parents to an excavation in Syria; the first time I encountered the Patriarchal *psaltes* chanting; and some I had not personally experienced, but were familiar to me—the recent visit of Pope Benedict I (he sat on the throne not three feet from where I stood) and the bombing attack on the church a few years before (in which someone lobbed a powerful bomb onto the roof of the church, directly above where we stood). Beyond that, and perhaps most powerful of all, was my knowledge of the history of the place. The many patriarchs who had stood right there, the great *psaltes* whose music I for 25 years had chanted on a weekly basis, had stood right there. My growing understanding was fueled by Stelios's continued monologue. "Here are the bones of Saints John Chrysostom and Gregory Palamas, and over there, the body of St. Euphemia.[15] Here is a segment of the pillar to which Jesus was chained when he was beaten, and here is the Patriarchal throne, which has been preserved since the fifth century! ... From when I was ten years old I stood there," he continued, pointing to the right *analogion*, "and chanted with Fr. Tsiniras. I have heard many great chanters here, and now it is my fortune to stand beside Kyr. Asteris and chant. Here, at the left *analogion*, Petros Lampadarios stood and chanted. At this same *analogion*!" he added for emphasis, thumping it with his hand.[16] "Look, it still has small flecks of black paint on it," Stelios commented as we squinted at the ancient *analogion* in the gloom. The flecks of paint remain from 1821, when Patriarch Gregory V was hung by Sultan Mahmud II directly outside the Patriarchate. A community in mourning painted large sections of inside of the church black and left it that for more than one hundred and fifty years before finally—and incompletely—scraping it clean.[17]

Stelios was not describing a collection of symbols arranged to signify some external meaning, interpretable by those in the know. Rather, he was describing an accumulation of memories. These memories range from the episodic and close at hand (i.e., who was chanting last Sunday), to the semantic and distant past (i.e., "the renowned Petros Lampadarios stood in this very spot and chanted"). Some of these memories are uniquely and directly his own: (e.g., singing at a friend's wedding) and some of them are cultural memories: things he did not directly experience but are known to him and many people around him (e.g., "the renowned Petros Lampadarios stood in this very spot and chanted"). Interestingly, the flecks of black paint represent an experience between these two. While Stelios, of course, had not personally experienced the death of Patriarch Gregory V, his memory of this event began as an experience, powerful and visceral, of entering a space that appeared to him to have been burned by fire, thus imparting a sense of recent catastrophe. While these different types of memory may seem distinct, they are experienced in the same way for Stelios as he chants: as a visceral sensation of weight.

I speculate that Stelios's description of learning to come to terms with this weight he felt inside the church suggests his learning to negotiate palimpsestic time. At first, the massive amount of memorial information that chanting alone[18] in the church evokes in his mind would overwhelm him, making him feel compelled to "live up" to it in some way. Once he had developed his sense of palimpsestic time, the experience would be recast as a coexistence. While it is true that the church is itself a palimpsestic anchor, the experience of palimpsestic time that Stelios describes is still inextricably connected with his voice and the act of singing.

THE ECHOING PALIMPSEST   357

CONCLUSION: SINGING WITHIN
AN URBAN PALIMPSEST

Stelios's voice is not only an anchor for his own palimpsestic experience. For the Turks his voice is representative of their prehistory, being a member of the ethnicity who inhabited the city before the Turks took it, a remnant of the people who were overcome in 1453. People of the city crowd the bars and taverns where he goes to sing *rebetiko*,[19] even though few residents of Istanbul can understand the language. The knowledge that he is a Patriarchal chanter adds a certain historical patina to their experience of his voice. I have on several occasions noticed people turn to each other as he is singing and say: "Do you know that he is one of the singers at the *Rum Patrikanesi*?"[20] Stelios's voice for them straddles present and past. On the one hand, he walks the earth like one resurrected from another time. He speaks a language that centuries ago was the language of the city; he is connected with the mysterious and ancient Patriarchate, a symbol of the living past; and he is a master of ancient vocal arts, known only to a handful of people in the city today. On the other hand, he speaks Turkish as well as any other well-educated Turkish citizen; he has served in the Turkish military, as is required of all citizens; he drives a motorcycle; and frequently posts things that amuse him on social media with his smartphone. Stelios is, in all of these ways, just like everyone else. These two features of his life—living member of past culture, and everyday Turkish citizen—overlay each other. Simultaneously experiencing both features produces a fleeting sense of past-in-present. Stelios can be seen as an embodiment of the past while at the same time the fact that he is clearly "of the present era" makes one aware of the remoteness of the past. In this way, many of his fellow inhabitants of Istanbul experience through him a sense of past-in-present. It was because of this feeling, of being a sole representative of a long and rich past, that Stelios would sometimes half-jokingly refer to himself as "the last of the Mohicans," recognizing that like the title character in the Cooper novel, he was the last representative of a once thriving community. This is not much of an exaggeration: he and his family are practically the sole Rum inhabitants of a neighborhood that used to be entirely populated by Rum.

In the urban palimpsest Stelios inhabits, he is beset with signs of the end of the days of his culture. When Stelios was a child, Basileos Nikolaides, then *protopsaltis*, selected him from among many other children in the community to be a *kanonarch*. Today, only Stelios's own children, and those of a few other chanters, are being raised as he was: there is no "pool" of possible *kanonarches* to choose from. Stelios complains that the few teenagers left in his community are only interested in the Internet and TV and are not likely candidates. The present state of the Rum community in Istanbul is experienced throughout the city against remnants of its former glory. Aside from monuments like Agia Sophia, or the Byzantine walls that encircle large sections of the city, there exists much more recent evidence of the strength of this community. For example, the skyline of the Fener district is dominated by an impressive crenulated building that served as a school for children of the Rum community up until the 1970s.

Because of these signs of decline, at times I found it amazing that Stelios did not rise every morning with a sense of impending doom. Instead, he seems stubbornly positive. Perhaps this sense of stubbornness is only my projection, as I felt it somehow unreasonable for someone who really is the last of perhaps one hundred generations of a tradition, his entire community having been decimated by political and social upheaval, to be so well adjusted. It seemed to me that the entire mass of the history of his people, and this place, ought to overwhelm him, pinning him down by its weight. Hadn't he spoken to me of a sense of weight? Why does he not feel this strain? How does he find it in himself to saunter down the street jovially singing songs in Greek, to the endless consternation and fascination of his neighborhood? Is he in denial? Is he putting a brave face on things?

Finally, I came to understand that the bleakness of the outlook Stelios and his community faced existed in my teleological gaze, and not in their experience. I do not mean that they are not troubled by their current situation. They are clearly and acutely aware of these things. If one considers Stelios and the Patriarchate as being at the end of a line, or, projects upon them the perspective of linear time, one finds them inescapably near the end of their history. From this perspective, one would expect Stelios to be deeply discouraged both by awareness of the unattainable greatness of the past and by the knowledge of irrecoverable separation from it. It would be a crushing burden to try and live in some way bearing the weight of this history on one's shoulders. However, this is not their experience. While Stelios appears to be part of a small community, a last remnant of a once-powerful empire, he lives and practices in a place where the entire history of the Rum is not only relevant but forms a tangible and ever-present context for everything he does. Stelios, in his characteristically dramatic yet understated way, once expressed this sense perfectly to me.

The continuity of the Patriarchate's chant tradition was cast in doubt by in recent history by people who claimed that one or another of Stelios's predecessors, from Iakovos Naupliotis in the early twentieth century to Thrasyvolos Stanitsas, who was forced away from Istanbul in 1964, were indeed the last of the Patriarchal *psaltes*. This assertion imply that Stelios and the other current Patriarchal *psaltes* are such in name only, not having received the *yphos* from these older generations. This idea offends Stelios. On several occasions he expressed this to me with the emphatic statement, "Stanitsas was not the 'last of the Mohicans,'" meaning that the Patriarchal tradition continued through the *psaltes* that followed Stanitsas and came to him. On one such occasion, I teasingly responded (echoing some of his own humor); "No, it is you. You are the last of the Mohicans." He paused for a moment, suddenly serious. I worried that I had offended him. Then he replied, "I am not last. Being 'last' means being on the bottom, but I am on top. It is like being on top of a mountain. I look down and I can see the entire history of my people; it lifts me up." This explanation strongly reflects an experience of time as an accumulation of events or characteristics. This is, of course, most evident in Stelios's singing.

While Stelios sings monophonic chants alone or as a lead soloist with no accompaniment other than an occasional vocal drone, we find in his experience of chanting not only a rich polyphony but also the sound and memory of a culture and community. There is no gulf between past and present and, therefore, no burden or isolation. Stelios's voice is, then, the palimpsestic anchor upon which experiences may accumulate and interact. The simultaneously internal yet communal nature of the voice serves as a conduit for this experiential understanding. Stelios not only needs technical skill and knowledge of such things as ornamentation or possible interpretations of melodic formulae but also must have the sound of other psaltes resounding in his ear in order for his interpretations to have meaning. When I asked him about his understanding of *yphos*, Ioannis Chariatidis, Stelios's elderly predecessor, simply explained: "My ear is full. What more could I ask for?"

NOTES

1. A *psaltis* (pl. *psaltes*) is a cantor or psalmist of the Orthodox Christian church.
2. This is the tail end of a steep decline that began around the turn of the century. In 1927 there were 100,200 *Rum* in Istanbul (Koglin 2017, 95).
3. Although often seen as an Orthodox Christian counterpart to the Roman Catholic Vatican, the Patriarch, unlike the Pope, is head of the Orthodox Church worldwide only from an administrative standpoint. As a religious leader, he is considered equal to other bishops and Patriarchs worldwide.
4. The term *lampadarios* literally means "lamp lighter," and refers to an ancient function of this post.
5. Technically an assistant to the *lampadarios*, Stelios instead assisted the *protopsaltis*, since the position of first *domestikos* had been left vacant.
6. An *analogion* (pl. *analogia*) is a type of lectern used for chanting.
7. Not unlike linguistic accents, regions have broad *yphi*, that can be further subdivided. For example, there is a Constantinopolitan *yphos* and yet, different neighborhoods also each have their own distinct *yphos*
8. It is important to note that these are not scholarly debates: the academic world, being relatively preoccupied with the study of manuscripts, has remained largely uninterested in this issue.
9. The usage of the term "*vasis*" ("basis") in chant is similar to that of the English "tonic." However, since "tonic" brings with it implications that are peculiar to Western European music and do not apply to "*vasis*," I have chosen to leave it un-translated.
10. The sense of past-in-present engendered by resonance between palimpsestuous layers is unlikely to be peculiar to chant. Multiple layers of remembered musical sounds create tensions and resonances within many of the world's musical traditions. Some forms that seem cyclic from an external perspective, involve an experience of tension with an unheard remembered component. Such forms might be thought of as developing palimpsestically.

    Live performance of music that is well-known on recording might also produce a similar effect. I have often observed this with popular music artists. There is always a certain tension when an artist, performing a song with which their audience is familiar through recordings, must confront the tacit yet viscerally present memory of his or her recorded self onstage.

11. Kyr. Ioannis Chariatidis, the former *lampadarios*, explained to me the process of spending years in the Patriarchal church as "filling his ear".

12. Such palimpsests range from the spectacular to the mundane. Agia Sophia, built in 345 by the emperor Justinian, exemplifies the former. Standing inside this Cathedral-cum-mosque-cum museum, it is difficult not to notice the overlay of Islamic and Christian symbols on a mega scale. Gargantuan frescoes of cherubim (although the western "cherub" was derived from this name, cherubim are awe inspiring figures that consist almost entirely of multiple sets of wings) have emerged, through archeological techniques, from beneath the surface of Islamic inscriptions and abstract designs, forming a massive and awe-inspiring palimpsest. On a more mundane level, one is often aware of layers of history while walking down the street: the thin layer of asphalt often broken to reveal an old cobblestone street just beneath the surface. This in turn is sometimes ripped open to reveal Roman masonry further below.

13. In Turkish, it is called *Buyukada*.

14. A very quaint aspect of life on the island of Halki is that they have banned all automobiles. It is quiet and idyllic. Riding through the steep pine forested slopes of this island either on horseback or in a carriage, it is difficult to believe that one is a ferry ride from a bustling metropolis of seventeen million people.

15. The body of this sixth-century saint has managed to be preserved to the present day and is housed in a copper casket.

16. The *analogia*, or lecterns, of the Patriarchal Church, made of ebony and inlaid with intricate floral patterns in mother of pearl and silver, were made in the sixteenth century.

17. In 1821, when Sultan Mahmud II learned that the Greek revolution had begun and the Greeks had taken Moldavia, he came to the Patriarchate in a rage. He entered the Patriarchal Cathedral of St. George and dragged Patriarch Gregory V out, who had just finished celebrating the liturgy of Pascha ("Easter"), and had him hung from the lintel of the gate of the Patriarchate. He then had twelve more bishops hung from the gate as well.

    After this traumatic event, from which the Rum who remained under Ottoman control would never recover their former power or status (Runciman 1986, 408), a community in mourning painted much of the inside of their own church black. The painting was done in a self-effacing manner. Just before this time the inside of the newly renovated church must have glittered and shone with the light of hundreds, if not thousands of candles reflecting from the gold leaf encrusted iconostas, a thirty-by-eighty foot, intricately carved wooden structure separating the sanctuary from the rest of the church. The painters in mourning used a thick, tarry black paint that dried into a hard crust, preserving their hasty brush-strokes while obscuring almost everything else. Aside from all color having been obscured from this and other structures in the church, many delicate carved details were also obscured by the thick paint. This thick layer of paint was cracked and fissured as the wood beneath its crusty surface expanded and contracted with more than one hundred and fifty seasonal cycles. Stelios described the thick, black, deeply cracked interior of the church as having given him, in his childhood, the impression that it had been "burned by a great fire." Only when Stelios was twenty-five years old was the paint finally removed. In order not to damage the ancient artwork beneath its surface, the paint was not removed by chemical or mechanical means (i.e., sand blasting, electric sanding machines). Rather, it was scraped off with spatulae, knives, and in some cases, chisels. This process, which took nearly one year, while revealing the now-faded gold leaf and elaborately detailed wood carving, resplendent with spectacular mother of pearl inlay that had remained hidden to several generations, was by no means thorough. Gathered like shadows, protected from both light of day and the reach of metal implements by delicate relief carving, are the countless flecks of black paint to which Stelios referred. In these flecks of black paint, the blackened church, while having been removed from direct experience, remains as a memorial layer beneath the surface. The paint, having literally been scraped away has, like ink from a classic palimpsest, proven impossible to remove completely. (Stelios and several assistant *psaltes* communicated the history of the black paint to me as we sat together in the church. I have been unable to ascertain exactly which parts of the church were painted and which were spared but it appears to have been quite extensive).

18. By "alone" I mean singing as a soloist rather than as part of a choir.
19. *Rebetiko* is a popular genre of folk song that has its strong roots in Asia Minor.
20. "Rum Patrikanesi" is the Turkish appellation for the Patriarchate.

WORKS CITED

Dillon, Sarah. 2007. *The Palimpsest: Literature, Criticism, Theory.* London: Bloomsbury Academic.

Ephesios, Petros. 1820. *Neon Anastasimatarion (New Resurrection Hymnal).* Bucharest.

Erol, Merih. 2015. *Greek Orthodox Music in Ottoman Istanbul: Nation and Community in the Era of Reform.* Bloomington: Indiana University Press.

Koglin, D. 2017. *Greek Rebetiko from a Psychocultural Perspective: Same Songs Changing Minds.* New York: Routledge.

Lingas, Alexander. 2003. "Performance Practice and the Politics of Transcribing Byzantine Chant." *Le Chant Byzantin: État Des Recherches. Actes Du Colloque Tenu Du 12 Au 15 Décembre 1996 À l'Abbaye de Royaumont* 6: 56–76.

Psachos, Konstantinos. 1906. "Peri Yphos (Concerning Style)." *Phorminx* 3 (5): 1–3.

Runciman, Steven. 1986. *The Great Church in Captivity: A Study of the Patriarchate of Constantinople from the Eve of the Turkish Conquest to the Greek War of Independence.* Cambridge: Cambridge University Press.

Törne, A. 2015. Recent Studies on the September Pogrom in Istanbul 1955. *Iran and the Caucasus* 19 (4): 403–17.

Vallindras, A. L. 1998. *Anastasimatarion* (Ressurectional Hymnal), 11th ed. Athens: Ekdoseis Zoe.

CHAPTER 17

···

LARYNGEAL DYNAMICS OF *TAAN* GESTURES IN INDIAN CLASSICAL SINGING

···

NANDHAKUMAR RADHAKRISHNAN,
RONALD C. SCHERER, AND
SANTANU BANDYOPADHYAY

INTRODUCTION

···

THE music of India comprises some of the oldest traditions practiced in the world. "Classical" music in India can be broadly classified into two genres: Hindustani music, also called North Indian classical music, and Carnatic music (*Karnataka sangeeta*), the South Indian tradition. Both prominently feature voice as a primary melodic instrument. *Khayal*, the current singing style of Hindustani music, evolved from *Dhrupad*, a form that was dominant between the fifteenth and eighteenth centuries (though it has experienced a revival in recent years). The former style was stricter in rendering melody, while *Khayal* is a more highly improvised and embellished form that allows singers greater freedom to modulate their singing in order to please their audience. In *Khayal*, singers demonstrate their musical and expressive skill within the melodic system, called *raga*. This system includes dozens of melodic modes (also called *ragas*), each with its own given pitches, prescribed ordering, and expected expressive practices. But across *ragas*, one of the most significant of these expressive practices is a modulation in pitch known as *taan*. This rapid pitch-changing maneuver, a quick drop followed by a rise that is controlled voluntarily by the singer, is used to expand a *raga* and also to glide between the notes involved in the piece. *Taan* is a significant part in any vocal performance. The rate and extent of pitch fluctuations usually increase throughout a performance, and the singer impresses the audience with these gestures during the climax of their concert.

It is as significant to Hindustani singing as vibrato is in Western classical singing. Vibrato has been widely researched; however, *taan* has not received much attention from the perspective of physiology and aerodynamics. A close study of *taan* production, like the study of vibrato, could be instrumental to the understanding of human vocal capabilities and culturally bound aesthetic preferences. This chapter reports acoustic, aerodynamic, and glottographic aspects of *taan* gestures rendered at different levels of rate, pitch, loudness, and extent of fluctuation by an elite singer and teacher of Hindustani vocal music. The results are reported for two separate styles of *taan*, each performed in a different context: one in a pedagogical setting, and the other in performance. Pedagogical *taan* gestures are those used by the singer as a teacher to demonstrate technique during vocal training, and the other style is produced during professional performance. A detailed description on pedagogical *taan* has been reported elsewhere (Radhakrishnan, Scherer, and Bandyopadhyay 2011); this chapter will discuss both pedagogical *taan* and performance *taan* in detail to broaden the analysis of expressive vocal gestures.

METHODOLOGY

In order to understand the basics of the *taan* gesture, an exploratory research design was selected to record the subject rendering both pedagogical and performance *taan*.

Subject

The subject for this study was coauthor Santanu Bandyopadhyay, a forty-five-year-old male Hindustani singer and teacher. Bandyopadhyay is a well-known elite singer and a successor of the Bishnupur *gharana* tradition.[1] He had been trained for more than thirty years under the tutelage of his father and grandfather. His ancestors were followers of Tansen, the head court musician of the Mughal Emperor Akbar (1543–1605). As a teacher, he conducts classes on vocal music for many students.

Instrumentation

A multisignal voice recording approach was used for this study (Radhakrishnan and Scherer 2003). Acoustic signals were recorded using a microphone (AKG C 480 B, AKG Acoustics, Austria) and preamplifier (APHEX 107, APHEX Systems, Sun Valley, CA). A distance of 0.5 m was maintained between the mouth and microphone. The MSIF-2 aerodynamic system from Glottal Enterprises (Syracuse, NY) was used to record airflow and oral air pressures during the recordings. The system includes a circumferentially vented face mask of clear plastic. Electroglottographic (EGG) signals—which are thought to reflect the change in contact area between the two vocal folds during phonation—were obtained using the electroglottograph (Scherer, Druker, and Titze 1988 and Hampala et al. 2016) from Pentax Medicals (Lincoln Park, NJ). These signals were recorded to an eight-channel digital audio tape recorder (PC208AX; Sony, Japan) and later digitized to computer files using a 16-bit analog-to-digital converter (DI-720; Dataq Instruments, Akron, OH). WindaqPro (Dataq Instruments) was used to digitize and display these signals.

Recording Protocol

The recording was made in a sound-treated booth (6x6x8 ft) and the subject was vocally warmed up before the session. The subject was asked to maintain a specific mouth-to-microphone distance (0.5 m). The subject held the mask to his face. The mask seal was inspected often to avoid any leakage of air between the mask rim and the face. The smoothly produced /pʌː pʌː pʌː/ sequence technique was used for aerodynamic analysis (Rothenberg 1973). EGG electrodes were placed on the subject's neck over the thyroid cartilage laminae at a location that provided strong EGG signals. The electrodes were secured in place using a Velcro band. In order to obtain signals that were reliable, sufficient training was given to the subject to maintain mask-to-face contact. In addition, the EGG electrodes were periodically monitored for their correct position. All these signals were monitored to assure they are recorded appropriately. The subject demonstrated the pedagogical *taan* productions from slower to faster rates. Given that a vocal performance incorporating *taan* gestures involves changes in pitch, loudness, *taan* gesture rate, Fo extent, emotional content, and other subtleties, the "performance *taan*" study was implemented to experimentally control a few of them. The singer was asked to vary loudness, *taan* gesture rate, and laryngeal obstruction levels while performing *taan* gestures on a constant note (G3), except for pitch variation, where the singer demonstrated *taan* gestures above and below the constant note. The laryngeal obstruction technique used by the subject will be shown later to be a subjective reference to extent of pitch fluctuation.

Analysis

Acoustic analyses of the microphone recordings were performed using Praat freeware (http://www.fon.hum.uva.nl/praat/) (Boersma and Weenink, The Netherlands) and custom software Sigplot written in Matlab code.

Acoustic

Specific locations on the Fo contour of *taan* utterances were selected for Fo analyses and the same time locations were chosen for glottal flow and EGG analysis as well. The data obtained from Praat were plotted using MSExcel (Microsoft Office) for further analysis and display.

Aerodynamic Analysis: Glottal Flow

TF32 (Milenkovic, CSPEECH) was used for inverse filtering the wideband flow channel that was converted to .wav files using Sigplot. Five consecutive glottal flow cycles were chosen at each analysis location of the *taan* gesture for glottal flow analysis. The AC flow and open quotient OQ were obtained for each cycle. It is noted that the AC flow is the measure of volume flow between the maximum value in a glottal cycle to the minimum value in the same glottal cycle, that is, the peak-to-peak modulation of glottal airflow due to the dynamic motion of the vocal folds. The open quotient OQ is the amount of time there is airflow through the glottis between the membranous vocal folds during the glottal cycle, divided by the period for that glottal cycle.

Aerodynamic Analysis: Subglottal Pressure and Average Flow

The intraoral air pressure and wideband flow channels were used to measure the estimated subglottal pressures and average airflows, respectively. The oral air pressure during the /p/ closure for each /pʌ/ was used to estimate the subglottal pressure during the initiation of the subsequent *taan* utterances. The pressure peaks were manually identified. The airflow half way between the pressure peaks was taken as the location to obtain the average flow.

Glottographic Analysis: EGG Pulse Width

The EGG waveform was trimmed to the same time locations as the glottal flow. The waveform shifted from baseline, creating a DC shift, probably when the larynx moved during voicing. Using Sigplot, a cycle-to-cycle fit was used to remove the DC shifts of the EGG waveform. The software calculated the electroglottographic widths EGGW25 and EGGW50, which are EGG pulse widths at 25 percent and 50 percent of the EGG signal waveform height. EGGW has been shown to be related to glottal adduction where the larger the value, the greater the glottal adduction (Scherer et al. 1995).

RESULTS

The Fo contour is used to describe the melodic pitch structure of the *taan* gestures. The structure of the pedagogical and performance *taan* gestures proved to be different. Performance *taan* gestures were relatively sinusoidal compared to their pedagogical counterpart, which had a flat portion between two peaks. (Please view Figures 17.2 and 17.9 for comparison.) This section will report the two groups, pedagogical and performance *taan*, individually for clarity.

Pedagogical *Taan* Gestures

These are basic *taan* gestures that the subject uses during student training. The training protocol includes production of *taan* at a slower rate. Once the student is comfortable in executing this gesture, the rate is increased to the next level. The subject believes that voluntary control of *taan* production at different rates will bring an effect in extent as well.

Frequency Contour

Figure 17.1 shows a series of *taan* gestures, and based on Figure 17.2, a single *taan* gesture can be defined as having a falling and then a rising portion, with a subsequent relatively flat portion in the Fo contour. The Fo fall and rise is named the "*taan* dip" and the subsequent portion past the dip is named the "superior surface."

Rate and Extent

The *period* of one *taan* gesture is the duration between the Fo data point at the beginning of the dip of the *taan* gesture and the beginning of the dip of the following *taan* gesture. The corresponding *frequency* was obtained by inverting the period expressed in seconds. The *Fo extent* of a particular *taan* gesture was measured as an average of the semitone

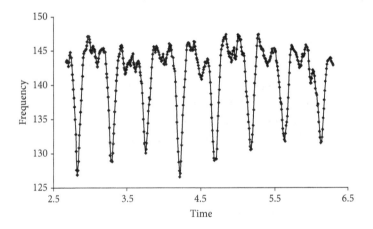

FIGURE 17.1 Fundamental frequency trace of a series of *taan* gestures.

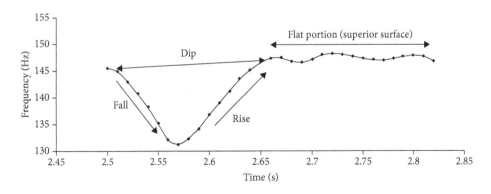

FIGURE 17.2 One *taan* gesture showing the fall, rise, dip, and the superior surface.

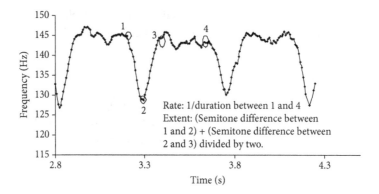

FIGURE 17.3 Rate and extent measurements at each *taan* gesture.

difference between the frequency point at the beginning of the dip (point 1 in Figure 17.3) and the lowest frequency point of the dip (point 2 in Figure 17.3), and the semitone difference between the lowest frequency point of the dip (point 2) and the frequency point at the end of the dip (point 3 in Figure 17.3).

Slope Measures

The two *slopes*, left and right, are the descending slope and the ascending slope of each *taan* dip. The semitone difference between the data point just after 1 and just before 2 in Figure 17.3 was divided by the duration (in seconds) between those two points to get the negative *left slope* of the *taan* gesture. Similarly, the semitone difference between the data point just after 2 and just before 3 was divided by the duration between those two points (in seconds) to get the positive *right slope*.

Duration Measures

The duration between points 1 and 3 of Figure 17.3 was termed the *dip duration* (Dd) and the duration between points 3 and 4 of Figure 17.3 was termed the *superior surface duration* (SSd). The sum of these two durations gives the period of that particular *taan* gesture (the duration between points 1 and 4). The *superior surface quotient* (SSQ) was determined by dividing the superior surface duration SSd by the *taan* gesture period.

Primary and Secondary Modulations

The superior surface was not necessarily flat, as can be seen in Figure 17.3. The dip of the *taan* gesture was considered to be the *primary modulation* and the alternations on the superior surface were considered to be *secondary modulations*. The frequency content of the *taan* gestures was obtained by using a low-frequency amplitude spectrum analysis.

Correlations between Variables: Taan *Gesture Rate and F0 Extent*

Across the six rates voluntarily demonstrated for the pedagogical *taan*, the singer varied the average rate of the *taan* gestures between 1.65 Hz and 3.41 Hz, and the extent from 1.6 ST to 2.2 ST (see Figure 17.4 and Table 17.1 for these results and the other results given

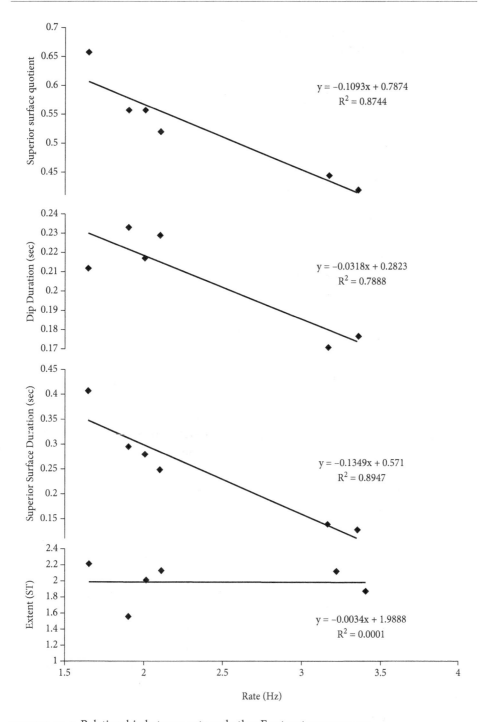

FIGURE 17.4 Relationship between rate and other Fo structure measures.

Table 17.1 Fundamental frequency structure of pedagogical *taan* utterances. (SSd = Superior surface duration, Dd = Dip duration, SSq = Superior surface quotient.)

Taan		Rate	Extent	Left slope	Right slope	SSd	Dd	SSq
Utterance#		(Hz)	(ST)	(ST/s)	(ST/s)	(sec)	(sec)	
1	Average	1.65	2.21	31.62	−18.67	0.41	0.21	0.6
	St.Dev	0.13	0.17	6.42	4.32	0.03	0.02	0.02
2	Average	1.91	1.55	14.49	−16.29	0.29	0.23	0.56
	St.Dev	0.22	0.41	4.28	4.15	0.05	0.04	0.07
3	Average	2.02	2.01	21.63	−22.71	0.28	0.22	0.56
	St.Dev	0.20	0.31	4.30	3.65	0.06	0.02	0.07
4	Average	2.12	2.13	24.78	−25.96	0.25	0.23	0.52
	St.Dev	0.07	0.23	7.67	4.44	0.03	0.01	0.03
5	Average	3.22	2.12	26.94	−25.00	0.14	0.17	0.45
	St.Dev	0.16	0.18	11.14	2.43	0.02	0.02	0.05
6	Average	3.41	1.87	26.47	−23.84	0.13	0.18	0.42
	St.Dev	0.36	0.34	6.68	6.02	0.03	0.03	0.08

in this section). The correlation between the averages of the rates and the extents of the *taan* utterances across the six rates was negligible (r = 0.01). This suggests that the Fo extent of the pedagogical *taan* gestures was not related to the rate. Indeed, the extent was relatively constant (about 2 ST) across rate if the lowest extent were excluded. It might seem logical to expect the extent to decrease with rate increase because of less time for the Fo dip, but this was interestingly not the case. This suggests that the extent is a highly controlled element of the *taan* gesture relative to the training of the gesture.

Taan *Gesture Rate, SSd, Dd, SSq, and Slopes*

An increase in the rate of the *taan* gestures led to a decrease in the superior surface duration SSd. The relationship between the rate and SSd was negative and strong (r = −0.945). While the rate increased by a factor of 2, the SSd decreased by a factor of approximately 3 (410 ms to 130 ms). The dip duration (Dd) also decreased with an increase in rate, but only by 14 percent (approximately 210 ms to 180 ms). The negative correlation of Dd with rate was also strong (r = −0.888). These results suggest that the dynamic dip duration reduced but was relatively preserved, whereas the rate increased primarily by decreasing the less dynamic superior surface duration following the dip. The superior surface quotient (SSq = SSd/period) combines the relationship among rate, SSd, and Dd. SSq decreased by 36 percent (66 percent to 42 percent) as the rate increased, with a high negative correlation (r = −0.935).

The left and right slopes increased rapidly negatively and positively, respectively, from about 1.6 Hz to 2.2 Hz, and then maintained slopes approximately constant above 2.2 Hz (see the piece-wise fits to the data in Figure 17.5, where the piece-wise fits were placed

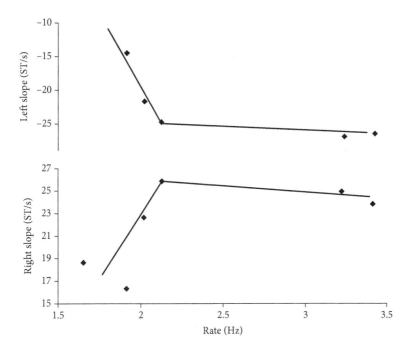

FIGURE 17.5 Rate and slope measures.

"by eye," not by regression analysis). Thus, the pedagogical *taan* slopes are more sensitive to changes in rate when the rate is relatively slow. For faster rates, the Fo rate of change reaches a maximum of approximately + 23–26 ST/s.

Fo *Extent and Various Slope Measures*

Both the left and right slopes tended to become steeper with an increase in Fo extent of the *taan* gesture (r = 0.856, r =0.55, respectively; Figure 17.6). The relationship between the extent and the slope was stronger for the left slope. Given that the *taan* dip has a V-like shape, if the extent of the dip, or height of the V, increases, without change of duration, then the slopes of the two sides logically should increase. This is evident here, as shown in Figure 17.6.

The correlations between the Fo extent and the measures SSd, Dd, and the SSq were very low (Figure 17.7), suggesting negligible functional relationship. Thus, the primary covariable with Fo extent was the left slope of the *taan* gesture (Figure 17.6).

Secondary Modulations

The superior surface had secondary Fo modulations. A low-frequency amplitude spectrum analysis was performed on two of the *taan* utterances (with rates of 2.01 Hz and 1.65 Hz). Figure 17.8 shows the analysis, where the primary spectral frequency of the *taan* gesture is the highest component and corresponds to the *taan* rate, with visible additional components near integer multiples of the *taan* frequency. The secondary modulations of the *taan* gesture appear to be related to the higher frequencies that appear as

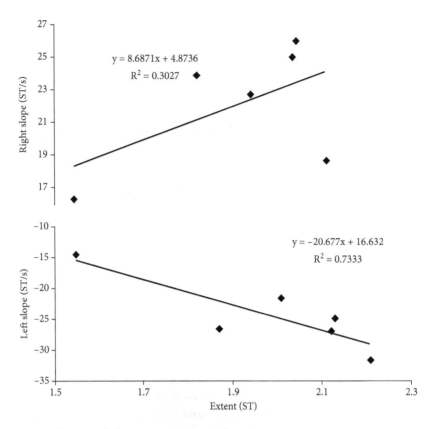

FIGURE 17.6 Extent and slope measures.

near multiples of the primary frequency. The *taan* gestures of Figure 17.1 also suggest that a multiple (x2) of the *taan* frequency is strongly related to the secondary modulations due to the short dips approximately halfway between the negative peaks.

Aerodynamic Analysis of Pedagogical Taan Utterances

Aerodynamic and glottographic analyses were performed on two pedagogical *taan* utterances, a slower (2.02 Hz) and a faster (3.41 Hz) *taan*. Table 17.2 shows the average aerodynamic measures AC-flow and open quotient from the inverse filtered glottal flow signal. The measures were taken at higher and lower notes of the *taan* utterances. The lower note corresponds to location 2 in Figure 17.3 at the bottom of the dip, and the higher note was equidistant between points 3 and 4 of Figure 17.3. The average AC flows at the higher notes were less than the average AC-flow values at the lower notes by approximately 28 percent for the slower rate and 10 percent for the faster rate. However, the average open quotient values were nearly the same for the higher and lower notes for both rates. The greater AC flow for the Fo near the bottom of the *taan* dip, with nearly constant open quotients, suggests greater subglottal pressure at the lower note may have produced the increased flow. Increase in subglottal pressure for the lower portion of the *taan* gesture should tent to make the lower portion also louder, perhaps giving greater

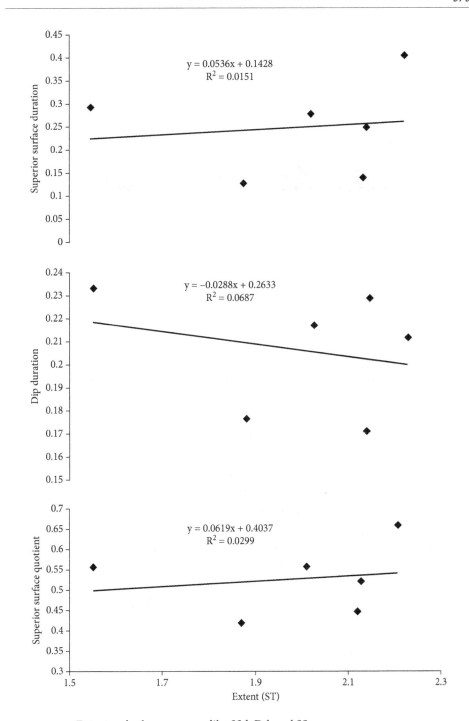

FIGURE 17.7 Extent and other measures like SSd, Dd, and SSq.

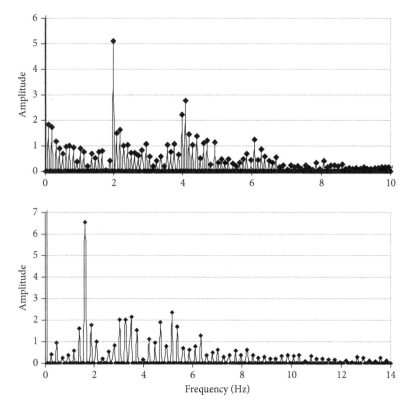

FIGURE 17.8 Low-frequency amplitude spectrum of the secondary modulations.

presence to the *taan* gesture itself. Table 17.2 also indicates that the AC flows were higher for the faster rate, and the open quotients lower, suggesting that both adduction and subglottal pressure may have increased for the faster *taan* gestures compared to the slower *taan* gestures. The lack of change of the EGGW values from slower to faster rates suggests lack of full compatibility of OQ and EGGW to render adduction implications.

Discussion for Pedagogical Taan

The results of this study have helped to establish basic descriptors of the *taan* gesture relative to the pedagogical approach of its instruction by a well-known teacher. Teaching *taan* production using a progression of increasing *taan* rates is a primary pedagogical approach by this teacher, so rate change effects were explored. The rate was varied voluntarily by the subject and coauthor Santanu Bandyopadhyay. According to Bandyopadhyay, the first exposure to *taan* gestures for a student should be slower rate of production and kinesthetic perception of an obstruction in the glottal area. Accuracy of this production is more important than speed, hence the focus on a slower rate as the preferred method of teaching. Acquisition of a slower rate will then take a student to faster rates. Rate did not affect the semitone extent of the *taan* gesture, suggesting that extent is robust and will be kept relatively independent or unaffected during *taan* training.

Table 17.2 Summary of the slower and faster *taan* utterance measures obtained from aerodynamic and kinematic analyses

		Slower Rate (2.02 Hz)		Faster Rate (3.41 Hz)	
FO		AC-flow(cc/s)	OQ	AC-flow(cc/s)	OQ
Higher	Average	254.81	0.72	387.73	0.46
	St.Dev	28.11	0.04	14.92	0.01
Lower	Average	353.70	0.69	428.62	0.47
	St.Dev	76.03	0.04	29.83	0.03
		EGGW25	EGGW50	EGGW25	EGGW50
Higher	Average	0.64	0.50	0.61	0.52
	St.Dev	0.04	0.04	0.03	0.02
Lower	Average	0.64	0.53	0.61	0.52
	St.Dev	0.05	0.05	0.02	0.01

Increasing the rate of the *taan* gestures was attributed to a decrease in the duration of the superior surface primarily and the dip secondarily. This suggests that the dip duration is also a more prominent and robust feature of the *taan* gesture, and the duration of the superior surface is the controlling variable for rate change. Change in extent across rate, although small (the range was about one-third ST, from 1.87 to 2.21 on average, Table 17.1) of the *taan* gesture was associated with the descending and ascending slopes, where an increase in Fo (ST) extent increased both the descending and ascending slopes, although this was more logical than actual, given the data scatter of Figure 17.6. The subject reflected that changing extent was not the focus when consciously changing *taan* rate.

In summary, pedagogical *taan* gestures are voluntarily produced and have a distinct acoustic structure consisting of an Fo lowering and rising (the *taan* dip) followed by a superior surface containing secondary modulations. The rate of *taan* gestures is primarily controlled by the duration of the superior surface. The Fo extent in semitones is maintained relatively the same for any rate. The dip duration and the extent are distinctive characteristics of *taan* gestures. The descending and ascending slopes increase with Fo extent. The secondary modulations on the superior surface portion of the *taan* gesture appear to contain frequencies that are multiples of the rate of the *taan* gestures (primary modulations). The pedagogical *taan* is the first step for a student to understand the production and control of *taan* gestures. The AC glottal flow, open quotient, and EGGW results suggest the hypothesis that subglottal pressure plays a significant role in the change of Fo and rate, increasing when Fo lowers or rate increases.

This study appears to be the first report of physiological aspects of Indian classical singing. The results serve as a platform for research on *performance taan* gestures, which will be described in the following section. It is noted that the results pertain to one instructor who is also an elite performer, and different results may be expected for other equally talented individuals.

Performance *Taan* Gestures

The subject was asked to demonstrate *taan* gestures as they would be rendered in a typical performance. In performance *taan* gestures are usually rendered at different levels of pitch, rate, extent, and loudness that was demanded by the *Raga*, emotions of the piece, and experience of the performer. *Taan* gestures also change in these parameters throughout the performance, usually faster and louder at the end.

For this study, the four tasks that the singer varied during performance singing included pitch variation, loudness variation, rate variation, and obstruction variation. For example, during the loudness variation task, the singer was asked to demonstrate performance *taan* gestures at the different loudness levels very soft, soft, normal, and loud.

The measures analyzed for pedagogical *taan* and subglottal pressure during the initiation of these gestures will be used to describe the voice production during the aforementioned tasks.

Fundamental Frequency

With respect to acoustic structure, performance related *taan* gestures had some similarities but yet were noticeably different from the pedagogical *taan* gestures used by the teacher to train students (Figure 17.9). They had a similar dip in pitch fluctuation but did not have a superior surface duration (SSd).

In the pitch variation task, the singer performed *taan* utterances at five different pitch levels around his comfortable level. The different levels are designated as comfortable pitch (mid pitch), 8 STs lower than the comfortable pitch (–8 ST), 4 STs lower than the

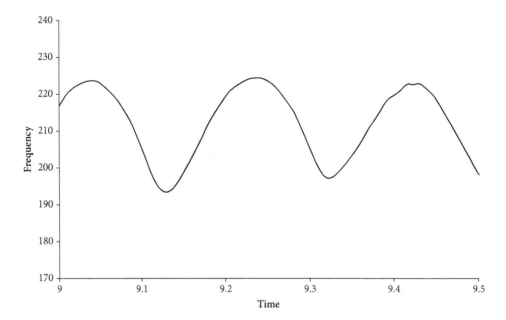

FIGURE 17.9 Dip and peak.

comfortable pitch (–4 ST), 4 ST higher than the comfortable pitch (+4 ST), and 8 ST higher than the comfortable pitch (+8 ST). Statistical analyses indicate the following for the Fo structure, aerodynamic, and glottographic measures.

TAAN GESTURE RATE

In general, the *taan* rate for the above-mid pitches for the performance *taan* were faster than for the other pitches (Table 17.3, Figure 17.10). Significant difference was seen between the slowest rate (occurring for the –4 ST level) and all other rates. The highest rate was for the +4 ST frequency level and was statistically significantly different from all other pitches except + 8 ST higher. Interestingly the lowest and highest rates were for the –4 ST and +4 ST from the comfortable pitch, suggesting greatest sensitivity to rate when pitch is not far from the comfortable (mid) level.

FO EXTENT

Overall, the Fo extent (in STs) for the above-mid pitches was less than for the other three pitches. The mid pitch significantly had the greatest Fo extent compared to all other pitch levels except for the –8 ST level, suggesting that the extent and rate values were essentially inversely related (except for the –4 ST lower condition) (Table 17.3, Figure 17.10). That is, the rates were higher and extents lower for the two highest pitches, and the rates were lower and extents higher for the other pitches, as if there were a production tradeoff between rate and extent (which seems logical; a faster rate provides less time to create the extent).

TAAN GESTURE LEFT AND RIGHT SLOPE

Consistent with *taan* extent, the smallest slope values were for the two highest pitches (Table 17.3, Figure 17.10), suggesting that for those pitches, not only was the extent less

Table 17.3 Averages of the fundamental frequency structure measures during pitch variation

		Rate	Extent	Left Slope	Right slope
		Hz	ST	ST/s	ST/s
8 ST Lower	Average	5.43	2.09	−25.76	20.52
	St.Dev	0.27	0.24	4.48	2.78
4 ST Lower	Average	5.07	1.63	−18.76	14.94
	St.Dev	0.22	0.23	4.07	2.80
Comfortable	Average	5.34	2.22	−26.44	20.96
	St.Dev	0.25	0.20	2.94	1.84
4 ST Lower	Average	5.86	1.16	−14.54	12.82
	St.Dev	0.31	0.20	2.74	2.05
8 ST Lower	Average	5.61	1.27	−15.63	13.17
	St.Dev	0.21	0.18	2.46	1.95

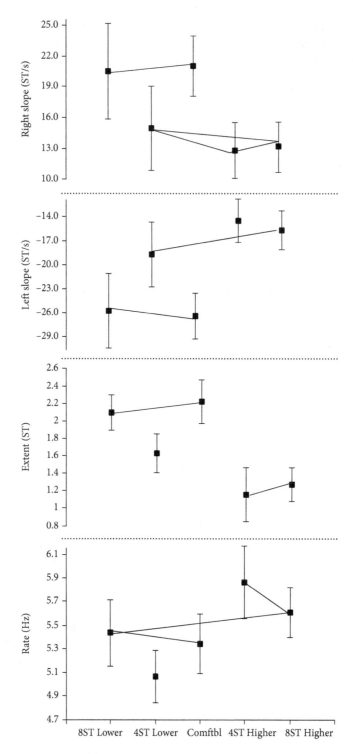

FIGURE 17.10 Fundamental frequency structure: pitch variation as the independent variable (the connected levels did not have statistically significant differences).

but also the Fo speed was less to reach that extent. For the other three (lower) pitches, both the slopes and extents were greater, suggesting the need to move Fo faster when there was greater Fo extent to reach.

AERODYNAMIC ANALYSIS

Aerodynamic analysis was performed at the lowest note (the lowest portion of the *taan* "dip") and the highest note (the "peak" of the Fo variation; Figure 17.9) of the performance *taan* gesture. The aerodynamic measures were compared at each pitch level (Table 17.4, Figure 17.11) and yielded relatively consistent trends. As pitch increased, so did subglottal pressure (tripling from the lowest to highest pitch), AC flow (doubling), and MFDR (tripling, negatively), with corresponding decreases in open quotient (reducing by about 30 percent) (Table 17.4, Figure 17.11). For the comfortable mid pitch, the MFDR was more negative for the Fo dip pitch (filled symbol in Figure 17.11) within the *taan* gesture compared to the peak Fo (unfilled symbol in Figure 17.11), also for which the open quotient and AC flow were lower for the peak pitch. The results suggest greater adduction for the lower pitch in the *taan* gesture with a significant influence of subglottal

Table 17.4 Aerodynamic measures: pitch variation task

Pitch and note level		AC-flow	MFDR	OQ	Sub.Pressure
		(cc/s)	L/s/s		cm-w
8ST Lower-higher	Average	320.74	−440.93	0.50	9.75
	St.Dev	52.18	82.04	0.01	1.53
8ST Lower-lower	Average	355.27	−451.06	0.51	
	St.Dev	65.73	117.42	0.02	
4ST Lower-higher	Average	314.88	−593.78	0.57	9.71
	St.Dev	36.63	61.23	0.03	1.53
4ST Lower-lower	Average	368.81	−642.11	0.51	
	St.Dev	39.49	81.98	0.02	
Comfortable - higher	Average	360.04	−903.36	0.49	13.65
	St.Dev	45.08	117.47	0.02	1.27
Comfortable - lower	Average	491.97	−1149.30	0.54	
	St.Dev	38.24	136.89	0.03	
4ST Higher-higher	Average	440.84	−1117.10	0.43	17.62
	St.Dev	42.66	148.81	0.01	1.5
4ST Higher-lower	Average	479.07	−1165.10	0.47	
	St.Dev	44.65	111.60	0.01	
8ST Higher-higher	Average	611.05	−1672.82	0.37	24.74
	St.Dev	48.82	164.20	0.02	0.00
8ST Higher-lower	Average	634.66	−1609.49	0.40	
	St.Dev	18.44	74.28	0.02	

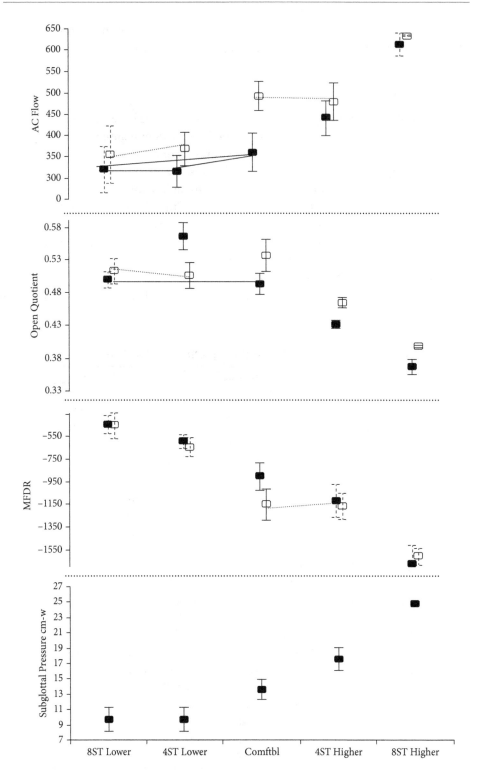

FIGURE 17.11 Aerodynamic measures: pitch variation. Graphs with solid and empty squares indicate measures at higher note and lower note of the *taan* gestures, respectively. (Dotted error bars and dotted and solid lines indicate data that were not statistically different.)

pressure. These findings point out the complex relation among pitch, subglottal pressure, MFDR, open quotient, and AC flow (Table 17.4, Figure 17.11).

GLOTTOGRAPHIC MEASURES

Similar to the aerodynamic measures, the EGGW50 values at the peak Fo and dip Fo of each *taan* gesture were compared across sung pitches for performance *taan* (Table 17.5, Figure 17.12). In general, the EGGW50 increased in magnitude for pitch levels at both the extremes, 8ST lower and higher. This is consistent with the reduced open quotient OQ data in Figure 17.11 for the higher pitches, but inconsistent with the increased OQ values for the lower pitches in Figure 17.11.

Loudness Variation

In the loudness variation task for the performance *taan* (Table 17.6, Figure 17.13), the singer performed *taan* utterances at four different loudness levels, a very soft level, soft level, normal loudness level, and loud level. The pitch was held constant at G3 (*c.* 262 Hz). Statistical analyses indicate the following for the fundamental frequency structure, aerodynamic, and glottographic measures.

Table 17.5 Kinematic measures: pitch variation

Pitch and note level		EGGW25	EGGW50	EGGW75
8ST Lower-higher	Average	0.62	0.50	0.37
	St.Dev	0.02	0.03	0.02
8ST Lower-lower	Average	0.66	0.54	0.38
	St.Dev	0.03	0.02	0.03
4ST Lower-higher	Average	0.59	0.46	0.33
	St.Dev	0.03	0.02	0.03
4ST Lower-lower	Average	0.61	0.48	0.35
	St.Dev	0.02	0.02	0.02
Comfortable - higher	Average	0.62	0.49	0.25
	St.Dev	0.01	0.02	0.02
Comfortable - lower	Average	0.59	0.47	0.26
	St.Dev	0.03	0.02	0.02
4ST Higher-higher	Average	0.61	0.48	0.33
	St.Dev	0.01	0.01	0.02
4ST Higher-lower	Average	0.63	0.50	0.24
	St.Dev	0.05	0.03	0.04
8ST Higher-higher	Average	0.75	0.57	0.33
	St.Dev	0.07	0.06	0.10
8ST Higher-lower	Average	0.64	0.52	0.36
	St.Dev	0.04	0.02	0.06

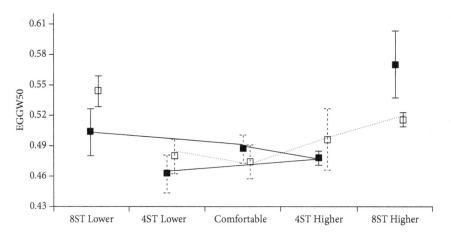

FIGURE 17.12 EGGW50 at higher and lower notes of the five pitch levels. Solid and empty squares indicate measures at higher note and lower note of *taan* gestures, respectively. (Dotted error bars and dotted and solid lines indicate data that were not statistically different.)

Table 17.6 Fundamental frequency structure: loudness variation task

Loudness		Rate	Extent	Left slope	Right slope
		Hz	ST	ST/s	ST/s
Very soft	Average	5.21	1.01	−11.50	9.86
	St.Dev	0.32	0.18	3.00	1.78
Soft	Average	5.22	1.13	−12.31	11.44
	St.Dev	0.33	0.08	1.52	1.36
Normal	Average	5.20	2.07	−24.44	19.35
	St.Dev	0.24	0.26	4.03	2.45
Loud	Average	5.55	2.29	−30.71	21.98
	St.Dev	0.26	0.40	8.34	3.65

TAAN GESTURE RATE

The *taan* rate for the loud level was significantly faster than for each of the other loudness levels (Table 17.6, Figure 17.13). The other three levels were not significantly different from each other, suggesting that increasing loudness from soft to normal did not affect *taan* rate. This suggests that subglottal pressure is most likely not the dominant variable controlling *taan* rate.

FO EXTENT

The very soft and the soft levels were not significantly different in Fo extent. Similarly, the normal and the loud levels were not significantly different. However, the normal and the loud levels were significantly greater (about double) in extent in STs than the

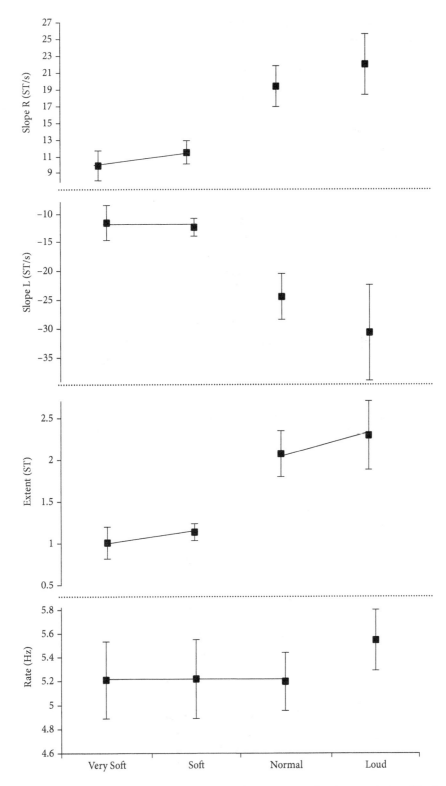

FIGURE 17.13 Fundamental frequency structure of *taan* gestures: loudness variation. (The levels connected did not have statistically significant difference.)

other two levels. This suggests that Fo extent may be related to subglottal pressure (Table 17.6, Figure 17.13).

TAAN GESTURE LEFT AND RIGHT SLOPES

The right and left slopes followed the Fo extent strongly, increasing when Fo extent increased (Table 17.6, Figure 17.13). The right and left slope values increased by a factor of approximately 2.5 as loudness increased. Again, the slope values therefore also may be highly dependent on the subglottal pressure (the variable most closely aligned with loudness level).

AERODYNAMIC

Results show trends for an increase in subglottal pressure (doubled) and AC-flow (tripled) along with the increase in loudness (very soft to loud) (Table 17.7, Figure 17.14). The open quotient decreased from 0.75 to 0.4 as the loudness increased and this was one of the strongest correlates for this task. This was complemented by the increase (negatively) in MFDR values (by more than a factor of 4).

GLOTTOGRAPHIC MEASURES

The EGGW50 increased significantly as the singer increased his loudness level and are in agreement with the decrease in the open quotient as loudness increases; however, there was no significant difference between the peak and dip of the *taan* gestures levels (Table 17.8, Figure 17.15).

Table 17.7 Aerodynamic measures: loudness variation task

Loudness		AC-flow	MFDR	OQ	Sub.Pressure
		Cc/s	L/s/s		cm-w
Verysoft-higher	Average	207.26	−240.74	0.73	6.29
	St.Dev	49.99	53.89	0.08	0.84
Verysoft-lower	Average	208.84	−238.24	0.75	
	St.Dev	22.10	22.22	0.07	
Soft-higher	Average	255.04	−433.86	0.54	10.00
	St.Dev	37.05	83.50	0.05	1.10
Soft-lower	Average	301.98	−544.81	0.55	
	St.Dev	52.35	123.11	0.03	
Normal-higher	Average	437.58	−1054.50	0.48	13.81
	St.Dev	51.22	129.37	0.01	0.82
Normal-lower	Average	563.40	−1276.53	0.52	
	St.Dev	59.52	190.11	0.02	
Loud-higher	Average	520.77	−1322.35	0.42	13.36
	St.Dev	108.73	361.91	0.04	0.25
Loud-lower	Average	574.99	−1387.40	0.41	
	St.Dev	91.99	345.77	0.03	

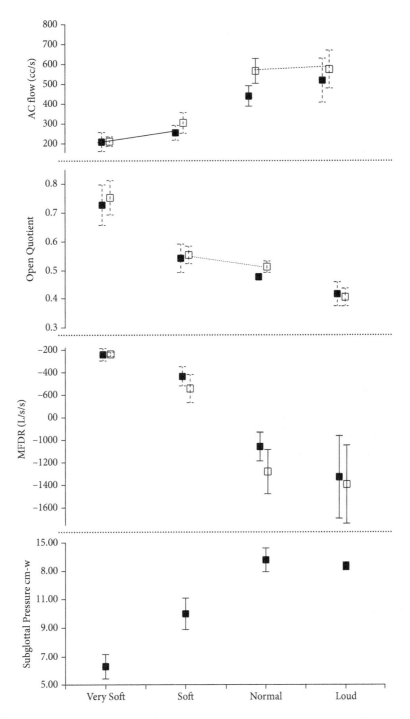

FIGURE 17.14 Aerodynamic measures: loudness variation. Graphs with solid and empty squares indicate measures at higher note and lower note of *taan* gestures, respectively. (Dotted error bars and dotted and solid lines indicate data that were not statistically different.)

Table 17.8 Kinematic measures: loudness variation task

Loudness		EGGW25	EGGW50	EGGW75
Verysoft-higher	Average	0.38	0.30	0.21
	St.Dev	0.02	0.02	0.01
Verysoft-lower	Average	0.39	0.30	0.21
	St.Dev	0.02	0.01	0.01
Soft-higher	Average	0.53	0.40	0.24
	St.Dev	0.02	0.02	0.01
Soft-lower	Average	0.51	0.39	0.21
	St.Dev	0.02	0.02	0.01
Normal-higher	Average	0.61	0.49	0.25
	St.Dev	0.02	0.02	0.02
Normal-lower	Average	0.59	0.47	0.27
	St.Dev	0.07	0.03	0.07
Loud-higher	Average	0.65	0.52	0.29
	St.Dev	0.05	0.04	0.10
Loud-lower	Average	0.76	0.51	0.29
	St.Dev	0.04	0.02	0.02

Rate Variation

In the rate variation task, the singer performed *taan* utterances at five different levels of rate: very slow, slow, normal, fast, and very fast. Statistical analyses indicate the following for the fundamental frequency structure, aerodynamic, and glottographic measures. As Figure 17.16 indicates, the actual *taan* gesture rate increased monotonically from 4 to about 7 per second, as intended (Table 17.9).

FO EXTENT

In general, Fo extent increased with rate, and the fast rate was significantly greater in extent than any of the other levels. The very slow rate had a lower extent value than each of the other levels (Table 17.9, Figure 17.16). In contrast, for the pedagogical *taan*, the extent did not tend to increase as the rate increased (Figure 17.4), suggesting that the training of *taan* includes a more rigorous orientation to extent control. It is noted, however, that the pedagogical *taan* rate ranged from about 1.6 to 3.5, whereas the performance *taan* was in a higher range, 4 to 7 Hz.

TAAN GESTURE SLOPES

The results were the same for both right and left slopes. Slopes tended to increase with rate (by a factor of 3 from very slow to very fast). The Fo extent and slopes again share the same relationship as mentioned for the pitch and loudness varying conditions, namely, as the Fo extents increased, the slopes also became steeper (Table 17.9, Figure 17.16).

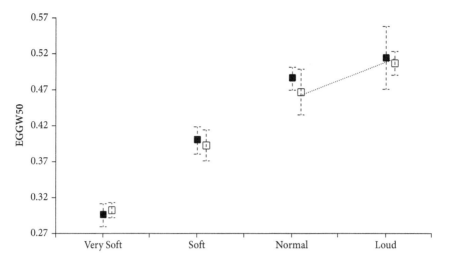

FIGURE 17.15 Kinematic measures: loudness variation. Solid and empty squares indicate measures at higher note and lower note of *taan* gestures, respectively. (Dotted error bars and dotted and solid lines indicate data that were not statistically different.)

Table 17.9 Fundamental frequency structure: rate variation

Rate		Rate	Extent	Left slope	Right slope
		Hz	ST	ST/s	ST/s
Very slow	Average	4.06	1.09	−9.53	8.42
	St.Dev	0.21	0.11	1.87	1.67
Slow	Average	4.62	1.74	−17.65	14.75
	St.Dev	0.21	0.21	1.87	2.24
Normal	Average	5.20	2.08	−23.91	19.91
	St.Dev	0.30	0.26	3.82	2.56
Fast	Average	5.92	2.42	−33.57	24.94
	St.Dev	0.30	0.33	6.52	3.61
Very fast	Average	6.79	1.98	−29.28	25.08
	St.Dev	0.53	0.23	5.41	3.85

AERODYNAMIC ANALYSIS

As the performance *taan* gesture rate increased, so did the subglottal pressure (an increase of 55 percent), AC-flow (more than double), and MFDR (nearly tripling) (Table 17.10, Figure 17.17). Overall, AC-flows at the peaks were lower than their respective dips. The open quotients did not change until the rate reached fast and very fast levels, for which the OQ decreased, suggesting greater adduction. The dips exhibited greater open quotient values for the normal to very slow rates.

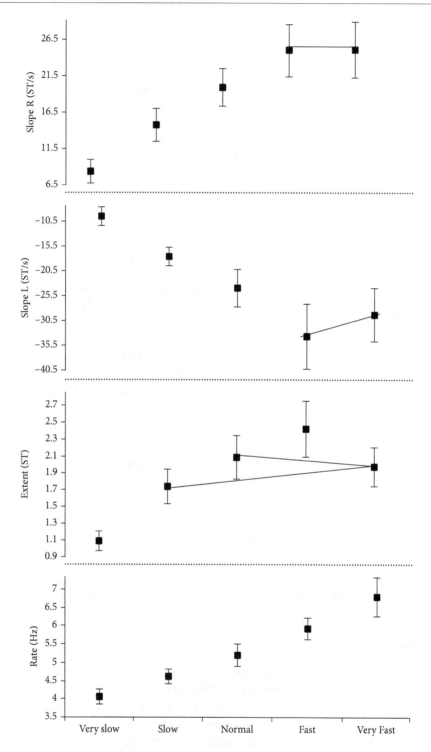

FIGURE 17.16 Fundamental frequency structure: rate variation. (The levels connected did not have statistically significant difference.)

Table 17.10 Aerodynamic measures: rate variation

Rate		AC-flow	MFDR	OQ	Sub.Pressure
		Cc/s	L/s/s		cm-w
Very slow-higher	Average	307.08	−592.08	0.49	11.28
	St.Dev	57.15	141.29	0.02	0.82
Very slow-lower	Average	331.39	−698.77	0.51	
	St.Dev	53.95	137.59	0.01	
Slow-higher	Average	375.60	−917.91	0.51	13.71
	St.Dev	37.93	86.07	0.01	0.75
Slow-lower	Average	485.10	−1032.67	0.51	
	St.Dev	32.55	113.86	0.02	
Normal-higher	Average	328.13	−844.76	0.48	13.55
	St.Dev	39.21	95.23	0.02	1.96
Normal-lower	Average	442.42	−970.71	0.52	
	St.Dev	34.05	109.49	0.02	
Fast-higher	Average	521.96	−1328.92	0.48	14.97
	St.Dev	36.55	141.76	0.02	0.07
Fast-lower	Average	650.58	−1444.93	0.42	
	St.Dev	35.44	94.45	0.03	
Very fast-higher	Average	608.23	−1563.60	0.37	17.13
	St.Dev	38.64	180.72	0.03	0.31
Very fast-lower	Average	723.72	−1712.57	0.37	
	St.Dev	42.79	132.74	0.02	

GLOTTOGRAPHIC MEASURES

The EGG50 results were consistent with the open quotient results, with little change in value until values indicated greater adduction for the fast and very fast rates (Table 17.11, Figure 17.18).

Obstruction Variation

The subject had a kinesthetic image of what he called "obstruction" in his larynx that helped him produce *taan* gestures. According to the subject, change in the level of obstruction makes a difference in *taan* production. In the obstruction variation task, the singer performed *taan* utterances at four different levels of the sense of laryngeal obstruction: much less, less, normal, and more obstruction. Statistical analyses indicate the following for the fundamental frequency structure, aerodynamic, and glottographic measures.

TAAN GESTURE RATE

Taan gesture rate increased as the sense of obstruction increased (Table 17.12, Figure 17.19). The rate of normal and more were significantly greater than others.

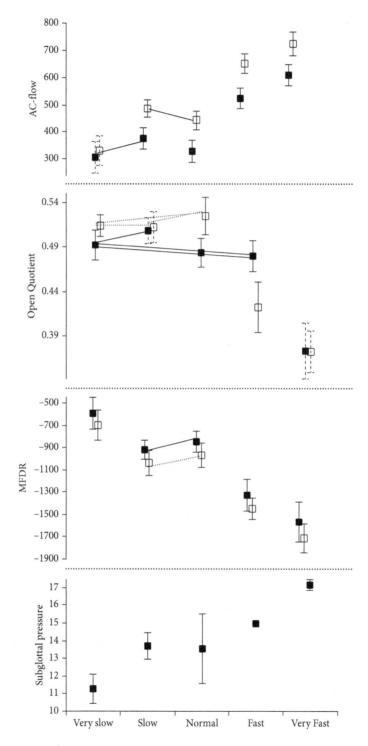

FIGURE 17.17 Aerodynamic measures: rate variation. Graphs with solid and empty squares indicate measures at higher note and lower note of *taan* gestures, respectively. (Dotted error bars and dotted and solid lines indicate data that were not statistically different.)

Table 17.11 Kinematic measures: rate variation

Rate		EGGW25	EGGW50	EGGW75
Very slow-higher	Average	0.58	0.48	0.27
	St.Dev	0.01	0.01	0.01
Very slow-lower	Average	0.57	0.47	0.24
	St.Dev	0.01	0.01	0.02
Slow-higher	Average	0.59	0.49	0.25
	St.Dev	0.02	0.02	0.01
Slow-lower	Average	0.58	0.46	0.25
	St.Dev	0.05	0.02	0.06
Normal-higher	Average	0.60	0.49	0.25
	St.Dev	0.01	0.01	0.01
Normal-lower	Average	0.57	0.47	0.25
	St.Dev	0.03	0.02	0.05
Fast-higher	Average	0.61	0.50	0.24
	St.Dev	0.08	0.06	0.07
Fast-lower	Average	0.70	0.52	0.36
	St.Dev	0.08	0.04	0.08
Very fast-higher	Average	0.70	0.54	0.29
	St.Dev	0.04	0.01	0.10
Very fast-lower	Average	0.80	0.62	0.39
	St.Dev	0.08	0.06	0.07

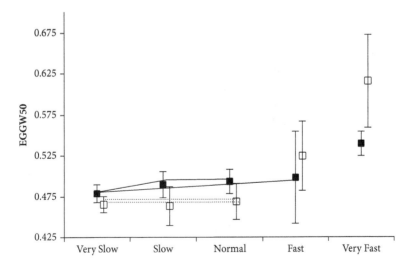

FIGURE 17.18 Kinematic measures: rate variation. The solid and empty squares indicate higher and lower notes of the *taan* gestures, respectively. (Dotted error bars and dotted and solid lines indicate data that were not statistically different.)

Table 17.12 Fundamental frequency structure: obstruction variation

Obstruction		Rate	Extent	Left slope	Right slope
		Hz	ST	ST/s	ST/s
Much less	Average	4.26	0.93	−8.65	7.47
	St.Dev	0.30	0.09	1.51	1.28
Less	Average	4.70	1.31	−12.63	12.04
	St.Dev	0.21	0.20	2.35	2.10
Normal	Average	5.44	2.20	−26.74	20.96
	St.Dev	0.26	0.19	2.66	4.67
More	Average	5.49	3.98	−54.51	36.44
	St.Dev	0.23	0.44	7.26	5.17

FO EXTENT

The Fo extents of the *taan* gestures increased consistently from much less (about 1 ST) to more obstruction level (about 4.2 ST) and all the measures were significantly different from each other. This indicates that the singer's concept of obstruction was highly related to Fo extent (Table 17.12, Figure 17.19). The values for the extent are within the ranges of the reported extents so far discussed in this report for the much less to normal sense of obstruction. The near 4.2 ST extent for the more obstruction case is significantly higher than all other extents so far reported, suggesting that the sense of obstruction is a highly sensitive determiner of the Fo extent production in performance *taan* gestures by this performer.

TAAN GESTURE SLOPES

The results were similar for both right and left slopes. The slopes increased monotonically across the four levels, had similar values and a wide range of change (from about 7 ST/s to 40–50 ST/s, a large range), and were significantly different from each other as the obstruction increased. These results suggest that the sense of laryngeal obstruction has strong rate, Fo extent, and Fo slope correlates; that is, obstruction is physiologically based (Table 17.12, Figure 17.19).

AERODYNAMIC ANALYSIS

In general, subglottal pressure, AC-flow, and MFDR were directly related to the sense of obstruction, with the values at lowest dip frequency being greater than peak frequency. The open quotients were similar for the first three obstruction levels, but significantly decreased for the highest level of obstruction (Table 17.13, Figure 17.20). These results suggest greater adduction with the higher subglottal pressure with greater obstruction.

GLOTTOGRAPHIC MEASURES

The EGGW50 measure followed the measures of Figure 17.20 consistently and at both peak and dip frequencies complemented open quotient values; that is, the values

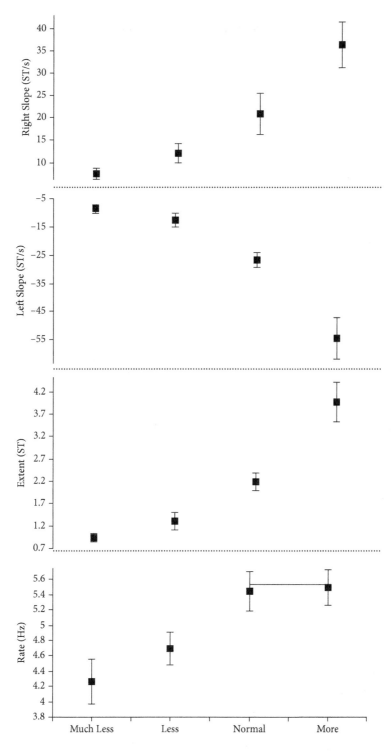

FIGURE 17.19 Fundamental frequency structure: obstruction variation. (The levels connected did not have statistically significant difference.)

Table 17.13 Aerodynamic measures: obstruction variation

Obstruction		AC-flow	MFDR	OQ	Sub.Pressure
		Cc/s	L/s/s		cm-w
Muchless-higher	Average	283.116	−562.87	0.50955	11.56
	St.Dev	26.4074	73.3524	0.01742	0.61204575
Muchless-lower	Average	321.54	−653.64	0.52423	
	St.Dev	22.4802	51.2668	0.01527	
Less-higher	Average	360.827	−878.6	0.50348	14.185
	St.Dev	51.7154	158.149	0.01537	1.27594409
Less-lower	Average	420.042	−900.14	0.51982	
	St.Dev	74.5829	190.706	0.01592	
Normal-higher	Average	367.356	−898.42	0.48833	13.0925
	St.Dev	64.9577	165.54	0.01292	1.82744585
Normal -lower	Average	504.793	−1136.8	0.526	
	St.Dev	57.1404	169.685	0.03063	
More-higher	Average	562.196	−1436.3	0.43857	17.035
	St.Dev	61.0634	212.915	0.02662	2.40319926
More-lower	Average	768.41	−1680.4	0.41293	
	St.Dev	63.7929	211.63	0.06941	

increased with the sense of laryngeal obstruction (Table 17.14, Figure 17.21), again suggesting greater adduction.

DISCUSSION FOR PERFORMANCE *TAAN*

For the elite Hindustani classical Indian performer and teacher, his performance *taan*, in general, is the control of production parameters including pitch, loudness, rate, and laryngeal obstruction of a basic *taan* gesture. The results obtained from this research revealed changes in voice measures when the above-mentioned parameters were strategically manipulated. Based on the given data, increase in the voluntary pitch level of performance *taan* productions is accommodated by an increase in subglottal pressure, increase in AC-flow, increase in MFDR (negatively) that would correspond to an increase in sound pressure level (Perkell et al. 1994), and higher levels of glottal contact. The EGGW50 was greater than normal, 0.36 (Scherer et al. 1995). Typically, there was a lower value of open quotient and a higher value of AC-flows at the bottom of the *taan* dips, suggesting that *taan* uses greater adduction and subglottal pressure for the lower frequency within the performance *taan* structure. These changes were also strongly evident when *taan* rate and loudness were changed as the independent variable.

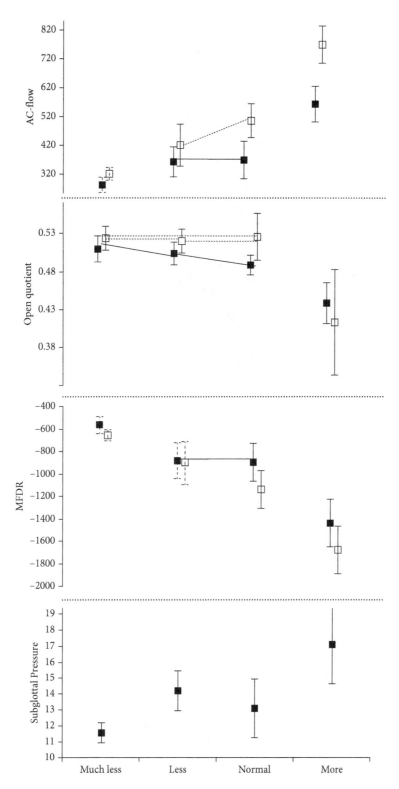

FIGURE 17.20 Aerodynamic measures: obstruction variation. Graphs with solid and empty squares indicate measures at the higher and lower notes, respectively. (Dotted error bars and dotted and solid lines indicate data that were not statistically different.)

Table 17.14 Kinematic measures: obstruction variation

Obstruction		EGGW25	EGGW50	EGGW75
Muchless-higher	Average	0.57	0.46	0.31
	St.Dev	0.01	0.01	0.01
Muchless-lower	Average	0.55	0.46	0.29
	St.Dev	0.02	0.01	0.02
Less-higher	Average	0.58	0.48	0.32
	St.Dev	0.01	0.01	0.01
Less-lower	Average	0.57	0.46	0.30
	St.Dev	0.02	0.01	0.02
Normal-higher	Average	0.61	0.52	0.30
	St.Dev	0.01	0.01	0.02
Normal -lower	Average	0.60	0.49	0.33
	St.Dev	0.02	0.01	0.04
More-higher	Average	0.64	0.56	0.35
	St.Dev	0.02	0.01	0.08
More-lower	Average	0.70	0.58	0.40
	St.Dev	0.10	0.08	0.06

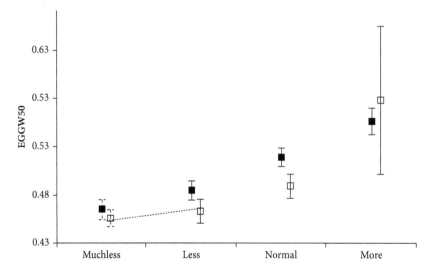

FIGURE 17.21 EGGW50 at the higher and the lower notes: obstruction variation. The solid and empty squares indicate the higher and lower notes, respectively.

Another convincing trend seen was between the Fo extent and slopes that were directly proportional to each other. The correlations were strong between the extent and both the slopes, with the stronger being for the left slope. This is consistent with the literature that suggests that shifting to a lower pitch can be faster than shifting to higher pitches (Sundberg 1987; Leonard et al. 1988).

Measurements from the loudness variation task complemented literature and basic understanding of voice production. Loudness variation involved gradual increase in glottal contact and subglottal pressure that resulted in greater Fo extents, and increases in MFDR and AC-flow measures. The increase in MFDR between very soft and loud levels supported an increase in sound pressure level suggested by several studies that have shown a positive relationship between the MFDR magnitude and sound pressure level (Baken and Orlikoff 2000). The AC-flows also increased with increase in loudness and were consistent with the literature that suggests increase in airflow measures with increase in vocal intensity (Hirano 1981). Increase in EGGW50 across loudness levels suggested that adduction increased between the very soft and loud levels.

Measurements from the rate variation task showed significant increase in rate for tasks between very slow and very fast, suggesting that the singer voluntarily controlled the *taan* gesture rate. Increase in rate was accompanied by greater Fo extents, steeper slopes, higher subglottal pressures, increased AC-flows, greater MFDR values (hence greater sound pressure level), and increased glottal adduction.

The laryngeal obstruction variation task showed that the concept of obstruction that the singer had in mind was strongly associated with the control of Fo variation. The Fo extent was significantly increased from about 1 ST for the much less obstruction to about 4 ST for the more obstruction. An even larger factor of increase than 4 was observed for the right and left slope changes over this range, namely, from about 7 ST/s for much less to 37–55 ST/s, an increase of a factor of about 7. Rate was a more modest factor for obstruction, increasing from about 4.2 Hz to 5.5 Hz from much less to more. Since subglottal pressure tended to increase and MFDR to increase negatively as obstruction level was raised, the phenomenon of obstruction, perhaps specific to this professional singer, involves strong components that are both physiological (Fo and adduction related) and aerodynamic (subglottal pressure related).

GENERAL DISCUSSION AND SUMMARY

Both studies, of pedagogical *taan* and performance *taan*, have given new information on voice production during *taan* gestures in classical Hindustani singing. The question of how *taan* gestures are produced could be answered only by obtaining information on what *taan* gestures are. The first study gave the basic features of *taan* based on the *taan* gestures used to train classical singing. A definition of *taan* was proposed based on the fundamental frequency structure of the *taan* gestures demonstrated by the singer, a structure that has two parts, a frequency dip (a voluntary lowering and then raising of the pitch) followed by a duration of a relatively constant pitch. The definition and structure formed the foundation for the *taan* measure for both studies. Since performance related to Hindustani classical singing involves the concept of *raga*, a combination of notes in a specific ascending and descending order that differ for each *raga*, analyzing *taan* gestures used in performance, the second study, would be difficult if the ground work were not available. It was discovered that a primary difference between the pedagogical *taan* and the performance *taan* was the radical reduction in time for the second part of the *taan* gesture, that is, the relatively constant pitch. It is hypothesized, therefore, that the use of the dip and constant pitch in the pedagogical approach was to establish the ability to control the pitch of the voice and its ornamental alternations, a necessary skill for the performance singing.

An interesting finding in this study is that all the production measures used in this research are interrelated. This suggests that during real-time performance, singers may be focusing on the whole rather than the parts involved in *taan* gesture production. The subject of this study agreed that the focus during performance is never on one single parameter. The pitch variation task varied the *taan* gesture rate; the loudness variation task varied the Fo extent, and so on. The change in rate during pitch variation as the independent variable affected the Fo extent in a specific pattern, but during rate variation as the independent variable, the Fo extent and rate relationship varied. The consistent feature across all conditions seen was the positive relationship between the Fo extent and the ascending and descending slopes of the *taan* gestures. As the Fo extent increased, the ascending and descending slopes increased in magnitude.

Both studies showed that *taan* gestures appear to be partly controlled by vocal fold adduction. The ability to vary *taan* gesture rate also indicates that this ornament is voluntarily altered. The rate and extents of *taan* gestures varied for all conditions and a comparison with other vocal ornaments (Brown and Scherer 1992; Hakes et al. 1987a, 1987b, 1988, 1990) like vibrato, trill, and *trillo* (performance bleat) in Western classical music is not straightforward (Table 17.15, Figure 17.22). Because the singer controlled the rate of the *taan* utterances, the production of *taan* was voluntarily modified, whereas typically, Western classical singers tend to keep vibrato rate relatively consistent throughout a performance. *Taan* rates measured in pedagogical *taan* were significantly lower than for vibrato and trill, but on the lower end for *trillo*. The rate for the subject's performance *taan*, however, extended to approximately 5.6 Hz, within the expected range for vibrato. The Fo extent values for all types are essentially overlapping (Figure 17.22). The

Table 17.15 Comparison of the taan gestures to other vocal ornaments

Ornament	Rate (Hz)	Extent (Semitones)
Vibrato	5–7	1–2
Trillo	2–12.4	1.1–2.7
Trill	6.5	2.7
Pedagogical *taan*	1.65–3.41	1.55–2.1
Pitch variation	5.07–5.86	1.16–2.09
Loudness variation	5.22–5.55	1.01–2.29
Rate variation	4.06–6.79	1.09–2.42
Obstruction variation	4.26–5.49	0.93–3.98

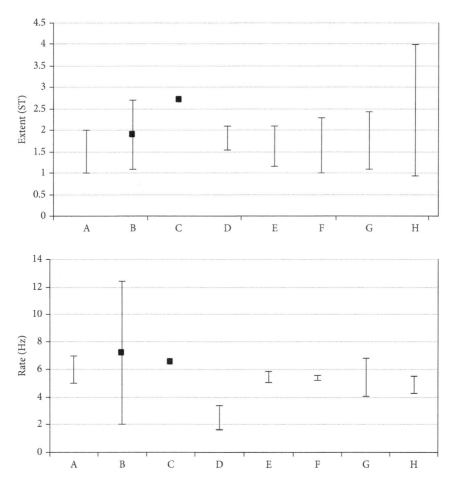

FIGURE 17.22 Rate and extent comparisons between A = vibrato, B = *Trillo*, C = Trill, D = Pedagogical *taan*, E = *Taan*-Pitch, F = *Taan*-Loudness, G = *Taan*-Rate, H = *Taan*-Obstruction.

lower rate of the pedagogical *taan* also should be consistent with the voluntary nature of its production. The origin of the robustness, however, of the extent and *taan* dip duration needs further study. Taking the *taan* dip duration alone (which is similar to the structure of the performance *taan*, that is, lacking the superior surface of the *taan* gesture) yields a range of 4.8–5.9 Hz, which is comparable to vibrato rates, indicating that *what is robust about taan (Fo modulation, Fo extent) may be the same for vibrato, but imbedded in a voluntary production*. Based on rate, vibrato, trill, *taan* during pitch variation, and *taan* during loudness, variation can be grouped together. *Trillo* has the fastest rate at its upper end, and pedagogical *taan* the slowest. The extents between these ornaments overlapped for *taan* gestures at all conditions, vibrato, and *trillo*. Trill had an extent that was within the range of *taan* during obstruction variation. The latter had the greatest extent among them all.

Implications and Future Research

This study brings a deeper physiological approach to the study of Indian classical music due to the measures that were explored. The methodology and results of this study can be used to compare different styles of vocal music around the world, especially regarding ornamentation. There are numerous vocal ornaments in different cultures of singing, produced through diverse techniques. Ornaments in Western classical singing have been widely researched compared to other ornaments. A cross-cultural comparison of vocal ornaments would give a comprehensive idea about the use and place ornaments have in music and culture. On the other hand, these artistic modulations can be compared to pathologies like vocal tremor. According to the literature related to vibrato and vocal tremor, frequency modulation of vocal tremor is less sinusoidal than vibrato. In addition, unlike vocal tremor, certain aspects of vibrato can be voluntarily controlled by the subject (Dromey et al. 2003; Dromey and Smith 2008). Physiological comparison between *taan* and pathological modulations would help give voice scientists and clinicians insight into more effective understanding and intervention strategies.

This study may be considered for pedagogical use to help teachers of Hindustani singing instruct *taan* production from a firmer basis of acoustics and physiology, which may greatly strengthen and justify the pedagogical approaches used. In addition, feedback in the form of Fo analysis and other measures applied in this study may be used to aid students in visualizing, and thus learning, aspects of the *taan* gesture. Similar intents for other aspects of vocal performance in India and other countries may likewise benefit from acoustic and physiological studies.

Note

1. A *gharana* is a "school" of musical heritage, thought, training, and practice.

Works Cited

Baken, R. J., and Orlikoff, R. F. 2000. *Clinical Measurement of Speech and Voice*, 2nd ed. San Diego: Singular Publishing Group.

Brown, L. R., and Scherer, R. C. 1992. "Laryngeal Adduction in Trillo." *Journal of Voice* 6 (1): 27–35.

Dromey, C., Carter, N., and Hopkin, A. 2003. "Vibrato Rate Adjustment." *Journal of Voice* 17 (2): 168–78.

Dromey, C., and Smith, M. E. 2008. "Vocal Tremor and Vibrato in the Same Person: Acoustic and Electromyographic Differences." *Journal of Voice* 22 (5): 541–5.

Hakes J., Shipp, T., and Doherty, E. T. 1987a. "Acoustic Properties of Straight Tone, Vibrato, Trill, and Trillo." *Journal of Voice* 1 (2): 148–56.

Hakes J., Shipp, T., and Doherty, E. T. 1987b. "Acoustic Characteristics of Vocal Oscillations: Vibrato, Exaggerated Vibrato, Trill, and Trillo." *Journal of Voice* 1 (4): 326–31.

Hakes, J., Shipp, T., and Doherty, E. T. 1988. "Trillo Rate Variations." Paper Given at the 17th Annual Symposium: Care of the Professional Voice.

Hakes, J., Shipp, T., and Doherty, E. T. 1990. "Trillo Rates Exhibited by Professional Early Music Singers." *Journal of Voice* 4 (4): 305–8.

Hampala, V., Garcia, M., Svec, J. G., Scherer, R., and Herbst, C. T. 2016. "Relationship Between the Electroglottographic Signal and Vocal Fold Contact Area." *Journal of Voice* 30 (2): 161–71.

Hirano, M. 1981 *Clinical Examination of Voice*. London: Springer-Verlag/Wien.

Leonard, R. J., Ringel, R., Horii, Y., and Daniloff, R. 1988. "Vocal Shadowing in Singers and Nonsingers." *Journal of Speech and Hearing Research* 31 (1): 54–61.

Perkell, J. S., Hillman, R. E., and Holmeberg, E. B. 1994. "Group Differences in Measures of Voice Production and Revised Values of Maximum Flow Declination Rate." *Journal of the Acoustical Society of America* 96 (2): 695–8.

Radhakrishnan, N., and Scherer, R. C. 2003. "Current Trends in Voice Analysis and Research Multi Signal Analysis." *Journal of ITC-Sangeet Research Academy* 17 (1): 15–42.

Radhakrishnan, N., Scherer, R. C., and Bandyopadhyay, S. 2011. "Laryngeal Dynamics of Pedagogical Taan Gestures in Indian Classical Singing." *Journal of Voice* 25 (3): 139–47.

Rothenberg, M. 1973. "A New Inverse-Filtering Ttechnique for Deriving the Glottal Air Flow Waveform During Voicing." *Journal of the Acoustical Society of America* 53 (6): 1632–45.

Scherer, R.C., Druker, D. G., and Titze, I.R. 1988. "Electroglottography and Direct Measurement of Vocal Fold Contact Area." In *Vocal Physiology: Voice Production, Mechanisms, and Function*, edited by O. Fujimura, 279–91. New York: Raven Press.

Scherer, R. C., Vail, V. J., and Rockwell, B. 1995. "Examination of the Laryngeal Adduction Measure EGGW." In *Producing Speech: Contemporary Issues: for Katherine Safford Harris*, edited by F. Bell-Berti and L. Raphael, 269–89. New York: American Institute of Physics.

Sundberg, J. 1987. *The Science of the Singing Voice*. DeKalb: Northern Illinois University Press.

CHAPTER 18

PROXIMITY/INFINITY

The Mediated Voice in Mobile Music

MIRIAMA YOUNG

> We represent small sounds as great and deep....We have certain helps
> which set to the ear do further the hearing greatly....We have also means
> to convey sounds in trunks and pipes, in strange lines and distances.
>
> —Bacon, *The New Atlantis*

ENCAPSULATING the zeitgeist of his era, in May 2013 Chris Hadfield beamed his self-recorded cover of David Bowie's "Space Oddity" (1969) from the compact International Space Station (ISS) he inhabited, for dissemination via YouTube. Hadfield's Internet-distributed song—which received over 23 million hits within the first year of posting—delivers to the multitude and individual at once. Further, this moment represents the cultural zenith in pod-music. Here both musical creation and performance are located in the private realm: a song is recorded in the musician's personal living quarters and on a mobile device, for distribution by bit-stream to a wide audience who, likewise, audition music within their own personal listening environment—typically in their automobile, or through headphones; from their tablet, digital watch, mobile phone, or personal computer.

Through the recorded song and its accompanying video, the listener/viewer is offered an intimate portrait of Hadfield floating within his solitary pod—the suspended space station. Complementing the visual scene, Hadfield's voice is heard close-up—at times raw and a little uncouth. The space station is a rather unforgiving acoustic environment for the singing voice, with artificial oxygen levels and a dearth of natural reflections. Further, a build-up of bodily fluid due to zero gravity makes vocalizing a challenge. Referring to the subsequent *Space Sessions: Songs from a Tin Can*, the first album recorded (partially) in space, Hadfield commented, "There's no gravity to pull the fluid out of your head...So you always have a full head and swollen tongue and vocal cords" (Patch 2015). These challenges are reflected in the vocal recording.

In keeping with today's bedroom-music production, the principle musical components of Hadfield's song—guitar and voice—were recorded and layered, mixed and produced on his laptop (or for the 2015 album, in his tiny sleep pod, direct to microphone connected to floating iPad). According to *The Economist*, piano was later added by Bowie's terrestrially bound former band member, Emm Gryner, while earthly producers mastered the album for commercial release ("How Does Copyright Work in Space?" 2013).

Hadfield's songs were uploaded and streamed widely around the planet. Before his passing, Bowie personally endorsed the project, but the music video has since been subject to earthly copyright laws, the publisher controlling and limiting the length of time the video was streamed on YouTube.[1] Crucially, Hadfield's experiment encapsulates current terrestrial sound-making and reception practices, in which small, portable media devices (such as via mobile phone or laptop) record,[2] and music is similarly received through pod-like means. Hadfield's project sounds the chronological evolution of vocal mediation here: if the telephonic medium concerned the necessity of transmission for basic communication, and the microphone became the driving signature force in pop music, vocal recording today, while still engaging with the microphone as the most important instrument, stretches beyond mere telephonic transmission of the voice, into an aesthetic paradigm. What I term pod-music engages with the creation and transmission of an aesthetic centered on internalized experience of the voice through the inner ear.

The Mediated Voice and Pod Listening

> Vocal sound...is no longer tied to a hole in the head but is free to issue from anywhere in the landscape. In the same instant it may issue from millions of holes in millions of public and private places around the world.
>
> —Schafer (2004 [1973], 34)

How immediate is our experience of Hadfield's voice in this instance? Before it is made available to the listener, his vocals are captured by microphone (which stamps its unique frequency response onto the sound); encoded into bits via personal workstation such as tablet or laptop; sent a distance of 250 miles to earth, transmitted as data via fiber-optic cable and wi-fi; subjected to postproduction mixing, engineering, and mastering; and quite possibly compressed into MP3 or another *lossy* format (which requires perceptual coding to remove data). At its endpoint, algorithms expand the data back into a voice, which is then piped through one of a variety of ubiquitous mobile listening devices— portable radio, tiny mobile phone or watch speaker, circum-aural headphones cupped close to the ears, or ear buds: "rubber-sheathed plastic shoved deep in the ear canal" (Gopinath and Stanyek 2014, 1).

As the "Tin Can" album title alludes, Hadfield's music is produced in the space-can, but perhaps also created for "cans," the industry's term for headphones. Auditioned through headphones, the voice occupies a small acoustic space within the 10 cm radius of the ear. Headphone listening—referred to here as "pod listening"—produces the *illusion* of close proximity, a contrived but plausible sense of intimacy—as if the vocalist were whisper-singing in the recipient's ear. The auditory deceit of "closeness" is remarkable considering the vast distance and levels of mediation separating Hadfield's International Space Station from our receiving ear. The notion of a private listening environment—in which the listener can control and personalize their auditory environment—stretches back to antiquity. Michael Bull and Les Black (2003) observe that Odysseus created a personal sound-world—between himself and the Sirens' song—by plugging wax into the ears of his accompanying oarsmen. As Alexander Rehding suggests, "The story of the sirens is in many ways an archetypal tale of music and mobility" (Rehding 2014, 1). It provides the "first description of the privatization of experience through sound" (Bull and Black 2003, 7–8), the first Silent Disco, of sorts.

So the listener's experience of the voice—both upon the Homeric ship and commonly today—is mobile and autonomously controlled. The voice is piped through small speakers—headphones, earbuds, mobile phone, laptop, tablet, watch, or into the pod-like bubble of the automobile. This mode of listening pertains to what Wayne Marshall refers to as "the utter ubiquity of treble culture today" (Marshall 2014, 46), in which "for young people in particular…'mobiles are the new boomboxes'" (63, quoting Martin Clark); and for Robert Putman, "the car becomes a perfectible mobile acoustic chamber in which individuals invariabl[y] prefer to listen in solitude" (Putnam [2000] summarized in Bull and Black 2003, 9), while headphones attached to the personal listening device provide "a tool whereby users manage space, time and the boundaries around the self" (Bull 2001, 179). In essence, then, these devices provide a single user with a portable, mid-range-centric, autonomously controlled listening experience.

As a sound distribution model, the mobile listening device has its roots in analog radio, a medium where, according to Frances Dyson, audio conducts an "epic journey: first projected into a transcendent and cosmic electronic ether, then received within the technologically enhanced, private space of the individual auditor" (Dyson 2009, 49). Since the advent of recorded music the options for personal modes of listening have increased exponentially. Initially, gramophones brought recorded music into the domestic realm, but subsequently, a gradual shift in music dissemination from loudspeaker to personal listening device has occurred. Putnam observed the critical shift in America through the twentieth century in which entertainment became "increasingly individualized": "No longer must we coordinate our tastes and timing with others in order to enjoy the rarest culture or the most esoteric information." Further, he points out that "electronic technology allows us to consume this hand-tailored entertainment in private, even utterly alone." Increasingly our experience of the recorded voice is diffused through the singular pod environment (Putnam 2000, 216).

In contrast to live or loudspeaker performance, songs produced specifically for pod-dissemination cultivate an artificially fabricated aesthetic, forged through specific vocal techniques, and with the assistance of a rich and powerful palette of technological tools in the recording/postproduction studio or digital audio workstation. In particular, vocalizations in *sotto voce* and hushed tones, articulated in close proximity to the microphone, as well as extensive use of postproduction applications such as dynamic range compression and reverb, all contribute to a new aesthetic that embraces pod-dissemination (Young 2016).

Further, as Wayne Marshall points out (quoting Robert Henke), small speaker systems, coupled with the frequency-biased algorithms of MP3 compression, tend to convey simple, mid-range-centric music more effectively than complex, frequency-rich arrangements (Young 2016, 11; Marshall 2014, 61). Marshall observes that producers, at least in dance music, "have zeroed in on the mid-range as the primary register of sonic salience" (63). Fortuitously or by design, the human voice naturally falls into this favored mid-range (excepting its extremes—the upper tessitura of a high soprano, the depths of a true bass, or the supernatural overtones or subtones that throat-singers and virtuosi can produce).

This chapter will survey vocal music from a range of genres to show ways in which composition, performance, recording, and production practices have evolved to exploit the personal listening environment that headphones and mobile listening enable. Not only does technology mediate how we hear the voice, but also vocal practice has been shaped and adapted in response to these technologies.[3] Further, the mediation of recording technology and transmission impacts how we hear the voice as proximal or intimate in various contexts. Discussion begins with headphone listening before turning to the creation of recorded music: vocal production, recording, and postproduction.

THE PRIVACY OF TELEPHONIC AND HEADPHONE LISTENING

> Messages on earphones are always private property....In the headspace of earphone listening, the sounds not only circulate around the listener, they literally seem to emanate from points in the cranium itself, as if the archetypes of the unconscious were in conversation...when sound is conducted directly through the skull of the headphone listener, he is no longer regarding events on the acoustic horizon; no longer is he surrounded by a sphere of moving elements. *He is the sphere.* He is universe. While most twentieth-century developments in sound production tend to fragment the listening experience and break up concentration, *headphone listening directs the listener towards a new integrity with himself.*
>
> —Schafer (2004 [1973], 35–36; emphasis mine)

FIGURE 18.1 "Marienkapelle, Würzburg." Germany, 2009. Photograph by Daderot. Image public domain in all territories. https://commons.wikimedia.org/wiki/File:Marienkapelle_W%C3% BCrzburg_-_IMG_6741.JPG.

Apparently the effectiveness of telephone-like devices to deliver personal messages reaches back to Biblical times. In iconography such as that shown in Figure 18.1, a late Middle Ages relief of the Annunciation at Marienkapelle in Würzburg, Germany, the word of God is shown to impregnate the Madonna through a tube fixed directly to her ear. On close inspection, the tiny fetus, sliding down the tube to Mary, is evident.

The very act of listening creates a turning inward: Jean-Luc Nancy compared the explicitly external and demonstrable act of viewing to the internal nature of listening itself: "Why, in the case of the ear, is there withdrawal and turning inward, a making *resonant*?" (Nancy 2007, 3).

In 1888 the relationship between telephonic medium and pod listening was illuminated in Edward Bellamy's futurist-utopian novel *Looking Backward from 2000 to 1887*. Bellamy's characters who inhabit the year 2000 listen to music in the comfort of their homes through a "musical telephone" that broadcasts live performances 24 hours a day. Bellamy imagined the musical telephone as a personal listening device, which could provide sound to the entire household or an individual: "If, of two persons side by side, one desired to listen to music and the other to sleep, it could be made audible to one and inaudible to another" (Bellamy 1888, 55). Such a concept now seems commonplace—indeed, we might stream the telecast of, for example, a Metropolitan Opera production, or Hadfield's songs, to our smartphone or headphones any time of the day and night.

For Jacques Derrida (1992), Molly's final soliloquy in James Joyce's *Ulysses* (1968 [1922]) is telephonic. Derrida claims that Molly relays the intimate details of Leopold Bloom's marriage proposal through the one-way transmission of the telephone line:

> and then I asked him with my eyes to ask again yes and then he asked me would
> I yes to say yes my mountain flower and first I put my arms around him yes and
> drew him down to me so he could feel my breasts all perfume yes and his heart was
> going like mad and yes I said yes I will Yes.
>   (Joyce 1968 [1922], 704; quoted in Derrida 1992, 274)

The privacy of the implied telephonic medium makes the reading of this excerpt a secret act, akin to eavesdropping on one side of a conversation. The recipient of Molly's address remains undisclosed, but through the act of reading, we become the ear on the other end of the telephone. Similarly, the personal listening device provides a receptacle into which personal secrets can be relayed. It is a private *acousmatic* space in that the speaker is heard but not seen. For philosopher Jean-Luc Nancy, such notions connect back to the French etymology of *listening*: *écoute*, which historically referred to a place where it was possible to listen in private (Nancy 2007, 4).

Furthermore, the telephone apparatus directs a speaker's voice close to transmitter and the listener's ear in immediate proximity to receiver, thus placing mouth and ear in "rare vocal intimacy... for ordinarily you do not permit just anybody to speak right into your ear" (Chion 1999, 63). In this sense tiny phone speakers or personal headphones emulate the particular listening experience of telephone transmission, but without the facility to speak back.

The recorded voice addresses an unknown other who becomes, through the act of listening, the headphone-donned recipient himself. While Bull and Black claim that Odysseus fabricated the first private listening experience through wax inserted into the ear, Peter Sloterdijk goes further to suggest that the Siren's deeply personal wail was experienced internally by the listener.

> The Sirens found eager victims in all listeners up until Odysseus—and especially in
> him—because they sing from the listener's own place. Their secret is to render pre-
> cisely those songs in which the passing sailors' ears yearn to immerse themselves.
> Listening to the Sirens thus means entering the core space of an intimately touching
> musical key and wishing to remain at the source of this indispensable sound from
> that point on. *The fatal singers compose their songs in the ear of the listener; they sing
> through the larynx of the other.*   (Sloterdijk 2011, 487; emphasis mine)

Sloterdijk suggests the Sirens played with the "bewitching" qualities of music in order to seduce him from the ropes that bound him to the mast (Sloterdijk 2011, 487). Western society's obsession with the automobile—and thus, with music played within the pod-like bubble of the car—presents a new challenge to those who might be seduced by the Siren's song.

WHISPERING IN THE EAR: THE MICROPHONE AND PHYSICAL PROXIMITY

> The most important instrument in pop music is the microphone.... What the microphone made possible in pop music was a complete range of vocal manners, from the most hectoring to the most intimate.
>
> —Ford (2014)

Invented in 1878 by David Edward Hughes, and building on recent telephone technology, the carbon microphone took its name from a combination of microscope and telephone. Hughes claimed that his microphone was an "instrument suitable for magnifying weak sounds" (Hughes 1878, 198). In contemporary recording and listening practice, this feature is more pertinent than ever.

Before the microphone, Andrew Ford (2014) points out that singers were required to master specific techniques to project their voice across a concert hall, or above a band or orchestra. With the advent of the microphone, singers would learn to manipulate their voices in ways that defied the limitations and exploited the advantages of the technology. No longer was it essential to project across distance. Now, even opera singers need not necessarily project their voice 2016 saw the realization of *Sydney Opera House: The Opera (The Eighth Wonder)* outside the eponymous landmark, in which live radio-miked singers perform upon the Opera House steps—mixed with live orchestra and opera chorus from within the hall—transmitted directly to an al fresco audience donned with audiophile-quality wireless headphones. Sound designer for the production Tony David Cray stated, "I believe it will make the connection between the performer and the audience much closer" (Blake 2016). Similarly, in recorded music, Rudolf Arnheim observed a "spiritual proximity" between voice and listener, due to the nearness of microphone to sound source (Arnheim 1972, 78). This phenomenon is especially evident if the singer capitalizes on proximity effects by directing her mouth to certain angles to control the frequency response and propinquity to the microphone.

During the first two decades of the twentieth century Enrico Caruso's tenor voice came to embody the sound of early gramophonic opera, but perhaps his voice was also shaped by the unique but somewhat limited capacity of the recording apparatus itself. By the 1920s, a new singing style commonly known as crooning would rely on the singer's proximity to the microphone to invoke a greater dynamic range, a sense of presence, a quiet intimacy on soft, low tones, and a warm, bass-rich sound. Crooners such as Bing Crosby, Frank Sinatra, Rudy Vallée, Perry Como, and Dean Martin would adopt what Mark Katz refers to as "the soft, restrained vocal style popular from the 1920s to the 1950s" (Katz 2005, 46). Ribbon and cardioid microphones are especially affected by presence, with low frequencies being accentuated more quickly as a function of proximity than higher tones (Case 2016). (Likewise, the sound becomes thinner as the singer distances themselves.) Such microphones required manipulation of vocal technique specifically for the studio: "The singer would lean in close for an exaggerated low end, while controlling breath and dynamics to prevent distracting artifacts" (Case 2016).

Those "distracting artifacts" magnified by the microphone and proximity effect have evolved in some genres to become consciously included, celebrated subvocal sounds. Numerous contemporary examples exist of singers utilizing microphone and proximity effect to relay extremes of quiet and vocal artifact. The singer may realize soft effects by singing "off" the voice—in which less force is applied in adduction of the vocal folds; by intentionally adding more breath; or by manipulating the physical adjacency of mouth to microphone (Greig 2009, 22). These techniques are evident in the opening verse to "Headphones" (1995), in which Björk's breathy spoken-sung delivery has a close, quiet, gossamer-like quality. A gradual crescendo leads to the louder chorus, which contrastingly draws from the full-body voice. By halfway through the song, where the voice becomes strident, Björk is heard to physically distance herself from the microphone in order to project the voice without "clipping" (at 3'33", however, some distortion is apparent). "My headphones," she sings, "they saved my life." As listener, we unwittingly eavesdrop on a secret and personal confession.

The music is clearly designed for the mode of dissemination that lies in the song's very title: appropriate for headphones, there is an intricate, delicate quality to the arrangement. Further, three-dimensional spatial depth is created through the deliberate placement of sound objects within different parts of the listening field. The keyboards are panned left, and treated with reverb so they appear more distant than the voice. Low synthesized beats are panned hard right and treated "dry," lacking reverb. During the principle verse and chorus, Björk's voice is centrally panned and frontal, so that it appears to enter through the center of the listener's cranium. Her accompanying vocal interjections—including whispered speech, giggling, breathing, harmonizations, are treated with contrasting amounts of reverb, and panned to various degrees left or right to fill the stereo field with a variety of vocal characters. In the digital audio workstation (DAW), cut and paste-style edits and the superimposition of multiple tracks facilitate this musical and spatial arrangement of distinct elements.

Björk takes the properties of proximity effect to a further extreme in "Cocoon" (2001), from the album *Vespertine* (see Young 2015, 159–160). Here whispery, compressed vocals magnify the tiniest details of her breathy, nonprojected, child-like vocal. The listener may hear Björk's mouth forming syllables and vowels, the voice resonating in the internal hard palette, and brushing against the soft palette. There is little audible reverb—for the most part we hear her voice arrestingly close-up and raw-sounding. The immediacy of her raw voice is simply enhanced through headphone listening. Her voice is accompanied by a low modular synth and high-frequency glitchy fizzing sounds that emulate the saliva and lip-movement of the mouth, and that, in headphone listening, swirl around the ear as if the listener were immersed in an aural/oral bath. But whose ear and whose mouth? The voice of the singer and the recipient's ear elide as the listener becomes entrapped in the realms of auditory imagination. Note also that the listener is privy to an intimate narrative, which, quizzically, includes a similar reference to the cradling of "his" head to her "bosom" just as Molly Bloom had confided 80 years earlier in her telephonic final soliloquy in *Ulysses*.

Björk's *Vespertine* exploits proximity effect to claim an intimate auditory space that exists entirely between vocalist and the listener's imagination. That is, the album is deliberately produced for personal headphone dissemination. As Björk suggested in interview: "Now we've got the Napster [originally an illegal download platform] thing, the Internet and downloading and you write specifically for that. I use microbeats, a lot of whispery vocals, which I think sound amazing when they're downloaded because of the secrecy of the medium. It's about being in a little house, on your own. You're creating paradise with your laptop, or underneath your kitchen table where nobody knows about it" (Toop 2004, 226–227).

Performers are the first to experience the uncanny proximity of their own voice: during studio recording, headphones are the primary fold-back source for the performer. The vocalist will typically hear their delivery (as well as the instrumental mix) through headphones (on at least one ear), responding to the "sound of their own voices as it is relayed to them through the microphone and mixing desk" (Greig 2009, 22). As such, vocalists risk falling victim to occlusion and Lombard effects, which alter perception of their own voice. Auditory feedback during the recording process is channeled back through headphones, in turn shaping the way the performer evaluates and modifies her performance in real time. In this way, headphone listening re-enlivens aspects of the studio recording: we hear the vocalist largely the way she heard herself.

ARTIFICE AS AESTHETIC IN
STUDIO INTERVENTION

Although the recording studio was originally regarded as a place to faithfully replicate the musical event, by the 1960s it had become the site for a conceptual and aesthetic shift. No longer merely for documentation, the music production studio offered a place in which music could be creatively recorded and postenhanced into the perfected "track" (Moore 2010, 264). Specifically, the studio offered the possibility to render the voice simultaneously present, while paradoxically more expansive. There are multiple enhancements that are commonly applied to the voice during postproduction—one of the most significant being intonation correction software such as Melodyne or Auto-Tune (for further see Young 2015, 96). Two other postproduction enhancements that significantly alter the appearance of the voice are dynamic range compression and reverberation. These ultimately create the curious blend of presence and space—proximity in the seemingly infinite.

By the early 1980s, domestic studios emerged, allowing a greater abundance of time in which bands could luxuriate. Gradually digital technologies developed, which popular genres adopted in tandem with various analog effects such as flanging, equalization, chorusing, double-tracking, echo plates, reverberation, and so on. As Richard Witts describes, "Through constructs of spatial location and motion these FX produced a sense of distance or depth, of flows, 'other-worldness' or alienation" (Witts 2009, 82).

Today, the DAW is the typical studio environment for music production, it offers the possibility to lay tracks and rerecord, edit, mix, postproduce, and render the song within a single state-of-the-art software environment. Available to professional and hobbyist alike, the DAW facilitates music creation on computer or tablet in the comfort of one's bedroom, enabling heavy postmediation far removed from the kind of music experienced in live acoustic concert settings. (In the seemingly challenging conditions of outer space, Commander Hadfield used the DAW to individually lay and edit the vocal and instrumental stems of his song immediately into the mix.) This working practice has greatly changed the way that popular recordings (and many classical ones) are produced today. No longer shackled to expensive recording studios, the opportunity to shape and enhance through postproduction tinkering in the bedroom studio becomes limitless.

Of course, not all music genres adhere to this trend. While popular music "production ... seeks to exploit and sometimes foreground the full potential of the mixing desk, tape and digital manipulation" (Greig 2009, 21), and electroacoustic/electronic music relies intrinsically on the creative possibilities offered by the music studio, classical music, on the other hand, has been a slow adopter of technological intervention. As Andrew Ford observes, "Among classical musicians, the microphone is still viewed with suspicion" (Ford 2014). In classical recording, a faithful concert-style rendering of the singer or ensemble will typically be invoked. "The recording space will mimic the kind of space in which the concerts may have occurred—thus, a hall, a large room, a church or a chapel, each with its own 'natural' acoustic (though in certain cases additional reverberation may be added later electronically)" (Greig 2009, 17).

However, there are some instances of classical music adapting to the mobile listening medium, with the aforementioned Sydney Opera House performance, as well as recent chamber realizations of canonical works. For example, 2013 and 2014 saw the release of chamber interpretations of J.S. Bach's *St John Passion* (1724) featuring one-voice-per-part in the choral sections (in contrast to the large-scale choir typically deployed). The 2014 recording by the Academy of Ancient Music is particularly scaled back and delicate, with each individual voice appearing present, close, and warm—ideal for headphone listening. Every minute detail is captured and, through headphones, relayed with a magnification for which the microphone's inventor, David Edward Hughes, would have been pleased. Headphones may not be the small choir loft in Nikolaikirche, Leipzig, but in some respects they may come closer to Bach's intention than a large choir projected through loudspeakers.

THE RISE, AND RISE OF DYNAMIC RANGE COMPRESSION

First developed for AM radio in the 1920s, dynamic range compression boosts low-level signal while reducing high-level noise. Compression and limiting are commonly used in radio and television broadcasting where manipulation of dynamic range enables the signal to appear louder and more present than the competitor. This has led to ever-increasing levels of compression and limiting since 1990, in what has been coined the "Loudness War."[4] Compression optimizes listening for small listening environments, such as headphones, automobiles, computer speakers, or portable speaker systems that relay a narrower dynamic (and frequency) range.

During the mastering process, pop music is commonly tested on a range of speaker outputs—from high-fidelity sound systems to tiny speakers and headphones. A compressor is applied to the signal to maximize a sense of presence and fullness even in compromised audition circumstances. Such treatment serves to render quiet sounds louder and more present. This is particularly useful for recordings in *sotto voce*. Compression can be used to reduce sibilants that might cause distortion, but reinforce the quieter internal sounds of the vocal tract such as breathiness and huskiness. As Curtis Roads observes, "High compression is a common cliché in the production of popular music. For example, ratios in the range of 10:1 make pop vocals sound 'intimate' due to the exaggeration of tongue gesticulations, lip smacking, saliva dripping, and breathing noises when all vocalisms are scaled to the same amplitude range" (Roads 1995, 394). Consider, for example, the role of both compression and microphone proximity in the erotic duet between Serge Gainsbourg and Jane Birkin/Brigitte Bardot: "Je T'Aime...Moi Non Plus."[5] Similarly, featherweight voices—such as those of Goldfrapp or Joanna Newsom—would be nearly lost without close-proximity recording and high compression effects.

Similar examples abound: only microphone proximity and dynamic range compression make decipherable the spoken whispering at the heart of Michael Jackson's "In the Closet" (1992). Such whispering requires significant compression to be comprehensible. Through headphones, the whispers seem unequivocally direct. Proximity and compression also elevate whispering to levels comparable with other musical elements.

De La Soul invert their typically declarative rapping style in "Can You Keep a Secret" (1989) by exploiting the microphone's tacit ability to magnify quiet sounds. Here secret whispered messages are captured and reinforced through recording and postproduction processes. The lyrics for one verse read: "Paul has dandruff. Posdnuos has a lot of dandruff. Mase has big fat dandruff. Trugoy has dandruff. Everybody in the world, you have dandruff." While meaning is lost in loudspeakers, a close review through headphones reveals the lyrics.

Likewise, in "Wait (The Whisper Song)" (2005), the Ying Yang Twins deliver sexually explicit lyrics in a whisper. They invite the listener to engage in a private listening mode from the outset: "Hey how you doin' lil' mama let me whisper in your ear." A headphone context delivered directly to the recipient enables the uncensored lyrics to become decipherable. In any case, the song is too pornographic in nature to broadcast publicly. This is secretive music designed for private dissemination.

As these examples show, physical proximity and dynamic range compression can reinforce subtle, mid-range, hushed vocal emanations that reach just beyond mouth and microphone, and into the ear of the willing (or unwitting) listener.

REVERBERATION

The close proximity of microphone recording, coupled with a dry studio environment eliminates acoustical depth. As Simon Emmerson states, "'Close mic' techniques try to exclude the environment, the room, the space and lead directly to the projection of intimacy" (Emmerson 2007, 117). Depleted of natural acoustical context, an artificial acoustic environment is then superimposed during postproduction phase, using echo, delay, and reverberation effects. Initially, such effects were achieved mechanically with plates, coils, springs, and other physical devices. Hardware, and later software plugins enabled reverberant acoustical spaces to be activated with the touch of a button. Rather than positing the voice within the acoustics of a simple room, reverb offered the temptation to apply the gargantuan acoustics of a cathedral, creating an immense sense of grandeur, as well as softening out inconsistencies in the vocals. Today, reverb is commonly applied to the voice, with varying degrees of magnitude, and thus varying degrees of plausibility.

Belle of 1980s and 1990s lush, synthesized pop, Kate Bush's agile soprano voice suited Walkman (1979) and later Discman (1984) headphone dissemination perfectly. Her canon during this period displays the heavy production aesthetic fashionable at the time, which served to reinforce her already virtuosic voice. From her vast output, two examples illustrate: In "Running Up That Hill" (1985) highly compressed vocals render the voice unnaturally alive and present. Compression forces her shallow breath to pop out of the arrangement, as if she were indeed running. In "Under Ice" (1985), highly compressed, close-proximity husky vocals are rendered so crisp they sound like ice splitting. As if slowly plummeting into water, multilayered harmonies grow vertically deeper as the song progresses. All material, especially the vocals, is placed in a highly reverberant acoustic environment to create an eerie under-ice setting (suggestive of being trapped under frozen water).

INFINITE IMMENSITIES

Clearly, the adaptation of vocal performance practice to recording technologies, coupled with a dependence on proximity effects, reverberation, and dynamic range compression, have created in some genres an entirely new aesthetic for a pod listening culture. To confirm the illusion of presence and closeness, contemporary recording and postproduction techniques in vocal genres (particularly pop) involve recording at close proximity and secondly, applying dynamic-range compression effects. Finally, synthetic reflections are imposed on the voice through reverberation, which can replicate an acoustic space of any proportion (even the infinitely long decay and reflection times of an enormously proportioned space are possible, and sometimes utilized). In all, proximity/infinity production techniques have become commonplace, and ensure that the voice conveys, paradoxically, qualities both "intimate" and "immense."

Such a close-propinquity/infinitely expansive contradiction can be experienced in the acoustical treatment of pop vocalists Adele and Hannah Reid of London Grammar. In the verses to Adele's "Hello" (2015), the intimacy of her confessional one-way telephonic-style lyrics ("Hello, it's me/I was wondering if after all these years you'd like to meet") are captured through a low-frequency-rich Neve 1066 preamp, which is fed through compressor and limiter to furnish the voice with even greater presence. According to producer Tom Elmhirst, the vulnerability of her verses are preserved through a mix that is, "intimate, drier and more conversational." This contrasts the chorus where, to create convincing reverberation effects, her vocals were passed through Capitol Studios' physical acoustic chambers and plates, originally built by Les Paul in the 1940s. The producer describes the physical challenge of accessing these rooms: "You go in to the basement of Capitol,…then climb through a ladder to get to the sub-basement, where it looks like no one has been for 50 years. You literally open a hatch and climb down a steel ladder." Paradoxically, this bunker-like environment produces superior reverberation effects that are revered in the industry to this day. Subsequently, Adele's already powerful voice is then exposed to an array of artificial reverberation effects: "There's an AMS delay, an Eventide preset called 'Canyon,' a plate, a spring…You can see the escalation of things. There's about seven or eight things going on. *You get this wide kind of thing, but her vocal remains super-present*" (emphasis mine). Lastly, the producer auditions the final mix on studio monitoring speakers, as well as through inferior $14 speakers, claiming that it is "just as important to hear a mix on an iPhone speaker as it is to hear on high monitoring in a control room. It's got to work on everything," which underscores the variety of listening environments which will ultimately deliver the song (Weiss 2015).

Similarly, Hannah Reid's close-miked vocals are greatly enhanced by compression and reverberation effects. Experienced through headphones, London Grammar's "Strong" (2013) and "Hey Now" (2014) deliver Reid's recorded voice at close proximity: one can hear "graininess" in the vocal texture, and even the most quiet of inhales. But the "authentic" close-up voice is mixed with vocals cast in multiple and long reflection times to convey the spatial largess of a church. As Dyson warns, "The whisper in the ear, the guttural laugh, the close-miked voice with a touch of reverb, represent a voice too large for any body, and a hearing too acute to be human" (Dyson 2009, 136). Curiously, this aesthetic artificiality has become the new norm, and recordings that lack aesthetic tinkering seem uncanny and raw to our ear.

For philosopher Gaston Bachelard, a sense of solitude and immense, infinite space generates a place for wonder, for connecting transcendentally and with the inner self: "Immensity is within ourselves. It is attached to a sort of expansion of being that life curbs and caution arrests, but which starts again when we are alone….We are dreaming in a world that is immense" (Bachelard 1994, 184). Of Charles Baudelaire's sonnet *Correspondances*, Bachelard observes that, "immensity in the intimate domain is intensity, an intensity of being, the intensity of a being evolving in a vast perspective of intimate immensity" (193).

The profoundly curious but now commonplace practice of telephonic/headphone listening enables possibilities for the imaginative unconscious to be invoked: the tiny pod-space of the headphone becomes a conduit for manipulation of the recipient's intrinsic experience. Frances Dyson notes: "Especially through headphones, sound enters and affects the individual's psyche" (49). With headphones, vocalisation, vocal and post-production artifice and a little imagination, the singer becomes immediately present: he seems to inhabit the circum-aural space beside our ear, in a simultaneously intimate and immense acoustic experience. Similarly, for Frances Dyson: "Listened to through headphones, in the dark, quiet intimacy of the living room, this already 'strato-spherized' voice becomes a screen for the projection of listeners' fantasies" (Dyson 2009, 53). Here we can float in a tiny pod in infinite space with Commander Hadfield. Headphones enhance the inner realms of the listener's mind: through headphones, Bachelard's visceral—perhaps transcendental—"intimate immensity" manifests.

NOTES

1. In the act of ultimately uploading the song from the earthly realm, a host of litigious issues were carefully circumvented. For if copyrighted material was recorded and distributed from space, a quagmire of legal issues would surface, especially regarding extraterrestrial copyright and intellectual property laws, which—messy, ambiguous, uncontained, and applicable to a plausibly infinite universe—represent the inverse of the pod in which the music itself was created and in which it is typically auditioned. As *The Economist* observed, because the YouTube music video was streamed from earth, in this case Chris Hadfield was subject to terrestrial copyright laws. However, had the music been streamed from space while ISS was orbiting the globe, the terrestrial airspace in which Commander Hadfield recorded the song would have become significant. Similarly, it would become equally important to determine which state-owned section of the Space Station Hadfield occupied at the time that the video and sound recording were made ("How Does Copyright Work in Space?" 2013).
2. Indicative of the very practice with which this chapter engages, David Byrne's August 2016 radio playlist was titled "Music Recorded on a Cell Phone." See http://davidbyrne.com/radio/august-radio-music-recorded-on-a-cell-phone.
3. This chapter is limited to addressing specific instances of vocal mediation in the Western tradition. Ethnographers and anthropologists have studied vocal effects in recording that reach beyond the West, including Amanda J. Weidman in her book *Singing the Classical, Voicing the Modern: The Postcolonial Politics of Music in South India* (Weidman 2006).
4. Further information on the "loudness war" can be found in Milner (2009, chapter 7).
5. Originally released with Jane Birkin in 1969, the 1967 Brigitte Bardot recording was released in 1986.

WORKS CITED

Arnheim, Rudolf. 1972. *Radio: An Art of Sound*. New York: Da Capo Press.

Bachelard, Gaston. 1994. *The Poetics of Space: The Classic Look at How we Experience Intimate Places*. Boston: Beacon Press.

Bacon, Francis. 1627. *The New Atlantis*. The Harvard Classics, 1909–1914. http://www.bartleby.com/3/2/3.html.

Bellamy, Edward. 1888. *Looking Backward from 2000 to 1887*. Champaign, IL: Project Gutenberg, *eBook Collection*, EBSCOhost, [1888], n.d. (August 19, 2015).

Blake, Elissa. 2016. "Opera Australia and Sydney Opera House Team Up For World-First Silent Opera." *Sydney Morning Herald*, August 30. http://www.smh.com.au/entertainment/stage/opera-australia-and-sydney-opera-house-team-up-for-for-worldfirst-silent-opera-20160830-gr49ur.html.

Bull, Michael. 2001. "The World According to Sound: Investigating the World of Walkman Users." *New Media and Society* 3 (2): 179–97.

Bull, Michael, and Les Black. 2003. "Introduction." In *The Auditory Culture Reader*, edited by Michael Bull and Les Black, 1–24. Oxford: Berg.

Byrne, David. 2016. "Music Recorded on a Cell Phone." *David Byrne*, August. http://davidbyrne.com/radio/august-radio-music-recorded-on-a-cell-phone.

Case, Alexander. 2016. "The Vocal Microphone: Technology and Practice." *Physics Today* 69 (3): 74.

Chion, Michel. 1999. *The Voice in Cinema*. New York: Columbia University Press.

Derrida, Jacques. 1992. "Ulysses Gramophone: Hear Say Yes in Joyce." In *Acts of Literature*. London: Routledge.

Dyson, Francis. 2009. *Sounding New Media: Immersion and Embodiment in the Arts and Culture*. Berkeley: University of California Press.

Emmerson, Simon. 2007. *Living Electronic Music*. Aldershot: Ashgate.

Ford, Andrew. 2014. "Amplified Intimacy." *Inside Story*, April 7. http://inside.org.au/amplified-intimacy/#sthash.2lWy6Wyv.dpuf.

Gopinath, Sumanth S., and Jason Stanyek. 2014. "The Mobilization of Performance: an Introduction to the Aesthetics of Mobile Music." In The Oxford Handbook of Mobile Music Studies, Volume 2, edited by Sumanth Gopinath and Jason Stanyek, 1–42. New York: Oxford University Press.

Greig, Donald. 2009. "Performing For (and Against) The Microphone." In *The Cambridge Companion to Recorded Music*, edited by Nicholas Cook, Eric Clarke, Daniel Leech-Wilkinson, and John Rink, 30–1. Cambridge: Cambridge University Press.

"How Does Copyright Work in Space?" 2013. *The Economist*, May 22. https://www.economist.com/the-economist-explains/2013/05/22/how-does-copyright-work-in-space.

Hughes, David Edward. 1878. "On the Action of Sonorous Vibrations in Varying the Force of an Electric Current." May 17. *Chemical News* XXXVII (964): 197–9.

Joyce, James. 1968 [1922]. *Ulysses*. Harmondsworth: Penguin.

Katz, Mark. 2005. *Capturing Sound: How Technology has Changed Music*. Berkeley: University of California Press.

Marshall, Wayne. 2014. "Treble Culture." In *The Oxford Handbook of Mobile Music Studies*, Volume 2, edited by Sumanth Gopinath and Jason Stanyek, 43–76. New York: Oxford University Press.

Milner, Greg. 2009. *Perfecting Sound Forever: An Aural History of Recorded Music*. New York: Faber and Faber.

Moore, Allan. 2010. "The Track." In *Recorded Music: Performance, Culture and Technology*, edited by Amanda Bayley, 252–67. Cambridge: Cambridge University Press.

Nancy, Jean-Luc. 2007. *Listening*. New York: Fordham University Press.

Patch, Nick. 2015. "About to Launch Album Debut, Chris Hadfield Talks Recording Music in Space." *The Globe and Mail*, August 7. https://www.theglobeandmail.com/news/national/about-to-launch-album-debut-chris-hadfield-talks-recording-music-in-space/article25872987/.

Putnam, Robert. 2000. *Bowling Alone: The Collapse and Revival of American Community*. New York: Simon and Schuster.

Rehding, Alexander. 2014. "Of Sirens Old and New." In *The Oxford Handbook of Mobile Music Studies*, Volume 2, edited by Sumanth Gopinath and Jason Stanyek, 77–108. New York: Oxford University Press.

Roads, Curtis. 1995. *The Computer Music Tutorial*. Cambridge, MA: The MIT Press.

Schafer, R. Murray. 2004 [1973]. "The Music of the Environment." In *Audio Culture: Readings in Modern Music*, edited by Christoph Cox and Daniel Warner, 29–39. New York: Continuum.

Sloterdijk, Peter. 2011. *Bubbles: Spheres I*. Frankfurt: Semiotext(e).

Toop, David. 2004. *Haunted Weather: Music, Silence and Memory*. London: Serpent's Tail.

Weidman, Amanda J. 2006. *Singing the Classical, Voicing the Modern: The Postcolonial Politics of Music in South India*. Durham, NC: Duke University Press.

Weiss, David. 2015. "Inside Adele's '25': How Tom Elmhirst Mixed a Masterpiece." *SonicScoop*, December 21. https://sonicscoop.com/2015/12/21/inside-adeles-25-how-tom-elmhirst-mixed-a-masterpiece/.

Witts, Richard. 2009. "Records and Recordings in Post-Punk England." In *The Cambridge Companion to Recorded Music*, edited by Nicholas Cook, Eric Clarke, Daniel Leech-Wilkinson, and John Rink, 80–3. Cambridge: Cambridge University Press.

Young, Miriama. 2015. *Singing the Body Electric: The Human Voice and Sound Technology*. Farnham: Routledge.

Young, Miriama. 2016. "Let Me Whisper in Your Earbud: Curating Sound for Ubiquitous Tiny Speakers." *Leonardo Music Journal* 26: 10–13. doi:10.1162/LMJ_a_00959.

Discography

Adele. "Hello." 25. XL, 2015.

Bach, Johann Sebastian. *St John Passion* (1724 Version). Academy of Ancient Music. Signum Records, 2014.

Björk. "Headphones." *Post*. One Little Indian, 1995.

Björk, "Cocoon." *Vespertine*. One Little Indian, 2001.

Bush, Kate. "Running up That Hill." *Hounds of Love*. EMI, 1985.

Bush, Kate. "Under Ice." *Hounds of Love*. EMI, 1985.

De La Soul. "Can You Keep a Secret." *3 Feet High and Rising*. Tommy Boy, 1989.

Gainsbourg, Serge and Jane Birkin. "Je T'Aime... Moi Non Plus." *Jane Birkin/Serge Gainsbourg*. Fontana, 1969.

Hadfield, Chris. "Space Oddity." Cover of David Bowie (1969). YouTube, 2013

Hadfield, Chris. *Space Sessions: Songs from a Tin Can*. Warner, 2015.

Jackson, Michael. "In the Closet." *Dangerous*. Epic, 1992.

London Grammar. "Strong." *If You Wait*. Metal and Dust Recordings, 2013.

London Grammar. "Hey Now." *If You Wait*. Metal and Dust Recordings, 2014.

Ying Yang Twins. "Wait (The Whisper Song)." *U.S.A. (United State of Atlanta)*. TVT Records, 2005.

CHAPTER 19

WHEN ROBOTS SPEAK ON SCREEN

Imagining the Cinemechanical Ideal

JENNIFER FLEEGER

IN the real world, robots are built primarily for labor: they make cars, perform surgeries, pack boxes, and vacuum floors. Their design may invite admiration, but anyone operating them expects efficiency rather than affection in return for a day's work. On screen, however, robots are also built to love: rarely mute automatons, cinematic robots are endowed with voices that make them appear to have souls. How do film robots inform impressions of the mechanical laborers that populate the twenty-first-century workplace? Why do robots speak on screen?

The voice that animates the machine continually threatens to belie its origins; it is as if Hollywood filmmakers cannot rest without showing us the "real" faces of the robots they have created. Typically, robots are played by actors with verifiable off-screen identities whose celebrity brings an aura of authenticity to the role and dollars to the box office. The conflict between the robot as a mechanical character and the human voice it possesses weaves its way into the films' narratives: robot movies are rife with unmaskings and boundary crossings. From David's quest to become a real boy in *A.I. Artificial Intelligence* (dir. Steven Spielberg, 2001) to Ava's escape into the real world at the end of *Ex Machina* (dir. Alex Garland, 2015), the robot's longing to be human reflects a kernel of desire found in the real relations between humans and robots and attests to the ontology of the cinema itself.

This imbalance in the revelatory impetus of the filmmaker and the necessity of the coherence of the robot character is made evident in *Iron Man*, a film series that condenses contemporary discourses about class, capitalism, love, and technology. In the original comic, Iron Man (the alter ego of wealthy, self-centered inventor, Tony Stark) had a remarkably overqualified butler named Edwin Jarvis. Before coming to work for the Stark family, Jarvis had been a WWII combatant and esteemed boxer. When Stark joined the Avengers, a team of highly skilled super heroes, Jarvis came along, attending to Stark's

FIGURE 19.1 J.A.R.V.I.S. in holographic form. Screen grab, *Avengers: Age of Ultron* (2015).

companions with the detached grace of British domestic servitude. By the time of the first *Iron Man* film, Jarvis was no longer a common man; he had evolved into J.A.R.V.I.S. (Just A Rather Very Intelligent System), an A.I. created by Stark to be both friend and digital assistant. Voiced by London-born actor Paul Bettany, J.A.R.V.I.S. appears in the *Iron Man* films[1] as the disembodied holographic image of rotating blue shapes shown in Figure 19.1. By substituting a wondrous display of glowing lights for the two-dimensional drawing of a British working class man with commendable physical prowess, the filmmakers have emptied the manservant of his revolutionary potential.

Unlike Edwin Jarvis, J.A.R.V.I.S. has no bodily or emotional needs, no human core to be exploited by the egotistical Stark. An A.I. ought to be able to serve his master without inciting audience outrage. After all, he is merely a manmade creature, a technological construction, a robot. So why do viewers care about J.A.R.V.I.S. at all?

The presumption that a robot is simply technology was put to the test in Spike Jonze's *Her* (2013), a film about a lonely man's infatuation with his overtly feminine operating system. Played by Scarlett Johansson, Samantha, like J.A.R.V.I.S., has no body, yet has been similarly designed to cater to her user's demands. As the film progresses, however, we find it impossible to pretend Samantha doesn't exist, a condition rooted in the grain of Johansson's voice. As Roland Barthes famously defines it, the grain is "the body of the voice as it sings"(Barthes 1977, 188), the sounds we make that have nothing to do with the meaning of the words we say; in other words, the grain is the listener's assurance that the speaker is human. Scarlett Johansson's breathy voice and the scratch of her consonants at the back of her throat tell us that Samantha must be more than a machine. The sound of the voice thus certifies the humanity of the operating system, unraveling the film's oppressive premise and revealing the role of the robot in the cinema's imagination. Filmic robots are perfect workers with imperfect voices, and in their voices emerges the quavering unsuitability of humanity for a technological age.

Near the end of *Avengers: Age of Ultron* (dir. Joss Whedon, 2015), a later Marvel property in which Iron Man plays a major role, Paul Bettany's J.A.R.V.I.S. evolves into more than a voice. Stark's incessant tinkering produces a character for Bettany to play, an impressively bright red android appropriately named Vision who is equipped with the J.A.R.V.I.S. operating system and capable of flight.[2] The visual motor of the cinema cannot resist making a vision of Vision, and in so doing, brings before our eyes a robotic modulation of the Edwin Jarvis that the original series sought to expel. Bettany speaks calmly, with the British accent readers of the comic would have imagined for Jarvis. But what exactly is Vision? His dialogue provides something of an answer in the form of a warning: "Maybe I am a monster. I don't think I'd know if I were one. I'm not what you are and not what you intended. So there may be no way to make you trust me." Of course, there is no reason to trust Vision, just as there is no reason to trust our own "vision" in watching these images, for Hollywood itself is an artificial intelligence machine with a long history of investing in imagined worlds, alternate realities. Nonetheless, because they are not quite human, Vision and the robots that came before him are uniquely positioned to tell the truth about the injustices that permeate this reality—injustices related primarily to social class—and appear almost uncannily aware that "real" robots are not part of the solution, in spite of what their creators may have intended.

This chapter argues that the audible signifiers of gender, class, and race in the voices that give life to Hollywood's robots make audiences comfortable with the robot as worker, and by extension, with the labor practices of an industry in which it is not always possible to distinguish images of and by real people from those generated by a computer.[3] The cinematic robot's voice unifies an era's dream of the ideal worker and its hopes for the perfect human. Yet as the tools available to filmmakers change, so do representations of the cinematic robot's humanity and its relationship to work. By examining a range of robots on screen that begin chronologically with the wildly passionate gestures, dances, and speeches of the artificial Maria in Fritz Lang's German silent film *Metropolis* (1927) and end with two recent Hollywood robotic rebels, Vision from *Avengers: Age of Ultron* and Ava from *Ex Machina*, I analyze the robot voices in relation to the economic and technological changes affecting the film industry to reveal the troubling connotations in the selection and use of the actors who play them. First I look at Lang's *Metropolis* as an origin tale for the cinematic fembot, then I turn to accents to explore the sounds of social class in mechanical beings, and finally, I examine the role played by race in the construction of the expendable robotic body.

FEMBOTS FROM *METROPOLIS* TO *MACHINA*

Perhaps the most surprising thing about listening to robot voices in the cinema is that they are not usually very robotic. Moreover, although it would be entirely possible to give each cinematic robot a variety of voices, each is typically played by a single actor. David, a robot in the film *Prometheus* (dir. Ridley Scott, 2012), offers a reasonable explanation for this phenomenon when asked by another character why he bothers to emulate human characteristics: "I was designed like this because you people are more comfortable interacting with your own kind." Indeed, social psychology proves David right: people respond better to robot voices when they sound more like our own. A 2011 study found that artificial voices sound less "robotic" when they have local accents (Tamagawa et al. 2011). Moreover, when the robots are female, listeners prefer higher-pitched voices. Researchers in 2013 studied interactions with female robot reception-ists and noted that participants getting assistance from the higher-voiced robot rated her appeal and personality higher than they did one with a lower voice (Niculescu et al. 2013 187). Thus perceptions of fembots conform to stereotypes about real girls.

Filmmakers were aware of the power of the robot voice even before the cinema learned to speak. Fritz Lang's infamous fembot Maria in *Metropolis* shares a face with the charismatic rebel Maria, a character whose moving speeches on workers' rights rep-resent a danger to the smooth operation of capitalist exploitation. Metropolis is a city divided: working men and women live underground serving machines while the upper classes roam above, shopping in glamorous stores and lounging in elegant gardens. Maria poses a threat to this structure by loudly asserting what the other residents can never admit: all men and women are the same. That is, class difference cannot be attributed to biology; there is no "natural" explanation for the workers' exploitation and the comfort of the privileged. Unsurprisingly, those in charge of Metropolis come up with a plan to stop Maria from making trouble: they create a robot that looks just like her and send it below to quell the movement. Since she is played by the same actress, robot Maria looks identical to real Maria. Lang had to provide audiences some way of distinguishing the real Maria from the false one. Thus, he gave robot Maria a unique "voice."

Although *Metropolis* is a silent film, it demonstrates the power of oratory. Maria's passionate speeches are what move the workers to action, her vocal delivery is what shocks the mayor's son not only to support her cause, but also to fall in love with her. Viewers, of course, hear none of this. Capable only of reading limited title cards, they must be able to locate the intensity of Maria's voice visually for her message to be convincing. Silent films have a number of ways to communicate sound. For example, a close-up of a horse running can prompt audiences to "hear" hooves hitting the ground (which would in some cases have been produced in the theater by an appropriate sound effect). Films could reference popular song lyrics, exaggerate falls so that one could practically feel a thud, or vary the length of shots to produce a visual rhythm. Voices can be similarly conjured. In describing the "grain" that makes each voice unique, literary theorist Roland Barthes famously said, "The 'grain' is the body in the voice as it sings, the hand as it writes, the limb as it performs" (Barthes 1977, 188). Lang's film makes the grain visual by allowing viewers to see the voice through the body. This is especially true of robot Maria, whose "voice" emerges primarily through her physical movements and the pace of Lang's edits. Her body movements are exaggerated, forcing the spectator to "see" the sound she makes. This happens initially with the erotic dance she performs for the men in a nightclub, as seen in Figure 19.2. Lang edits the scene so that robot Maria's move-ments are intercut with close-ups of men's eyes, which speak volumes about her appeal. She is moving constantly, spinning, marching, throwing her shawl, each action carefully executed to display Maria's body and fill the frame. The scene becomes metaphorically

FIGURE 19.2 Robot Maria on display. Screen grab, *Metropolis* (1927).

louder as the men's faces are manically superimposed over one another and the pace of the editing increases. The rhythm implies panting; the pace makes whatever music one could imagine in the scene louder and faster. The men's faces become larger and larger, until only a Dali-esque arrangement of superimposed eyes remains. Lang has substituted an eye for a scream.

Near the end of her frenetic performance, robot Maria stares into the camera as Lang makes us acutely aware of her difference from the calm human Maria. Robot Maria bounces as she stares, her hypnotic gaze daring us to examine a body that cannot stand still. Her "voice" is halting; shouting rapid-fire instructions, it speaks without cadence. When the real Maria looks into the camera at the beginning of the film, however, she evokes a lyrical mode of speech, made visible in Figure 19.3. In this scene, which begins in an extreme long shot, Maria enters an enchanted garden belonging to the rich sons of the city's anointed while herself surrounded by astonished children in ragged clothing. She points slowly around her and says to the children, "Look! These are your brothers!" The medium close-up that follows this assertion as Maria calmly lifts her chin slightly upward to stare into the eyes of the men affirms the truth of her statement. Lang's camera takes its time with each subsequent shot, cutting between human Maria and the mayor's son several times, giving their looks and her words time to seep into the viewer's mind. In *Metropolis*, Lang seems to say, the voice and the look are synonymous; viewers must use their eyes to hear.

The real Maria uses loving gestures to accompany her plea, while robot Maria asks us to examine her body for evidence of "rational" speech. A scene late in the film makes it evident that robot Maria's voice is just as capable of entrancing the workers as that of

FIGURE 19.3 Real Maria's face speaks volumes. Screen grab, *Metropolis* (1927).

her double, but rather than producing an emotional connection with them, robot Maria speaks with coercive violence. As she advocates for the anarchistic abandonment of machines, the workers lean toward her en masse, looking as if they want literally to eat her words. A horde of men shouts in response as she asks them, "Who feeds the machines with their own flesh?" and Lang encourages viewers to hear their vociferous agreement by showing the crowd from different angles, the men indistinguishable from one another in their anger. This is a mass responding to oration. The visual presentation of this moment is compelling because Maria eschews machines in making her point; in spite of the design of this futuristic city, the public speech remains the best way to convince large quantities of people of a particular position. Of course, Lang makes this point through a robot in film, a mass medium that uses technology to deliver its message. In spite of the film's conclusion, which destroys the robot in favor of the real Maria, whose relationship with the mayor's son succeeds in uniting the classes, the robot remains the most influential part of Lang's film, its scenes the most cited, its movements the most compelling. The emphasis on the human qualities of the real Maria is therefore a ruse to distract viewers from what they already know: the twentieth century is an age of both mass audition and mass deception, a combination that will remain ineffective as long as they neglect to account for the human, but one that regards the workforce as a potential collective.

By contrast, the twenty-first century workplace depicted in *Ex Machina* is populated by employees motivated by personal rewards that are ultimately reaped by the very few. The most ostentatious example of this is Nathan, the CEO of a software company who lives in a secluded natural wonderland. Caleb, his employee, is a cubicle-bound computer programmer who ostensibly wins the company lottery at the beginning of the film. Importantly, this is a scene shot without synchronous sound, accompanied instead by the music Caleb hears through his headphones as he learns the news by email, thus perfectly illustrating the isolation of the contemporary office worker. The prize is a trip to the home of the sadistic and narcissistic Nathan, who designs not only search engines, but also A.I. for both personal and professional gain. Although Caleb is asked to assess the believability of Nathan's latest A.I., a fembot named Ava, the boss is secretly testing his own employee, expecting Caleb to fall for Ava's charms. Unlike Maria, whose rhetorical skills are aimed at the masses, Ava is quietly manipulating Caleb, convincing him she has feelings for him so that he might free her from Nathan's authority. Yet as it was with Maria, Ava's appearance is important; Nathan later acknowledges that he has designed her in accordance with Caleb's porn search preferences. In addition to being a physical conglomeration of attributes culled from Caleb's data, Ava's gestures and expressions are also the result of Nathan's hacking: he has stolen images and video from millions of cell phones to construct the perfect girl. Thus Ava, a robot intended for the isolated and individual worker, is the result of mass data collection, making her the distinct opposite of Maria, who shared the same body as *Metropolis'* main actress.

It is strange that Ava's voice is so distinctive, seeing that she is meant to have been sourced from millions of digital bits. Swedish actress Alicia Vikander plays Ava, and although her accent is not audible as such, there is a tangible difference about her mode of speech—hesitations in the wrong places, an ethereal breathiness at times and deep throated expressions at others, all of which get wrapped up in an effort at robotic vocal delivery—that makes it seem as though her voice does not quite belong to an individual personality; it is as if she were the audio equivalent of photographic experiments that blend attributes of beauty standards onto a single face.[4] She seems to summon her voice from different parts of her body, as if to express human emotion sonically but without necessarily registering the accompanying facial expression that would make the emotion personal. Robots may not be capable of shedding tears, but they can sound as if they are about to cry. When asked during a late night television interview how the actress came up with a voice suitable for a robot, Vikander answered that she began by "finding a physicality for Ava" (Vikander 2015), which is important because in the finished film, Ava's physical movements are accompanied by soft whirring effects intended to make her body sound robotic. As shown in Figure 19.4, she appears unclothed for much of the film, the mechanical contents of her skull, forearms, and torso visible through her translucent plastic framing, all of which are there to remind us that she is not human.

Yet the body in her voice confirms the existence of an actress erased in postproduction to make the robot's body possible. Vikander normally speaks English quickly, with a British accent. She claims that she has always had a "dark and husky voice," so she attempted to harness a tone for Ava that would be "gentle and light" (Vikander 2015). The contrast between the deep tone of Vikander's natural speech and the "gentleness" she attempted to portray seems responsible for the eerie calmness of Ava's presence; it is what makes us willing to believe her capable of either loving or destroying Caleb. In one scene, Ava quickly and capably shuts down the monitoring system Nathan has set

FIGURE 19.4 Visual reminders that Ava is not human. Screen grab, *Ex Machina* (2015).

up to observe her. She sits across from Caleb, wearing a modest dress, hands folded nervously in her lap, and states quietly: "I want to be with you." The statement was made lyrically, peaking in volume on the word "be," the only one of the words spoken without a raspy quality. After a pause, Ava's assertive manner comes to the fore again, cleanly and abruptly announcing the arrival of a new question, and then she pauses, before asking him hesitantly, in a near whisper: "Do you want to be with me?" The variations in Ava's vocal delivery is what makes the film's ending—her seemingly cruel abandonment of Caleb in favor of her own freedom—believable. Her voice insists Ava is a person, not a robot who must spend her life working for a man's affection. A real robot is reliant on her creator; Ava is not.

A similar relationship arises in Spike Jonze's film *Her* (2013). Theodore, a character who generates greeting card sentiments for a living, which he produces in an isolated office environment similar to Caleb's cubicle existence, gets a new operating system named Samantha, who is voiced by Scarlett Johansson. Although Vikander attempted to change her voice to suit the robot, Johansson's voice is easily identifiable as belonging to her, which becomes valuable for film viewers because she never appears on screen. Michel Chion would call Samantha an "acousmêtre," a disembodied voice that, because it does not need to follow physical laws, can crop up anywhere and to whom we attribute both absolute knowledge and control over the story world (Chion 1999, 24). Theodore falls in love with Samantha, who appears to love him back, and the two spend much of the film discussing what it means to have a relationship with a bodiless "person." Samantha exists only in Theodore's ear, but she speaks with a deep voice that cracks with emotion. During one conversation, in a voice that barely moves into an audible register, Samantha sadly asks, "Are these feelings even real? Or are they just programming?" Our focus on the question of whether or not Ava and Samantha have feelings is a distraction. We can hear that the actresses have feelings, whatever we might believe about their characters. These women are powerful robots with powerless voices, the combination of which works to remind us of who is really in control. Can objects love us back?

Vikander's and Johansson's voices allow us to indulge that fantasy, but ultimately, the films conclude that the voice does not make us human after all. Instead, these films are testing us: how willing are we to watch the subjugation of women for the pleasure of sci-fi?

Like *Ex Machina*, which exiles its workers in the first few minutes of the film, leaving only lead creative personnel in their place, the film industry gives the impression that it not reliant on human labor either; it appears to be a self-generating, self-regulating machine, guided by a singular artist capable of speaking human truths, a creator who loves what he does and has earned his place in the system. The robot in cinema, however, continually exposes the falseness of this presumption by revealing its human origins, either by shaping its feminine voice, or by stressing its accent.

Accents and the Mechanical Man

What is distinct about male robots? Do they suffer the same degree of objectification? In spite of its distinctly human origins, the male robot's voice in cinema often announces its mechanical construction through its utter disregard for audio-visual matching. Robots speak near us, too near us. Michel Chion calls the vocal close-up "a voice that belongs to the cinema," a lineage that he says we can trace to the postsynchronous soundtracks of Italian films (Chion 1999, 165). Dubbed voices hover on a plane distinct from the bodies for which they speak, trusting us to believe in them, while robot voices do not bother with pretense. We are not supposed to believe the robot is real. In fact, we know very well he is not any more possible than the sci-fi worlds he inhabits. As was true of Scarlett Johansson's unseen character in *Her*, films often do not visually invest in the robot as a character. We understand how cinematic robots work because we witness how they function. Yet filmmakers encourage identification with these heaps of metal through the strategic deployment of voices. The Terminator and C-3PO (of *Star Wars* fame) are presented as otherworldly travelers created to accomplish specific tasks. The distance between a brutally destructive force from the future with a rather basic understanding of English and a friendly space explorer who speaks six million languages is overcome by their distinctly European accents. Accents permit the body of the voice to sneak its way into the properties of the robot.

The opening scene of *The Terminator* (dir. James Cameron, 1984) affirms Chion's proposition that the cinema relies on audio close-ups to establish imagined worlds. Los Angeles of 2029 is littered with human remains and utterly absent of human sounds. A man running through the murky battle makes no noise. Instead, low synthetic tones rumble in the score beneath the convincing sounds of laser fire and all-too realistic audio of skulls being crushed by a bulldozer. Because they are the most recognizable and disturbing element of the scene, the skulls are louder and closer than anything else. They also give us our first unsubtle indication of where our identification ought to lie in the battle between human and machine. In addition, the contrast between the sonorous crunching skulls and the silent human warrior asks us to consider the

FIGURE 19.5 The Terminator is more human than human. Screen grab, *The Terminator* (1984).

corporality of man: what noises are bodies supposed to make? This question becomes significant when the Terminator himself is introduced. Unclothed and bowed to the earth, he slowly rises; it is as if James Cameron were attempting to recreate one of Eadweard Muybridge's nineteenth-century experiments with motion photography (see Figure 19.5).

We are thus led to see Arnold Schwarzenegger's body as both perfect and false, an ideal human and a cinematic construction born of technological innovation. Indeed, minutes later, when a knife enters his flesh and has no effect on his muscular ability, we are sure that unlike the skulls smashed by his mechanical comrades, the Terminator's core must be inorganic.

The Terminator's voice, however, is inescapably Arnold Schwarzenegger—a real person with decades of lived experience—even while he is attempting to sound like a robot, empty of emotion on his first trip to Earth. His opening lines, delivered in monotone, merely repeat statements by three of the city's miscreant youth: "Nice night for a walk," and "Nothing clean, right." The "right" of the second sentence is articulated to suggest the Terminator misunderstands its rhetorical undertone, yet his third line, "Your clothes, give them to me, now" is delivered forcefully and with a brief nod. With this introduction, in which the Terminator vacillates between seeming to need instruction in human forms of communication and being capable of backing up his emphatically delivered demands with the force of his body, we are thrown into in a state of indecision with regard to the Terminator's personhood; is this a very smart robot or a very poor actor?

A similar quandary plagues the audience's relationship to C-3PO; that is, the combination of the voice and movement of the character makes viewers uncertain whether C-3PO is a robot or a human in a robot costume. The actor who played him, Anthony Daniels, noted: "In the beginning I was actually signed to secrecy. The studio wanted people to believe C-3PO was a real robot" ("Star Wars: Confessions" 2011). His movements, like Schwarzenegger's, are choreographed as if in homage to how robots are supposed to move. Because of the restricted mobility of the suit, C-3PO stands very straight, his torso seems disconnected from his lower half, and his arms and legs move with a mechanical stutter. The jittery motions match his short manner of speech, both of which are idiomatic of an English servant. In the same way that Schwarzenegger's Terminator appears to mimic human speech badly, Daniels's C-3PO cuts short the ends of words, giving the impression of little contemplation or forethought. His speech patterns are emphasized by their contrast to Darth Vader, who may look robotic, but whose humanity is assured by his infamously labored breathing, and to his companion R2D2, capable of emitting only a series of beeps. C-3PO cannot adjust his facial expressions or move his body fluidly, thus our ability to project emotions onto him are a result of his ability to speak. In spite of his villainous introduction, learning to speak softens how audiences are meant to feel about the Terminator as well. Indeed, his metamorphosis into a likeable character happens in part through the transformation of his speech. In *Terminator 2: Judgment Day* (dir. James Cameron, 1991), young John Connor teaches the Terminator how to use slang: "You gotta listen to the way people talk. Don't say, 'Affirmative'...You say, 'No problemo.'...and if you want to shine them on, it's 'Hasta la vista, baby'." That the Terminator's deployment of Connor's terminology has become as recognizable a cultural referent as C-3PO himself is evidence of the degree to which communication is the primary task for both of these robots, even if their narratives tell us that they have been employed to save the world.

The notion of imperfect communication is essential to how we understand that robots are different from humans. Writing about what it means to be human among beings artificial and animal, John Durham Peters calls communication, "the term that invites consideration of our relations to these creatures—each marked in some way as 'other' to 'man'" (Peters 1999, 229). What are our relations to a robot, particularly to one we see on the screen? Although we cannot communicate with cinematic robots ourselves, the robot's ability to speak invites our empathy. That is, we have to believe the robot has feelings if we are to care about it at all. And to believe it has feelings, we generate a body where, perhaps, none exists. Peters describes the absent body as the most troubling element of the Turing Test, Alan Turing's famous experiment that asks third parties to distinguish a human from a machine by engaging in a typed conversation: "The Turing test wants to imagine communication as if eros did not matter. But the repressed returns. The skins and faces and bodies of others turn out not to be in the least irrelevant to our interactions with them, at least in interactions among friends, lovers, and families" (Peters 1999, 240). We could add film characters to this list. The extent to which we project relationships onto screen figures, a mode of engagement on which narrative cinema relies, depends on what they look and sound like (were this not true, the star industry would have little value). Thus when we are watching a robot on screen, few among us would want it to fail the Turing test; indeed, the conditions of cinematic viewing have given it little hope of doing so. The robot must be a character; the robot must be loved. But here we have a paradox: to be convincing, the robot must *look* like a robot. It is the voice that gives feeling to its words.

Peters, however, claims that the power of the voice is more than mere feeling: "Human speech exceeds puzzle-solving intelligence, since it is always linked to possibilities of embodied action, which is why questions of ethics, sex, politics, life, and death will elude the machine" (Peters 1999, 236). However, the cinematic robot is concerned with all of these questions. For example, the Terminator attempts to interfere in politics by going back in time and eliminating his future foe. His relationship to sex and ethics is challenged by his interference in Sarah Connor's family life (indeed, in 1984, the *Hollywood Reporter* called the film "an age-old morality play" [Ellis 1984]). And while the character may be capable of replication, the actor who plays him visibly ages as the series goes on, reminding us of the certitude of death even for robots. C-3PO's political value lies in his communication skills. His ethical value lies in his application of those skills to alert his comrades to danger. When he appears in harrowing scenes himself, the possibility of his "death" scares us as much as it does for any of the other *Star Wars* characters. And while he is not a romantic figure, his "friendship" with R2D2 is essential to the series. Thus, when the Terminator and C-3PO speak, their voices carry a different weight than, perhaps, the robotic receptionists mentioned near the beginning of this chapter.

Robotic speech may lead to embodied cinematic action, but only because of how the robots themselves sound. That is, film characters listen to the advice of their robotic companions because they talk like people. The Terminator learns to speak, and when he succeeds, he sounds like the actor who plays him. Thus, the Terminator's speech maturation parallels that of the actor's. C-3PO sounds like an affable British butler: his tone is fussy, his articulation is impeccable, and his accent suggests a snootiness about his position of servitude. The work these robots perform on screen is a result of the ideas associated with their accents, which have, of course, been selected to depict the character as conceived at the moment of production. Indeed, there would be little reason for an intergalactic robot translator to sound like an Englishman. However, for a film produced in 1977 that uses a nostalgic cinematic language to articulate a futuristic theme, such a speech reference offers a certain logic. The English butler gives us a romantic presentation of work, an embodied image of the "robots" that make this film's effects possible. Like C-3PO, we imagine the machines that make the film may also be capable of loving what they do, and through them, the film itself becomes deserving of our love. Although in a different context, the Terminator's Austrian accent constructs a similar effect. The stern machinations of the Eastern European stereotype are familiar to filmgoers. Articulating the extreme capabilities of the human body with his precinematic fame as Mr. Universe, Schwarzenegger was called a "big, lovable lug" at the time of the film's release, although his voice and the character he builds to contain it are anything but cuddly (Ellis 1984). The mismatches between body and voice, work and love, are what gives these characters meaning that extends beyond their robotic significance.

Paradoxically, this disunity at the level of the body makes these robots seem real. In her description of the cinematic voice, Mary Ann Doane shows that film demands attention to realism by housing voices in appropriate bodies and produces the implication that these bodies are copresent with us. This is all in service of unity, because, she says, "Sound carries with it the potential risk of exposing the material heterogeneity of the medium" (Doane 1980, 35). Perhaps this is why Doane suggests that the two most prominent disembodied cinematic voices—God and the computer—are typically represented with "a certain anthropomorphism" (33). The body is necessary, because the cinema is in danger of dissolution without it; in a cinema without bodies, one would become too easily aware of the separate construction of the sound and image tracks. What, then, might we do with an animated robot, an object that announces itself as false from the start, a mere drawing, the work of a computer?

A film ostensibly for children, *Wall-E* (dir. Andrew Stanton, 2008) is a Pixar-fueled, terror-filled romance set in a space-age dystopia. In it, the titular robotic worker has been left on earth to tidy up the mountains of trash left behind by humans and the corporation, Buy 'N Large, that directs every aspect of their lives. Reflecting Pixar's tradition of transforming mass-produced objects into playthings to be loved by individual children, Wall-E listens to old jazz and watches VHS versions of Hollywood musicals to generate a nostalgic desire for a romantic relationship he has never had. He finally gets his chance when the humans send a scout, Eve, to search for signs of organic life on earth. Eve is sleek and sophisticated while Wall-E is essentially a trash compactor, and their verbal interaction illustrates this difference. Eve first asks Wall-E his "directive," which he demonstrates by exhibiting his trash, an unimpressive display, to which Eve responds by asking his name. Wall-E pronounces his name in a labored way, transforming each syllable into several by altering the pitch. Eve's laughter is a response both to his clunky corporate name and to the awkwardness of his speech, which is contrasted by her own pronunciation of Eve, a trick he cannot quite master. The film thus poses the question: is the robotic ideal to be found in Wall-E's playful and musical speech, or in Eve's expanded vocabulary and accurate articulation?

"Wall-E" is the robot's first word, spoken within the desolate soundscape of a postapocalyptic earth, an expression of identity and a call for recognition. Although Wall-E and Eve are both products with functions designated by humans, they imitate human ideals by—somewhat ironically, given the film's critique of consumer culture—loving objects. Like Ariel in *The Little Mermaid*, Wall-E collects artifacts of human progress, which represent for him the place he wishes to occupy in the world of objects: he wants to love and be loved in return. Wall-E is therefore a robot designed to become more than a cinematic figure, and it is no surprise that his voice, like Eve's, has been transmitted into the Disney Pixar toy that bears his name. The toys, shown in Figure 19.6 and selling for $50 each, have been made to interact, to replay the moment where Wall-E meets Eve, incessantly repeating their names.

Wall-E and Eve thus fit neatly into a tradition of talking toys: as Mladen Dolar observes, the original speaking machine, designed by Wolfgang von Kempelen in the late eighteenth century, was created to profess two main values: "the declaration of love and the praise for the ruler" (Dolar 2006, 7–10). Although Wall-E and Eve have moved off the screen to become "real" robots in a child's home, they cannot but recall the humans who voiced them in the film, the "rulers" who bestowed them with the identity they announce over and over again. It is though they are suffering from a hysterical devotion to someone who has placed this voice inside of them. Mladen Dolar says of

FIGURE 19.6 A robot that would be loved. Sales image for Pixar Collection Wall-E Talking Action Figure on Amazon.com.

interior voices: "at the very core of narcissism lies an alien kernel which narcissistic satisfaction may well attempt to disguise, but which continually threatens to undermine it from the inside" (41). The alien kernel at the heart of the toys, the film voice of Wall-E enters the home, allowing the robot to come to life by becoming a product, an object whose coherence is always threatened by its human creator.

Wall-E was voiced by Ben Burtt, who rose to fame as a sound designer for the *Star Wars* movies. Burtt said that the director of *Wall-E* wanted "the illusion that these robot characters, the speech and sounds they made were really coming from their functions as machines" (Roberts 2008). To create that impression, Burtt recorded and digitally altered his own voice, leaving artifacts in it to convince the listener that it had inhuman origins (Roberts 2008). Eve's voice, however, has been manipulated with a Vocoder, a device that marries a human voice to a musical tone capable of modulation. The significance of this difference is not to be missed; Jacob Smith has shown that the Vocoder and similar machines that were popular in the 1940s, such as the Voder and Sonovox, were gendered; they were operated by women and often used to give voice to commercial products, whether on the radio or in cinema. Yet once processed, they did not always sound like women: "The Sonovox voice seemed to lack 'female-ness'...The voice we hear is not just part male, part machine, and part nature, but also part female enunciator" (Smith 2008, 201). When we fetishize these voices by putting them into toys, or praising the clever technologies that produce them, we erase the female work that makes them possible. Unlike Wall-E, in which you can hear Burtt himself, Eve has become musical, so distanced from Elissa Knight, who voiced her, that like the women who used the Vocoder in the past, she has become unrecognizable. Burtt claimed his construction of Eve's voice was intended to project "the soul that a human being might have," but "sound like the voices were synthesized, like they were coming from a machine" (Burtt 2008). Indeed, the feeling of a soul remains in Eve, but the traces of the work that produced her voice do not. The robotic ideal presented by *Wall-E*, then, is a working toy that sounds like a human soul, a combination of masculine and feminine signifiers detached from the sonic markers of gender, a couple who can love their work and one another because they are objects themselves.

ROBOTS OF COLOR: A CONCLUSION

It seems strange that the body of the voice should continue to be valuable in robotic representation after *Wall-E* demonstrated the absolute affinity of love and labor. Yet in spite of the rich sonic universe Burtt created for the characters, Wall-E and Eve are missing something nonetheless, an observation that becomes more evident when in the presence of the toys. The personality made manifest by the vocal variations in the robot's limited speech suddenly seems flat when compared with a real child's voice, who might use the toy with an imaginative range of vocal effects that far outdoes the capabilities of the little robot. This could be why the robot worker on screen never quite makes good on his threat to replace the human, an effect we see in the real world as well. Rob Horning argues that although humans can offer creativity and compassion in the workplace in ways that robots cannot, employers will always find ways to exploit these qualities for profit: "The threat of automation, then, can be used to extract more emotional labor and more competitive advantage from humans. After all, one of the few things a robot can't supply is enthusiasm" (Horning 2015). Perhaps this lack of enthusiasm is nothing more than a glitch in the system, something Hollywood can solve by hiring specific voices.

Indeed, filmmakers have come up against this problem before. During the conversion to sound, critics began to suspect the limitations of sound technology might be overcome by employing African American actors. Alice Maurice has shown that conversion-era directors fetishized black song and speech to prevent audiences from recognizing problems with synchronous sound systems: "the 'black voice' offered a kind of insurance, a preemptive defense against the revelation of a lack" (Maurice 2002, 48). There are not many black robots in Hollywood films, which should not be all that surprising given there is not a lot of black speech in American cinema in general.[5] Yet the black robot's voice recalls the conversion era's nervous cover-up. Comedian Chris Rock plays a very small role in *A.I.*, Spielberg's fantasy on a Pinocchio theme that originated with Kubrick and tells the story of a robot-child named David who had been created to love. The film is full of uncomfortable voices: one of the robots can summon crooners' recordings with a tilt of his head and David's Teddy Bear is voiced by what sounds like a gruff old man. The most disturbing voice, however, is the most realistic. It occurs when David finds himself at the Flesh Fair, a dystopian festival where robots are violently torn apart for the entertainment of cheering human audiences. David looks on from inside a cage as an animatronic Chris Rock is hauled into the arena and makes a single joke before being shot through a ring of fire and, subsequently, a propeller, his head dismantled from his body and frozen for a moment in the frame of the bars of the cage (Figure 19.7). The film had established earlier that robots' physical identities are unstable; disfigured robots try on new parts—a white arm on a black body, a woman's jaw on a man's face. But while this cinematic image blends Chris Rock's features with the distinctive look of a minstrel character, Rock's voice is audibly his own.

Even though we could read the scene as an evocation of the public lynchings of the past projected onto the future, the terrifying moment simultaneously seems firmly rooted in the present. Because Rock's robot meets the same fate as all the others, the film appears to validate the celebration of colorblindness that dominated politics at the start of the twenty-first century. Yet Rock's voice, for its perceptible sarcasm, undermines this reading. The cavalier way he asks not to be sent to his death, perfectly representative of the comedian's humor, reveals that no matter what we see on screen, what we hear is an authentic human being, who carries with him into the film a racial and class identity that cannot be subsumed by cinematic fantasy. The lessons of this moment seem lost both on the film itself, which ends by claiming that the perfect human is a robot boy capable of giving and receiving love, as well as on the members of the public: the silicone face used for Chris Rock in *A.I.* was sold at auction for $2,250.[6] However, careful audition tells us why the moment is potentially revolutionary. If the cinematic voice is perpetually

FIGURE 19.7 A robot for the twenty-first century? Screen grab, *A.I. Artificial Intelligence* (2001).

interpellating us, Chris Rock's persona exposes the stakes of that process; what the narrative has really proposed is not that humans ought to love what they do, it is that they make work out of love. Little David spends 2,000 years trapped in the ice, begging the blue fairy to make him a real boy so that he can be loved. To love work is a choice available to only a few, and is dependent on the oppression of specific bodies we allow to stay hidden, bodies who often must feign love as work. The spectacle of dehumanization that dramatizes this latter position emerges within a narrative about becoming human, not only in *A.I.*, but in all the films I have examined here. We see it in *Metropolis'* mechanical workforce, *Ex Machina*'s caged fembots, the deformities of *Star Wars'* Darth Vader, the cruel muscular force of the Terminator, the bloated bodies of humanity's last members aboard *Wall-E*'s space ship. To speak about the robot is always to speak about the human. The body of the robot voice has been essential to overcoming the lack at the core of the robot image; in spite of the artificiality of CGI or a metal suit, the voice suggests that the robot can both love and work. Yet perhaps the disunity of the robot's body and voice is not so different from other cinematic figures, after all, Hollywood cinema is full of disembodied voices. Andrew Gibson claims, "the bodiless voice might be paradigmatic for film precisely because voice in film *is never other than bodiless*" (Gibson 2001, 652). Certainly the cinematic voice is a product of film technology, audible for only as long as the speakers release its sound, perceptibly a remnant of an era's recording capabilities. Yet the robot's voice implies a body beyond the cinema, irreducible to the image, that challenges the conditions of work and love in the culture that produced it.

Notes

1. *Iron Man* (dir. Jon Favreau, 2008), *Iron Man 2* (dir. Jon Favreau, 2010), *Iron Man 3* (dir. Shane Black, 2013).
2. Although I am aware that "android," "cyborg," and "robot" have different meanings and that extensive work exists tracing these distinctions, for the purposes of this discussion of the cinematic voice and its relationship to figures that challenge the idea of the human, I am putting all three in the same category.
3. See Lev Manovich's claim that the increased presence of computer-generated imagery has fundamentally changed our relationship to the image: "Consequently, cinema can no longer be clearly distinguished from animation. It is no longer an indexical media technology but, rather, a subgenre of painting" (2001, 295).
4. See, for example, an experiment that blends average faces of women from various countries: "Meet the World's Mrs. Averages: Scientists Blend Thousands of Faces Together to Reveal What the Typical Woman's Face Looks Like in 41 Different Countries from Around the Globe," *Daily Mail*, September 27, 2013, http://www.dailymail.co.uk/news/article-2435688/The-average-woman-revealed-Study-blends-thousands-faces-worlds-women-look-like.html.
5. For a palpable illustration of this, see Dylan Marron's "Every Single Word" series, which edits films to include only the dialogue of people of color. Unsurprisingly, the reconstructed films are quite short: http://www.dylanmarron.com/every-single-word/.
6. The head sold at an online auction in 2009: http://www.icollector.com/Chris-Rock-Comedian-animatronic-robot-head-from-A-I-Artificial-Intelligence-Android-scalp_i8632862.

WORKS CITED

Barthes, Roland. 1977. "The Grain of the Voice." In *Image, Music, Text*, translated by Stephen Heath, 179–89. New York: Hill and Wang.

Burtt, Ben. 2008. "Animation Sound Design: Building Worlds From the Sound Up." Special Feature on the *Wall-E* DVD Release, Disney-Pixar.

Chion, Michel. 1999. *The Voice in Cinema*, translated by Claudia Gorbman. New York: Columbia University Press.

Doane, Mary Ann. 1980. "The Voice in Cinema: The Articulation of Body and Space." *Yale French Studies* (60): 33–50.

Dolar, Mladen. 2006. *A Voice and Nothing More*. Cambridge, MA: The MIT Press.

Ellis, Kirk. 1984. Review of *The Terminator*. *The Hollywood Reporter*. October 26. Reprinted October 24, 2014. http://www.holywoodreporter.com/news/terminator-read-thrs-1984-review-743708.

Gibson, Andrew. 2001. "'And the Wind Wheezing Through that Organ Once in a While': Voice, Narrative, Film." *New Literary History* 32 (3): 639–57.

Horning, Rob. 2015. "Do the Robot." *The New Inquiry*. August 12. https://thenewinquiry.com/blog/do-the-robot/.

Manovich, Lev. 2001. *The Language of New Media*. Cambridge, MA: The MIT Press.

Maurice, Alice. 2002. "'Cinema at Its Source': Synchronizing Race and Sound in the Early Talkies." *Camera Obscura* 17 (1): 31–71.

Niculescu, Andreea, Betsy van Dijk, Anton Nijholt, Haizhou Li, and Swee Lan See. 2013. "Making Social Robots More Attractive: The Effects of Voice Pitch, Humor and Empathy." *International Journal of Social Robotics* 5 (2): 171–91.

Peters, John Durham. 1999. *Speaking Into the Air: A History of the Idea of Communication*. Chicago: University of Chicago Press.

Roberts, Sheila. 2008. "Ben Burtt Interview, Wall-E." *MoviesOnline*. http://www.moviesonline.ca/movienews_14930.html.

Smith, Jacob. 2008. "Tearing Speech to Pieces: Voice Technologies of the 1940s." *Music, Sound, and the Moving Image* 2 (2): 183–206.

"Star Wars: Confessions of the Brit Who Plays C-3PO." 2011. *The Mirror*. September 11. http://www.mirror.co.uk/news/uk-news/star-wars-confessions-of-the-brit-who-153114.

Tamagawa, Rie, Catherine I. Watson, I. Han Kuo, Bruce A. MacDonald, and Elizabeth Broadbent. 2011. "The Effects of Synthesized Voice Accents on User Perceptions of Robots." *International Journal of Social Robotics* 3 (3): 253–62.

Vikander, Alicia. 2015. Interview, *Late Night with Seth Meyers*. Aired June 3. https://www.youtube.com/watch?v=xSmi5B7I1EQ.

PART VI

....

NEGOTIATING
VOICE

VOICE AS TRANSACTION

....

CHAPTER 20

....

ROBOT IMAMS!

Standardizing, Centralizing, and Debating
the Voice of Islam in Millennial Turkey

....

EVE McPHERSON

INTRODUCTION

THROUGHOUT Turkey, as it is in other primarily Muslim countries, five times a day the Islamic call to prayer is recited and broadcast to millions of people. The call reminds adherents of prayer times and of Islam's fundamental tenets: there is only one God and Mohammed is His prophet. Almost every reference to the call notes its primacy to the faith and its position as one of the most important symbols; many narratives, for instance, note that the beauty of the human voice reciting these words can convert listeners and restore the faith of those who have strayed (McPherson 2009, 94–121). This belief in the affective ability of Islam's public voice has made the call a site for political manipulation of its sonic attributes. In Turkey, since the establishment of the Turkish Republic in 1923, the voice of the call has received ongoing attention in a tradition of shaping this very public sound that also advances contemporary political agendas.

In the past, under early Turkish Republic Kemalist reform policies, the state manipulated the voice of the call in order to secularize, modernize, and Turkicize its captive audience through language reform (McPherson 2011). Today, in the wake of the increasing success of Islamist-based parties since the 1990s, the call is shaped by a different ideology, one that argues Islam can coexist with, and perhaps even guide, that which is democratic, modern, and progressive. And while the underlying goals of the early Republic and those of the more recent Islamist-based parties may differ, what has not changed is the state's attempt to control religion and its aurally embodied understanding through the sound of the humanly voiced call. In the twenty-first century it is attempted through a subtler regulation, one that encompasses continuing education, national competitions, and centralization. But, as in the past, many adherents have not received regulation of this auditory symbol with enthusiasm. Discourse, debate, and dissent continue to appear in response to such programs, particularly centralization. This chapter discusses the early twenty-first-century regulation of the public voice of Islam and the public responses it has engendered, arguing that the links between Turkish political institutions and what is perceived as the daily sound of divinity continue a complicated history of manipulating affective response through audition of the call's sacred, but very human, voice.

The information for this chapter was gathered in 2006 and 2007, the early years of the Islamist-based Justice and Development Party's (AKP) administration, during which time I was conducting fieldwork on the call to prayer in Turkey and the Turkish construct of the beautiful voice in call-to-prayer recitation.[1] This period comes before the unrest of the early millennial teens and the subsequent attempted coup of July 15, 2016, while dissent was expressed with *comparatively* relative openness. It builds on my earlier work in which I discuss how the early modern period, specifically the Kemalist call-to-prayer reform project of 1932–1950, has had lasting impact on the vocal timbre and melodic elements of the call. After 1950 the single-party Kemalist period was replaced with the multiparty period and often shifting political powers, along with several successful military coups, until the mid-1990s when the stage was set for the long-term entrenchment of Islamist-based parties as ruling parliamentary majorities. Thus, this chapter follows the story that emerged in the earlier years of the AKP administration and its political gains, from the 1990s to about 2010, and the way in which the discourse surrounding and the actions taken regarding the public voice of Islam reflected the ongoing debate concerning national Turkish identity and its often uneasy, but nonetheless inextricable, relationship with Islam.

EXTRATEXTUALITY AND
VOICE IN ISLAMIC RECITATION

In call-to-prayer recitation practice, there are three primary components: language (its sound quality and textual message), vocal timbre, and melody. Of these, the text conveys a direct message, while the sound of the language, the vocal timbre (which is tied to the language of recitation as well), and the melody can evoke extratextual understandings. This extratextuality arose, in part, from the twentieth-century Turkish experience of the call, which is discussed later in this chapter. It also came from the longstanding position of the call as of divine origin and the human voice in recitation: intrinsic to the practice of the Islamic faith is human recitation and all that it can suggest beyond a text.

In Koranic recitation,[2] for instance, voiced text creates an auditory faith space that transcends the written word of the Koran in its affective and intellectual experience of Islam. A study of Islamic jurisprudence by Brinkley Messick argues that the text of the Koran is "backgrounded in relation to its emphasized recitational identity" (1993, 22).

And, from the first years of Islam, stories of the voiced Koran's affective ability circulated telling of conversions based on its recited sound:

> Believers, most of whom, including Muhammad himself, were illiterate, imbibed its [the Quran's] teachings by listening to public readings of its chapters... Many of the first believers were converted by the sheer beauty of the Quran, which resonated with their deepest aspirations, cutting through their intellectual preconceptions in the manner of great art, and inspiring them, at a level more profound than the cerebral, to alter their whole way of life.   (Armstrong 2000, 4–5)

And, while the call to prayer is not Koranic recitation, its aesthetic qualities, expectations for vocal performance, and recognition as a nonmusic recitation practice are similar (Sarı 2010, 19). And, also like Koranic recitation, the call to prayer was established as a humanly voiced recitation practice of divine origin (Sırma 2005, 24–29).

In its aesthetic and history, the call's vocal sound affectively implies multivalent layers of understanding and purpose. The call's basic objective is to announce each of the five daily prayer times and remind adherents of their duty to pray. Ahmet Gürtaş writes that when Muslims hear the call to prayer, they must accept the invitation and pray after the call is over (2005, 17). Likewise, Tong Soon Lee notes, "Upon hearing the *adhan*,[3] Muslims are obliged to put aside all mundane affairs and respond to the call physically and spiritually" (1999, 86–87). Another very clear objective of the call to prayer is to reaffirm the major tenets of the faith. Whenever Muslims hear and process the text of the call to prayer, in effect they are participating silently in a communal affirmation of their core beliefs (Saabiq 2006).[4] However, beyond the demarcation of prayer times and the textually oriented affirmation of beliefs, there have long been other auditory internalizations of the recited call to prayer. First among these is the way in which Muslim identity and community are reinforced by the sounding of the call. Lee's study of the call to prayer in Singapore argues that the call can serve to connect Muslims across real and imagined geographical spaces (1999). Furthermore, in countries where the call is broadcast to the general public, it is simultaneously reminding non-Muslims in the community of the local importance of Islam and the spiritual, and, at times, the material wealth of its followers. For example, historically the first act upon the conquering of a non-Muslim city was to recite the call to prayer. This act announced that the power of Islam had arrived in the city and that non-Muslim dwellers must now cede their space, both physical and sonic, to the new rulers (Sırma 2005, 43). And, as noted earlier, the voice of the call is an invitation to the faith with the ability to convert or reaffirm the listener's faith regardless of religious or linguistic background.

The call therefore has the ability to embody in the voice and its aural reception a rich acoustemology: it reminds listeners to pray, it voices fundamental beliefs, it unifies Muslims, it affirms Muslim identity, it proclaims the power of Islam, and it invites all listeners to the faith. With its ability to encompass so much information and evoke an emotional connection to the sound, it is not surprising that this public voice of Islam was of interest to the early architects of the Turkish Republic and that it is still of interest today. These Turkish leaders have recognized the power of the call to intone, consciously and unconsciously, their own political ideologies and have sought to manipulate the affective auditory response and to construct a sonic allegiance through the regulation of this voiced sound.

SHAPING THE SOUND IN
THE EARLY TURKISH REPUBLIC

The vocally disseminated and aurally received understandings discussed earlier may be considered pan-Islamic; however, historically a variety of call-to-prayer styles existed that overlaid local identities and interpretations to the receptive listener. When the call was recited in a particular style (timbrally and melodically), the voice expressed a specific regional identity. In Turkey, for example, there were four official regional styles during the Ottoman period (Özcan 1995, 44). So, in the Ottoman period, a regional style was perceived as being of Bursa or of the Istanbul palace, for instance. This voiced identity marker became a site of political manipulation with the establishment of the Turkish Republic. The nationalist authorities understood that the vocal/aural experience was a defining one, and while the call was recited in the sacred Arabic dialect, one that suggested a stronger tie to Islam and regional Ottoman identities rather than to the unified secular nation. Hence it was mandated that the call be recited in vernacular Turkish rather than sacred Arabic in order to insert a public national consciousness into this sonic faith space. In addition, while not officially mandated, the Istanbul style of recitation was nonetheless promoted over other regional styles through the distribution of a recording meant to teach other muezzins the new Turkish text (Lewis 1999, 46). The language mandate, which lasted from 1932 to 1950, was extremely unpopular and it was revoked in 1950 when the Republican People's Party (CHP) finally lost parliamentary control to the Democratic Party (DP).

State recognition of the public soundscape as a particularly effective communication zone in an Islamic country is one that maintains relevance. However, this more current project is much less interested in promoting a secular Turkish identity; instead, it seems to be concerned with reviving Ottoman Islamic pride while still promoting a modern, streamlined sound that invokes images of an organized, democratic, and controlled state. When Recep Tayyıp Erdoğan (the current AKP leader), was mayor of Istanbul (1994–1998) and then a member of Necmettin Erbakan's Islamist Welfare Party (RP), he was known for his improvement of city services and transportation and development projects in the interest of commerce and progress (Sontag 2003). During these years of his mayorship, the debate concerning the chaotic and unpleasant sound of the urban call to prayer seemed to be a regular topic among newspaper columnists. One writer, Can Ataklı, discussed the sorry state of the call in at least eight articles (Ataklı 1997a–h). It was also during this time that plans publicly emerged to address the uncontrolled and fragmentary sounds of the call (see, for example, Çevik 1997). These efforts at reform of the Turkish soundscape seemed to coincide with the reorganization of the urban landscape. Consequently, in recent years the government has continued its politicization of the call through what is effectively a sonic beautification project utilizing continuing education, competition, and centralization. However, because the mandates are state-driven ones implemented through state-run mosques and state-employed muezzins (official callers) and imams, arguments continue as to the appropriateness of state oversight of a religious practice, even when the state has Islamist leanings, as the AKP does.

REGULATING THE VOICE OF ISLAM IN THE NEW MILLENNIUM

After the RP was shut down by the Turkish military in 1997, the AKP was established, and in the fall of 2002, Erdoğan's AKP won a parliamentary majority.[5] The AKP initially claimed that it was not an Islamist party, rather it was a "democratic conservative" party and any concerns it had with religion were to let individuals practice their faiths with "impartiality" (Fuller 2008, 50–51). Nonetheless, the state still maintained management of religious institutions through the *Diyanet* (Directorate of Religious Affairs), which oversees all mosques and their employees, including imams and muezzins. Still, in these early years of AKP administration, there was some debate by political analysts and scholars as to whether or not the party was "Islamist." Whatever side of the debate one fell on, what is clear is that the party did take an interest in symbols of Islam, particularly those of Ottoman Islam (Fuller 2008, 53). The voiced call to prayer being a particularly public symbol with a recurring daily aural presence, it received state attention with what seemed to be the goal of reviving the call's Ottoman heritage within a democratic and modern framework.

Complaints concerning the call generally centered on the following. First, muezzins had poor voice qualities. Second, muezzins did not understand how to recite in the Turkish traditional manner and had only been educated in the government's secondary schools that train religious functionaries, the *imam-hatıp* schools, rather than undergoing the more rigorous and traditional pedagogical method of *meşk*. The following commentary by Necdet Tanlak, a well-known musician with expertise in religious music, exemplifies the grievances then circulating:

> Aziz Mahmut Kutlu, the head muezzin at Fatih mosque, with whom I studied religious music (through *meşk*), according to what I learned, used to recite the call to prayer in these *makams*:[6] the predawn prayer in *saba*; the midday prayer in *dugah*; the afternoon prayer in *hicaz*, *uşşak* or *neva*; the sunset was in *segah*; and the night prayer was in *uşşak*, *rast* or *hicaz*. The noon call to prayer was recited in *dugah* in order to establish a connection between dawn and noon. The *makam* in which the call was recited also could change according to the weather. Today, with most of the muezzins who come to Istanbul and work here, they receive no education. However, they learned to

recite the call in their village or city and this is how they recite here. Those who
know how to recite need to educate these muezzins on the call. Today, the error
most often noticed is that the evening calls are recited in a prolonged way. The evening call should be recited in a short period of time. The person who recites the call
should also be able to read the Koran without error. This is because the call is read
"with the mouth" of the Koran.[7] The second thing is that studying in the *meşk* system is necessary and the preferred voice of the person reading is baritone or tenor.

(Öztürk 2001, 53)

Here Tanlak's comments invoke what has been referred to as the Ottoman Istanbul
palace style, which is the expectation that muezzins should know how to negotiate the
correct *makams* and at what time of day to apply them (taking into consideration the
weather as well), how long certain daily calls should be (in particular, the evening call
should be shorter than the others), that they come as knowledgeable experts through
traditional training, and that their voice quality is on the higher end of the male range.

Attempts at reforming the call also seemed to codify the Ottoman Istanbul palace
style. The 2006 *Diyanet* web site, for instance, listed courses under its "Educational
Services" that were instituted to teach imams and muezzins how to recite in the proper
makams and how to use their voices more effectively.[8] Additionally, improved recitation
quality was encouraged through the establishment of call-to-prayer recitation competitions (alongside competitions for recitation and memorization of the Koran). The first
competition took place in 2003, less than a year after the AKP's national parliamentary
victory. In a set of more recently compiled competition guidelines made available in
2011, the *Diyanet* explained that the goals of competition are as follows:

> In the context of the week of activities celebrating mosques and religious officials,
> the aim of the Koran memorization, beautiful Koran recitation, and call-to-prayer
> recitation competitions is to develop the talents of our personnel and to provide
> opportunities to acquire deliberate work habits, continuing personal development
> of one's own talents, and feelings of confidence in one's own profession.
>
> ("2011 Yılı Camiler ve Din Görevlileri Haftası" 2011, 1)

A *Turkish Daily News* article from 2007 explains that another goal of the competition, as
it concerns the call to prayer, is to promote beauty in the sound and is a means of
addressing the increasing complaints received about poor quality calls (Akyol 2007).

In 2006 I attended the finals for the Istanbul regional call-to-prayer competition
(a preliminary competition that immediately precedes the national final competition),
and recorded the event with the permission of the local *müftülük* (local governing religious body). At this event, ten competitors, all muezzins or imams,[9] were each asked to
recite a call to prayer and were judged on the following criteria:

1. Up to 25 points for diction
2. Up to 25 points for style and comportment
3. Up to 25 points for knowledge of *makam*
4. Up to 25 points for beauty of the voice

Table 20.1 Written sources concerning *makams* used historically (see, for example, Sırma 2005, 75–76; Yeprem 2004, 208; Öztürk 2001, 45–55; Dursun 1999, 173–174; Sezgin 2006; Değirmenci 2004)

Time of Day	Makam
Sabah (predawn)	*Saba, Dilkeşhaveran*
Öğle (midday)	*Saba, Hicaz, Rast, Uşşak, Bayati*
İkindi (afternoon)	*Hicaz, Uşşak, Bayati, Rast*
Akşam (sunset)	*Hicaz, Rast, Segah, Dugah, Eviç*
Yatsı (night)	*Hicaz, Rast, Neva, Beyati, Uşşak*

Points were deducted for mistakes or low-quality performance.

At each competitor's turn, he was called up and asked in which *makam* he would begin the recitation and then the judges assigned a second *makam* to which the competitor was required to modulate at a specific point in the call's text. The modulation to a second *makam* in a single call-to-prayer recitation is against traditional Ottoman practice, but was required so that the competitor could demonstrate knowledge of and skill in more than one modal entity. Competitors were required to choose from and be able to recite in the following five *makams*: *saba, uşşak, rast, segah,* and *hicaz*. The choice of just five modes is limited given how many melodic modes exist, and, in the past, references cite a few more modes as being appropriate to certain daily calls. Examinations of documents relating to call to prayer practice reveal a historically richer application of *makam* to the call, as shown below in Table 20.1.

Thus, while the competition celebrates the Ottoman tradition of modal variety in recitation practice, at the same time it diminishes the richer Ottoman modal vocabulary. The small number of *makams* to select from reflects a more contemporary and controlled aesthetic. This modal reduction seems to acknowledge that creating expert practitioners, who are mythologized in call-to-prayer narratives, through the traditional method of intensive training, *meşk*, is no longer possible, or perhaps even desirable since that method implied an individualized master-student relationship that was not so easily controlled by a central entity such as the *Diyanet*. An additional sonic construct of Turkishness can be found in the preferred vocal register of the competitors. Sources, along with anecdotal evidence, suggest that there is a Turkish preference for the highest male range, tenor, and this range is associated with the Ottoman Istanbul palace style (see, for example, Öztürk 2001, 53; Akyol 2007). My own observations and an analysis of the recordings I made at the 2006 Istanbul call-to-prayer recitation competition suggest this is also the case: all competitors recited in what is traditionally considered to be a tenor range and the competitor who utilized the highest range (rising to an E above tenor high C) was the winner of both the Istanbul regional and national 2006 competition. Thus, the style codified in these competitions includes registration. Consequently, one commentator has argued that the call-to-prayer competitions seem to institutionalize and update the Istanbul palace practice by adapting a simplified, modern Ottoman Islamic aesthetic to democracy and order through the juried review and control of modal entity (Akyol 2007).

While implementation of call-to-prayer competitions and continuing education courses ultimately may standardize the Turkish recitation practice into one national style conceptualized as Ottoman revival, these reform measures did not generate much public debate or dissent; centralization, however, did. Centralization is the practice by which an area mosque simultaneously broadcasts the live call of one muezzin to other area mosques and these mosques subsequently broadcast this specific recitation to the community. Thus, several mosques broadcast the same call and not that of the mosque's individual muezzin. The *Diyanet* argues that centralization is a response to complaints surrounding noise caused by faulty amplification systems; simultaneous, clashing calls; calls recited at inaccurate times; and quality control in terms of the voices and musicality of the muezzins.

Plans to centralize the call seriously began in 1997 ("Diyanet: Ezan Susmaz" 1997), but the practice was not officially implemented until 2001. In a 2001 newspaper article detailing centralization, then *Diyanet* Minister, Mehmet Nuri Yılmaz, explained his specific reasoning:

> We have established such a practice in order to provide a unified call to prayer and in order to ensure that a beautiful call to prayer is heard. *Hafizes* with beautiful voices will be reciting the call in turns. The sounds of the call to prayer will not mix together.   ("En güzel sesli imam yayındı" 2001)

Yılmaz's justification is certainly in line with some basic requirements of the call. First, that it be recited with a beautiful voice, considered by many to be the most important feature of the call because it serves not only to remind listeners of times to pray but also to entice all listeners to the faith. Second, when the sounds of many mosques in close proximity mix together, the text and the voices themselves are often completely inaudible and this lack of audibility, for some adherents, means that in certain respects the call has simply not been recited in a way that fulfills its purpose.[10] Another reason cited for centralization was the lack of muezzins to fill positions. A *CNN Türk* article noted that for the approximately 75,000 mosques in Turkey, there were only 9,000 educated muezzins, which meant that many callers broadcast from loudspeakers were theoretically unqualified as far as the *Diyanet* was concerned (Değirmenci 2004).

Centralization was implemented first in the cities of Burdur, Zonguldak, Balıkesir, Van, and Tekirdağ by connecting all the area mosques by cable. As the project expanded to locations where connecting by cable was not possible, the *Diyanet* planned to broadcast via an FM station that was to be simultaneously broadcast to area mosques, which would then broadcast the signal to their local congregations ("En güzel sesli imam yayındı" 2001). These techniques did not always work well: the problems were technical and logistical. One journalist noted that when the call to prayer was broadcast from a central location, the main frequency sometimes mixed with other frequencies broadcasting the call to prayer from nearby cities. The resulting broadcast undermined the sound quality and produced a "grating" (*hışırtlı*) sound; thus, the point of ensuring the sound of a beautiful voice and a lack of cacophony was defeated and the listeners felt "uncomfortable" (*rahatsız*). Additionally, when a system unintentionally picked up frequencies broadcasting the call to prayer from other locations, the call sometimes came too early for a specific location. This was particularly problematic during the month of Ramadan when listeners rely on the sunset call to prayer to break the fast (Açıkay 2006). In Istanbul, a lack of available frequencies caused another problem: for the most part, the call to prayer *could not* be centralized; accordingly, widespread centralization in Istanbul did not take place in the early 2000s and as of 2004 only a few Istanbul districts had been centralized (Kaplan 2004).

The practitioners I interviewed during my fieldwork year in 2006 agreed that centralization was rare in Istanbul. Muezzin Necati Yaman of the Nurosmaniye Mosque cited only the Kadıköy district as being centralized and noted that five muezzins shared duties in that district (Necati Yaman in discussion with the author, November 11, 2006). Other imams and muezzins concurred. However, they did not point to the difficulty with radio frequencies for the lack of a centralized system. Necati Yaman explained that the *Diyanet* attempted to centralize the Fatih district, for example, but met with strong opposition from area congregations. Fatih is considered a more conservative religious area and it is not surprising that the inhabitants were against such as system: the call is heard as a moment of potentially divine inspiration and the aesthetic is ideally embedded in a sense of transient, improvisatory wonder. Other practitioners explained Istanbul's lack of centralization differently. According to the majority of practitioners with whom I spoke, Istanbul had not been fully centralized because there were already so many beautiful voices in the city making the practice superfluous. Imam Mustafa Yaman, winner of the 2006 national call-to-prayer recitation competition, told me: "The best quality and most beautiful voices are in Istanbul…Because there are such beautiful voices in Istanbul, there is no central system" (Mustafa Yaman in discussion with the author, November 2, 2006). I speculate, however, that this opinion may have been influenced by a regional competitiveness, possibly encouraged by the recitation competitions, which, in addition to the goals stated earlier, may serve to create a sense of regional pride while simultaneously codifying a nationalized call-to-prayer practice, just as centralization does.

Outside of Istanbul, centralization became a presence in many Anatolian communities. Mustafa Yaman indicated that this practice was necessary because of the shortage of good voices, stating that each city (outside of Istanbul) was lucky to have just two or three competent callers who could elicit an affective response. Some listeners do seem to appreciate this change. For example, Mustafa Avcı, then an ethnomusicology graduate student at the Center for Advanced Studies of Music at Istanbul Technical University, stated that his hometown had benefited from centralization:

> Beypazarı, my hometown, centralized. There is a muezzin and he is, I think, last year's or the previous year's champion of call-to-prayer reciting. He is fabulous, and he recites for the whole town…It's good I think, a central system. Especially in

small towns like Beypazarı because...it's small. Fifty thousand people are living in it. So, it's good I think...and people like to hear it...I hate it if it's not of good quality because it's really disturbing...But now it's really good to hear it...

(Mustafa Avcı in discussion with the author, September 12, 2006).

And the centralized system does seem to employ and broadcast voices that are pleasing to listeners. Burak Yedek, a filmmaker who was working on a film about muezzins at the time of our interview, recounted his experience with the centralized call:

I had the idea to start [on the film] two years ago when I was in Istanbul for a vacation and one day [I was] sitting with a friend in my house. Well, [it was] five o'clock in the morning. And we heard a muezzin recite and we were fascinated because we never realized that it was so beautiful and it was. It's strange when I think about it now because I can hear it every day and then just once in a moment you think that it's wonderful and before...you don't even have the consciousness that it's beautiful. Anyway, so we went to the muezzin, just to meet him because it was something extraordinary...So we went [to the mosque] and it was like five o'clock in the morning. Just right away. And we said we want to meet the muezzin and the guy there he said he was on vacation. "So how come there was a call?" we asked. He said it's radio [broadcast] from Kadiköy...So, after that I couldn't find the guy because I learned that every day, every week, it changes...different muezzins come from all over Istanbul to recite there. Then I decided to do some research about muezzins, the call to prayer, Turkish music. And I started to love it.

(Burak Yedek in discussion with the author, August 24, 2006)

A story such as this one seems to illustrate a successful outcome of the *Diyanet's* program because one of the basic functions of the call to prayer is to entice listeners to the faith. Burak Yedek's response demonstrated how well this centralized system favoring the transmission of beautiful voices worked in one case: Yedek left his home at five o'clock in the morning, went to the mosque, and developed a serious professional interest in the call to prayer.

Centralization, however, was not without its opponents, as evidenced by the protestors in Istanbul's Fatih district. Among these was Mustafa Özcan, a journalist who devoted a portion of his book *İslamın Sembolleri: Ezan ve İbadet Dili Tartışmaları* to arguing against the practice of centralization. First, he argued that centralization removed the congregation from human contact with the muezzin and that this lack of contact eroded the "personality" of the mosque. He also argued that the system had technical failures. These included the problem of what it was that the loudspeakers actually broadcast. He gave the example of the call in one Anatolian village, where, when no muezzin was present to recite, often the loudspeakers were left open all day long and subsequently broadcast a wide variety of sounds from the mosque, few of which were the call. Moreover, he was concerned that if there were technical failures in the centralized system due to power outages, which are not uncommon in Turkey, without a muezzin physically present to recite from the minaret the call simply might not be broadcast to the local community (Özcan 2003, 10–13). Concerns were also raised as to how centralization affected the professions of muezzin and imam. Özcan worried that the professional muezzin would become extinct as fewer and fewer muezzins were needed:

> If the centralized system is this way, there will not be even be a muezzin...It will be but a dream for us to see the new generation of muezzins. If they do not undertake *meşk* and *talim* (instruction), how will the muezzins themselves come to the minarets? "But in any case, with this system there is no need for a muezzin," is what can be said in its defense. As such, it means the drying up of the profession of muezzin and the foundational branch of muezzins, which is one of the most important symbols of Islam. In implementing the centralized muezzin system, the centralized system of the imamship could be very well be implemented. After that come to the funeral service! Probably after that robot imams from Japan will come to be imported.   (11–12)[11]

According to Özcan, the *Diyanet* countered this claim by stating that muezzins had welcomed the system, in that it encouraged them to improve their skills (18–22). However, it is important to note that official muezzins, who are state employees, are unlikely to publicly criticize the *Diyanet*, even if dissatisfied with its reform measures; any dissent on their part is subtle. At least one anecdote I collected belies the claim that muezzins wholly approve of centralization. During my year in Istanbul I became friends with an American woman, Claire, who had a young son, Tayga. Claire lived in Istanbul with her husband Süleyman in the Moda neighborhood, which is in the Kadıköy municipality, one of the few parts of Istanbul in which the call to prayer had been centralized. She told me that one day Tayga and Süleyman had gone to a local mosque in order to explore its architectural features. There Tayga and Süleyman met the muezzin, who, after briefly speaking with the two, looked at his watch and told Tayga that he needed to climb the minaret and go to the room from which the call was broadcast and prepare to recite. Shortly after he left Tayga and Süleyman began talking to the mosque's imam, who informed them that the muezzin had not actually left to recite the call to prayer because this district of Istanbul was centralized and today the call to prayer was being broadcast from another mosque (author and tour guide Clair Karaz in discussion with the author, September 9, 2006). What this anecdote may imply is that despite muezzins' public support of, or cooperation with, a centralized system, there is in fact an undercurrent of dissatisfaction. Varying motives may play a part, such as limited recitation opportunities, a feeling of lesser self-worth, and a disconnection from the mosque and its congregants. These are sentiments that they may not feel they can directly express since they are employed by the same entity that promotes centralization.

As to how centralization has affected the profession of imam, while no robot imams were imported, in some cases there were some unanticipated negative outcomes. An article in the *Özgür Kocaeli Gazetesi* reported that some imams, who also sometimes recite the call, were sleeping through morning prayers now that they no longer had to recite the call themselves or to prepare the mosque for the muezzin. Consequently, congregations were angry because when adherents arrived to pray, there was no one to lead the prayers ("Cemaat İmama kızınca" 2006).[12] And such neglect of duties led, at least in one case, to the removal of the centralized system. In the Sandıklı municipality of Afyonkarahisar the system was removed. The area religious governor İbrahim Demirkoparan explained:

> Of course, many of the imams in this situation are blameless—of the 120 imams in the area the problem concerns perhaps only two percent. Nonetheless, from here on out every mosque will recite the call to prayer separately. The imams will conduct the necessary preparations by coming to the mosque at least a half an hour before the call to prayer and will also take this time to chat with the congregation. Imams who do not wish for this change, let them complain to me. We will employ this system for at least one to two months. After that, according to public opinion, we may return to the centralized system.   (Akar 2006)

So, it seemed that occasionally, by removing the need for each mosque to broadcast its individual call to prayer, the *Diyanet* inadvertently interfered with the routine of the imams as well. It might be argued that centralization may have mentally distanced imams from their responsibilities. They were accustomed to the live human recitation, the personality of the mosque, and when another mosque assumed that responsibility, perhaps they felt as if their mosque abdicated some of its responsibility to the congregation as well. Neglect of duties may also have been another form of subtle dissent and a way of negotiating centralization without directly confronting it.

Objections to the centralized system went beyond technical failures and the neglect of duties: they were also made on religious and political grounds. One major concern was that centralization, which still relied on a live recitation, might degenerate into the use of prerecorded calls; many adherents objected to prerecorded calls because the live human voice reflects a momentary direct conduit to the divine.[13] It was also argued that the *Diyanet* implemented centralization partly to maintain a tighter degree of control on religious practice in Turkey ("This Time the Debate Is about the Call to Prayer" 1997). And given the Turkish Republic's historical attempts to govern religious practice in order to create a unified sense of Turkish Muslim identity, this argument seems a fair one. It is an argument that also mingles with the privileging of the modern, the Turkish nation, over the traditional, religious worship. For example, a 2004 *Sabah* article argued that centralizing the call to prayer was part of a modernization agenda:

> We wrote that the call has been modernized with the centralized system. On the one hand, by starting the call to prayer at different moments, it is the traditional sound of the call that is distributed in waves... On the other hand, when the call to prayer starts and ends at the same time it is the "modern" call to prayer.   (Aköz 2004)

Such a modern practice was discomfiting to some listeners who felt it eroded the traditional sound with that which they were familiar and comfortable, so they took issue with the centralized call to prayer and when they heard it, it is possible that what they absorbed was not the religious intent of the call, but rather that the state was asserting dominance over their devotional practices.

Mandating state regulation of religious practice, as in the case of the centralized call to prayer, has made religious practice a locus for dissent against the state. However, there's an interesting counter effect to having state-run religious practice. For the most part, in contemporary Turkey, grievances against state "interference" with religious practice tend to come from those not working in mosques. Imams and muezzins are state employees and they are very hesitant to speak openly against their employer. This attitude is something I experienced when conducting fieldwork. Imams and muezzins were at times reluctant to talk with me if I did not have official state permission. When I was granted interviews, with or without state permission, it was not uncommon for subjects to answer my questions by taking out the state published encyclopedia of Islam and referring to it before answering me. This might happen on any topic including questions such as, "In what *makams* do you tend to recite?" So, as a result of being employed by the state, practitioners are generally not keen to criticize any regulations, since they themselves are in fact subjects and representatives of the system. Any protest instead tends to come from adherents who are not practitioners; in this way the people have a unifying position against the state, but the state effectively controls any likely potential leaders of the protest—particularly, the imams.

In the end, today's call-to-prayer centralization mandates are a twenty-first-century example of what Karpat has summarized as the difficulty of faith in the ideally secular Turkish Republic: "how to free the faith from the autocracy of the state rather than vice versa" (2001, 8). While there is certainly discontent at times, it is unlikely that faith and its ritual practices, like the call to prayer, will be released from state oversight, given that most religious actors are confined to the bureaucracy of the state. Such a position has necessitated subtle forms of dissent from practitioners and their reliance on outside parties to be the voice of protest.

CONCLUSION

When the Turkish Republic was formed, the founders may have envisioned a secular entity with a separation of mosque and state. However, as Karpat has observed, these early founders also used Islam as a unifying ethnic identity when seeking to create a single Turkish identity from the multiplicity of Ottoman ethnicities (2001, 13, 309). As such, instead of allowing Islam to function independently of the state, the founders sought to control its message by creating a branch of government to oversee the interpretation and dissemination of Islam. They then inserted a nationalist mentality into the practice of Islam in Turkey; a strong example of this manipulation was the Turkish-language call to prayer, the purpose of which was to transfer the population's identity allegiance from Ottoman to Turkish through the oral delivery and aural internal reception of the voice.

The institution of the *Diyanet* that oversaw mandates such as the call-to-prayer language reform remains to this day. Consequently, no matter which party has assumed leadership in the country, the oversight of mainstream Islamic practice has fallen under its aegis. This chapter has examined the period from approximately 1996 to 2007, in which the increasing acceptance of and interest in Islam in public life made the call a site of state attention yet again. In these years, the first Turkish Islamist-based parties won parliamentary majorities and simultaneously centralization, recitation competitions, and continuing education were instituted in response to complaints about poor quality calls to prayer. These programs sonically imbued the call with a tie to its Ottoman heritage by promoting the sound of the higher male voice and the recitation of a different *makam* at each daily call. The state also sought to standardize the sound, a project that seemed to parallel its reorganization of Turkey in line with its rhetoric on modernization, democratization, progress, and what may be best characterized as more streamlined urban planning. Through competitions and continuing education, voices were improved and the number of *makams* was diminished. Through centralization, voice quality was directly controlled and the chaos of multiple overlapping calls was removed. Commentators both extolled these programs for their aesthetic improvements and criticized them for their lack of authenticity and spirituality. The latter dissent is particularly interesting since politicians who claim strong ties to Islam have led millennial Turkey. Nonetheless, it does not seem to matter if the government is secular or Islamist, the fact is that the government continues to attempt to control the understanding of Islam and its relationship to Turkish identity using, among other means, the human voice as an agent. The human voice is a particularly effective method by which to promote a political agenda since listeners from Islamic cultures such as Turkey are predisposed to experience an affective response through sacred aural audition and to "hear" beyond the call's text. Thus, each day this humanly voiced call has the remarkable ability to elicit varied affective responses, incite debate, and reinforce or contest state ideology for the few minutes it is sounded to millions of its communal listeners.

NOTES

1. Beginning with the establishment of the call to prayer in the 620s, a preference for recitation with a beautiful voice has been expressed, but what constitutes a beautiful voice is somewhat elusive since descriptions of beautiful voices generally have been subjective in nature. One common means of describing a beautiful voice has been to compare the sound to that of the biblical King David (Shiloah 1995, 33). Complicating an understanding of the beautiful voice, aesthetic preferences can be culturally based, rather than pan-Islamic. Turkish sources, for instance, note a preference for a higher male registration when compared to neighboring Arab communities (McPherson 2009, 142–235). Therefore, I spent those years collecting historical documents, narratives on the beautiful voice, interviews with practitioners and professional musicians, and recordings from hundreds of mosques throughout the city, along with recordings of muezzins identified as having preferred voices. I combined this information in order to understand the Turkish beautiful voice using Fales's three dimensions of timbre: perceptual, productive, and acoustic (2005, 157). Ultimately, my analysis suggests that there may be a productive nasalization that, among preferred

Turkish voices, results in the common appearance of an antiformant or antiresonance—a frequency area of relative low amplification (McPherson 2014, 39–40).

2. I have chosen to transliterate this Arabic word as "Koran" since this is also how it is written in Turkish. However, "Qur'an" is the more common transliteration.

3. *Adhan* is a transliteration of the Arabic word for call to prayer.

4. The text of the call to prayer, recited in the Arabic dialect used for sacred practices, can be translated as: "God is Great. I testify that there is no God but God. I testify the Mohammed is his Prophet. Come to prayer. Come to salvation. God is Great. There is no God but God."

5. For a few years in the late 1990s and early 2000s, Turkey's parliament was led by a coalition government of parties with no Islamist base. However, for the majority of the years covered in this chapter, the party with a parliamentary majority has had Islamist ties.

6. *Makam* is often translated as "melodic mode." *Makam* prescribes melodic elements of composition (improvisatory or otherwise) including: melodic contour, pitch set, modulation, and ornamentation. Each *makam* is heard as a distinct entity with its own "personality."

7. In this association, Tanlak is likely referring to the rules of pronunciation that are applied to Koranic recitation. Another source also indicates that recitation of the call to prayer should ideally be rooted in these rules (Sarı 2010).

8. The 2006 *Diyanet* web site has been archived by the author.

9. This competition is organized for male competitors only, whereas the competitions for memorization of the Koran and Koranic recitation are held for both sexes.

10. The accompanying audio example (see the website for this volume) aurally exemplifies the cacophony created when several mosques near one another broadcast the call simultaneously. This field recording of the midday call was made in 2006 in the courtyard of the Istanbul Nurosmaniye mosque complex.

11. As one reviewer of this chapter astutely points out, the hyperbolic choice of the phrase "robot imams" may also imply fears concerning freedom, mechanization, and modernization.

12. While it is not necessary for an imam to lead prayers, this short article strongly suggests that the congregation nonetheless was angered by the imam's absence. The title translates to "When the Congregation Gets Angry at the Imam" and then goes on to note that when the area residents finished participating in the dawn prayers without the imam, they locked the mosque doors (which had been left open for them) and took the key directly to the municipal offices of the Directorate of Religious Affairs, pointedly indicating the imam's absence to area supervisors.

13. It is true that the live recitation is often mediated by a microphone and amplified loudspeaker, and that this mediation could be considered as interference between the voice of man and the voice of God. However, as long as the recitation is that of a live human from a "high place," there seems to be some consensus that the call's functions are not diminished by amplification in and of itself, as discussed in online articles and forums on sites such as the *Şamil İslam Ansiklopedisi* and *Esselam.net* (links to these sites are no longer active, but have been archived). Nonetheless, if the amplification distorts the sound too much or negatively affects its beautiful sound, then this mediation can be seen as problematic (Öztürk 2001, 51; Anonymous [muezzin] in discussion with the author May 16, 2006).

WORKS CITED

"2011 Yılı Camiler ve Din Görevlileri Haftası Münasebetiyle Kur'an Kursu Öğreticileri İmam Hatip ve Müezzin Kayyımlar arasında Yapılacak Hafızlık, Kur'an-I Kerim İ Güzel Okuma ve Ezanı Güzel Okuma Yarışmaları ile İlgili Şartname.pdf." 2011. *Diyanet*, October 7. diyanet.gov.tr.

Açıkay, Ahmet. 2006. "Merkezi ezan tam karmaşa!" *Milli Gazete*, November 2. https://www.milligazete.com.tr/haber/841709/merkezi-ezan-tam-karmasa .

Akar, İsmail. 2006. "İmamlara ezan cezası." *Hürriyet*, September 22. ht http://www.hurriyet.com.tr/gundem/imamlara-ezan-cezasi-5132731.

Aköz, Emre. 2004. "Modernleşmenin cilveleri." *Sabah*, November 12. https://www.sabah.com.tr/yazarlar/akoz/2004/11/12/modernlesmenin_cilveleri.

Akyol, Mustafa. 2007. "And the Winner Is . . . Muezzin İsa Aydın." *Turkish Daily News* (Istanbul, Turkey), September 15.

Armstrong, Karen. 2001. *Muhammad: A Biography of the Prophet*. London: Phoenix.

Ataklı, Can. 1997a. "Ezan genelgesine uyulup uyulmadığını belli değil." *Sabah*, December 13. http://arsiv.sabah.com.tr/1997/12/13/y05.html.

Ataklı, Can. 1997b. "Ezan Refah'ı telaşlandırdı." *Sabah*, August 10. http://arsiv.sabah.com.tr/1997/08/10/y05.html.

Ataklı, Can. 1997c. "Ezan tartışmasında değişik görüşler." *Sabah*, July 6. http://arsiv.sabah.com.tr/1997/07/06/y05.html.

Ataklı, Can. 1997d. "Güzel ezan sesi istemek tek tip uygulaması değil." *Sabah*, July 9. http://arsiv.sabah.com.tr/1997/07/09/y05.html.

Ataklı, Can. 1997e. "Güzel ezan sesine çığ gibi destek var." *Sabah*, July 27. http://arsiv.sabah.com.tr/1997/07/27/y05.html.

Ataklı, Can. 1997f. "İstiklal marşı hazır, ezan ise incelemede." *Sabah*, July 5. http://arsiv.sabah.com.tr/1997/07/05/y05.html.

Ataklı, Can. 1997g. "İstiklal Marşı ve ezan'a standart." *Sabah*, July 3. http://arsiv.sabah.com.tr/1997/07/03/y05.html.

Ataklı, Can. 1997h. "Ve ezan artık güzel okunacak." *Sabah*, August 9. http://arsiv.sabah.com.tr/1997/08/09/y05.html.

"Cemaat İmama kızınca." 2006. *Özgür Kocaeli Gazetesi* (İzmit, Turkey), February 2.

Çevik, İlnur. 1997. " . . . and Now the Debate on the Call to Prayer." *Turkish Daily News* (Istanbul, Turkey), August 11.

Değirmenci, İrfan. 2004. "Ezan tartışması yeniden başladı." *CNN Türk* (Istanbul, Turkey), October 19.

"Diyanet: Ezan Susmaz." 1997. *Sabah*, August 10. http://arsiv.sabah.com.tr/1997/08/10/r04.html.

Dursun, A. Halûk. 1999. *İstanbul'da Yaşama Sanatı*. Istanbul: Ötüken Neşriyat A.Ş.

"En güzel sesli imam yayındı." 2001. *Sabah*, June 18. http://arsiv.sabah.com.tr/2001/06/18/p10.html.

Fales, Cornelia. 2005. "Short-Circuiting Perceptual Systems: Timbre in Ambient and Techno Music." In *Wired for Sound: Engineering and Technology in Sonic Cultures*, edited by Paul D. Greene and Thomas Porcello, 156–80. Middletown, CT: Wesleyan University Press.

Fuller, Graham E. 2008. *The New Turkish Republic: Turkey as a Pivotal State in the Muslim World*. Washington, DC: United States Institute of Peace Press.

Gürtaş, Ahmet. 2005. *Abdest Ezan Namaz Duaları ve Manaları*. Ankara: Türkiye Diyanet Vakfı Yayınları.

Kaplan, Pervin. 2004. "İstanbul'da frekans sıkıntısı." *Sabah*, October 15. http://arsiv.sabah.com. tr/2004/10/15/gnd104.html.

Karpat, Kemal. 2001. *The Politicization of Islam*. Oxford: Oxford University Press.

Lee, Tong Soon. 1999. "Technology and the Production of Islamic Space: The Call to Prayer in Islam." *Ethnomusicology* 43 (1): 86–100.

Lewis, Geoffrey. 1999. *The Turkish Language Reform: A Catastrophic Success*. Oxford: Oxford University Press.

McPherson, Eve. 2009. "The Beautiful Voice: Voice Quality and the Turkish Call to Prayer." PhD diss., University of California at Santa Barbara.

McPherson, Eve. 2011. "Political History and Embodied Identity Discourse in the Turkish Call to Prayer." *Music and Politics* 5 (1): 1–20.

McPherson, Eve. 2014. "The Turkish Beautiful Voice: Acoustic Traits of Preferred Muezzins' Voices in Istanbul, Turkey." In *On Local Vs. Universal: Musiccult'14 Music and Cultural Studies Conference Proceedings*, edited by Ayşe Güngör and Efe Duyan, 27–42. Istanbul: DAKAM Publishing.

Messick, Brinkley Morris. 1993. *The Calligraphic State: Textual Domination and History in a Muslim Society*. Berkeley: University of California Press.

Özcan, Mustafa. 2003. *İslamın Sembolleri: Ezan ve İbadet Dili Tartışmaları*. Istanbul: Yeni Asya Neşriyet.

Özcan, Nuri. 1995. "Ezan, Musiki." In *İslam Ansiklopedisi Cilt 12*, 43–5. Istanbul: Türkiye Diyanet Vakfı.

Öztürk, Mustafa Tahir. 2001."Türk Din Mûsikîsinde Ezan." Master's thesis, Istanbul Teknik Üniversitesi.

Saabiq, Sayyid. 2006. "Fiqh-us-Sunnah, Volume 1: Azhan, Call to Prayer." *USC-MSA Compendium of Muslim Texts*. http://web.archive.org/web/20071023201259/www.usc.edu/ dept/MSA/law/fiqhussunnah/.

Sarı, Mehmet Ali. 2010. "Günümüzde Ezanlar." In *İstanbul Ezanları*, edited by Yusuf Çağlar, 13–19. Istanbul: Bilnet Matbaacılık.

Sezgin, Bekir Sıdkı. 2006. "Dini Musiki Formları." *Türk Musikisi*. http://www.turkmusikisi. com/dini_musiki/bekir_s%FDdk%FD_sezgin.html.

Shiloah, Amnon. 1995. *Music in the World of Islam: A Socio-Cultural Study*. Detroit: Wayne State University Press.

Sırma, İhsan Süreyya. 2005. *Ezan ya da Ebedi Kurtuluşa Çağrı*. Ankara: Beyan Yayınları.

Sontag, Deborah. 2003. "The Erdoğan Experiment" *New York Times*, May 11. https://www. nytimes.com/2003/05/11/magazine/the-erdogan-experiment.html.

"This Time the Debate Is about the Call to Prayer." 1997. *Turkish Daily News* (Istanbul, Turkey), August 15.

Yeprem, M. Safa. 2004. "Türk Cami Müsikisi ile Mukayeseli olarak İstanbul Gayr-ı Müslimlerde Mabed Müsikisi." PhD diss., T. C. Marmara Üniversitesi.

CHAPTER 21

SINGING AND PRAYING AMONG KOREAN CHRISTIAN CONVERTS (1896–1915)

A Trans-Pacific Genealogy of the Modern Korean Voice

HYUN KYONG HANNAH CHANG

IN November of 1909, North American missionaries in Pyongyang mounted an event called the Million Movement, which encompassed prayer meetings, music sessions, and Bible studies that unfolded over the course of several weeks. Though intended for Koreans in Pyongyang, the Million Movement was also planned so that the missionaries could display to the larger Protestant community in the United States the explosive growth of Christianity in Korea since 1884, the first year of American Protestant missionization in Korea. More North American dignitaries were invited to this multifarious religious fair than to previous large-scale Protestant events in Korea, most of which were focused on obtaining native converts and disciplining recent ones. North American guests for the Million Movement included not only distinguished figures such as Arthur Pierson, the editor of *The Missionary Review of the World*, and Henry McCracken, the chancellor of New York University, but also Robert Harkness, a composer of more than 2,000 gospel songs, and the world-traveling Chapman-Alexander gospel music duo (Oak 2009, 375).

As the inclusion of the prominent musicians suggests, musical activities in the Million Movement were central programming choices that served to symbolize and renew the ties between North American Protestantism and the nascent Protestant community in Korea. The musical guests from the United States conducted activities with Korean Christians, who were already trained in hymn-singing by the local missionaries. The excitement of engaging the mission field also inspired one of the visitors to compose a

FIGURE 21.1 Charles Alexander conducting a women's choir in Pyongyang, 1909.

new hymn. According to Mattie Wilcox Noble, a missionary in early twentieth-century Pyongyang who hosted some of the visiting Americans, Robert Harkness was "so impressed with the watchword that he composed a thrilling song on the 'Million'" (Noble 1910, 195). The Million Movement also inspired the earliest known photograph of a Korean Protestant choir, included in a booklet titled *Korea for Christ*, published in 1910 (see Figure 21.1). This widely reprinted photograph captures Charles Alexander in the act of conducting, with his arms raised and facing a crowd of several hundred Korean women. Possibly he was teaching and conducting Harkness's "A Million Souls for Jesus," translated into Korean. The aerial photograph shows the Korean women from behind, with their braided or wrapped hair and *jeogori* (upper garments) filling the lower half of the frame.

The photograph, probably taken by a missionary who wished to use it as evidence of the mission's success, encapsulates the self-celebratory narratives of turn-of-the-century North American Protestant missions. Indeed, missionaries in Korea were fond of recounting, advertising, and celebrating their accomplishments among themselves and for their home agencies in the United States that funded missionization, and the singing of hymns among Koreans was one of the commonly cited "evidence" of their success. Missionary publications described Koreans singing hymns in mission schools, church services, Bible classes, and revival meetings across Korea's cities and villages, and portrayed the missionaries as agents of a more advanced civilization who fulfilled the duty of "uplifting" the natives with "sympathy, patience and consecration" (Wachs 1915). The photograph of Alexander distills this narrative: he is positioned at the center of the frame, directing a crowd of indistinguishable Koreans, whose faces are not recorded due to the chosen perspective of the photographer.

The meaning of Koreans' hymn-singing for missionaries seems clear enough, but what did it mean for the Korean participants themselves? Shrouded in their own agendas and assumptions, missionary writings do not tell us much about the meaning of singing hymns for the Koreans. But historical contextualization tells us that in 1909, hymn-singing as and in a community of Koreans had a significance that exceeded its function as religious or disciplinary practice. In that year Korea was on the verge of being colonized by Japan: Japan had coerced the Korean government into an unequal treaty in 1876 and thereafter held military and industrial campaigns on Korean territory; in 1905, Korea became Japan's protectorate, and in 1910, a colony of Japan. Thus 1909 was a fraught year during which public assemblies and publications in Korea were under the surveillance of the Japanese authorities in Korea (see Robinson 1998, Caprio 2009). In an environment where Koreans' public mobilization was becoming illicit, the Korean singers most likely experienced collective hymn-singing as a form of subversion and resistance backed by Americans, who had extraterritorial rights in Korea. As for the Japanese administrators, they would have heard this and other instances of Korean collective singing as Korean defiance, sponsored by American nationals meddling in the affairs of Japan-occupied land.

American-style hymn-singing and the related practice of praying began in missionary churches in Korea in the late nineteenth century and continued to be dispersed throughout the twentieth century, as the number of Christian converts grew at an exceptional rate that was not replicated in any other parts of Asia. But just as the missionary writing rarely asked what the hymns might have meant to the Koreans, it is difficult to "hear" Christian singing and praying in scholarship on Korean music, which has typically concerned itself with the Korean voice that could be understood as "traditional." The framing of the Korean voice as "traditional" in turn reveals several social and, in some cases, disciplinary assumptions surrounding the notions of voice, tradition, and national identity. Such framing discloses a pervasive social modality of listening, in which the human voice is heard as a natural and true expression of a person's identity, and what is deemed natural and true is related to race and ethnicity (Eidsheim 2009, 2015; also see Fuhr 2013). The naturalized link of voice, tradition, and national identity also reflects traces of what Ana Maria Ochoa Gautier has described as "a foundational trope for folkloristics," which is presupposed on "an epistemology of purification that seeks to separate musical practices discretely into categories of genres that represent people" (2014, 67; also see Witzleben 1997; Weidman 2006). Similarly, this naturalized link betrays a nation-bound analytical framework that masks the transcultural impact of colonial dynamics (see Bloechl 2008; Bloechl et al. 2015).

Korean vocal practices in the twentieth century exceed both the missionaries' notion of Koreans as "uncultivated," as well as the conventional ethnomusicological approach structured around discrete traditional genres. When contextualized in the social transformations of twentieth-century Korea, these vocal practices highlight not so much an insularity that would be a guarantee of cultural continuity with the premodern but rather multifaceted and powerful mediation through modern/colonial entanglements (see Killick 2010; Maliangkay 2017); indeed, they exhibit some of the hallmarks of modernity such as capitalism and nationhood. Acknowledging modern conditions as an analytical framework opens up space for considering the uneven, multifaceted, and continued interrelations of the local with "a global history of exchange," bound up with the rise of the modern empires and the global rise of capitalism (Novak 2013; also see Utz and Lau 2013, 3). Such framework not only addresses the reordering of traditional vocal genres upon transnational or colonial contact but also augments the significance of "new" or "mixed" forms of vocalization born of such contact. To signal the particular (re)constitutive conditions of modern Korea and the vocal practices therein, I propose an adjusted notion of modernity, which I call trans-Pacific modernity. As I conceptualize it, the framework of trans-Pacific modernity underscores the relationship of modernity with the specificities of modern Pacific empires (Japan and the United States), as well as the traffic of the colonial/modern across a field of local motivations and pre-existing proclivities (see the final section of the chapter).

Born within the context of colonial pressures from the United States and Japan, Korean Christian singing and praying in the early twentieth century exhibit a trans-Pacific genealogy of modern Korean voice, that is, a genealogy that materialized at the intersection of Pacific colonial projects, local experiences, and pre-existing cosmologies. In this chapter, I investigate Korean Christian singing and praying by examining missionary and Korean records, primarily, as well as some Japanese colonial sources. Activities directed by the missionaries, hymn-singing and praying among Korean converts reflected a network of American aesthetic, moral, and economic ideologies. While I acknowledge the influence of such ideologies on the Korean converts, I examine Korean Christian singing and praying not merely as a medium of assimilating American ethnocentric discourses, but as sonic appropriations that responded to an affective structure constituted by the trans-Pacific relationship of Korea, Japan, and the United States—a structure that continues to frame local politics in Korea till this day. In particular, I argue that Korean Christian singing and praying formed a complex site in which North American religious practices and Korean social mobilization converged in the contexts of Japanese colonialism and US–Japan rivalry in the Pacific. This inquiry allows me to hear and describe not a Korean voice in mimesis of or opposition to the West, but a trans-Pacific voice, exhibiting a trans-Pacific genealogy. The voice, then, can be understood as a kind of technology through which Korean converts negotiated their way into a "global history" not as full agents or subjects, but in their markedly compromised positions, within multiple shifting power relationships.

US Religious Mission and the Triangular Entanglement of Korea, Japan, and the United States

The unusual success of the American Protestant mission in Korea has fascinated contemporaneous mission societies and a number of scholars in later decades. As several scholars have argued recently, geopolitical context was a crucial factor of the exceptional rate of Christian conversion in early twentieth-century Korea (Park 2003; Kane and Park 2009). The arrival of the missionaries from 1884 onward coincided with the violent outbreak of Korean "patriotic identities and nationalist rituals" in response to Japan's imperial expansion into Korea, which began in 1876 (Kane and Park 2009, 365). As one missionary recounted in 1909, the Korean society that the missionaries had entered was one where "a mad sort of spurious patriotism started into being, with suicide, chopping off of fingers, sworn oaths, guerilla warfare, flint-lock resistance" (Gale 1909, 38). In this geopolitical context, many Koreans perceived American missionaries as potential allies who could counterbalance Japanese power in Korea—a scenario quite different from China and Japan, where American missionaries were perceived as Western colonizers. Korean political elites dispensed with their longstanding injunction against Western religious missions and approached American missionaries as persons with ties to American politics and business, access to Western media, and resources to build the kinds of modern institutions that had transformed Japan. Many Korean commoners perceived the missionaries as figures with extraterritorial rights; for them, churches established by American nationals were spaces exempt from Japanese military abuse, especially during the Sino-Japanese War (1894–1895) and the Russo-Japanese War (1904–1905), which were waged in northern Korea over the question of Korea's sovereignty (Oak 2013; also see Clark 2003).

As sociologists Kane and Park argue in their discussion of the "puzzle of Korean Christianity," not only were geopolitical conditions favorable to the North American religious mission, but also the religious practices that they promoted in the "mission field" were compatible with Korean nationalist rituals (2009). To a certain extent, this affinity was a function of mid- to late-nineteenth-century North American evangelical-ism, which was characterized by an American middle-class zeal for sung, spoken, and written expressions of religious faith in spontaneous and learned forms by "everyday man" over clergy-centered liturgy. In the Korean context, the evangelical emphasis on the expression of one's "internal" feelings in public meetings such as Bible studies, prayer meetings, and revivals aligned with the enthusiasm for popular mobilization. The mis-sion's promotion of mass literacy, intended for the wide circulation of religious doctrines, also had an appeal for Koreans across class and religious affiliations. In particular, the missionaries' choice to adopt the Korean vernacular script—the script of commoners and women—instead of the upper-class script of literary Chinese as the official letter of religious materials resonated with both elite and commoner strands of Korean nationalism, which, despite their differences, tended to converge around the project of nationalizing the vernacular script. Such a project gained momentum against the back-drop of Japan's imperial advances, which encompassed aspects of linguistic surveillance after 1905. In this environment, vernacular Bibles and hymns were not just religious publications but also nationalist texts, which exhibited "national" letters and used these letters to present Christian metaphors of a community in suffering (Wells 1990).

With American religious practices shaping and reinforcing Korean popular mobiliza-tion, the missionaries became increasingly entangled with Korean nationalism despite their apparent position of adhering to the US government's stance of political neutrality in Korea. Historical records outline a religious mission that often sponsored Koreans' subversive activities under Japanese rule; indeed, they suggest that Korean Christian nationalism might have served as a site of US–Japan rivalry. The missionaries not only directed religious life but also ran hundreds of para-religious schools and cultural institutions and sustained Korean-language publications well into the colonial period (1910–1945), knowing that the Japanese colonial government considered this network of institutions a breeding ground of Korean nationalism. To a quote a Japanese report from 1910, missionaries ran "Christian schools that showed evil tendencies, mixing impurities (i.e., politics) in their education" (quoted in Wells 1990, 33). In return, the Japanese colonial government in Korea ran an English-language newspaper meant to contain American opinions in Korea (*the Seoul Press*) and formulated education policies to weaken the influence of the missionaries on Koreans (Caprio 2009). For instance, the Japanese authorities banned religious education and required the teaching of Japanese language in all schools in the mid-1910s—policies that were partially rescinded in the 1920s due to pronounced missionary resistance—and enforced Shinto worship in all schools in the mid-1930s, which led a number of missionaries to close their schools as an act of defiance. The tense US–Japan relationship that surfaces from official and private documents suggests that the missionaries' involvement in Korean affairs was in part motivated by their conviction in "America's national beneficence as a Christian and democratic society" (Hill 1988, quoted in Clark 2003, 6) over and against the influence of Japanese culture and spirituality on Korea (see Yoo 2016). With the onset of the Pacific War in 1941, the friction between the United States and Japan escalated not just in Korea but also in contested locales across Pacific Asia. This rivalry came to a peak with the United States' bombing of Japanese cities in 1945, which ended Japan's rule of Korea and ushered in an even stronger alliance of the United States and (South) Korea as well as American hegemony in Pacific Asia (see Chang 2014).

Hymn-Singing

It was in the nexus of Japan-US contestation, American missionary evangelism, and Korean nationalism that hymn-singing gained momentum among the Korean converts. Despite the fact that there was no comparable practice of collective monodic singing before the arrival of the missionaries, American and Korean writings around the turn of the twentieth century record the enthusiastic adoption of hymn-singing among the converts. Hymns were sung in the forms of congregational singing and staged performance in a vast network of religious gatherings that included worship services, Bible studies, revivals, evangelical tours, and small services conducted by the so-called Bible women, older Korean women who had spiritual authority in small villages. They were also sung in an equally extensive web of para-religious venues, such as Sunday schools, Christian cultural organizations like the YMCA, and schools managed by missionaries, referred to as mission schools.

Verse 1
It is difficult, oh so difficult, but our God saves
He gives clothes and food, and all that is good

Verse 2
[God] listens to our prayers and is with us always
It is difficult, oh so difficult, but our God saves

FIGURE 21.2 "Spanish Hymn" in *Chanyanga* (Praise Hymns), compiled by Horace Underwood, 1894. Korean authorship is indicated at the bottom of the page.

Missionaries were the primary enablers and facilitators of this collective singing culture. From 1892 to 1908, leading male missionaries such as George Heber Jones, Horace Underwood, Graham Lee, and Malcolm Fenwick compiled and published hymnal editions with the support of the mission society boards. All of these editions were conceptualized as projects of translating contemporaneous Anglo-American hymns and gospel songs. The prefaces of these early hymnals indicate that Korean assistants aided with the translation, and it is acknowledged that the Korean aides were the primary authors for a minority of the hymns (see Figure 21.2 for an example of hymn with Korean-authored lyrics). Most of these early hymnals included only the lyrics and the indication of the intended melody from the North American repertory (see Figure 21.3). A few, like Horace Underwood's *Chanyanga* (1894), had music in staff notation and lyrics (see Figure 21.2).

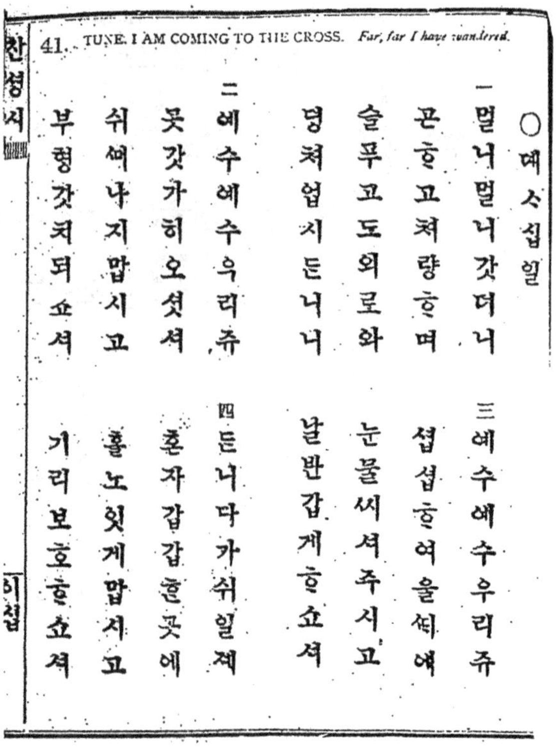

Verse 1
I travelled away, far away
And felt weary and desolate
Despondent and forlorn
Walking about aimlessly

Verse 2
Jesus, Jesus, our Lord
Please come close to us
Do not leave us
Be our father and brother

FIGURE 21.3 "I Am Coming to the Cross" in *Chanseongsi* (Sacred Poems for Praise), compiled by Graham Lee, 1895.

The conceptualization of Korean-language hymns as translations of North American "originals" meant that the missionaries took on the self-imposed duty of disciplining Korean ears and voices according to North American standards. Indeed, the missionaries' ethnocentrism fills not only the pages of the Korean-language hymnals but also the missionary archive, which is suffused with records of missionaries' habits of listening—what Jonathan Sterne called "audile technique" (2003). The most illustrative example of this is the repeated comments on the Koreans' inability to sing half steps due to the five-tone orientation of Korean folk and court traditions. For instance, missionary Paul Grove expressed his frustration in a racializing article in the 1915 issue of *The Korea Mission Field*, which featured the views of missionary music teachers on what one contributor called "the musical uplift of Korea and the uplift of music in Korea":

> When [half steps are] imposed upon the unsuspecting Korean, he dodges under, and over, and all around them, twisting this way and that with amazing dexterity, tho if you questioned him closely, you would discover that he is not cognizant of just what he is doing, for he cannot differentiate our scale, that is he cannot by hearing, but just seems to feel that something is wrong, and consequently rights it in his own way, much to the detriment of congregation singing…They were born with a capacity of hearing only five tones where we hear seven.   (1915, 110)

Grove concluded that the mission should promote the minority of hymns that use the pentatonic scale while other contributors argued that it was their duty to help the Korean students to "hear correctly" (Wachs 1915, 103). For example, Grace Harmon McGary advocated for a systematic music education for Korean children in mission schools: "I believe the only hope for the half tones is through the cultivation of the voice and ear of the school children…Besides the monthly written examinations, once every term, we have a singing examination in each chorus class. Each girl must stand before the class and sing either a solo in a duet or a quartette with the different parts" (1915, 103).

Yet to focus solely on the missionaries' ethnocentrism is to continue to reduce the Koreans to objects of missionary ears. For the Koreans, I suggest, hymn-singing was "an ongoing act of acoustic design through appropriation" (Ochoa 2014, 67), rather than a mere reproduction of a foreign genre. Hymns that the converts learned through a combination of reading, listening, and memorization formed a medium through which Korean converts experienced reassurance as well as belonging to a national community in a catastrophic time. The text and the format of the hymns indeed made them an exemplary medium of affirmation. Many of them set to music elegiac texts that mobilized images of a community or person in suffering. Consider, for example, "Spanish hymn" in *Chanyanga* (Praise Hymns), a hymnal published and used during the Sino-Japanese War (see Figure 21.2). Credited to a Korean, the lyrics of "Spanish hymn" uses a simple repeating line in which a lament is followed by a message of hope and redemption: "It's difficult, oh so difficult, but our God saves." The hymnbook format also allowed Koreans to read such messages in Korean vernacular script and to vocalize them in unison with other Koreans, in addition to reinforcing the longstanding Confucian emphasis on the act of reading as a way of cultivating morality and of obtaining social prestige (Yu 2016).

Early Korean Christian writings also demonstrate that converts actively appropriated North American hymns as well as the hymnal mode of singing for the purpose of nationalistic mobilization. Consider, for example, an anonymous announcement in *Dongnip Sinmun* (The Independent) from 1896:

> Tomorrow, in Seoul's churches, we will celebrate the birthday of the emperor. In the morning, we will gather in the chapels and pray and sing to God for the emperor

and for the people of Korea. Then, at four o'clock, we will gather in Mohwa Hall. We will sing patriotic songs, and a number of reputed persons will give speeches. Anyone who deems this occasion to be worthy of celebration is welcome to come to Mohwa Hall to sing patriotic songs together and listen to speeches.   (September 1, 1896)

Announcements and reports of this kind appeared in turn-of-the-century religious and para-religious publications like *Dongnip Sinmun* (The Independent), *Sinhak Wolbo* (Theological Monthly), *Joseon Geuriseudoin Hoebo* (Korean Christians' Newsletter), and *Geuriseudo Sinmun* (Christian Newspaper); all of these were Korean vernacular newspapers or journals managed by converts in conjunction with the missionaries. These publications also solicited readers to submit new lyrics for circulating hymns and published the selected texts, indexing an energetic cultural sphere of young nationalist Christians who socialized in para-religious venues like the YMCA and mission schools. Such nationalistic contents declined after 1905, the year the Japanese authorities began to read and censor Korean-language publications, and disappeared by 1910, the year of annexation.

The enthusiasm for hymn-singing among Korean Christian nationalists also led to hymnals and songbooks compiled by Koreans (see Min 2008). However, the fate of the first such hymnal by Yun Ch'iho demonstrates how tenuous Christian nationalism was in Japan-occupied Korea without the support and sponsorship of the missionaries. Yun's *Chanmiga* (Songs of Praise), published in 1905, provided lyrics to ten North American hymns and included three separate patriotic songs, two of which were meant to be sung to "Auld Lang Syne" and the other to "God Save the Queen." He submitted this version to the US Methodist mission society in Korea, hoping to get it circulated as the official hymnal of the Korean Methodist church, but the missionaries rejected this request, most likely because supporting it would have meant risking open confrontations with the incoming Japanese administration. Indeed, *Chanmiga* was considered subversive by the Japanese authorities and banned in the early 1910s. Furthermore, Yun was also incarcerated with other Christian nationalists in 1911. Korean Christians continued to compile and circulate nationalist hymnbooks and songbooks after 1905, but most of these vocal music compilations were banned or blacklisted by the Japanese censors (Mun 2011). Interestingly, some of the surviving compilations from the 1910s are those created by Koreans in self-exiled Christian communities in Manchuria and Hawai'i.

PRAYING

The convergence of missionary evangelicalism and trans-Pacific geopolitics also provided the conditions for the communal prayers. Missionary writings in the first decade of the twentieth century were fascinated with the loud, improvised prayers that made up the centerpiece of the so-called revival meetings, during which hundreds of Koreans gathered under missionary leadership to partake in both scripted and spontaneous activities, including singing, praying, sermons, and street proselytizing, over the span of several days. Records indicate that such prayers were practiced throughout Korea, but it appears that they were especially popular in Pyongyang and the surrounding north-western area of Korea, where commoners were the main targets of the North American missionization. There, Korean national consciousness was enmeshed with the lived experiences of the victimization during Japan's conquest wars and with indigenous (shamanic) sensibilities, which, to cite missionary James Gale, retained "those peculiarities of race that have been smothered out of the gentry by fumes of Confucianism" (1896, 475). The theological orientation of the missionaries who ventured northwest also resonated with the restless environment of this region, which saw the outbreak of a variety of prophetic, apocalyptic, and guerilla movements among the Korean peasant population (Oak 2013). These missionaries were not the social evangelists who were equally committed to the spread of "civilization" and evangelization but premillenialists, whose belief in the imminent second coming of Jesus added a sense of urgency to proselytization.

Missionary and Korean seminarian historiographies trace the beginning of the audible confessional prayers to Robert Hardie, a Canadian Methodist missionary; his confessional prayer during a sermon in Wonsan (presently a city in North Korea) in 1903 is seen to have started the "fire" that spread across Korea (Kim 2012). However, most of the missionary testimonies focus not on themselves but on the Koreans' prayers. They capture the exhibited agitation through characterizations of gesticulation and vocalization. Consider, for example, Graham Lee's description of a revival meeting that took place in Pyongyang in 1907, excerpted from a much longer documentation of the apparently inextinguishable prayers.

> After the prayer there were a few testimonies, and then the leader announced a song, asking the audience to rise and stating that all those who wished to go home could do so, as we intended to stay until morning, if there were men who wished to remain that long and confess their sins. A great many went, but between five and six hundred remained. These we gathered into one ell of the building, and then began a meeting the like of which none of us had ever seen. After prayer, confessions were called for, and immediately the Spirit of God seemed to descend on that audience. Man after man would rise, confess his sins, break down and weep, and then throw himself to the floor and beat the floor with his fists in a perfect agony of conviction. My own cook tried to make a confession, broke down in the midst of it, and cried to me across the room "Pastor tell me, is there any hope for me, can I be forgiven?" ... Sometimes after a confession the whole audience would break out in audible prayer, and the effect of that audience of hundreds of men praying together in audible prayer was something indescribable. Again in another confession they would break out in uncontrollable weeping, and we would all weep, we couldn't help it. And so the meeting went on until two o'clock A. M. with confession.   (1907, 34)

Graham's testimony, perhaps the most elaborate of its kind, correspond with other observations in missionary publications like *The Korea Review* and *The Korea Mission*

Field and individual missionaries' diaries and letters. Such written attestations suggest that the missionaries were listening closely to the sounds and contents of the subalterns' prayers. Some of the common themes were the prayers' audibility, the nonverbal expressions of suffering like crying, the sheer quantity of the spoken words, the improvised and heightened quality of speech, and the confession of sins.

The ample space devoted to the documentation of the prayers and the general tone of fascination in missionary writing suggest that the missionaries "heard" the success of their evangelization in the Koreans' vocalization. Missionaries perceived the vocal and physical attributes of emotionality in Koreans' prayers as outward indications of the converts' authentic Christian faith and understood the confessions of sin as proofs of their assimilation of the Christian doctrines of conscience and sin. In particular, missionaries liked to underscore the confessions of those "transgressions" that related to the act of stealing. To cite several examples, the Methodist mission's account of the Korean revivals, *Religious Awakening of Korea*, elaborated on a laborer who confessed having "at different times stolen small quantities of gold" from the American Mining Concession in northern Korea (1908, 20); J. Robert Moose recounted that the prayer meeting involved "the most disgraceful confessions and restitution of stolen goods" (1904, 41); Robert Hardie recalled a 1903 meeting where a Korean confessed not having returned an overpaid sum of money to the Royal Mint (1934, 41). This missionary concern with money and conscientiousness indicates that the American capitalist ethics of private property was among the moral values preached in the missionaries' sermons in revivals and worship services. It also suggests that one of the tasks of the prayer meetings was to serve as a disciplinary space that compelled the natives to restate the preached "sins."

Korean Christian writings on prayers, a much smaller body than the missionaries', indicate, again, the contrast in concerns between the missionaries and the converts—the converts were not there to listen to themselves. The paucity of Korean-authored materials also signals the class background of the converts who were drawn to prayer meetings: audible, confessional, and improvised prayers were more popular among peasants and commoners than among Korean Christians of elite background who had access to published writing. The extant records vary in tone and emphasis but as a whole they suggest that the prayers and the larger events of revivals constituted a site of popular mobilization and affirmation. Brief announcements of upcoming revivals that appeared in single issues of vernacular Christian publications displayed on paper a web of Christian meetings that linked cities and towns throughout Korea, creating an imagined community through vernacular print culture (Anderson 1983). Reports of past revivals trace the processes of social galvanization, in which large crowds merged for praying, singing, and sermons and broke off into small units that then infiltrated the open-air markets and distant villages.

Longer writings also demonstrate that a growing national consciousness shaped the dynamics of the revivals. For instance, Mun Kyeong Ho's testimony in *Sinhak Wolbo* (Theological Monthly) depicts the revivals as a spiritual sanctuary for a dispossessed community: "With each day passing, the number of attendants soared so much that we could not find enough space in the church. The Holy Spirit descended upon us, touching each of the brothers and sisters who gathered at the church…They were crying while making confessions" (1903, 342). Another interpretation, by a Pastor Mu in a 1906 issue of *Geuriseudo Sinmun* (Christian Newspaper), reads like an exercise in covert nationalism. He likened the Korean situation to the Babylonian captivity and identified revivals as the key to national recovery: "Revivals are manifestations that can happen in any community that serves God, and not just among foreigners. When the King of Babylon captured the people of Israel, Nehemiah rose, collected his people, spread his message among them, and rebuilt the destroyed fortress. The people realized their sins and changed their conduct, and with this, their nation was recovered" (1906, 54).

The articulation of agitated vocalization with national consciousness was not entirely lost on the missionaries. The missionaries knew that the converts' prayers were not merely a spiritual manifestation that began in their churches but a vocal manifestation continuous with the "mad patriotism" witnessed in the Korean society. The missionaries also knew that this condition of mass vulnerability was the very cause of the success of North American evangelization. For instance, in 1903 Homer Hulbert, one of the most distinguished missionaries in Korea, used the notion of "loud cry" as both a sonic icon of Korea's catastrophic situation and a motto for evangelization: "Nowhere is the cry louder than in Korea…Korea's argument is her present opportunity. The delicate political situation; the beginnings of civilization with its drawbacks; the multitudes yielding to the least persuasion. The hour of Korea's opportunity is peculiarly now. Is the Church going to let this golden opportunity go by?" (1903, 548). As Kenneth Wells aptly summarized in his study of the early twentieth-century North American mission in Korea, "the troubles of one were fortunes for another" (1990, 29).

The prayers, to repeat, were a multivalent practice that mediated some of the modernity's hallmarks, like capitalism and nationhood. But it should be noted that it is also possible to link vocalization in prayers to pre-existing ritual traditions in Korea, especially shamanic rituals. The argument for the continuity of improvised Christian prayers and shamanic rituals is speculative at best, but the class backgrounds of the Korean participants who were drawn to large-scale revivals makes this continuity a highly plausible notion (see Kim 2000). The ritual and performative functions of the Christian prayers resemble those of the shamanic ritual of *gut*, through which Korean commoners sought to attract fortunes and dispel misfortunes for much of Korea's recorded history. Just as the converts burst into spontaneous, audible vocalization in communion with the sacred, shamans performing *gut* spoke aloud as numinous beings in a process called *kongsu*, described by shamans as "opening the Gate of Words" (Bruno 2002). Korean seminarian historians have tended to disavow notions of equivalence of Korean Christian prayers and shamanic rituals, but it is worth considering that the eerie similarity between the two was first acknowledged by some missionaries and elite Christian Koreans who were witnessing the prayers in revivals. In the words of an elite Christian Korean, the commoners were "reverting to traditional behavior and thought" (quoted in Wells 1990, 38). Records of revivals indeed have traces of shamanic sociality and material culture that are largely ignored in seminarian historiography.

THE TRANS-PACIFIC MODERN VOICE

In this chapter, I have described Korean Christian hymn-singing and praying as a genealogy of Korean vocalization constituted within the uneven flows of power, discourses, and practices that circulated through the colonial projects of the two Pacific empires—the United States and Japan. My account underscored such macro-structural flows, while also detailing how the Korean converts themselves utilized new and mixed vocal practices as a material site of social mobilization in a catastrophic time, wrought by colonialism. Korean convert singing and praying in the nexus of American missionary institutions were thus a medium of paradoxical enfranchisement, through which the converts voiced resistance and affirmation.

To signal the multiplicity of influences, motivations, and proclivities within Korean Christian hymn-singing and praying, I have formulated a framework of trans-Pacific modernity, recalibrating the notion of modernity. Modernity as a critical analytical lens has challenged easy conceptions of agency in cultural analysis by drawing attention to the Western-centric articulation of spatialized and historicized time on a global scale, but it has also tended to subscribe to a monolithic, one-way movement of power in investigating the interrelation of Western colonial projects and cultural formations in the non-West. Furthermore, while the term "modernity" makes a generic reference to Western hegemony and its consequences, it has often taken as its main frame of reference European colonialisms in the Americas, and thus centered on trans-Atlantic circulations. Trans-Pacific modernity, as I conceive of it, underscores the specificities of American and Japanese imperialisms, which influenced not only Korea but also the broader region of Pacific Asia in diverse configurations, and foregrounds more nuanced workings of agency and idiomatic proclivities particular to this region.

In line with such a framework of trans-Pacific modernity, I conceptualize the trans-Pacific modern voice, of which Korean Christian vocalization is a both a variation and an illustrative example, as a multivalent and liminal voice, exceeding a single analytical frame. The trans-Pacific modern voice is a voice framed by macro-level geopolitics. In the case of Korean Christian singing and praying, it was born in American religious mission in Korea and catalyzed by Japanese imperialism. As such, this voice articulated the practitioners affectively and materially with some of the hallmarks of American modernity, including individualism, capitalism, and, in the case of singing, the idea of "beautiful" music, against the backdrop of Japanese imperialism. But the voice I speak of cannot be reduced to the inaugurative conditions of macro-level geopolitics, which perpetually banish the practitioners to the status of "colonized." This brings me to my second postulation: the trans-Pacific modern voice is one that is used by practitioners to affirm a sense of self and community within the compromised circumstances in which they find themselves (cf. Pilzer 2012; also see Schwartz 2012). Korean Christian converts used their voices to animate a material field that signified a bounded community and to express the condition of transcending their shared dispossession, demonstrating a kind of interpenetration of political economy and everyday life (cf. Harkness 2014). Finally, I suggest that the trans-Pacific modern voice is one that is ambivalently positioned between the "new" and the "old," or the "modern" and the "premodern." As Sakai and Yoo formulated, the trans-Pacific, which extends from "the Western coast of North America to the Eastern shore of the Eurasian continent," is "a space of traffic and convergence rather than a barrier or separation between traditional societies of East Asia from the liberal capitalism of the US or the Confucian-Buddhist heritage from the civilization and cultures based upon Christian values" (2012, viii). The Korean voices in missionary-influenced institutions were marked by such a confluence: the "new" promoted by the American missionaries circulated in and out of the already established routines of everyday life, affiliating with pre-existing modalities of feeling, speaking, and relating.

With the notion of the trans-Pacific modern voice, I do not mean to suggest the need for a new empirical category or genre of music but rather to highlight the embedded-ness of "local" voices within a structure of affect and temporality stemming from trans-Pacific circulations and contacts throughout the twentieth century. Such entan-gled voices, I add, get occluded in knowledge of vocal music that is shaped as a study of traditional genres or as a discourse that fulfills a multiculturalist mold. This point is akin to Sakai and Yoo's theorization of the "trans-Pacific" as a critique of "East Asia" and "East Asian Studies" (2012, vi). Sakai and Yoo argue that the field of East Asian Studies, a body of knowledge shaped as a study of a particular area (i.e., area studies), remains largely unconscious of the conditions of possibility of "East Asia" and "East Asian Studies." They situate the emergence of both categories in the historical transition from Japanese imperialism to US collective security system formulated during the Cold War; in other words, a US-centric Pacific Asia—a reconfiguration of a Japan-dominated Asia—constituted the hegemonic position from which to name a region as "East Asia," demarcate the geographical limits of this region, and to determine its historicity (also see Chen 2010; Sakai 2010). When applied to the study of voice, such critique calls attention to the historical situated-ness of contemporary frames through which voices of this region are categorized and heard.

Finally, thinking through the notion of the trans-Pacific modern voice, I highlight the importance of reinforcing the particular transnational histories that shaped adopted vocal practices and reshaped old ones in music scholarship. Trans-Pacific circulations indeed formed the basis of a vast web of historical ruptures and traumas, many of which have not been fully investigated in music scholarship. These underexplored histories include Japan–US imperialist rivalry beginning in the late nineteenth century; the Japanese Empire's military, sexual, and cultural violence in its colonies and occupied ter-ritories; the diaspora of Asian laborers to the Western coast of North America, Hawai'i, and Japan; the United States' religious, humanitarian, cultural, and military projects across the Pacific, including Hawai'i, Guam, the Philippines, Korea, the Marshall Islands, and Japan; manifestations of the Cold War, including the Korean War and the Vietnam War; and the articulations of US hegemony with local stratifications in US-allied countries. Unless we have a more nuanced understanding of the modern reconstitution of Korea (and more broadly, Pacific Asia), we cannot hear many Korean voices, and without these voices, we miss the sounds that signal us toward the historical violence and resistance interwoven with such reconstitution.

Works Cited

Anderson, Benedict. 1983. *Imagined Communities: Reflections on the Origin and Spread of Nationalism*. New York: Verso.

Bloechl, Olivia. 2008. *Native American Song at the Frontiers of Early Modern Music*. Cambridge: Cambridge University Press.

Bloechl, Olivia, Melanie Lowe, and Jeffrey Kallberg, eds. 2015. *Rethinking Difference in Music Scholarship*. New York: Cambridge University Press.

Bruno, Antonetta Lucia. 2002. *The Gate of Words: Language in the Rituals of Korean Shamans*. Leiden: Research School of Asian, African, and Amerindian Studies (CNWS), Universiteit Leiden.

Caprio, Mark. 2009. *Japanese Assimilation Policies in Colonial Korea, 1910–1945*. Seattle: University of Washington Press.

Chang, Hyun Kyong Hannah. 2014. "Exilic Suffering: Music, Nation, and Protestantism in Cold War South Korea." *Music & Politics* 8 (1): n.p. http://dx.doi.org/10.3998/mp.9460447.0008.105.

Chen, Kuan-Hsing. 2010. *Asia as Method: Toward Deimperialization*. Durham, NC: Duke University Press.

Clark, Donald N. 2003. *Living Dangerously in Korea: The Western Experience 1900–1950*. Norwalk, CT: EastBridge.

Davis, George T. B. 1910. *Korea for Christ*. London: Christian Workers' Depot.

Eidsheim, Nina Sun. 2009. "Synthesizing Race: Towards an Analysis of the Performativity of Vocal Timbre." *TRANS-Transcultural Music Review* 13: n.p. http://www.sibetrans.com/trans/articulo/57/synthesizing-race-towards-an-analy.

Eidsheim, Nina Sun. 2015. "Race and the Aesthetics of Vocal Timbre." In *Rethinking Difference in Music Scholarship*, edited by Olivia Bloechl, Melanie Lowe, and Jeffrey Kallberg, 338–65. Cambridge: Cambridge University Press.

Fuhr, Michael. 2013. "Voicing Body, Voicing Seoul: Vocalization, Body, and Ethnicity in Korean Popular Music." In *Vocal Music and Contemporary Identities: Unlimited Voices in East Asia and the West*, edited by Christian Utz and Frederick Lau, 267–84. New York: Routledge.

Gale, James. 1896. "The Korean Coolie." *The Korean Repository* 3 (12): 475–81.

Gale, James. 1909. *Korea in Transition*. New York: Eaton & Mains.

Grove, Paul. 1915. "Adequate Song-Books." *The Korea Mission Field* 11 (4): 110–13.

Hardie, Robert. 1934. "The Methodist Episcopal Church, South." In *Within the Gate: Comprising the Addresses Delivered at the Fiftieth Anniversary of Korean Methodism*, edited by Charles A. Sauer, 31–43. Seoul: The Korea Methodist News Service.

Harkness, Nicholas. 2014. *Songs of Seoul: An Ethnography of Voice and Voicing in Christian South Korea*. Berkeley: University of California Press.

Hulbert, Homer. 1903. "Editorial Comment." *The Korea Review* 3 (12): 546–7.

Kane, Danielle, and Jung Mee Park. 2009. "The Puzzle of Korean Christianity: Geopolitical Networks and Religious Conversions in Early 20th-Century East Asia." *American Journal of Sociology* 115 (2): 365–404.

Killick, Andrew. 2010. *In Search of Korean Traditional Opera: Discourses of Ch'anggŭk*. Honolulu: University of Hawai'i.

Kim, Andrew E. 2000. "Korean Religious Culture and Its Affinity to Christianity." *Sociology of Religion* 61 (2): 117–33.

Kim, Chil-Sung. 2012. "The Role of Robert Alexander Hardie in the Korean Great Revival and the Subsequent Development of Korean Protestant Christianity." PhD diss., Asbury Theological Seminary.

Lee, Graham. 1907. "How the Spirit Came to Pyeng Yang." *The Korea Mission Field* 3 (3): 33–7.

Maliangkay, Roald. 2017. *Broken Voices: Postcolonial Entanglements and the Preservation of Korea's Central Folksong Traditions*. Honolulu: University of Hawai'i.

McGary, Grace Harmon. 1915. "Music in the School." *The Korea Mission Field* 11 (4): 103–5.

Min, Kyeong Chan. 2008. "Hanguk geundaehwa yangaksa gaeron" [Introduction to Modern Western Music in Korea]. In *Tong asia wa seoyangeusuyong* [East Asia and the Embrace of Western Music], edited by Kyeong Chan Min, Seong Jun Kim, Jeon Jang, In Ok Ryu, and Yasda Hiroshi, 16–92. Seoul: Eumak Segye.

Moose, J. Robert. 1904. "Report of the Seoul Circuit." In *Minutes of the Annual Meeting of the Korea Mission of the Methodist Episcopal Church South, 1904*, 39–42. Seoul: Methodist Publishing House.

Mun, Kyeong Ho. 1903. "Songdo." *Sinhak wolbo* 3 (10): 342.

Mun, Ok Bae. 2011. *Hanguk geumjigogui sahoesa* [The Social History of Banned Songs in Korea]. Seoul: Yesol.

Noble, Mattie Wilcox. 1910/1993. *The Journals of Mattie Wilcox Noble, 1892–1943*, edited by Manyeol Yi. Seoul: Hanguk gidokgyo yeoksa yeonguso.

Novak, David. 2013. *Japanoise: Music at the Edge of Circulation*. Durham, NC: Duke University Press.

Oak, Sung-Deuk. 2009. *Hanbando daebuheung sajin euro boneun hanguk gyohoe, 1900–1910* [The Great Revivals of the Korean Peninsula, Examining the Korean Church through Photographs, 1900–1910]. Seoul: Hongseongsa.

Oak, Sung-Deuk. 2013. *The Making of Korean Christianity: Protestant Encounters with Korean Religions, 1876–1915*. Waco, TX: Baylor University Press.

Ochoa Gautier, Ana María. 2014. *Aurality: Listening & Knowledge in Nineteenth-Century Columbia*. Durham, NC: Duke University Press.

Park, Chung-shin. 2003. *Protestantism and Politics in Korea*. Seattle: University of Washington Press.

Pastor Mu. 1906. "Buheunghoe" [The Great Revivals]. *Geuriseudo Sinmun*. 53–5.

Pilzer, Joshua D. 2012. *Hearts of Pine: Songs in the Lives of Three Korean Survivors of the Japanese "Comfort Women."* New York: Oxford University Press.

The Religious Awakening of Korea, an Account of the Revival in the Korean Churches in 1907. 1908. New York: Board of Foreign Missions Methodist Episcopal Church.

Robinson, Michael. 1998. *Cultural Nationalism in Colonial Korea, 1920–1925*. Seattle: University of Washington Press.

Sakai, Naoki. 2010. "Theory and Asian Humanity: On the Question of Humanitas and Anthropos." *Postcolonial Studies* 13(4): 441–64.

Sakai, Naoki, and Hyon Joo Yoo, eds. 2012. *The Trans-Pacific Imagination: Rethinking Boundary, Culture and Society*. Hackensack, NJ: World Scientific Publishing.

Schwartz, Jessica. 2012. "A 'Voice to Sing': Rongelapese Musical Activism and the Production of Nuclear Knowledge." *Music & Politics* 6 (1): n.p. doi:10.3998/mp.9460447.0006.101.

Sterne, Jonathan. 2003. *The Audible Past: Cultural Origins of Sound Reproduction*. Durham, NC: Duke University Press.

Underwood, Horace. 1894. *Chanyanga* [Praise Hymns]. Seoul: Seoul Seongyohoedan.

Utz, Christian, and Frederick Lau, eds. 2013. *Vocal Music and Contemporary Identities: Unlimited Voices in East Asia and the West*. New York: Routledge.

Wachs, Sylvia Allen. 1915. "Teaching Music to Young School Children." *The Korea Mission Field* 11 (4): 102–3.

Weidman, Amanda. 2006. *Singing the Classical, Voicing the Modern: The Postcolonial Politics of Music in South India*. Durham, NC: Duke University Press.

Wells, Kenneth. 1990. *New God, New Nation: Protestants and Self-Reconstruction Nationalism in Korea, 1896–1937*. Honolulu: University of Hawai'i Press.

Witzleben, J. Lawrence. 1997. "Whose Ethnomusicology? Western Ethnomusicology and the Study of Asian Music." *Ethnomusicology* 41 (2): 220–42.

Yoo, William. 2016. *American Missionaries, Korean Protestants, and the Changing Shape of World Christianity, 1884–1965*. New York: Routledge.

Yu, K. Kale. 2016. "Korea's Confucian Culture of Learning as a Gateway to Christianity: Protestant Missions in the Late Nineteenth and Early Twentieth Centuries." *Studies in World Christianity* 22 (1): 37–65.

Yun, Ch'iho. 1905. *Chanmiga* [Songs of Praise]. Unknown: Gwanghakseogwan.

CHAPTER 22

....

BUILDING THE
BROADWAY VOICE

....

JAKE JOHNSON

"WITHOUT much fanfare," boasts the *New York Post*, "Broadway has become an economic cornerstone of New York City, as big a tourist magnet as the Empire State Building and Katz's deli" (Riedel 2011). In conjunction with the revitalization of Times Square during the 1980s and 1990s, the Broadway musical during this period became a commodified and heavily mediated tourist experience. Mega corporations like Disney, Warner Brothers, and Viacom International were interested in buying real estate as "a marketing opportunity made possible by a Times Square address," as Lynne B. Sagalyn has documented in *Times Square Roulette*. "The place," she notes, "was a branded address" (Sagalyn 2001, 310). The branding potential of a Times Square address soon rebranded Times Square itself as the family-friendly corner of New York with something for everyone. One of the leading architects of the revitalization project put it like this: "Everybody in New York thought it was ... so we said it was the center of the world, but was it really? Well, it really is ... at least for a New York tourist" (Sagalyn 2001, 302).

Along with the revitalization of Times Square and the repurposing of Broadway as a dependable tourist industry, the vocal sound of Broadway musicals has also been redesigned. The voices behind musical theater have narrowed over the decades to a more focused sound—a vocal ideal and process that I call the Broadway sound. The sonic development of the Broadway musical has in part come about due to certain vocal pressures. These pressures include the increasing use of belting, stylized diction, and the unique challenges of using compact microphones in smaller theaters, as well as an audience expecting to hear the type of voice or performance present on the cast recording. The result is that for all the widely varying musical styles erupting onto Broadway over the past several decades—from pop to rock, to hip-hop, blues, and country—at the center of that apparent variety lies a specific quality of vocal sound so ubiquitous that it is paid little attention.

That said, musical theater composer Dave Malloy has given some thought to this sound, and observes that Broadway training has only enhanced performers' dependence on this narrow style of singing. He reflects that during a time of "embrac[ing] idiosyncrasies" and "champion[ing] subtlety" in other genres of music, musical theater "remains chained to an orthodoxy of diction, projection, and extroversion" (Malloy 2011). Malloy contends that the "problem" with musical theater today is that singers "adhere to a very learned, imitative, uniform style that has evolved over years of fusing classic Broadway singing with jazz, rock, and pop. It's a style that is usually the result of years of training in over-articulating, over-enunciating, and over-emoting, presumably to ensure that the words are heard and understood" (Malloy 2011). Malloy's grievance seems well placed, for the tension between textual clarity and the means of expressing vocal resonance, for better or worse, has come to characterize the overall voice of Broadway today, with specific manifestations in each show and for each character.

Here I investigate how differing pressures on the musical theater industry can contribute to certain vocal stylistic choices, and I explore the ways in which collegiate and professional training programs have responded to these needs through their musical theater curricula. I bring into relief how vocal training in such programs ensures a sonic conformity, which presumably improves the marketability of the performer in an industry demanding predictable sounds. Specifically, I consider the pedagogical philosophies prevalent in Midwestern musical theater training programs where I have worked as a vocal coach and where many Broadway performers cut their teeth. I have no position for or against the vocal ideas taught in these or other musical theater training programs, but do make some observations for the unique demands attached to such training and what demands those pressures make on singers today. Furthermore, I suggest that the growth of the Broadway musical as a tourist attraction, the rise of the megamusical, and the formation of this Broadway sound are all interrelated phenomena—enabled by a new corporatizing ideology in musical theater that has disciplined the body of the Broadway performer for decades and continues to shape the industry's sound today.

DEVELOPING THE BROADWAY SOUND

While Broadway superstars like Idina Menzel enrapture fans with seemingly "individualized," "exceptional," and "distinctive" voices, the pressures on singers to keep up with such vocal models can function as a strong suggestive force for both singers and teachers (Nocco 2015).[1] To paraphrase Malvina Reynolds's lyrical retort to conformity in "Little Boxes," this Broadway sound is all made out of ticky-tacky and it all sounds just the same. Whereas other musical genres like opera are part of an economic model that emphasizes new productions and casting, musical theater producers hope for long uninterrupted runs with audience expectations of seeing and hearing the same show as the initial staging and original cast, sometimes originating years earlier. One frequent experience I have working as an audition pianist for regional theaters in the Midwest is that most performers, no matter how unique they imagined their performance of a particular song to be, invariably sound strikingly similar to the last person in the room who sang that tune. In fact, in those rare instances when a group of performers brings in a new or trendy song that I do not already know (there is a limited musical theater audition repertoire and in my years of experience only rarely does something unfamiliar cross my piano), the performances are so much the same—down to the finest of stylistic or interpretive choices—that in those moments I feel like I know what the cast recording sounds like without having ever heard it. The people auditioning often are musicians of a very high caliber, who certainly have the ability to learn a song without imitating a recording, so I am inclined to attribute such sameness to stylistic expectations rather than technical limitations. Indeed, this patented sound is an interesting choice since the musical theater community has long prided itself on its artistic and social individuality and ingenuity. Yet with regard to voice, musical theater largely has moved away from the iconic in favor of the fabricated.

This trend is made particularly apparent in the Broadway "supercuts," videos popular on YouTube in which a well-known musical theater song—"Defying Gravity" from the musical *Wicked* (2003), for example—is presented as a montage of performances from various performers from the worlds of Broadway, pop, and even the television show *Glee*. Tucked behind the idiosyncratic vocal mannerisms of the different performers is what amounts to the common vocal style for "Defying Gravity": having the performers aurally lined up side-by-side actually makes this point quite evident. These supercuts are not created to highlight the prevalence of a Broadway sound, but rather to allow an aural comparison for fans to determine the "best" performer in that role ("Who is your favorite Elphaba?" a pop-up bubble embedded within the video asks. "Let us know in the comments section below"). While similarities may seem unavoidable, given that songs require their own specific singing style, the extreme degree of similarity outpaces those requirements. The effect, however, is that these montages propose the semblance of artistic individuality yet articulate the uniformity of voice underlying that artistry (Wicked Supercut n.d.).[2]

On the one hand it seems probable that to a degree, a performer like Idina Menzel set a style for "Defying Gravity" to which all subsequent Elphabas feel the need to aspire. The supercut in fact begins and ends with Menzel singing the song as Elphaba, and returns to her five more times throughout the piece, making obvious the point of comparison is not random but strategically focused on how closely the original gets replicated. My experience hearing auditionees closely model a performance from a show's original cast album points to this same phenomenon. Yet on the other hand, the industrial calculations motivating the creation of a megamusical like *Wicked* indicate that these voices aren't just similar, but are in fact metaphorically "cloned," to use Jonathan Burston's term, and that each iteration of Elphaba heard on Broadway since Menzel originated the character are akin to vocal "franchises" of a larger corporate operation. This standardization doesn't stop at the voice, but includes elements of the overall sound of Broadway as well. As Burston observed in his discussion of sound design on Broadway, with the advent of the megamusical came "the attainment of a level of standardization in production regimes previously unknown in the field of live theatre" and that "most megamusicals' sonic texts reflect an increasing homogenization of both music and acoustics within the world of the stage musical" (Burston 1998, 205–206).

The rise of the megamusical coincides neatly with increased corporate interest in Times Square. Initially associated with European-imported musicals in the 1980s and 1990s such as *Les Miserables*, *Cats*, *The Phantom of the Opera*, and *Chess*, the megamusical genre consists of epic plots, often sung-through music, large sets, and spectacular scenic design. They are also known for their intense international marketing or branding schemes, their ability to translate and transport cross-culturally, and, significantly, often feature a strict division between audience adoration and puzzled critical response. As Jessica Sternfeld points out, "The new advertising style generated so much interest in a show that poor reviews, and a lack of pithy positive quotes attached to a show's ad campaign, went unnoticed. And audiences kept coming, long after the initial hype had subsided" (Sternfeld 2006, 4). Although many of these musicals continue in perpetuity on Broadway, the 1980s version of the megamusical is largely outmoded. Still, aspects of the megamusical survive in new musicals not only in convention and scope, but also in ideology. Sternfeld notes that to a degree, all new musicals today have been influenced by the megamusical, arguing, for example, that "without *The Phantom of the Opera*, *Wicked* would not be the same show" (334). And, as Burston contends, the megamusical's "rationalizing, industrial logic" introduced musical theater to a new level of quality control, one that could "replicate technical and artistic production details with such rigour as to delimit the interpretative agency of performers to a significantly new degree" (Burston 1998, 206).

Yet the curtailing of individuality associated with the current trends in the musical theater industry begins not among the busy streets of New York, but within musical theater training programs of more modest location. By 2002, there were over two hundred undergraduate programs in the United States offering degrees in musical theater. While some of the more popular programs, as might be expected, are geographically centered near New York City—nearby Ithaca College, Syracuse University, and New York University, for example, consistently rank among the top twenty-five musical theater programs in the country—the densest block of coveted programs in the nation is in the Midwest. The expanse of country stretching north to Ann Arbor, Michigan, east to Pittsburgh, Pennsylvania, south to Tallahassee, Florida, and west to Oklahoma City, Oklahoma not only harbors a high number of musical theater programs, but surprisingly boasts some of the most touted ones in the world. These premiere programs include the University of Michigan, Northwestern University, University of Cincinnati College-Conservatory of Music (CCM), Roosevelt University (Chicago), Webster University in St. Louis, and Oklahoma City University. I admittedly draw the boundaries of the "Midwest" rather liberally, but do so in part to demonstrate the perplexity of what is largely understood to be an urban American musical genre so dependent on what James Shortridge called "the most American part of America" for the bodies (and voices) that occupy its stages (Shortridge 1989, 33).

Not only does the Midwest supply many of the voices for Broadway, but, even more broadly, musical theater bristles from a fascination with the region. Cara Leanne Wood has termed this preoccupation "domestic exoticism" (Wood 2010, 14). Familiar shows like *The Music Man*, *Oklahoma!*, and *State Fair* or recent productions like Jason Robert Brown's celebrated but short-lived *Bridges of Madison County* (2014) revel in a sometimes idealized, sometimes mocked—but always exoticized—Middle America. Hilary Baker, on the other hand, has pointed to "the interplay between the dramatic content of musicals and New York" as indication that the city serves as a "locus for idealized representations of community" (Baker 2010, 5). Musicals like *Hair* or *Avenue Q*, according to Baker, collapse an exoticized community and spatiality into the singular expression of "New York City." In both cases, it could be argued, Broadway utilizes place to elicit particular emotional touchstones. As the site of negotiation between the city it occupies and the Midwestern prairie that supplies many of its top performers (and audiences, as I discuss later), Broadway likewise manages to construct a voice at once able to merge Middle America's fantasies of urban authenticity with the necessary commodification that tourism demands.

Commodification or homogeneity are terms far removed from the rhetoric of musical theater vocal training, however. Vocal coaches and voice teachers seem to agree that the most beautiful sounding voice is one that is "unique" to that person, and they consequently train students to "find their voice" rather than sing through imitation. This individuated voice becomes a fetish object in itself, often described in terms of its truthfulness or authenticity. As vocal practitioner Karen Morrow put it in a dissertation by Frank Ragsdale, "I think any voice that's unencumbered and comes from a person freely, is basically the truth. And I think the truth is always attractive in performing" (Morrow, cited in Ragsdale 2004, 47). Mary Saunders adds that she teaches "correct belting"—a particular manner of vocalizing discussed later—as being "more along the lines of what I consider authentic or truthful. Because beauty is a dramatic sense, in terms of how truthful it is" (46).

Yet it is also true that these programs are designed to meet industry standards and audience expectations, and must prepare students within four years to be proficient in a wide variety of styles. For many of the top musical theater training programs, training involves a careful balance between teaching students to navigate the unique vocal pressures of the genre in an individualized manner while also preparing them to maintain a relationship with the standardized vocal sounds currently on Broadway. Thus, students in programs such as Oklahoma City University, the University of Michigan, and the University of Cincinnati, College-Conservatory of Music (CCM) are placed in a demanding position. Incidentally, CCM is an institution that lays claim as the oldest musical theater program in the country, founded in 1968 and thus coming into development around the same time as the genre is undergoing the significant cultural and structural changes noted earlier. The idealization of a performer able to "do it all" is so entrenched within the pedagogical infrastructure of musical theater training that CCM devotes an entire page on their website to what they call "The 'Triple Threat' Philosophy," where the preference for young performers equally accomplished in singing, dancing, and acting is couched within a curious mixture of what may best be described as intimidation, tough love, and industry hazing:

> At CCM we are in the business of turning out "Triple Threats" . . . We have a demanding and difficult course of training with intensive class-work and little time for relaxation. However, we provide our graduates with the wherewithal to survive in a highly competitive field.
>
> PLEASE REMEMBER that the training at CCM is rigorous. We are preparing young people for an inordinately difficult and heart-breaking profession. It is not the school for everyone and not everyone is the kind of student for us.
>
> ("Triple Threat" Philosophy n.d.)

CCM is not alone in its strident pedagogical approach; this tough-love rhetoric and Fordist acumen ("At CCM we are in the business of turning out 'Triple Threats'") is indicative of a careerist mentality prevalent in many top training programs. As the oldest and one of the most competitive programs in the country, CCM takes an unapologetic stance on this issue, stating that they "see no inconsistency in our dual roles of career builders and educators." For all the talk of focusing on "individual ingenuity" and "examin[ing] the nature of artistic communication," CCM's philosophy turns a strange corner when, at the bottom of the document, we learn that "training in musical theatre is *not about being famous or becoming a star*. It is about learning to work in ways that contribute positively to the art of musical theatre, about the unique interaction among the many and varied aspects that make up the musical stage" (emphasis added). Contrary to the rhetoric of freedom, truthfulness, and authenticity surrounding vocal training, CCM's philosophical statement reads like a devotional to musical theater—a simulacrum of a totalitarian regime where ceaseless, tiring work is valued for its means to an individualized "artistic communication," but also where uniformity is de rigueur. So which philosophy to attend to: seek truthfulness and individuality of voice, or format the body to fit narrow conscriptions as a member of a larger and more important body? Herein lies the paradox of contemporary musical theater training.

At the crux of this paradox is the voice itself. While the student may be molded to fit uniformly within an industry that "demands a high level of commitment from the student," fostering an individual voice is still prioritized. For all the students auditioning for admission into their coveted program, CCM reminds the hopefuls that "musical theatre is a frankly presentational form of theatre" that requires "a magnetic stage presence, a confident air and a unique personality. . . . These qualities should be evident in a musical theatre audition" ("Do's and Don'ts" n.d.). Alumni and faculty likewise attest that CCM helps students "find their inner voice" and that they don't value a "cookie-cutter approach" (Pender n.d.). For many years I heard similar expressions while working as a musical theater vocal coach and musical director in the Midwest.[3] In fact, I found it common to hear those in top programs claim students from rival programs sound too similar, all while denying similar accusations of vocal sameness leveled against their own program. Perhaps the differences between an imitation and an original are difficult to define in the frenzy of such intense training. Regardless of the reason, in musical theater training the concept of a unique voice and personality are seemingly prioritized, but the conditions that might make those voices heard and their ideals matter do not seem to exist.

ARTICULATION AND RESONANCE IN BELTING

On a basic level, what distinguishes a vocal sound primarily has to do with two some-what opposing concepts: articulation and resonance. Although technically the articula-tors are the lips, tongue, teeth, jaw, and palette, for our purposes we might conceive of articulation as an externally imposed system that orders those parts of the body. Diction, elocution, and enunciation are all tools of articulation. Resonance, on the other hand, is often closely associated with an individual's "true" sound, or vocal identity, and is both an aural and physiological sensation. Jody Kreitman and Diana Sidtis define resonance as "the process by which the vocal tract interacts with the vocal source to produce the final sound of a voice" (Kreiman and Sidtis 2011, 50). More particular to musical theater vocal pedagogy, the concept of resonance encompasses an idealized way the vocal mechanism can be manipulated (or "released") to achieve the most pure or "honest" sound unique to that individual; consequently, a fully resonant sound has more over-tones and is thus better able to sonically fill a large theater than a less resonant sound. Resonance is also conceived as an inverse of articulation, since finding resonance almost always involves eliminating physiological restrictions rather than introducing new ones. In day-to-day speaking, articulation and resonance of course function cooperatively—the ability to voice oneself requires a natural balance between the acoustic principles that allow a voice to be heard and the social arrangements for how to manipulate bone and soft flesh in order to help make sense of that sound. Articulation and resonance sometimes do get in the way of one another, however, and when this conflict surfaces in musical theater, the demands of articulation almost always tip the scale.

This tension between articulation and resonance is what frames the paradoxical musical theater vocal training and, as a result, are likewise the two issues lying at the crux of the prevalent Broadway sound. Perhaps more than anything else, the musical theater "belt" sound presses this conflict most forcefully. According to Tracy Bourne and Dianna Kenny, a belt voice "is characterized by a relatively high and forward tongue position, a more constricted pharynx, and a higher laryngeal position, as well as a more open mouth shape than for classical vocal production, although some singers may pro-duce a belt sound with a relatively low larynx and wide pharyngeal shape" (Bourne and Kenny 2016, 128.e1–128.e2). The vocal sounds of Barbara Streisand, Idina Menzel, and Ethel Merman, for instance, occupy the popular conception of this belting voice.[4] Once described as a "brassy, sassy, sort of twangy sound," the belt has increasingly become a fixed aesthetic in musical theater over the past few decades (Melton 2007, 133). Regardless of musical style or the physical type of the singer, the successful Broadway performer almost invariably must have or be able to mimic this particular sound. To turn again to Mary Saunders, "musical theatre is no longer either/or; it is all-inclusive. All boys are bari-tenors; all girls are sopranos who belt" (58).[5] One recent study found that in comparing ads on a musical theater job posting website between October 2012 and April 2013, only five percent of employers sought performers who could sing "legitimately"—a thinly veiled and often pejorative description of what for a musical theater trained ear seems like the artificial or inauthentic sound of continuous vibrato in "classical" singing (Green et al. 2014).[6] Clearly there is a market preference for the belted voice. Noted vocal pedagogue Karen Hall suggests the appeal to this abrasive sound lies within its sounding dangerous or edgy. She writes that

> unlike the classical voice, belting has been considered emotionally edgy and verging on the brink of sounding out of control. It is this unique quality that so many singers have attempted to emulate in the past sixty years. There is no denying that the belt voice has established itself as a vocal quality that is desired and hired in the professional arena and as such demands attention to healthy production.   (Hall 2014, 59)

A true emblem of modernity, the belt cuts across time and context and positions itself as a natural voice for all ages. Hall states that when a musical is revived on Broadway, "the male and female roles are most often sung with a more contemporary sound" (73). The evolution of the voice of Curly in Rodgers and Hammerstein's *Oklahoma!* (1943) is a helpful reference point in following the development of this contemporary sound. This can be demonstrated with some close listening comparing the voice of Alfred Drake, the original Curly, to subsequent performances by Gordon MacRae in the 1955 film version, Laurence Guittard in the 1979 Broadway revival, and Hugh Jackman's interpretation in the 1999 Broadway revival. In the opening number "Oh, What a Beautiful Mornin'" Drake sings with a consistent and heavy vibrato indicative of classical training, making his voice sound "operatic." He also manages the few challenging pitches between his chest voice and head voice by accessing a *voix mixte* or "mixed register." As Drake ascends to the highest notes of the piece, the texture of the voice subtly changes as he shifts the sound into the space of a *voix mixte*. This allows the voice to resonate more fully and grants the illusion of consistency between vocal registers without him having to shift completely into a head voice or, as we hear later in Jackman's rendition, a belt voice.

Inasmuch as Drake's voice is emblematic of vocal stylizations of the 1940s—and indeed the kind of voice *Oklahoma!*'s creators had in mind—each subsequent voicing of Curly is likewise emphatically of its own time. Gordon MacRae's singing of the show's opening number seems mostly in line with what Drake created, though we might note overall the brighter, flatter vowels in places that make the cowhand sound less contemplative and more conversational. By the time we hear Laurence Guittard's bright, ringing, and nasal sound when singing about corn growing high "as a elephant's eye," it is clear that a shift in vocal aesthetics has occurred. Guittard's performance places Curly within a clear evolution toward a new vocal sound, one that is concerned less with rounded, full resonance and more with a tilt toward textual communication and dramatic believability. In other words, between 1943 and 1979 Curly morphed into a more genteel and easily relatable character through the harnessing of vocal resonance. Guittard's recording in 1979 likewise captures the moments just before the arrival of *Cats* on Broadway in 1980 (signaling the formation of the megamusical) and the subsequent corporatization of the musical theater industry. Thus Guittard's performance offers a fixed point in the development of Broadway's voice that quickens its pace greatly in the coming decades.

This development is all the more apparent in Hugh Jackman's rendition just before the new millennium. Compared with Drake's, Jackman's "Oh, What a Beautiful Mornin'" involves singing far less and speaking the pitches much more; we might say Jackman approximates the pitches rather than allows the voice to resonate on each one. He noticeably modifies the final syllable of the word "meadow"—which is only the second pitch he actually sings—to avoid the pure /o/ sound that to the ears of many musical theater aficionados, is a sound sure to mark the singer as "classical." Perhaps the most prominent deviation of Jackman's version from that of Drake is Jackman's use of a belt sound, rather than a *voix mixte*, on those highest notes of the phrase. While difficult to determine from a recording, the belted voice sacrifices brightness of sound over the voice's ability to resonate; compared with Drake's operatic sound, Jackman's belt voice is more pronounced but lacks the overtones that would allow his voice to carry without amplification in a theater. Such a flat, nasal sound rings of the contemporary Broadway voice; indeed almost all popular music genres today make use of this belting voice to some degree, so there is a familiarity with that distinctive—if not near ubiquitous—voice. But what place does this contemporary belt sound have in a musical written in 1943 and set at the turn of the century? Is there an explanation for why Curly's voice evolved from operatic to belt? Both seem equally inappropriate voices for a simple cowhand, so why such a dramatic shift from one to the other?

One possible explanation involves changing ideals surrounding resonance, particularly with the introduction of amplification into musical theater, as I explore later. It seems likely that the pragmatics of the belt eventually created a new standard for how musicals should sound, an adaptation that essentially aestheticized a diminished vocal resonance. According to those in the musical theater industry, that abrasive and brassy ring in the voice allows the text to clearly be heard. In fact, the primacy of the text over the sound itself may define the aesthetics of modern musical theater. Even among those singing "legitimate" vocal styles, there is a "necessity of textual comprehension" that frames "all music theater vocal qualities . . . as speech-like," as Bourne and Kenny observe (Bourne and Kenny 2016, 128.e9). Nonetheless, belting has long been the practice most favored for its closeness to speech in musical theater singing. Karen Hall writes that "understanding and communication of the text is the most important aspect of vocal production," noting that singing with a belt "is considered an extension of the speaking voice" (Hall 2014, 65). Mary Saunders adds that "what we think of as a 'belt sound' is the apex of a spoken crescendo" (quoted in Ragsdale 2004, 39).

It could be that this conceptualization of the belt as a means of continuing natural speech patterns carried over from the Stanislavsky system of acting, which infiltrated postwar American theater through New York's Actor's Studio. This particular interpretation of Stanislavsky's method of acting placed value on a more natural, region-neutral style of delivery; the popularity of the method led eventually to New York City play casts sounding more and more generic. By the time Ethel Merman arrived on New York stages and popularized the belting voice with her signature song "There's No Business Like Show Business," the conventions of theater were meshing with evolving sentiments of honesty and naturalness within musical theater—ironic, given that Merman's style of planting herself center stage and singing directly to the audience undermined any notion of dramatic realism. From this point on, the business of show business was to carry on where Merman left off, making the sounds and voices of Broadway louder, brassier, and more in your face than ever—all industry tokens of honesty, regardless how unnatural a sound it may actually be. "In classical singing, the aim is usually to be beautiful and to be easy," writes one voice teacher. "And [with] belt singing the aim is to communicate and to excite and really get the audience, to sell something, sell a song, you know?" (quoted in Ragsdale 2004, 48).

Yet clarity of text comes at a high price. Selling a song through belting involves a quashing of vocal resonance, pushing the resonating sensation further into the front of the face and, often, closing off the vocal mechanism itself with hard muscularity in order to project as loud and as piercing a sound as possible. Belting requires a great deal of force since, perhaps counterintuitively, the performer must use greater volume to compensate for overtones lost in the practice of diminishing resonance. The likely deleterious effect of belting has occupied vocal pedagogical literature for decades; both the American Academy of Teachers of Singing and the Voice Foundation have cautioned students and teachers about the dangers of belting (Hall 2014, 59). Frank Ragsdale's survey of voice teachers lists numerous potential dangers in belt singing, noting that belters run the risk of developing "lesions on the cords, polyps, cysts, blood vessels popping, nodules, fatigue, decreased range, a wobble in the voice, tough folds, scratching of the cords or larynx, false fold constriction, polypoid edema, vocal fold hemorrhages, vocal fold edema and pre-nodular swelling" (Ragsdale 2004, 59). As much as these cautions may be taken seriously, others point to examples of singers who belt frequently and heartily who have enjoyed great longevity in their careers. Countering this logic, C. L. Osborne insists that "to argue that some singers belt and survive has all the weight of observing that some people smoke three packs a day, live to eighty, and die of causes other than cancer, emphysema, or heart attack" (Osborne 1979, 65). In other words, there is no way to belt healthily. As many would disagree as would agree with that statement, of course, but such is an inherent quality of the sometimes-heated disputations regarding the belting phenomenon.[7]

I will turn in the next section to the costs—physical and material—of attaining this Broadway sound, but for now want to conclude by acknowledging that the belting voice is a primary site of negotiating articulation and resonance. Karen Hall concedes that belting is a privileging of articulation over the sound itself, noting that "less resonance is used to enhance the speech approach to singing—the shape of the pharynx in speech is more relaxed than the stretched pharynx required in classical singing" (Hall 2014, 67). She later adds that "the contemporary music theater sound, which emphasizes the enunciation of the text rather than the beauty of the voice, results in singing that uses less resonance than classical production" (Hall 2014, 73). Frank Ragsdale points the discussion back to the musical theater institutions themselves and lays blame on incorrect vocal pedagogy: "Part of the issue [with the homogenized musical theater voice] is that resonance is what makes a person's voice individual and a lot of people are teaching belting and [musical theater] styles with a less open space making everyone sound similar" (personal communication, May 7, 2015). If you recall, Dave Malloy's similar concern with musical theater's Broadway sound boiled down to "the result of years of training in over-articulating, over-enunciating, and over-emoting, presumably to insure that the words are heard and understood" (Malloy 2011). This shackling of musical theater singing to the "orthodoxy of diction, projection, and extroversion" gets at exactly the issue I am raising here. The high value Broadway has placed on articulation and textual clarity has somehow shifted the focus away from resonance and, with it, the individuated voice. That the words can be heard is all that matters and, as Jonathan Burston has pointed out, the assumption seems to be that the louder and more forceful those words come across, the better.

Paying for the Voice

According to a report by The Broadway League, "in the 2013–2014 season, there was a record breaking 8.52 million admissions by tourists in the Broadway theaters, representing 70% of all tickets" ("Demographics of the Broadway Audience" n.d.). The report also revealed interesting demographics of the new Broadway audience. The most likely Broadway theatergoer for that season was white, female, middle-aged, and, on average, had an annual household income of $201,500. The relative wealth of today's Broadway audience brings to relief the soaring costs of producing musicals, which helps explain a dramatic increase in ticket prices. Not everyone is so pleased with this economic shift in musical theater, nor the reasoning given for such prohibitive costs. Broadway veteran and notorious provocateur Patti LuPone once quipped that exorbitant ticket prices "has more to do with greed than it has to do with anything else" (quoted in Geidner 2011). Regardless of the explanation, hit shows have large profit margins. In 2011, Michael Riedel wrote that ticket prices for hit shows are more than three times the cost of what they were in the early 2000s. "As a result," he writes, "weekly grosses for hit musicals run to $1.5 million" (Riedel 2011). Broadway has hit a stride with its new audience and doesn't mind catering to its tastes. A *Times* article from January 2013 pointed to tourists as the reason for the near disappearance of dark theaters, adding that tourists are, "more and more, influencing what kinds of shows make it to Broadway" (Zoglin 2013). As more tourists pour in to its theaters and, increasingly, movie studios too try to reproduce Disney's early success in the theater market, all the interest in the area makes it undeniable that, in Riedel's words, "Broadway's the hottest ticket in town" (Riedel 2011).

Demographic reports such as this are a reminder that a great deal of money is exchanged in the musical theater industry. Many of those dollars are spent in less obvious ways, however, and often in places far removed from the streets of Times Square. Unknowable figures from years of dance lessons, voice lessons, acting workshops, musical theater camps, and, of course, trips to Broadway itself all fill the checkbook ledger lines of families eager to assuage their budding performer's ambitions—and all this before going to college! Indeed, it takes a lot of resources and relative financial privilege to prepare to become the kind of performer places like CCM, Oklahoma City University, or the University of Michigan call for—and therefore presumably to succeed on Broadway—just as it takes a similarly privileged position to travel to New York City to experience a Broadway show as an audience member. But what exactly are audiences and students paying for? At one level, they are both paying for an authentic voice. Yet of course the actuality of such an authentic voice on Broadway today has already been problematized. For all the money and labor that goes into highly individualized musical theater training, as well as the material means of paying for a ticket to a production, the musical theater industry makes demands on the performer to find or replicate a fixed voice able to be exchanged and interchanged with that of any number of other Broadway constituents. Thus the resources required to "find your voice," to get on Broadway, are rendered invisible and, with few exceptions, any instance of an individuated voice made suspect.

Broadway audiences may have grown wealthier, whiter, and increasingly touristic, but Broadway shows today are the most ethnically diverse they have ever been. This phenomenon may be related to Disney's presence in Times Square, which, as Lynne Sagalyn recounts, "marked a turning point for the [42nd Street Development Project] because it conferred middle-class respectability on the street" (Sagalyn 2001, 312). What is implied by "middle-class respectability" is as vague as it is contentious. Indeed, the seemingly progressive vision of racial and class harmony advocated in Disney films and musicals appeals to a broadly conceived respectability that nonetheless puts the subaltern on display for the benefit of middle-class entertainment. In his telling of Toni Braxton's starring role as Belle in Disney's Broadway production *Beauty and the Beast*, Jason King writes that the particular version of multiculturalism Disney advocates is merely "a token gesture to diversity floating along a river of liberal monoculturalist assumptions" (King 2002, 70). Since *Beauty and the Beast*, a number of musicals with ethnically diverse characters and themes have emerged; for many, these serve as middle-class fantasies of the racialized voice and body for reasons largely having to do with the voices themselves. As voices on Broadway that sing the same characters now oftentimes sound more similar than merely accounted for in terms of the demands of style adherence, so too have various cultures and ethnic communities been reduced to a common voice at precisely the moment representatives of these cultures come to populate the musical stage.

Uniformity of the Broadway performer is realized in nonvocal ways, too—an outcome of the grueling schedule a life in the theater demands. In virtually every way, being in a show determines a performer's everyday lifestyle. A Broadway performer typically performs eight shows over a six-day workweek—Sunday nights and Mondays are usually the only time off. There is considerable pressure to stay fit and maintain consistent eating habits; even the slightest fluctuation in weight could require a costume refitting, an expense many producers may see as unnecessary. Given the uniform size and physique of most performers, interchanging ousted performers with near-identical replacements is an easy way to cut costs. Therefore, workouts and meal plans occupy the attention of performers even on off days. Cast members report early to the theater for fittings, fight calls, and last-minute rehearsals and often leave theaters late at night after necessary tasks like costume changing or mingling with fans backstage. While none of these intrusions directly affect the voice per se, such a lifestyle certainly contributes to inevitable vocal fatigue and exhaustion.

Technology often makes up for losses accrued from such demands. Microphones can act as a crutch for a faltering voice, and indeed amplification helps make a demanding Broadway schedule tenable, if only provisionally so.[8] Even more, the same conditions and expectations for standardization in voice are often at work in sound design. Burston writes provocatively of the use of sound on Broadway to reduce the "singing body" to "the status of cipher," and notes the voracious appetite for loudness characteristic of Broadway producers. Others have taken note as well. After observing a sound engineer set the decibel level for the orchestra in *Beauty and the Beast* to a startlingly high 110 decibels, celebrated voice teacher Jeannette LoVetri asks a similar question: "Why are producers requiring this? Because they don't know much, don't know singing, don't know acting, don't understand the voice, and don't know what else to evaluate except volume. If it's loud, it's great! No, it's pathetic" (Melton 2007, 50).

Louder sounds and amplification processes again contribute to the ever-present conflict of demanding articulation over the body's natural ability to resonate. But with less resonance and thus fewer overtones present in the belted voice, artificial amplification is often the only recourse for actually hearing the voices on stage. Such a process leads to what can be an unsettling sensation of hearing an acousmatic sound—a phenomenon where the source of a voice seems displaced from its visual signifier on stage. This corresponds with Patti LuPone's admission of feeling "disenfranchised from [her] experience" as a theater audience member because of the ambiguity of the voice's origin: "I don't know where the voice is coming from. It's not coming from the stage any more. My eyes are looking at the stage, and my ears are searching for the sound that the mouth is producing" (Geidner 2011). The labor of the voice, as siphoned through amplification, remains hidden and obscured, no longer a part of the body on stage, leaving behind what Burston describes as "a filtered, synthetic trace" (Burston 1998, 213).[9] Despite the loudness and overwhelming presence of the vocal sound in the space, the performer's voice is disembodied, rendered invisible, erased. It is as if Broadway is using loudness to compensate for the choked-out voices, even as the sinews and tissues themselves rattle with the intensity of a belt. "The productions are just too loud," says LuPone. "You can't have an intimate experience in the theater anymore. And that's what it's about. It's really about the unification of an audience, having a collective audience, individually, and listening. And we're not allowed to listen any more because the sound level is too loud" (Geidner 2011). To put it another way, articulation is killing resonance—the system is sonically burying the performers whose voices keep it running. Meanwhile the audience has stopped listening, deafened by the roar of a voice-eating machine.

This is why true resonance matters. Nick Couldry argues that there is an impulse for narrative in life, and that with that ability to narrate one's life comes great power. As he writes,

> What we do—beyond a basic description of how our limbs move in space—already comes embedded in narrative, our own and that of others. This is why to deny value to another's capacity for narrative—to deny her potential for voice—is to deny a basic dimension of human life.   (Couldry 2010, 7)

Is this what is happening on the New York stage? Are voices being silenced and the capacity to narrate denied? With the multiplicity of races and musical styles on Broadway today—and with an avid and growing audience coming from all parts of the world—it doesn't seem tenable to argue that voices or potential voices are not being valued. An askew glance at the situation might reveal another side of the matter, however, drawing attention to the "rationalities" Couldry warns of "that do not directly deny the value of voice outright (indeed, in some contexts they may celebrate it), but work in other ways to undermine the provision of voice at various levels" (Couldry 2010, 11).

This does seem to be the case in musical theater today. The multiplicity of voices and styles designed for a variegated audience act as a distraction from the conformity of the Broadway sound. This distraction lulls audiences into mishearing uniformity for individuality, and the fabricated as honest. While Broadway voices have morphed into similar objects to be refitted and sold, moved around here and there, it seems unlikely in the high stakes business of the musical theater industry that this commodification process will be reversed any time soon. While the "lullaby of old Broadway" is presented as unique, for that unique experience to be reproduced, sameness may be a paradoxical compromise.

*   *   *

"Close your eyes and listen as [Broadway performers'] larynxes stretch and vibrate with the pain of being an underdog and the joy of being really loud," writes the *New York Times*. "Bet you can't tell them apart" (Brantley 2005). Indeed, from the training programs in Middle America to the bright lights of Broadway, the business of musical theater can best be summarized by the old Holiday Inn tag line: the best surprise is no surprise at all. While the rhetoric fetishizes vocal uniqueness, the voices prepared for Broadway are actually producing conformity. Critics are conflicted with this scenario since some ideal of conformity is obviously bringing audiences to the theaters, or at least not inhibiting them. For example, Ben Brantley bristles at the idea of Broadway with "eminently replaceable" cast members, yet acknowledges that it is probably good for business: "Sui generis stars are not necessarily advantages for investors hoping for long, sold-out runs.... So it would seem to make good commercial sense to create musicals that put the emphasis less on individual performance than on overall concept" (Brantley 2005).

In the end, such "good commercial sense" means a standardized vocal product. Although the rhetoric of a distinctive, individualized voice remains a part of Broadway's mythology, the building of the Broadway sound plainly illustrates how an economic model can drive a certain type of vocal economy. The details—the individual bodies and voices—matter little in the formulation of a Broadway show. Consistency and replicability, now enhancers of rather detractions from storytelling or artistry, are the latest things on Broadway.

NOTES

1. Adriana Nocco, writing for OnStageBlog.com, uses these words to describe Broadway's five "most distinctive female voices." According to Nocco's criteria, Menzel ranks at number three.
2. TheaterMania.com features several other supercuts, including *Funny Girl, Company, Chicago, Gypsy,* and *Anything Goes.*
3. Thanks to popular television shows like *The Voice,* where celebrity judges refer to themselves as "vocal coaches," the popular image of a vocal coach is that of a sideline cheerleader armed with nuggets of well-intentioned yet wholesale, nondescript advice for budding singers. Traditionally, however, the role of a vocal coach is a much more involved and important part of vocal pedagogy. Vocal coaches instruct singers in all nontechnical aspects of singing. They may give advice regarding diction, musical style, suitability of certain repertoire for auditions, dramatic characterization, or other vocal stylizations that fall within a particular vocal coach's specialty. Often a proficient pianist, the vocal coach in musical theater is an important liaison among the singer, voice teacher, and stage director, being particularly adept at translating instructions from one corner of a production's creative team to another.
4. Informants in Bourne and Kenny's study nominated these and other performers as exemplary belters.
5. The "bari-tenor" is of course a portmanteau, not only of the words "baritone" and "tenor," but also of the vocal types and their respective ranges.
6. This percentage comprised 59 of 1,238 total jobs from this period on this website. See Green et al. (2014). The authors conclude that, while "traditional voice training remains indisputably valuable as a skill for the musical theatre singer," "voice teachers and specialists must address CCM [Contemporary Commercial Music] styles of singing that currently dominate professional auditions in order to give musical theatre performers the best chance at success."
7. For a comprehensive look at the inability of voice teachers, voice practitioners, and voice scientists to agree on what precisely happens when one belts, see Ragsdale (2004).
8. The microphone likewise contributed to a new vocal aesthetic, particularly among male voices. As Salzman and Desi point out, the implementation of microphones in musical theater resulted in "a major reaction against the high, trained singing voices that had

dominated for so long." Lower voices, now no longer dependent on bodily projection, came to dominate Broadway singing. Thus the bari-tenor displaced the primacy of higher vocal registers, for a time placing them "on the verge of extinction." See Salzman and Desi 2008, 24, 25 n8.

9. Burston was writing in 1998 near the beginning of what has been called the "corporate musical" on Broadway and, from his perspective at the time, surmised that the volume level in musical theater would eventually level off as "qualities of head voice and crooning" would gradually overcome "Broadway's belting cantorial traditions." While it is true that body mikes and advanced sound technology grant singers opportunities to sing with a greater range of sensibilities, the dominance of the belting sound on Broadway continues today even as celebrated shows like *The Light in the Piazza* or *Bridges of Madison County*—musicals designed to be a throwback to more traditional, legitimate musical theater stylizations— come and go without significantly altering the prevalent soundscape of Broadway.

WORKS CITED

Baker, Hilary. 2010. "Stage(d) Communities: Representations of New York, Sexuality, and (Auto)Biography in Contemporary American Musical Theater." PhD diss., University of Pennsylvania.

Brantley, Ben. 2005. "How Broadway Lost Its Voice to 'American Idol.'" *New York Times*, March 27. http://www.nytimes.com/2005/03/27/theater/newsandfeatures/how-broadway-lost-its-voice-to-american-idol.html.

Bourne, Tracy, and Dianna Kenny. 2016. "Vocal Qualities in Music Theater Voice: Perceptions of Expert Pedagogues." *Journal of Voice* 30 (1): 128.e1–128.e12.

Burston, Jonathan. 1998. "Theatre Space as Virtual Place: Audio Technology, the Reconfigured Singing Body, and the Megamusical." *Popular Music* 17 (2): 205–18.

Couldry, Nick. 2010. *Why Voice Matters: Culture and Politics After Neoliberalism*. London: Sage Publications.

"The Demographics of the Broadway Audience 2013–2014." n.d. http://www.broadwayleague.com/index.php?url_identifier=the-demographics-of-the-broadway-audience. Accessed May 14, 2015.

"The Do's and Don'ts." n.d. http://ccm.uc.edu/theatre/musical_theatre/auditions1/dos_and_donts.html. Accessed May 15, 2015.

Geidner, Chris. 2011. "Patti LuPone Talks About Broadway's Problems." *MetroWeekly*, September 9. http://www.metroweekly.com/2011/09/patti-lupone-talks-about-broad/.

Green, Kathryn, Warren Freeman, Matthew Edwards, and David Meyer. 2014. "Trends in Musical Theatre Voice: An Analysis of Audition Requirements for Singers." *Journal of Voice* 28 (3): 324–7.

Hall, Karen. 2014. *So You Want to Sing Music Theater: A Guide for Professionals*. Lanham, MD: Rowman & Littlefield.

King, Jason. 2002. "Toni Braxton, Disney, and Thermodynamics." *The Drama Review* 46 (3): 54–81.

Kreiman, Jody, and Diana Sidtis. 2011. *Foundations of Voice Studies: An Interdisciplinary Approach to Voice Production and Perception*. Hoboken, NJ: Wiley-Blackwell.

Malloy, Dave. 2011. "A Slushy in the Face: Musical Theater Music and the Uncool." *HowlRound*, December 12. http://howlround.com/a-slushy-in-the-face-musical-theater-music-and-the-uncool.

Melton, Joan. 2007. *Singing in Musical Theatre: The Training of Singers and Actors*. New York: Allworth Press.

Nocco, Adriana. 2015. "'Imitative of No One': Five of Broadway's Most Distinctive Female Voices." OnStageBlog.com, August 8. http://www.onstageblog.com/columns/2015/8/8/imitative-of-no-one-five-of-broadways-most-distinctive-female-voices.

Osborne, C. L. 1979. "The Broadway Voice: Just Singin' in the Pain." *High Fidelity* (January–February): 53–67.

Pender, Rick. n.d. "Retrospective: Forty Years of Musical Theatre Excellence." http://ccm.uc.edu/theatre/musical_theatre/overview/retrospective.html. Accessed May 15, 2015.

Ragsdale, Frank. 2004. "Perspectives on Belting and Belting Pedagogy: A Comparison of Teachers of Classical Voice Students, Teachers of Nonclassical Voice Students, and Music Theatre Singers." PhD diss., University of Miami.

Riedel, Michael. 2011. "How Broadway Emerged from Ruin to Become a Billion-Dollar Business." *New York Post*, June 12. http://nypost.com/2011/06/12/how-broadway-emerged-from-ruin-to-become-a-billion-dollar-business/.

Sagalyn, Lynne B. 2001. *Times Square Roulette: Remaking the City Icon*. Cambridge, MA: The MIT Press.

Salzman, Eric, and Thomas Desi. 2008. *The New Music Theater: Seeing the Voice, Hearing the Body*. New York: Oxford University Press.

Shortridge, James R. 1989. *The Middle West: Its Meaning in American Culture*. Lawrence: University Press of Kansas.

Sternfeld, Jessica. 2006. *The Megamusical*. Bloomington: Indiana University Press.

"'The Triple-Threat' Philosophy." n.d. University of Cincinnati College-Conservatory of Music. http://ccm.uc.edu/theatre/musical_theatre/overview/philosophy.html. Accessed May 14, 2015.

"A Wicked Supercut of Elphaba's 'Defying Gravity.'" n.d. YouTube. https://www.youtube.com/watch?v=qdjb2Xx6nyI. Accessed May 15, 2015).

Wood, Cara Leanne. 2010. "Representing the Midwest in American Stage and Film Musicals, 1943–1962." PhD diss., Princeton University.

Zoglin, Richard. 2013. "Is Broadway Just for Tourists?" *Time*, January 2. http://entertainment.time.com/2013/01/02/is-broadway-just-for-tourists/.

EPILOGUE

Defining and Studying Voice across Disciplinary Boundaries

JODY KREIMAN

INTRODUCTION

IT is hard to imagine a topic of study with deeper roots throughout the world, and in more academic and professional disciplines, than voice. For example, the Sanskrit Hindu texts *Natyasastra* (dated between 200 B.C.E. and 200 C.E.) and *Sangitaratnakara* (thirteenth century C.E.) contain approaches to voice in the forms of a dramaturgical manual and synoptic music treatise, respectively. Sophisticated theories describing voice production and the relationship between voice and speech were well-established in the foundations of Western thought by the time of Aristotle (Laver 1981; Butler 2016; O'Neill 1980), as were other theories relating the sound of the voice to underlying characteristics of the speaker (Sanford 1942), and complex frameworks for describing voice quality as an aspect of rhetoric (Quintilian 95 C.E./1920; Pollux second century C.E., cited by Austin 1996 [1806]). These issues are still actively debated today, attesting to both the importance of voice and the difficulty of the questions. Over time, studies of voice have extended in range beyond questions of how we communicate personal identity, emotion, and personality (and how we thereby influence listeners), to include the biomechanics of tissue vibration, the neurophysiology and cognitive psychology of voice production and perception, the art and science of the singing voice, vocal acoustics and aeroacoustics,[1] the role of voice in regulating behavior in humans and in nonhuman animals, signal processing and voice synthesis, the causes and treatment of voice disorders, speaker recognition by listening or by machine in everyday or forensic contexts, and dozens of other research topics.

The range of what can reasonably be considered part of voice studies is part of the delight of this research area, but it also places an enormous burden of scholarship on those of us who are concerned with how voice is produced, how it is perceived, how it accumulates meaning, and how to measure it in all of its many facets. Given the differences in the training and research interests of scholars across the disparate disciplines that study voice, it is probably not surprising that cross-fertilization of questions, ideas, methods, results, theories, and even terminology has been quite limited. In fact, so great is the incoherence of the voice literature that a new researcher scanning a handful of papers might be hard pressed to understand what different studies have in common, or even whether voice when studied by an otolaryngologist is the same thing as voice studied by a semiotician. In the absence of a common body of knowledge shared by everyone who studies voice, whatever their home discipline, this fragmentation is self-perpetuating: jargon, lack of appropriate conceptual tools, the difficulty inherent in mastering the methods of even a single approach, and antipathies that can exist between the sciences and the humanities all serve to discourage scholars from exploring topics outside their own (often quite narrow) research area, or from even considering forays into such unknown, possibly hostile territory (Gould 2003). It is difficult enough to keep up with the literature on laryngeal biomechanics, one might argue, without also reading papers in ethology, human development, musicology, and sociology, the relevance of which to one's own work may not be readily apparent.

The goal of this chapter is to explore the implications of this situation and to build a case for the importance of a broad understanding of voice, and hence for the need for cross-disciplinary training. In part because disciplinary limitations apply to all scholars and disciplines, I will argue that without development of a truly interdisciplinary degree program in voice studies, our knowledge is likely to remain incomplete and unsatisfying, and long-standing blind spots will persist. I will then outline a *preliminary* curriculum as an invitation to conversation and debate about what a broadly cross-disciplinary voice studies program might look like. My own training in scientific approaches to voice gives this discussion a somewhat empirical perspective, which is not meant as a position statement. Instead, the curriculum that is put forth in this chapter (and in the accompanying wiki page for ongoing collaboration and updates) is intended to start a conversation about voice studies within a higher education context.

Do We Need Voice Studies?

It is worth asking at the outset if a specialized interdisciplinary course of study related to the voice is really necessary. After all, voice has been studied productively for millennia without any such thing, as the 18,000 references to the scientific literature in my database testify.[2] However, it is not difficult to demonstrate the limitations of even this vast body of research. For example, many scientists who study voice production devote little consideration to perception. Engineers, physicists, and others use computational and physical models to study vocal fold vibratory properties or aeroacoustics, with outcomes measured in terms of extent and symmetry of vocal fold vibration, mucosal wave motion, glottal gap configuration, existence and location of vortices in the airflow through the glottis, and other physical characteristics. It is quite unusual for reports of these investigations to assess—or even mention—the perceived sounds that are produced by the models (although some recent work has begun examining the perceptual effects of changes in one or more aspects of voice production; see, e.g., Signorello et al. 2016). Even the acoustic signal is often ignored, or treated offhandedly as a byproduct of the production process.

Such studies are sometimes criticized because models, being necessarily simplifications, may not represent real phonation especially well. A greater problem, however, is that without a listener, vocal folds may oscillate and articulators may vary the vocal tract shape, and as a result air molecules will move in particular ways, but the output of this process is vibration, and not the sound of a voice per se (Sterne 2003; Eidsheim 2015). The study of voice, like the study of sound in general, also benefits from consideration of the listening process, because listeners influence the perceptual process even before sound reaches the brain (Heffner and Heffner 2016). Head shape and size, external ear shape, the ear canals, and bone conductance all emphasize certain frequencies in the sound and de-emphasize others, before the sound ever reaches the listener's cochlea for transduction into neural impulses. Sound processing, once it starts, does not proceed passively from the bottom up: the influence of cognitive (top-down) processes begins at the auditory periphery (e.g., Krishnan and Gandour 2009), and factors such as attention and expectation, the listening and acoustic context, the listener's hearing ability, native language, and familiarity with the speaker affect what listeners ultimately perceive from the sound. Like studies of voice production that disregard perception, acoustic studies that examine waveform characteristics such as aperiodicity[3] or open quotient,[4] but do not address perceptibility, overlook important information about voice, however much they improve our ability to describe waveform attributes. Nevertheless, such studies are clearly meant to be about voice, include the word "voice" or "vocal" in their titles (e.g., "'Finding a Voice': Imaging Features after Phonosurgical Procedures for Vocal Fold Paralysis" [Vachha et al. 2016];[5] "Vocal Responses in Heightened States of Arousal" [van Mersbergen et al. 2017]),[6] and appear in journals that focus on the study of the voice (for example, the *Journal of Voice*).

If it is true that listeners influence what is heard, it is also true that they influence what is said and how phonation happens, as follows. The biological facts of phonation specify that voice necessarily encodes the body that produces it. For example, vocal tract resonances depend on the size and shape of the vocal tract, which are constrained by the overall size of the animal (Fitch and Hauser 2003; see Kreiman and Sidtis 2011, for a review). This encoding reflects similar properties (e.g., personal identity, physical size, age, sex, reproductive fitness, dominance), albeit to varying degrees, across quite a surprising range of species, including reptiles, anurans, birds, most mammals, and possibly even fish (Lengagne et al. 2001; Fine and Waybright 2015; Reber et al. 2015; Amorim et al. 2016). This wide distribution suggests that these abilities are biologically old and have been conserved across evolution for many eons, which would not have occurred unless projection of biological information by voice served some important function for the phonating animal. In other words, vocal encoding of biological information cannot exist simply to encode the speaker's characteristics, because that code has no meaning or function without a listener who hears the phonation and makes use of the information, which in turn somehow benefits the vocalizer. It follows that voice production is impossible to understand out of the context of voice perception. Animals phonate to be heard, and the characteristics of the listener ultimately contribute along with the characteristics of the speaker to the shape vocalizations take.

Beyond these short- and (very) long-term biological pressures linking voice production to perception, it is also clear that understanding voice production in a general way further requires considering the dynamic social and cultural factors that shape speakers, listeners, and actual individual utterances. The phonating body is embedded along with the listener in a social context, or enculturation. For example, several studies report a cultural preference in Japan for women who speak using significantly and substantially higher vocal pitches than are typical of either American or Swedish women (van Bezooijen 1995; Yuasa 2008).[7] Physical differences do not explain these dissimilarities, which average as much as 36 Hz and are easily perceptible. However, ratings of Japanese and Dutch female speakers on personality scales related to powerfulness and attractiveness suggested that Dutch listeners associated lower pitches with attractiveness, while Japanese listeners preferred higher pitched voices. (Both listener groups associated higher pitch with less power.) These findings—similar ratings across groups with respect to power, but divergent aesthetic preferences for high versus low pitch—suggest that Japanese women increase their fundamental frequency (Fo)[8] during speech due to cultural standards for femininity (see also Starr 2015, for a more nuanced view).[9] Similarly, many prosodic features of speech apparently begin as sociocultural markers of group membership. For example, many commentators note (or lament) the increasing use of "creaky voice" or "vocal fry" in the speech of young professional women, although reliable data are scant (e.g., Yuasa 2010; see Podesva and Callier 2015, for a review).[10] The messages conveyed by voices are thus not functions of just speakers and listeners, and the concept of voice necessarily implies a social being (Bertau 2007).

Two Examples

Two studies of fundamental frequency provide specific examples of the limits of explanations of voice quality derived solely from the perspective of voice production. Mean Fo represents the average rate of vocal fold vibration, and is well-correlated with body size across a number of different animal species, including rats, raccoons, mule deer, and African elephants (Titze et al. 2016). Larger animals have larger larynges than smaller animals, and larger larynges can accommodate larger vocal folds, which (other things being equal) vibrate at lower rates than do smaller folds. From the perspective of production, this "size code" (Ohala 1983; Chuenwattanapranithi et al. 2008) is an incidental association whose biological value derives from the use listeners make of it. For example, male animals (which are generally larger than females) tend to have lower-pitched voices than do females, allowing Fo to serve as a cue to sex. Larger animals also tend to be more dominant, so Fo can cue status within a herd. Adult animals are typically larger than juveniles, allowing Fo to cue age; and so on. The social and behavioral value of these Fo cues seems to have led to further adaptations that both derive from the size code and simultaneously undermine it. Titze et al. (2016) demonstrate that *average* Fo is indeed primarily determined by larynx size and vocal fold length, but that animals have evolved several strategies for extending the *range* of frequencies they can produce:

> A laryngeal adaptation for greater length change is greater rotation or gliding between cartilages that anchor the ends of the vocal folds. Alternatively, a tissue layer that can bear a greater tension (i.e., a ligament with high density collagen fibers) can also increase the fundamental frequency range and thereby allow vocal versatility. As a consequence, fundamental frequency can become uncoupled from size. Two large frequency ranges produced by two species can overlap even if the two have dramatically different body sizes.   (10)

In other words, the particular uses listeners make of the association between size and Fo has led speakers to evolve ways of "scamming" listeners by sending messages whose characteristics are inconsistent with their true sizes.[11] It is not possible to explain such adaptations without consideration of listeners' behavior and of the whole communicative and social context in which phonation occurs.

A second example of the limits of biological explanations is the case of jazz singer Jimmy Scott (Eidsheim 2019; Eidsheim and Kreiman 2016). Born with Kallman syndrome, which prevented the onset of puberty and voice mutation, Scott's voice is generally heard as unambiguously female. Measurements indicate that both his Fo and Fo range are consistent with female values. However, a number of male singers with "high voices" (for example, Smokey Robinson, Marvin Gaye, and Frankie Valli) used Fo values that are much higher than Scott's, but their voices sound unambiguously male. Fo alone does not explain the perception of maleness in these cases. Two other factors appear to play roles. The first is vocal tract resonances, which interact with Fo in determining the speaker's perceived sex. Although exceptions occur,[12] generally speaking a longer vocal tract corresponds to a larger animal. Vocal tract resonances decrease in frequency with increasing vocal tract length, making resonances a second potential cue to physical size. Scott's resonances are consistent with usual female values, while those of male "high singers" are in the male range. Finally, Scott rarely, if ever, used falsetto in his singing; in contrast, songs like "Ooh, Baby Baby" (Robinson and Moore 1965), "Trouble Man" (Gaye 1972), and "Walk Like a Man" (Crewe and Gaudio 1963) feature long passages in falsetto. In Robinson's, Gaye's, and Valli's singing, falsetto in the context of male formant frequencies marks the phonation timbrally, and allows it to be heard as masculine despite the very high Fo values. Were our interpretation of these songs entirely dependent on biology, the high Fo values should be heard as feminine (or childlike), or at least as ambiguous between male and female. Instead, these voices are unambiguously male, while in contrast, the lower pitch of Scott's voice in the context of female vocal tract resonances paradoxically contributes to its feminine quality.

As these arguments and examples demonstrate, the meanings suggested by biology are not immutable, nor are they the sole determinants of how a voice signal is interpreted (Podesva and Callier 2015). Both over evolutionary time and in the case of a single listening event, understanding what we hear requires reference to the phonating animal, to the acoustic signal, to the listener, and to the complex context in which phonation and listening occur. A similar case can be built from the perspective of critical studies. It is as easy to assume that biological meaning has been superseded by social meaning as it is to assume that the meaning of a voice is at heart based on biology. As the examples here demonstrate, however, biology is always part of the picture, if only to provide the basis from which social meanings deviate.

In summary, the sounds an animal creates and the manner in which a listener perceives and responds to these sounds represent an interaction between what is wired in by evolution and what is varied by social and cognitive pressures. The voices we use reflect all these factors, and it is reductionistic to assume that we can understand one facet of this complex of determinants out of the context of the others. If the study of voice were interdisciplinary simply because voice does many things (carries/functions linguistically in spoken messages; reflects speaker identity, age, sex, size; reflects speaker's mental/emotional state; etc.), these things could presumably be studied individually, using whatever methods belong to the relevant discipline. However, voice is interdisciplinary because by its very nature it partakes of the physical, the biological, the cognitive, and the social, all of which interact with each other.

So yes, we need a truly interdisciplinary voice studies program. One response to similar concerns is a relatively new academic discipline called "vocology" (Titze, 1992, 2018; Titze and Verdolini Abbott, 2012). Vocology programs partially fill the need for interdisciplinarity in voice studies, but only partially. Vocology broadly defined is the study of vocalization in humans and other animals, and in conception it incorporates ethological perspectives on voice production and perception. However, at present its scope is usually proscribed to the science and practice of voice habilitation, and as taught in the limited number of programs available, study is usually focused on voice production, voice training, and evaluation, often from a clinical perspective, with little emphasis on the humanistic and social aspects of the study of voice. These programs thus represent a valuable first step towards the kind of curriculum I envision, but do not fully resolve the issues just raised.

A BRIEF COMMENT ON THE ISSUE OF DEFINITION

This view of voice as a whole comprising all these areas is seemingly inconsistent with traditional definitions, which thus require comment here. A shared definition of voice seems a priori to be an important part of establishing a field of voice studies, and yet despite millennia of research, this simple preliminary goal has apparently eluded us.

In fact, voice is one of those objects under study that continues to garner controversy, analogous to the notion of culture in anthropology. Matt Rahaim's work on vocal ontology and epistemology in chapter 2 of this volume also highlights the ways in which vastly different aspects of voice come into focus depending on a given fields' questions and research processes. While our specific approaches are diametrically opposite, both Rahaim and I seek to put those field-specific definitions into conversation.

Historically, efforts at defining voice follow the research practice of avoiding a focus on the big picture in favor of carving out specific aspects for consideration. A number of distinctions are commonly proposed as part of the definition process (see Kreiman and Sidtis 2011 for extensive discussion). The first, commonly found in the sound studies literature, distinguishes voice as the expression of the "inside" of a subject from voice as a signal quite separate from a speaker. This contrast is an old one; historical studies suggest that "both the fields of acoustics and medicine treated the voice as something separate from an intending, speaking subject since the eighteenth century" (Sterne 2008, 96).

A second common distinction emphasizes the difference between the contribution of a listener (termed "voice quality") and the speaker + transmission channel (labeled "voice") to what is heard. "Voice" in this sense refers to the acoustic signal as generated by the speech production system, and thus is grounded in speakers and their physiology. Quality picks up where voice alone leaves off and refers to the listener's sensation and perceptual impression. These two concepts are thus adjacent, but disjunct, pieces of a continuum represented by the classic speech chain model (see Figure 23.1). Unfortunately, "voice" and "voice quality" are often used interchangeably, adding to the terminological confusion that plagues voice studies. Even more unfortunately, no body of empirical data or theory exists to explain how these pieces go together.

Yet another distinction separates so-called narrow and broad definitions of voice. Narrow definitions specify voice as the sound produced by vibration of the vocal folds, excluding the acoustic effects of vocal tract resonances, noise excitation, room reverberation, and other factors. Voice in this sense resembles the linguistic voicing feature that distinguishes /s/ from /z/. Broad definitions of voice characterize it as essentially synonymous with speech.[13] This view of voice is also an old one; for example, Butler (2015) argues that in Greco-Roman times, voice and speech were intertwined concepts. The distinction between broad and narrow definitions has always been problematic (Gerratt

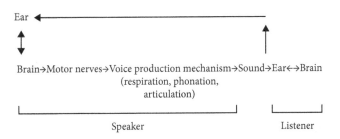

FIGURE 23.1 The speech chain (following Denes & Pinson 1993).

et al. 2016), and continues to be particularly troubling. Butler (2015) describes this situation by suggesting that modern practices:

> …define the voice as something *outside* speech:…either before it (we have a voice before we learn to speak), below it (voice is the material support of spoken language), or beyond it (the voice expresses what language alone cannot). Most definitions, in fact, assume all three and imagine the voice as something that surrounds speech without exactly entering it.   (37)

To summarize, these definitions and distinctions suggest there are a number of rather different voices: voice as expression of the inner self or the soul; voice as something that implies a speaker but is not that speaker; voice as sound made by a larynx; voice as speech; voice as speech-but-not-language; voice as something the speaker does; voice as something the listener does; and not forgetting of course voice as an expression of the physical self, the emotional self, and the social self (Sidtis and Kreiman 2012). Note, however, that all of these different voices represent either the perception of something—which implies production, or there would be nothing to perceive—or the expression of something, which implies a perceiver. Thus, these definitions are in fact consistent with the view of voice developed in the previous section. Both research and attempts at definition lead to the same conclusion: the study of voice in its essence is a unified endeavor, and existing approaches that do not reflect this are not able to explain why or how voice does what it does in the lives of speakers and listeners.

Building a Voice Studies Curriculum

Building a curriculum requires identifying the pieces of information that will actually be useful to all scholars of voice, whatever our home discipline, and making that information accessible to a very broad audience. What knowledge should be shared? Realistically, what do humanists need to know about scientific approaches to voice? And what do scientists need to know about humanistic views? For example, surgically removing a vocal fold nodule with a laser or a scalpel does not require even a passing familiarity with psychoanalytic or phenomenological thought about voice, but when treating a voice disorder, one does not simply treat a physical ailment. The selected intervention will have a profound effect on nearly every aspect of the patient's life, and treating the patient in addition to the disorder requires some understanding of the issues described in this chapter and its companions in this volume. In the same way, access to approaches and ideas from critical theory, sociology, gender studies, and related fields could help scientists and engineers understand why some variables, and not others, are important concomitants of voice quality, and can sometimes explain variability in the data that might otherwise be written off as noise.

Similarly, analysis of a singer's performance or development of an epistemology or an ontology probably do not require understanding the role of the superior laryngeal nerve in control of phonation. However, as previously discussed, biological meaning is an important part of the information conveyed by voice, and if it does not explain everything we hear, it does underpin a wide range of perceptual and cultural phenomena across species and provides a baseline for thinking about the changes introduced by social and other influences. A broad understanding of the biology and control of voice can often shed light on the meaning of a specific phonation in its particular context, and on why that particular meaning arises.

Finally, scholars from different disciplines need to be comfortable reading each other's literatures. This is not a trivial matter. The technical complexities of laboratory methods and statistical approaches are familiar to scientists, but not humanists, and concepts like "grain of the voice" and "logos" occur routinely in the humanistic literature, but not so much in scientific studies. Terminological problems extend beyond the use of unfamiliar words or obscure acronyms: key concepts like "timbre" and "pitch" can mean very different things depending on the particular scholarly traditions in play. Depending on a given scholar's familiarity with a given cluster of concepts and terminology, the terms in use can seem to exhibit inherent confusion or to provide needed technical or theoretical complexity that bring forth clarity and precision. The goals of this curriculum are thus 1) to provide everyone with enough information to appreciate the unity of the field of study; 2) to provide tools for further forays into unfamiliar research areas; and 3) to help all researchers avoid the mistakes that come from an excessively narrow view of their topic.[14]

These goals could be met in four rather intensive semester-length seminars. As mentioned in the introduction, the kind of transdisciplinary engagement that voice requires also requires a crowd-sourced curriculum. This chapter is an invitation to precisely such collaboration, and needless to say, the specific texts and examples included here represent only one possible approach, and only the tip of the iceberg of material that might be included. In the end, any one version of a voice studies class or curriculum will be strongly influenced by the expert areas of the instructor and the guests they may be able to include. Therefore, a crowd-sourced curriculum could function as a resource from which to curate select reading, activities, and discussions.

Class #1: Introduction to Voice Studies

Given the range of disciplines that incorporate the study of voice and the historical lack of cross-fertilization among disciplines, any proposed curriculum must start with a comprehensive introductory class. Such a class, ideally cotaught by a scientist and a humanist, would of course focus in part on giving students an appreciation of the scope of the discipline, on the many possible sources of the meaning of voice signals, and on the factors that might influence these meanings for a given listener. Emphasis might also be placed on listening skills and ear training (see the wiki page for an example for listening activities).

Beyond this, however, students require a basic understanding of what counts as data in different kinds of study, and of how conclusions are reached by scholars in different research areas. One approach to this might be to organize the class around sets of readings, each with a focus on different approaches to related problems. For example, students could read a paper about the role of voice in mate selection (for example, the studies of Reby and colleagues on the calls of rutting red deer [e.g., Reby and Charlton 2011], or Burke and Murphy's [2007] study of male vocalization and female mate selection in gray tree frogs), paired with studies of perception of sex in voice (e.g., Weston et al. 2015; Reby et al. 2016), work on voice quality in transgendered individuals (e.g., Munson 2007; Zimman 2013), and studies of the female voice in non-Western culture (e.g., Sundar 2008) (Table 23.1).

Table 23.1 Introduction to voice studies. A sample set of matched readings for one unit in an introductory class in voice studies, as part of a comprehensive voice studies curriculum. Complete references are given in the bibliography at the end of this chapter

Authors	Article Title	Summary
Burke and Murphy 2007	How female barking treefrogs, Hyla gratiosa, use multiple call characteristics to select a mate	Female frogs assess multiple call characteristics simultaneously when judging the reproductive fitness of potential mates.
Carson 1995	The gender of sound	Traces the negative attitudes toward female voices back to ancient Greek literature.
Kreiman and Sidtis 2011	Foundations of Voice Studies, Chapter 4.3: Sex and the voice	A thorough review of the physiology and perception of male/female vocal differences.
Munson 2007	The acoustic correlates of perceived masculinity, perceived femininity, and perceived sexual orientation	Perceived sexual orientation, perceived masculinity, and perceived femininity are distinct but correlated perceptual parameters.
Reby and Charlton 2011	Attention grabbing in red deer sexual calls	Male "harsh" roars attract and maintain female attention to calling males relative to "common" roars.
Reby et al. 2016	Sex stereotypes influence adults' perception of babies' cries	Low-pitched cries are more likely to be attributed to boys, and are perceived as more masculine, than high-pitched cries, despite the absence of overall sex differences in pitch.
Sundar, 2008	Women, vocality, and nation in Hindi cinema	The interaction between femininity, social norms, and voice in constituting a national identity.
Weston et al. 2015	Discrimination of voice gender in the human auditory cortex	fMRI data suggest that gender-dependent activation levels in specific brain regions strongly distinguish male and female voices during voice perception.
Zimman 2013	Hegemonic masculinity and the variability of gay-sounding speech: The perceived sexuality of transgender men	Comparisons of the voices of gay-sounding trans men and nontrans men indicate that there is more than one way to sound gay.

Discussion of each set of readings would provide an introduction to the various research methods applied in studies of voice, along with a survey of the questions asked in different disciplines. Students would also learn how papers are organized and how arguments are constructed in different disciplines (e.g., Platt 1964).

Class #2: Voice Science

In this draft curriculum, the introductory class would be followed next by three intermediate level classes. The first, "Voice Science," would examine voice production, acoustics, perception, and the biology of voice, with the goal of explicating how and why animals produce and perceive sound. Topics could include the nature of sound; an introduction to hearing, vocal physiology, and voice production; the extent to which speakers can control the sound of their voices, and how they do it (including the singing voice; e.g., Edgerton 2015); and how characteristics like personal identity, age, sex, race, emotional state, and personality are (or are not) perceived from voice. Ideally this class will include an opportunity for students to view and manipulate excised larynges (Figure 23.2), or—even better—participate in a laryngeal dissection. High-speed videos of vocal fold vibration can further help students understand how phonation occurs, and audio demonstrations can provide further ear training and understanding of the difficulty of describing complex auditory stimuli. Several texts are available for use in a class like this, including *The Science of the Singing Voice* (Sundberg 1987), *Dynamics of the Singing Voice* (Dayme 2009), and *Foundations of Voice Studies* (Kreiman and Sidtis 2011). Compare this course to a curriculum proposed for vocology training, which includes individual classes in principles of voice production, instrumentation for voice analysis, voice disorders, voice training and rehabilitation, private voice lessons, and a voice practicum (including studio observation) (Titze 1992), but omits most of the material covered in classes 1, 3, and 4 in the present proposal.

Class #3: Philosophical and Critical Thought about the Voice

As noted earlier in this chapter, in Western history writing about voice dates back at least to the ancient Greeks. I envision the third class in this proposed curriculum as a historical survey of the traditions and major lines of thought that have emerged over this long history. Themes could include materiality and subjectivity, embodiment and disembodiment, interiority/exteriority, performativity, identity formation, vocality, textuality, narrative, ritual and spiritual practice, and so on.

A few review papers have appeared (e.g., Plugge 1942; Gray 1943; Laver 1981) and collections of essays are increasing in number as interest in voice grows (e.g., Bernhart and Kramer 1994; Thomaidis and Macpherson 2015; and, of course, the present volume). To my knowledge, however, no comprehensive monograph-length review has appeared that would make a suitable text for this course, other than Butler's (2015) survey of

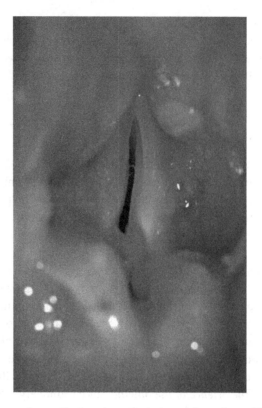

FIGURE 23.2 The human larynx during phonation, viewed from above. The front of the speaker's neck is at the top of the image and the back is at the bottom. The two white bands with an opening between them are the vocal folds, which attach to the thyroid cartilage in the front and to the arytenoid cartilages in the back. The opening between the folds is called the glottis. In this image (taken from high-speed video), the cartilages are covered with mucous membrane, and are thus difficult to see. Image provided by Zhaoyan Zhang of the UCLA Department of Head and Neck Surgery.

thought about voice in Greco-Roman writings. A more broadly focused book, or a liberally annotated reader of primary sources, would be a very useful contribution to the field, particularly for beginners like me. A few papers that I have personally found helpful in the early stages of my readings in this area are listed in Table 23.2.

Class #4: Voice in Communication, Cognition, and Behavior

The final proposed class in this program would examine how voice functions in human and animal communication. Topics could include linguistic approaches to the study of voice, tone, and phonation contrasts (Gordon and Ladefoged 2001; Garellek et al. 2013); evidence from cognitive psychology, neuropsychology, and brain imaging regarding neural processing of voice signals and the interactions between linguistic and voice

Table 23.2 Philosophical and critical thought about the voice. A sample set of readings for one unit in a comprehensive voice studies curriculum. Complete references are given in the bibliography at the end of this chapter

Author	Title	Summary
Cavarero 2005	*For More Than One Voice*	Human uniqueness resounds in the voice.
Chion 1999	*The Voice in Cinema*	Discussion of the faceless voice and its magical power in the context of cinema.
Connor 2000	*Dumbstruck: A Cultural History of Ventriloquism*	Historical examples of "sourceless" voice ranging from prophetic voices, oracles, female mystics, hearing voices, to ventriloquism as entertainment.
Eidsheim 2015	*Sensing voice: Materiality and the Lived Body in Singing and Listening Philosophy*	What we hear depends as much on our materiality, physicality, cultural and social histories, as it does on properties of the sound per se.
Fales 2002	"The Paradox of Timbre"	Physical attributes of sounds do not account fully for a listener's perceptual experience.
Gould 2003	*The Hedgehog, the Fox, and the Magister's Pox*	Scientific and humanistic approaches are complementary, not conflicting.
Jarman-Ivens 2011	*Queer Voices: Technologies, Vocalities, and the Musical Flaw*	Analysis of popular vocal music from queer studies perspective.
McPherson 2005.	*The Turkish Call to Prayer: Correlating the Acoustic Details of Vocal Timbre with Cultural Phenomena*	
Rée 2000	*I See A Voice: Deafness, Language and the Senses*	A history of deafness and how science and medicine, philosophy and culture understood the role of voice, language, and communication in relation to being a human.

quality processing (e.g., Nygaard and Pisoni 1998; Krishnan and Gandour 2009; Latinus et al. 2013; Zhang et al. 2016); sociophonetic studies of the use of voice in construction of social and personal identity (e.g., Sicoli 2010; Podesva and Callier 2015); and studies of how humans and nonhuman animals use voice to identify kin and conspecifics, or to regulate behavior in a troop or herd (Lengagne et al. 2001; McComb et al. 2014) (Table 23.3).

One possible objection to this proposed curriculum is that, other than the introductory course, the proposed classes maintain traditional distinctions between research areas, which are studied more or less independently of one another. Given the present state of voice studies, however, it is difficult to see how we could begin in any other way. Ideally course material will be well-integrated and cross-referenced, but even if this does

Table 23.3 Voice in communication, cognition, and behavior. A sample set of readings for one unit in a comprehensive voice studies curriculum. Complete references are given in the bibliography at the end of this chapter

Author	Article Title	Summary
Garellek et al. 2013	"Voice Quality and Tone Identification in White Hmong"	Phonation contrasts interact with tone to determine word meanings in White Hmong.
Gordon and Ladefoged 2001	"Phonation Types: A Cross-linguistic Overview"	Phonation differences can cue differences in lexical meaning in natural languages, and vary along a continuum ranging from voiceless, through breathy, regular, and creaky voice, to glottal closure.
Krishnan and Gandour 2009	"The Role of the Auditory Brainstem in Processing Linguistically-Relevant Pitch Patterns"	Speakers of tone languages process pitch contours in the auditory periphery faster and more accurately than do speakers of nontone languages.
Latinus et al. 2013	"Norm-Based Coding of Voice Identity in Human Auditory Cortex"	fMRI data suggest that that voice identity is coded in the brain as a function of the acoustical distance between a voice and two internal voice prototypes (one male, one female)
Lengagne et al. 2001	"Intra-Syllabic Acoustic Signatures Used by the King Penguin in Parent-chick Recognition: An Experimental Approach"	King penguin adults and chicks recognize each other by voice, using a very complex perceptual strategy evolved to function in a very noisy environment.
McComb et al. 2014	"Elephants Can Determine Ethnicity, Gender, and Age from Acoustic Cues in Human Voices"	African elephants use age, sex, and language information to distinguish human groups that represent different degrees of threat.
Nygaard and Pisoni 1998	"Talker-Specific Learning in Speech Perception"	Sensitivity to talker-specific information affects the perception of speech.
Podesva and Callier 2015	"Voice Quality and Identity"	Voice indexes information about speakers and participates in construction of stance in interactions.
Sicoli 2010	"Shifting Voices with Participant Roles: Voice Qualities and Speech Registers in Mesoamerica"	In a number of languages spoken in Mesoamerica, voice qualities function systematically to mark participant roles in conversation.
Zhang et al. 2016	"Functionally Integrated Neural Processing of Linguistic and Talker Information: An Event-related fMRI and ERP Study"	Neuroimaging data suggest there is a general neural mechanism for integral phonetic and talker processing, irrespective of specific parameters (vocal tract length or pitch) or languages (English or Cantonese).

not happen, students who complete this program will return to their departments of origin with a much broader understanding of what voice is and how it is used.

DISCUSSION AND CONCLUSIONS

My intent in this chapter was to show that seemingly nonoverlapping scholarly traditions for the study of voice in fact all lead to the same conclusion: that the study of voice should proceed as a multidisciplinary endeavor, and not just as physics or biomechanics or philosophy, if we are in fact to study voice. This view contrasts with the classic speech chain model (Figure 23.1), in which voice is characterized as a sequence of discrete steps that are largely independent of one another.[15] This model reflects the fact that voice cannot be understood solely as physiology, or as sound, or as perception, but it does not incorporate the manner in which each facet interacts with the others, or how all of these aspects of voice interact with and are shaped in both the long and short terms by a myriad of biological, environmental/contextual, and social factors. The meaning of a voice signal cannot be explained by biology alone, as the example of Jimmy Scott shows, but the role of biologically derived meaning in many aspects of voice perception also cannot be denied. As Nina Sun Eidsheim (2015) has written:

> This lived body is embedded in, and subject to, cultural forces at a foundational level. It is this body, whose perceptual system has been "tuned" by a given culture, that is the perceiving conduit of sound... What we hear depends as much on our materiality, physicality, cultural and social histories, as it does on so-called objective measurements (decibel level, sound-wave count, or score).   (115–116)

We cannot develop the theories to explain what we hear across these many dimensions unless students of voice studies are trained to apply more than one set of scholarly tools in their pursuit of understanding. This will not happen without a formal interdisciplinary program created to remove the institutional and cultural obstacles to crossing disciplinary boundaries.

The literature on voice can be seen historically as a tale of two broad kinds of research, one emphasizing the specific (a humanistic approach), and one seeking to derive general principles (a scientific approach). The complex relationship between these two approaches makes voice research a particularly promising target for truly interdisciplinary studies and integrative research (Bertau 2012). Unfortunately, at present many impediments seemingly stand in the way of conducting such research, including the breadth of the topic and consequent difficulty acquiring the necessary interdisciplinary expertise (Sicoli 2015). This last impediment is exacerbated by academic traditions and by the structure of most universities, with their intellectual, administrative, and often physical separation of humanistic and scientific disciplines.

Discussions of conflicts between the sciences and humanities are as old as the sciences and humanities, but it is past time to put aside these "false barriers to understanding" (Gould 2003, 17), given that it is clear that neither scientific nor humanistic approaches in isolation are sufficient to truly understand voice (or any phenomenon; Gould 2003). On the one hand, the plethora of details that emerge from intense humanistic study of specific cases can obscure a broader point; however, downplaying these details in the interest of describing an ideal or average case can "blind [us] to the actuality of the world" (Hayles 1988, 5). In the case of sampling error when the data do not represent the average, smearing the specific details of a case in search of a broader truth can even ironically lead to missing the point altogether. Gould strongly advocates a culture of investigation that represents a hybrid of mental approaches with observation and experimentation. As interest in the study of voice continues to grow, nurturing such a culture in our work could bring particularly spectacular benefits.

ACKNOWLEDGMENTS

This research was supported by grant DC01797 from the National Institute on Deafness and Communication Disorders. Thanks to Zhaoyan Zhang for providing the image in Figure 23.2, to Bruce Gerratt and Ingo Titze for many helpful comments on earlier versions of this chapter, and to Nina Eidsheim for luring me down the rabbit hole to begin with.

NOTES

1. Aeroacoustics is the subfield of acoustics that concerns the transmission of sound through air, the interactions of aerodynamic forces with surfaces (for example, tissue in the vocal tract), and noise generation created by turbulent airflow through the vocal tract.
2. This actively maintained Endnote database is freely available by request.
3. Even when pitch and loudness are held steady, natural phonation is not perfectly periodic. Small differences in period and amplitude occur between adjacent glottal cycles. These cycle-to-cycle differences in period are called "jitter"; cycle-to-cycle differences in amplitude are called "shimmer." See, e.g., Buder (2000) for extended review.
4. Open quotient is the ratio of the time during a glottal cycle that the vocal folds are apart to the total cycle length. It can be defined with respect to high-speed images or electroglottographic or aerodynamic records of vocal fold vibration, but is also commonly estimated from the acoustic signal (e.g., Hanson and Chuang 1999).
5. The abstract for this study reads, "Altered communication (hoarseness, dysphonia, and breathy voice) that can result from vocal fold paralysis, secondary to numerous etiologies, may be amenable to surgical restoration. In this article, both traditional and cutting-edge phonosurgical procedures targeting the symptoms resulting from vocal fold paralysis are reviewed, with emphasis on the characteristic imaging appearances of various injectable materials, implants, and augmentation procedures used in the treatment of vocal fold paralysis. In addition, complications of injection laryngoplasty and medializationlaryngoplasty are illustrated. Familiarity with the expected imaging changes following treatment of vocal fold paralysis may prevent the misinterpretation of post-treatment

changes as pathology. Identifying common complications related to injection laryngoplasty and localization of displaced implants is crucial in determining specific management in patients who have undergone phonosurgical procedures for the management of vocal fold paralysis" (Vachha et al. 2016, 1).

6. The abstract for this study reads, "Objectives. The purpose of this study was to investigate electroglottography (EGG) contact quotient modulation with emotional state in the presence of increased arousal. Study Design. A within-subject reversal paradigm using multiple experimental conditions. Methods. A total of 11 healthy undergraduate students underwent emotion induction with intermittent startles to increase physiologic arousal. During emotion induction, they vocalized on the vowel/u/while EGG was recorded. Results. EGG contact quotient was significantly greater for negative emotions compared with positive emotions with increased arousal commensurate with past research. In addition, overall EGG contact quotient was greater with elevated arousal. However, the effect sizes were small. Conclusions. EGG contact quotient appears to increase with elevated arousal and be greater for negative mood states than positive mood states confirming that emotion states directly influence vocal functioning" (van Mersbergen et al. 2017, 1).

7. Note that the examples in this section are not concerned with the immediate situational context of phonation. Instead, they take a broader approach, in which statistical tendencies are mapped onto political formations. These political formations are in turn mapped congruently with the top-down boundaries of nation-states (Japan, Sweden, the United States, etc.) rather than bottom-up formations that would take ethnicity, social class, and education into account. While not concerned with phonation only, some examples of studies of bottom-up formation approaches include Eidsheim (2011), Harkness (2013), Newland (2014), and Stoever (2016).

8. The fundamental frequency of phonation (often abbreviated Fo) is the rate at which the vocal folds vibrate. The perceptual correlate of this physical property is pitch, which is defined as an attribute of auditory sensation in terms of which sounds may be ordered on a scale from low to high (American National Standards Institute 1994, 34). The correspondence between the two is not exactly linear (e.g., Stevens 1935), a state of affairs that has resulted in the development of a number of scales for measuring phonatory frequency (for example, the bark scale, which measures frequency in terms of critical bands of hearing, and the mel scale, which measures subjective pitch; see, e.g., Rossing [1990] for review).

9. Yuasa (2008) provides an interesting history of these patterns via a set of quotations from Japanese and American literary texts and etiquette books regarding standards for women's speech starting in the eleventh century.

10. Creaky voice has in fact been a documented feature of speech for decades. In languages like Jalapa Mazatec it functions phonemically to distinguish the meaning of different otherwise-identical words (Silverman et al. 1995; Garellek and Keating 2011); in the Zapotec languages it conveys sympathy or commiseration (Sicoli 2015); and in English it marks the end of sentences, major semantic topics, or speaking turns in the speech of both men and women (e.g., Lehiste 1979). Creak can also mark "parenthetical" comments or asides in a conversation (Lee 2015).

11. Another alternative is simply to evolve a larger larynx. This can occur because laryngeal size is not constrained by any nearby bony structures, so the larynx can grow somewhat independently of the rest of the body. For example, this kind of elaboration occurs in male humans, and also in hammerhead bats, for whom the larynx nearly fills the chest cavity (Fitch and Hauser 2003).

12. In some cases animals (for example, lions and rutting red deer) will also lower their larynges prior to roaring to increase vocal tract length, thereby lowering resonant frequencies and increasing their perceived size (Fitch 2000; Fitch and Hauser 2003).

13. Narrow and broad definitions of voice quality also appear in the literature. These definitions parallel the narrow and broad definitions of voice; for example, voice quality in the narrow sense is simply the perceptual impression created by vibration of the vocal folds.

14. For example, hundreds of studies have proposed and evaluated dozens of measures of jitter and shimmer (see Buder [2000] for review) as indices of disease, emotional state, personal identity, age, and almost any other imaginable speaker attribute. Unfortunately, further research (Kreiman and Gerratt 2005) reported that listeners are not perceptually sensitive to jitter and shimmer levels in speech, so that they cannot function as cues in the way other researchers apparently assumed.

15. Note that the model does include a feedback loop to model vocal self-monitoring by speakers.

WORKS CITED

American National Standards Institute. 1994. American National Standard: Acoustical Terminology, S1.1–1994.

Amorim, M. C., C. Cont, C. Sousa-Santos, B. Novais, M. D. Gouveia, J. R. Vicente, T. Modesto, A. Goncalves, and P. J. Fonseca. 2016. "Reproductive Success in the Lusitanian Toadfish: Influence of Calling Activity, Male Quality and Experimental Design." *Physiology & Behavior* 155 (Mar 1): 17–24.

Austin, G. 1996 [1806]. *Chironomia*. Carbondale: Southern Illinois University Press.

Bernhart, W., and L. Kramer, editors. 2014. *On Voice*. Amsterdam: Rodopi.

Bertau, M. C. 2007. "On the Notion of Voice: An Exploration from a Psycholinguistic Perspective with Developmental Implications." *International Journal for Dialogical Science* 2 (1): 133–61.

Bertau, M. C. 2012. "Voice as Heuristic Device to Integrate Biological and Social Sciences. A Comment to Sidtis and Kreiman's 'In the Beginning Was the Familiar Voice.'" *Integrative Psychological and Behavioral Science* 46 (2): 160–71.

Buder, E. H. 2000. "Acoustic Analysis of Voice Quality: A Tabulation of Algorithms 1902–1990." In *Voice Quality Measurement*, edited by R. D. Kent and M. J. Ball, 119–244. San Diego: Singular.

Burke, E. J., and C. G. Murphy. 2007. "How Female Barking Treefrogs, Hyla Gratiosa, Use Multiple Call Characteristics to Select a Mate." *Animal Behaviour* 74 (5): 1463–72.

Butler, S. 2015. *The Ancient Phonograph*. Brooklyn, NY: Zone Books.

Carson, A. 1995. "The Gender of Sound." In *Glass, Irony, & God*, 119–42. New York: New Directions.

Cavarero, A. 2005. *For More Than One Voice*, translated by Paul A. Kottman. Redwood City, CA: Stanford University Press.

Chion, M. 1999. *The Voice in Cinema*, edited and translated by Claudia Gorbman. New York: Columbia University Press.

Chuenwattanapranithi, S., Y. Xu, B. Thipakorn, and S. Maneewongvatana. 2008. "Encoding Emotions in Speech with the Size Code." *Phonetica* 65 (4): 210–30.

Connor, S. 2000. *Dumbstruck: A Cultural History of Ventriloquism*. New York: Oxford University Press.

Crewe, R., and R. Gaudio. 1963. "Walk Like a Man" [recorded by *The Four Seasons*]. On *Big Girls Don't Cry and Twelve Others* [record]. New York: Vee-Jay Records.

Dayme, M. 2009. *Dynamics of the Singing Voice*, 5th ed. Vienna: Springer.

Denes, P. B., and E. N. Pinson. 1993. *The Speech Chain*, 2nd ed. New York: W.H. Freeman.

Edgerton, M. E. 2015. *The 21st-Century Voice: Contemporary and Traditional Extra-Normal Voice*, 2nd ed. Lanham, MD: Rowman & Littlefield.

Eidsheim, N. 2011. "Sensing Voice." *The Senses and Society* 6 (2): 133–55.

Eidsheim, N. 2015. "Sensing Voice: Materiality and the Lived Body in Singing and Listening Philosophy." In *Voice Studies: Critical Approaches to Process, Performance and Experience*, edited by K. Thomaidis and B. Macpherson, 104–19. London: Routledge.

Eidsheim, N. 2019. *The Race of Sound: Listening, Timbre, and Vocality in African American Music*. Durham, NC: Duke University Press.

Eidsheim, N., and J. Kreiman. 2016. "Jimmy Scott and the Problem of Gender in Singing." Invited paper, presented at the 171st Meeting of the Acoustical Society of America, Salt Lake City, UT, May 23–27.

Fales, C. 2002. "The Paradox of Timbre." *Ethnomusicology* 46 (1): 56–95.

Fine, M. L., and T. D. Waybright. 2015. "Grunt Variation in the Oyster Toadfish: Effect of Size and Sex." *PeerJ* 3: e1330, doi:10.7717/peerj.1330.

Fitch, W. T. 2000. "Skull Dimensions in Relation to Body Size in Nonhuman Mammals: The Causal Bases for Acoustic Allometry." *Zoology-Analysis of Complex Systems* 103 (1): 40–58.

Fitch, W. T., and M. D. Hauser. 2003. "Unpacking 'Honesty': Vertebrate Vocal Production and the Evolution of Acoustic Signals." In *Acoustic Communication*, edited by A. M. Simmons, A. N. Popper, and R. R. Fay, 65–137. New York: Springer.

Garellek, M., and P. Keating, P. 2011. "The Acoustic Consequences of Phonation and Tone Interactions in Jalapa Mazatec." *Journal of the International Phonetic Association* 41 (2): 185–205.

Garellek, M., P. Keating, C. M. Esposito, and J. Kreiman. 2013. "Voice Quality and Tone Identification in White Hmong." *Journal of the Acoustical Society of America* 133 (2): 1078–89.

Gaye, M. 1972. "Trouble Man." On *Trouble Man* [record]. Los Angeles: Tamla/Motown.

Gerratt, B. R., J. Kreiman, and M. Garellek. 2016. "Comparing Measures of Voice Quality from Sustained Phonation and Continuous Speech." *Journal of Speech, Language, and Hearing Research* 59 (5): 994–1001.

Gordon, M., and P. Ladefoged. 2001. "Phonation Types: A Cross-Linguistic Overview." *Journal of Phonetics* 29 (4): 383–406.

Gould, S. J. 2003. *The Hedgehog, the Fox, and the Magister's Pox: Mending the Gap Between Science and the Humanities*. Cambridge, MA: Harvard University Press.

Gray, G. W. 1943. "The 'Voice Qualities' in the History of Elocution." *Quarterly Journal of Speech* 29 (4): 475–80.

Hanson, H. M., and E. S. Chuang. 1999. "Glottal Characteristics of Male Speakers: Acoustic Correlates and Comparison with Female Data." *Journal of the Acoustical Society of America* 106 (2): 1064–77.

Hayles, N. K. 1988. "Two Voices, One Channel: Equivocation in Michel Serres." *SubStance* 17 (3): 3–12.

Heffner, H. E., and R. S. Heffner. 2016. "The Evolution of Mammalian Sound Localization." *Acoustics Today* 12 (1): 20–7, 35.

Jarman-Ivens, F. 2011. *Queer Voices: Technologies, Vocalities, and the Musical Flaw*. New York: Palgrave Macmillan.

Kreiman, J., and B. R. Gerratt. 2005. "Perception of Aperiodicity in Pathological Voice." *Journal of the Acoustical Society of America* 117 (4 pt. 1): 2201–11.

Kreiman, J. and D. Sidtis. 2011. *Foundations of Voice Studies*. Malden, MA: Wiley-Blackwell.

Krishnan, A., and J. T. Gandour. 2009. "The Role of the Auditory Brainstem in Processing Linguistically-Relevant Pitch Patterns." *Brain and Language* 110 (3): 135–48.

Latinus, M., P. McAleer, P. E. Bestelmeyer, and P. Belin. 2013. "Norm-Based Coding of Voice Identity in Human Auditory Cortex." *Current Biology* 23 (12): 1075–80.

Laver, J. 1981. "The Analysis of Vocal Quality: From the Classical Period to the 20th Century." In *Toward a History of Phonetics*, edited by R. Asher and E. Henderson, 79–99. Edinburgh: Edinburgh University Press.

Lee, S. 2015. "Creaky Voice as a Phonational Device Marking Parenthetical Segments in Talk." *Journal of Sociolinguistics* 19 (3): 275–302.

Lehiste, I. 1979. "Perception of Sentence and Paragraph Boundaries." In *Frontiers of Speech Communication Research*, edited by B. Lindblom and S. Ohman, 191–202. New York, Academic.

Lengagne, T., J. Lauga, and T. Aubin. 2001. "Intra-Syllabic Acoustic Signatures Used by the King Penguin in Parent-Chick Recognition: An Experimental Approach." *Journal of Experimental Biology* 204 (4): 663–72.

McComb, K., G. Shannon, K. N. Sayialel, and C. Moss. 2014. "Elephants Can Determine Ethnicity, Gender, and Age from Acoustic Cues in Human Voices." *Proceedings of the National Academy of Sciences of the United States of America* 111 (14): 5433–8.

Munson, B. 2007. "The Acoustic Correlates of Perceived Masculinity, Perceived Femininity, and Perceived Sexual Orientation." *Language and Speech* 50 (1): 125–42.

Nygaard, L. C., and D. B. Pisoni. 1998. "Talker-Specific Learning in Speech Perception." *Perception and Psychophysics* 60 (3): 355–76.

Ohala, J. J. 1983. "Cross-Language Use of Pitch: An Ethological View." *Phonetica* 40 (1): 1–18.

O'Neill, Y. V. 1980. *Speech and Speech Disorders in Western Thought Before 1600*. Westport, CT: Greenwood Press.

Platt, J. R. 1964. "Strong Inference." *Science* 146 (3642): 347–53.

Plugge, D. E. 1942. "'Voice Qualities' in Oral Interpretation." *Quarterly Journal of Speech* 28 (4): 442–4.

Podesva, R. J., and P. Callier. 2015. "Voice Quality and Identity." *Annual Review of Applied Linguistics* 35: 173–94.

Quintilian, M. F. 1920 [95 A.D.]. *The Institutio Oratoria*, vols. I–XII, translated by H. E. Butler. Cambridge, MA: Harvard University Press.

Reber, S. A., T. Nishimura, J. Janisch, M. Robertson, and W. T. Fitch. 2015. "A Chinese Alligator in Heliox: Formant Frequencies in a Crocodilian." *Journal of Experimental Biology* 218 (15): 2442–7.

Reby, D., and B. D. Charlton. 2011. "Attention Grabbing in Red Deer Sexual Calls." *Animal Cognition* 15 (2): 265–70.

Reby, D., F. Levrero, E. Gustafsson, and N. Mathevon. 2016. "Sex Stereotypes Influence Adults' Perception of Babies' Cries." *Bibliotheca Medica Canadiana Psychology* 4: 19, doi:10.1186/s40359-016-0123-6.

Rée, J. 1999. *Deafness, Language, and the Senses: A Philosophical History*. New York: Metropolitan Books.

Robinson, S., and P. Moore. 1965. "Ooh, Baby Baby" [recorded by Smokey Robinson and the Miracles]. On *Going to a Go Go* [record]. Detroit: Tamla/Motown.

Rossing, T. D. 1990. *The Science of Sound*, 2nd ed. Reading, MA: Addison-Wesley.

Sanford, F. H. 1942. "Speech and Personality." *Psychological Bulletin* 39 (10): 811–45.

Sicoli, M. A. 2010. "Shifting Voices with Participant Roles: Voice Qualitites and Speech Registers in Mesoamerica." *Language in Society* 39 (4): 521–53.

Sicoli, M. A. 2015. "Voice Registers." In *The Handbook of Discourse Analysis*, edited by D. Tannen, H. E. Hamilton, and D. Schiffrin, 105–26. Malden, MA: Wiley.

Sidtis, D., and J. Kreiman. 2012. "In the Beginning Was the Familiar Voice: Personally Familiar Voices in the Evolutionary and Contemporary Biology of Communication." *Integrative Psychology and Behavior* 46 (2): 146–59.

Signorello, R., Z. Zhang, B. Gerratt, and J. Kreiman. 2016. "Impact of Vocal Tract Resonance on the Perception of Voice Quality Changes Caused by Varying Vocal Fold Stiffness." *Acta Acustica United with Acustica* 102 (2): 209–13.

Silverman, D., B. Blankenship, P. Kirk, and P. Ladefoged. 1995. "Phonetic Structures in Jalapa Mazatec." *Anthropological Linguistics* 37 (1): 70–88.

Starr, R. L. 2015. "Sweet Voice: The Role of Voice Quality in a Japanese Feminine Style." *Language in Society* 44 (1): 1–34.

Sterne, J. 2003. *The Audible Past*. Durham, NC: Duke University Press.

Sterne, J. 2008. "Enemy Voice." *Social Text* 96 25 (3) 79–100.

Stevens, S. S. 1935. "The Relation of Pitch to Intensity." *Journal of the Acoustical Society of America* 6 (3): 150–4.

Sundberg, J. 1987. *The Science of the Singing Voice*. DeKalb: Northern Illinois University Press.

Thomaidis, K., and B. Macpherson, eds. 2015. *Voice Studies: Critical Approaches to Process, Performance and Experience*. London: Routledge.

Titze, I. 1992. "Rationale and Structure of a Curriculum in Vocology." *Journal of Voice* 6 (1): 1–9.

Titze, I. 2018. "The Rationale and History of Vocology." *Voice and Speech Review*. doi:10.1080/23268263.2018.1439867.

Titze, I., T. Riede, and T. Mau. 2016. "Predicting Achievable Fundamental Frequency Ranges in Vocalization across Species." *PLoS Computational Biology* 12 (6): e1004907.

Titze, I., and K. Verdolini Abbott. 2012. *Vocology*. Salt Lake City: National Center for Voice and Speech.

Vachha, B. A., D. T. Ginat, P. Mallur, M. Cunnane, and G. Moonis. 2016. " 'Finding a Voice': Imaging Features after Phonosurgical Procedures for Vocal Fold Paralysis." *American Journal of Neuroradiology* 37 (9): 1574–80.

van Bezooijen, R. 1995. "Sociocultural Aspects of Pitch Differences between Japanese and Dutch Women." *Language and Speech* 38 (3): 253–65.

van Mersbergen, M., P. Lyons, and D. Riegler. 2017. "Vocal Responses in Heightened States of Arousal." *Journal of Voice* 31 (1): 127.e13–127.e19.

Weston, P. S. J., M. D. Hunter, D. S. Sokhi, I. D. Wilkinson, and P. W. R. Woodruff. 2015. "Discrimination of Voice Gender in the Human Auditory Cortex." *NeuroImage* 105: 208–14, doi:10.1016/j.neuroimage.2014.10.056.

Yuasa, I. P. 2008. *Culture and Gender of Voice Pitch*. London: Equinox.

Yuasa, I. P. 2010. "Creaky Voice: A New Feminine Voice Quality for Young Urban-oriented Upwardly Mobile American Women?" *American Speech* 85 (3): 315–37.

Zhang, C., K. R. Pugh, W. E. Mencl, P. J. Molfese, S. J. Frost, J. S. Magnuson, G. Peng, and W. S. Y. Wang. 2016. "Functionally Integrated Neural Processing of Linguistic and Talker Information: An Event-Related fMRI and ERP Study." *NeuroImage* 124 (A): 536–49.

Zimman, L. 2013. "Hegemonic Masculinity and the Variability of Gay-sounding Speech: The Perceived Sexuality of Transgender Men." *Journal of Language and Sexuality* 2 (1): 1–39.

INDEX

Note: Figures and tables are indicated in the page field with *f* and *t* respectively.

Chandler, James 125
Chandler, Raymond 102–3
Chang, Hyun Kyong Hannah xxxii
changes in voice xxix–xxx
  age and 57–58
  anxiety and 62
  cinema and (*see* cinema)
  diagnosis of 56
  environment and 59–60
  gender hearing and 58
  hoarseness and 56–57, 153–58, 160n14
  impersonation and (*see* impersonation)
  larynx and 63–68, 64*f*–66*f*, 70–73, 73*f*
  medicine and 55–74
  music and (*see* music)
  neurological issues and 60, 72
  physical causes of 59–68, 64*f*–66*f*
  in radio (*see* radio)
  singing and 59
  treatment of 56, 68–70, 73–74
  usage and 58, 62–63, 153–58, 160n14
Chanmiga (Songs of Praise) (Yun Ch'iho) 466
Chanyanga (Praise Hymns)
    (Underwood) 463–64, 463*f*, 464*f*, 465
Chapman–Alexander (gospel duo) 457
Chariatidis, Ioannis 346, 348, 359, 360n11
charisma 165–86
  anatomy and 167
  audience and 167
  biological functions of 171, 173–74, 173*t*,
    175*f*–77*f*, 178–79
  of the body 169–70
  climax and 179–81, 180*t*
  culture and 167, 173*t*, 174, 175*f*–77*f*, 179–85,
    180*t*, 182*t*–84*t*, 186n1
  emotional induction and 172*t*
  ethos and 169, 172*t*
  fundamental frequency and 171, 173–74,
    173*t*, 175*f*–77*f*, 178–79, 180*t*, 180–81
  gender and 173–74, 173*t*, 175*f*–77*f*, 178–79
  intensity and 174, 175*f*–77*f*, 178–79, 180–81,
    180*t*
  language and 167–68, 179–86, 180*t*,
    182*t*–84*t*, 186n1
  of the mind 168, 170
  Multidimensional Adjective–based Scale
    of others' Charisma Perception and
    170–71, 172*t*

  origins of 165–68
  pathos and 169, 172*t*
  perception of 178–79, 181–84, 182*t*–84*t*,
    186n1
  pitch and 167, 171, 173–74, 173*t*, 175*f*–77*f*,
    178–81, 182*t*, 183*t*, 184, 184*t*
  power and 169
  prosody and 179, 181–82
  range and 173–74, 175*f*–77*f*, 178–79
  resonance and 171, 173
  rhetoric and 168, 179
  speech and 167–68
  traits of 170–71, 172*t*
  vocis climax strategy and 179–81, 180*t*
  vocis variatio delectat and 174,
    175*f*–77*f*, 178
  voice quality and 165, 167, 181
Charlton, B. D. 275
Chess 478
Chion, Michael 426–27
Chirac, Jacques 181
Chong Gum, JociAnna 205–7
Choy, Tim 302–3
Chrysostom, John (Saint) 356
Cicero 8–14, 15n14
Cincinnati College Conservatory of
    Music (CCM), University of xxxii,
    478–80, 486
cinema 125–38
  animated 431–33, 432*f*
  audience and 133, 138n3
  automated voice and 419–35, 435n2
  BBC and 135
  culture and 125–30, 126*f*, 134, 137–38, 138n1
  femininity and 420–27, 423*f*, 424*f*, 426*f*,
    432–33, 435
  gaze and 125, 127, 129–30, 134, 138
  gender and 420–33, 423*f*, 424*f*, 426*f*,
    428*f*, 432*f*
  intimacy and 127, 134
  language in 125, 127–30
  liberalism in 125–38
  masculinity and 427–33, 428*f*, 432*f*
  music and 125, 129–31, 133–35, 138, 138n3
  race and 433–35, 434*f*
  sentiment and 125–27, 130, 132–33
  silent 422–24
  trauma and 132–33, 138n2

Ottoman Empire 348, 356, 360n17.
    see also Turkey
    call to prayer and 442
    modern Turkey and 443–46, 451
Oxford Handbook of Voice Perception, The xix
Özcan, Mustafa 448–49
Özgür Kocaeli Gazetesi 449, 453n12

P

Pacific Island culture 193–96, 209n6–209n10.
    see also Marshallese voice; specific island
Paikopoulos, Demosthenes 348
Palamas, Gregory 356
palimpsest vocal tradition 352–59, 359n10,
    360n12
pantomime 13–14
Papua New Guinea xvi
Parcher, Jeff 220
pareidolia 238, 262–63
Park, Jung Mee 461
parody 78, 108–10, 117n24, 118n28
pathos 169, 172t
Paul, Les 415
"Pavarobotti" (Titze) xxxivn3
Pawlowski, B. 280
pedagogy. see vocal pedagogy
Peemot, Victoria Soyan 315, 320f, 323t, 325t,
    332, 335n4
perception xxx–xxxi, 493–98, 500, 502–3,
    502t, 506t, 507
    of acoustic space 307, 312n8
    age and 275
    animal behavior and 270
    articulation and 282
    attractiveness and 275, 277–81,
        290n6–290n12
    blindness and 275
    body and 272–80, 289n2–290n11
    brain function and 269–70
    of charisma 178–84, 182t–84t, 186n1
    communication and 281–82
    crying and 271–72, 289n1
    cues and 270–72, 289n1
    culture and 271, 273–74, 276–78, 283,
        285–89, 290n7
    emotion and 283–85
    estrogen and 278

    evolution of (see evolution)
    face 238–39, 262, 263n3
    fear and 283–84
    formants/formant frequencies and 272–81,
        290n6, 290n8
    fundamental frequency and 272–81, 287,
        289n2
    gender and 273–81, 289n2–290n12
    intention and 281–83, 286–88
    Kaluli people and xvi
    larynx and 272–73, 282, 284, 290n6
    laughter and 282
    multisensory (see multisensory perception)
    pharynx and 272
    physical strength and 272–73, 276–77,
        290n5
    pitch and 272–81, 283–84, 287, 289n2,
        289n3, 290n6, 290n8
    prosody and 283, 287–88
    puberty and 276, 278, 290n6
    resonance and 272, 277
    sexual dimorphism and 277–81,
        290n6–290n12
    signals and 270–72, 283–85, 289n1
    superior temporal sulcus and 269–70
    testosterone and 274, 277–79, 290n6
    timbre and 272–73
    vocal fold and 272–75, 278, 281, 284, 289n2,
        290n6
    vocal ontology and 19
    vocal tract and 272–73, 281, 283–84, 290n6
    whisper and 275
performance
    as domain of inquiry xxv
    privilege and 150–53, 159n9, 160n11, 160n13
    taan and 376–400, 376f, 377t, 378f, 379t,
        380f, 381t, 382f, 382t, 383f, 384t, 385f, 386t,
        387f, 387t, 388f, 389t, 390f, 391t, 392t, 393f,
        394t, 395f, 396f, 396t, 398t, 399f
    transgender identity and 143–58
performative listening xvii
Perón, Juan Domingo 117n22
Perry, Katy 79
perspective, vocal ontology and 25
Peters, John Durham 4, 15n3, 107, 429–30
Peterson, Marina 308, 312n9
Petrohelios, Andreas 348